DEC   2003

B WASSERMAN, E.
Sharp,
Mr. & M
Edie an

P9-DVY-547

WITHDR

MR. & MRS. HOLLYWOOD

MR. & MRS. HOLLYWOOD

Edie And Lew Wasserman

And Their

Entertainment Empire

KATHLEEN SHARP

CARROLL & GRAF PUBLISHERS
NEW YORK

ALAMEDA FREE LIBRARY
2200-A CENTRAL AVENUE
ALAMEDA, CA 94501

MR. & MRS. HOLLYWOOD
Carroll & Graf Publishers
An Imprint of Avalon Publishing Group Inc.
245 West 17th St., 11th Floor
New York, NY 10011

Copyright © 2003 by Kathleen Sharp

All rights reserved. No part of this book may be reproduced in whole or in part without written permission from the publisher, except by reviewers who may quote brief excerpts in connection with a review in a newspaper, magazine, or electronic publication; nor may any part of this book be reproduced, stored in a retrieval system, or transmitted in any form or by any means electronic, mechanical, photocopying, recording, or other, without written permission from the publisher.

Library of Congress Cataloging-in-Publication Data is available.

ISBN: 0-7867-1220-1

Designed by Paul Paddock
Printed in the United States of America
Distributed by Publishers Group West

ALAMEDA FREE LIBRARY
2200-A CENTRAL AVENUE
ALAMEDA, CA 94501

CONTENTS

To Raymond, James, Emily, and Timothy, and in loving
memory of my sister, Peggy Sharp Patterson

MR. & MRS. HOLLYWOOD

PROLOGUE

ON THE LAST DAY OF OCTOBER 1998, some of the most formidable people in Hollywood were gathered at what was once a forty-acre orange grove in Woodland Hills, California. The day was unusually warm, and the three-hundred guests waited congenially in the shade at the Motion Picture & Television Fund (MPTF) home, where Johnny Weissmuller of Tarzan fame and Mary Astor of *The Maltese Falcon* lived out their final days. The place was the town's signature charity, the result of a kind of social stewardship not generally associated with Armani-clad agents. And in attendance were some of the fund's biggest patrons: Steven Spielberg; his partner in DreamWorks Studio, Jeffrey Katzenberg; Robert Daly, co-chairman of Warner Brothers; Ron Meyer, president of Universal Studios; and Sid Sheinberg, former chief executive officer of MCA, which owned Universal.

Suddenly the air stirred, and the guests of honor arrived like the royalty they were. At eighty-five, Lew Wasserman was very much the lion in winter, his white hair still luxuriant, his broad-shouldered frame sleek in a tawny sport coat. On his arm was his eighty-two-year-old wife and partner, Edie, resplendent in a suit of canary yellow, her neck ringed with a strand of large pearls. The modern-day court of chiefs and directors surrounded the couple. Lew greeted them, nodding to each one. Edie smiled and chatted, basking in the attention. The Wassermans were still the unassailable rulers of twentieth-century Hollywood, the singular duo who had miraculously survived a series of cultural whirlwinds and political storms. As Katzenberg remarked later that day, "As I look around me today, I don't know two people who have lived bigger than Edie and Lew." Their lives had paralleled the development of the world's entertainment industry.

They seemed unlikely conquerors—Cleveland natives who fell in love at the nadir of the Great Depression. In 1935 Edie was the spoiled daughter of a German-Jewish millionaire who had lost his American fortune in scandal and speculation. Lew was a grubber and showman's apprentice, the son of Russian-Jewish immigrants who had risked their lives to sail here in steerage class. When Edie and Lew first met that summer, she was dancing to the bands that he booked in a lavish, mob-owned nightclub. The two were drawn together by a mutual love of music and a passion for the ritz—the theatrical pageantry and grand spectacle that can lift almost any spirit. "On their first date," said Suzanne Pleshette, "Edie decided to marry him and Lew didn't have a chance." One summer night, the showman and his dancing partner eloped. Six months later, in 1936, the newlyweds boarded a train to Chicago, where Lew began an entry-level job at the Music Corporation of America (MCA), and Edie forged her own way behind the scenes.

Lew's accomplishments form a string of exciting ventures. He represented top stars during Hollywood's second Golden Age, including Gregory Peck, Joan Crawford, and Kirk Douglas. He became the first Hollywood agent to buy a movie studio, and the first man to parlay a studio tour into a $1 billion-a-year theme-park business. Early on he envisioned the possibilities of TV and went on to invent several television formats: the first 90-minute TV show, *The Virginian;* the first made-for-TV movie; the first miniseries, *Rich Man, Poor Man;* and the first time slot that rotated series and stars. His studio gave several important directors their American feature debuts: George Lucas (*American Graffiti*); Milos Forman (*Taking Off*); Steven Spielberg (*Jaws*); Ivan Reitman (*Animal House*); Constantin Costa-Gavras (*Missing*); Amy Heckerling (*Fast Times at Ridgemont High*); Joel Schumacher (*Car Wash*), among others. He even built Hollywood's first studio conglomerate, from the ground up.

He was that rare mogul who personally introduced technological change. In the 1950s, he owned a pay-TV entity, PhoneVision—thirty years before the concept caught on. In the late 1970s, he and some other studios formed a cable TV channel—now known as the Premiere Movie Channel. Wasserman and MCA attorneys made copyright case law when they fought the Japanese video cassette recorder, while simultaneously inventing the precursor to the DVD—DiscoVision. He and Edie forged the political campaign footpath that now runs like a freeway between Hollywood and Washington, D.C. And it is Wasserman, more than any other industry figure, who lifted American show business to the world stage, where it dominates global pop culture.

This book opens on the night that Wasserman became a studio landlord by quickly buying Universal Studio's property. It follows Edie and Lew as they shed their agency habits and slip into their new roles as mogul and wife. At times, the book explores their childhoods and early days as a means of understanding their actions and motivation in contemporary Hollywood. The two obtain their prize, fortify their positions, and safeguard their turf until they achieve what appears to be the culmination of their dreams.

But I'm getting ahead of the story.

When I started to write this book, it was 1996, and media-averse MCA had been on the front page many times in the previous year. In 1990 Wasserman had sold his company to the Japanese, who after five years had sold it to the Canadians, who five years later would sell it again, this time to the French, who would sell it yet again. Apparently, no one at any global corporation could manage for a few years the company that Lew had spent almost sixty years building—perhaps because no one had the counselor he had in Edie. "I'm sure he consulted her on everything he did," her longtime confidante Wendy Goldberg told me.

If Lew's accomplishments were legendary in the annals of business—and they were—Edie's achievements were relayed among insiders by word of mouth. Lew had turned a mere band-booking agency into the top Hollywood talent house while Edie waltzed new clients to his door. When Lew built the biggest TV production facility in town, Edie persuaded film actors to try the new medium. But aside from their prolific deal-making, who were the Wassermans? And how did they plant their flag on so many beachheads? From the original Hollywood wives' club to *The Man in the Gray Flannel Suit*, from The Beaver to The Extraterrestrial, from the "A" list to the White House, they made their mark, comprising the most successful, longest-running management team in the history of entertainment. Writing a book about two such giants was not that difficult, but getting to the heart of Edie and Lew was the real challenge.

The conventional wisdom was that the two never gave interviews, that none of their friends and family would speak on the record, and that it was impossible to discern fact from the fiction that had enveloped Edie and Lew. None of that turned out to be true. Yes, it's always tricky writing about a powerful duo, and the late-twentieth-century tendency to sanctify CEOs was exacerbated by Hollywood's predilection for hype. But slowly a few windows opened.

During my six years of research, I kept both Edie and Lew Wasserman abreast of my progress, either through notes and letters or via intermediaries such as Sid Sheinberg, Steven Spielberg, and Tom Pollock, former president of Universal Studios. Every now and then, I'd make another interview request of them, always receiving polite demurrals. I continued interviewing what grew to be 450 sources. Several of my sources asked Edie and Lew for their blessing before they agreed to talk to me, and the couple began to grant permission.

At my request, Wasserman gave me access to some records inside Universal Studios. I spent time in the studio's musty basement files, where I found a few gems, and hours in MCA's corporate finance department, where I reviewed every annual report since MCA's first, in 1958. I was given access to a few personal collections held by associates of Edie and Lew's.

The first breakthrough occurred while I was covering the dedication of the Wasserman Campus at the MPTF, Edie's favorite charity. That October day, I greeted several sources whom I'd already interviewed for this book, including Jack Valenti, chief of the Motion Picture Association, the studios' lobbying arm. "I can't think of any other industry in the world where two people have contributed so much to their own," he said. As if to underline those words, the Wassermans then announced to the crowd a multimillion-dollar donation to build a hospital and wing for the retirement home. They also pledged to match every dollar donated by all of the studios, which surprised the group and shamed the other moguls, especially those who were absent.

To celebrate, we were ushered into a banquet room, set with silverware and flowers. But then I was halted abruptly by a burly bodyguard and pulled out of the line. The guard escorted me to a separate space, where I sat on a folding chair alone in front of a closed-circuit TV monitor. I was the only person accorded such treatment, and for the next hour or so, I sipped water and took notes while the other guests lunched on roast chicken and white wine. Later, when I inquired about my solitary confinement, I was told that the arrangements had been made at the request of Edie Wasserman. I realized that this was an example of what a few sources had been trying to convey to me: the art of an Edie snub. The incident left me with the distinct impression that Edie was not happy with my book project. Yet I was fascinated by this form of Hollywood hazing, which seemed to speak volumes about the powerful woman who ordered it. I recalled former Universal Studio chief Ed Muhl warning me: "Women in this town can be very astute about money and position. They might say they like you," he said, "but don't fool with their turf or possessions. If you do, they'll turn mean." Muhl had been describing Lana Turner and Bette Davis, but he might as well have been talking about Edith Beckerman Wasserman. After all, I was scrutinizing her crown in the reflected glow of filmdom's other jewels.

As Lew himself later told me, "They take everything in Hollywood for granted," and topping the list of those taken for granted was Edie Wasserman. Yet her influence upon America's star system has been profound if subtle. When the young actor Jimmy Stewart needed help in 1939, he was a lowly contract player at MGM. He had just met Lew Wasserman, who was new to town, and Edie, who recognized a creative spirit in the young actor. "Jimmy lived at Edie and Lew's place for six months after he came to L.A.," actress Janet Leigh told me. With Edie bolstering his morale, Stewart took on his breakout film in 1939, *Mr. Smith Goes to Washington*, which earned him his first Oscar nomination and his own address. Fifty-five years later, Stewart was again at a loss, this time over the death of his wife, Gloria. "Edie and I went over to see him but he refused to leave the house," said Leigh. Edie eventually took her old friend to dinner, but she could not cheer him up. Three years later, in 1997, Stewart died, and Edie tried to console her own husband, who called the actor "my favorite friend."

During World War II, one of Wasserman's most important clients, Bette Davis, formed the Hollywood Canteen, which boosted the morale of American servicemen and became a model for USO clubs. Davis and MCA client John Garfield staged canteen shows inside a converted barn near Sunset and Cahuenga boulevards. It functioned like a nightclub filled with famous singers and musicians where screen stars gladly danced every night with servicemen. Davis had cajoled MCA chairman Jules Stein into managing the canteen's finances, but it was Edie who corralled the stars and enlisted Hollywood union members, who donated their labor to refurbish the barn. "She was a driving force behind the canteen and worked there almost every night," said Julie Payne, daughter of Edie's bosom friend, child actress Anne Shirley. Edie made sure that bandleader Kay Kyser, Bud Abbott, and Lou Costello headlined the canteen's grand opening on October 3, 1942. She dressed in black gowns, sapphire earrings, and swept her hair up, à la Betty Grable. Edie, Marlene Dietrich, and Rita Hayworth spent hours dancing with thousands of GIs before they were shipped to the front lines. "Edie was the belle of the ball," said a longtime reporter. She led bond rallies, planted victory gardens, and performed any service to fund the war effort—though she rarely received credit. "I think those were the happiest times of her life," Payne told me. Edie loved working backstage for big causes.

After the war, she went on to gather her Hollywood wives' club—a coterie of spouses of MCA agents and female stars. An independent woman, she had love affairs with talented men, shaping their films and boosting her husband's client list. Her political instincts were so strong that she willingly buried the hatchet in order to advance MCA's future. She did this several times—in 1965 with former Attorney General Robert F. Kennedy, who had forced Lew to disband his agency, and in 1967 with then-California Governor Ronald Reagan, the political protégé of Taft Schreiber, Lew's MCA nemesis. She gathered intelligence from studio publicists and celebrity doctors like a modern-day Mata Hari. She trained several generations of Beverly Hills hostesses, who went on to entertain statesmen and elders, albeit without Edie's verve or vision.

"Today, the so-called Hollywood wives have nothing to offer," columnist Rex Reed told me. "They have little to say and offer no class, glamour, or legacy. They may get $10 million a picture or be married to the studio chairman, but they do not affect our times."

Edie shaped several epochs while playing her most visible role: Lew's protector.

Yet the mogul did not always bend to his wife's will, which is how this project received its second wind. Nine months after experiencing Edie's Hollywood-style hazing, I attended another charity event, this one at the Jules Stein Eye Institute. A few of Stein's relatives already knew that I was the niece of Dr. Sherman Mellinkoff, the first dean of UCLA Medical School, who had helped persuade Jules Stein to build his institute at UCLA. My uncle by marriage, Mellinkoff, had sat on the institute's board with Stein and Wasserman, sharing duties and mutual esteem. That night I was introduced to Wasserman with that preamble. "So, your uncle is Sherman Mellinkoff?" Lew Wasserman asked me. Why didn't you say so? he seemed to imply. Because, I thought, my work should stand on its own. Then I experienced the flip side of the Wasserman power: Lew's gallant charm. Before I left that night, he warmly told me to call his secretary to arrange an interview.

A few weeks later, on June 22, 1999, I passed through the Universal Studio gates and was directed to Wasserman's suite at the top of the tower. As I waited to see the chairman emeritus, I watched his three secretaries as they typed letters and answered telephones. I was amazed that their eighty-six-year-old boss could keep three efficient women so busy. I was quickly ushered into Lew's large office, where the aging mogul stood and greeted me, leaning on a gold-headed cane. Behind him stretched enormous windows that opened onto a gloomy June day. As expected, there would be no free-spirited discussion here; Wasserman had already set the ground rules by limiting my questions to Jules Stein, his late mentor. Before we began our talk, Wasserman glanced at his side table, which held a small clock. We wasted no time in the next seventy-five minutes or so.

Once, during the 1940s, Wasserman visited Stein at his hilltop mansion, where he was playing tennis with a machine that spewed balls. Stein ordered his assistant to turn off the machine, but

Wasserman didn't know how. "I had never seen one of those before," he told me. An exasperated Stein finally turned it off himself, and Lew spent the next forty minutes retrieving the boss's spent balls. "Why don't you hire an instructor?" Lew asked Stein. "Because the machine is better and faster." Wasserman was like Stein's machine, better and faster than most men, a formidable package, two for the price of one. Lew's stories told me more than he had intended.

Over the course of our interviews, Wasserman started to deviate from his own rule. He loved talking about the early agency days and relished one particular story about Isham Jones, a famous song-writer. In the 1920s, Jones was earning $2,500 a week and Jules Stein was a thirty-year-old wannabe agent, "a short but very swag-gering figure," as Lew described him. Stein hounded Jones, who finally agreed to sign with MCA—if he received a certified check for $10,000, a Pierce Arrow stretch limousine, and letters from hotels guaranteeing fine lodging. Four days later, Stein delivered all three requirements, and Jones went on tour. "But on the way back to Chicago, it started raining, his car skidded off the road, and he had to wait overnight for a towing car," Wasserman explained. "Isham stood in the rain and said, 'MCA—mud, clay and abuse.'"

I laughed several times at his tales, often in spite of myself. Wasserman sometimes answered questions in a flippant manner, prompting me to recall what former MCA agent Merle Jacobs had told me: "Lew was the snottiest guy I ever met." His arrogance and cavalier attitude surfaced during our talks. For example, I had been told that when Wasserman finally opened the formal Universal Studio Tour, a line of guests waited to get in. "We didn't have a line the first day," he corrected me. "It was the second day." When I asked him what advice he'd give to young people today, he retorted: "Think. Just think. You'll find a subject." Some of his responses were refreshingly, even brutally, frank. Toward the end of one meeting, he told me: "You've got five minutes."

Other times, he warmed up considerably. Wasserman clearly

respected and, I think, adored his boss, Jules Stein. He was enormously proud of the stars he represented. As I listened, he once recited fifty marquee names from a list he had tucked into his breast pocket a few weeks earlier. Yet, when I attempted to broach a controversial topic, he flashed me a withering look. "Well, we're not going to get into that, are we?" We did not.

I was struck by several of his traits. Wasserman was generous in giving credit to his men, and acknowledged his good luck freely. He was not introspective, preferring to inspect his buffed and polished nails rather than reflect on his emotions. He took great pride knowing that he had lived close to the action. In his heyday, he was not only surrounded by people who sparkled with glamour, panache, and prestige, he arranged their lives. "By the way," he asked me, "who are the stars today?" I couldn't name one whom I knew would satisfy his exacting standards. "Well, we once managed them all, and they were all class acts."

During our last significant meeting, he reminisced more openly—but his memory faltered. Some of his stories didn't ring true in light of the timing or the numbers I had come to know. A few were actually refuted by other sources. No doubt some of the discrepancies can be attributed to Wasserman's age. But the more he talked, the more I realized that some of his yarns were the result of habit. He—and his clients in this make-believe business—had been telling and retelling the same old chestnuts for so long that they'd become part of the town's lore. By the time I met him, Wasserman had reined for so many decades that his decrees were sacrosanct. None of his men had ever challenged his version of history, so who was I to try?

Yet, in the end, untangling the legend from the man and the woman became the biggest obstacle in completing the project. The studio-based conglomerates in the past half-century have boomed into America's largest exporters, capable of great good and immeasurable harm. The Wassermans, the movie stars, and the studio conglomerates have benefited handsomely from decades of public adulation and assistance. Federal revenue bills, state budgets, public airwaves, and tax loopholes are just a few reasons behind the industry's fabulous wealth—some $135 billion in annual revenues. That's why this book belongs to Mr. and Mrs. John Q. Public as much as it describes Edie and Lew Wasserman, entertainment royalty who never forgot where they came from even as they became synonymous with America's most glittering spot: Mr. and Mrs. Hollywood.

PART I
Obtaining the Prize:
1958–1962

ONE

A WEEK BEFORE THANKSGIVING 1958, a red-and-black Buick snaked up Cahuenga Pass, over the backbone of the Hollywood Hills, and dropped into the tangle of burr clover and brush that covered the San Fernando Valley. Bathed in moonlight, the sedan sped to the birthplace of modern California, a panoramic spot sheltered by a crescent of mountains and skirted by fields. For centuries, this location had served as the backdrop for blood feuds, land grabs, and audacious power plays. Tonight would be no different.

Inside the car sat Hollywood kingpin Lew R. Wasserman and three tight-lipped colleagues from the Music Corporation of America—the biggest, most ruthless talent agency in the world. If Wasserman, MCA's president, succeeded in executing his plan, those on the other side of these hills would witness yet another cunning blow, "a deal" that would prove so masterly that Hollywood—and the world—would never be the same.

The car's destination was a chicken-ranch-turned-film-factory—Universal Studios—that had become the butt of industry jokes. The studio hadn't won an Oscar in nearly thirty years, and most of its features were formulaic or derivative, according to Bernard Dick, a studio historian. "Universal was the sixth of seven studios," he said. It was hemorrhaging $2 million a year in 1958. But Wasserman was a true believer in the resiliency of show business, and, really, he had to be. For if the world's oldest and largest film studio slipped into bankruptcy, others would soon follow. And then where would Wasserman and his army of agents peddle their high-priced movie-star clients?

"Wasserman had no historic sense at all," said Ed Muhl, the executive vice president of Universal Pictures at the time. "Lew was all about money." Though Wasserman had no interest in preserving tradition, he possessed an uncanny sense of timing, which made everything he accomplished seem effortless. Indeed, his achievements were so extraordinary that he could afford to dismiss their magnitude with a wave of his hand. Forty years later, Wasserman would recall this particular night, cock his head, and say in his modest manner and gravel voice: "It was either courage or stupidity that led [me] to Universal." In fact, it was far more complicated than that.

As soon as the car pulled into Universal's parking lot that night, Wasserman and his three companions jumped out and walked toward the studio. The short man in the pack was Jules Stein, the tight-fisted, schooner-nosed chairman of MCA. He looked like the type of man who would sell his brother for room and board—and that's precisely what he had done in 1915, when he booked Billy Stein, a gifted soprano, into a Michigan summer resort. That job helped launch the Stein brothers' musical ventures and, eventually, its band-booking agency in Prohibition-era Chicago. By the 1940s, MCA represented every top musician, big band, singer, and comedian in the nation. It also produced and sold most of America's hit radio shows, which featured, not coincidentally, MCA acts. The agency grew so big that during World War II, Stein and MCA were prosecuted for operating an illegal monopoly. The presiding federal district judge was so appalled at MCA's grip on the band business that he called the agency an octopus. The term stuck.

Stein had spent years perfecting his mercenary style, accumulating a trove of treasures that were often buried in paper trusts and foreign accounts. He studied tax and finance, and his knowledge of estate planning became a key factor in luring stars to MCA. When big stars like Fred MacMurray and Milton Berle had no pensions or portfolios, they invested in commercial real estate, thanks to Julius Caesar Stein. But when it came to coaxing and coddling sensitive artists, Stein fell short. "Jules had no charm and could be a real son-of-a-bitch," said one MCA executive. That's why the dragoon counted on his suave and handsome protégé, Lew Wasserman.

At 6'2", Wasserman towered over most men. The forty-five-year-old was MCA's president and the town's agent provocateur. He had risen rapidly, beginning in 1939, when Stein ordered the twenty-six-year-old Lew to start signing big-screen names to MCA's all-music roster. "The whole power and success of an agent is who they have to sell," said former MCA executive Berle Adams, who worked with Wasserman for twenty years. "Lew decided he was going to go out and take a shot at every star." Initially, Hollywood ridiculed Lew as just another flesh peddler, "a bloodsucker" angling for ten percent, and that bothered him, said producer J. B. Lesser. Prior to Lew's arrival, the town's agents had a "Jewish gentlemen's agreement" that said there was plenty of business for all to share. "We didn't need to cut each other's throats to succeed," explained a rival agent. "But Lew—he went out for blood." Wasserman poached stars from rival agents by promising them better roles and bigger pay. Longtime agent Sam Jaffe was stunned by Lew's aggression. "He stole a lot of my clients, like Joan Crawford. He romanced Bette Davis by telling her how much MCA could improve her career." If necessary, Wasserman would give his 10 percent commission to a star's former agent until the old contract expired. Then he'd negotiate a new contract worth many times more than that. "If Lew did that once, he did it twenty times," said one producer. He quickly grew into the town's most powerful talent broker.

Because of Wasserman, MCA soon represented an unheard-of 60 percent of the industry's bankable talent—from screenwriters to directors to leading men and ladies. By 1955, the firm packaged and produced most of the country's entertainment shows, from the big screen to the little one, from Broadway to Las Vegas. On any given day, MCA employed 1,000 clients, said Ronnie Lubin, a former MCA agent. "Not every actor got his hallelujahs, but they were too scared to leave MCA." Few people left the fold as long as Wasserman and his men kept negotiating ever-higher prices for talent, beginning with his first $1 million contract in 1939 to his latest 1958 movie package for $2 million—$13 million in today's dollars.

By 1958, most of the legendary studio founders were either geriatric—like stubborn Jack Warner or Paramount's avuncular Barney Balaban—or dead—such as Harry Warner, Columbia's Harry Cohn, and MGM's L. B. Mayer. The industry had fallen into such a depression that studios that had once employed 2,500 people now limped along with 75, said Frank Price, a former MCA executive, and later, president of Columbia Studios. "You could drive through Beverly Hills and see 'For Sale' signs all over the place." The number of movie ticket sales had plummeted from 90 million during the Great Depression—when 75 percent of the nation took in a weekly movie—to barely 40 million in 1958—when only 20 percent of the population did. That year marked the film industry's nadir, which confounded the moguls, since the rest of the country was enjoying an unprecedented postwar boom. During the 1950s, people had started raising families, purchasing automobiles, and buying homes in the suburbs away from urban theaters. "By the time people turned twenty-four, they were too busy to go to the movies," said Price. "The movie audience had changed into a dating audience, but the moguls didn't realize that. They were used to dealing with the entire audience, and that was called television."

Wasserman had already built a TV subsidiary that was producing more hours of film than any other studio. This made him not simply a formidable agent, but the dominant producer of prime-time shows and therefore Hollywood's most powerful man.

"Lew became like a god," explained Lubin. But Wasserman didn't act like a deity, at least not in public. He never appeared in the spotlight and was seldom photographed. He rarely bothered to explain his cardinal rules, the first of which was "Avoid the press." "No interviews. No panels. No speeches. No comments," he ordered his agents. "Stay out of the spotlight. It fades your suit." He hardly spoke, but when he did, people leaned in to catch his brusque words. His gait was deceptively slow, the effect of big, splayed feet that threatened to trip him. Yet he ambled with purpose, his coiled, feral energy sucking up space and stealing attention. "Under his smooth, ingratiating surface, Lew was a cold, calculating fellow holding to no purpose other than power and the money it can bring," said John Weber, a William Morris agent. "But mostly power."

On this November night in 1958, Wasserman was hoping to expand his already-sizable empire by sneaking a modern-day Trojan horse—escrow papers—inside the studio gates. He hoped to buy the broken-down facilities and grounds of Universal Studios—but not the studio itself, at least not yet. "We were only buying the real estate," said Al Dorskind, an MCA attorney. Wasserman and his men would rule the studio as landlords, exercising their right to tear down Universal buildings, inspect its storehouses, and probe its financial statements. Lew would examine the studio's credit and debt, its holdings and prospects. Then, when the time was right, Wasserman would reveal his real intention. He would buy Universal Studios, its rich intellectual property, and its holding company, the top-ranked Decca Records. As Bernard Dick explained years later: "MCA had designs on Universal as early as 1950. Its long-range plan had always been to be the ultimate media colossus."

Stein had started his plan by buying 25,000 shares of Decca stock in the late 1940s. He had received a tip that a shady Russian-born banker named Serge Semenenko was advising Decca in its acquisition of Universal Studios, said Decca executive Joe Delaney. On

Halloween, 1951—nine months before Decca Records acquired Universal Studios—Stein bought a chunk of Universal Studios stock, priced at $1 per share. As Delaney explained: "Stein made a deal with Semenenko. If Jules would help Semenenko down the line, Stein could eventually control the two companies."

But in 1958 Stein and Wasserman were agents; legally, they could not own a studio *and* a talent agency. For now, MCA would simply buy the studio's real estate. It would appear to be an innocent enough property deal. But actually it would become one of a series of suspect moves whereby MCA would someday own the publicly held Decca, its main subsidiary, Universal Studios, and all of their rich intellectual assets. Stein and Wasserman kept their long-term plan secret even from some of their own advisers.

As Lew walked toward Universal's adobe headquarters that night, his brilliantined black hair glistened in the light and his white shirt contrasted sharply with his trademark suit. Elegant and cunning, he advanced upon his goal.

Accompanying Stein and Wasserman that night were two other MCA executives. Vice president Taft Schreiber wore bottle-thick glasses and had an upright, almost sanctimonious bearing. Most employees were hard-pressed to describe what Schreiber actually did at MCA. But he was Stein's very first employee, hired in 1926, and therefore his longest-serving consigliere. On the other flank was Al Dorskind, the lawyer, with stooped shoulders and dachshund eyes. He had spent most of the year fine-tuning the real estate contract that the men hoped to sign later that night. In lockstep, the four marched into the administration building that was once occupied by Carl Laemmle, the world's most famous studio mogul. His lair now smelled faintly of horsehair and glue. Indeed, the office, the nocturnal visit, and the property deal about to go down all shared the same unseemly odor. As one Universal executive said later: "The whole thing stunk."

• • •

The studio executives welcomed the agents, and Wasserman, Schreiber, and Dorskind extended their hands in an uncharacteristically friendly manner. Studio manager Ed Muhl wasn't sure whether the gesture signified friendship or some sleight of hand, but he didn't care. It was the studio's eleventh hour, he said. "Wasserman was coming to save us. To me, it was lovely."

Wasserman greeted Nate Blumberg, chairman of Universal Pictures, the studio's parent company. With his thick dark eyebrows and bushy white hair, Blumberg looked like a silent film character, right down to his broad grin. Next to him was the hulking Milton Rackmil, president of Decca Records. Dorskind walked past Rackmil to the large wooden desk, where he placed a thick document. He could see a pile of termite droppings under the desk, a sign of rotting structures. "The deal almost didn't go through because of the enormous amount of termite damage," said a studio executive.

All Hollywood studios were desperate in 1958. Income at Paramount Studios had fallen so low that it had been forced to sell some assets. The three Warner brothers no longer owned their eponymous studio, and the company barely eked out a living producing cheap television shows; it was about to record its first annual loss since 1934. RKO Studios had been mismanaged so grossly by tycoon Howard Hughes that its film days were over. It was now a TV production company owned by ex-RKO star Lucille Ball and her husband Desi Arnaz. Twentieth Century Fox had almost escaped its competitors' fate, thanks to MCA client Marilyn Monroe and her movies, including *The Seven Year Itch* (1955). But the studio's film magic had disappeared now, too, and it was trying to sell 260 acres of its 334-acre back lot. Columbia Pictures had raised money by selling 1,000 of its pre-1948 movies, which could be seen on late-night TV when most stations aired test signals. And the most glamorous studio of all, Metro-Goldwyn-Mayer, could barely post a profit. Its founder, the paternalistic L. B. Mayer, had just been laid to rest in a standing-room-only funeral scripted and produced by David O. Selznick. The movie veteran had once quipped that "Hollywood is like Egypt, full of crumbling pyramids." If so, then Universal was the great pyramid of Cheops.

The biggest studio was worse off than any other. Known for producing second-rate westerns (*Ride a Crooked Trail*) and science-fiction horrors (*Monster on the Campus*), Universal had ridden a roller-coaster decade of booms and busts. Now it needed $3 million a year just to maintain its 500 outdoor sets, 367 acres, 30 soundstages, and warehouses of props. During the financial slide, Decca chief Rackmil had grown increasingly creative in his search for capital. In 1957 he had signed an $18 million deal to lease 500 of Universal's pre-1948 films to Screen Gems (owned by Columbia Pictures). But, despite this cash influx, the studio soon fell back into dire financial straits. Rackmil had tried to sell the studio and land for $25 million to Walter O'Malley, owner of the Dodgers baseball team. When O'Malley hesitated, Rackmil said he could have it for $15 million—if the film studio could remain. But that deal fell through, and Rackmil had begun contemplating renting out his enormous facility to independent filmmakers.

In early 1958, Rackmil ordered Universal to cut back film production, which further squeezed its income. "Those guys didn't understand the business," groused Muhl. A Universal employee since the advent of talkies, Muhl had survived four ownership changes. With his hooded eyes and widow's peak, he looked as if he'd been born cranky; but, like Wasserman, he had a soft spot for show business and a steady hand for management. While Rackmil contemplated bankruptcy, Muhl continued producing motion pictures.

For several years, Wasserman's TV subsidiary, Revue Productions, had been renting Universal's soundstages, bolstering its sagging fortunes. To Muhl, MCA was not just a talent agency, it was primarily a TV producer. In 1950 Wasserman had flouted union rules by forming Revue, which later made prime-time TV series such as *Bachelor Father* and *Tales of Wells Fargo.* "We were producing a great many television shows at that time," Wasserman explained. Between 1954 and 1958, Revue accounted for about half of TV shows. Few insiders realized just how rich the stealthy Revue Productions had become: By 1958, it was raking in *six times the money* that MCA the agency collected in talent commissions— some $50 million a year. As Berle Adams said, in an understatement: "We were making a fortune."

But Wasserman wanted more. Faced with dwindling studio demand for his agency's movie talent, Wasserman needed to increase Revue's activity. "It was a very good arrangement for MCA to have both the talent agency and the production company," said Frank Price, who worked at Revue. Producers customized TV shows for MCA clients who might otherwise go without work. And to produce its cheap, lucrative TV fare, Revue had to lease stages every week—not just at Universal, but at five other studios, stretching from Culver City to the Valley. As long as TV boomed, Wasserman needed to acquire more stages to remain at the top of the industry pile. "Lew always wanted to consolidate his TV operations," said Dorskind. Universal's 367 acres offered him a splendid solution.

The pairing of the land-rich, cash-poor Universal with the ambitious, cash-rich MCA made sense, Muhl explained. "There were only a few outfits in town that had enough money to buy us, and MCA was one of them."

In Universal's termite-ridden office that night, Wasserman and his agents quibbled with the studio men over details of the real estate deal. Wasserman finally moved toward the document on the desk, and the haggling stopped. Dorskind expected Wasserman to sign first. Instead, he turned and extended his arm to Rackmil, indicating that the president of Universal's holding company should precede him.

Rackmil faced Dorskind. "What's the weakest part of the deal for me?" he demanded.

"Oh, no," said Dorskind. He couldn't believe this was happening now, when they were so close. He'd spent most of the year nailing down the agreement, and further discussion could kill the deal. "I'm not going to answer that. Not after all this time and work." He crossed his arms.

Wasserman moved close to Dorskind and said, "The man asked you. Go ahead. Tell him."

Dorskind took a deep breath. Then he listed the terms by memory, his words spilling like beans from a sack. "MCA is buying your land, all 367 acres, for $11.25 million. You and your studio can stay as our tenant," he said. "For rent, you pay us $1 million now. Then $1 million a year, every year, for the next ten years." He continued, "The worst thing that can happen to you is that at the end of ten years, we can kick you out. Or we can renegotiate your rent so sky-high, you have to leave. And you'll have no say in the matter."

Rackmil was silent.

Wasserman spoke up: "What's the weakest part of the deal for me?"

Now Dorskind was dumbstruck. He realized that his boss was nervous about assuming so much liability. Dorskind answered carefully. "With all this land and equipment, you now have an overhead of $7 million a year, including taxes and insurance. Lord knows what it will be a decade from now. Plus, you're no longer only in the agency business." Dorskind left unspoken the riskiest part of all: Lew Wasserman must now accomplish what no other, more-experienced studio landowner had been able to do: *salvage a money-losing business in a dying industry.*

Wasserman was quiet. Just then, Stein, Schreiber, Rackmil, and the attorneys all started yelling.

Suddenly Nate Blumberg burst out laughing. "You guys are foolish, you know that?" The men fell silent. Blumberg looked genially at the two camps that had formed. "What are you arguing about?" he asked, spreading his hands wide. "If either one of you gets into trouble ten years down the line, you can merge. Besides"—he looked at Rackmil—"Universal has to sell, and"—he turned to Wasserman—"MCA needs to buy."

Wasserman glanced at Stein. "[Stein] could have stopped the deal if he wanted to," Wasserman told me many years later. "But he didn't." Wasserman walked to the papers and signed them. His signature was even, without a flourish and utterly indecipherable. One by one, the others scribbled their names, too. At last, Dorskind stooped over the papers, found his name, and blinked. "That's when I knew I had been promoted to vice president and treasurer, because that's what my title read." He turned to Wasserman, who congratulated him.

The MCA men then walked out of the room without ceremony. It was nearly midnight, and an exhausted Dorskind fumbled for his car keys. The agents weren't much for gravitas, so they didn't care that they were standing on historical ground. This was the site of the original Rancho Cahuenga de Ramirez land grant, given in 1795 to the loyal subjects of Charles IV of Spain, whose soldiers brutally stole it from the Gabriela and Fernandeño Indians; and where Mexican General Andres Pico and the power-hungry American Lieutenant Colonel John C. Fremont signed the 1847 treaty that ended their nation's hostilities and sold out the Mexican people. This is where freebooter Isaac Lankershim paid $115,000 for this plot of 60,000 acres—just 90 cents an acre—to the state's last Mexican governor in another steal of a deal. Generations later, Lankhershim's son, "Colonel J.B.," made a killing by subdividing it into the pricey townships of Van Nuys, Sherman Oaks, and Encino. And here is where "Uncle" Carl Laemmle landed in 1914, seeking sanctuary from the Edison Trust, which extorted money from moviemakers and exhibitors for the "right" to handle filmstrips. Laemmle had come here to build his studio beyond the grasp of those East Coast bullies.

Now this was Lew Wasserman's land. Soon he'd stand accused of building an illegal trust. As it was, Wasserman and MCA were already the focus of two federal investigations and one grand jury 3,000 miles away. It would take years for some of the details of Wasserman's shrewd deals to be revealed; by then, he'd be untouchable. At the end of the century, entertainment would rank as America's largest export, and Wasserman's empire would dwarf those built by Colenel Fremont or the king of Spain. By signing his name that night, Wasserman seeded a global enterprise that would exceed the others not only in scope but in impact. His realm would eventually be part of an enormous cultural kingdom that would produce goods and services $535 billion dollars a year—more than the Gross National Product of most European nations.

Wasserman and the men waited in the chilly night air until Dorskind found his keys. They piled into his Buick, which climbed Cahuenga Pass, crested the hill, and dropped to the other side of the mountains. The car skirted the old Fox studio and passed the rusting gates of Columbia, Paramount, and the once-glorious RKO. Dorskind mentally reviewed how he had fine-tuned every clause and term. He marveled how Wasserman had negotiated the sale, cleaving the price from $25 million down to $15 million, and finally to $11.25 million.

Even better, the purchase was funded 90 percent by the seller. Once the deal closed on December 15, 1958, MCA would begin to pay off the balance of the mortgage over the next ten years, without using *any more of its own cash*. MCA had paid $1 million in cash for the world's biggest studio lot—367 acres. Universal would now pay MCA $1 million in rent every year for the next decade and MCA would essentially return the check, giving Universal its $1 million annual installment on the ten-year note. "It was a hell of a deal," marveled one producer.

Wasserman's deal was less a triumph than grand larceny, said a Universal executive. "It was unconscionable how cheaply Lew got all of that real estate and equipment." The Internal Revenue Service would audit MCA—repeatedly over the years—but it would never find a reason to levy a fine. As Dorskind drove his car through the near-empty streets, one of the men finally spoke. "Jesus Christ," he whispered. "We've just bought a damn studio." At that, the four agents hooted. Now that MCA was the studio's overseer, it could surreptitiously begin to run the place as if it were its own.

"From then on," said Ed Muhl, "we didn't have to worry about the leaks in the roof, the cracking corner of the stage, labor negotiations, or overhead." Wasserman took care of it all, he said. Although Rackmil and Muhl still technically headed the studio, MCA exerted actual control. As one Decca Records manager explained, "Wasserman knew how to handle Rackmil."

That night, the agents celebrated. "The whole bunch of us were laughing and shouting and whistling. We were like little boys who had stumbled onto a new playing field or something," said Dorskind. "It was really quite a moment."

Now, if Wasserman could fend off the investigators from the East, he might be able to execute the rest of his plan.

TWO

THE WIZARDS OF HOLLYWOOD'S DARK ART—agenting—worked most days in an incongruous-looking antebellum-style manse. MCA's home was made of white bricks, green shutters, and Corinthian porticoes and was surrounded by clipped shrubs and white roses. It boasted a two-story columned entrance crowned by a cream-colored cupola. Located in the heart of Beverly Hill's Golden Triangle, the building straddled the thoroughfare of Little Santa Monica Boulevard and leafy Burton Way, and it transcended the area's more modest displays of concrete, wood, and stucco. Perhaps most telling was the agency's street address—MCA Square—which was embossed on a discreet brass plate. There was no square, but the agency's architecture, address, and location all conveyed one message: arrogance, wealth, and pretentious class.

Lew Wasserman usually arrived at work before his men. At 7:00 A.M., he'd climb the Tara-like staircase to the second floor and pass beneath the $50,000 cut-crystal chandelier that was always lit. One of his two secretaries would be typing a document and they'd exchange a brief greeting before he disappeared into his vast suite. "I knew his mind was going a million miles a second," said Shirley Kory, one of his secretaries. "Everything always had to be done yesterday."

This was especially true in late 1958, when Wasserman was orchestrating his duties like a circus ringleader. There were the usual problems associated with a farm system—the same talent issues that preoccupied agents at the William Morris Agency or General Amusement Corp. (GAC), MCA's bigger rivals. During this time, MCA client Judy Garland was stumbling on the grueling performance schedule MCA had arranged for her. "She was very difficult—drunk and stoned all the time," said MCA agent Daniel Welkes. Joan Crawford was calling her agent in the wee hours to complain about her hotel room. Charles Bronson had grown so upset at the B-movie roles that MCA kept tossing him, he had left for another agency. Then there were the domestic problems of such gifted people as Oscar Levant, the pianist, composer, and manic-depressive wit who in 1958 hosted *The Oscar Levant Show*. The police would often run into Levant in the middle of the night—either at his home, fighting with his young wife and costar, June, or sitting in his parked car, after being shot full of Demerol or phenobarbital.

The chief of the Beverly Hills Police Department, Clinton Anderson, often buried such incidents and "secrets in a confidential file," so as not to embarrass MCA or its stars. According to several ex-officers, Wasserman also worked closely with the Los Angeles Police Department, particularly LAPD's Captain Jim Hamilton, and later, Captain Hal Yarnell. Once, the police discovered MCA client Eddie Fisher in a compromising situation. "Some guy was shaking him down for money, which was scaring the hell out of Fisher," said Roger Otis, a former LAPD deputy. The thug had threatened to beat Fisher so badly, he'd be unable to host his network TV show—a Revue production. "Captain Hamilton had assigned us to watch Fisher," said Otis. The captain debriefed Wasserman—as he did in most matters regarding MCA employees and clients.

Stein had deliberately built his Hollywood headquarters across the street from the Beverly Hills Police Department. He didn't want any thieves or agents breaking into his office to pilfer MCA contracts and ledgers. His fears were not paranoia; his own MCA agents had done just that to at least one rival. In 1948 Edie Wasserman, the wife of MCA's chief, had stumbled onto a hilarious new act, Dean Martin and Jerry Lewis. She introduced her husband to the two comedians, but they were already represented by New York agent Abbey Greshler. One night, two of Lew's men broke into Greshler's office and lifted the Martin and Lewis contract, according to a lawsuit filed by Greshler. A few days later, Wasserman used the contract to make a counteroffer to the comedians. A short time later, Martin and Lewis left Greshler and joined MCA. "That hurt my father deeply," said Francine Greshler Feldmann. Greshler sued MCA and Edie and Lew Wasserman for trespassing and robbery, but eventually settled for a huge sum.

MCA was now the world's top talent agency, "with more stars than there are in heaven," as the once-illustrious MGM Studio used to boast of itself. But Wasserman's work was not glamorous. Most days, he sat at his desk, taking phone calls, approving movie deals, and collecting reports from his spies and soldiers. "Lew had maybe 250 agents all over the world, and he knew what they were doing

every day, from [their efforts] on the smallest act to the biggest one,"
said Freddie Fields, a former MCA agent and golden boy. "Nothing
was hidden from Lew. Nothing happened without him knowing
about it." Some producers suspected that Wasserman hired spies to
work in the town's typing pools. How else to explain his knack for
picking up movie scripts before the studio had started casting? The
agency seemed omniscient. Rivals joked that "if MCA isn't God, no
one in the company knows it."

Yet Wasserman was also reviled because of his unfair advantage
over competitors. MCA was able to buy and sell talent—the only
agency able to do so—because of a deal Lew had engineered with
the Screen Actors Guild in 1952. At that time, film actors were
losing jobs to TV performers, and most studios were cutting production from fifty films a year to twenty-five or so. Wasserman had
promised SAG that his TV unit would create jobs for Hollywood
actors, and the union let his talent agency produce TV shows. "The
SAG deal became key to how MCA grew into such a monster firm,"
said GAC chief Henry Miller. From that point on, MCA hired its
own stable of writers, directors, and actors to work in Revue's TV
productions.

However, managing both the "buy" side of Revue and the "sell"
side of MCA created problems. While other Hollywood agents concentrated on "getting the best possible deal for our clients," Miller
explained, "MCA was focusing on its own production facilities."
Wasserman believed that his rivals were simply jealous. "We were
just too damn good, that's all," Dorskind explained. What MCA
executives refused to admit to its rivals was that MCA's sweetheart
union waiver allowed it to dominate both sides of the producer's
table. "MCA and Revue had a huge conflict of interest and we all
knew it," snapped Miller. "It was crooked."

Wasserman ignored the complaints. "Work hard," he told his
agents. "There are no shortcuts, and if there are, they don't last very
long." In between meetings and deals, he'd work quietly in his

office, reading through stacks of papers that his secretaries delivered. Sometimes the sunlight would stream through the venetian blinds and soften the forty-five-year-old's features. His nose resembled a raptor's beak—prominent, rounded, and hooked. He had a large, wide forehead and full, fleshy lips. His neck was thick as a meat-cutter's and his ham-size hands moved continuously.

Wasserman's wood-paneled office was furnished with eighteenth-century English antiques that were owned by Stein and arranged by Stein's wife, Doris. "A lot of the executives hated it," said Myrle Wages, a former MCA secretary. "They wanted to put their feet on the tables—and probably did, when no one was looking. But Mr. Wasserman loved it." He reveled in the luxury and used the elegant surroundings as a secret psychological weapon. "MCA's offices always had an air and atmosphere, which subconsciously influenced many a deal," said Karl Kramer, one of MCA's first hires. With its framed oils of parliamentary lords, the décor signified quiet, well-mannered wealth. Wasserman's motto was "Dress British, think Yiddish." He'd welcome visitors warmly, seat them in a straight-backed chair, and offer them whiskey from Waterford crystal. Then he'd negotiate a cruel, lopsided deal so smoothly that the other party would suspect nothing until it was too late. Studio chiefs braced themselves before meeting Wasserman. Nick Schenck, the president of MGM's parent company, once confessed: "I never see him after twelve noon. I'm too slow to take him on after that."

During his meetings with his agents, Wasserman took off the gloves. Secretaries used to buy cookies for these sessions, but "few men had the stomach for sweets when Lew was looming over them," Wages recalled. Wasserman assigned agents to monitor each of the seven studios. They were expected to keep MCA clients happy on movie sets, to check in with producers and learn which pictures were moving forward, and to drop by the front office to nose around. Every week he demanded full reports detailing all studios' projects, and if an agent didn't know more than Wasserman about a studio, he'd be replaced. "Lew would ask you what was happening at Twentieth Century Fox, but he'd know more about the studio that you were supposed to be on top of," said one agent. These briefings were so brutal and conniving, they were called "Fagin meetings," after the Charles Dickens thief who trained young thieves.

Wasserman would angrily throw sharp-pointed pencils at his men. He once compared his management style to that of a man who kicks his dog every day. "If one day you stop kicking the dog, it will wonder why you stopped loving it." So he kicked his men. Once, during a Fagin meeting, he zeroed in on agent Harry Friedman, who was sandwiched on a couch between two other men. Wasserman paced. "What did you do last night, Harry?" The man said he'd had dinner with his wife. "Where were you? I couldn't get hold of you." Friedman slouched lower on the couch while his companions inched away. "Lew yelled at the poor guy because one of his clients was in trouble that night, and Lew couldn't find him," said one man. As Wasserman continued screaming, Friedman sank lower until he hit the floor. "Then, Lew got down on his knees and in the guy's face and continued shouting at him," said the man. "It was awful."

Wasserman once ranted at an agent until he fainted. Then he stood over the man until he regained consciousness, and resumed his tirade. "Why don't you just quit now?" he bellowed. After these humiliating sessions, Wasserman would later call the victim into his office, put his arm around his shoulders, and offer him a drink or dinner. But this technique wore on even the best of men. Top agent Herman Citron developed an ulcer. Arthur Park collapsed and was forced to take a month's medical leave. Several men had nervous breakdowns, and some never returned. As one producer explained, "Many people died serving Lew Wasserman. This was war, and he was very demanding."

But Wasserman berated his men in order to make a point. "He had a temper, but it was always coming from some logical point of view," said Freddie Fields. One time, while Wasserman was expanding Revue Productions on Universal's lot, he walked into a meeting room and sat in the back. His men were matching MCA clients with Revue shows that needed talent. A TV producer wanted a certain star for his show and asked the star's agent, "Why can't your client be on my show?"

"Because he doesn't do well on that type of show. It's not his style." The producer pressed, and the agent argued until Wasserman stood up and marched to the front of the room, recalled agent Roy Gerber.

Wasserman asked the assembly. "Who knows what 'fiduciary' means?"

No one spoke.

Wasserman asked the star's agent if he knew the definition. He did not.

"You're fired," Wasserman said. The agent's face froze—but he left, said Gerber. "Lew could be very cold. But he didn't like that guy and used the incident as an excuse to get rid of him."

Wasserman recessed the meeting quickly. The agents rushed out to their desks and grabbed dictionaries to look up the word. But no one knew how to spell "fiduciary." Someone's secretary telephoned the Beverly Hills Library across the street and got the definition. "It meant a bond of trust," said veteran MCA agent Jim Murray. "Lew had given us a break to learn the word. What he was saying is that it wasn't our place to say who would do well on which TV show and who wouldn't.

"Our duty was to sell."

And that's what Wasserman told his men after reconvening the meeting. They needed to keep their agency clients working and their Revue productions staffed. "After that, we damn well knew what 'fiduciary' meant," said Gerber.

Wasserman may have believed he was making a valid point, but he was actually underscoring the built-in conflict that he cultivated within his talent agency/TV production firm. As he illustrated that day, a man couldn't serve two masters. Either MCA's agency or its production firm would gain the upper hand, but the two entities could not remain equal.

The incident had a second, unintended consequence: The fired agent now joined the growing list of Wasserman enemies. Whether it was a disgruntled ex-employee, as some believe, or one of MCA's rivals, as others claimed, someone in Hollywood began making a federal case—literally—out of MCA's rapacious growth. "There were at least three guys who were trying to get MCA," said a junior agent. One was William Morris chief Abe Lastfogel, who believed that MCA abused its power, said Bob Goldfarb, a Morris employee. "I'm sure Abe got the antitrust action going." Another critic was the late Ted Ashley, an agent and MCA rival. Then there was Herb Siegel of GAC. "He kept calling the government and asking, 'Why does MCA have permission to get into TV and we don't?' " said Gerber.

By yearend 1958, after news spread of MCA's purchase of Universal's property, the decibel level rose. "A lot of people were outraged," said Goldfarb. Wasserman was now dominating three sectors of show business: the talent side, the TV production side, and the studio realty arena. Federal investigators who had been trying for years to pry loose evidence of MCA's skulduggery were now deluged with telephone calls and tips. Offers to bear witness against MCA began to pile up, according to a prosecutor for the U.S. Department of Justice. Many of the complaints repeated the same allegations. As GAC chief Miller explained, "It was inevitable that MCA and Wasserman would someday be curbed."

THREE

At five o'clock—cocktail hour in Beverly Hills—a circle of witty Hollywood women headed toward a modest home on Sierra Drive, right below Sunset Boulevard. Young and glamorous, they were MCA agents' wives, MCA actresses, or MCA publicists. All were visiting Edie Wasserman, Lew's wife. Most weekdays, Edie hosted a late-afternoon happy hour for friends, said Jackie Gershwin, wife of MCA agent Jerry. "It was like clockwork. About seven or eight of us would meet at Edie's house for drinks.

"It was the only place where we could just let our hair down."

Edie was not simply married to the town's most powerful man; she was a force in her own right. At forty-three, she had more zest and energy than most of the twenty- and thirty-year-olds she protected. Respected and feared, she certainly had more experience than most other women in town. Her friends often sought—and took—her sage counsel. "Edie was not our diva exactly, but she was our reigning queen," said actress Janet Leigh, a regular at Edie's house. According to MCA agent Jay Kanter, Edie had more brains and savvy than did the typical Hollywood executive. "She knew what she was doing. People at MCA would go to her for advice. *I* would go to her for advice."

Petite and vivacious, Edie wore her short brown hair in a permanent wave, as was the fashion in the winter of 1958. She had an alabaster complexion, broad cheeks, and small, twinkling eyes, though she was not considered beautiful. But Edie knew how to dazzle. "She was always a peppy girl, full of vim and vigor," said Merle Jacobs, who had dated Edie when she was a sixteen-year-old in Ohio. "She could be a flirt."

While Lew spent his days commanding MCA Square—located ten blocks west—Edie held court in her colonial-style house, perched on the eastern edge of Beverly Hills, one block west of Hollywood. Tucked behind a white picket fence and skirted by a green lawn, the Wasserman house was a smaller version of the brick-and-stone mansion in which Edie had lived as a youngster in the leafy suburb of Cleveland Heights, Ohio. The beige walls and modest rooms of her California home invoked Norman Rockwell feelings in its bohemian guests, said Jackie Gershwin. "I loved that house. It was always so warm."

The interior decor was unassuming, as though Edie was determined *not* to let her lofty standing intimidate the greenest guild member or the newest MCA hire. The home featured a large walnut dining room table, a few deep-cushioned, flower-print sofas, and some kitschy paintings of saucer-eyed waifs. "She didn't have refined tastes, exactly," explained couturier Luis Estevez. But her political instincts were uncanny.

Most mornings, she'd tour the town's business circuit, arm in arm with an MCA consort. "She'd lunch with a studio wife or a rising star," said Leigh. Occasionally, Edie would reserve a table at The Bistro, where she'd conduct her affairs in a leather booth set against a red-papered wall. Or she'd spend an afternoon perched on a bar stool at the Cock 'n' Bull. With her charm and sexuality, she would extract the latest scuttlebutt and act as a go-between for her deal-maker husband. "Edie was a strong right hand for Lew and often brought him information," explained Leigh. "His work was her work." Her tidbit became his bargaining chip, and her handiwork was stitched inside dozens of MCA deals. She lobbied for a movie starring her dear friend Tony Curtis and his idol, Cary Grant, which grew into *Operation Petticoat* (1959), said Curtis. Though the granddaughter of two rabbis, Edie opposed any film that seemed "too Jewish," for fear of depicting Hollywood in an unflattering way to the rest of the country, said several agents. That's why Wasserman never turned Budd Schulberg's novel *What Makes Sammy Run?* into a film package—despite several overtures. To him, the tale of the Hollywood hustler Sammy Glick was "too negative." What few people realized is that Edie Wasserman protected and advanced not just the interests of her husband and MCA, she furthered her own agenda, too.

In the late afternoon, Edie usually hurried home to fill the ice bucket at her well-stocked bar. Come five o'clock, her "girls" would drop in on their way home, after spending the day shopping on Rodeo Drive or working on studio sets. Edie considered these women to be her loyal retinue, and she shielded and guided them. In return, they brought her gossip. "No one understood how important wives were in the MCA culture," said Herb Rosenthal, an MCA executive. But Edie did; she used them as MCA's secret agents.

The first one through Edie's door was often Jackie Gershwin. The young blonde had been inducted into the inner circle in 1955. At the time, her husband, Jerry Gershwin, was handling MCA stars Martin and Lewis, and the comedians appeared on *The Colgate Comedy Hour.* A girls' vocal group opened the show and Jackie stood out as one of The Skylarks' singers. Jerry fell in love with Jackie, and within the year, Edie was organizing their wedding and Lew was escorting the bride down the aisle.

Now Jackie was trying to master her new job. "Edie took me under her wing and taught me how to be an agent's wife, what with the long hours, cold dinners, and such," she explained.

Another member of Edie's court was Teme Brenner, a studio publicist who was married to MCA agent Herb. "We called him 'Pass-the-buck' Brenner," explained one MCA secretary. "Anything that was wrong at the office was never his fault." But his wife, Teme, was a go-getter. She collected leads from city newsrooms and movie sets and shared them with Edie. At night, she and Edie would dress to the nines and hit the nightclubs—often accompanied by young men. Edie and Teme loved to dance, and between the two of them, they wined, dined, and waltzed some twenty actors up to MCA's door.

Janet Leigh had been befriended by Edie after signing with MCA in 1946. "I was so unhappy with my roles that Edie must have seen that," said Leigh. Edie sat beside her one day during a tennis match, and the struggling starlet poured her heart out. Later, Edie repeated the conversation to Lew and urged him to talk to the actress. Lew not only telephoned Leigh, he made sure she started getting bigger and better roles. "That was very impressive to me," said Leigh. Edie had been crucial in launching the actress's career, and in return, Leigh pledged her undying loyalty.

Sometimes Jeanne Martin joined the klatches. Her husband, Dean Martin, was one of MCA's biggest clients and Lew's latest cinematic triumph. Martin had been frustrated in his attempt to land the serious movie roles he wanted so desperately. Lew had stepped in on his behalf. He had already signed his clients Marlon Brando and Montgomery Clift to a Twentieth Century Fox film, *The Young Lions*, that included Fox contract player Tony Randall in a supporting role. Days before the $4 million film started shooting, Wasserman warned the studio that Brando and Clift wanted Dean Martin—not Randall—in the picture. Rather than lose the two stars, Fox dropped its own actor and brought in Martin. By late 1958, the crooner was landing rave reviews for his first dramatic performance, and Revue was producing *The Dean Martin Show*. Meanwhile, Jeannie was raising the couple's three children in addition to four others from Martin's first marriage.

Then there was Polly Bergen, hostess of one of MCA's most popular TV series that year, *The Polly Bergen Show*. It was earning MCA top dollar in syndication fees and building the actress into a national brand name. "It was verboten for MCA agents to date their clients," said Jackie Gershwin. But Bergen had been secretly dating her agent, Freddie Fields. Edie frowned on the forbidden liaison, but Lew decided to spare Fields, whom he considered invaluable. The actress and agent married quickly, and Bergen became even more valuable to MCA—as an agent's wife, star actress, and TV performer.

Rounding out the circle was Judy Balaban Kanter, a diminutive redhead whose husband, Jay, was another top MCA agent and Lew confidant. More than any other lady in Edie's court, Balaban Kanter was Hollywood royalty. Her father was Barney Balaban, an Eastern European immigrant who in 1915 had started a chain of ornate theater palaces. Now he was chief of Paramount Studios and one of

MCA's regular buyers of film talent. Balaban Kanter had been raised in Hollywood and knew all of its social rites and unwritten codes. "You don't repeat family conversations," she recited. "You make people feel comfortable. And you always listen." She was Grace Kelly's best friend and had been a bridesmaid at Kelly's storybook wedding to Prince Rainier.

Most afternoons, Balaban Kanter would breeze into Edie's house, occasionally with her three-year-old in tow. Once, Edie asked the little girl if she wanted a glass of ginger ale.

"No thanks, Aunt Edie. That stuff goes right through me."

Edie spent hours chatting with members of her brood and pouring them vodka tonics. While they nibbled on crackers and cheese, Edie lit their cigarettes and complimented them on their new lacquered hairstyles. "Basically, show business is an unhappy business with a lot of unhappy people," said Jim Murray. "Everybody kisses everybody, but underneath, it's a desperate way to live." Edie's friends were performers whose worth was measured by ratings and box-office numbers. Her husband collected at least 10 percent from these performers' salaries—which over the years amounted to millions of dollars. His TV subsidiary charged 30 percent or more for producing their TV shows and network specials. Publicly, Edie's friends were marquee names and *Silver Screen* cover girls; privately, they were anxious and vulnerable. Some suffered from low self-esteem that had been tweaked neurotically by years of too much fickle adulation, said Merrill Park, wife of MCA agent Arthur Park. "But Edie knew how to handle such people." She stroked their egos, assuaged their fears, and clucked over them as their own mothers never had.

Amid rings of cigarette smoke and the scent of Chanel No. 5, the women confided in one another. "I realized I could say anything," said Leigh. Often, Edie's entourage dressed in the "same mandatory uniform," said Balaban Kanter. They wore tight-crotch slacks bought from Jax's, bright-colored crop tops, and the same style of high heel. "We favored the 'low vamp' look," she explained.

"We had our babies delivered by the same gynecologist, Dr. Kron," said Gershwin. The Jewish mothers checked in at Cedars-Sinai near Beverly Hills, while the Catholics and Protestants booked rooms at St. John's Hospital in Santa Monica. When Leigh was pregnant with her second child, she had "a really rough time." First, she suffered a kidney infection, which placed the baby in danger. Then Leigh's father-in-law (Tony Curtis's dad) died. When their baby was expected to be born any minute, they had only one car, which Curtis took to the set. Edie offered to drive Leigh to the hospital the minute she felt labor pains, then made alternate arrangements in case Edie was absent. "Edie made sure there was a second car in the driveway *and a driver,* in case I started labor," said Leigh. Finally, Jamie Lee Curtis was born.

After an MCA wife or client delivered a baby, she'd receive bouquets of flowers and catered dinners from Chasen's, served bedside by a tuxedoed waiter—with congratulations from Edie and Lew. "They were godparents to all of our children," said Gershwin. Edie and Lew Wasserman gave every one of the MCA babies a cash gift or, later, company stock. The gifts were placed in a trust so the children couldn't touch them until they turned eighteen. "You have no idea how valuable that was for my Gina, later, after all the troubles began," said Gershwin.

At the time, no one wanted to believe that the catered dinners, the special treatment, and the long afternoons on Sierra Drive would ever end. Yet, some afternoons, the women sensed trouble at the edge of their circle. By the second round of drinks, one of the girls would let something slip. "I know that Janet talked to Edie a lot," said Tony Curtis. He and his wife were featured in movie fanzines as the "Ideal Hollywood Couple," and, for a time, they actually were. Yet, after the second baby, Leigh confessed to Edie that life at home was rocky. The babies, the movie schedules, and publicity shots were becoming too difficult to juggle.

It became Edie's job—her obsession, really—to keep her group together. Gershwin recalled the time when Edie threw the "most glamorous baby shower imaginable" for two MCA "preggo" clients: Janet Leigh and Rosemary Clooney, who was married to MCA client Jose Ferrer. It was not a typical, girls-only shower, but a full-blown coed party, with music, dancing, and catered food arrayed around an enormous ice sculpture of a stork. "Edie wasn't that close with Rose," said Balaban Kanter. But she assumed the responsibility of keeping MCA's pool of rich talent stable, if not happy.

MCA syndicated *The Rosemary Clooney Show*, which Lew and his men filmed at Revue Studios. Even though Ferrer openly cheated on his wife, TV appearances had to be maintained. MCA agents made sure that Clooney's show opened with the estranged couple singing a duet of "Love and Marriage," as though everything was ducky. Clooney's series of thirty-nine half-hour black-and-white shows generated an estimated $2.5 million in fees and commissions—*before* MCA peddled the reruns for millions of dollars.

In 1958 Clooney starred in a Ford television special that was produced, packaged, and sold by MCA. *Look* magazine gave it the annual Best Musical Show Award. She also starred in the *Lux Show*, a high-caliber variety show with a rich national sponsor (Colgate Palmolive's Lux Soap, Rinso Blue) and a slate of MCA clients, including Nelson Eddy and Carol Channing. The $4.5 million series was a smash, leaving Revue with an estimated $1 million cut—not including rerun income.

Clooney's private life, however, was deteriorating. She had just delivered her fourth baby in three and a half years—in between personal appearances and a grueling TV schedule. "I couldn't take it," she said. She grew so miserable she started using sleeping pills. Edie and the girls whispered about her bizarre behavior, but they left her alone. As Balaban Kanter said: "Rose was so erratic in those days, we never knew what was the matter with her."

The happy hours, late nights, and early-morning feedings were taking a toll; the business was changing, and the studios were sputtering, too. But Edie urged her friends to keep it up. Maintain those appearances, please your husbands, and flash those gorgeous smiles. By the end of the 1950s, some of Edie's girls were breaking their manicured nails trying to nail down the loose ends of their lives. With the party pace and work hours, "things became socio-manic," said Balaban Kanter. The women soldiered on—but they were slowly losing control.

FOUR

AS THE 1958 YULETIDE SEASON BEGAN, Edie and Lew Wasserman traveled to New York, where Manhattan's streets were brighter than ever. Park Avenue at 52nd Street glowed from the light of the new bronze Seagram Building which, was sheathed with 12,000 Christmas lights, and Edie had to see it. Commissioned by Edgar Bronfman, Sr., and designed by architect Mies van der Rohe, the structure resembled a giant bar of gold bullion. Edie reveled in the sight. "She loved New York, and Edie traveled with Lew whenever she could," said Jackie Gershwin. The Wassermans usually stayed at the exclusive Sherry-Netherland Hotel. The swank Fifth Avenue hostelry overlooked the southern edge of Central Park, just three blocks north of MCA's office. Edie made sure that their eighteenth-floor suite was higher than the rooms of other MCA officers, many of whom were in also in town that week.

Edie and Lew's visit was partly social—Jules and Doris Stein were about to marry off their eldest daughter. With MCA's TV interests about to explode into a full-blown scandal, the trip was also business. That week, Lew visited MCA's stately offices at 57th Street and Madison. Stein had bought the building and distinguished it proudly with a sculpture that depicted MCA's sprawling empire in the Western Hemisphere. Lew rode the elevator to the top, where MCA's mahogany-and-brass suites occupied the eighteenth and nineteenth floors.

The scandal that Wasserman had to contain was all over the *New York Post* and the *New York Times,* which were having a field day with the so-called "fixed game shows." The papers had printed allegations about TV's two biggest hits: *The $64,000 Question,* where MCA had placed several of its star clients; and *Twenty One,* produced by MCA mega-clients Jack Barry and Dan Enright. Barry/Enright Productions was the most prolific creators of game-show fare during the 1950s, and MCA earned millions of dollars representing them and their product. The producers had created *Tic Tac Dough, High-Low,* and the misogynists' favorite—*Do You Trust Your Wife?*—hosted by MCA client Edgar Bergen. The game shows were easy to execute and scored high in the ratings. By 1957, MCA was packaging or producing one-third of the twenty-two quiz shows on network TV.

However, that fall, a New York grand jury had started to investigate allegations of fraud and "fixes" in quiz shows. New York prosecutors had already contacted MCA's office, demanding documents and depositions. So, in December, Wasserman paid a visit to David Werblin, head of MCA's New York office.

Unlike Wasserman, Werblin was a college graduate and a former football player from Rutgers University. Everyone called him Sonny, as in money, and he had worked at MCA his entire career, beginning in 1932, when MCA rented two rooms and barely made payroll. Now the agency owned an entire building, and Sonny barked at his men to ring up fat expense accounts. "He was the most social of the top guys in the company," said Daniel Welkes, who worked for Werblin. "All the Madison Avenue guys were his friends." Short, balding, and bullish, Werblin regularly met his network and advertising buddies at the Stork Club or some other high-class eatery. "Wasserman wasn't social like that," said Welkes. "Sonny was the man."

Werblin had been a shoo-in for president of MCA until he suffered a heart attack at age twenty-eight. He took a medical leave in
1938. During that year, a new hire, Wasserman, proved to be "the
biggest, toughest Jew" in the business, Stein later claimed. When
Werblin returned to work, he was shocked to learn that Wasserman
was now his peer, an executive vice president, in charge of the fledgling West Coast office. Seven years later, in 1946, Werblin was
stunned again when Wasserman leapfrogged over him to become
chief of MCA. "Sonny always felt that he had been pushed back by
Wasserman," said Welkes. Added Freddie Fields: "The only executive who had any visible resentment of Lew was Sonny."

Upon becoming president, Wasserman visited all of MCA's
offices. In New York, the cocky thirty-three-year-old breezed past
MCA's receptionist on his way in to see the thirty-six-year-old
Werblin. "Wait a minute sir! You can't go in there," the receptionist
objected. The office fell silent as people eyed the newcomer, said
Charlton Heston, then a fledgling actor in New York. "Lew looked
about nineteen, with his black hair brushed back and his suit well-
pressed." Wasserman froze, eyed the stern receptionist, and hissed
under his breath: "I'm head of this company." Then he strode into
Werblin's lair.

"Someone whispered, 'That's the president,' and we could not
believe it," said Jim Murray. "The guy had a lisp and walked like a
duck." That day in 1946, Wasserman laid down his law in Werblin's
office. No more "bold look," with MCA agents wearing multicol-
ored striped shirts and jackets with wide lapels; the dress code was
black suits and white shirts from now on. "He straightened us out
and was gone in about twenty minutes," said Murray.

Werblin and Wasserman butted heads in those early years. But
Wasserman needed Werblin, whose excellent New York connections
stretched back to MCA's big-band radio shows from the 1930s.
Manhattan was the nation's broadcast center and home to corporate
merchants like American Tobacco, Coca-Cola, and Alcoa. They paid

handsomely to advertise on MCA's radio shows and, later, on Revue's TV productions. New York was also home to Madison Avenue advertising agencies and the network chiefs at NBC, CBS, and ABC, which aired Revue-produced and MCA-packaged shows. Sonny knew them all. He and his agents brokered the million-dollar deals between the corporate sponsors, the advertisers who financed the shows, and the network guys who aired them.

"Sonny was pushing and go getting all the time. He wouldn't take no for an answer," said Welkes. "He never quite dictated, but he held big sway over the networks and the agencies." Werblin and Wasserman grew to depend on each other, said Fields. "Sonny had a charming ego and eventually became very supportive of Lew."

After Wasserman formed Revue Productions, he named Werblin head of Revue's parent, MCA-TV. Now, seven years later, in 1958, Werblin's operation was contributing $50 million to the coffers. A full-blown scandal could threaten all of MCA's TV operations, and "Lew and Sonny knew that," said Albert Freedman, a producer at Barry/Enright. He, Werblin, and Fred Stettner, another Barry/Enright producer, had already been contacted by investigating attorneys. That December, Wasserman and Werblin met behind closed doors to figure out a way to limit the damage.

On Friday afternoon, December 5, 1958, Lew and Edie pulled up in front of St. Patrick's Cathedral in New York. Edie and the MCA women thought it odd that a Jewish duchess such as Jean Babette Stein would marry outside a synagogue. But the groom, William J. vanden Heuvel, was a practicing Catholic and Cornell University alumnus, and the wedding was the social event of the year. The fact that it took place 3,000 miles away from Hollywood simply added to its cachet: "I hope that I'll be invited," Hollywood columnist Louella O. Parsons wrote coyly. And she was, along with several hundred society mavens and corporate captains.

Wasserman had joked that this was the biggest production since

MGM's 1952 epic, *Quo Vadis*—the Roman Empire extravaganza packaged by MCA. The main difference was that security for Stein's production was tighter; Lew had taken pains to make sure that few guests would notice the plainclothesmen lurking in the shadows. Edie had offered help, too, but Doris Stein was running this show. Jules Stein escorted the bride down the aisle. She wore an empire gown of French white satin, and her mother had helped select the veil of heirloom lace. Jean Stein had been educated at the best private schools—from Switzerland to the Sorbonne—and it showed. Doris was delighted that her daughter, at age twenty-four, was finally marrying a blue-blooded suitor—and an Ivy League graduate, to boot. To Jean's girlfriends, the ceremony in the cathedral's side altar in the Lady Chapel was dreamy, if forbidden. "I remember us girls thought the priest [Father Vincent Donovan] was so cute," said Jean's cousin Patsy Miller. "I couldn't take my eyes off him."

Later, the wedding party took on the St. Regis Roof—the same place where the bride had made her debut at a 1951 dinner dance. "It was odd for a Jewish girl to have a debutante ball, but Jean did," said Judy Balaban Kanter. "Doris didn't want many people from MCA at her parties." She denigrated her husband's business and "thought so many of his agents were loud and crass," according to one woman. "She preferred the blue-chip crowd," added Eleanor Phillips, former editor of *Vogue*. And that's who she invited to her daughter's reception: socialite Babe Paley and her husband, William Paley, chairman of CBS; Vincent Astor and his wife, Brooke; former New York Governor W. Averell Harriman; and powerful Senator Jacob Javits, with his young wife, Marion.

"[The wedding] was one of the most prestigious invitations that year," gushed the *Hollywood Reporter*. Champagne and caviar fed not just business and social movers but politicians, diplomats, and a few spies. Stein's new son-in-law was an U.S. Air Force captain who had served as an assistant to General William "Wild Bill" Donovan, director of the Office of Strategic Services—the espionage unit that became the Central Intelligence Agency (CIA). The groom's close friend and best man was Angier Biddle Duke, a descendant of the founders of Duke University and the Wall Street house of Drexel Harriman Ripley. One of the groom's ushers was Robert S. Salzmann, who would later become associate director of the Office of National Drug Control Policy. There were former ambassadors, men who would later advise leaders in Central America and the Middle East. Stein's new son-in-law would soon join the prestigious law firm of Javits, Moore and Trubin in New York, and Jules welcomed the new connection.

The global powers and brokers partied and drank that evening, high atop the landmark hotel overlooking Fifth Avenue. Doris and Jules circulated among their guests, but neither of them could escape the shadow of the quiz-show scandal. Everyone was talking about it. CBS chief Frank Stanton would later claim, rather disingenuously, that he didn't know a thing about his networks' fixed game show—CBS aired *The $64,000 Question* —until that fall, when he heard gossip about program irregularities. But that year's highest-rated game show of them all had been on NBC: *Twenty-One,* produced by MCA's clients. The shows were intellectual parlor games for the public and gold mines for the corporate sponsors and talent agencies—not exactly criminal operations. "No one imagined that anything would come from the allegations," said Fred Stettner.

But the New York District Attorney had impaneled a grand jury to investigate the shows, and executives at MCA, NBC, CBS, and other New York media firms had been contacted. That fall, CBS had canceled its show, as had NBC. The district attorney had just indicted Al Freedman, former MCA client and a writer/producer of *Twenty-One.* The wedding guests were buzzing about what the grand jury would learn in the coming months from its 150 witnesses. The real $64,000 question: Who else would be indicted?

Quiz shows had been a staple on radio since the 1930s, but they didn't light up TV until 1955, with the debut of *The $64,000 Question.* That show became CBS's top-rated program and doubled the sales of its sponsor, Revlon. After that hit, every consumer company clamored to sponsor a game show, and few producers were better at developing them than Jack Barry and Dan Enright. Barry was a dark-haired, photogenic show host; Enright was the mild-tempered business manager. Barry/Enright Productions employed a large staff on the fourteenth floor of a building at 667 Madison Avenue, four blocks north of their agents at MCA.

"We were a bustling place, with people working on several different shows," said Freedman. Soft-spoken and courtly, Freedman had an easygoing manner that put contestants at ease. "At one point, I was caught at both ends of the fad, working on *Juvenile Jury* and *Life Begins at Eighty,*" he explained. MCA sold most of these shows, primarily to NBC. They were inexpensive, because they used nonprofessional actors, had no costumes, and used only one set. Yet, they entailed more work because producers had to coach the contestants to speak clearly, act naturally, and watch for stage cues. "All radio and TV quiz shows had to exert some controls on their contestants," said Freedman. "Otherwise, the shows would flop."

As commercial TV grew more lucrative, the controls became tighter. Game show producers chose which contestant should win and which on-air question he or she would answer. Since neither the Federal Communications Commission (FCC), which governed the airwaves, nor New York's criminal code outlawed such practices, they became de rigueur.

When CBS's show topped the ratings, the perennial second-place network NBC wanted a hit game show, too. At the time, NBC chief Robert Sarnoff was acting as programming chief. He asked his old MCA friend Sonny Werblin to help him devise a hit. Werblin turned to his impresarios—Barry and Enright—and called them to his office to discuss NBC's request. MCA agent Herb Rosenthal had already found a corporate sponsor, Pharmaceuticals Inc., the parent company of Geritol. That afternoon, Barry, Enright, and producer Fred Stettner gathered in Werblin's office and listened as their agents laid out the proposal. The producers said they'd return later with a plan.

They devised a show based on the card game twenty-one, or blackjack, only with higher stakes. Two contestants would sit in separate isolation booths and take turns choosing categories of questions. A correct answer earned a certain number of points; a wrong one subtracted points. The first player to get twenty-one points would win—unless there was a tie. Most important, the winner could supposedly collect an unlimited jackpot—though, in fact, Geritol had capped the winnings.

"There was lots of support and contact with our agents during this time," said Freedman. The program was fine-tuned and aired on September 15, 1956. *Twenty-One* sputtered immediately. "After the third or fourth week, we had a couple of people who missed almost every question," Barry later said. "Ratings were so low, it was painful," said Freedman.

The president of Pharmaceuticals, Matty Rosenhaus, was so upset he complained to Barry about his show, said Freedman. Werblin rang in, too. "MCA had sold the show to NBC, and they weren't happy at all," added Stettner, who happened to be Enright's brother-in-law. The network, the sponsor, and the agents all warned that the show was about to be canceled.

In October 1956, Werblin summoned Barry, Enright, and Stettner to another meeting. Werblin and Rosenthal instructed the producers how to stage their show professionally. "This is television, fellows," Werblin said. "People have to look good and be all-American types." The program needed suspense and sympathetic characters for whom the audience could root. The agents went down their list, said Stettner. "But most important," Freedman added, "they told us there had to be winners and tie games where the contestants could vie against each other for more than one program." Before the producers left, Werblin told them: "You guys have to make this work."

The producers started drilling contestants, rather than coaching them. They taught them how to pause before answering, how to miss a question, how to look puzzled and act stumped. If a guest answered correctly, he was to look into the camera. If he won, he should flash a big smile. Some contestants were given answers ahead of time, a ruse that was perfectly legal, though deceptive.

After the next well-orchestrated broadcast of *Twenty-One*, Barry and Enright received congratulatory calls from their agents, the sponsor, and the network. The men not only liked the show, they offered thinly veiled advice. "When they called us, we all knew that we'd better act on their comments," said Freedman. "We all took orders from the people at the top."

Twenty-One attracted higher ratings, and not simply because of improved performances. The show gave away more money than any other program—as much as $220,000, or $1.4 million in today's dollars. It featured sharply drawn characters, such as Herb Stempel, a working-class graduate of New York's City College. He became the show's first big money winner, and quizmaster Barry built suspense by exhorting viewers to watch the genius. Would the poor boy triumph? Soon the rumpled Stempel was being stopped in the streets by admiring strangers. He didn't hail from Brooklyn, as Barry claimed, and he could have worn a new suit if Enright had allowed it. But Stempel played his role well.

In November, ratings slipped, and everyone agreed that the show had to change again. By then, Freedman had found an "all-American type," a Waspish face to play opposite the Jewish character. Charles Van Doren was the opposite of Stempel, a handsome English professor at Columbia University, son of a Pulitzer Prize–winning poet. The visage of the modest, fair-haired Van Doren catapulted *Twenty-One* above the schlockyard of TV game shows and turned the quiz format into profound moral theater. "People loved Charlie," said Stettner, and the show's ratings soared.

One day, Enright told Stempel that he'd have to lose the next round against Van Doren. Stempel was angry but agreed reluctantly. On December 5, 1956, Stempel and Van Doren played their last match—a real nail-biter. As Stempel sweated, Van Doren mastered his questions gracefully until the last round, when finally Stempel missed a question deliberately. Wasserman watched the show, along with 32 percent of TV viewers that night. The episode pushed NBC's *Twenty-One* neck-and-neck in the ratings with CBS's *$64,000 Question*.

The next year, 1957, was a banner one for *Twenty-One* and its sponsor. Sales of Geritol zoomed 50 percent to nearly $13 million— half of its parent company's total revenue. The producers had a hit. "No one really thought anything was wrong," said Freedman. "The guys who were putting up the money for the contestants [Geritol] were thrilled; the guys who were selling the show [MCA] were thrilled; the guys at NBC who sold [commercial] time before and after the show were thrilled." The show became so valuable that MCA "always had a guy present on the set," said Stettner.

When the courtly Van Doren lost his last match on March 11, 1957, Wasserman, Werblin, and their men were elated. The show scored a 51 percent rating—far more than the 39 percent claimed by the season's top program, *I Love Lucy*. By then, MCA and their producer clients were charging NBC and the sponsor $3.5 million in annual production costs for *Twenty-One*. Somehow, the once-cheap show had developed exorbitant fees. MCA collected at least $350,000 in commissions, another meaty sum. "NBC thought they could save money by bringing [the show] under their control," explained Stettner. In early 1957, Sarnoff and his new programming chief, Robert Kintner, offered to buy Barry/Enright Productions. The NBC executives and their lawyers began negotiating a deal with Barry, Enright, Werblin, Rosenthal, and their attorneys.

The only glitch was Stempel. He had gambled away thousands of dollars in the past year. When he was a contestant, he'd been able to borrow advances against his *Twenty-One* winnings. But now he'd fallen deeper into debt. "He was so bitter and mad about getting bumped off the show that he threatened to blow the whistle on us," said Stettner. In March 1957—a few weeks after MCA started negotiating with NBC—Stempel and a hoodlum friend barged into Enright's office. They told the producer that if he didn't pay Stempel $50,000, the former game-show contestant would sell his tale about the fix at *Twenty-One*. Enright told Stempel he'd discuss it with Barry. Stempel left, and Enright sought advice.

He visited Werblin to relay Stempel's blackmail attempt. An oft-repeated tale about this visit paints Enright confessing to Werblin *for the first time* that the producers had scripted *Twenty-One*. But Stettner, Freedman, and Howard Felsher, another B/E producer, claim that Werblin and MCA executives had helped instigate the fix. "They all knew the shows were rigged, including Wasserman," said Felsher. Wasserman called Werblin regularly for progress reports on MCA's projects—and *Twenty-One* was its most lucrative prize. Lew knew what was going on with the show.

That day, Enright filled Werblin in about Stempel's extortion attempt, said Stettner. "Dan told him that Stempel was trying to blackmail them and might go to the press." But Werblin wasn't concerned about a has-been contestant with credibility problems. Werblin asked Enright: "Have I ever asked you if the show was rigged?" No, said Enright.

"Do you know why we haven't asked? Because we don't want to know!"

Although it was not illegal to "throw" a TV game, Werblin knew that if viewers learned the truth, they'd stop watching. NBC would yank the show, and MCA would lose some $350,000 in commissions. Worse, the multimillion-dollar sale of Barry/Enright Productions that Werblin was negotiating would wither, too. Werblin and Barry agreed that if Stempel went public, they'd simply deny his accusations. "Besides, this was show biz," said Stettner. Everyone knows the magician doesn't really saw the lady in half, right?

A few days later, when Stempel returned to Enright's office to discuss his payoff, the producers were ready to entrap him. Stettner had hidden a tape recorder in Enright's office. But then Stempel backed down. With the tape running, he said he regretted his blackmail attempt. He signed a declaration stating that he had never been given any questions or answers for *Twenty-One*. For the time being, Wasserman, Werblin, and their clients had averted a crisis.

On May 2, 1957, with *Twenty-One* flying high, NBC and MCA finally signed the agreement that transferred Barry/Enright—and all of its game shows—to the network. The sale price was $2.222 million. "That was huge money in those days," added Stettner. The sales contract ran one hundred pages and covered every detail—except whether the contestants had been coached. "No one had ever thought of bringing up the issue," said Howard Felsher, who produced Barry/Enright shows. MCA received at least $222,000 in the sale. "Plus, it received 10 percent of whatever NBC got for the show, as long as it aired," said Stettner. "MCA's entire goal was to keep us on the air and continue collecting those commissions," added Felsher. For another few TV seasons, the money piled up. MCA's commissions from *Twenty-One* continued for eighteen months or so, until the fall of 1958. By then, the show's run had ended, upstaged by the news of the grand jury and the front-page photographs of the district attorney and his subpoenas.

In December 1958, Barry and Enright were among those who had talked with the district attorney, denying any knowledge of "fixes." Al Freedman had been fired and indicted for perjury. Felsher and Stettner had been summoned, as had dozens of contestants—including a very angry Herbie Stempel.

Few of the Stein family's wedding guests knew about all of this—perhaps only the network executives, Wasserman, and some attorneys. But that didn't stop the rooftop crowd at the St. Regis from making wagers and predictions. That evening, Edie and Lew heard the murmurs. Meanwhile, Wasserman attended to some select MCA clients like Grace Kelly and her husband, Prince Rainier of Monaco. MCA actress Ethel Merman sang, and after supper Guy Lombardo trotted over from the Roosevelt Hotel, where Stein had signed him to a twenty-year contract. "It was a sentimental, sweet moment," when he struck up his dance tunes, said one guest.

But as the party wore on, Edie felt more like kitchen help than a guest. "Mrs. Stein was a real snob," said an MCA former secretary. "She was full of airs. And Edie would never put on airs." Doris let it be known that she and Edie "weren't really in the same class," said Eleanor Phillips. "The Wassermans worked for the Steins, my dear, so it was a different circle." Sometime during the party, Doris snubbed Edie for the umpteenth time, although no one seemed to recall the mortifying details. "I saw Edie later, and she was fuming about Doris's high-and-mighty ways," said one of Edie's friends.

Around midnight, the reception broke up, and the tipsy crowd moved to the city's nightspots. Some remarked on the contretemps between Edie and Doris, but the meatiest gossip by far centered on the quiz shows. Wasserman, Werblin, Stein, and their agency were now under increased scrutiny on two fronts. As some guests undoubtedly knew, the U.S. Justice Department's Antitrust Division had acquired information detailing the alleged monopolistic practices of a handful of companies—including the networks and MCA—that had put several TV producers out of business. And now there was the grand jury. As Freedman said: "None of us imagined this would become so huge."

Wasserman was in double jeopardy.

FIVE

After Wasserman returned to the West Coast, he redoubled his efforts to build up his TV business. The year 1959 would inaugurate several stunning achievements for him, but Edie decided he needed a break from work. One afternoon, she told her husband she was inviting some friends over for an impromptu dinner—nothing fancy. The change of pace would do him good. Edie called a handful of friends—including her protégée, Judy Balaban Kanter.

Balaban Kanter was weary and didn't want to leave the house. "I hadn't done my hair, and I looked a mess," she said. But Edie pleaded with her. "Come on. Who cares how you look? You ought to come over."

Balaban Kanter gave in. She dispensed with her usual curl-comb-and-spray routine, tied a scarf around her head, and walked out the door. Minutes later, she was sitting at the Wasserman bar. The younger woman wore slacks and an ordinary blouse and looked more disheveled than Edie had ever seen her. "Edie took one look at me and started in. She looked me right in the eye and wagged that rigid, red-nailed finger right in my face."

"Judy, you look awful," she said. "You should never, *ever* leave the house with your hair looking like that."

Balaban Kanter was stunned. "I couldn't even say anything." She got up, walked out the door, and drove off, hurt and angry.

On her way home, Balaban Kanter felt lower than dirt. But when she pulled into her own driveway, she was surprised to see Lew, leaning against the side of the house, waiting for her. Kanter got out of the car and walked up to him. "Come back, Judy," he said softly. "Edie didn't mean it. She feels awful about what she said to you."

The young woman wavered. Lew put his hand on her shoulder. "C'mon, Judy Bird. Let's go back." So she did.

Wasserman had a soft spot for Balaban Kanter, who was like family. Indeed, MCA had a long and storied connection with her father, Barney Balaban, chief of Paramount Studios and one of MCA's biggest clients. The connection between MCA and Paramount stretched back to 1926 Chicago, when Jules Stein was a fledgling band agent and Balaban a wealthy theater owner. Stein rented offices in Balaban's Oriental Theater, which was part of a regional theater chain Balaban had just sold to Paramount Studios. The Chicago building became MCA's "real spiritual home, if I can use such a word," said one old-time agent. When Stein opened his New York office two years later, he rented space in Paramount's Tin Pan Alley building. Stein and Balaban grew even closer after the 1929 stock-market crash. Paramount fell into bankruptcy, Balaban became head of the reorganized company in 1936, and Stein promptly bought 20,000 shares of its stock, paying $11 a share. To avoid brokerage commissions on this purchase, Stein also bought a seat on the New York Stock Exchange and soon owned shares in most of the studio companies.

When Wasserman arrived in Hollywood in 1939, he knew little about the business. But Uncle Barney taught great lessons. Paramount, like all the studios, employed actors, writers, and directors full-time. It made several pictures a week, and showed them in theaters it owned across the country. From creation and assembly to exhibition, studios dominated the movie pipeline. By the mid-1940s, Paramount was churning out about 400 films a year just to satisfy its gluttonous theater chain.

Balaban and the moguls booked their best films through their own theaters, throwing leftovers to the few independent exhibitors. Wasserman knew that they sold the small theaters "bundles" of good and bad films. They demanded that the independents buy the bundles sight unseen—a practice called "blind booking." They also sold them in yearlong packages—"block booking"—and set minimum admission prices so independents couldn't undercut their chains. By the time Lew came to Hollywood, the government had filed an antitrust suit against the Big Five—Paramount, Warner Brothers, RKO, MGM, and Twentieth Century Fox—which became known as the Paramount case. Wasserman closely followed its twenty-year odyssey through the courts.

The moguls fought the suit, but eventually the Supreme Court outlawed bundling, blind booking, and block booking. In 1948 it forced the studios to shed their theaters, although full divestiture would take a decade. Nevertheless, the cataclysmic decision strangled the studio's feudal system. Without a guaranteed audience inside their theaters, they had to compete for box-office receipts. Income plummeted. Almost overnight, the moguls freed their stables of contract players and unshackled hundreds of actors, directors, and writers. Independent talent now needed agents to negotiate per-picture salaries, and MCA agents were standing by. "Lew Wasserman would never have landed in his position if the Paramount decision hadn't come down," said studio historian Douglas Gomery. Suddenly Lew and his men were calling the shots, not the studio chiefs.

The Paramount decision elevated Wasserman in another way. Before the court's ruling, many studios had already applied for FCC licenses to own and operate TV stations. Paramount Pictures had on its lot one of Los Angeles' first TV stations—KTLA. But the FCC could refuse a license to any firm that had been convicted of a crime, and since studios had already been guilty of monopoly, they weren't about to ask for permission. As for TV production, Paramount's Balaban wasn't sure where that road would lead. "My father was scared to death the government would come after him if he got too deep into TV," said Balaban Kanter.

Wasserman, however, jumped into the void. Right after the high court's decision in 1948, Wasserman moved ahead with MCA's first TV show. In March 1949, he arranged a TV simulcast of NBC's radio show, *Your Hit Parade,* an MCA package of vocalists. In September, Revue produced the half-hour show *Starring Boris Karloff.* Revue produced more shows in 1950, including the episodic *Stars Over Hollywood.* Then it landed a huge contract from Coca-Cola for a year's package of half-hour children's western shows, which became *The Adventures of Kit Carson.* Wasserman scrambled to fill that order, borrowing money from the Teamsters to ramp up production and cajoling underemployed actors and union members. The agent started building MCA's Revue into a purveyor of unremarkable low-budget TV shows. Wasserman's shop was not known for the sort of luminous, heartwarming films that Paramount had made during its heyday as The Continental Studio. But maybe Lew could buy its old films and thereby possess a piece of their wit and sophistication.

In 1958 Jules Stein was the second largest shareholder at Paramount, with voting power and privileges. His stake had grown tenfold since 1936 and was now worth $2.2 million. Lew coveted Paramount's film library—gems like Preston Sturges's *The Lady Eve* and Billy Wilder's *The Major and the Minor.* "He wanted more product to sell to independent TV stations and overseas TV," said Berle Adams. Wasserman had hired the wiry, curly-haired man in 1950 to market Revue's TV shows. Adams had plugged songs and built Mercury Records. Now he hustled to build Revue's syndication business.

Those metal canisters of old celluloid were hot commodities. TV networks and stations viewed them as inexpensive product to fill non-prime-time viewing hours, especially in early-morning and late-night slots. Other studios opened their vaults for sale: In January 1956, Columbia Pictures allowed its subsidiary, Screen Gems, to rent feature films to TV stations for an instant $5 million. That March, Warner Brothers sold its films to Associated Artists syndicate for $21 million. In August, MGM sold its pre-1948 films for an amazing $34 million to CBS, which began regularly showing one of the most beloved movies of all time—*The Wizard of Oz* (1939).

But Paramount had so far held on to its film legacy. "Paramount was one of the last untouched vintage libraries in town," said Adams, and Balaban wanted top dollar for it. "But Barney was running out of money, and Lew knew it."

In late 1957, Wasserman and Stein learned that the National

Telefilms Association was negotiating to buy Paramount's old films. Such a deal would vault NTA into a bigger syndication business, in competition with MCA. So, while Paramount's board considered NTA's offer, Wasserman moved in. He and Stein contacted a friend, Paramount director Eli Weisl, and asked him to hand-deliver MCA's counteroffer.

Wasserman offered to buy the TV rights to 700 of Paramount Studios' Golden Age films, for a $10 million down payment. It pledged to pay another $25 million over a ten-year period—for a total cash price of $35 million. If MCA collected more than $51 million on its movies' sales during the next fifteen years, MCA would pay Paramount another $15 million. That way, Balaban could collect $50 million, and MCA wouldn't risk more than it could sell. "We were sweating bullets, because no one really knew if it was a good deal," said Al Dorskind.

But Wasserman knew. Some 300 of Paramount's old films were "A" fare, including the classic Bob Hope–Bing Crosby "Road" comedies, the Oscar-winning *The Lost Weekend,* and some luscious Barbara Stanwyck films, such as *Double Indemnity.* Independent TV stations were eager to run these high-quality films because they could charge more for commercial time.

In early 1958, Balaban and Wasserman signed a deal. Before the ink had dried, Wasserman told Adams to start selling films to TV stations. "We had no trouble making money with it," Adams said. MCA bundled inferior "B" and "C" films along with the "A" features. It sold the films sight unseen in blind bookings, wrote long-term contracts—ironically, block blocking for TV—and offered the deals on a take-it-or-leave-it basis. Though similar practices had landed the film studios in legal trouble a decade earlier, the courts had said nothing about applying them to TV syndicators. Wasserman got away with it—at least initially.

He made sure his men sold every one of those 700 films to every TV station in each of the then-100 major American markets.

Independent stations even paid twice the money for the golden oldies that the networks paid. The Paramount backlist became another brilliant Wasserman deal.

Balaban was pleased, too. At the end of 1958, he gloated that the studio had made more in that one deal than it had earned in a decade of movie-making. But a year later, Barney looked like a goat. Wasserman had already sold nearly $35 million of the films, and the shareholders' deal didn't look so sweet. MCA was making so much money selling Paramount's discards that Wasserman contractually would have to pay the studio its third and last installment—$15 million—in late 1961, a dozen years before Balaban anticipated. Wasserman's $50 million investment would return $100 million to MCA's coffers within just a few years. Over the decades, MCA would sell and resell the same 700 films to thousands of foreign and domestic TV stations, earning approximately $2 billion. By 1982, MCA would turn this cinematic trove into the foundation of the world's most valuable film library, worth $1.6 billion.

Wasserman's deal earned him another enemy, too. National Telefilms was so angry about his interference that its vice president complained to authorities. Assistant Attorney General Victor R. Hansen wrote Jules Stein a letter a few weeks after the sale, saying the Paramount deal raised "certain questions under the [antitrust] laws." MCA was not simply an agency, it was a TV producer. And now it was a distributor. It was becoming a vertically integrated player in the entertainment field, and Hansen politely asked Stein to promptly provide him with all the documents pertaining to the Paramount sale.

Stein ignored the letter.

Wasserman, however, picked up the telephone. He knew that Werblin and his guys were, at that very moment, sitting in the Hotel Pierre, wheeling out the beverage cart for CBS executives, who were about to buy a huge package of Paramount films. The network men were ordering drinks when Wasserman called from Beverly Hills, insisting that Sonny break up the meeting—now. Werblin objected, but Wasserman pressed him. "We knew the government was starting to breathe down our necks, and Lew wanted us to know it, too," said Berle Adams. Not even a sale was worth a federal case.

Werblin hung up the phone and sheepishly told his network pals that the meeting was over. A CBS executive asked sarcastically, "Is it okay if we stay for a drink?"

Wasserman and Werblin were walking a bicoastal tightrope. As they moved aggressively to expand business, they edged ever closer to violating the law. Five months after Assistant Attorney General Hansen asked MCA to send details of its Paramount deal, neither Stein nor Wasserman had responded. Hansen turned to the FCC, which gave him the files on all licensed TV stations that did business with MCA. As soon as Wasserman and Stein got wind of that, they brought in corporate attorney Cyrus Vance of Simpson, Thacher & Bartlett in New York. "We had to watch our Ps and Qs," said Adams. But this was not a schoolroom. The Justice Department was getting ready to authorize a full-fledged investigation into MCA for restraining trade, and Lew and his men had to analyze every move they made.

SIX

IN THE SPRING OF 1959, Wasserman ordered his men to pack up Revue's props and equipment, which were scattered around town. He was moving most of them to their new home at Universal Studios. For weeks, trucks pulled up to rented TV facilities, loaded up crates, then rumbled down to the pastoral Valley. Universal was still owned by Decca Records and Milton Rackmil, and it was still managed by the plodding Ed Muhl. But now, amid the wild rabbits and tumbleweeds on the range appeared dozens of sallow-faced agents, staking MCA's claim.

Inside the studio gates sat twenty-five charming bungalows, surrounded by overgrown lawns and lazy oaks. The quaint cottages, which included kitchens, offices, and other homey touches, had been part of the contracts that Wasserman had negotiated years earlier for clients Jimmy Stewart, Marlon Brando, and Doris Day. After a day of shooting, the actors would lounge on their front porches, soak up the late-afternoon sun, and rib one another across the breezeways. Cary Grant, Tony Curtis, and Rock Hudson had ringside views of Revue's "moveover," as they called it, and they wisecracked about the parade of Teamsters, groaning under heavy loads, taking terse direction from thin-lipped suits.

Universal Studios was making films like *Pillow Talk* and *Spartacus,* packaged with MCA stars and talent, on land and stages leased from its new landlord, the same MCA. On the same grounds, the agency's production arm was also churning out TV shows, such as *Leave It to Beaver, The Adventures of Ozzie and Harriet, Wagon Train, Tales of Wells Fargo, Bachelor Father, and Frontier Circus.*

Not every Revue show moved to Universal that spring, but enough did to redraw the studio map. Wasserman erected a fence to separate Universal's film activities from Revue's work; the TV side was loud and frenetic while the movie section remained languid and collegial. Universal released only eleven films in 1959—or about 22 hours. Revue was churning out twenty-seven half-hours of weekly comedies, mysteries, and adventures, much of it violent and mediocre. "We were doing specials with Fred Astaire, Gene Kelly, and Dinah Shore," said Berle Adams. "We had shows on TV five days a week, every week." Revue's crew was producing about half of all the network evening shows that season. The volume, pace, and uniformity of Revue's fare was so exhaustive that crewmen called it The Factory. By autumn, its assembly line was churning out $33 million worth of TV shows—an all-time high for network production.

Despite the load, Wasserman viewed nearly all of the dailies for every show. "We were producing twelve or fourteen shows a week—

and a lot of it was top rated," he proudly told me years later. He couldn't afford to lose one program, given the $11.25 million he had just spent on the Universal property—plus the payroll and overhead he now carried. "MCA was all about money," said Muhl. "Lew's idea was that production had to be bigger, quicker, and leaner." Wasserman *needed* to keep his buyers happy; there was always a network guy or adman who threatened to cancel a show. At one point, a dramatic anthology, *Thriller*, was on the endangered list. Hosted by the eerie Boris Karloff, its hour-long dramas featured moody black-and-white photography, creepy scripts, and stars like Cloris Leachman and Conrad Nagel. The show would later be hailed as one of the better anthologies of its time; some called it the scariest TV show ever made.

But a number of *Thriller*'s early episodes appealed to old folks, and NBC wanted younger viewers, said Jo Swerling, Jr., a young, fair-headed production assistant who worked on *Thriller* and attended its show meetings. "Lew commented more than once on the fact that he thought there was a sameness to the shows, especially with old-lady characters appearing in so many episodes," he said. Wasserman had just fired one director and brought in veteran William Frye.

Frye's first *Thriller* episode featured a cast of older women.

After viewing the dailies, Wasserman was appalled. His secretary called Swerling, who had no clue about the boss's mood. She asked Swerling, "Could you please come to Mr. Wasserman's office right away?"

Swerling walked over to a makeshift office in a bungalow, where Wasserman waited, along with Revue executive Alan "Pinky" Miller. Wasserman addressed Swerling calmly:

"What did you think of the dailies?"

"I thought they were okay."

"You've been in all of these meetings we've had with [the producers]."

Swerling had.

Wasserman said, "Haven't I said, on repeated occasions, that there was a similarity with the same bunch of old ladies?" Swerling agreed. "And didn't you see that in today's dailies?" He said he had.

"So, what do you do here, Jo?" Wasserman asked.

"I watch the budget, time the scripts, help the producers, and—"

"No, that's not what I mean," said Wasserman, watching the young man squirm.

"Let me tell you what you do," he continued. "You are the eyes and ears of this man." Wasserman gestured to Miller. "When you are on the set, and you see something that upper management has objected to, your job is to get on the phone and let him know immediately, so he can address it."

Lew paused, and his wolfish eyes narrowed. "Why didn't you do that?"

Swerling was tempted to answer that since the show's new director, Bill Frye, was experienced, and since Frye had liked the dailies, Swerling thought the episode was swell, too. But something inside him warned, "Don't pass the buck."

Instead, Swerling looked Wasserman in the eye and said, "I'm sorry, Mr. Wasserman. I screwed up."

Wasserman relaxed. "Well, I wonder how much of my money has been thrown away by guys like you who screw up."

"It will never happen again."

"It better not. Good-bye," Wasserman said.

Swerling walked out of the bungalow in a "state of shock." But he learned a lesson that day. "I believe that if I had passed the buck in that meeting, I would have been fired. But because I owned up to my mistake, Lew gave me another chance." Wasserman expected his men to stand accountable for their errors. If you did, he'd give you a second chance—but not a third.

"From then on," said Swerling, "I performed exactly the way he wanted me to, and we never had another problem." Swerling stayed at MCA for twenty-four years.

Wasserman was alert to TV script problems, even though the president of Revue Productions was Taft Schreiber. "Taft was really smart and a very good salesman," said Jay Kanter. "He had a great deal of contacts among network people and the sponsors." Slim, dark, and handsome, Schreiber had spent twenty-three years working for MCA, toiling six days a week, from morning to midnight. During radio's heyday, he had been a major deal-maker, said Kanter.

In those early days, Schreiber had worked with Wasserman on innovative and lucrative contract arrangements for Jack Benny, Red Skelton, Edgar Bergen, and Bing Crosby. "Taft came up with the idea of selling *Amos and Andy* to CBS as a corporation, not as individual actors," said Adams. That way, the talent wouldn't have to pay 77 percent of its income in taxes, but a lower corporate rate of only 25 percent. "Taft would start with an idea like that, then jump ahead and say something that, to others, didn't make sense." But Lew understood him perfectly. Lew helped simplify the idea, refined it, and slipped it into MCA's armory of weapons. Schreiber and Wasserman used the new package to move dozens of radio clients from NBC to CBS—and back again. The performers and agents made more money in the corporate shelters than they'd ever made before.

Wasserman and Schreiber did not forge the most amicable relationship, but they learned to work together as good cop, bad cop. Then a new technology appeared on the horizon—television—and it dazzled the twenty-six-year-old Wasserman. When he arrived in Los Angeles in 1939, he was amazed to find himself in a hotbed of experimental TV. He was fascinated by what he called "vaudeo," and he bought himself a TV—one of only two sets sold in California at the time. He'd spend hours in his office, peering at his one-inch-by-one-inch TV picture, trying to find a way to capitalize on this wonderful invention. "I bought one and the whole thing started," he later boasted to me.

Actually, it had been going on for a few years, at least in Los Angeles. As early as 1930, Don Lee had created a nine-station hookup along the West Coast, calling his audience "lookers." Wasserman admired Lee, who took cameras into airplanes and beamed down aerial shots. Wasserman also met Klaus Landsberg, the German genius who had broadcast the 1936 Berlin Olympics on early TV and now managed KTLA. The agent loved his telecasts of charade programs, dog shows, wrestling matches, jalopy derbies, and cooking lessons. The older music agents at MCA Square thought young Wasserman was a bit daffy. But he always believed that TV embodied the future of entertainment.

"I was lucky, that's all," he said sixty years later. "I was very bullish on television. Still am."

When the budding—and commercially cheap—medium began to erode MCA's radio business in the 1940s, Wasserman seized the moment. "By then, [Stein] had kicked me upstairs, and it was my decision to go into TV," he recalled. Lew turned MCA's radio show sponsors into TV sponsors, becoming the most prolific producer of corporate programming. Before long, these big-budget company shows transmitted the shiny new 1950s message: Big Business was an upstanding citizen, possessed of cultured tastes, human emotions, and great stories with happy endings. The companies' names topped the opening credits: *The Alcoa Hour, Chrysler Theater, The Kaiser Aluminum Hour,* and *General Electric Theater.*

Kraft Foods Inc. sold the concept of "gracious living." U.S. Steel promoted its "family team." And General Electric was the grand ad master of them all, acutely aware of image. G.E. sponsored dramatic shows that featured "realism with a modest moral" and tightly controlled each episode to spoon out message-morsels about products, in the guise of progress.

But these shows needed pitchmen, and no respectable film actor would stoop to become a glorified corporate vendor. "Radio shows had real stars, while TV had nobodies," said film archivist Ronnie

James. It used actors who were on their way up, or on their way down, like Ronald Reagan.

Reagan was one of hundreds of actors in MCA's stable, and the top echelon of MCA rarely dealt with him. "You have to understand the hierarchy at MCA," said Adams. "There were men who were deal-makers and men who were service agents." The deal-makers were Stein, Wasserman, and Schreiber, who negotiated the talent and production deals with studios, networks, and other buyers. Wasserman never really represented Reagan in the actor's career. His agent was Arthur Park, and in 1950 Park was trying to resuscitate Reagan's failing career while Schreiber was looking for a G.E. show host.

In 1953 the forty-three-year-old actor had just flopped in the third remake of *Law and Order,* a low-budget western. The actor had two children from his first marriage and a new wife and baby; he was running out of income and was willing to consider TV. Schreiber and G.E. signed a desperate Reagan to the show, and on September 26, 1954, he began hosting *General Electric Theater,* summarizing story lessons at the beginning and end of each episode. The program ended the season twentieth in the ratings. "Reagan's role was such a big shtick," said TV producer Laird Koening. "But no one did it better than him."

Reagan made $125,000 a year—more money than he had made in the previous six years of movie acting. And each year G.E. renewed its Revue contract. In 1955 *G.E. Theater* rose to number ten in the ratings, and Park and Schreiber negotiated a bonus for Reagan. "Art got General Electric to give Ronnie an all-electric kitchen," said Art's widow, Merrill Park. "Taft worked on it, too, but from behind the scenes."

Reagan's Pacific Palisades ranch house became the template for a modern American home. It was refitted with an intercom system, a retractable canopy roof for outdoor dining, a film projection room, light dimmers, a heated swimming pool, plus the electronic kitchen—all for free. "Later, Nancy and Ronnie always said that it was Lew who negotiated the G.E. gadgets, but that wasn't true," said Park.

Reagan gained more from his affiliation with G.E. than he had in twenty years of studio work—or fifteen years of activism for the powerful Screen Actors Guild. In 1955 Schreiber got Reagan a producer's credit on some G.E. shows, which gave the actor even more money, if not prestige. Although SAG prohibited producers from holding office, Reagan ignored the conflict-of-interest rule and in November of that year ran for a three-year term on SAG's board. He became third vice president of SAG, weighing in on union matters that, ethically and legally, he should not have. But his union position enhanced his value to MCA, and Schreiber and Reagan grew close. By 1957, *G.E. Theater* was the country's third-most-popular TV show.

In February 1959, Schreiber negotiated a permanent producer's credit on all G.E. shows for Reagan. Schreiber also got the actor—now a SAG director—a 25 percent interest in the show's reruns. A few months later, Schreiber and Wasserman were preparing for some bitter union talks. SAG was demanding that its members be paid reuse fees for old movies sold to TV. If they didn't get what they wanted, they could strike, and that would cripple Revue and its multimillion-dollar production schedule. Schreiber and Wasserman were counting on having a friend at the bargaining session. Reagan, ever willing to assist old friends, would surely help them keep Revue's engine humming.

An invitation to Misty Mountain was like a summons to Mount Olympus. The Stein manse was perched at the end of winding Angelo Road, atop Bel Air Estates. From Jules and Doris's picture windows, one could see the Southern California basin from the San Gabriel Mountains to the port of Los Angeles. To the east was Hollywood, old-money Hancock Park, and the silver skyscrapers of downtown Los Angeles. In the opposite direction were the manicured suburbs of Westwood and Brentwood, and Malibu, where the movie colony summered.

On party nights, Doris and her friends would step outside to admire the magnificent purple cityscape below. They'd sip and prattle, never noticing the deer that ventured down from the hills to sip from their two swimming pools.

"I learned very quickly that Jules and Doris Stein's home was a center of power," said famed couturier Luis Estevez. As Doris often said, "Some people will go to the opening of the door." But she was selective and had spent years cultivating a circle of friends. "Doris adored Santa Anita [racetrack]," said Eleanor Phillips, the onetime wife of Sam Colt, heir to the gun fortune. She liked to mix guests from both ends of L.A.'s social spectrum—Hancock's old money and Hollywood's nouveau riche. "She knew how to blend people together, which wasn't done much in those days," said Phillips.

She invited entrepreneur millionaires just like her husband. Henry Salvatori was an Italian immigrant who made a fortune selling oil rigs to speculators. Holmes Tuttle had sold used cars before he built his network of car dealerships—Rolls-Royce, Ford, and Lincoln Mercury—in four western states. Tuttle's partner, Charles E. Cook, was an Oklahoma boy who had founded Community Bank of Los Angeles—at age twenty-six. And there was Asa V. Call, "Mr. Big" in California politics and chief of Pacific Mutual Life Insurance Company.

"Mother organized all of Stein's parties," said Gerald Oppenheimer, Doris's son by her first marriage. "Here was Jules, in the agency business, and he didn't like to socialize much." Yet she insisted that he learn. "It was a great benefit to Jules to have a wife who was so social and loved to entertain," Oppenheimer explained. "She really helped him and his business. She didn't get enough credit for what she did."

In 1959 Doris and Jules Stein were in a party mood. For the past three years, they had been waiting for The End. "Dr. Stein had a death scare in 1958," Wasserman said, still using his mentor's honorific many years later. A few years earlier, Stein had undergone abdominal surgery to remove intestinal cancer. But adhesions had built up and blocked his colon, causing so much pain that Stein went under the knife again. They found cancer of the rectum, said Wasserman. He was very concerned, as it was quite serious. He tried several cures, but the doctors couldn't help him. He started to plan for his departure from the firm. "Actually," added Wasserman, "we started to plan for his funeral in 1958."

But Stein had miraculously recovered. Whatever had been eating away at him had subsided, and Doris sent out invitations. Several times that summer, a fleet of Rolls-Royces paraded up to the top of Angelo Drive, said Estevez. Wearing long gowns and black tie, guests emerged from their limousines and strolled up to the Steins' massive front door, where they were greeted by one of William Randolph Hearst's former butlers. In this milieu, two butlers signified real money, and "the Steins always had two butlers," said Estevez.

Between the parties, Stein, Schreiber, and Wasserman discussed reorganizing MCA. "Schreiber was Jules's adviser, a sort of Mr. Inside," said Berle Adams. Like Wasserman, Schreiber knew what secrets lay hidden beneath which floorboards—and who could unearth them. But he was a mystery man. "No one really knew him," explained former secretary Jane Rosenbaum. "He wasn't one of the guys you kidded around with at the office. He was more of a power behind the throne." Technically, Wasserman was Schreiber's superior, but Schreiber did not always report to the MCA chief. Sometimes he went directly to Stein, which grated on Wasserman.

That year, MCA's men were dealing with a particularly contentious issue: how to move MCA up to the next plateau. "Jules wanted to go public for estate and tax purposes, but Lew didn't want him to," said Oppenheimer. Wasserman believed it best to keep

MCA shrouded from public eyes, and he pressed his case. MCA had a fiduciary relationship with clients and should not reveal its business, he argued.

"Lew was always talking about fiduciary duty," said Roy Gerber. But Wasserman took the ancient trust law to extremes, using it to justify his penchant for clandestine moves. His "fiduciary duty" compelled him to keep secret MCA's TV sales, its agents' competitive methods, and even whom it represented. While federal investigators worked overtime to count the arms of Hollywood's notorious octopus, Wasserman did everything to thwart them. Said Oppenheimer: "Lew really wanted to keep the agency private."

Schreiber disagreed adamantly. If MCA went public, it would be listed on the New York Stock Exchange, the oldest and most respected roster of blue-chip companies. Schreiber and others stood to make a killing on MCA's rising value—gross revenues had nearly tripled in the previous four years from $17 million to $48 million. An initial public offering would also allow Schreiber and a dozen other agents to cash in. But even this did not sway the secretive Wasserman.

Ultimately, it was Stein's decision. His brush with death had placed his multimillion-dollar corporation in a vulnerable spot. Without planning, his death would cost his family huge estate taxes. An initial public offering would solve the problem.

"There was gossip in the air about MCA's stock going public soon, but it wasn't something polite people talked about at the dinner table," said Estevez. Rather, the long-necked women and ham-fisted men whispered about the Steins' growing fortune: Did you know that Jules owns all of the buildings that house MCA offices, including those in Paris and London? Or that he collects $250,000 a year by renting them back to his own company? Or that he bought the preeminent New York antique dealer—Stair & Co.—so he could avoid paying customs taxes on the collectibles he regularly imports?

"Most of the parties started in the library, where Jules was most comfortable," said Estevez. That's where before the party, Stein would often meet with Schreiber while Wasserman still toiled below at MCA Square. When necessary, Stein would bring Wasserman in on their talks through a squawk box, or, years later, a private phone that was wired from Jules's library to Lew's antique desk. The box sat on Stein's desk, where he once demonstrated its power to Artie Shaw. Stein pressed a button on the box.

Shaw recognized Lew's voice: "What's going on?"

"I'm here with Artie," Stein said, checking for Shaw's reaction.

"Oh, you're showing him the gimmick?" Wasserman asked.

"Yeah."

"See you later," said Wasserman, who hung up.

Stein would often "talk to Lew on that extension at nights and during parties," said Shaw. "He'd walk around the room, talking about some deal." Sometimes Schreiber would be in the room. Most of the time Wasserman would be absent.

Meanwhile, Doris would be entertaining her guests in the front room. There would be Dolly Green, whose father had founded Beverly Hills in 1907. A frequent guest was Rosalind Russell, the exceptional MCA client who was not just an actress but an East Coast debutante. Roz and actress Irene Dunne often led conga lines through Doris's residence, shedding articles of clothing like so many snakeskins. Gene Kelly, David Niven, Robert Montgomery, and other dapper stars enlivened the evenings, too.

Stein preferred the company of Walter Annenberg, head of Triangle Publications, a Philadelphia publishing empire, whose wife, Lee, was a niece of Columbia Pictures' czar Harry Cohn. He spent time with Armand "Artie" Deutsch, heir to the Sears, Roebuck fortune, and his wife, Harriet; and Alfred Bloomingdale, scion of the East Coast department store chain, and wife Betsy, a native Angeleno and well-known clotheshorse. There was Justin Dart, head of Rexall Drug and renowned as ex-finance chair for Dwight

Eisenhower's campaign. Rounding out Stein's library club were A. C. "Cy" Rubel, the chairman of Union Oil Co., and steel magnate Earle Jorgenson. "They loved to talk politics," said Oppenheimer. They backed GOP candidates to run in local, state, and national races and were renowned for their political clout. In just a few years, Stein, Schreiber, and their cohorts would throw their weight behind Ronald Reagan and make up his informal Kitchen Cabinet. Wasserman would not be included.

In 1959, as several of Stein's friends began reorganizing their affairs so that they could retire, Stein streamlined, too. In October, he formally changed the name of his company from Music Corp. of America to MCA—which is what everyone called it, anyway. He consolidated MCA's thirty units into twenty subsidiaries—the most important of which were Revue Productions; MCA Artists, the agency; Music Corp. of America, which represented variety and music acts; and MCA TV, which sold television shows.

Then he took MCA public—selling only 400,000 shares of common stock, priced at $17.50. That increased the number of shares outstanding to 4 million—most of which were already owned by MCA employees. The company realized only $7 million, which was peanuts compared to its $15 million revolving loan from First National Bank of Chicago and its $30 million in cash. The initial public offering was so tiny, it was oversubscribed. The stock ran up to $38 a share and made several men paper millionaires. The second-richest of them all was Lew R. Wasserman, who held 715,000 shares, worth about $12.5 million.

Wasserman did not like his new status as chief of a public company. He felt exposed. "But years later, Lew was glad it was public," recalled Oppenheimer. "He admitted that Jules had been right all along." He didn't mention Schreiber.

SEVEN

LEW LOOKED EXHAUSTED. He was working even longer hours than his usual herculean schedule required, and Edie grew worried about his health, said Jackie Gershwin. "His hair started graying a lot." His shoulders began to hunch forward, and he was losing weight. The forty-six-year-old chief was putting in seventy hours a week, rising at 5:00 A.M. to talk with Sonny Werblin in New York and check with MCA's attorneys in Washington. Then he'd dress and drive the twelve blocks to his office. Around midnight, he'd come home and collapse on the sofa in the den outside Edie's bedroom. "Lew was silent and seemed preoccupied," said Roy Brewer, the former president of the International Alliance of Theatrical Stage Employees (IATSE).

One weekend, to divert his attention, Edie rang up some of Lew's favorite clients. "All the chummy-chums are meeting here for a barbecue," she told them. "Come over Sunday afternoon."

Edie's middle-aged devotion to her friends was like a schoolgirl's fierce affection for her clique. "The first thing she'd do is get out her cut-crystal decanter and fill it with ice," said Jackie Gershwin. Then she'd dust off the drinking glasses that she had had engraved with her chummy-chums' first names. She'd put some music on the hi-fi, something for the girls, like "Gigi," sung by MCA client Louis Jourdan or—to cheer her husband—the rakish "Volare," sung by his devil-may-care client Dean Martin. "Edie always thought of everyone," said Jackie.

Come Sunday, she'd have everything ready. Then she'd light a cigarette and wait. Usually the Gershwins would arrive first. "We'd pull up to their driveway and there'd be Lew, standing at the front door," said Jackie. He looked like the new suburban man, surveying his green lawn, picket fence, and freshly painted two-story home. "He'd be smiling and waiting to greet his friends as they came up the walkway." Jerry would clasp Lew's hand, then joke about how he almost didn't recognize his chief and leader without the usual undertaker's garb.

On these occasions, Wasserman wore an open-collar sports shirt and soft, dark creased slacks. "He never wore jeans, and never, ever shorts," said Jackie. He'd pad around in soft leather loafers, holding a glass of iced tea until he'd melt into the old Lew—a relaxed, easygoing guy with a quick, bright smile.

Jerry Gershwin usually assumed the job of entertaining Lew's guests, acting as court jester. "He kept everybody laughing, and Lew loved that about him," said Jackie. "Jerry was 'on' all the time so Lew could relax." Soft and pudgy around the middle, yet hard and cruel on the edges, the thirty-three-year-old Jerry had a quick laugh and glib manner. Tony Curtis and some other MCA clients didn't quite trust their agent. "I knew from the moment I met him what a jerk Jerry could be," said Curtis. But any acts of betrayal lay far in the future.

In those halcyon days on Sierra Drive, Gershwin never mistreated Curtis or any other top client. Besides, Lew was obviously fond of his goofy aide-de-camp, so no one spoke against him. Gershwin also represented Jerry Lewis, who was now solo and starring in *The Bellboy* and *Cinderfella*—which would break box-office records. "Jerry and Jerry were an act unto themselves, volatile and darling," said Curtis bitingly. Gershwin also represented Dean Martin, who so detested his ex-partner Lewis that he could barely say his name. That caused problems for Curtis and his wife—not to mention Lew—who remained friendly with both the singer and the clown.

"It was all part of the family," said Curtis.

Cheerful and debonair in his own right, Curtis adored Wasserman and treated him with affection and respect. He'd arrive tardy, dressed in the latest fashion. He'd shake Lew's hand, pass through the front door, and glide out to the backyard, where he'd buss Edie on both cheeks. Meanwhile, Lew would bend down and peck Janet Leigh, before sending her through the door. "He'd always give the girls a kiss or a hug and made everyone feel welcome," said Jackie.

Then came Jay and Judy Kanter. Jay was one of Lew's chosen ones and considered to be one of MCA's finer agents. He represented hot young talent and had a better reputation than Gershwin—at least beyond MCA's orbit. Kanter's clients adored the diminutive, energetic man, and he had an affinity for artists. He was shrewd and protective of them. Marlon Brando considered him a trusted adviser. Marilyn Monroe depended heavily on him. Former client Grace Kelly called him "Jay Bird" and served as maid of honor when he married "Judy Bird." Kelly counted the couple among her best friends, even though she was now away from the industry.

Sometimes Dean and Jeanne Martin showed up at Wasserman's home. In 1959 Dean was at the top of his professional form, and Jeanne was his devoted blond spouse. The suave playboy was the idol of young men and the heartthrob of women—which caused no little strain at home. The Martins were going through a rough patch in their marriage, but Edie and the chummy-chums figured they just needed time together. Dinner at Edie and Lew's seemed like the perfect antidote.

Sometimes actress Barbara Rush and her husband, Warren Cowan, would drop by, as would publicist Teme Brenner and husband, Herb; or Kirk and Anne Douglas. Edie's mother, Tillie, would wander through, talking a blue streak with her favorite movie stars. The widow was known for her chopped liver, and she'd ask Curtis when he had last visited his "Mama," who lived in the Fairfax District. "My mother made these huge Hungarian dinners for Lew, Edie, and Tillie and they loved it," said Curtis. Wasserman had moved his own immigrant Russian parents from Cleveland to the Westside, but they had been dead now for ten years. Lew enjoyed the fuss that Curtis's mother made over him, and he savored these occasional respites from the narcissistic tedium of show business. Said Curtis: "Lew didn't go in for ostentation and his house was very simple, even if his life wasn't. And nobody was invited to those inti-mate afternoons except a few of us."

So, as the gang gathered, Edie poured vodka tonics for the girls and bourbon or whiskey for the guys. "Everybody usually had a cocktail in their hands except Lew," said Jackie. "I never saw him take a drink in all those years." He kept himself under strict control.

There was a lot of history—and money—in this group. At thirty-four, Curtis was a marquee name. Yet when he arrived in Hollywood in 1948, he had no agent. He played bit roles in Universal films such as *Criss Cross* and *Winchester '73*. When his handsome face started appearing in fan magazines, Jerry Gershwin noticed and invited the young actor to drop by MCA. "I love your looks, Tony," he said. Curtis walked into MCA's marble foyer, where Gershwin introduced him to the top MCA agents. He was then ushered into the lair of the lion, where he met Wasserman himself. "I remember that first meeting so well." The blue-eyed actor noticed Lew's clean, paperless desktop. When the agency chief stood up and greeted the unknown actor as if *he* were nobility, Curtis was really impressed. "What an aristocrat! What a gentleman," he thought.

Without any chitchat, Wasserman sat down and presented Curtis with a few hard facts: "If you want to be a major star in the movies, you've got to put in ten years of heavy work. Don't raise your head for a while. Just go from one year to the next." Curtis agreed and signed with MCA that very day. "Lew could see my potential."

Wasserman helped groom Curtis for stardom, squiring him around to dinner tables at Romanoff's, where he met Clark Gable, Gary Cooper, Gregory Peck, and Cary Grant. "All of these guys reached out to me," said Curtis. They taught the young actor how to wear a tuxedo, how to pull out a chair for a lady, and "how to sip Jack Daniel's from an old-fashioned glass. Lew was the leader of these stars," Curtis said. "He was the most considerate, most out-standing host you ever saw in your life."

Wasserman was even better at making deals, Curtis learned. The cagey agent got Curtis starring roles in a few Universal movies: *The Prince Who Was a Thief* (1951), *Son of Ali Baba* (1952), and *All American* (1953). Made in a few months for about $150,000 each, these movies went on to gross $1 million or more, delighting the studio. Wasserman then cajoled Universal into lending out his client so he could work in a 1953 Paramount film, *Houdini,* with Curtis's new wife, Janet Leigh. Both studios and the agency made a lot of money on that film, while the newlyweds made their regular salaries. It would be the first of five films the couple would make together, earning them the reputation as one of "Hollywood's Great Love Teams." At ages twenty-eight and twenty-six, Tony and Janet became the elite of America's milkshake set. "Nothing compared to my numbers at the time," said Curtis. Soon Lew made sure Curtis got top billing in all of his films. "I only started doing really well when I found Lew."

As Curtis's star rose, so did his agent's demands. Curtis was so eager to please, that if a director asked, the actor would agree to star in his film. But when the producer would call Wasserman and say: "We made a deal with Tony Curtis and we're ready to start filming," Lew wouldn't miss a beat. "Is that so?" he'd say. "I don't believe we have a signed contract to that effect." Wasserman took these calls so often that he ordered special business cards for Curtis, which read: "To whom it may concern: Don't listen to Tony Curtis. To discuss a deal, call MCA."

"Lew told me to pass these out whenever I felt an urge to say yes," Curtis explained.

The agent's strategy was to place Curtis in films he didn't have to carry. "He always paired me with big names." Ernest Borgnine (*The Square Jungle*), Sidney Poitier (*The Defiant Ones*), Kirk Douglas (*The Vikings*), and Frank Sinatra (*Kings Go Forth*) were his costars. "After a while, I realized my career had a nice string of good films. And that was all Lew."

After every film, Wasserman complimented Curtis, but pushed

him. "Now, what we need, Tony, is a broader audience." Wasserman arranged it so Curtis could do more films outside of Universal. In 1956 Wasserman convinced his client, Burt Lancaster, to use Curtis for *Trapeze*. "It was quite a coup for me to star in a movie with Burt," said Curtis. Lew also made sure that Curtis got a piece of the movie's gross. "By the time I was thirty, I got this unbelievable deal—I think it was 10 percent of the gross. Nobody in town believed it. This was in the mid 1950s, remember, before they played games with gross and net numbers."

From then on, Lew made sure his protégé got a piece of every film: *Some Like It Hot* (5 percent of gross), *The Vikings* (7 percent), and others. "I still retain those rights," Curtis said fifty years later.

Dean Martin also owed a lot to Wasserman. "After Dean split with Jerry [Lewis], a lot of people thought that Dean was the weak link," said Leigh. Indeed, Martin's first solo movie project was MGM's *Ten Thousand Bedrooms*—and it bombed. Wasserman, however, was undeterred. "Lew knew that Dean had something special," Leigh explained. "So he tried to surround him with solid actors— just like he did with me and Tony."

Wasserman pulled strings to get Martin the next supporting role in *The Young Lions*, and *Variety* called the film "one of the standout pictures of the year." Said one wag: "Thank goodness Dean got the part as it probably saved his career." Martin shrugged off the raves, saying that he had just played himself—"a likable coward." There was truth in his words, but he knew that Wasserman and MCA were steering his now-booming career.

"Those days seemed like paradise," Jackie said. In Edie's backyard, the air smelled of orange blossoms and jasmine. In Lew's sunny kingdom, the young couples basked in the reflected light. The strings, percussion, vodka, and scotch made everyone's eyes sparkle— not always at one another, but at the bounty that MCA always delivered. Here was a private universe whose novas and stars revolved around Lew, the sun, and Edie, the empathetic moon.

"Lew was totally different with us than he was around the office," explained Jackie. "In the office, he was always the boss. But at home, he was so relaxed and close to his pals, you'd think he was your best friend."

After a second round of drinks, Lew would start teasing Jackie, Judy, and Janet. "He'd toss the girls into the water, but never the men," said Jackie. "We loved it," explained Leigh. "You think of him as all wheely-dealy. I mean, Lew is brilliant. But I always loved those times because he became so human. That's why I loved those Sundays. That's why I loved that Lew."

Eventually, Edie would bring out the steaks or, sometimes, a tray of hot dogs and hamburgers. The Wassermans had built a "really wonderful barbecue grill" in the backyard, and Lew would light the coals. "He loved steaks," said Leigh. While he tended the coals, he talked with Tony, Jerry, and Dean. "Lew knew Beverly Hills inside and out," said Curtis. "He knew which houses were leased and which were paid off." And Edie knew who was sleeping in which bed and with how many.

All the while, "Edie was thinking about Lew at these barbecues, making sure he was relaxing," said Jackie. She had only one Sunday rule, Leigh recalled. "No business! Not on Sunday," she'd say. She might as well have ordered them all to stop breathing. Show business was what bound them together. Edie may not have wanted any deals done in her house, but her guests freely passed industry gossip around like condiments at the table. "We were always asking each other: 'What do you think about so-and-so on that show?'" said Jackie. "Or 'How about that producer or director?'"

In 1959 many of Lew's troubles were becoming apparent, but not one of the chummy-chums asked about Charles Van Doren, or *Twenty-One*. They didn't want to know why the FBI was nosing around Sunset Boulevard, asking questions about MCA. "Keep the mood light," was the Sunday dictum. "Lew was so full of fun during those times," said Jackie. No one wanted to break the spell.

Still, the town was throbbing from all the war drums and their anti-MCA messages. "I knew that a lot of people were pissed off at Lew," said Curtis. "They were mad at Lew and at MCA, and I couldn't understand why. Lew was the most honorable man I'd ever known. But you didn't want to cross Lew. Because if you did, that was it. You'd never work in this town again." It was hard for Wasserman and his inner circle to believe, but a line of disgruntled actors, fired employees, and rival agents was about to advance against the chief.

EIGHT

IN THE SUMMER OF 1959, a car carrying a few FBI agents pulled up to MCA's curved driveway. The government investigators were already perspiring as they got out of the car in their ill-fitting, off-the-rack suits. They had learned plenty about MCA, Stein, and Wasserman, including how Stein had bought these Corinthian columns cheaply from the estate of Marion Davies, mistress of newspaper tycoon William Randolph Hearst. They couldn't believe that MCA's building was known as "The White House" and Stein's suite was called "The Oval Office." To the FBI, MCA's overweening arrogance was ridiculous, if not appalling. As one agent groused, "What upsets me most is the way people tell me that MCA says, 'Nobody in Washington can touch us.'"

That day in July, the FBI tried to prove otherwise. They burst into MCA's lobby armed with subpoenas giving them access to agency files. This angered Wasserman, who believed the raid was unnecessary. But he held his tongue; this moment had been a long time coming. The Justice Department had been looking at MCA as far back as 1938, when bandleaders first complained about Stein's stronghold on orchestras. J. Edgar Hoover began keeping files on

Wasserman and his Hollywood operation as early as 1954, when complaints started piling up like dry matchsticks. The common wail was that MCA and William Morris had built themselves by raiding clients from smaller agencies. Indeed, that's exactly how Stein broke into Hollywood in 1937. "That was Jules's entire philosophy," said Berle Adams. "He didn't like to start companies. He liked to buy them out."

Now Wasserman and his men had to deal with FBI agents and crusading attorney Leonard Posner. The lawyer had spent most of his career with the Justice Department, where he had prosecuted theater chains for selling "C" movies with "A" films in take-it-or-leave-it packages. Posner knew something about show business's predatory practices, and he recognized several of them in MCA's ploys. Arthur Park considered Posner to be a rude lout, adding: "He was insulting and intimidated you." But juries and the attorneys' coworkers admired him. He came across like a nice guy who worked on behalf of the average Joe against big business simply because it was the right thing to do. For several years now, Posner had been interviewing people about Hollywood's White House; some had spoken anonymously for fear of reprisals. But others were quite open.

Among them were MCA clients who felt pressured to appear on MCA-produced shows. Revue made variety shows for Perry Como, Bob Hope, Dinah Shore, Rosemary Clooney, Dean Martin, and others. But the same entertainers kept appearing on the same shows. Hosts even started appearing as guests on competitors' shows. Vic Damone, Eddie Fisher, and Hope had complained to MCA about Revue's "variety" shows turning into one long, monotonous series. But MCA controlled the hosts, performers, networks, and sponsors, and whatever the shows lacked in spark or quality, they made up in agency profits.

Sonny Werblin and Terence Clyne, of the McCann-Erickson advertising agency, often devised ideas for these shows. Clyne represented Coca-Cola, Chesterfield cigarettes, and General Motors and reportedly bought more TV time than anyone else. Werblin and Clyne decided that Fisher should cohost a variety show with MCA's taciturn comedian George Gobel. Fisher hated the idea, but Werblin cajoled him: "Just do this one thirteen-week segment. If you're not happy with it, you'll do it alone."

The show flopped, and Fisher asked MCA's New York chief to change it. But Clyne and Werblin told him forget it; it was too late. Fisher had to soldier on until MCA's contract with NBC expired. "What bothered me most about the whole episode was that I had no one to fight for me," Fisher later told investigators.

Tensions escalated between Fisher and his agency. Revue wanted Fisher to hire MCA clients Kate Smith and Charles Laughton for his show, but Fisher knew they'd appeared recently with Rosemary Clooney and Bob Hope. "I want stars who haven't been overexposed," he explained. The issue came up during a "Fagin" meeting, when Wasserman and his agents decided to "show the little bastard who the boss really is." Fisher was forced not only to invite the same old MCA artists onto his TV show, but also to pay a premium price for them. His friend Dean Martin said he would appear on *The Eddie Fisher Show,* but MCA raised Martin's fee from the already-agreed-upon $7,000 to $11,000—and when Fisher hollered—to $25,000. Martin played along, and Fisher was furious. Twenty-five thousand zaps for an appearance on a show!

When Fisher's MCA contract expired in 1959, he did not renew. MCA veteran agent Johnny Dugan invited Fisher to a meeting at the Beverly Hills Hotel, where Fisher was summoned to a suite and buttonholed by four top executives. "If you leave MCA, we'll see to it that you never work again," Dugan threatened.

"Well, I guess I won't work again," he said.

Sure enough, Fisher lost his TV show, his record sales, and many of his bookings. But he went on to perform in the Oscar-winning *Butterfield 8*—with his new wife, Elizabeth Taylor, one of the few stars not in MCA's stable.

Cary Grant felt MCA's squeeze, too. When his own agent, Frank Vincent, died in 1946, Grant allowed Wasserman to represent him, alongside Grant's trusted attorney, Stanley Fox. Grant never signed an agency agreement, but Wasserman agreed to split his 10 percent commission with Fox. Grant usually got whatever role he wanted, and when he read the script for *Bell, Book and Candle,* he believed the role was tailor-made for him. But Wasserman said that Columbia Studios had already given the lead to Jimmy Stewart—one of Wasserman's friends—and Grant was crestfallen. When the movie premiered in October 1958, it received tepid reviews, partly because of the lack of sparks between the twenty-five-year-old Novak and fifty-year-old Stewart.

The following year, however, the situation between the two actors was reversed. Stewart had all but begged for the lead in MGM's *North by Northwest,* to be directed by Alfred Hitchcock, another of Lew's favored clients. But Hitch claimed that Stewart's age had hurt the box-office receipts of the director's previous film, *Vertigo,* and Wasserman could not sway the director. Instead, Hitchcock wanted Cary Grant, who was actually four years older than Stewart but more suave and appealing to women. Wasserman, with Grant's attorney, brokered Grant's deal for a then-substantial salary of $450,000, plus a percentage of gross profits.

The film, which debuted in the summer of 1959, was a smash, and Wasserman quickly set up a meeting with Grant to discuss his glowing future. Surrounded by several top MCA agents, Grant sat as Wasserman announced it was time to create *The Cary Grant Show.* Grant abhorred TV and had said so many times. "Do you *really* think I should appear on television?" Grant asked. Oh, yes, said Wasserman, and the agents explained their concept. Grant realized that the agency's other arm would be producing the expensive show—thereby wringing more cash from the actor's talents than they already grabbed. Grant stood up and ended the meeting summarily.

Producer Walter Seltzer, an MCA client himself, felt his agent's heavy hand when he tried to make a movie with MCA clients Paul Newman and Joanne Woodward. Seltzer was trying to hire a director to start filming *Paris Blues* in 1961 when suddenly, "I couldn't get my phone calls returned by Lew," by Newman, or by Woodward, he explained. "It was a delicate situation." Finally Seltzer went to Lew's office and asked, "What do I need to do?" All Seltzer had to do was hire Marty Ritt, another MCA client, as director. "Marty was fine, but we had to surrender artistic control to MCA," said Seltzer, who had to explain this to his own first choice.

Stars like Montgomery Clift began to undercut their MCA agents. When director Stanley Kramer asked Clift to appear in *Judgment at Nuremberg*, about the Nazi war-crimes trial, the actor readily agreed. Kramer offered him a small, weeklong part for $75,000— but MCA demanded $300,000, which was Clift's usual starring-role fee. Kramer looked elsewhere until Clift offered to work for free. That way, the actor explained, he could "take a big, empty paper bag, tie a blue ribbon around it, and send it to MCA with a note, saying 'Your commission is inside.'" Ironically, Clift's supporting role in that 1961 film landed the actor his fourth Oscar nomination.

More damaging were reports from MCA's rivals. "Let me tell you the cutest story," Berle Adams said. He had long wanted to represent Andy Williams, the era's hottest singer. But Williams belonged to rival GAC, where agent Alan Bregnan handled him. Williams wanted his own TV show, but GAC had difficulty landing one. GAC's Bregnan finally asked Adams if MCA wanted an Andy Williams show. "I sure do," said Adams. "Come around and bring Andy's GAC contract." Bregnan showed up, and Adams scanned the document. He saw that GAC represented Andy Williams as a performer only. "It wasn't an all-inclusive contract, like ours." Adams told the GAC agent: "I don't want to represent Andy Williams, I want to represent his corporation."

MCA helped Williams form Barnaby Productions, named after

the singer's dog. "We sold the show to NBC for about $150,000," explained Adams. "The corporation paid Andy a salary of $5,000, and GAC got $500 or 10 percent of that," said Adams. MCA, however, pocketed at least $15,000—10 percent commission on the show's sale. Then, as the show's producer, it took *another* 20 percent for "overhead" and about 55 percent for studio rental, camera crew, film, and other expenses. After MCA and Revue had subtracted all of its sundry fees and costs, about 25 percent of the total remained. That figure—$37,000—was just enough to pay salaries for the guest talent—many of whom were MCA clients.

"Isn't that cute?" asked Adams. GAC agents did not think so, but they never said a word to MCA. "Maybe they realized their mistake in not having all-inclusive contracts." *The Andy Williams Show* debuted in 1957 as a summer show, appeared for three more summer seasons, and finally became a regular year-round show, enjoying ten years of high ratings and financial success. GAC's top agent, Henry Miller, was flabbergasted at MCA's chutzpah. But neither he nor his boss, GAC chief Herb Siegel, could prevent MCA from packaging a show for the GAC client.

Soon even big-name TV performers outside of MCA were crying foul. Steve Allen was a glib master of innovative television who appeared weekly on NBC. But he found it increasingly difficult to book the stars he wanted, whether they were clients of his own or some other agency. There were too many instances when Allen would arrange for a guest to appear only to have him back out at the last minute and appear on the rival MCA-produced *The Ed Sullivan Show.* "We all knew that Sullivan played unfair hardball, and we knew that his agency was behind it," he told me. Allen grew so angry with MCA that he complained to the local district attorney. "We got a message that someone from the Justice Department was talking to some guys at MCA." That was music to Allen's ears, but the showman concluded that nothing would ever come of the government's case. "It's highly unlikely that anyone in the entertainment industry would be willing [to talk] about the power of Lew Wasserman." He was too big.

But the FBI was giving it a go. From that moment in July when federal agents burst into MCA's vestibule waving subpoenas until December 1959, they spent nearly every day reviewing MCA's files. Wasserman hardly gave the men free rein. They had to request certain files, then wait for a secretary or mail boy to deliver the files to a room that had been set aside for them. The G-men quickly ran into obstacles. Many files had been destroyed a few months earlier. Nor could they touch the papers of Wasserman or Stein—supposedly, neither man kept files.

After a few weeks inside MCA, any veteran detective could sense the chilling parallels between Wasserman's outfit and an organized-crime syndicate. There was the uniform. "I had so many black ties, I had to label each one for every day of the month," said one MCA agent. There was the rigid code of discipline. "Once you left MCA, Lew never let you back in," said agent Ned Tanen. Wasserman believed that any attempt to succeed outside of his office was an act of aggression. Like Mafiosi, early MCA agents came primarily from one socioeconomic background: They were children of Jewish immigrants who had been unable to find many open routes to wealth and never attended college. Early on, MCA discriminated against other ethnic groups. "They didn't want Italians," said Jim Murray, who booked MCA acts in Las Vegas. Irish and Polish guys were okay, but Sicilians were anathema. "I had to change my name from Fusco to Murray."

Wasserman placed a premium on loyalty, honesty, and a respect for leaders—"norms [that] are stressed in the society of organized criminals." MCA had unwritten rules: Number One? "Don't discuss business outside the family." Meanwhile, agents filed daily reports on the organization's clients, patrons, and activities, spied on MCA's enemies and rivals, and pumped their operatives about the ever-shifting alliances behind studio gates and network doors. Intelligence was gathered up and passed on to the chief. As Swifty Lazar once complained, "You have a Mafia-type routine here, Lew, with all of these guys reporting to you." Swifty did not last long at MCA.

What really interested the government, though, was how MCA exerted its economic and political forces to overwhelm and wipe out rivals. MCA seemed to control all of show business's legitimate activities. It also engaged in racketeering, which is the "systematic extortion of money from persons or organizations." It relentlessly sought more power to build its monopoly and control labor-management battles—just like a criminal syndicate. The secrecy that shrouded MCA's operations made for a difficult antitrust case. Even so, Leonard Posner and the FBI culled enough information to learn that MCA represented about 75 percent of the top talent in the motion picture, television, and radio industries—most of which it had obtained through "predatory practices," said Posner.

He told his supervisors that MCA had been less than cooperative with the government. MCA responded through its Washington, D.C., attorney, Cyrus Vance, that, from now on, the agency would cooperate fully. Still, Wasserman tried to limit the government's scrutiny by narrowing its review to the years 1957–1958—and by offering files from only six of its twenty divisions—and by forbidding the government to look at its foreign offices. In the end, the Oval Office in Hollywood had to bow to Capitol Hill and hand it all over. But whenever FBI agents requested certain files—especially those from Revue—the documents seemed to get misrouted or were lost en route.

In MCA's first annual report, in 1959, Wasserman told shareholders that the Department of Justice was investigating talent agencies—including MCA—for violating antitrust laws. "In [our] opinion," he wrote, "no such violations have existed or do exist."

However, too many government-department heads had heard of Wasserman. Though the quiz-show grand jury had folded—the jury had not charged anyone, and a New York judge had sealed the jury's findings because he found no violation of law—Senator Warren Magnuson, chairman of the Senate Interstate and Foreign Commerce Committee, among others, had received copies of the report. In late 1959, Senator Magnuson suddenly wanted to review the grand jury's findings on the quiz-show matter, especially those at *Twenty-One.* And another lawyer in the antitrust division, Charles Whittinghill, wanted to impanel yet another grand jury in New York—this time to investigate possible violations of the Sherman Antitrust Act arising out of alleged tie-in sales by NBC and CBS of network time and shows. Among the tie-ins were MCA's "extremely close relationship with NBC, to which it supplies numerous 'live' properties." The FCC was trying to determine exactly how many of its licensed TV stations bought properties from this so-called talent agency.

Now Wasserman had several bombs ticking under his desk. The loudest were sent by Hollywood's unions. In October 1959, the Writers Guild of America (WGA) announced a strike against independent film producers that was expanded to include TV producers, such as Revue. At the same time, SAG was heading into difficult negotiations with producers, including Revue. "We knew there was going to be a big fight," said Jack Dales, executive director of SAG. Wasserman's problem was how to work things out with SAG's president, Howard Keel, who recalled: "I was no fan of Lew Wasserman."

NINE

Howard Keel had not forgotten the last conversation he had with Lew Wasserman. At the time, Keel was working on *Kiss Me Kate* (1954), and his MCA agent sent him an awful script: *Rose Marie.* "I decided I wouldn't do the movie," said Keel. But as he completed the first musical, his agent called and told him to report for the next project. Keel told his agent that he didn't want any part of it. The next day, Keel was suspended by MGM studio chief Dore Schary.

Unknown to Keel, Schary and Wasserman went way back. After Schary had been fired from a B-unit production job, Wasserman bagged him a lucrative contract with David Selznick's Vanguard Films in 1944. Schary went on to produce *Crossfire, The Farmer's Daughter*, and other hits, and by 1951 he headed MGM. Now Schary traded regularly with Wasserman, swapping talent for dollars like buckets of fish. But Keel was unaware of this history. The suspended actor was worried about appearing alone at a showdown with Schary and three studio executives. Since Keel's talents had enriched his agents at MCA, for the first time he called on Wasserman for support: "I'd like someone from the agency to be with me at this meeting."

"We don't do that," said Wasserman. "You're on your own."

Keel could not believe his ears. "Well, then," he sputtered. "You can take me off your list. I don't need your kind of representation."

Wasserman hung up. Eventually, Jack Cummings, a sympathetic producer, ordered rewrites for *Rose Marie* (1954), hired director Mervyn LeRoy, and persuaded Keel to star. "But I had no use for MCA after that." Keel's opinion hadn't changed by 1959. "I think Lew had gotten awfully big for his pants by then. I didn't like his attitude towards me at all. I was a client, but I was nothing as far as he was concerned. I found him rude and unprofessional," said Keel. "He was a gutsy agent. But I never trusted him."

Wasserman and Revue—and Hollywood—needed SAG's trust if they were to maintain labor peace and production. SAG's contract with movie producers was scheduled to expire on January 31, 1960, only a few months away. SAG's executive director, Jack Dales, had announced that union members wanted to be paid residuals for their work in the old movies that were now playing on TV. Television had boomed, swallowing up most of Hollywood's creative energy, yet those who benefited most from the bonanza were not directors, writers, or actors—but salesmen like those at MCA who peddled some of the 15,000 old films in circulation. If the actors didn't get a few shekels out of this gold mine, they would strike. They also wanted a pension and welfare fund, which several Hollywood craft unions already had. The possibility of a labor shutdown threatened Lew in several ways. Wasserman's biggest tenant, Universal, would have to shut down if SAG called a strike. And Revue's production could also halt, once its contract with SAG ended on March 31, 1960. That could cripple Revue. MCA needed a SAG friend.

Two months before the SAG contract expired, Keel was offered an out-of-town role. Several of MCA's top clients were about to launch a Broadway production of *Saratoga,* said Keel. "Johnny Mercer and Harold Arlen asked me to join." Keel took the role and prepared to leave Hollywood.

SAG needed a replacement, and quick. Dales met with a few leaders—including MCA clients Dana Andrews, Rosemary De Camp, and George Chandler. Most of SAG's fifty board members were either MCA or Revue employees, including Walter Pidgeon, Leon Ames, James Garner, Charlton Heston, and Conrad Nagel, said Dales. So was Ronald Reagan, even though he was a producer, too. His name came up as a replacement for Keel, which was fine with the Broadway-bound actor. "I knew that Reagan had helped in the past."

Indeed, in 1952, Reagan had helped SAG broker its most controversial deal ever. At the time, the floundering actor was an MCA client, divorced, broke, and hungry for better movie roles. He was also president of SAG. Wasserman, as chief of MCA, was in a position to help Reagan, but he needed help himself. Wasserman's growing TV production company was already violating SAG's rule that barred agents from producing shows. That year, Reagan, Dales, Wasserman, and his attorney, Larry Beilenson, who had helped found SAG, hammered out a secret deal. It gave MCA—and no other agency—a waiver (until December 1959) to the rule prohibiting agents from acting as TV producers. It was a sweetheart deal—and a blatant conflict of interest. Yet without that waiver, it's unlikely that Wasserman's Revue would have grown into a $50 million giant. And it was that cozy deal, more than any studio contract, that drew Reagan and the agency chief together, said Berle Adams. "Lew got close to Reagan on that SAG deal."

In 1954 Wasserman needed another Reagan favor. SAG planned to pass a blanket rule forbidding all agents from acting as TV producers. MCA's lanky chief again went to Reagan, who was sitting on SAG's negotiating committee that year. Wasserman reminded him that MCA had to be excluded from the rule—Reagan and Dales had guaranteed that two years earlier. SAG's board went into closed session and exempted MCA. At Lew's request, the waiver was then extended until 1960. "Ronnie Reagan had done Lew another good turn," said TV producer Henry Denker. From 1954 on, MCA was the *only* agency to get a blanket production waiver from the unions. "No one ever expected Revue Productions to be as successful as it was," said Chet Migden, an executive secretary of SAG. "If we had known, perhaps we would have put more conditions on MCA."

The town believed that Reagan had gotten something in return for extending SAG's "sweetheart deal." As Revue boomed, the rumors grew louder. "The relationship with Reagan was always very murky," said Walter Seltzer, producer of the science-fiction classic *Soylent Green.* "Money changed hands when he was president of the guild or there were contract deals. Somehow, he got favorable treatment." Even the government would suspect a bribe, but what was the quid pro quo?

Wasserman called such talk "nonsense. It's always been nonsense."

Absurd or not, no one argued that Reagan and the SAG waiver had put Revue in the captain's chair. Now, in late 1959, Lew needed another favor from SAG. Who better to help MCA than its loyal soldier, the genial host of *General Electric Theater?*

• • •

Dales and SAG executives thought Ronald Reagan was a natural choice to lead SAG into its pivotal labor negotiations. Dales asked Reagan if he would take the helm. Reagan first discussed the matter with Taft Schreiber, the man who had got him the *General Electric Theater* job five years earlier. Dales explained: "Reagan was really closer to Taft Schreiber than he was to Lew." After being encouraged by both Schreiber and Wasserman, Reagan again assumed the union's presidency on November 16, 1959. In doing so, Reagan continued to ignore the SAG rule that prohibited an actor/producer from holding a SAG post. But, as he later told a grand jury: "I naturally had a loyalty to the fellows at Revue." And the fellows at Revue surely needed him.

The guild's 14,000 members elected the unopposed Reagan; about 800 attended the meeting. A few gave him a standing ovation, but several SAG members criticized Reagan for hiding his producer's status. Reagan lied by denying he had a producing role, and Dales supported him, lashing out at the "vile and unscrupulous" allegations in SAG's December 1959 newsletter. Dales repeated what Reagan had told him: "[Reagan] has no ownership interest, percentage, participation or otherwise in the *General Electric Theater.*" Reagan never corrected the record, and his critics were hushed for a few months.

Talks began with the Association of Motion Picture Producers (AMPP), whose members faced SAG negotiators over a polished thirty-foot-long table. Reagan, Dales, and others sat across from Paramount's Balaban, MGM's Joe Vogel, Jack Warner, and Spyros Skouras of Twentieth Century Fox, who acted as the AMPP's spokesman. As soon as the talks began, tensions arose over TV residuals.

Reagan told the studio chiefs that his union was adamant about getting the money. In 1960, however, movie reruns on TV were about the only thing keeping studios afloat, said Dales. "I'll never forget Skouras at one meeting." The son of a poor Greek shepherd, Skouras had spent the past decade trying to rescue Fox and the industry from TV's grip. He had almost succeeded, too, by introducing CinemaScope in *The Robe* (1953). Viewers were drawn in by the film's pageantry and the wide-screen technology. Going to the movie theater became an event again. The $5 million film grossed $36 million, but seven years later, the cash-strapped Fox had to sell its back lot.

Skouras detailed his studio's woes. "Speaking in a heavy Greek accent, he told us how important it was that the studios get what they wanted. Then he actually started crying," said Dales. Through his crocodile tears, Spyros appealed to Reagan: If he gave away the studio's remaining asset, shareholders would run him out of town. "Spyros was silly and not impressive at all." Reagan pressed him: Surely Fox could afford a penny of every TV dollar? The studio chief turned stony and replied: "We won't discuss it. It's nonnegotiable."

After a few exchanges like this, Reagan recommended that SAG strike—and members did on March 7, 1960. None of SAG's 14,000 members broke ranks—nor did any other union brethren—even though some 3,500 workers were sidelined. Most of the big studios halted work, which affected eight major pictures and several minor ones.

Soon Wasserman and his agents were flooded with calls from film stars—notably those working on the MCA package *Let's Make Love* (1960). Norman Krasna's script had been revised by Arthur Miller so his wife, Marilyn Monroe, could get more time in front of the camera. But now that set was dark.

"Once we were in strike mode, producers started coming around," said Dales. But even before the strike, Reagan had negotiated with some producers behind the scenes—including Milton Rackmil at Universal. According to Ed Muhl, Wasserman often advised his "tenant" Rackmil: "Lew was the kind of guy who had a sturdy pencil—that's all he did," while Rackmil had only a rudimentary grasp of the film business. "Rackmil was ideal for

Wasserman, who could handle him smoothly," added former Decca Records executive Joe Delaney.

At Wasserman's urging, Rackmil offered to pay residuals of 6 percent of net TV sales—minus 40 percent for distribution, advertising, and prints—for films made from 1948 to 1960. The offer spared Universal from the actors' walkout, which would have devastated the struggling studio. It also saved MCA's $1 million rent payment. After Universal's pact, United Artists and about sixty independent producers signed the same deal, too. But the deal was contingent on the union's securing agreements with the other studios.

This prompted the rest of the majors to reconsider their policy on residuals, "but then, they changed their minds," said SAG historian Valerie Yaros. Instead, they offered to seed SAG's pension fund with $4 million. By spring, Reagan's SAG was no longer pushing for residuals, which angered some members. It got so that Richard Walsh, head of the International Alliance of Theatrical Stage Employees, accused SAG of "wrecking the business," and claimed that he could get his union people three times whatever Reagan got SAG. So many craft workers and low-level union members viewed Reagan as a management patsy that Bob Hope, acting as emcee of the 1960 Academy Awards, joked onstage: "The only person working in Hollywood today is Ronald Reagan." Sure enough, Revue was still filming *G.E. Theater* and its other series, said Dales, because Schreiber had already approached Reagan and SAG, which agreed to extend the TV producers' contracts until May 31.

But the movie producers turned tough. They abruptly canceled two meetings without explanation and let stand their last offer: no residuals, but they would kick in to a pension fund. In response, SAG called a pivotal meeting on April 18, 1960, and two camps formed. One side called for Reagan's resignation, claiming he was selling out to management by dropping their demand for residuals. Other members were eager to return to work. That night, SAG voted to approve management's offer—though it had sunk even lower than it had been a few weeks earlier. Somehow, Reagan had managed to weaken—not strengthen—labor's bargaining power. In the end, producers paid $2.65 million to SAG's pension fund—about 65 percent of the original $4 million offer.

"Reagan sold us down the river," actor Gary Merrill said at the time. "We were on strike and . . . then all of a sudden it was called off because the studios said they would contribute so many millions of dollars to a pension fund. I felt that Reagan kind of sold the idea to the union."

"Reagan didn't pump for residuals at all," said Gene Kelly, but neither did the rest of SAG's board. There was much bitterness over this deal, as actors such as Mickey Rooney, Ann Sheridan, Bing Crosby, June Lockhart, and Robert Mitchum, along with hundreds of lesser-known professionals, had spent their careers making movies before 1960. While studios reaped millions from the actors' work, the artists would end up with little or nothing—all because of what became known as Reagan's "Great Giveaway." Compounded over forty years, the settlement cost actors an estimated $100 million in residuals. "But we got a pension fund," said Keel.

At SAG's next meeting in May, an angry member accused Reagan of negotiating in bad faith, since he had been a producer all along. Reagan hotly denied the charge, until someone waved a General Electric letterhead that listed Reagan as a producer. On June 6, Reagan resigned as SAG's chief due to his "upcoming producer's status," even though he had been a producer all along. He remained on the board in violation of union rules as SAG tried to negotiate a new TV contract, "particularly with Taft Schreiber of Revue," according to SAG's minutes. "After several meetings, on July 6 Revue agreed to recommend to the producers that a deal be approved." Together, Schreiber and Reagan hammered a union TV contract. A few days later, on July 9, Reagan resigned as a SAG officer, upset at growing criticism from his guild colleagues. "[T]he only role [I] could possibly play as far as they're concerned is a slick lawyer from the East."

But Schreiber lessened the sting. Six months later, Revue's chief managed to renew Reagan's contract for *General Electric Theater*, though its ratings had fallen considerably.

Meanwhile, Wasserman moved to settle the strike at the Writers Guild of America (WGA). The union had walked out on independent film producers on October 10, 1959, and then, on January 16, 1960, struck major studios and TV producers over the issue of TV film residuals. "We were very aggressive in trying to work something out," said Michael Franklin, the guild's executive director at the time. Wasserman had picked Schreiber to bargain with WGA, too, said Franklin, but talks had bogged down. So Wasserman himself attended a guild meeting held inside the Rexall Building on La Cienega. Standing in front of a group of suspicious and anxiously unhappy writers, Wasserman "laid out his concept of a royalty plan for us," said Franklin. "It made a great deal of sense." Essentially, Lew proposed that WGA ask the studios for a percent of gross revenues from their licensing of old films to TV. His 4 percent formula applied only to shows after their first broadcast and first rerun. After that, the formula kicked in, said Franklin. "He gave us the very basis of working out what eventually became the solution at that time."

The so-called "Wasserman formula" broke the deadlock. Again, at Lew's urging, Universal Studios was the first to break ranks from the other studios. Ed Muhl approached Franklin and "made a separate deal with us," said Franklin. That prompted other studios to settle, too. WGA members finally received their first residual payments—but only for post-1960 work. Separately, the studios paid lump sums to individuals for works created prior to the strike, but the numbers were minuscule. For example, Julius Epstein, author of thirty-five pre-1960 movies, including *Casablanca*, was paid only $1,500 for *all of his films*—certainly not enough to support an aging man. William Ludwig, who wrote *Oklahoma!* and *Love Finds Andy Hardy* —the 1938 film that introduced Judy Garland, Lana Turner, and Mickey Rooney—received a paltry residual of $74. Ludwig would spend the next forty years agitating for more money from his work—which by 1999 could be viewed on foreign TV stations, on cable, satellite TV, video, DVD, and the Internet. But he never succeeded, and died in a nursing home while MGM continued raking in a fortune, rerunning his films and selling, among other things, "Andy Hardy" video sets for $20 a apiece.

Once WGA gave up residuals on the old movies, the studios welcomed them into an industry-wide health and pension plan. But the studios gave the writers' fund even less than they had given the actors—a puny $300,000. Years later, many WGA members would rue the day they ever settled the 1960 strike. At the time, however, few artists could imagine that entire cable networks like Turner Classic Movies would be dedicated to showing old movies. Or that *I Love Lucy* episodes would be replayed into the twenty-first century. "In 1960 we agreed that motion pictures broadcast on television would not be paid residuals," said Margaret Cone, lobbyist for Committee for a Fair Deal. "But we never gave away the rights to any other market." One executive would say that paying writers residuals on old works would have cost each studio about $1 million over twenty years—or "peanuts."

The eight-month strike finally ended on June 15, 1960, and with it the town's labor turmoil—at least for a while. WGA's action had been the longest strike in Hollywood history—and Wasserman had been instrumental in settling it.

TEN

AS WASSERMAN GRAPPLED WITH HOLLYWOOD UNIONS, he could take comfort in the belief that the quiz-show scandals were dead. Then Washington lawmakers resuscitated the affair. Congressman Oren Harris of Arkansas declared an immediate investigation of the quiz shows. As chairman of the House Subcommittee on Legislative Oversight, Harris called the issue a national problem that was "a proper concern of federal government." He scheduled his hearings for a week in October and a week in November 1959, with a three-week intermission that he filled with newspaper stories quoting him. His hearings triggered a fresh wave of flashbulb-popping features on the "quizlings," much to the horror of the TV industry, including MCA, whose clients Jack Barry and Dan Enright were still churning out TV game shows for NBC—and still paying commission fees to their agent.

Harris's investigation was an effective way to draw attention away from his own scandal. In 1958 the new Special Subcommittee on Legislative Oversight had uncovered the politician's financial interest in a TV station within his own district—a blatant conflict of interest. The exposé caused such a commotion that Harris was forced to sell his share in the station. He desperately wanted to transform his image and help fellow Democrats retain control of the House in the upcoming election. What better way than to crack open the grand-jury report on the popular TV quiz shows for all to see?

Harris's subcommittee sent Richard Goodwin, a young attorney, to collect the sealed records from the New York court. Goodwin promised the judge that he'd keep secret all testimony and would ask jury witnesses to appear before Congress on a voluntary basis. But according to the New York Assistant District Attorney Joseph Stone, who oversaw the jury, Goodwin terrorized producers and contestants by "brandishing blank subpoenas signed by Harris." Goodwin tracked down Al Freedman in Mexico, the only place the producer could find work, and threatened him. If *Twenty-One*'s producer didn't cooperate, he'd never return home again. Goodwin actually had no such authority, but he frightened Freedman into cooperating, said the producer.

By then, reporters and photographers were camped outside the pilastered Caucus Room of the Old House Office Building in Washington. "It became like the Army-McCarthy hearings," said Fred Stettner, referring to Joe McCarthy's witch-hunt for alleged Communists. When Harris finally opened his hearings, there was standing room only. In the audience sat Stone, who slowly realized that Harris was orchestrating the entire show like "a three-ring circus." The hearings were not televised but "were heavily scripted," said Stettner. In fact, the entire proceedings seemed as rigged as any TV game show.

"Goodwin was an unscrupulous person," said Stettner. "He'd tell you what to say and told you what the committee members were going to ask you." If that sounded like "coaching" witnesses, the irony wasn't lost on Freedman, Stettner, and the others. However, said Stettner, "you'd get to the table and find out that Goodwin had lied. The congressmen would grill you on something entirely different than what he had told you." Several witnesses considered Goodwin untrustworthy. "We called him the Sammy Glick of Washington," said Stettner, referring to the fictional Hollywood huckster.

The lawmakers played to the headlines and "pretended it was a crime to give answers, when it never was," said Freedman. "And they all knew it wasn't." But they focused on the producers—including Howard Felsher, who supervised *Tic Tac Dough*. "The inquisitors really had no mercy on me or any of the other producers. I was drawn and quartered." Felsher did not name any contestants for fear they would be unfairly tarred, and he refused to answer questions involving any particular match. He was asked about tests, retests, and other game-show controls—but nothing about corporate controls, network fixes, or agent manipulations.

Those omissions bothered Felsher. During a break, he resolved to tell the congressmen about far more insidious practices in network TV. For example, *Tic Tac Dough*, originally sold by MCA, was sponsored by Tender Leaf Iced Tea. Yet the sponsor routinely misrepresented its product during live commercials. In order to make Tender Leaf Iced Tea, one had to brew the tea, then let it cool—which took too much time for a commercial break. A competitor's product, White Rose Iced Tea, could be mixed with water and served easily on live TV. So Tender Leaf execs ordered producers to use White Rose instead. This was a clear violation of law, said Felsher. "Companies tricked the consumer when they asked him to buy their deceptively presented product." If such practices were exposed, company chiefs, admen, and talent agents might be brought down—not just lowly producers.

Felsher waited for the hearings to resume. Just then, Congressman Harris came up to him and smiled in a conciliatory manner.

"I hope you're not too upset at our treatment of you," Harris told him. "I'm sure you must know what wonderful publicity this is for our committee."

Felsher stood up, angry at the lawmaker's comment. "Do you mean to tell me that you're ruining peoples' lives so you can have some wonderful publicity?"

The politician turned and walked away.

The encounter strengthened Felsher's resolve. When the hearings resumed, the producer took his seat. Harris asked him about a quiz-show script, and Felsher replied:

"Before I answer that question, I'd like to say something about what I believe are crooked commercials. . . ."

Harris pounded his gavel several times and drowned out Felsher's words. He sternly ordered the witness to answer the question.

Years later, Felsher explained: "I knew that day that the committee didn't want to hear what was really going on. The phony commercials and dishonest products were really costing the consumers money, but no one wanted to hear about that fraud." Even worse was how game-show sponsors used wiretaps and deceit to steal concepts for popular quiz shows from one another, which is what

Revlon had done with *The $64,000 Question*. It had allegedly wire-tapped its archrival to obtain trade secrets and snatch away the game-show sponsorship idea just before its rival signed a deal. Con-testants paid talent agents to get on the shows, retailers paid pro-ducers to plug their products for free, and CBS and NBC had formed entire departments to procure gifts for "giveaway" shows—which struck some lawmakers as "plugola." Harris's subcommittee possessed evidence and reports of all these illegal practices, along with proof that Revlon and its agency had actually ordered the rigs, Stone wrote in his account.

"MCA and its corporate sponsors weren't any different," said Freedman. "We got calls from these guys all the time, telling us what they wanted. They all knew it was rigged. Bob Kintner and the guys at NBC knew it. Sonny Werblin knew it. And Lew Wasserman knew about it."

But these findings did not surface in the public hearings.

Instead, the cameras focused on another MCA client: Charles Van Doren. "Where's Charlie?" the headlines screamed. Wasserman and his men had found a high-profile job for Van Doren, who now appeared regularly on NBC's *Today Show*, reciting poetry or dis-cussing non-Euclidean geometry every day in his five-minute spot. Van Doren was so popular that MCA agents were scouring Holly-wood to land him a feature-movie role. Van Doren's answers to the committee would dictate the direction of his budding show-business career. How much would the young man reveal in this inquisition?

On November 2, 1959, Van Doren took the stand in a room packed with 1,000 spectators. In the most dramatic scene of the hearings, Van Doren admitted that, yes, he had seen quiz answers before the show. "I was involved, deeply involved, in a deception." He said, "I'd would give almost anything I have to reverse the course of my life in the last three years." That day, Van Doren lost his beloved teaching job, his high-profile TV job, and a bright future in the movies.

Now it was the networks' turn in the spotlight. Many TV executives feared a federal antitrust suit, a tax audit, or a full-fledged investigation. So when Harris summoned them, they appeared contrite, especially Robert Kintner, who had recently become president of NBC. After Kintner's promotion in July 1958, Wasserman had thrown a surprise party for the executive in Beverly Hills, calling him "my very good friend."

Now the NBC executive arrived at the hearings wielding an awesome display of paper, including notarized depositions from his men, who swore they had had no knowledge of any fix. "We were just as much a victim of the quiz-show frauds as the public," Kintner said. Some congressmen questioned his ignorance, but no one pressed him. "The network guys were treated with a lot of deference," said Felsher. Ultimately, Congress did not pursue the executives or their agents, whom they suspected of giving evasive, contradictory, or—what they later discovered to be—false testimony.

NBC, however, fired Felsher summarily. Behind the scenes, the network and MCA worked feverishly to contain the damage. Kintner washed his hands of Barry and Enright, paying off the pair quietly, then canceling the $2.2 million contract that MCA had negotiated for them. The two producers were banished from network TV for years, yet NBC kept their show, *Concentration*, running until 1979. "And MCA kept getting its 10 percent and royalties from syndication," said Stettner. "Lew never walked away from cash."

In July 1960, the New York District Attorney convened yet *another* grand jury—this time to consider charges of perjury, subornation of perjury, obstruction of justice, and conspiracy in connection with the earlier quiz-show investigation. Prosecutors hauled out the same hapless contestants and mid-level producers who had been grilled by the first grand jury, and then by the House leaders. Only those contestants who had recanted and told the truth during subcommittee hearings were charged with perjury. About eighteen *Twenty-One* winners pled guilty and, in 1962, received suspended sentences. In October of that year, Freedman, who had gone above and beyond his duty in helping the grand juries and congressional hearings, had his perjury charges dismissed. However, he would never be able to work in TV again, even though he had broken no law. "It was like some bad joke that wouldn't end," said Freedman.

However, Wasserman and his TV associates feared potential new FCC regulations. It appeared as if lawmakers were about to wrest back control of the public airwaves from the agencies and their clients. Harris's subcommittee recommended new laws that would give the FCC more powers to regulate broadcasting, but the networks, sponsors, and agencies lobbied quietly against them. In the summer of 1960, Congress passed a law making it a crime to give or take assistance on quiz shows. Since that time, some pundits have said that *Twenty-One*'s demise marked the end of TV's Golden Era. But you don't hear that from *Twenty-One*'s producers. "We didn't lose our innocence in the 1950s quiz-show scandal, and it's rubbish to say so," scoffed Freedman. "The entertainment field from time immemorial has been based on showmanship, spectacle, and illusion."

And that's pretty much how Wasserman felt.

But the hearings triggered a sea change for MCA. Soon there would be no more single sponsorship of a program. From now on, networks would have to sell commercial TV time to advertising agencies and corporations—in two- and one-minute chunks. The fees for such time would be set by networks, depending on the show's ratings, rather than by production companies like MCA's Revue. But instead of one company selling its message during a TV hour, many competing vendors would be shouting for the viewers' attention, assaulting them with more hype and noise. Madison Avenue and advertisers would no longer hold direct sway, but certainly indirect. And the power to dictate programming lay with the networks—and independent producers like Revue.

The dramatic quiz shows, once valued for their esoteric questions and educational quality, disappeared and were replaced by more fluff and schlock, such as *The Dating Game*, or *Hollywood Squares*. These shows were no longer broadcast live, but were videotaped, creating even more syndicated product for packagers like MCA to sell and resell. Lawyers assumed larger roles in deciding what played on TV, becoming arbiters of taste and safe programming. After 1960, the TV dial was gripped even tighter by corporate interests in New York and Hollywood. When all was said and done, the average citizen lost even more control of what was supposed to be publicly owned airwaves.

On a dark set at Universal Studios, high-pitched giggles answered a husky plea. A trousered voice . . . a nylon sigh . . . and the air was infused with an itchy sexuality. Breath quickened, temperatures rose, and slow moans betrayed the rhythm of a horizontal bop. These were the scenes played with increasing frequency by members of Edie's circle in late 1960.

While Lew was slowly gaining more power, Edie felt hers slipping away. This was an uneasy time in Hollywood, when the social girdle of the Eisenhower era was sliding off, about to be discarded. The fear, depression, and restlessness that motivated many actors was rising to the surface. Tony Curtis, for one, was married, with children, yet he acted like a swinging bachelor. He was making love to starlets and script girls in his dressing room, in his automobile, and in the home of his friend, restaurateur Nicky Blair. The actor's illicit trysts at Blair's hideaway in Laurel Canyon were so well known that they became the plot of *The Apartment* (1960), directed by Billy Wilder. "There were so many beautiful girls who were bit players and I wanted . . . them all," Curtis said. He boasted that his agent, Lew, made sure that all of Curtis's contracts included a key clause: "Tony can get laid anytime he wants." And the star exercised his clause rigorously.

By 1960, Curtis's indiscretions were becoming more than Edie could bear. She had a vested interest in the success of both Tony and his wife. Edie's success pairing Curtis and Cary Grant had led to *Operation Petticoat* (1960), which became Universal's most profitable film at the time, grossing $10 million. Meanwhile, she was trying to reassure an insecure Janet Leigh, for whom Lew had negotiated a movie deal. "Edie was close to Janet, but she still treated MCA's clients with great respect, like they were her clients," said Jackie Gershwin. Edie instinctively knew how to juggle the conflicting roles of friend and secret agent. She'd listen to Leigh unload her problems, stroke her arm, say, "Don't worry, Janet. You're a star. A real star." Still, the business was paramount.

Leigh told Edie about Tony's growing list of affairs, and Edie reacted by hunting him down. She backed the philanderer into a corner and aimed her finger at him like a cocked and loaded gun. "Control yourself," she hissed. "At least be discreet!" Curtis tried to discuss *his* feelings and *his* problems. "But it was to no avail," he said. Edie would just grow madder and order him to treat his wife better. "Have your affairs if you want. But don't ignore your wife!"

Meanwhile, the wives turned aggressive. Within Edie's closed circle, everybody was now flirting. Some of it was the European, "sophisticated sort that never goes anywhere but makes an evening more amusing," said Judy Balaban Kanter. Witty repartees and snappy one-liners were considered as artful as a Preston Sturges script. But Edie couldn't help but notice that, lately, the flirting had gotten randier—and more apt to backfire. A new parlor game—called sardines—carried unexpectedly stiff penalties. This was a grown-up version of hide-and-seek, but a wife might find that her husband wound up in the closet with her best friend. Or a husband might catch his wife playing kissy-face in the kitchen with his agent. The object of sardines was to "out" an illicit affair that most everyone knew about, anyway. It was played for kicks, but it destroyed relationships.

Edie was at the center of these games, equal parts den mother and social director. Everybody—the MCA agents, their wives, their clients and spouses—all knew the cardinal rule: "You never flirted—or went any farther—with a ringer or outsider," said Balaban Kanter. As long as it stayed *en famille,* the circle would survive.

But fissures appeared. Dean and Jeanne Martin, who had separated several times during the 1950s, were going through another rocky round. "Jeannie had all those children and Dean traveled a lot," explained Gershwin. Though Lew had just gotten Dean Martin another plum role—this one in *Rio Bravo*—Martin had begun popping Percodan like breath mints; he and Jeanne were no longer living together.

Cary Grant and his wife, actress Betsy Drake, were living apart, too, and receiving therapy with Dr. Mortimer Hartman. The doctor worked out of a small, dark office on Lasky Drive off Rodeo. It had a backstreet entrance where patients could come and go without being spotted. Hartman was one of several doctors in Los Angeles who was experimenting on patients with the drug lysergic acid. A number of Edie's acquaintances were under Hartman's care, including Esther Williams, Judy Balaban Kanter, and Grant. Some were taking LSD as often as three times a week, trusting that the doctor knew what he was doing. Reclining on Hartman's couch, with the blackout drapes drawn, stars and agents embarked on personal journeys that would end in breakthroughs, breakups, or breakdowns. Grant was thrilled with his trips, which he said made him a better actor and human being. Williams called LSD an "instant psychoanalyst." But others found the experience too dark and disturbing.

"Jay and I begin living two separate lives in the same house," said Balaban Kanter. She, too, was succumbing to the atmosphere of sexuality. Once, at Chasen's, she met Tony Franciosa and his wife, Shelley Winters. An electric current passed between her and the actor, and warning bells clanged. "My attraction to Tony was dangerous" because he was not part of Edie's circle, she said. He exuded a raw energy that was not controlled by the mores of her "movie mob." When Edie heard about this, she warned Judy and took action.

Whenever a chum had news—good or bad—Edie threw a party. Once, she invited all of MCA's music combos to entertain her guests. Her backyard pool was covered with lilies and floating candles, said Gershwin. There was a huge dance floor, where Cyd Charisse, June Allyson, and Jane Russell stole the show in eye-popping evening gowns. To the side, Gary Cooper, Clark Gable, and Jimmy Stewart sipped champagne.

Gable was one of Edie's favorite actors and was among Lew's early idols. Wasserman had grown up watching the matinee star, who was probably the most romantic star Hollywood every produced, loved by women and admired by men. As a talent agent in the 1940s, Wasserman and his wife were on a first-name basis with Gable, who one night invited them to a dinner party at his home. During the evening, the gallant actor noticed Edie fuming as her husband fended off producers who wanted to make deals. "I never make a deal at a party," Lew demurred. Finally Gable interrupted the cocktail chatter and announced: "Ladies and gentlemen, Lew Wasserman is my guest tonight. If you'd like to discuss business, please call him at the office." Edie wanted to hug him for that, and later borrowed Clark's line as her house rule.

"At one party, lyricist Jule Styne played the piano, Dean Martin sang a song, and Rita Hayworth hiked up her gown to play the drums, which all of us thought very funny," recalled Gershwin. Edie always had her parties catered by Chasen's—serving rare steaks, succulent shrimp, and its famous chili. Her bar was as busy as the swank club The Mocombo. Dress designers Orry-Kelly, Oleg Cassini, and Edith Head were known to vamp, primarily for one another. Producers like Walter and Marvin Mirisch, Daryl Zanuck, and David Brown chatted with Lew, but never cornered him there.

"You heard such great conversations," said Charlton Heston,

quite a raconteur himself. One party night, MCA directors Billy Wilder and William Wyler were trawling at the edge of the revelry when they stopped to chat. Billy Wilder complained to "Willie" Wyler: "They keep confusing our work. The other day, some producer called me Willie. I hear he calls you Billy. Willie, Billy—why can't they get us straight?"

Wyler looked at the curmudgeonly Wilder and shrugged. "Monet. Manet. What's the difference?" he said and walked off.

By the end of 1960, even Edie's party carousel could not quite keep the chummy-chums together. Rosemary Clooney was popping pretty colored pills called Seconal, Miltown, and Tuinal—"sunshine, lipstick and snowdrift," she called them. But it was her way of handling her pain and sorrow, she later explained. "I knew all too well that my marriage was crumbling." Shelley Winters was out on her front lawn in Beverly Hills, hollering about Tony Franciosa's infidelity. Cary and Betsy were splitting up; so were Tony and Janet, and Dean and Jeanne. Even Judy Bird and Jay Bird were in trouble, and Edie was trying to talk Balaban Kanter out of a divorce.

So, when a handsome young Democratic senator came to town that season stumping for votes, it was a welcome respite. The game of politics, the town discovered, could be more exciting than a round of sardines.

ELEVEN

WASSERMAN HAD BEEN ASKED BY JACK WARNER to contribute to the 1960 presidential campaign of then-Vice President Richard Nixon. Instead, Lew and Edie laid money on Nixon's Democratic rival, John F. Kennedy. Wasserman donated a few thousand dollars to the Kennedy-Johnson campaign as Democratic Party fever swept through Lew's circle.

"Getting involved in politics wasn't always of our own choosing," said Tony Curtis. But it seemed like a natural thing for actors to do. It helped that Kennedy's sister Patricia was married to actor Peter Lawford, so when Lawford asked Curtis to host a luncheon for JKF, he and Janet Leigh said, "Of course!" The lunch included drinks and grew into a pep rally, recalled Jackie Gershwin. Later, Leigh got to dance with JFK himself at Lawford's Malibu Beach house. "I was dazzled," she said. Rosemary Clooney sang at fundraising events, Zsa Zsa Gabor volunteered, and MCA starlets worked at campaign head-quarters. Frank Sinatra became a big Kennedy fan, drawing in Sammy Davis, Jr., Nat King Cole, and Bobby Darin. As for the Hol-lywood wives, said Balaban Kanter, "Kennedy stirred our latent social consciousness. For the first time, a lot of us felt inspired to act."

There was something about the dashing Irish Catholic that stirred these liberal Jewish artists. Even Presbyterians felt his heat. "He seemed different than the cigar-smoking politicians we were used to," said Leigh. He had charisma and substance, "which inspired in us an idealism about politics," she said.

Wasserman had been rubbing elbows with the Kennedys for decades. Years later, he told me: "I had the privilege of knowing them all, including JFK's father." Joseph Kennedy had made a for-tune in bootleg liquor, doing business with Moe Dalitz, chief of the Cleveland syndicate and Wasserman's early employer. When Lew joined MCA in 1936, the Kennedy patriarch was spending time in Hollywood, playing house with Gloria Swanson and advising Para-mount Pictures how to restructure. "Joseph Kennedy [Sr.] was in show business, and so was I," Wasserman explained. Later, whenever Jules Stein traveled to England, he tried to see Kennedy, who was the ambassador to England from 1937 to 1940. But Wasserman made a point of staying out of national politics in MCA's early days. "Lew and Jules thought it was bad for business," explained Berle Adams.

Wasserman's first step toward that door was his support for

Franklin Roosevelt's vice president, he said. "I had a party at the house for Harry Truman," in 1944. "I invited anybody who would come." When Roosevelt suddenly died in office in 1945, and Truman became president, Wasserman admired how quickly the former Missouri haberdasher grew into a capable leader. However, the agent didn't work to raise campaign funds. "Money was different in those days," he remarked. Cash didn't dominate the election process like it would decades later, after Wasserman had become a Democratic fundraiser par excellence.

John F. Kennedy, as it turned out, had many advantages—including money. Wasserman had heard reports that Joe Kennedy paid *Time* magazine $75,000 to put his son on its cover. Certainly, the magazine cover boosted John's profile and positioned him well for the 1960 presidential campaign. He was telegenic, hardworking, and young—all qualities Wasserman looked for in any rising star. Best of all, Kennedy understood the holy trinity of favors, funds, and friendships.

By the time Wasserman's close friend, Beverly Hills labor attorney Paul Ziffren, landed the Democratic National Convention for Los Angeles, American politics was ready for the big-screen treatment. Statecraft and stagecraft merged as the convention put glamorous Los Angeles on the map politically. Studio moguls ran tour buses from the Ambassador Hotel to their back lots. Disneyland drew more conventioneers than the city's nightclubs. When Kennedy was nominated on the Democratic ticket, the Hollywood crowd went berserk. Joe Kennedy monitored it all from a Beverly Hills mansion once owned by starlet Marion Davies, William Randolph Hearst's longtime companion.

In January 1961, Edie, Lew, and several other MCA executives and clients traveled to Washington for Kennedy's inauguration. "We were so excited to be included," said Jay Kanter. The ceremony took place on a freezing day, but nothing broke the MCA contingent's esprit de corps. That night, Sinatra, Lawford, Dean Martin, and other Rat Pack members put on a lavish show for the inaugural ball. The youthful president embodied enough vigor and hope to thaw a long cold war. The first lady brought a sense of style and grace to the Pennsylvania Avenue White House, and the movie veterans felt elated about the future, said Kanter. They had played a part in the president's narrow victory. To Edie, Lew, and their friends, that accomplishment was more thrilling than any box-office hit. The Wassermans had high hopes for this administration, but they would soon come crashing down.

After Kennedy's snowy swearing-in, the FCC ordered MCA executives to appear at a hearing, set for March 1961. The new administration was keenly interested in MCA and its rival, talent agency William Morris. Between them, they controlled most of the entertainment business, the FCC discovered.

One witness recalled watching a group of men march out of MCA's White House. They wore dark suits and gray hats; one executive brandished an unlit cigar. "They were all balding, except Lew," said Bill Gardner, who for years had tried to get a job at MCA. He admired the way the men tucked down the brim of their hats slightly and how they walked with such purpose. He envied their crisp white Sulka shirts, their tailored suits by Sy Devore—haberdasher to the stars—and their 14-karat gold links glinting from their cuffs.

"They were elegant, tall Jews who projected this great image," said Gardner. Wasserman agents had more panache, said Gardner, than those at William Morris, whose chief, Abe Lastfogel, was only five feet one inch tall. "He didn't want anybody to tower over him, so he hired short people." But at MCA, several men stood six-feet-plus, and their height didn't faze the six-foot-two-inch boss. Wasserman towered over everyone, anyway, given his stature in the industry. As Berle Adams said: "Lew was big and imposing, and he used that to his advantage whenever possible."

That spring, Wasserman needed every advantage he could muster. The Justice Department had been circling MCA since 1954. "It is well-known that the anti-trust (sic) division had for several years been investigating MCA," *Variety* reported in 1960. Now the Kennedy administration was picking up the scent. The FCC wanted to learn how Hollywood used the airwaves. It had subpoenaed executives at both William Morris and MCA, demanding documents related to TV shows they owned, packaged, or sold. The Morris agents had complied quickly. They brought not only documents to the hearings but also flowcharts and graphs to explain their business. They had stressed repeatedly: "We own no part of any package. We only package and sell shows—for a customary 10 percent."

But MCA had fought the summons. So the FCC had gone around them, retrieving details of agency deals from its TV licensees and gradually piecing together a breathtaking picture. Whereas William Morris had annual revenues of about $10 million, MCA had taken in $82 million. And while Morris rarely took more than 10 percent commission from its TV deals, MCA took 10 percent only when it sold network first-run shows. It went on to grab 20 percent from network reruns, 30 percent from regional TV networks, 40 percent from local stations, and 50 percent for foreign distribution. It collected about 30 percent in fees and overhead from the TV shows it produced, in addition to $17 million from selling old movies to TV every year and $1 million by renting its former sets and stages back to Universal Studios.

The commission subpoenaed Schreiber to learn more about this. He arrived that March day to testify, flanked by an entourage. "You'd think this was a funeral," said one witness.

The proceedings immediately took on a strained note. When Schreiber took the stand, he was asked to hand over the list of network shows Revue owned. He did. But when asked for a list of shows that MCA had packaged or sold, Schreiber intoned: "We'd be happy to produce it on the basis of it being kept confidential." A jolt ran through the panel; Schreiber's request went against the most basic tenet of democracy. This was an open meeting of a public agency, yet Schreiber refused to play by the rules. The FCC pressed, Schreiber repeated his position, and the two sides volleyed for a minute.

Then Schreiber pulled out a typed sheet, which he had vetted earlier with Stein and Wasserman. He read aloud: "It has been the policy of our company not to give out this information." Schreiber repeated his objection and added that the FCC's request is "outside the scope of its investigation." At that, the room erupted. FCC attorneys objected, MCA's attorney yelled, and the commissioner ordered Schreiber to answer. Instead, the TV salesman and his attorney packed their briefcases and walked out of the hearing room.

Schreiber's arrogance and contempt triggered one of the more fascinating corporate showdowns between Washington and Hollywood. Back at headquarters, FCC officials turned apoplectic. Its new chairman, Newton Minow, asked Attorney General Robert Kennedy to sue Schreiber for criminal contempt. But Kennedy had other things in mind. The Department of Justice dropped William Morris from its antitrust case and focused on MCA.

Meanwhile, government attorney Leonard Posner finally learned one secret of Wasserman's power. One day over lunch, entertainment attorney Gunther Schiff explained that, ten years earlier, MCA had made a "sweetheart deal" with SAG: "Ronnie Reagan gave MCA a waiver, and he managed to capitalize on it nicely," Schiff told the federal prosecutor. "There's no question that Reagan was not that successful. All of a sudden, he gives MCA a waiver, and they give him a huge job." Posner's new information, combined with Schreiber's stiff arm to Congress, was reason enough for the new attorney general to step up his investigation.

MCA's clients were becoming especially needy. Marlon Brando called his agent, Jay Kanter, every day to check in. Judy Garland was falling-down drunk before performances. Marilyn Monroe was showing up at the office in shabby dresses, with hair like straw. "She looked like she was homeless," said MCA secretary Myrle Wages. Tony Curtis agreed: "Everybody in town thought I was giving a bum rap to Marilyn, but she was in trouble and I knew it." The actress struggled with drugs and alcohol, yet her agents seemed unable to help. "Marilyn only did [*Some Like It Hot*] because she needed money to help her husband [Arthur Miller] with his legal bills from HUAC," said Curtis. The Pulitzer Prize–winning Miller had appeared in front of the House Un-American Activities Committee in 1956—without his MCA agent. He had admitted attending a few political meetings, but denied that he was a Communist. Congress cited him for contempt, forcing Miller and Monroe to spend money clearing his name.

MCA had recently sold a Miller screenplay for *The Misfits* (1961), which would feature Montgomery Clift, Clark Gable, and Monroe. But Monroe was showing up late, stalling production, and she was caught with her paramour and previous costar, Yves Montand, while her husband worked on the set. The project was so messy that Robert Mitchum warned director John Huston, "You're going to kill Gable with this film. I saw him the other day at lunch, and he had the brandy tremors." Two weeks after production wrapped, the fifty-nine-year-old Gable died of a massive heart attack. Edie and Lew grieved at his funeral, and over the next eighteen months, they'd mourn the deaths of other MCA clients—Jeff Chandler, Gary Cooper, and the troubled Monroe as well.

Wasserman was now forty-eight years old and tired of the business. He'd been an agent for twenty-five years—in Hollywood for twenty-one of those years—and through it all, he had kept a low profile. This was partly because his boss Stein had demanded it and partly because he knew what publicity consisted of. "It's primarily ego," he told me—whether a star's ego, a mogul's ego, or even an agent's ego: "It's ego on the part of everyone involved." He'd become the ego wrangler par excellence, the unrivaled handler of legends and names. "You either know how to handle stars or you don't," he explained. Wasserman had the knack. He had worked hard to perfect his touch, using an iron fist, kid gloves, or sleight of hand, depending on what was needed. How had he represented so many fragile talents for so long? "With care," he answered wearily. Patient, loving care.

So, too, with MCA. Wasserman had grown the agency by cajoling and pushing his agents away from their early reliance on band-booking fees. Now he had movie stars, scriptwriters, and screen directors on his roster. He worked with unions, producers, and networks, and owned TV shows, reruns, and old movies. The only thing in town he didn't have was a major film studio.

Wasserman knew that Posner was inquiring about MCA and the studios. "If you're talking about links, what about the one between Universal and MCA?" one actor teased Posner. MCA's purchase of the land at Universal Studios was an obvious connection. Before the sale, Milton Rackmil had cut its slate to 12 films. Some 100 MCA actors were under contract at Universal, and after MCA's deal, its biggest projects were MCA's packages. There was Doris Day and Rock Hudson in *Pillow Talk* (1959); Cary Grant and Tony Curtis in *Operation Petticoat* (1960); Burt Lancaster, Kirk Douglas, and Tony Curtis in *Spartacus* (1960); Janet Leigh, Vera Miles, John Gavin, and Anthony Perkins in Alfred Hitchcock's *Psycho* (1960); Henry Koster, director of *Flower Drum Song* (1961); Gregory Peck and Robert Duvall in *To Kill a Mockingbird* (1962). Now Wasserman was drawing plans to develop the 410-acre lot.

In fact, the ties between MCA and Universal went back before the real estate sale, to a series of deals in the 1950s that Wasserman had negotiated for his clients. In 1950 he and Jimmy Stewart waived the actor's $200,000 salary in return for half the potential profits on one Universal film *Winchester '73*. Stewart worked for nothing; the film became a hit and went on to net $2 million—half of which belonged to Stewart. "Everyone called [studio chief Leo] Spitz and Lew Wasserman geniuses," said Ed Muhl. Wasserman had the confidence that his client would make a hit, and Spitz jumped at the chance to sign a star without paying cash up front. But that deal also included a contract for a Universal picture, *Harvey*, one of Stewart's favorite films. He happily waived his salary to star in the movie, but this time, it flopped. Wasserman had won half of his two-part gamble, and Universal had gotten one hit and one free star performance.

Whenever MCA needed to park a fading star, Universal obliged. For example, when MCA client Ronald Reagan couldn't get a studio contract elsewhere, Universal gave him a five-picture deal in 1950 at half his previous salary. When one of MCA's grande dames wanted a job, Universal accommodated—as it did with Joan Crawford in *Female on the Beach* (1955) and June Allyson in *A Stranger in My Arms* (1959). It got so that Universal was called the agents' studio, run by Jules Stein, rather than by Milton Rackmil.

The relationship between Rackmil and Stein had started through their banker, Serge Semenenko. "He ran a bank within a bank," said Berle Adams. The Russian had arranged as much as $2 billion worth of loans to movie-industry people over the years. He told Stein and Decca's founder Jack Knapp the same thing said Joe Delaney: "In order to grow bigger, we had to control all aspects of show business in the postwar economy." But Knapp wasn't interested, although his executive Rackmil was. In a series of stealth stock purchases, made through nonprofit foundations and holding companies, Semenenko helped Stein acquire stock in Decca in 1946 and in Universal in 1951. When Knapp died, Semenenko also helped Rackmil take over Decca in 1949 and Universal in 1952. "They all had a deal," Delaney insisted. One day, Stein could control Decca and Universal.

Rackmil presided over the decline of Universal. In 1955 the studio's profits were $4 million, but by 1957 income had dropped to $2.5 million, and that turned into a $2 million loss the following year. "We thought the money was going to Mexico, or something," said one Universal executive. Times were tough all over town, but no other studio performed as poorly—or so quickly—as Universal did. It even dragged down the value of its parent, Decca Records.

That set up the sale in 1958 of Decca's main asset: the real estate at Universal Studios. "The reason for all of this was that Wasserman all along was planning to get into movie production," said Hollywood historian Bernard Dick. But everything had to click together—the union contracts, the SAG waiver, and the network business. Through Semenenko, Wasserman and Stein could manipulate the timing of when they acquired the Decca/Universal asset. But neither one of them had counted on the new chief at the Department of Justice. "All I remember is that Bobby Kennedy was sure after us," said Berle Adams. "He thought that MCA was mob-controlled."

TWELVE

A BLACK TINTED-WINDOW LIMOUSINE glided up to the Desert Inn Hotel and Casino in Las Vegas and stopped. Lew and Edie Wasserman stepped out, followed by a swarm of black-suited men wearing sunglasses. It was around 1960, and the couple strode into the lobby and looked for a familiar face. This rose-colored casino was owned by their friend, the head of Cleveland's Jewish Mafia—Moe Dalitz—a lean, dapper man. "Moe was the unofficial referee," said George Riff, a former Stardust executive who was close to Dalitz. "He kept peace among the competing Mafia families and was called the 'first among equals.'" Dalitz was in the midst of acquiring The Stardust casino after its owner had mysteriously dropped dead in the Desert Inn. Dalitz was also under surveillance by the FBI, which considered him "armed and dangerous." Yet the sixty-year-old Dalitz was avuncular and gracious as he greeted the old Cleveland sweethearts, Edie and Lew Wasserman.

Wasserman's hair was now graying and his towering frame carried more weight than it had twenty-five years ago in Cleveland. Edie still wore her dark hair at chin length and hadn't lost any of her energetic sparkle. Dalitz disappeared, Lew sent Edie into the casino, and he crossed the lobby to whisper to his men, Jerry "The Ear" Gershwin and Alan "Pinky" Miller. A woman watched Lew, attracted to his vitality yet repelled by his sotto voce style. "I thought he was Mafia," she said. "He certainly looked the part."

The Wassermans often stayed in one of the Desert Inn's best suites, said Roy Gerber. Dalitz made sure their room was filled with flowers, fruits, and liquor. "Lew was always friendly with Dalitz," said Gerber. "Everyone thought that because of Lew we had an 'in' in Las Vegas." Hollywood's elite assumed that Lew Wasserman was connected to the mob, even though few could explain his ties. But MCA's connections were an open secret, said Robert Mitchum. "Everyone knew that Stein worked for Al Capone in Chicago. That's how MCA got into the band business."

During the Great Depression, Lew worked for Dalitz and his gang, promoting their most lavish nightclub, the Mayfair Casino, located in downtown Cleveland. The syndicate had spent more than $250,000 on the club. When it opened in October 1935, Wasserman boasted that it had the world's longest bar, Ohio's biggest dance floor, and the best acts in town. "Practically everybody was there . . . or everybody who had the money," said one wag. Ohio politicians, judges, lawyers, industrialists, socialites, and gangsters crowded the bar. Part of Mayfair's appeal was its secret back room, where the rich played illegal roulette and craps. "It was always a hush-hush thing, and you had to be in the know," said Marge LaRonge, who frequented the den. "But you can't hide things like that in a small town, and soon everyone knew about it."

The Mayfair was just one of six fancy gambling clubs that Dalitz owned in the Midwest, and it drew the attention of Eliot Ness, leader of the "Untouchables." Ness had made his name closing Capone's breweries during Prohibition. In 1935 he became Cleveland's safety director, charged with stamping out mob-owned whiskey mills and shutting down bars that violated post-Prohibition liquor laws. That spring, he raided the Mayfair early Sunday morning—the only day it was illegal to sell alcohol, and at a time when Saturday-night patrons were still swinging. Wasserman was there when Ness also discovered that the liquor served at the Mayfair's bar was bootleg—the specialty of the house, made illicitly by Dalitz and his gang.

Another time, Ness and seven detectives raided the nightclub, searching for trapdoors, secret rooms, or any sign of gambling. They never found any, but returned several more times, said LaRonge. Before each visit, someone at the precinct would alert Dalitz or his men. That would give the Mayfair crew time to camouflage the gambling den and return to the floor—just as Ness and his squad burst through the doors. LaRonge, who was there during one raid, noted that through it all, "Lew kept his ears and eyes open but his mouth shut."

Dalitz claimed with a straight face that he had no idea that gambling clubs were illegal. "There were so many judges and politicians in them, I figured they had to be all right," he often said. He was sly and subtle; more than any other mob, the Cleveland syndicate preferred the bribe to the bullet. Its members led quiet personal lives, earning them the nickname the Silent Syndicate. But payoffs and bribes didn't always work. By the fall of 1936, Dalitz's men inside the Ohio legislature had failed to pass a bill legalizing gambling and the Mayfair's days were numbered.

Dalitz prepared to sell his casino to two New York gangsters: Louis Blumenthal and Jacob "Gurrah" Shapiro. The two men were better known as part of Murder Inc., the enforcement arm of the national syndicate. By the time the sale was completed in December, Wasserman was en route to Chicago, where he took a $40-a-week cut in pay to work as the publicist for Jules Stein's music agency.

By the mid-1940s, when gangsters from the East started to build lavish casinos in the middle of the Nevada desert, Lew had become MCA's chief, selling the entertainment that lured big spenders. When New York's Meyer Lansky and his minion Bugsy Siegel opened The Flamingo in December 1946, Wasserman sent his client Xavier Cugat to headline opening night. When Dalitz opened the Desert Inn in 1950, Wasserman assembled Edgar Bergen, the Donn Arden Dancers, and the Ray Noble Orchestra as headliner acts. He also sent MCA clients Van Heflin, Bud Abbott, and Lou Costello to sit in the audience. "That's when all of the gangsters started coming," said Barbara Greenspun, publisher of the *Las Vegas Sun*. After the Desert Inn's success, the Detroit, New York, and New Jersey gangs streamed into town, hungry for bands and acts to enliven their own casinos.

William Morris and other agencies sold to the casinos, but only after MCA arrived, said Roy Gerber. "I remember driving around town one day and realizing that we handled every major headliner, supporting act, and lounge show in Las Vegas," he said. In March 1956, Edie and Lew watched MCA clients Martin and Lewis climb onstage at The Sands, where the crowd gave them a standing ovation that lasted for several minutes. Wasserman had negotiated a record-breaking performance fee of $250,000 a night. By 1958, his agency acts were earning $1 million for six months of work. Two years later, MCA was ringing up $50,000 a week in Las Vegas sales—or $2.6 million, an awesome amount. That meant Wasserman was collecting at least $265,000 in annual commissions from the mobsters' casinos—far more than any other agency. "It was staggering," said Gerber.

By 1961, Wasserman was the top seller of Las Vegas entertainment, known to the casino mobsters as the go-to guy for orchestras, singers, comedians, and chorus girls. "The people who owned the hotels and casinos didn't want to talk to some agent from Las Vegas," he explained to me. "They wanted to talk to someone important in New York or Los Angeles. Of course, they wanted to talk to the big guys." Of course, they wanted to talk to Lew.

And Wasserman returned the favor, holding annual MCA meetings in Las Vegas, where he, Werblin, and Schreiber would gather their men. "We had so many acts in Las Vegas that Lew thought it made sense to patronize our clients," said Jim Murray. One year they'd stay at Sidney Korshak's place, The Riviera; another year they'd stay at The Sands. "They never stayed at The Flamingo because of the thing with Bugsy Siegel," said Seymour Heller, another agent. The "thing" was Siegel's 1947 murder. Many believed that Siegel was shot because he was skimming casino money. But Wasserman knew that Dalitz had him killed because Siegel was beating up Virginia Hill, one of Dalitz's old flames.

As Las Vegas flourished, Wasserman found himself walking a thin line. He continued to do business with the mob in 1961, when it became particularly risky for him to do so. But some of his agents thought Lew had no alternative. "We had to deal with these guys if we wanted to do business," explained Murray. "Besides, they never lied or cheated." MCA agents never used attorneys when they contracted with casino owners. "Sometimes I'd even write deals on a cocktail napkin, and show it to the crooked noses," said Murray. "They'd make handshake deals on the spot, and the bosses would lean in and whisper: 'If there's a mistake somewhere, I know you'll correct it.' " No more needed to be said. Murray and Gerber became so trusted, they could walk into the mobsters' inner sanctum. One day, Murray and Gerber accidentally wandered into the Desert Inn's counting room—Dalitz skimmed at least $400,000 a month, and that was just from the one-arm bandits. Murray's eyes bulged when he saw the enormous piles of money being tallied. Dalitz's counters saw the two intruders, froze, and studied their faces for a minute, then coolly returned to their calculations. "That was rare, let me tell you," said Murray. "We could have gotten killed one hundred times over. But we were never hurt. We were Lew's boys."

Still, Wasserman had to protect MCA and his own career. "Lew always had a passion for keeping MCA's reputation clean," said Jay Stein, an MCA executive. "He didn't want to be too closely associated with gambling, bookmaking, and such and was always very sensitive about that." Yet his life intersected with those who lived in that world.

Meyer Lansky, Moe Dalitz, and Sidney Korshak were public names, part of Lew's past, present . . . and future. The FBI suspected that Dalitz had recently taken over The Riviera by ordering his men—with Sidney Korshak's blessings—to slit the throat of owner Gus Greenbaum. The bureau also noted that Dalitz took over The Stardust after owner Tony Cornero dropped dead inside the Desert Inn, a victim of either sudden heart failure or poisoning.

Bobby Kennedy also suspected the worst of Dalitz, Korshak, and now Lew Wasserman, too.

Before becoming attorney general, Kennedy had been a staff member of the Senate Labor Rackets Committee, chaired by Senator John McClellan (D-Ark.). Kennedy helped untangle organized crime ties to labor unions, including those to the Teamsters and its Central States Pension Fund. The committee had assembled a spectacular lineup of witnesses, "plug-ugly Teamsters" who had lent money to mob figures such as Moe Dalitz. The mobster had used union funds to build the Desert Inn, The Stardust Hotel, and much of Las Vegas. Yet, despite the committee's evidence, neither the Justice Department nor its investigative arm, the FBI, indicted anyone.

But Kennedy had learned something about criminal enterprises, unions, and sweetheart contracts. So when his staff stumbled across the waiver that Reagan and SAG had given to MCA, they connected the dots. In the years that MCA/Revue had boomed—1952 to 1961—SAG had extended several favors to MCA only. By comparison, it had given other agencies only *limited* waivers, good for just a TV project or two. Kennedy and his staff noted how MCA's annual revenues had jumped—by 27 percent, then 40 percent, and in 1961 by 80 percent. Even non-agents could see the wild injustice in the union deal.

That spring, the pressure on MCA rose a notch. FCC chief Newton Minow gave a tongue-lashing to a conference of national advertisers. In a speech that has since become famous, he called television a "vast wasteland [full] of game shows, audience participation shows, formula comedies about totally unbelievable families, blood and thunder, mayhem, violence and cartoons. And endlessly, the commercials—many screaming, cajoling and offending." A few days later, an adman sent Kennedy a note saying that if Minow thought TV was bad, he should scrutinize Sonny Werblin of MCA, whose "incredible power over talent and booking is the source of much of the mediocrity on America's TV screens."

Kennedy authorized a federal grand jury to probe MCA. This was war. He requested all of MCA's tax returns for the previous few years and began developing a criminal-conspiracy theory that involved MCA, NBC, SAG, and other unions. That anyone would consider Stein's agency a crime syndicate infuriated Jules and Doris. After all, they had tried to do their part for the new administration. When Jacqueline Kennedy announced her plans to refurbish the White House, Doris offered to lend her valuable eighteenth-century antiques to grace the reception hall in the first family's quarters. The loan was announced as the Steins' "gift to the nation." Unfortunately, the first lady had to decline the museum-quality gift because of MCA's federal investigation. The Steins were embarrassed until, a few weeks later, Mrs. Kennedy accepted the very same pieces from Alastair Stair—an antiques dealer and Jules's partner in the prestigious Stair & Co. of New York. At least, Doris could finally tell her social peers that, oh yes, the first lady *did* borrow a few old things from her collection.

But Kennedy and the grand jury tightened their net. Suddenly, MCA's longtime advertising clients and network friends began to shun their agency pals. The company's stock price, which had been flying at 78, slid to 33. Washroom tidbits circulated all over New York and Los Angeles, and wafted back to Wasserman. "We heard the company was breaking up totally, that the government was after us, that some people were going to jail," said Daniel Welkes. Others believed that Kennedy was going to jail Wasserman, Stein, and Schreiber. "Word was, we were going to merge with Paramount—or with some other studio. But no one really knew." Every week, Wasserman briefed his men in the baronial meeting room. "Go about your business," he ordered his men. Pay no mind to the gossip. "We'll let you know what's going on soon enough."

In New York, the grand jury made little progress because "witnesses were frightened to death," said one prosecutor. Joseph Cotten had been threatened, Betty Grable had been bribed, and now even investigators were being warned about Werblin and Wasserman, supposed masters of skulduggery. "If you go after [MCA] too hard, watch out for the concrete shoes," one federal attorney general was told. Before long, the Antitrust Division moved the grand jury to Los Angeles. That's when the gloves came off, said Malcolm D. MacArthur, one of the federal attorneys. "This became a huge knock-down, drag-out investigation with no holds barred."

From the sidelines, MCA's archrival, GAC chief Herb Siegel, stepped up his efforts to obtain a SAG production waiver, too. Siegel and his attorney Abe Fortas (a future U.S. Supreme Court justice) invited SAG staff member Chet Migden to New York. "I thought it was going to be a nice friendly lunch," said Migden. Instead, Fortas blasted Migden and his union friends for giving MCA an unfair advantage. Fortas insisted that the secret backroom deal was not only dishonest, it had hurt his client. If SAG didn't extend the same deal to GAC, the union would face dire consequences. "He threatened us with a lawsuit and other kinds of nonsense," said Migden. The union official returned to Los Angeles and told SAG officers of GAC's request.

On October 10, 1961, SAG finally came through with a waiver for GAC—good for three months only. After that, Migden told GAC agents, "nobody's going to get any waivers." The guild intended to cancel all production waivers by December 1 of that year. Not even MCA would be allowed to produce TV shows under SAG bylaws. If a firm continued acting as both agent and producer, SAG would cancel the agency's franchise by the following June, and the agency would cease to exist.

The news shocked Hollywood—no one more than Wasserman. He tried to wheedle his way around the new rule, insisting that MCA needed more time to respond. Jack Dales, SAG's director, told Lew to make up his mind: Was he an agent or a producer? Wasserman explained that he had contracts with networks, studios, and employees. He couldn't possibly close his agency, or Revue, in a scant six months—not without violating existing agreements. Besides, he told Dales, SAG had guaranteed him that this wouldn't happen. Angrily, Dales told Lew that federal attorneys were at that moment reviewing SAG's files on the history of MCA's ten-year-old waiver.

"This is it, Lew. It's the end," he said.

Even so, Wasserman managed to extract an extension to July 31, 1962. And a few weeks later, SAG announced that MCA would receive yet *another* extension—this one to September 30, 1962. Wasserman now had more than a year to decide if he was going to remain in the annual $9 million agency business—or pursue his $72 million-a-year Revue operation. He pledged to make his choice before the fall 1962 TV season. Dales issued a press release: "During the transition period, MCA will be permitted to prepare for theatrical production, although no actual production may take place."

Lew was not about to reveal his grand-slam plan—at least not before taking care of his stable of star clients.

THIRTEEN

BACK AT MCA SQUARE, Wasserman chewed over his dilemma and hit upon a brilliant solution. He would preempt Kennedy's antitrust case, while protecting his stellar agency. "Lew had it all figured out," said Daniel Welkes.

Wasserman outlined his idea during one of his meetings. He intended to spin off the talent agency to his key employees. Long-time agent Larry Barnett would be chairman, obedient George Chasin would be president, and Lew would name the other officers in due course. Wasserman christened the new agency Management Corporation of America—or MCA—which drew a few wicked chortles. He planned to transfer all of MCA's performer contracts to the new talent agency so that the same agents would continue representing the same stars. "Now, this was wonderful," said Welkes. Several agents had worried that if Wasserman dissolved the agency, they would have to compete for clients. Of course, that's what the government wanted. But Wasserman was trumping Jack Dales and Robert Kennedy by shifting the agency's assets to a shell. He could still control the agency *and* Revue without violating any SAG agreement.

Best of all, Welkes added, Wasserman was going to give the entire $9 million agency to his men—for free. "Now, MCA was many things, but altruistic wasn't one of them," said rival agent Henry Miller. Wasserman's "gift" sent cheers through the meeting that day—and howls through the town.

When Dales heard about this, he cursed. The agency "spin-off" was a sham, he felt, since it would still be under Lew's control and still retain the same people. Revue would still have a direct pipeline to TV talent and would probably still secure special deals and packages. Lew's strategy was a flagrant disregard of SAG rules. But Dales did not relish confronting him over the issue.

Wasserman then went a step further. He, Stein, and twenty-nine other MCA agents began applying for agent licenses from the California Labor Commission. They would use their new state licenses to get new SAG franchises and open a new MCA. Dales and SAG's board—packed with MCA clients and employees—tried to wrestle with Wasserman's latest maneuver. "We didn't know what to do about this new wrinkle," Dales said. "I knew it was a problem. But what was the solution?"

In the fall of 1961, attorney Leonard Posner and the grand jury began calling witnesses in Los Angeles. The jury's mandate was to consider criminal charges against MCA, its executives, and union officials. The FBI had talked to 300 witnesses and possessed some 20,000 documents. The jury and antitrust attorneys were about to interview 150 more witnesses, including MCA rivals, clients, and labor leaders. One day, while Reagan was on the set of *General Electric Theater*, the jury served him with a subpoena. In February 1962, the panel listened as the former SAG president explained his reasons for granting MCA its unusual waivers. The actor did little to squelch the jury's suspicions, and his evasive answers, fuzzy memory, and contradictory testimony made him appear either incompetent or dishonest. The antitrust division and jury members suspected that Reagan had somehow been paid off by MCA. They subpoenaed the IRS to retrieve his and his second wife's income-tax returns, as well as those of Dales, Migden, and others. Hollywood could barely contain its intense curiosity. What was the government going to find?

General Electric did not wait to find out. The corporation could not afford to have its spokesman named in a federal lawsuit. In March, after eight successful seasons of *General Electric Theater*, the company did not to renew its contract with Reagan or Revue.

By now the actor had become quite wealthy. But he had no job with G.E. or Revue and no position with SAG. His agent, Arthur Park, circulated his résumé, but producers were underwhelmed by the fifty-one-year-old, former TV show host. Reagan turned to Schreiber but with no luck. In desperation, he called Wasserman. The superagent minced no words: "You've been around this business long enough to know that I can't force someone on a producer if he doesn't want to use him." Merrill Park spoke to him later: "Ronnie was hurt and devastated. But after all, what did he expect?"

Reagan naturally expected MCA to bail him out—as it had so many times before. Aside from several instances when MCA had rescued Reagan's faltering career, there was the matter of the ranch.

In 1951 Reagan and his former wife, Jane Wyman, sold the eight-acre Northridge Horse Farm that they had owned together. The divorced actor had two young children in private school and was strapped for cash, yet he made a surprisingly extravagant purchase. He bought a ranch 36 times bigger than the one he had just sold— a 290-acre horse-breeding farm in Malibu Canyon—and named it Yearling Row Ranch, after the two films he and Wyman made during their union (*The Yearling* and *Kings Row*). Part of the $85,000 purchase price allegedly came from the sale of the small Northridge spread. But where did Reagan get the rest of the money? "Some people in Hollywood said that Stein had bought him the ranch in return for the SAG waiver," said William Link, a TV writer. Added another: "*That* was the payoff."

Such a transaction was right in character for Stein, who was notorious for giving money and gifts to clients in exchange for something else. In the 1930s, Stein gave Mutual Broadcasting a nonreturnable $50,000 loan so it could extend its radio hookups west. Mutual repaid MCA by broadcasting its dance bands at no charge until Mutual had worked off the loan. In 1943 Stein tried to lure actor Laird Cregar (*The Lodger*) to MCA by lending him $14,000 for a ranch, but the actor died soon after and never repaid the loan. MCA offered Jayne Mansfield $50,000 in cash and Rock Hudson a Bel Air home—if only they'd sign with MCA. Given Stein's long-standing practice, it would have been surprising if he had *not* given Reagan money or land for the waiver.

The Antitrust Division would look for—but never find—such a gift. It had Reagan's IRS filings for the years 1952 through 1962—the period of MCA's waiver. But it never studied his filings for 1951—the year Reagan actually bought his Malibu property. In December 1966, Stein and Schreiber—acting as trustees—would quickly sell 236 of its 290 acres. The land would go to Twentieth Century Fox, then owned by Darryl Zanuck, a supporter of Reagan's political career. At nearly $2 million, the price of the property seemed inflated; 3,000 percent higher than it had been fifteen years earlier, when Reagan bought it for a low $85,000. The county appraised the land at $118,000. But Reagan kept his windfall, and Fox explained the high price by claiming it was moving its studio headquarters to the isolated ranch—just as Reagan was about to become California governor. Fox never did move its studios, and the series of deals looked like a daisy chain that enriched MCA's loyal client. As Reagan himself later explained, the inflated sale had been planned for years: "I could not have run for office [as governor] unless I sold the ranch."

As the government looked for evidence of corruption, Wasserman prepared to spin off his agency. "We had the best meeting ever one day, and we were all elated," said Welkes, who was named vice president of the new agency. The agents were moving to a new space on Wilshire Boulevard, and their client contracts were going with them. Wasserman had arranged to transfer MCA's profit-sharing trust, pension plan, and benefits to the new MCA. "That way, we wouldn't lose a beat in switching over," said Welkes. "We were ecstatic."

In April 1962, as the Los Angeles grand jury was still hearing witnesses in Los Angeles, MCA made a bold announcement. It intended to buy Decca Records and its subsidiary, Universal Studios. "Lew indulged in a calculated risk," said one observer. "He and Jules knew they were poking the devil." It would soon own the world's biggest record company and the largest film studio, completing a decades-old plan that had started in 1950, with Stein purchasing Decca and Universal stock, and had advanced in 1958, with Wasserman buying Universal's land. In June 1962 Stein and Wasserman completed their acquisition of Decca/Universal.

At last, Wasserman was ready to hand over his agency—the one he had spent twenty-six years of his life building. He invited reporters to MCA's very first—and last—press conference. Inside the white mansion at MCA Square, Wasserman intended to introduce the new MCA and its officers—five days before MCA was to surrender its SAG franchise. Wasserman believed that the spin-off would blunt Kennedy's case and make it harder for the government to press its case. If MCA no longer legally owned a talent agency—and was just a producer—how could Kennedy argue that MCA dominated the industry?

Now it was Bobby Kennedy's turn. Hours before Lew's scheduled press conference, the attorney general made his move. On July 13, 1962, in a downtown Los Angeles courthouse, he sued MCA under the Sherman Antitrust Act. He also sued SAG and WGA and claimed that MCA had allegedly gained a unfair advantage because of its "unique dual" role as both a talent agent and TV producer. Furthermore, the complaint alleged that MCA's acquisition of Decca violated the Celler-Kefauver Antimerger Act. After acquiring Decca and all of Universal Studios, it now owned 1,000 feature films, 2,500 TV programs, a record company, and a studio—not to mention its land, and most of the industry's talent.

Kennedy then delivered his coup de grâce. A government attorney called Wasserman and said: "Don't make any announcements just yet." He drove to Beverly Hills and served Lew with a temporary restraining order that barred MCA from transferring its performer contracts to the new talent agency.

Wasserman was stymied. Later, he'd admit that the suit was "the major surprise of my life. It was a useless, unwarranted act."

Three days later, on July 16, MCA went to court to fight the restraining order. The next day, a judge denied the agency's motion. For the next week or so, Wasserman, Stein, and Schreiber considered their options. On the eve of the SAG waiver's expiration, Wasserman called an emergency meeting in MCA's wood-paneled theater. He announced to all the agents: "We are still in court. We are fighting it out. But if you care to resign, your act will not be treated as disloyalty." The room buzzed with questions. Was Lew surrendering his new agency plan? "That's what he was saying, which was a major shock to us," said Welkes. Wasserman quieted the room and gestured to a table piled with resignation papers, ready for signatures. Wasserman repeated: "If anyone wants to resign, you may do so now."

One man rose, walked to the table, and took a form, then walked past Lew. Another man did the same, and soon dozens of others filed by in somber procession. Wasserman stood still, said Welkes. There were no lawyers present—"Lew was our attorney. I watched these guys as they signed their papers, still not quite believing what was happening," Welkes said. How could Lew give up without a fight? Welkes and several others were angry at the government. "If we have done something wrong, that's one thing," said one man. "But we didn't." Many believed that MCA was being persecuted only because of its long-running success. Others wanted to go to trial so MCA could clear its good name. But that option entailed legal fees and public scrutiny. It might even expose some of the agency's many secrets.

After the meeting, the office imploded. Some agents crashed through the halls in panic, like wounded animals. "What are we going to do?" wailed Harry Friedman. A few guys walked across the street to the Beverly Hills library, where they sat in the stacks to ponder the future. "They looked so sad," said a producer. A few composed themselves long enough to pick up the telephone, dial a rival, and inquire awkwardly about job openings. When Herb Siegel of GAC heard the news, he reportedly took the next plane to Los Angeles and snapped up a few good men. "It was a madhouse," said Henry Miller. "We were all scrambling to get MCA's clients, and it was very exciting." Another rival walked into the lobby and shouted: "Bus for William Morris leaving in five minutes."

The firm had two weeks to leave the premises. During that time, men were expected to wind down their affairs and pack up their personal items. Two burly security guards stood at the entrance to make sure no one hauled off any files or documents. "There were a lot of guys who didn't know what to do," added Roy Gerber. "The agency breakup was more like a breakdown."

On July 23, 1962, MCA and Wasserman agreed to dissolve the agency and never return to the business again. By August 8, he had to surrender all of MCA's contracts with stars, guilds, unions, and employees—and report his progress to Justice Department lawyers. Still on the table was Kennedy's threat to prohibit MCA's acquisition of Decca and Universal. By then, however, Wasserman was besieged with teary requests from his clients. "Can't you do something?" asked Gene Kelly. Brando demanded to be treated as a federal exception. Zsa Zsa Gabor and Kim Novak became hysterical. "I want my MCA," Janet Leigh cried. "I was like a baby, sucking my thumb and wailing. MCA was all I had ever known."

Weary, Wasserman met with attorneys, and clients, and bid goodbye to most of his men. For two decades, he and his staff had been feared and reviled, managing the unruly town like no agency ever had. "There had been a lot of jealousy, envy, and dislike directed at us," said Berle Adams. So when Wasserman and his men were knocked down, hallelujahs rose from some corners.

As an agency, MCA was dead. As a production arm, Revue was

wounded. As for Universal Studios? It hadn't made an award-winning film since 1930. Conventional wisdom said that Wasserman was buying a weed-choked sarcophagus somewhere beyond Sunset Boulevard. Sources chortled to the *New York Times*: "We'll see if he is as a shrewd a buyer as he was a seller."

On one of Wasserman's last official days at MCA Square, he drove around town and turned onto La Cienega Boulevard, a former swamp turned Hollywood artery. The street was home to several hot spots, including a comedy showroom called The Losers Club. Most weeks, the club posted a large sandwich board outside its door that displayed coming attractions and a joke or two. On the day Wasserman passed The Losers Club, he glanced at the poster. Written in big bold letters was: "Loser of The Week—MCA."

It was a humiliating moment, but just one of several jibes directed at Lew. "We were the laughingstock of the industry that summer, and Lew knew it," said Gerber. MCA's stunning court defeat, the newspaper headlines, and industry cracks hurt Wasserman. But he vowed to prove his detractors wrong. "We'll see if Hollywood will become a desert," he said, echoing Selznick's famous comparison of the falling studio system to ancient Egypt. But in this next round, the stakes would be much higher, and Lew's enemies would not be so obvious.

PART II
Rising to the Test: 1962–1969

FOURTEEN

THE DAY AFTER LEW WASSERMAN SIGNED the government's consent decree, agreeing to give up the agency business, he moved tons of heavy machinery onto Universal's lot. On September 19, 1962, bulldozers picked up acres of earth, giant crushers knocked down the termite-ridden structures, and steel jaws spit out chunks of plaster like so many broken teeth. Wasserman stood on a hill with a few of his executives and proclaimed to one reporter: "We've already spent $10 million to improve the lot and will now spend $15 million more. That's a $25 million investment that the big studios will last," he said, then added: "They'd better." The trade papers called Lew "crazy" for investing in Hollywood at a time when Rome, London, and Tokyo ranked higher in film production. More than any other man, Wasserman was responsible for chasing the movie business overseas. During the past decade, he and his MCA agents had championed and exploited tax loopholes, Liechtenstein subsidiaries, and capital-gains shelters, making it financially attractive for talent to flee abroad. So, who better than Wasserman to bring it all back home again? As he explained: "I hadn't been burned in movies as other companies had." And so, jackhammers, backhoes, and piling rigs would add to the cacophony as Lew tried to resurrect not just Universal Studios but the entire industry. Initially, he would spend $25 million to prove his dream, but his expenditure would balloon higher as the years rolled by. Right now, however, he was erecting a few buildings.

Wasserman's purchase of Decca and Universal had finally been allowed to stand, and MCA was no longer in the agency business. But Wasserman still had some loose ends dangling from his consent decree with the government. For one thing, Wasserman had to lease or sell most of Universal's 229 old films and was allowed to keep only 14 movies. He and his attorneys met with Leonard Posner and Malcolm MacArthur to discuss their progress in selling this inventory; Wasserman indicated that a Canadian TV production firm, Seven Arts, had the inside track on the post-1948 film library. Seven Arts was one of three companies owned by Louis Chesler, a client of financier Serge Semenenko's. The deal included a $7.5 million initial payment to MCA with more to come as Seven Arts rented out the films. Eventually, MCA would collect $24 million from this arrangement, and Seven Arts millions more. To the U.S. attorneys, it all seemed fair and square.

The battle between Wasserman and Kennedy had been one of the nastier antitrust fights in recent memory. "It was the most monumental piece of litigation in the country at the time," recalled Rick Ray, a TV producer. MCA never admitted to any wrongdoing, although the government claimed it had been operating an illegal monopoly since 1938. The Justice Department did extract several concessions. One was that Wasserman couldn't buy another major TV, motion picture, or record company for seven years—until 1969. MCA also had to stop its "tie-in" sales, in which it forced a client to contract for shows, movies, or records the buyer didn't want in order to get what it was really after. The Justice Department could also demand to see MCA's ledgers over the next few years, and if it had any suspicions, Wasserman pledged to address them in writing.

It had been a long case, with the grand jury working an unusually arduous four days a week. Posner had called it "the finest grand jury I've ever worked with." Around Halloween, the jury was disbanded, and a short time later, Lew extended an unusual invitation. "After the smoke had cleared, Wasserman invited us all to his office, along with two MCA attorneys," said MacArthur. "It was a very cordial thing, really. It was very unusual for something like that to happen."

Posner, MacArthur, and a few of the other lawyers drove to the studio and met their adversary in a bungalow that was then his makeshift office. At first the men felt awkward, but Wasserman welcomed them in and even showed them a few old movie sets. "This was after all the shooting was done and the government had no intention of pursuing anything further," said MacArthur. "Wasserman had never met any of the people involved." The prosecutors has heard that Wasserman had a photographic memory. "Posner has a photographic memory, too," someone let slip. They'd heard of Lew's charm and manners; Posner unleashed his social graces. The former enemies chitchatted like old friends.

After a few inane questions about movie lore and stars, the federal attorneys rose from their chairs and said good-bye. "Wasserman had nothing to gain by the visit," said MacArthur. "Maybe he did it for goodwill. Or maybe he wanted to see these monsters that had broken up his agency. But to me, the visit was meaningless— although it was rather nice to see his offices."

The case had taken its toll on Wasserman. His large beefy frame had shrunk a bit. "He used to watch his weight," said one of his secretaries, and now he developed a soft paunch. His once-black hair started graying, and his face looked a decade older than his forty-nine years. His smile wasn't as quick or frequent as it used to be, said Jackie Gershwin. But Wasserman allowed himself a few pleasures. He now drove a Bentley four-seat roadster, which was a small, sporty car for such a big, serious guy.

Wasserman lay awake at night, fretting about owning so much real estate, said Al Dorskind. At the time, Twentieth Century Fox,

MGM, and Columbia were selling some of their property to raise cash. Yet here was MCA, developing a vast kingdom. Universal City had its own post office, fire department, and sewer system. It cost $7 million a year just to maintain the property, pay insurance and taxes, and keep services running. At one point, Dorskind blurted out to his boss: "Jesus, we have a lot of land. For a Brooklyn boy like me, it's mind-blowing to see all this acreage."

"Land is a liability," Wasserman responded. "You have to pay taxes, kids could break into the buildings, you could have a fire, and it would all be destroyed." He recognized the changed landscape. As owner of a studio, Wasserman was now responsible for all the hard, tangible expenses that depended on the elusive magic of a hit movie. His new market was an amorphous faceless audience, made up of 180 million individuals scattered across fifty states, with different tastes, religions, and backgrounds.

Dorskind told Wasserman that land was also an asset and should be improved. But he understood his boss. "If MCA couldn't support the studio, it wouldn't survive, and Lew knew that," said Dorskind. "At his core, Lew was a risk-averse person. Lew was a Depression baby. I came up the hard way, too, but Lew was scarred by that time, and he still carries around those scars."

Wasserman had been born on Cleveland's east side, in the Woodland neighborhood. Just beyond downtown, the area's industrial warehouses and gritty factories straddled the dirty Cuyahoga River and ran along the railroad tracks up to 55th Street. In 1913, the year of Lew's birth, the district contained some of the city's worst housing. Once-attractive single-family dwellings were packed with three and four families of Jewish, Italian, or African-American descent. Sanitation was poor; garbage was plentiful, and rodents and lice flourished. Decent-paying jobs were rare and health care was scarce. Lew's father, Isaac Wasserman, was an immigrant who had been a bookbinder in Russia. After he and his wife emigrated to America, Isaac worked odd jobs that, for one reason or another, he could never keep. "He always dressed nicely, but I never knew him to work," said one of Lew's classmates, Paul Beck. Lew's mother, Minnie, was known for her gefilte fish and matzoh-ball soup, said Lewis Ratener, another family friend. "She was a wonderful cook." Over the years, the Wassermans operated several diners along Woodland Avenue, often with partners. By 1925, the family had finally purchased its own restaurant and hoped to turn a comfortable profit and someday pay off the debt.

Louis Wasserman was the youngest of the couple's three sons. His parents enrolled him in a public school a few miles from his run-down home. Every day, Louis walked out of the slum to Patrick Henry Junior High on the edge of Cleveland's city limits. By the time he turned twelve, he was expected to work, too. "Everybody worked at that time, or you were nothing," said Merle Jacobs, who grew up near the Wassermans. "To be a boy without a job at twelve or fourteen was shameful in our time." Some boys sold two-penny newspapers on street corners, but that work required more muscle than skinny Louis had. At the time, the circulation manager at the *Cleveland News* paid a gang of Italian toughs to beat up knickered boys who were selling competing broadsheets. Some boys, such as Al Polizzi and Tony Milano, would grow up to form Cleveland's Mafia, the Mayfield Road gang, and partner with Dalitz's Jewish syndicate.

Louis landed a job selling candy at a burlesque house in the tenderloin district. "You had to be pretty hard to sell candy in theaters," said Al Setnick, one of Lew's boyhood friends. "It wasn't a nice job for a Jewish boy." After school ended, Wasserman would walk four miles to his job, past speakeasies, gambling halls, and whorehouses. At the theater, he'd grab a tray of unwrapped chocolates and treats. From the shadows, he'd watch scantily clad women cavort onstage while grown men whistled and jeered. "This was a place where only men could go," said Ronald Brown, who frequented the city's burlesque houses. "The girls onstage weren't wearing much, but at least they had something on." At intermission, Louis would walk up and down the sticky aisle, yelling "Buy your fresh candy. Get your ice creams." The job paid a few coins a day and ended around midnight, whereupon Wasserman would walk fifty blocks home, fall onto a makeshift bed, and sleep a few hours. At sunrise, the twelve-year-old would awake and start the routine all over again.

Between his job and school, Louis put in sixteen hours of work almost every day. Later he'd find better jobs, but he'd never stop scrimping and saving. He wanted his father to pay off the property loan and own the restaurant outright. But a real estate crash in 1927 killed those dreams. One day a banker came to repossess Isaac Wasserman's property, and the family lost the little savings it had.

The forty-four-year-old Isaac seemed adrift after that. The family rented a two-story apartment on East 105th Street, closer to their sons' school, Glenville High. Isaac spent his days chatting with store-owners and arguing politics with older Jews. Meanwhile, his sons continued to work and Minnie redoubled her efforts. Their apartment had three bedrooms, one of which was used by the parents. But rather than give the other two to her sons, Minnie rented them out to male boarders. When Louis returned from his long day at school and work, he'd sleep on the floor or on a couch—adopting a habit he'd never break completely. To supplement her income, Minnie used her culinary skills. "She'd prepare three- and four-course meals for a regular stable of a half-dozen mostly male customers," said Paul Beck. "For years, this was how she fended for her family." And this was even before the onset of the Great Depression.

The family's shattered dreams—and the painful sacrifices Louis had made for the dream—affected him profoundly. Wasserman hid his heartbreak so well that only one of his friends ever glimpsed it. One day, Louis visited the large two-story home of his friend, Paul Beck. Louis started explaining his frustration with his father and his deep hurt, when suddenly he broke down. "He was crying like a baby." Beck tried to console his friend, but it was no use. "He was sobbing uncontrollably, with copious tears streaming down his face." Wasserman would later change his name to Lewis or "Lew," and he'd leave Cleveland far behind, but he'd never shake the memories of his early grinding poverty. Fear of failure fueled Wasserman's drive as surely as his ambitions did. Dorskind did not know the details of his boss's childhood, but he sensed its residue. "Lew believed in putting your eggs into one basket and watching them like a hawk."

The year MCA completed its Decca-Universal buyout, its revenues more than doubled from $82 million to $188 million, yet its income rose only 18 percent from $11 million $13 million. It would have been higher if not for the antitrust battle, but all Wasserman told shareholders was that the case had been settled. "Nineteen sixty-two was the most eventful year for your company in its entire history," he reported. Then he set about shaping its future.

Jerry Gershwin accompanied Wasserman on his demolition rounds. With a pad and pencil, the jovial Gershwin took down Lew's instructions and memorized all of his conversations. In case Lew died, at least there would be a record of his last order—Stein had already taken out a $5 million insurance policy on Lew, listing MCA as beneficiary. But to some agents, Gershwin seemed more like Lew's bodyguard or scout. "He acted as Lew's eyes and ears," said Ned Tanen. Explained Jackie Gershwin: "That's because Lew was grooming Jerry to be president."

The younger man clearly idolized his boss. One day, Gershwin and his wife sat in front of the renovated commissary, which was surrounded by piles of dirt. "It was such a mess from the rains and mud," said Jackie. The next day, the mud pit was covered with a rolling lawn of grass. A group of employees walked past the new landscape, did a double take, and marveled at the change. Gershwin said with a grin: "And on the seventh day, Lew said, 'Let there be grass.' "

Every morning, the two men would review the previous day's progress until nearly every structure had been demolished.

Wasserman left only one stage standing: the set built in 1925 for
Phantom of the Opera. During that film's wrap party, a gypsy fortune-teller had warned studio founder Carl Laemmle that whoever
destroyed this set would be cursed forever. Wasserman was not
about to tempt fate.

But the agent who had once extracted sky-high salaries for his
clients now squeezed every one of the studio's nickels. To keep the
grass short during the summer fire season, Wasserman allowed a
neighbor's flock of sheep to graze on his land. "They later bought
the sheep for fifty cents a head rather than pay some gardeners to do
the job," said one executive. To level miles of steep rocky terrain,
Wasserman struck a deal with the California Department of Trans-
portation. Cal-Trans was trying to finish the Hollywood Freeway on
the west edge of Universal Studios, and it needed tons of crushed
granite. Dorskind arranged for the state to quarry the rock and
granite—and pay MCA for the privilege. The state ended up buying
650,000 cubic yards of dirt at top dollar. Dorskind also convinced
the state to irrigate and landscape some 100 acres of Universal's
property as part of its freeway project. As a bonus, the company
secured an off-ramp from the new freeway that led right to Universal City and its new parking lot. "We really lucked out on that
one," Dorskind said grinning.

When Jules Stein discovered that his studio lot abutted a golfing
range owned by Bob Hope, he proposed a deal. Stein and Hope
drove around the city for a day so Hope could select a property of
Stein's to trade for his driving range. The tax-free deal gave
Wasserman a total of 420 contiguous acres.

Dorskind learned that the studio commissary had been run like a
private dining room. Former studio chief William Goetz had
installed his personal chef to cook there, and it charged very little for
excellent food. "For some people it was the best meal of the day, as
there were no restaurants for miles around," said film editor Ernie
Nims. Before MCA acquired the studio, Dorskind told Wasserman

that the commissary was losing $100,000 a year and advised him to cut Universal's $11.25 million purchase price. "I can't do that," Wasserman objected. "I gave them my word." But after MCA took possession, Dorskind fired the commissary's top chef. Then he ordered the sous-chef to fire the four men under him, which produced more savings. When Dorskind learned that former studio executives had been taking home choice meats every night, he had food deliveries pass through the gate at Lankershim Boulevard, where it was weighed and accounted for. "It was little things like that that saved us money," Dorskind said.

Wasserman wanted to run an efficient plant at full capacity, so he and Dorskind contracted with engineers at MIT and Caltech to study the studio's efficiency ratio—something unheard of in Hollywood at the time. "They looked at traffic flow, where labor was invested, and measured how many times people did the same thing," Dorskind said. Wasserman didn't think Universal's financial reporting system was as fast as it should be, so he bought an enormous Honeywell Systems computer that kept inventories of cameras, lenses, and other things. "We kept budgets and compared it to what movies were made and how many made money, and how much," said Dorskind. They measured what time a director took his first camera shot, how much footage he shot, and how many shots were made per page of script. Most important, the printouts detailed how close each film and TV show stuck to budget.

But the chief's pet project was his new headquarters. To replace the studio's quaint bungalows, he hired architects from the San Francisco firm of Skidmore, Owings & Merrill—disciples of the new international school of architecture. Wasserman wanted the design to bear his imprint, just as the old "White House" had displayed Stein's taste. "Mr. Wasserman wanted an image that conveyed something different from the rest of Hollywood," said Sam Carson, then a young architect with the firm. "He wanted it corporate, all business, buttoned-down, and pulled together. There was an attempt to imitate taste and class."

The early drawings showed a white building, but Wasserman sent them back. At one point, he flew to San Francisco to confer with the architects. The firm had prepared a meeting room with soft music, gentle lighting, and soft drinks. "Then these dark suits come in and sweep the place," said Carson. They turned off the music and brought up the lights just as Wasserman arrived "with an entourage of thirty people and a few guys who looked like bodyguards."

Wasserman originally wanted two asymmetrical towers and a disconnected courtyard off to the side. "It would have looked weird," said Carson. The young man timidly suggested that Wasserman consider linking the two asymmetrical buildings with the courtyard. "There was dead silence, as no one *ever* said anything against the boss," Carson said. After what seemed like minutes, Wasserman looked at him and said, "You may have a point there." From then on, the two men got along so well that Wasserman started calling him "boychik," a Yiddish endearment. Carson shrugged: "I'm not sure what that meant, but it was always friendly.

"I never met a nicer person. He was always a gentleman who treated me with more respect than I deserved."

Before long, a fourteen-story, $8.5 million edifice rose like a stylized, postwar box, made of smoked glass and anodized aluminum. "Jules hated the tower, and hated its black and gray shades," said one executive. Stein had wanted variegated red Pietrasanta marble that gave off a rosy Italianate glow. But, to his credit, he held back and gave Wasserman free rein. "Lew was the heart and soul of the company and Jules knew that," said producer Walter Seltzer. Let the tower be as austere and sleek as Wasserman, Stein decided. But he so loved his old Beverly Hills building that he and Taft Schreiber wanted Lew to move it to Universal's grounds. Stein figured he could cut the building into twelve pieces, load them onto trailers, and deposit them there for reassembly. Stein would have had his white plantation manse sit opposite Wasserman's modern black tower. Lew talked his boss out of the idea, but it didn't take a fortune-teller to see that someday their two radically different styles would clash.

Most weekends, Wasserman took home the floor plans to review. He made sure his new building had no thirteenth floor. He once found a door missing on the fourteenth-story executive floor. To avoid such embarrassing mistakes in the future, Wasserman made sure his assistant Bert Tuttle called the architect the night before meetings "to compare notes," said Carson.

"Wasserman was always crazy for two of everything. He thought it was cheaper that way, as you didn't have to pay full price," Carson recalled. As his building took shape, Lew began to contemplate finishing touches. "Stein had a small Henry Moore sculpture," said Carson, referring to the English artist who had become well known for his monumental outdoor bronzes. Wasserman carried his blueprints to England and asked the sixty-two-year-old sculptor how much it would cost to make a piece for MCA's lobby. The artist quoted $250,000. "How much for two?" asked Wasserman. The reply was $400,000. Wasserman ordered two. "Down the line, our firm started designing a corporate building in San Francisco," Carson said. "Mr. Wasserman called and asked, 'What sculpture are you going to use?'" The architects hadn't decided yet.

Wasserman proposed: "I'll give you a Henry Moore for $300,000." The firm accepted quickly. "So Wasserman got his own sculpture for $100,000."

Carson constructed a three-story mock-up of MCA's building "because Wasserman wanted to see what it would look like." After Wasserman inspected it, he said: "Let's put it on the back lot, in the New York street scene." The mock-up became a free backdrop for Revue's TV shows and was used for years. "It seemed like I saw it on every third show I watched," Carson said.

By 1963, the lot had a new windowless commissary, a post office, and a bank. Finally, the Black Tower, as it was called, opened high above Universal City. Wasserman had designed every executive suite to be roughly the same size. "The office tower is inefficient," remarked one executive. "It has offices on the outside of the building, so everyone can have a window, but the center is all elevators and empty space." Its carpet was so thick that a visitor could twist his ankle in the plush pile—which would have muffled his screams. "It was eerie walking on that carpet, as you always felt the earth was shaking," said screenwriter Gavin Lambert. The interior decor was based on beige colors, light wood, and sleek lines. Wasserman furnished the modern offices with Stein's gorgeous dark antiques, which certainly looked odd. But Lew did so in deference to Stein, who was now selling his cherished MCA building on Burton Square.

At the top of Lew's tower were the executive offices. Wasserman's desk was situated in front of an enormous picture window. He would sit with his back to the glass while visitors faced the panoramic view. By late afternoon, the sun would stream in and blind visitors. It was said that he purposely scheduled unpleasant appointments late in the day so recalcitrants would squirm or leave. If so, Wasserman was borrowing a trick from the old-style tycoons like Harry Cohn, who used to sit on an elevated platform so he could look down on his intimidated visitors.

Stein, however, refused to work in an austere beige environment. He imported his walls and ceiling from an English castle. "His office was gorgeous," said Carson. Even so, the Anglophile collector could not forget that he was working on a former chicken ranch. Said his stepson, Jerry Oppenheimer, "He hated it."

FIFTEEN

EDIE WASSERMAN, FOR HER PART, was consciously molding herself into a mogul's wife. She had become a very rich woman. Six months after MCA's public offering, the Wassermans' stock had nearly doubled, making them worth about $24 million. The antitrust unpleasantness halved that value, but MCA's share price was rebounding by 1963. Her stake in MCA's profit-sharing plan had also doubled. Two years after her husband had taken over Universal's lot in 1958, Edie had begun looking for a bigger and better home. Their modest red-brick colonial home had served her well for some twenty-two years. But it no longer matched her new image and future status.

Edie shopped for months, running real estate agents through their paces as she inspected some 150 properties. "I hated everything I looked at," she said. The only home she did like was not for sale. It was big—6,400 square feet—and recently built, but not ostentatious and it sat on a spacious, green two-acre lot. When it suddenly became available due to a death in the owner's family, Edie flew into action. The Wassermans bought the place for $400,000. Lew considered the price excessive, but his wife was adamant. Forty years later, the property would be worth $12 million, and he and Edie would say that they'd bought it for a bargain.

In 1961 the couple moved to the manicured heart of Beverly Hills on an incline above Sunset Boulevard. "No one was building French chateaux and English traditionals anymore," said Bruce Nelson, a veteran realtor in Beverly Hills. "Everything was lean, one-story and contemporary." And Edie's new home, built by Harold Levitt, who was popular with Los Angeles's new aristocrats, was a masterpiece of that style, with flowing, open spaces and floor-to-ceiling glass. It had only one bedroom, which was primarily Edie's. Wasserman slept most nights on a couch in the den, so he wouldn't disturb his wife when he came home late. Up by 5:00 A.M., he was calling his men in New York to find out the latest box-office receipts before anyone else on the West Coast. As Edie entered a new stage in her life, her intense marriage to Lew changed, too. Said Artie Shaw: "Theirs was not a marriage, it was an arrangement."

Edie was a sexual politician. "She always struck me as a power wife, a woman who was just as driven as her husband," said Gavin Lambert. "She pushed him, I think. And the power thing succeeded sex. Power is where both of them got their real kicks."

If Edie Wasserman had been born a few decades later, she might have been a career woman leading a Fortune 500 company. Had she been born in an earlier century, she might have been a top courtesan, controlling kings and emperors with her seductive mix of political brinkmanship and boudoir intelligence. Edie was no beauty by Hollywood standards. She was rather plain-looking, a middle-aged woman who wore her hair bobbed at the chin and parted in the middle. She dressed impeccably, preferring classic tailored designs. "Edie was loud, tough, and her voice was lowish. Yet, there was something very flirtatious about her," explained Lambert. Still, for better and worse, for nearly thirty years, she had remained the only Mrs. Lew Wasserman. "She was the wife of a powerful man, and that's all anybody needed to know about her," said Ed Muhl.

Edie had weathered many storms in her marriage. "There were some bad times between the tenth and twentieth years," she told her friend Dominick Dunne. Lew had never stopped working during the 1940s and 1950s, and "I think she felt neglected," said Jay Kanter. "I was surprised that Edie admitted marital problems," Dunne later confided. But her indiscretions were legion, and women, in particular, criticized her behind her back. "The fact that they weren't together, I understood that due to Lew's work," said Tony Curtis. "But there were always those rumors and innuendos . . . ," he added, his voice trailing off. Hollywood affairs are as common as white lies. But in Edie's case, extramarital affairs became a way to exert her strength and independence, while masking her own heartbreak and unhappiness.

Like Lew, Edith Beckerman grew up in Cleveland; she was the baby in a family with two older boys. In 1935, when she was twenty years old, she was considered a brainy girl who never scored top grades but had loads of dates. Headstrong and quick-witted, Edie was always garrulous and good company, said Merle Jacobs, who would take her to the theater in downtown Cleveland then treat her to a midnight supper. "She liked to go to one restaurant that was a hot spot for us young bloods," he said. "She loved to dance." Edie was an orchestra groupie who flirted shamelessly with musicians. One night, she and her friends were preparing to see "The Waltz King," orchestra leader Wayne King. When Edie discovered a pimple on her face, she asked Dorothy Barton for help, pleading, "Wayne King will throw a fit when he sees this." Barton helped the young woman conceal her blemish but thought, "As if Wayne King is going to notice."

Among the nightspots Edie frequented was the Mayfair Casino. During one late-night round of club hopping, Edie spied a handsome young man at the Mayfair. He was twice her height and wore a striking pin-striped suit with a red silk kerchief in his breast pocket. She asked a newspaper columnist to introduce her. The lanky twenty-two-year-old was Louis Wasserman, who had been working for the club owners since about 1934, earning just enough money to dress like a boulevardier, which he did. The swain made Edie's heart skip, recalled Seymour Heller, a friend. "Lew was a smart operator who knew all the movers and shakers in town," he explained. Swarms of young women hung on his arms and words. Edie was obviously impressed by him, too. So, when Wasserman nonchalantly tossed her two free show passes, she practically swooned. Edie returned a few nights later with a girlfriend. But she missed the performance because her eyes were on Lew, who roamed the floor like a sentry on duty. "I chased him for a year until he caught me," she later joked.

Their friends were puzzled by what appeared to be an odd couple, said Barton. "They seemed altogether different." He was taciturn and aloof, even snobbish, while she was giddy and sociable. He was tall, she was stout. He came from poor Russian immigrant stock, while her family were well-to-do German-American Jews. His father was chronically unemployed, hers was a well-known attorney. Edie lived with her folks in an affluent part of Cleveland Heights with her own car and bedroom, while he came from an entirely different world. To Wasserman, perky little Edie Beckerman seemed to have it all. A year after they met, they married. On the Fourth of July weekend in 1936, her parents threw a garden wedding reception with 100 guests, including Dorothy Barton. "We always wondered why he married her. Maybe it was because she had money."

Wasserman moved into the Beckerman family's home near Rockefeller Gardens and lived, for several months, in the three-story, twelve-room house. It had polished wood floors, custom-made stair railings, and chandeliers. It had a garage, a den, a formal dining room, a family room, a living room, and a two-room eat-in kitchen. Wasserman and his bride shared a spacious bedroom on the upper floor, where they had a private bathroom. For a young man who had spent a lifetime sleeping on the floor while boarders occupied the few bedrooms, this place must have seemed like a palace.

His bride was supported by her parents, although she clerked at the May Company and earned $18 a week. He supported his parents and pulled down $100 a week at a time when most publicists pulled down only $38. Later that year, when Wasserman went to Chicago to interview with MCA founders Jules and Billy Stein, Lew borrowed money from the Bartons, and Edie stayed with Dorothy. "I remember she had all these beautiful nightclothes," said Dorothy Barton. In December, Lew Wasserman landed the publicity job at MCA, and he and his bride prepared to leave Cleveland. They didn't take much with them, Barton recalled. The Cleveland girl who had never left her hometown was throwing in her lot with this young man and heading to the Midwest's biggest city.

In Chicago, Edie and Lew shared a furnished apartment with an MCA agent. They slept in a pull-out Murphy bed. Lew spent his days at the office, while Edie fended for herself. At night, she accompanied her husband on his nightclub rounds, but after a few months, Lew was sent to New York and Edie went with him. Again she fended for herself during the day and trailed along with her husband at night when possible. Several months later, however, when Jules Stein wanted Lew to move once more, Edie put her foot down. She'd had enough, said Al Dorskind. "So Lew went to Hollywood and Edie went to Florida," where her brother lived and her parents vacationed. Eventually, however, the bride followed her husband west. By 1939, she had reunited with him—only to find herself alone again.

"I think it was very hard for her, given all the hours Lew put in at work," said Janet Leigh. Edie was vivacious, a little spoiled, and certainly starved for affection, her friends agree. Many afternoons, she'd flirt with actors from a barstool at the Cock 'n' Bull on Rodeo Drive, said one film producer. "Or she'd be at Scandia drinking for hours, picking up men," he said. Errol Flynn and Frank Sinatra were among her many alleged conquests. "Edie was madly in love with my uncle Sidney Buchman" (screenwriter for *Mr. Smith Goes to Washington*), said Virginia Korshak. Robert Stack, and record executive Manie Sachs were among her quarries. She went through a phase of dating quiet, loner-type men, said Robert Mitchum. "She had a penchant for cowboys who worked as extras in some of the movies I made." She even enjoyed a few flings with MCA agents. "Once three different fellows told me they had a thing with Edie, and I thought they were joking," said Myrle Wages. "But it turned out to be true. She was one very busy lady." Added Tony Curtis: "I never understood the relationship Edie had with Lew, but I didn't even go *near* the gossip."

One of Edie's biggest loves was the gifted director Nicholas Ray, who certainly cared for her. The script for the director's most acclaimed work, *Rebel Without a Cause*, grew out of a dinner with Edie and Lew at Ray's house in September 1954. The three old friends were enjoying dinner and watching *Dragnet* on TV, Ray told a biographer. They started discussing Ray's next project. At the time, Edie and Lew's daughter Lynne was having the usual teenager problems. "Nick was always interested in troubled juveniles," explained Gavin Lambert, Ray's assistant at the time. Ray insisted that his next picture would have to be something he really cared about. "What's important to you?" Lew asked. "Kids," said Ray. "Young people growing up. Their problems."

The next day, Wasserman sent Ray to Warner Brothers, which had purchased a nonfiction book published by Dr. Robert M. Lindner, *Rebel Without a Cause: The Story of a Criminal Psychopath,* which revolved around the abnormal psychology of the son of a poor family. Ray didn't like the story, but he loved the title. The director thought of himself as a rebel and artist, who was grossly misunderstood in commercial Hollywood. Ray used the title, but his movie focused on ordinary kids whose delinquency was a way for them to get attention from adults.

His 1955 film caused a huge sensation and struck a chord with teen audiences, who identified with its theme of loneliness and alienation. Edie fell in love with Ray—"partly because of his power," said Lambert. She visited him at his bungalow at the Chateau Marmont, where the Norman turrets, romantic spires, and utter privacy made a perfect trysting spot. "Edie was in love with Nick, absolutely," said Lambert, who saw her visit him. "There was something masculine about her manner and voice" when she talked to other people. But as soon as she'd see Ray, she'd turned "soft and feminine," he explained. Ray made Edie feel like a woman, handling her in a kind and gentle way. He was the silent type who could be, at turns, rough, adventurous, and bisexual. "Ray was very talented but conflicted," said Lambert. "He wanted it both ways. He wanted to be an offbeat art director while being ferried to the set in limos."

While Edie was playing muse for Ray, Lew was striking film deals for the director. "I think that Lew knew that Edie was very interested [in Ray]," said Lambert. "He must have heard the rumors, too." Edie's love affair grew so intense that she reportedly considered leaving her husband for the rebel filmmaker. "But Nick never had any intention of marrying Edie, I'm sure of that," said Lambert. It would have been too difficult for the director to steal the wife of the biggest gun in town. "Nick could have been blacklisted from film lots. He knew the score."

Instead, Nick Ray married a young dancer in late 1958 and fell into an unhappy marriage. Years later, his reputation took on cult status, but none of his subsequent films ever landed him the cash or prestige that *Rebel* had. He always needed money for alimony, child support, and gambling debts, and slowly, he descended into alcohol and hard drugs, before dying in 1979.

Meanwhile, Edie made peace with her past—and her husband. "Edie realized that Lew knew what he was doing and she actively supported him in every way she could," said Jack Dales. Having sacrificed enormously in the name of marriage, she was adamantly opposed to divorce. At Edie's urging, Janet Leigh and Tony Curtis papered over their marital difficulties and threw a party for their tenth anniversary. Edie helped invite 250 guests, including Kirk Douglas and his second wife, Anne; Gregory Peck and his second wife, Veronique; Bob Wagner and his doe-eyed wife, Natalie Wood—who had also had an affair with Nicholas Ray, as she had had with Dennis Hopper and Warren Beatty, other party guests. Everyone seemed to be having a wonderful time at the anniversary bash—except for Curtis and his wife. "I was never so miserable in my life," said Leigh. "My marriage was gone, and I was getting disillusioned with Hollywood," added Curtis. Within a year, the couple would divorce, and Edie would shun Curtis for years afterward. But she and Lew never would forget his two daughters, their godchildren. "Every Christmas and birthday, we'd get a pearl from my godmother, Edie, so that by the time I was sixteen, I had a necklace," Jamie Lee Curtis said. None of Edie and Lew's other godchildren—the Gershwins, the Kanters, or the others—would be forgotten, either.

But the circle was coming apart. Marlon Brando and his wife, Anna Kashfi; Rosemary Clooney and Jose Ferrer; Natalie Wood and Bob Wagner . . . many of the MCA star marriages were crumbling. For the Wassermans, one of the most painful breakups was that of Jay Kanter and his wife, Judy, who had fallen in love with Tony Franciosa. "I told Edie that I was divorcing Jay, and that I couldn't live like this any longer," Balaban Kanter recalled. "Edie spent most of the night trying to talk me out of it, but it was no use." The young woman left her marriage—and Edie's circle. "Edie didn't speak to me for a few years," she said. "I think it hurt her very much." To Edie, it was an act of disloyalty.

At her husband's insistence, Edie furnished her new home like MCA's new offices—with Stein's eighteenth-century English furniture. The couple shared a partners desk that enabled them to face each other while keeping up with their private correspondence. Edie discarded the kitschy paintings and began buying Impressionist works by Degas, Matisse, and Picasso. After Wasserman and MCA purchased Universal Studios, Edie started her own construction project. In 1962 she brought back architect Harold Levitt and hired him to design a projection room across her driveway; it had a sliding aluminum roof and more seat-side controls than a jet's cockpit. She adorned her private theater with a collection of antique cameras and silent-picture posters from Universal. When she placed a Henry Moore sculpture beside her driveway and a Chaim Soutine painting in the dining room, the town took note.

Meanwhile, Edie turned her sights on Jackie Gershwin, arranging for the Gershwins to purchase the old Wasserman house for $85,000—the going market rate. "She knew that we would be entertaining clients, and they both wanted us to have a nice place," said Jackie Gershwin. The younger woman tried to emulate Edie by throwing parties catered by Chasen's restaurant and peopled by MCA faces. "When Tony and Janet got divorced, Tony stayed at our house. When Janet got remarried, I was a witness at her marriage," said Gershwin. One Sunday morning, Jackie looked out her window and saw Jeanne Martin and Janet Leigh on the porch. "My doorbell would ring, and Gene Kelly would be there, like he was visiting Edie," said Gershwin. Only now, MCA's clients were visiting the Wassermans' heirs apparent. "Sometimes, people would come looking for Edie and Lew. But when they found out it was Jerry and Jackie, they'd come in anyway," she said. "We entertained guests on the same nice patio." As the years progressed, this stand-in routine grew a little eerie. The old MCA agents no longer worked under one roof, but competed viciously against one another. Their new spouses were not as committed to their husband's careers as Edie's Hollywood wives had been. With few exceptions, these women did not work to advance MCA's strategies or champion the town's causes as much as they began to promote their own agendas. "It slowly started to change," said Hollywood columnist Rex Reed. "It changed in the quality of the women who ran around town, their glamour, and their offscreen lives."

Edie would seize on that change and use it to expand her influence. To maintain her home's privacy and unobstructed views, she bought an adjoining lot from Billy Wilder. Years later, she'd welcome back to her fold old flame and former MCA client Frank Sinatra, who had moved up the street on Foothill Drive. Edie's circle slowly added new links, but she did not forget past slights. While Wasserman reconstructed his MCA empire in the San Fernando Valley, she fumed over the humiliations wrought by the attorney general. "There was great antipathy between Wasserman and Robert Kennedy after the breakup," said Walter Seltzer. Publicly, Edie said nothing. Privately, she nursed her grudge. As far as she was concerned, the enemy was Kennedy, said Seltzer. "You cannot mention his name to either Edie or Lew without their going apoplectic." Forty years later, Seltzer said, "the anger still exists."

Her outrage was exacerbated by the fact that Wasserman had acted as President Kennedy's illicit escort service while Bobby had been treating Lew like a white-collar criminal. John Kennedy had fallen for Angie Dickinson, a former MCA client and unofficial member of the Rat Pack. "When Lew went to a political function for Kennedy, he didn't always take Edie," said Frank Price. "He'd escort Angie, who at the time was having an affair with Kennedy." Price recalled one night when Wasserman walked into an event with Dickinson, but left alone. Meanwhile, "Angie was ushered through a side door, where some of the president's men whisked her off," he said. The affair was so famous around Universal Studios that even TV crew members knew about it. One day, a hairdresser working on Dickinson's blond tresses explained that he wanted to style her hair in a Jackie Kennedy bouffant. Immediately, the hairdresser froze. "No one said anything, and it was an awkward moment," said Price. "The hairdresser realized what he had said, and felt embarrassed. But Angie didn't say anything. We all knew that Lew was the beard for Angie and Kennedy."

By early 1963, Wasserman had passed on these duties to his assistants, according to Sam Carson. One night, Bert Tuttle was driving the young architect to the airport when Tuttle detoured and picked up Dickinson from her apartment. The trio then drove to the basement parking lot of the Beverly Hilton Hotel, where they rode an elevator to a large suite filled with men. As Dickinson entered the suite, Carson saw President Kennedy. Tuttle said, "Good night, Angie," and the door closed. Carson added, "I'm sure Angie Dickinson was visiting Jack Kennedy that night."

These late-night presidential favors could not ensure that MCA and the Wassermans remain immune to federal prosecution. They were too hush-hush confidential. Edie once told a Universal executive that an administration official must never again ambush her husband. But how to prevent such a repeat? While Edie contemplated her dilemma, a solution was emerging from miles away. Almost by happenstance, the Wassermans would soon slip into their new official roles as Hollywood ambassadors to Washington czars.

SIXTEEN

WHEN WASSERMAN WALKED ONTO THE STUDIO LOT as its new mogul, he was not embraced. "When he came in, the good old days were gone," said a film editor. Wasserman fired many old-timers but kept a few chiefs. Perhaps his wisest decision was to keep studio manager Ed Muhl, the long-suffering, no-nonsense executive who had worked at Universal since the advent of talkies. During the 1950s, Muhl had helped crank out unimaginative pictures such as the Ma and Pa Kettle series, Audie Murphy horse operas, and sci-fi horror classics like *The Creature from the Black Lagoon* (1954). Many of these films made a lot of money. Under Muhl's prudent management, the studio had also employed such consistently talented producers as Aaron Rosenberg of *The Glenn Miller Story* (1954) and *To Hell and Back* (1955), and Albert Zugsmith of *Written on the Wind* (1957) and *The Incredible Shrinking Man* (1957). The studio made money from these films, too, said Muhl. But the top-grossing producer was Ross Hunter, a former Cleveland schoolteacher known for glossy tearjerkers, such as *The Magnificent Obsession* (1954) and *Imitation of Life* (1959). It wasn't Oscar fare, but his pieces were entertaining, never extravagantly budgeted, and often lovingly told. These men stayed on.

A less logical move, at least to Universal watchers, was Wasserman's promotion of Milton Rackmil to vice chairman of MCA Inc., which now encompassed Revue Productions, Universal Studios, and Decca Records, among other subsidiaries. During Rackmil's ten years as studio overseer, he had not earned respect from those in the back office, said Muhl. "Rackmil was smart enough to understand that he didn't know a thing about Hollywood. He once asked me if he should develop personal relationships with stars in order to be a good studio manager." Muhl responded bluntly: "No. All you need are two kinds of books: a good screenplay and a fat checkbook." In fifty years, Universal had never really possessed either one.

Muhl and other studio veterans suspected that Wasserman and MCA had rigged a dishonest deal when they bought Universal. "It was a giveaway; the sale was flat-out robbery," said Ernie Nims, a Universal employee. "Lew bought the studio from Rackmil, who got a big job out of the deal." Rackmil received an unusually long ten-year contract as well as a substantial salary, Nims noted. "Of course he'd give the studio away." When MCA bought Universal, it *was* losing money, said Muhl, but not as much money as Rackmil reported. A third executive insisted that the studio was actually *making* money. "We all knew that Universal was profitable, but no one knew where the money was going," he said. "And the only guy who wanted to sell was Rackmil." The studio had never been advertised for sale or offered out to competitive bidding, which made MCA's abrupt deal surprising. "Universal was sold to MCA before anyone knew much about it," said Nims. "It was like a bombshell, and we all thought it very strange."

Perhaps that was naïve. In fact, Wasserman had been cleaning Universal's house since he became its landlord in 1958. He even pushed out a few directors, Orson Welles, for one. Welles was working on *Touch of Evil* (1958) from a bungalow, staying up late, drinking, and "supposedly talking about the picture," said Nims. "He'd do his magic tricks and carouse with crew members." His moody film noir masterpiece dealt with police corruption on the U.S.-Mexico border and starred Charlton Heston as a Mexican cop, Janet Leigh as his wife, Marlene Dietrich as a fortune-teller, and Welles as her former lover and detective. Welles ended up banned from Universal's editing room, though he tried to finish his work via teletypes to Nims. In one epistle, he lamented: "I was not given the ordinary courtesy of consultation on the matter." The artist also sent a 58-page memo to Muhl, detailing changes. But the studio diluted the film's bold edits, sweetened the love story between the cop and his wife, and released it as a conventional B movie. "Welles was cut off at the knees," said Nims. His movie failed to arouse much interest in the United States, but won a prize at the 1958 Brussels World Fair and has since been reconstructed according to the director's instructions.

Universal also lost Stanley Kubrick, the thirty-one-year-old director of *Spartacus*. While still working as an agent, Wasserman had sold the project for client Kirk Douglas, who was coproducer. Unbeknownst to MCA, the script was written by Dalton Trumbo, who had been blacklisted and jailed during the McCarthy era. An anti-Communist organization discovered Trumbo's role just as the film was about to wrap. "They threatened [Muhl] by saying if he didn't remove Dalton, they were going to spill the beans," and ruin the film, said MCA agent Ronnie Lubin. Muhl called Wasserman, who asked Lubin if it was true. It was, Lubin responded. "What do you think we should do?" asked Wasserman. The film was already months over schedule, 250 percent over budget, and approaching the then-astronomical sum of $12 million. "It's too far gone to tell the client to remove himself," Lubin responded. "And it would be very bad for the studio to do anything at this juncture. Besides, I don't think the anti-Communist group will do anything."

Wasserman repeated that to Muhl, said Lubin. "He put the whole thing on the studio's shoulders, and they never got exposed for that." But the film, which focused on one man's courageous struggle for freedom against tyranny, was a baptism by fire for Kubrick. He didn't like the script's moralizing tone, argued with the cinematographer, and fought often with Douglas. At one point, the star rode his white stallion right up to the director, pushing him farther and farther into a corner. Then Douglas turned his horse and galloped away, leaving Kubrick humiliated and dusty in front of his own crew.

In 1961, the film won four Oscars, two Golden Globes, a WGA award for Trumbo, and a British Oscar for Kubrick. But Kubrick was repelled by his experience at Universal and left Hollywood for

England, where he made *Lolita* (1962), *Dr. Strangelove* (1964), and several other great films. He eventually built a studio of his own to maintain artistic control over his projects. When he died in 1999, he was a hero to most film aficionados as an auteur par excellence.

Douglas stayed on at Universal. The MCA client made *Lonely Are the Brave* (1962), which some critics hailed as his best work. Yet he complained that the studio treated it like a cheap western. The actor pleaded with Wasserman to roll out the film gradually in art houses and college theaters, but Wasserman handled it like commercial fare. The picture did poorly at the box office, and Douglas blamed the studio's marketing.

By then Wasserman had built thirty-six soundstages, and all of them were busy. In 1963 he approved budgets for fourteen new films—more than any other studio at that time. One of them was the classic *To Kill a Mockingbird* (1963), directed by Robert Mulligan and starring former MCA client Peck, who won an Oscar. Otherwise, the studio's assembly-line output was uneven. Wasserman and Muhl simply continued tapping the lot's existing talent, greenlighting Ross Hunter's formulaic *Tammy and the Doctor* (1963), with Sandra Dee and Peter Fonda, and *The Art of Love* (1965), a farce with too many disparate elements. But at least Hunter's films made money.

Lew's penny-pinching approach extended to film editing. Traditionally, much of what a director filmed ended up on the cutting-room floor. That cost the studio time and money. However, Ernie Nims started the practice of editing film abstractly. He'd take home a script and read it at night. "As I read, I'd see the picture in my head," he explained. "Whenever the picture was dull or blank, I'd cross out that part of the script." Having seen the movie in his mind's eye, he'd carry the script back to the director and suggest changes. Nims used this technique to eliminate the first fourteen pages of Welles's script for *Touch of Evil*. Nims called his technique "pre-editing," and became so well respected that Wasserman gave him the power to cut scenes—even when a producer argued. In that case, Nims was supposed to settle the disagreement with the producer and Muhl, who pledged to back Nims. "But I never had to call in the chief, because the producers and directors would always see the logic of what I was saying."

Wasserman liked Nims's talent and, in 1962, told him: "We want to tie you up for a few years." He offered the editor a seven-year contract—unusually long for that time. The salary would remain unchanged, which gave Nims pause. But the editor had a son with polio, who lived in an iron lung, and Wasserman was firing studio people. Nims agreed to the salary as a form of security for his family. "Maybe Lew took advantage of that, I don't know," he said. "I never did get as much money as I should have for all the films I did (*Father Goose*, 1965; *Shenandoah*, 1965; *The Day of the Jackal*, 1973). Each year, though, Wasserman made sure Nims received a new car which, every Friday was waxed and gassed for his personal weekend use, and Wasserman eventually promoted Nims to vice president in charge of editing.

Meanwhile, the camaraderie that had once marked Universal slowly bled out of its lot. The old studio "was family," said Nims, "and there was a real spirit of teamwork. You knew that no one was trying to get your job or stab you in the back." Muhl summed up the new studio best: "MCA was all about money."

Wasserman had little use for archives. He gave away or threw out the studio's valuable papers from its early days. "I was so mad at him, I could have socked him in the nose," groused Muhl. But Wasserman had his own sense of history and his place in it. Undoubtedly, he enjoyed the irony that he, an accused monopolist, had purchased a studio founded by Hollywood's first and only trustbuster.

Carl Laemmle was a German immigrant who started in 1906

with a few nickelodeons in Wisconsin. While building his chain of theaters, he bought a print of a discarded film for $96 and rented it out. He soon owned enough discarded film to open his own distribution unit. At the time, the Motion Picture Patents Company, a trust headed by Thomas Edison, controlled the camera industry, projection machines, and celluloid film. The trust decided who could make motion pictures and convinced Eastman Kodak to sell raw film stock only to nine licensees. It also charged exhibitors a steep $2 a week to show these films. The trust enforced its rules with brutal tactics, and those who broke ranks were left without films. This infuriated independent exhibitors like Laemmle, who fled the East—the trust was based in New York—and set up shop in Cuba, Mexico, and California. In 1909 Laemmle released his first film, *Hiawatha,* and followed it with others. He lampooned the trust in advertisements and in cartoons published in the press. As the public tide began to turn in Laemmle's favor, he became the trust's biggest and best-known target, named in some 289 lawsuits.

A pivotal case accused Laemmle of infringing on a trust patent that covered the continuous feed of perforated film on a sprocket, which looped the film through a projector. Laemmle and his attorneys had only one day to produce evidence that this perforation existed in another form, or he could lose his studio. The day before his court appearance, he and his attorneys racked their brains for an example but were running out of time. At one point, a young aide retired to the bathroom. When he reached for the toilet paper, he saw the answer to their problems. He emerged from the privy, all but yelling "Eureka!" And in court the next day, Laemmle proved his case by unspooling a roll of perforated toilet paper. The judge ruled in his favor, and the trust was found guilty of violating the Sherman Antitrust Act.

Laemmle always considered his biggest achievement not the creation of his studio but the crushing of the trust, said his son-in-law Stanley Bergerman. From then on, "Uncle" Carl became one of the best-known and best-liked moguls in the land.

Laemmle and Wasserman had many stylistic and philosophical differences, yet they both envisioned a vast Universal City. In the golden days of the 1930s, studios functioned like medieval villages, occupying 40 acres or so of land and employing 1,000 to 3,000 workers. Laemmle had turned Universal into an efficient compound whose dimensions dwarfed any other factory in California, with its own telegraph room, blacksmith shop, sawmill, barbershop, electrical department, zoo, cavalry barracks, horse stables, and a hospital.

Wasserman took Uncle Carl's blueprints to a whole new level. His property was nearly twice the size of Laemmle's. It, too, was a municipality with its own post office, phone-exchange prefix, hospital, film lab, mayor, city council, police department, firehouse, development arm, brokerage houses, and state and federal lobbyists. Wasserman acquired his own bank, Columbia Savings & Loan of Denver, Colorado. "There were a few chuckles in town when we bought that," said Al Dorskind. MCA already had two $25 million credit lines from two other banks, and the Denver thrift seemed like a hokey acquisition. But after MCA's old client, Jack Benny, became its spokesman, the savings and loan flourished. Three years after its purchase, the thrift with $65 million in assets had doubled in size and income.

Wasserman constructed a complex of buildings around Universal City Plaza, then struck long-term leases with E. F. Hutton, Bank of America, and Technicolor Corporation of America to fill them. His film laboratory employed the most advanced film-processing techniques of its time, and by 1965 it would process film for the entire entertainment industry. Wasserman then acquired a major music publisher, Leeds Music Corporation, which had a huge catalog of popular and classical sheet music. Leeds would form the base of what would soon blossom into MCA Music Group—later Universal Music Group, the world's dominant recording conglomerate.

Wasserman borrowed another idea from Uncle Carl, although it took him a while to realize it. The commissary that had plagued him and Dorskind with insurmountable losses suddenly had commercial possibilities, thanks to a ride Sam Carson and Dorskind happened to take around the lot one day. Their golf cart almost ran over Fred Astaire. After apologizing, Carson told Dorskind: "Say, this is really something! People come to California every year to see Disneyland. Why don't you let them tour Universal City and see real stars?" Dorskind laughed. "But you could see the light go on in his head," according to Carson.

That weekend, Dorskind took his two children to Farmers Market, where he noticed a tour bus unload dozens of tourists. That sight, along with Carson's comment, encouraged him to try a Universal tour. Dorskind called a few tour operators and inquired: "Would you like to ferry tourists to Universal Studios for a tour of the back lot?" Tourists could see real movie sets and lunch at the commissary, where they might spy Rock Hudson or Doris Day. The tour guides agreed, and so did Wasserman.

"We can't take credit for that idea," Wasserman said to me years later. "There is a photograph in our files, shot in 1919, of a group standing on Lankershim Boulevard, waiting to walk up a flight of stairs. They're posing next to a sign that said, 'Watch them make movies for 25 cents,' " he explained.

In 1915, when Laemmle opened his studio, he invited the public to a two-day party. People squeezed into jalopies that clogged the two-lane country road leading to Universal. On March 15, some 20,000 guests streamed through the gates, greeted by silent-screen star Lon Chaney and mixing with guests such as Laemmle's nemesis, Thomas Edison. Uncle Carl had built a two-story-high grandstand so people, for a quarter each, could watch directors make films. He also offered guided tours of Universal's movie sets.

Wasserman lifted Laemmle's concept to a much higher level— although he was cautious at first. "He wanted to make sure that the tourists wouldn't get in the way of his [3,000] employees," said

Dorskind. Wasserman was not hosting a party, he was conducting business. Still, he knew he had something special in this tour idea, said MCA publicist Herb Steinberg. "In those days, you could never get on a lot unless you knew someone." Dorskind added 150 quick-service seats to the commissary, jacked up food prices 20 percent, and charged the tour-bus lines 50 cents a head. In 1963 Gray Line began with a few busloads of tourists a day—about 250 people— who kept waitresses busy. Before long, the studio tour reservations jumped 200 percent, said Steinberg, and Wasserman's commissary finally made money.

"That first year we started the tour, we had 30,000 people," Wasserman said proudly. "We eventually got it up to 5 million a day, so I guess we didn't do so bad."

Uncle Carl lost his beloved studio to a loan shark during the Great Depression and spent his final days roaming his huge Beverly Hills mansion, feeling lost and nostalgic, said his son-in-law. Wasserman had no intention of following suit. He had already lost an agency. He knew that safeguarding assets was just as crucial as building them. In 1963 he formed an MCA corporate-film division to cater to business and government leaders. "Our job was to produce films and tapes for major corporations," said Bill Burch, head of the unit. General Motors, Ford, and "all of the major concerns" paid top dollar for MCA to produce short films that executives could show to employees, customers, and Wall Street analysts. The office was located across from the Black Tower because "Wasserman charged us so darn much money to use his lot. Besides," added Burch, "he wanted us to make a profit. But the aim of this particular division was not only to collect income but cachet as well.

"We got contracts with the federal government, like the Energy Department," he explained. "The division lent a bit more prestige to MCA's image and provided access to major corporations." Executives, thrilled that their films were being produced by a motion-picture company, were often happy to do a good deed for MCA. "The division also gave Wasserman entrée to government people, and, over the years, it grew to be quite important," said Burch. "But it didn't happen overnight."

Other political connections were strengthening, too. The Wassermans were invited into the elite fundraising circle of the Democratic Party by Arthur Krim, the chief of United Artists. Krim and his partner Robert S. Benjamin were major supporters of President Kennedy. In May 1962, they threw the notorious fundraising party at Madison Square Garden where Marilyn Monroe appeared in a skintight dress and breathlessly sang "Happy Birthday, Mr. President." The event raised a few eyebrows and an astounding $1 million. And it was at a small party at Krim's town house later that night that Robert Kennedy reportedly initiated an affair with Monroe, according to several published accounts.

To raise even more money for pro-Kennedy congressional leaders, Krim founded the President's Club. For $1,000 each, members received special briefings from Cabinet members, gold-engraved cards, photo opportunities, and invitations to Washington's legislative backrooms. Krim, who worked out of New York, needed a West Coast counterpart. In the spring of 1963, Wasserman agreed to head the California chapter of the President's Club. Among his first duties was to help host a fundraiser for President Kennedy on June 7, 1963. "We had to use the rooftop of the Beverly Hilton Hotel because of a [high-school] prom," said Joe Cerrell, then executive director of the state's Democratic party. Wasserman did not chair the event, said Cerrell, but he micromanaged it. He and Edie supervised the seating, menu, and flower arrangements, said Herb Steinberg. "Kennedy was starstruck, and Wasserman made some of them available for fundraisers," he said. One such star was Jane Wyman, ex-MCA client, formerly Mrs. Ronald Reagan, and now an avid Kennedy supporter. Another of Wasserman's contributions was to place an eleventh chair at each ten-person table so that the president could sit at each one during the meal. "That way, the president could meet everyone in the room," explained Steinberg. The eleventh chair was so successful that it became a staple at other political fundraisers.

The dinner raised about $250,000 and garnered Wasserman a personal thank-you note from Kennedy. That night, Edie confided to one of her dinner companions: "We will never be investigated again. From now on, we will always know what's going on in the White House." The Wassermans were within arm's reach of Washington's inner sanctum, where they would soon flourish.

SEVENTEEN

The twenty-six-year-old writer sat nervously at the edge of the conference table, waiting for his studio boss. Frank Price wondered why he had been summoned here to meet the president. As Wasserman walked into the room, Price stood, shook his hand, then guessed the purpose of this visit. Wasserman was carrying one of Price's recent TV scripts. "Lew had marked up the pages quite a lot," said Price, and the writer girded himself.

Wasserman had just read the young man's script for Revue's most ambitious series ever—*The Virginian.* The show was based on the 1902 Owen Wister novel about a rancher in Wyoming Territory. The nameless lead character had a mysterious past and fought nature, Indians, and shifty white men. "He had traits that drew on the mythology of the Western hero," Price explained. The script that Wasserman placed on the table was titled *The Drifter,* and it was the Virginian's backstory. This lone cowboy figure evidently resonated with Wasserman, said Price, for during the next twenty minutes, Wasserman critiqued the piece, explaining why the script did not accurately reflect the TV hero's emotional makeup. As the mogul flipped through the pages, he read his notes, pointing out the story's flaws and contradictions. Price said, "Lew was incredibly logical listing his problems with the story."

Nervously, the young man took down Wasserman's concerns, while fighting a growing urge to engage the chief in a philosophical discussion. Price wanted to lean over the long wooden table and discuss the meaning of the fictional cattle ranch, Shiloh. He wanted to debate the magic of storytelling, and explain why hero myths are anything but rational. But Price dared not interrupt the president of MCA. He said, "If you are the neophyte working on a new show, and the head of the company points out some problems, you listen to him very, very carefully."

After the meeting, Price returned to his office and rewrote the script. "I tried to incorporate all of Lew's suggestions. But in order to plug every hole, I realized I'd be killing the story." So he put aside the script. Twelve weeks later, in midseason, "while Wasserman and everyone else was looking the other way," Price slipped *The Drifter* into the series schedule. The episode later scored the highest rating for the series that year, and Wasserman never said another word about it.

It was not unusual for Wasserman to pay such close attention to his TV product. In the early 1960s, MCA still dominated the television production sector—but not much else—because of Revue. "Television *was* MCA," Price explained. Until Wasserman could build up his film or music division, all of MCA's eggs were sitting in the TV basket. It couldn't afford to lose even one show contract. "If Lew wanted to stay in business, he had to keep the client happy." And so the mogul eyeballed nearly every script and production before it left his back lot. "You had this transition period when Lew was very strongly involved in motion pictures and television product—much more so than he'd ever been," said Price.

Wasserman was fighting other forces, too, such as network censorship. As late as 1963, TV executives were still skittish about content that might be labeled as subversive. One of Revue's many western series was *The Tall Man*. Price had written a provocative episode for that show and hired the then-unknown Sydney Pollack to direct it. Sheriff Pat Garrett had gone to Mexico to find a prisoner and return him to jail. On the way home, the lawman and prisoner stopped in a poor Mexican village, where the chained prisoner pointed to the sheriff's horse, fancy saddle, and shiny gun. Price explained, "He's trying to incite the villagers to attack the sheriff, and he succeeds." But after robbing the sheriff and leaving him for dead, the villagers kill the prisoner, too. Said Price, "We were trying to do something offbeat, rather than the usual western fare."

When NBC executives saw the dailies, they "thought it was Communist propaganda because it incited the poor to take from the rich," said Price. NBC president Robert Kintner called Wasserman and told him to replace the episode with something tamer. "And don't do anything too emotional," Kintner pleaded. Wasserman hung up the phone and walked out of his office, his arms pumping like pistons. He strode angrily to the office of the show's executive producer, Revue veteran Nat Holt, glared at him, and started to roar. Employees in the area froze as Wasserman's vitriolic words rattled the rafters. "Lew was really beating up on this old guy pretty well, and you could hear it a mile away," Price said. The studio chief threatened to fire Holt, who had produced some of MCA's more successful shows during the 1950s. Producer Dick Irving later managed to calm Wasserman down, and Holt kept his job. Price continued sneaking in offbeat stories, though, and Pollack soon left Universal to direct his first feature at Paramount Studios. A short time later, NBC canceled *The Tall Man*.

Wasserman also had to kowtow to *Red Channels*, the bible of TV's blacklist, which published rumors and innuendo about dubious writers and actors who either belonged to the Communist Party or had "bad associations, such as a former membership in a tainted Boy Scouts troop," said Price. For more than a decade, *Red Channels* had ruined careers, and the newsletter was still read by the network men and sponsors in commercial TV, who had to give their okay to any TV talent Wasserman's men wanted to hire. Said Price: "I had to list which writers we were considering using and what they had done, before I could get their approval. It was a fearsome thing, really."

Wasserman's TV operation even had to battle its own recipe for success. Radio star Fred Allen originated the comment: "Television is called a medium because it is neither rare nor well done." That summarized Revue Productions. While Gore Vidal, David Susskind, and Paddy Chayevsky were producing award-winning TV dramas, Revue was reheating schlock and passing it off as new series. *Frontier Circus, Riverboat, Laramie, Tales of Wells Fargo, Wagon Train, The Deputy*—none of these shows did much to advance TV as an art form, and many of them blurred into one another. Sidney Sheinberg noticed this after he joined Revue in 1958. "The company had a reputation for making real garbage, very cheap syndicated product." Only after audiences began demanding more sophisticated fare was Revue forced to raise the quality of its shows.

By 1963, Wasserman had assembled an impressive collection of creative producers. There was Jack Webb and his *Dragnet* team, the senior residents. Wasserman had bought Webb's production company, Mark VII, in 1954 for $5 million. Webb had essentially invented the cop show—a genre that would be reinvigorated in the future in such programs as *Hill Street Blues, NYPD Blue,* and *Law and Order.* Webb was the producer and director of the half-hour documentary-style series. With his basset-hound eyes and droopy jowls, the actor played the humorless Sergeant Joe Friday, and his weary "Just the facts, ma'am," conveyed grim reality. *Dragnet's* tales were borrowed from real police cases, said former LAPD chief Ed Davis. "He'd solicit stories from our men and investigators." Off-duty officers would frequently drop by Webb's studio, said Charles Reese, a patrol inspector. "I'd go out to the studio, and he'd pour me whiskey with both hands. He was authentic and would pay well for stories." Webb became such a fixture at the precinct, filming scenes at the front desk and shaking hands with the brass, that Chief Davis felt like decorating him with ribbons and medals. "Jack Webb always appeared to be one of our men," he said.

However, young writers had a hard time cracking Webb's unit. "They wrote stuff by the book, and it was hard to break into their little group," said TV writer Stephen Cannell. "They didn't deviate much from their success." *Dragnet's* bungalow had heavy drapes that were often drawn tight in the afternoon. Cops would sprawl at the writers' table, which was cluttered with closed case files, ashtrays of burning cigarettes, and a bottle of Crown Royal. Wasserman so valued *Dragnet* that he ordered Al Dorskind to shadow Webb, who was fond of women and booze. "You signed the purchase deal—you see to it that Jack stays on the straight and narrow." Like a detective, Dorskind made regular surveillance reports to his chief. "I stuck close to Webb and whoever was his Queen for a Day."

Also on the lot was Alfred Hitchcock. The English filmmaker had been quite happy making Paramount films such as *Rear Window* (1954) and *To Catch a Thief* (1955). And Wasserman had seen to it that his friend Hitchcock—not Paramount—retained the rights to these films, which made the director a rich man. In 1955 Wasserman wanted him to do a Revue TV series, which appalled the director. TV meant no stars, no Technicolor, and no dazzling camera angles, said his daughter Patricia Hitchcock O'Connell. "He didn't know whether TV was the right thing to do for his career." But Wasserman outlined his concept carefully: The series would be produced by a unit housed on the Universal lot, where Revue was renting space in 1955. The half-hour shows would bear Hitchcock's name and likeness, and he wouldn't have to direct or write them. "That appealed to him," because Hitch preferred to work on films, said O'Connell. The TV series would be an anthology of mysteries and thrillers that would capitalize on Hitch's name and style, and he'd earn a percentage and residuals. But only after Revue sold the idea to CBS and Bristol-Myers, at $129,000 per half-hour show, did Hitch consider it seriously. After the show's initial broadcast, Hitch would own all rights, a lucrative prospect indeed. Still, Hitch worried. "Do you really think I should do this?" he asked his agent. Wasserman nodded. "Very definitely."

"That set a new standard for TV and was one of Lew's masterstrokes," said Gavin Lambert. But years later, Wasserman waved away any notion of artistic motivation. "I told [Hitchcock] he had to go into television because we needed the commission. For thirty years, we managed him, and maybe more when you think about it," Wasserman recalled. "He never said no." Hitchcock trusted the agent. "I had a lot of clients who trusted me—I hope most of them did," he said.

Once Hitch had committed to the TV show, he designed the series logo, using a pen-and-ink silhouette of himself. He chose the impish theme music—Charles Gounod's "Funeral March of a Marionette"—and opened and closed each episode with a droll setup and explanation. When the series debuted on CBS, it rocketed to sixth place in the Nielsen ratings and was an immediate success. Said his daughter, "Dad loved doing it and was glad he had listened to Lew." Alfred Hitchcock became a household name, and his company, Shamley Productions, turned into a cottage industry that produced other series in addition to *Alfred Hitchcock Presents*. "It was the only show on the lot that was produced by a woman, Joan Harrison, and it was the best," said Jerry Adler, the executive producer. Wasserman often stopped by Hitch's bungalow, making sure all was well. "Even though Hitch owned it, we treated the company like it was our own," said Adler.

Wasserman also employed a group of radio writers from the 1940s who had transferred their skills to TV. Among them was Dick Irving, known for producing cheap TV shows very quickly. "Dick loved Lew, and Lew leaned on him a lot," said *Columbo* cocreator William Link. "Lew considered him a troubleshooter, and if there was an actor who was being difficult, Lew would ask Dick to talk to that person and calm him down." Don Siegel was another stalwart, a master of action sequences but prone to choose violent material. (He later produced the "Dirty Harry" series with Clint Eastwood.) As soon as Wasserman gave Siegel too long a leash, the cultural gate-keepers were on the phone.

Then there was Roy Huggins, who had come to Universal after creating *Maverick* (1957–1962), *Cheyenne* (1955–1963), and *77 Sunset Strip* (1958–1964). Wasserman so prized the writer that he gave him a large bungalow filled with Stein's antiques. Huggins could be seen striding across the lot, gesturing like an orchestra conductor, with sheaves of TV script pages flying in the breeze and a flock of earnest assistants trailing behind, jotting down his ideas. Among Huggins's many protégés was writer Frank Price, who married his daughter, actress Katherine Huggins.

In 1962 most TV revolved around the half-hour show. But Wasserman always believed that TV was visual enough to sustain longer forms. "Lew's philosophy, which drove the TV division, was that he didn't want to play by everyone else's rules," said Price. "If you could come up with new rules, then you could control the field. Then you're in a much better position to win the game." While other TV producers were thinking, "How can I sell a half-hour series?" the guys at Revue were asking, "How can we come up with a different concept—then dominate that format?"

That's how *The Virginian* was born in 1962. Revue was about to renew its NBC contract for *Wagon Train,* which had debuted in 1957 and scored high ratings every season that followed. Now its five-year contract was set to expire. Although NBC wanted to renew it, Revue salesman and veteran agent Jennings Lang figured he could sell it to another network at twice the price. "Much to the consternation of NBC, Jennings sold the series to ABC one night over drinks," said Price. The next morning, NBC executives were livid, but Lang said he had something *even better* for them. He remembered that Price and Huggins had sketched some ideas about a Wyoming rancher. Okay, said NBC. But how is that better?

Because, Lang responded, grabbing at straws, "It will be the first ninety-minute TV series ever, and NBC will make broadcast history when it buys this one." When Price heard this, he laughed. "It was a neat little trick on Jennings's part, since the concept would give NBC something to boast about." When *The Virginian* aired with Lee J. Cobb and Roberta Stone, it attracted a 37 percent rating (compared to today's 13 percent to qualify for a "hit"). *Wagon Train,* once the highest-rated show, fell off the Nielsen charts while *The Virginian* rose, running every season until 1971 and becoming a prototype for the modern TV western.

Pitching shows to the networks was ostensibly the job of Sonny Werblin. He was still heading the New York office, meeting with programmers and advertisers, as he'd been doing for three decades. But Lang began to encroach on his turf—much to Werblin's annoyance. Yet Wasserman didn't intercede. "Lew left Jennings alone more than he did the others," recalled Ned Tanen.

Lang ate, drank, and lived large and had a face like an open ham sandwich—fleshy and flushed pink. "He was a legitimate Hollywood character from the old Ciro's and Trocadero nightclub days," Tanen explained. In the 1940s, Lang was a habitué of those casually decadent, *toujours glamour* clubs that lined Sunset Boulevard. "He was one of those guys who would chase someone's wife down the hallway, screaming like a drunk lecher." In 1951 Lang had been involved in a scandal after producer Walter Wanger (*Reckless Moment*, 1949) found the agent with his wife, MCA client Joan Bennett. After confronting the adulterers in the agency's parking lot, Wanger shot Lang in the groin. The lurid incident became front-page news, and Wanger was eventually sentenced to four months in jail. Bennett never starred in a major film again, and Lang lost one testicle. "That never affected his performance," his second wife, Monica Lewis Lang, insisted. "Our son is proof." Though Taft

Schreiber demanded that Wasserman fire the agent, Wasserman refused. "Lew realized that Lang had a lot going for him, including being terribly loyal to Lew," said Lang's wife. But Lang's transgression would come back to haunt Wasserman, who from then on called Lang the "one-ball wonder."

"Jennings could sell you anything," explained Jerry Freedman, an MCA TV writer. "He schmoozed with network and advertising executives," just like Werblin, said Price. He'd lounge in fine restaurants, order martinis and rare steaks, and toss out ideas for grandiose shows. Then he'd fly back to Los Angeles, where he'd meet with Price or another writer. "Whenever Jennings came up with a creative idea," said Price, "I had to make it work within a twenty-six-week format, so that he could take it back to New York a few days later, and say, 'See, we actually have it all worked out.' " Lang's ideas were either brilliant or foolish; they rarely fell anywhere in between. Once, Lang gave $2,000 to Freedman and musician Jimmy Webb, composer of the hit song "Wichita Lineman," and ordered them to produce a theatrical musical about Noah's ark. "It didn't go anywhere because it was too ridiculous," said Freedman. When Lang lived on a street named Bristol, he told Price to write three half-hour comedies about three apartment renters; *90 Bristol Court* made it to prime-time TV, said Price. "But it was tough to find a format for three people in half-hour comedies." After a while, the show was canceled.

After a boozy late-night meal with his network friends, Lang would telephone Wasserman from New York, jubilant at making a big sale. "But then he'd return to work the next day, hung over, and couldn't remember what he had done," said Price. This happened often enough that an exasperated Wasserman finally found Lang an assistant, Sidney Sheinberg. The young Texas attorney was teaching at UCLA Law School when MCA hired him in 1958. Wasserman had seen enough of Sheinberg's direct style to know he wouldn't clash with Lang's profane exuberance. Besides, Wasserman liked the attorney's attention to detail. Said Sheinberg, "Lew always feared that something horribly irrational would take place with Lang's deals. Jennings was one of those people who went through town like a hurricane. I had to clean up after him, which was hard. He'd tell you, 'Three for one, three for one,' and then call you an idiot because you didn't understand that what he *really* meant was just the opposite." In time, the lawyer learned to translate.

Huggins and Price fine-tuned *The Virginian,* and it became TV's first ninety-minute TV show—and a huge hit. Now Wasserman wanted a high-profile star vehicle to boost Revue's reputation. In 1963, while Jules Stein was swapping real estate with Bob Hope, Wasserman inserted his own rider onto the deal. He asked Hope to host a show for Revue, and the comedian agreed. That same day, Wasserman called the head of the Young & Rubicam advertising agency and sold a lavish package called *Bob Hope Presents Chrysler Theater.* "Lew promised the moon and stars on that one, far more than we could deliver," said Jerry Adler. "But he bit the bullet, lost money, and started producing a high-quality show."

Hope hosted and sometimes starred in the anthology series that featured award-winning dramas with Shelley Winters, Ginger Rogers, and Suzanne Pleshette. Sometimes Hope would also host a one-hour variety special. It raised Revue's profile, but was very expensive, said Adler. "Whatever the purchase price was, it wasn't enough, and Lew knew it. But it was important for him to make a quality statement. He'd never admit it, but it's a fact. And it was exactly the right thing to do at the time."

Suddenly, there was a new form of competition. The studios had now sold or leased some 4,000 old films for about $200 million. In September 1961, NBC kicked off its season with *Saturday Night at the Movies,* which showed such glamorous fare as *How to Marry a Millionaire* (1953). The Fox film, which starred Marilyn Monroe, Betty Grable, and Lauren Bacall, stole viewers from CBS's *Gunsmoke* and ABC's *Lawrence Welk.* To retaliate, the two other networks started their own *Saturday Night at the Movies*—ABC in April 1962 and CBS in September 1965. Advertisers were paying as much as $1 million to sponsor prime-time broadcasts of old, Oscar-winning films. "Lew wanted that money," said Price, and pushed his men to devise new ways of getting it.

"Imagine what MCA could earn if we showed *new* movies on prime-time TV," Lang told his boss one day. Revue was already spewing forth seven hours of TV programs a week—collecting between $200,000 and $500,000 per show—and processing enough film footage to make forty-five movies a month. It was already making a ninety-minutes series. How much tougher could it be to produce two-hour movies? "Sell it," Wasserman told Lang. To their surprise, the networks were timid. "It was a very, very radical idea at the time, because most critics felt that people wouldn't watch these movies," said Price. "They wanted *real* movies. It seems ridiculous now, but that was the prevailing thought." Stubbornly, Wasserman approved a few pilots under the code name *Project 120,* signifying the length of the programs. Lang kept pushing the idea on NBC. "You can make broadcast history again, this time by airing the first made-for-TV-movie," he'd say. But the network didn't bite—not until Wasserman learned that NBC's parent, RCA, was about to introduce the first color television set. When Lang pledged to produce quality color movies, NBC signed up.

The first project was *The Killers,* a Don Siegel work based on a Hemingway story and starring John Cassavetes, Lee Marvin, and Angie Dickinson. The story revolved around two thugs who murder a man and then piece together his background. The network considered the finished product too violent, and Wasserman released it in the theaters. The second effort, *See How They Run,* fared better. This film posed a new and different problem, said Adler. "We had never negotiated to buy a book for a two-hour movie, and we couldn't afford it. Plus, the author, Michael Blankfort, had one of the toughest agents in town, and I didn't want to deal with him."

But Blankfort's son-in-law dearly wanted to direct a film. Adler offered to find a job for the would-be director in return for the movie rights. "That was the first time I ever heard the term 'quid pro quo,' and I had already done it, without even knowing." The film starred John Forsythe and Senta Berger and aired October 1964 to modest ratings. However, the critics sneered.

"You have no idea how big a deal it was," said Sheinberg. "Today you can laugh, and say, 'Ah, what's he talking about?' But making a movie for television was oxymoronic at that time. Movies were in theaters, not on television." ABC and CBS were gloating over MCA's missteps, and Wasserman took umbrage. "One major executive in our industry told me at the time that I was an idiot to make the deal," for TV movies, he later told a reporter. Behind his back, the town whispered that Wasserman was selling movies for too low a price—and they were right.

Six weeks later, NBC broadcast the third experiment, *The Hanged Man* (1964), again directed by Siegel. The tightly edited, charged film centered on a gunman who set out to kill the people who had murdered his friend. Set in New Orleans, it starred Robert Culp, Edmond O'Brien, Vera Miles, and Edgar Bergen (all former MCA clients). Once again, critics ridiculed the film, but now viewers were watching. The ratings climbed. "Lew said it was time to get a contract," said Sheinberg. By 1965, Universal had an NBC agreement in which the studio would deliver weekly TV movies over the next four years for $195 million. "That was a major deal," said Price, and it boosted MCA higher

By this time, Revue had changed its name to Universal TV. Wasserman's television units still created low-brow but popular fare such as *McHale's Navy,* though it started making quality programs, too. Along with the *Bob Hope Chrysler Theater,* the division made classy shows such as *Big Three Golf,* a weekly match that featured Arnold Palmer, Jack Nicklaus, and Gary Player. *The Virginian* started climbing the charts while *The Jack Benny Program, Alfred Hitchcock Presents,* and *Dragnet* continued bringing in revenues.

"We started developing a reputation for putting MCA on the quality map," said Sheinberg. Universal TV had some two dozen programs on the air every week, and TV was paying Universal Studio's overhead, said Price. Wasserman was not about to congratulate his men on their achievements—not yet. Not one of these hits scored higher than a 35 percent rating. Wasserman told his men that TV, at its peak viewing hour, had maybe 80 million viewers, or half the nation's population. "But that means 80 million people aren't watching TV," he'd grouse. The chief goaded, hollered at, and threatened his men. He wanted all American eyeballs glued to Universal TV shows.

EIGHTEEN

Having survived government investigations and high-profile lawsuits, Stein, Wasserman, and Schreiber continued working to elevate their influence onto higher, more prestigious planes. Democratic politics, Republican campaigns, and scientific philanthropy were the tools they used to conjure MCA's subtle, masterful transformation from avaricious show-biz merchants to humanitarian kingmakers. Stein thought it best to have his top men working both sides of the political aisle while he operated invisibly behind the curtain. "Stein was a genius to see that he could have two people in his organization represent both political parties," said Ronnie Lubin. "And that's what eventually happened."

MCA's two-party policy was deliberate and pragmatic, according to several sources. "It was all Stein's idea," said TV producer and published novelist Henry Denker. "That way, MCA would have friends no matter who was in power." One Universal executive agreed: "We had a joke on the lot that if you were running for dogcatcher, MCA would kick in some money for your campaign." Long before any other studio had an executive vice president of government affairs, MCA had two ward bosses.

Stein had watched his Republican friends underwrite GOP causes for years. His frequent dinner guests Asa Call and Justin Dart had raised enormous amounts of cash for President Dwight Eisenhower in 1956. Henry Salvatori was finance chair for the California Republican Party, and Holmes Tuttle was a delegate to the 1964 Republican National Convention. Stein had introduced his friends to Schreiber, who shared their pro-business agenda. Said Lubin, "Schreiber became very big in the Republican party during Kennedy's rise."

At first, Schreiber and Stein tried to push their photogenic clients toward high office. For a decade, Schreiber had cultivated George Murphy and Robert Montgomery, both of whom were former SAG presidents, MCA clients, and political conservatives, said Lubin. In 1952 Montgomery had coached Eisenhower for his presidential campaign, written his speeches, and directed his public appearances and televised spot commercials. By the time of Ike's TV debate, the former general appeared confident and relaxed. "A lot of people in Hollywood took notice of that," said Lubin. Eisenhower appointed Montgomery as his "special consultant," but the actor wasn't interested in holding office himself.

But George Murphy was. The actor and hoofer had played supporting roles in musicals such as *For Me and My Gal* (1943), hosted the NBC radio quiz show *Hollywood Calling*, and cofounded the Hollywood Republican Committee. He was also a California delegate to the 1952 Republican National Convention. By the early 1960s, Murphy had talked to Schreiber and Stein about running for the U.S. Senate. "Nothing was a coincidence with Stein," said one MCA executive. "Schreiber encouraged Murphy," agreed Lubin, and the hoofer was backed with money from Jules Stein and his friends.

In 1964 Murphy was the GOP's favorite in a Senate race against

Pierre Salinger, former press secretary to President Kennedy. Competition was tense inside and outside of MCA. While Schreiber helped Murphy's campaign, Wasserman worked on Salinger's, and his grown daughter, Lynne, volunteered for the Democratic candidate. Political consultants noticed MCA. "They used to talk about how Taft was the Republican counterbalance to Wasserman," the Democrats' warhorse, said Joe Cerrell, a California Democratic Party official. "He was supposed to be the Republican answer to Lew." When the gamesmanship between the two MCA executives turned personal, Stein acted as the swing vote, backing one man over the other, said Lubin. Otherwise, Stein didn't mediate the increasing rancor. "Jules could be a real son-of-a-bitch," said Berle Adams. He'd sit back and watch his men duke it out. "It was smart business to play both sides of the fence, but it divided the company," said a publicist. The political races simply ratcheted up MCA's long-simmering internal tensions. When Schreiber's guy Murphy resoundingly trumped Wasserman's man Salinger, it was a harbinger of things to come. Wasserman had to work harder to guard his flank.

Edie and Lew were still on the edge of Democratic circles in 1963, helping arrange functions in Los Angeles, but never taking the lead. They enlisted studio employees to help. "You were never hired," said MCA executive Bob Raines. "You were assigned and your politics were assumed." Before an event at the Ambassador Hotel's Coconut Grove, Wasserman had invited a few members of the President's Club to meet Kennedy at a cocktail party. The press was not invited, but when the group moved into the ballroom for a larger event, Lew spied newspaper columnist Walter Winchell, who demanded to interview the president, then began pushing his way through the crowd. Studio aides were about to physically remove Winchell when they heard Wasserman: "Don't hit him, boys. He's older than you." The Secret Service men accosted the columnist and, later, Wasserman reminded his men: "Never fight with the press. They always have the last word."

The relationship between Wasserman and John Kennedy, however, was short-lived. When the president was assassinated on November 22, 1963, "Lew was heartbroken," said Herb Steinberg. He added that Wasserman was so upset that he closed down Universal Studios, but no one else recalls that. "I know I was working," said Frank Price. Later, the story grew into the tale that Wasserman had ordered all of Hollywood to shut down for the day, a fabrication that would be quoted ever after. Steinberg and his publicists were doing their jobs in the town's best time-honored tradition. They were building a mogul into a granite business legend, a giant who could also claim a soft, vulnerable side and so fulfill the unscripted needs of the most besotted movie fan of all: Hollywood itself.

When Wasserman hired Steinberg in 1963, he gave the former Paramount star handler no specific job. "Lew really put me into what he called 'Executive in Charge of Special Projects.' That was my title," he recalled. Steinberg assumed the job of organizing Wasserman's political efforts. "I did Everything That Nobody Else Wanted to Do," he told me, and he grew close to both Edie and Lew.

Before Kennedy's death, Wasserman had submitted an idea to build a Kennedy Cultural Center in the nation's capitol, to be funded in a most unusual way. He suggested that the president designate for the nation a Monday night in April as Kennedy Cultural Center night. Every one of the country's arts venues—ballet productions, theaters, motion-picture houses, and music clubs—would be asked to donate that night's proceeds to the center; the public would be asked to patronize their favorite entertainment that night. The effort could raise several million dollars, Wasserman estimated, enough to build the facility. Before his death, Kennedy had approved the idea, and in 1964, President Johnson agreed, although Wasserman's idea would evolve further.

After Kennedy's tragic death consumed the country, Edie and Lew threw themselves into political fundraising. In June 1964 they helped organize a dinner for marquee guest President Johnson, held at the Hollywood Palladium and, later that night, at the Ambassador Hotel. Wasserman had invited shoe magnate Harry Karl, the husband of Debbie Reynolds, but the businessman was impatient for a glass of champagne. "The waiter wasn't moving fast enough for him, so Karl reached over, grabbed the iced bottle," and started to open it, said Joe Cerrell. It fell to the floor and uncorked with a bang. "I never saw so many guns drawn in my life," said Cerrell, "and everybody was on top of Johnson," including Wasserman. Six months after Kennedy's murder, Hollywood was still jittery.

Wasserman, along with attorney Eugene Wyman, started to raise the profile of the California chapter of the President's Club. Two years after the mogul assumed control, the California chapter had more than 500 members in the group, more than Johnson's home state of Texas and second only to New York. In 1964 it raised $155,000 for campaigns—about $1 million in today's dollars—which was then a stunning amount. And the Wassermans' $28,000 donation ranked among the largest of fifteen checks nationally. Edie and Lew were taking out insurance against future liabilities like government antitrust suits, said Doug Gomery, a studio historian. "Lew knew that he needed access to the powers that be." He also wanted a smooth, friendly path to Capitol Hill to pick up favors not just for Universal but for all of the entertainment industry, said political consultant Pat Caddell.

Wasserman also believed in the Democratic party's ideals—just as Schreiber fervently adhered to those of the GOP. Unlike most contributors, Wasserman did not give his money on a quid pro quo basis. Said Cerrell, "If I asked Lew for money, I don't think he expected anything in return." As time went on, that characteristic set Wasserman apart from most other wealthy patrons. But initially, his chief distinction was collecting so much California cash.

Johnson noticed this talent, and after he won the 1964 presidential election, an LBJ advisor asked Wasserman if he'd become the president's unofficial ambassador in California. "I'd like that," Wasserman said. He flew east to meet the president, and the two men hit it off immediately, said Steinberg. "Johnson absolutely fell in love with Lew." They were similar in many ways. Both were strong and decisive; they were ruthless, relentless, and very driven. "They were big guys who didn't sleep much," said Berle Adams. "Johnson admired Lew for his sound judgment," explained Jack Valenti, a Johnson aide. "Lew exercised good judgment instinctively." LBJ liked Wasserman's candor. "Lew never lied or dissembled." And Wasserman liked LBJ's direct style. Both men were wily negotiators, and Edie and Lew began to develop a relationship and, later, a genuine friendship with LBJ and Lady Bird. The Hollywood couple soon had the ear of the president of the United States—while Schreiber did not.

Jules and Doris Stein were in the midst of reconsidering their role as show-business operators. "Jules had approached a point in his life when he wanted a change," said one of his associates. He wanted to leave something behind, and the Music Corporation of America was not enough. In 1959 the Steins had visited New York's Lighthouse for the Blind, a favorite charity of their Upper East Side friends. Following its founding in 1905, the Lighthouse had grown into a major provider of vision care, treating low-income people and teaching them self-sufficiency. Doris was touched by its work, but Stein didn't want to give his millions to someone else's organization. He envisioned his own foundation, one that would reflect his personal, early endeavors unrelated to his agency fame.

Stein graduated from high school in 1912 at age sixteen, earned a degree in philosophy from the University of Chicago at age nineteen, and applied to many medical schools. His invalid mother had always wanted her son to be a doctor, and in October 1917, he was admitted to Rush Medical College. But he and his older brother Billy supported themselves by playing in orchestras, booking bands in clubs, and pocketing 20 or even 50 percent as commission. When

Prohibition dawned in 1919, the Stein brothers were working on the South Side of Chicago, the turf of Big Jim Colosimo and, later, Al Capone. To their service menu, the Stein brothers added chorus girls, ashtrays, confetti, cocktail stirrers, napkins, tablecloths, and even bootleg whiskey, said Gerald Oppenheimer.

At night, Stein met the mobsters who ran the clubs. By day, he concentrated on his studies, eventually serving an internship at Cook County Hospital. In June 1922 Stein graduated and took off for a three-month stint at the University of Vienna. He worked in an eye clinic there, then returned to Chicago in January 1923 and continued working the band circuit.

By that time, Stein had two partners—his brother Billy and his friend Bill Goodheart. Those two sweated to keep the band-booking business running while Stein took another internship, this one at the Michael Reese Hospital Dispensary, where he had access to opium, morphine, cocaine used for optical surgeries, and other legal medicinal drugs. According to a few sources, Stein used his pharmaceutical connection to gain an edge in the mob's nightclubs. "Stein ran drugs for the mob in the early days," said Robert Mitchum, who knew Stein. "That's how he got into Capone's nightclubs"—by supplying drugs to the dance clubs, opium dens, and prostitution houses that the mob operated. As MCA's first publicist, Karl Kramer, later wrote: "Any tactics were justifiable so long as a sale was consummated and you were clever enough to solve the difficulty when it came up." Stein and his cofounders agreed: "There was nothing wrong if you didn't get caught."

But Stein didn't abandon his medical career. Around 1923, he began working as an assistant to Dr. Henry Gradle, an eye doctor in Chicago's Loop. He and Gradle wrote a treatise on "telescopic magnifiers" for Zeiss Optical Company, the well-known lens maker. But Stein grew disenchanted with his doctor's salary. He was making $50 a week—substantial by 1924 standards—but not enough to satisfy the grand designs of Julius Caesar Stein.

Down the hall from Gradle's medical office, Stein noticed a thriving music agency. "He saw all these top orchestra leaders and trombone players, black and white, coming into the office at all hours," said GAC agent Henry Miller. Stein bought Ernie Young's Music Corporation for $10,000—an enormous sum at the time—and in August 1924 formed the Music Corporation of America. A year later, he quit medicine for good. Stein could be seen tooling around Chicago, driving a rakish Stutz Bearcat, wearing a raccoon coat and pince-nez spectacles, bragging about drinking liquor from a lady's slipper. His agency struck a sweetheart deal with the head of the American Federation of Musicians union, so MCA could represent bands *and* produce their radio shows. Ten years later, in the midst of the Great Depression, Stein was rich and famous. "Everyone knew that he was an eye doctor," Wasserman told me years later. That's part of what attracted Lew to MCA. "I knew who he was and what he had done. He was very unusual."

But Stein grew wealthy by peddling talent, which to Doris was a tawdry line of work. Now, as Stein approached his sixty-fifth birthday, he realized that he didn't want to be known just for building MCA. Besides, many of his peers were forming their eponymous foundations. At his wife's urging, Stein searched for a new cause. He paid for the first national public-opinion poll on eyesight and found that Americans feared blindness more than most physical afflictions. Even so, "nothing was being done to prevent blindness," said Dr. Bradley Straatsma, a Stein associate. In 1960 Stein founded a foundation—Research to Prevent Blindness—but it lay dormant until Wasserman acted.

In April 1961 the MCA president was pondering what to give his boss for his sixty-fifth birthday. "Several executives had already asked me, 'What the hell are we going to give him for his birthday?' It was not an easy chore," Wasserman recalled, since Stein was richer than Solomon. "So I asked what he wanted." Stein desired some contributions to his RPB foundation, he said. Wasserman called together MCA's top men and he, Taft Schreiber, Sonny Werblin, and seven others donated about $100,000 each. "The next day, we gave him a check for $1 million," said Wasserman.

Stein matched the gift with $1 million of his own, and the total offering catapulted RFB to prominence. Now he wanted to build his own research center, preferably at an elite East Coast university. But Harvard, Yale, and Johns Hopkins all turned him down. Instead, a few administrators from the University of California at Los Angeles started courting Stein. Initially, the MCA chairman wasn't impressed with the young Westwood-based institution; its medical school had graduated its first doctors only five years earlier, in 1955. But UCLA was in the midst of a postwar boom. Once Stein finally agreed to meet with its leaders, he realized UCLA's potential. "The more Jules learned about our university, the more impressed he became," said Straatsma.

Two things clinched Stein's support. One day, Straatsma took him on his medical rounds. "I introduced my patient to Dr. Jules Stein, which really pleased him," said Straatsma. From then on, Jules started calling himself Dr. Stein. The deciding factor was that if Stein built his facility at UCLA, he and Doris could look down upon it from their Misty Mountain castle. "That had a lot to do with his decision," said Straatsma.

In 1963 Stein introduced the Jules Stein Eye Institute (JSEI), which would soon become the world's leader in vision research, education, and treatment. It would sit prominently beside the UCLA Medical School, and have its own clinic, hospital, and research staff. Doris and Jules threw themselves into their noble project. Jules buttonholed his friends to raise $5 million for his five-story facility. Doris selected architects, artists, and craftspeople to build her new Los Angeles landmark. Between Jules's exacting standards and his wife's exquisite taste, the price tag would quickly triple to more than $15 million.

When the Steins finally broke ground on September 22, 1964—a few months before the Senate and presidential elections, 350 people were on hand. Stein's first movie-star client, Bette Davis, hailed him as "a maker of dreams come true." Bob Hope quipped that his pal just might "cure a lot of the eye disorders caused by his television programs." Walt Disney, Sam Goldwyn, Norton Simon, and Henry Ford II, among others, donated to the Steins' new production.

It was quite an achievement in just three years. As Gerald Oppenheimer explained, "Jules wanted to be sure he'd be remembered more for his efforts in curing blindness than for his work in show business." He was now a major philanthropist.

NINETEEN

IN THE EARLY 1960S, with Jules Stein building his eye clinic, Wasserman started moving more freely, as though a weight had fallen from his shoulders. "When Lew took over the studio, he was a different sort of person," Jerry Gershwin once said. He no longer confined himself to the background; he started wearing jewelry and displaying his wealth a little more. The vanity plates on his Bentley read MCA 1—in case there was any doubt who was boss. "Lew was like a kid in a candy store, and he was determined to be a studio creator," said Ned Tanen.

Wasserman had come of age with movies. When he was fourteen—in 1927, the year Warner Brothers released the first talkie, *The Jazz Singer*—Lew started working in a popular Cleveland movie theater. He stood guard at Keith's 105th Street Theater east of downtown. "It was a beautiful place that we loved to be in," said Al Setnik, one of Wasserman's coworkers. The theater boasted an ivory and gilt-trimmed lobby, lots of mirrors, and 3,000 rose velvet seats. "It was *the* place to be on a Saturday night, a major social center," said a Cleveland historian. And Louis Wasserman was its gatekeeper, greeting the grownups and handling the youngsters. He got the job because he was tall and looked older than his years, said his friend Paul Beck. "That helped his early career."

Wasserman loved wearing his usher's uniform; the brass buttons and gold-braid trim were so much smarter-looking than his hand-me-down clothes. As a doorman, the teenager became more confident and started projecting an image of being a guy "in the know," said his acquaintances. He could tell them which movies were popular, which studio produced them, and which one was coming next. After selling candy in a burlesque house, his new post felt more like an honor than a duty. He gave patrons a smile and a quip as they passed through his doors.

The Jazz Singer affected Wasserman on another level. The story revolved around an aging Jewish cantor and his young assimilated son, who yearns to be in show business. It mirrored the conflicts that were unfolding in the homes of thousands of Jewish immigrant families— including Wasserman's. Indeed, the parallels between the Wasserman family and the film family were eerie: Lou's dad was a devout Jew who objected to his son's secular ways. The young man worked on the Sabbath and didn't attend temple, while his parents followed religious law. Like the movie's fictional son, Lou aspired to climb out of his marginal life and onto the new American scene. After *The Jazz Singer*, Wasserman and his friends could at least identify some of the reasons they struggled with their fathers, said Lewis Ratener, a family friend. "His parents didn't know anything about theaters, and to them, movies were mysterious."

But to Wasserman, they were liberating. "We'd watch Clark Gable and Gary Cooper and memorize the best lines," said Setnik. Wasserman borrowed Gable's style and took to wearing ascots even though he was built more like the tall, laconic Cooper. Escapist stories, with their happy endings, offered a welcome respite from the boys' seven-day work schedules.

Wasserman recalled those golden memories thirty-five years later. "When I was a boy, the movie house was a thing of beauty," he said after taking over Universal. "We're getting back to that now." He borrowed a page from the old studio system and opened a school for new actors. Soon he had 100 fledgling stars under contract, including Carrie Snodgrass, Burt Reynolds, and James Brolin. They all worked in Universal TV shows until they had gained enough experience for feature films. Wasserman backed Broadway shows in the hope that one of them might become a hit; his men scouted for material on college campuses and in community theaters; the mogul doubled the slate of Universal movies to twenty-five a year, a sign of his faith in the business.

Universal had already released some respectable films by the time Wasserman took over: *Cape Fear* (1962) with Gregory Peck, Polly Bergen, and Robert Mitchum; *Freud* (1962) with Montgomery Clift; and *That Touch of Mink* (1962), a Ross Hunter production with Doris Day and Cary Grant. "Ross was one of the few producers who would come to your office with a yellow pad," recalled Ed Muhl. "When you talked, he took notes. He was unegotistical that way." Hunter had a knack for turning out hits, which is why Universal had given him a $75 million, seven-year contract.

Wasserman brought Alfred Hitchcock back to the film studio after a twenty-year hiatus. For Universal, Hitch had directed *Saboteur* (1942), followed by *Shadow of a Doubt* (1943), starring Joseph Cotten as a guilty uncle and Teresa Wright as his suspicious niece. The film deftly juxtaposed evil and innocence, and Hitchcock often said it was his favorite. In 1960 Wasserman made sure that the director, who was under contract at Paramount, made *Psycho* at Universal, where the two studios split the film's low $800,000 cost. On that film, Hitch used the same quick black-and-white production techniques that had made Revue so rich. Young movie audiences who had been weaned on Revue TV shows thrilled to *Psycho,* which made an astounding $15 million.

At Wasserman's behest, Hitch then made a full-fledged return to Universal, consolidating his TV and movie projects on the same lot. For Wasserman's Universal Studio, Hitch transformed a Daphne du Maurier story into a suitably creepy script. He signed Evan Hunter, aka detective novelist Ed McBain, to write the script for *The Birds* (1963), and shot it primarily in Bodega Bay, a coastal town north of San Francisco. The director spent a week filming the scene where actress Tippi Hedren is descended upon and ravaged by birds; he added to the terror by tying the creatures to Hedren's clothes with nylon threads. When the birds tried to fly away, they would panic and attack the actress over and over. At one point, the birds cut Hedren's face, and she broke down in tears. But the only time Wasserman put his foot down was when Hitchcock wanted to shoot his last scene on the Golden Gate Bridge, which would be covered with thousands of black birds. The mogul convinced the director that would be too expensive, said Jerry Adler. The film was acclaimed as a masterpiece of control and manipulation, although it brought in just one-third of *Psycho*'s take—$5 million.

Hitch's next film was *Marnie* (1964), a tale about a frigid kleptomaniac (Hedren) and her wealthy boss (Sean Connery), who falls in love with her and marries her. The film's overwhelming mood was frustration—both intentional and subconscious. Hitch grew so possessive of his star that he forbade her to travel. By midway through the movie, the director and his leading lady were not speaking, and Hitch had to direct her through intermediaries. Wasserman used his Honeywell computer to crunch the numbers of each film being made—including *Marnie*. "Every movie director had to get going early in the morning, like 6:30 or 7:00," said Al Dorskind. "But they couldn't just stand around and get coffee. They had to get their shot in, right away." Daily reports reflected the number of camera shots, total minutes per shot, number of employees, and even the length of their coffee breaks. Directors knew that their careers rested on these dot-matrix sheets—and many studied their computerized figures so they could improve them. One day, Louise Latham, a supporting actress in *Marnie,* spied a production assistant scanning his report. "My God, your days *really* are controlled, aren't they?" she said.

In *Marnie*'s case, that control tightened the film's suspense. Every camera angle and move, every actor's expression, and every object's placement seemed so purposeful that one still marvels at its focus. But Wasserman's mainframe Honeywell, whirring in an air-conditioned corner of the tower, became the butt of many jokes, said Latham. "People would laugh and say, 'The suits can't figure out what makes a hit movie, so they're feeding information into that computer to find the right formula.'" Laughable or not, Wasserman's practices stream-lined the production of Hollywood movies—and were years ahead of their time.

Despite the pressure, Wasserman and Hitch grew closer and even exchanged gifts. In 1962 Hitch traded his rights to *Psycho* and the 268 telefilms of *Alfred Hitchcock Presents* for a huge block of MCA stock, which made him the third-largest shareholder. Hitchcock became the most envied director in town, the only one with an equity stake in a studio. The value of MCA's copyright of Hitch's properties would someday surpass that of MCA's stock, but at the time, it was a magnanimous present. Hitch also gave Lew a chilling work of art. He commissioned French impressionist Bernard Buffet to paint a portrait of the studio head. Buffet was known for his tragic subjects and abhorrence of war and technology. Using angular strokes and bleak colors, he depicted the mogul as a skeleton wearing a black suit, white shirt, dark tie, and black-rimmed glasses. It was not unkind, although Wasserman's hands are crossed over his chest like that of a corpse. His fingers are prominent and bone white, his face is sculpted with hollows and crags, and his eyes are large and opaque. "Lew had made a fortune for Hitchcock by syn-dicating his shows," said Tanen. "And Hitch, who had never had much money, really took care of Lew. You could see that someone with a dark sense of humor spent a lot of money on that piece. It's a frightening portrait, totally Hitchcockian." Wasserman hung the portrait in his foyer at home, where it was the first thing that greeted guests.

Wasserman brought another old friend to the studio, former client Jimmy Stewart. Stewart agreed to play against type by starring in *Shenandoah* (1965), a heartbreaking film about a widower who tries to ignore the Civil War. After his son is captured, he cannot help but get involved. The film starred Doug McClure, Rosemary Forsyth, and contract player Katharine Ross in her film debut. "It was a strong antiwar film that was filmed at the height of the Vietnam War," said Ed Muhl. "There was a lot of pacifist propaganda in it." The film was nominated for several awards but did only moderate box-office business. Even so, it had a lingering impact on Wasserman. Nearly two years after it was released, a woman whose son was in Vietnam wrote a letter to the studio chief, saying she was still haunted by the film. Wasserman passed the note on to Muhl, who considered it one of the better films of this era. Two years later, in 1969, Jimmy Stewart's stepson Ronald was killed fighting in Vietnam, which devastated the actor and made the film even more poignant to those who had worked with him.

Wasserman hired producer Walter Seltzer, who began making a $3 million movie. *The War Lord* (1965) was a realistic medieval tale that starred Charlton Heston and Richard Boone, but during its production, Seltzer felt increasingly hampered by the studio's dictates. His next project, *Beau Geste* (1966), was the third remake of a classic tale about brotherly devotion and the French Foreign Legion. Other producers on the lot recalled Wasserman's heavy hand in that film. "Lew was very actively involved in that picture and it became his personal project," said one MCA executive. Wasserman found the director-scriptwriter, Douglas Hayes, who performed the two jobs for very little money. The studio chief also made sure that Guy

Stockwell was cast in the same role that Ronald Colman had played in the silent version in 1926 and Gary Cooper had portrayed in 1939. Wasserman made decisions about dialogue, story, and scenes—all of which preempted Seltzer's duties. Said the MCA executive, "Everyone on the lot knew that this was Lew's movie, and it was just dreadful." But critics blasted Seltzer when they panned the movie, which did not do well at the box office. By then, Seltzer had decided to leave. "It was too regimented and stifling for me," he said. Although Wasserman asked him to stay, Seltzer declined. "I wanted to do my own thing."

It was becoming apparent to Hollywood insiders that MCA was having a hard time manufacturing creativity. "I don't think they realized how tough it would be," said one producer. Universal turned out several congenial surprises: Cary Grant appeared as a slovenly drunk in *Father Goose* (1964), and the film won an Oscar for best screenplay—but sputtered at the box office. The amiable western *War Wagon* (1967) starred John Wayne and Kirk Douglas, with Howard Keel playing an unlikely wisecracking Indian. Ross Hunter made *I'd Rather Be Rich* (1964), starring Sandra Dee and Maurice Chevalier, and *The Art of Love* (1965), starring Ethel Merman and Dick Van Dyke. None of these, however, were riveting movies about the day's issues: the Vietnam War, racial strife, and other controversies were sweeping the country.

"A lot of the people who joined the new regime were guys from the same old paradigm," said Roy Gerber. They used the same old stars and same old stories they had sold when they were agents, explained Jim Murray. "So why shouldn't they use the same formula?" The studio had not been very successful in the past, "but it was less successful when we got there," said Tanen. A little risk-taking would have distinguished Universal from the other studios. But Wasserman wasn't ready for creative risks. As one producer remarked, "The best we had going was John Wayne in a cowboy hat or Doris Day grinning at the screen."

By 1964, MCA's gross revenues were $192.7 million—double what they had been three years earlier. Profits were at an all-time high of $14.8 million. "I plead guilty to being commercial," Wasserman confessed at the time. Let the others tackle social issues—he'd continue developing real estate at Universal City, making hit TV shows, and bringing efficiency to the art of movie-making. *Time* magazine hailed him as "a new kind of cinema king," a corporate president who manufactures movies. Industry deal-makers started calling him "Lew, baby." They copied his personal style and took to wearing large gold pinkie rings and oversized glasses. By 1965, the town respected Wasserman again—even if they didn't think much of his movies.

Perhaps if Wasserman had been forced to deal with cunning agents, Universal Studio might have released some higher-quality films. If brokers had insisted that their client directors and writers maintain creative control, Wasserman would have had to loosen his grip. "He never should have been making decisions about script dialogue and such," said Frank Price. But no other agency had filled MCA's old agency spot in the hierarchy. Some 200 agents had been thrown out of MCA Square; it had taken months before studios could locate some of MCA's 1,500 clients and a few more months before they could determine who represented them. Many agents had started boutique firms: Art Park and Herman Citron formed Park-Citron; Jerry Perenchio formed United Talent Management; David Baum-garten created Artists Performing Agency. Others had joined William Morris, General Amusement Corporation, or Freddie Fields's agency, Creative Management Associates.

MCA agents who had once chafed under Wasserman's rules now missed the good old rigid days. Some men had never liked Lew's edict to answer the phone by saying "MCA," rather than their own names. They thought they were important enough not to have to use his agency's name. But these men learned otherwise. After leaving MCA, not even those who had been Wasserman's best men could get their calls returned, said Murray. "Those initials M-C-A were magic. A lot of guys couldn't get jobs because they weren't as good as they thought they were."

The exiled kept in touch, passing on leads. Stories about Wasserman took on malevolent shadings. Several agents believed that, contrary to news reports, Wasserman had not been forced to break up his agency. Rather, he had secretly orchestrated the breakup in conjunction with the government. "I always felt that the antitrust thing was a big setup," Murray explained. "Lew really wanted to be out of the agency business, but how could he do that without alienating the clients?" Added Gerber: "It's my firm belief that MCA set up their own bust, as it was a gracious way to get out of the business without angering their clients." After they learned that Wasserman had ordered his lawyers to destroy the antitrust case files, they grew certain of this. "I think there was incriminating evidence against MCA, and Lew ordered that all of it be destroyed," said Gerber.

Malcolm MacArthur, one of the government prosecutors on the case, dismissed the notion of a conspiracy. "To think that MCA had gone to Washington, D.C., to arrange it all is ludicrous," he said. But the agents believed otherwise. On one level, it didn't matter if Wasserman had plotted with Kennedy or not. That so many loyal MCA vassals thought that their leader could organize such a Machiavellian plot was telling in itself. "I wouldn't put it past Lew to do something like that," said one man. Tanen agreed: "I think there was collusion between Kennedy and Lew, and I'm not the only one who believes that."

The agency breakup was cataclysmic for both the agents and the industry. "Unconsciously, MCA set the patterns for the entire agency business and gave the industry a strong backbone," said Chet Migden, a SAG official. "Lew deserves a lot of credit for elevating the agency business. His was a real class act." MCA's strength had always been its Midas touch with its clients' taxes and contracts; after it closed, lawyers and accountants handled those duties. In a few years, pods of entertainment lawyers would proliferate along Wilshire Boulevard. In their reputations and client lists, Park, Citron, and Fields would rival Wasserman in his agency heyday. But no other agent would build a house to match Wasserman's former agency in stature or clout—at least, not for another decade or so.

When Wasserman had arrived in town in 1939, the agent had emphasized the importance of talent. But once he became head of a studio, he believed in the supremacy of the script. "Wasserman didn't discover this, but he changed his philosophy a little," said former agent Stanley Bergerman. As the nation rode a wave of unparalleled prosperity in the 1960s, neither Wasserman nor any other studio head was filming scripts that really captured audiences. Although the price of a movie ticket was about a dollar—the cost of two loaves of bread—people were not paying to see Hollywood movies. They were watching Universal TV shows or listening to bands called The Animals, The Byrds, and The Beatles. Wasserman, meanwhile, kept tinkering with scripts and formulas, seeking a way to get to the core of the country's popular imagination. Increasingly, his job depended on this.

But by mid-decade, the most exciting movies were being produced in Europe, not in America. "That was the period when London was 'It,' " said Jay Kanter. "Music, fashion, theater, films, art, everything was happening there." *A Hard Day's Night* (1964) was made for $560,000 and earned $7 million. *Help!* (1965) cost $1.5 million and made $6 million. *The Pink Panther* (1964) hit an $11 million jackpot and spawned a series of lucrative films and cartoons. The Italian director Sergio Leone made *Per un Pugno di Dollari (A Fistful of Dollars)* (1964)—with a then-unknown actor named Clint Eastwood. After United Artists acquired the film's world rights outside of Italy, it helped launch a successful string of spaghetti westerns. The association between the film's producer, Alberto Grimaldi, and United Artists would eventually lead to more prestigious films, such as Federico Fellini's *Satyricon* (1969).

Two of Wasserman's protégés wanted to help the boss produce

better films. "Lew was always looking for a boy, whether it was Jay [Kanter] or Jerry [Gershwin]," said Al Dorskind. Gershwin was eager to try his own hand at filmmaking, and he asked Wasserman for permission to produce. "But Lew said no. He thought it was beneath Jerry," said Jackie Gershwin. "Lew wanted Jerry to be an executive and maybe take over his job someday." Wasserman told Gershwin to be patient, he'd find him the right position.

Kanter told his boss that Universal needed a European presence. "If you're going to make European films, use the best European talent—or forget it." Wasserman looked at his aide and said, "Why don't you do it for us?" Kanter agreed, which stung Gershwin. But Wasserman told his other "son" to hold on. He thought Kanter would stay in London six months or so, then return to the studio. As it happened, Kanter remained there for seven years, signing European directors, writers, and actors to make what were supposed to be groundbreaking Universal films. Instead, the studio made the confusing thriller *Arabesque,* starring a miscast Gregory Peck with Sophia Loren. Wasserman thought he had a hit with *The Pad and How to Use It,* but it bombed. The sixth incarnation of *Madame X* (1966), starring Lana Turner, had been melodramatic in 1909, a film that was even more so now, under director Ross Hunter's heavy hand. "Lew thought he could get these movies for much less money than he could in America and wouldn't this be wonderful," said Tanen. "But the only problem is that you had every person in Europe unloading their steamer trunk with all the screenplays they'd always wanted to make, but couldn't. And that's the stuff that got made."

TWENTY

THE UNIVERSAL STUDIOS LOT no longer resembled a construction site but a bustling film lot. More than 6,000 actors and technicians worked at the studio now, and on any given day they were scurrying across stages and asphalt, trying to beat tight production schedules. Cranes, dollies, and camera equipment rolled on walkways like robots on a mission. Women wheeled wardrobe racks from one set to another. Craft workers wearing tool belts disappeared inside cavernous soundstages while, from the opposite direction, a gaggle of suits walked toward the commissary arguing about cost overruns. Threading in and out of the commotion was the Glam Tram, full of camera-wielding tourists. In only two years, the Universal City Tour had grown to one of the top ten tourist attractions on the entire West Coast—a triumph by any measure.

Wasserman was reaching to use every inch of his lot. He had installed a push-button waterfall on one of seven small lakes, where Joe Friday could find a murder victim. There was a man-made hydraulic quicksand pit that could complicate *The Virginian's* life and an "ocean" where *McHale's Navy* sailed its PT boats. Golf carts delivered staples to *My Three Sons'* cast and freakish props to *The Munsters.* And, somewhere, on an urban street set, stood the architectural model of Wasserman's Black Tower, now being used in several TV series.

Al Dorskind's experiment with a studio tour had gone so well that Wasserman agreed to open it officially in the summer of 1964. First he pulled together some of his key men on the project, including Herb Steinberg, Jerry Gershwin, and Dorskind, and said, "You've got to remember three things with this tour. One, give the people their money's worth. I don't want them to come to me when I'm having breakfast at Nate and Al's, and hear: 'You ripped us off.' Two, you can't interrupt TV or film production. If you do, it will cost more money than we'll ever make with the tour. And three, *don't lose money.*"

Wasserman expected no more than a few hundred people a day during peak season. On the tour's first day, Jules Stein went downstairs to mingle anonymously with the crowd. An hour later, he barged into Wasserman's office, where a meeting was in session. With no apology, Stein interrupted and spoke directly to Wasserman: "I want to compliment you for thinking of the tour. I decided to stand in line like anyone else to see what it was like. But no one took my ticket." He warned that unless the ticket takers did a better job, tourists could reuse their tickets, give them away, or sell them on the street. "Think of all the money we'd lose. You better fix that problem right away," Stein ordered. "By the way," he added. "You owe me fifty cents."

"What for?" asked Wasserman.

"I bought some milk from a vending machine, and it didn't come out."

Wasserman stood up, reached into his pocket, and gave the tycoon two quarters. Stein disappeared.

Actors and directors were not happy about the distraction. Although the Glam Tram was not supposed to interrupt production, tourists sometimes sought out stars, at least in the beginning. Once, Shirley MacLaine pulled down her pants and mooned a busload of tourists. "The most amazing thing is we did the tour for the first eighteen months without paying for any advertising," said Steinberg. The publicist dialed a handful of syndicated columnists, including Bob Thomas of the Associated Press, and passed along a hot tip for readers: They could tour a real studio for only $3 apiece. Dozens of newspapers printed Steinberg's item, and "we got millions of dollars of publicity for nothing." During the tour's first full year, two drivers, two guides, and one ticket taker ushered some 425,000 visitors through the gates. The following year, the number nearly doubled to 800,000. "We had a phenomenon on our hands," said Steinberg. The tour even made money.

Visitors got to shake hands with members of the Munster family. They peeked into Lana Turner's dressing room and saw racks of old costumes. They visited soundstages, including the one used for the 1925 movie *The Phantom of the Opera*, which still contained its props. They traveled to Killer Canyon, where Universal's silent-film actors used to corral old horses and put them out of their misery. After ninety minutes of sightseeing, they disembarked at the Tour Entertainment Center, where people moved through exhibits about moviemaking, watched stuntmen perform, and paid inflated prices for T-shirts. Then they ate lunch at the commissary, where Rock Hudson or another star might be graciously signing autographs.

Wasserman and Dorskind intended to eventually develop all 400 acres of the lot. MCA had hired consultants who told them to build hotels, restaurants, and apartment complexes along the Los Angeles River. Wasserman didn't buy all of their suggestions, but he incorporated some. The jewel of the plan was to be an 1,800-room "hotel of the stars." Wasserman had already borrowed $25 million to construct the tourist facilities and upgrade the studio. In 1966 he borrowed another $25 million. For the first time in its history, MCA was accumulating debt—a lot of it.

Wasserman's political clout was also piling up. High-ranking Democrats on both coasts had come to respect him. White House staff knew that the studio chief didn't need to ride in the president's limousine nor did he expect any display of affection. "He was content to know that his president needed and counted on him," explained Jack Valenti. In late 1964, after Lyndon Johnson won the election, he asked a favor of Wasserman, which Steinberg recalled. "Edie and I were in New York," he said. Wasserman had flown to Washington to meet Johnson; he planned to meet Edie and Steinberg for dinner that day at '21.' By the time Wasserman arrived at the New York restaurant, his face was flushed. He slipped into a chair. "Herb, why don't you go to the bar for a minute and let me talk with Edie." Alone with his wife, Wasserman leaned over the table and talked with her for a few minutes. Then he waved Steinberg back to the table. "Herb," he announced. "The president asked me to join his cabinet as Secretary of Commerce. I turned it down."

Steinberg was flabbergasted.

Over dinner, the three discussed the matter further. "Lew was leery of taking the job," Steinberg said. "He didn't want to get into Washington . . . he didn't trust it. And he knew Edie would be uncomfortable. There was just no way he would do it."

"Lew was a political animal in the sense that he could smell which way the wind was going to blow," Dorskind explained. In Washington, he'd be one of several cabinet members. He'd lose his job as soon as the president stepped down, in eight years at most. If he left MCA, Stein would appoint some other chief, and Wasserman wasn't sure he'd be allowed to return. In Hollywood, however, Wasserman was the biggest of six studio moguls, a man who still ruled the industry with little interference. At the time, he believed that if he remained, he could keep his job forever—a dangerous assumption in such a fickle business. Even so, Wasserman had weighed his present value against an unknown future and decided to stay.

He later told Dorskind, "As long as I'm here, the president is working for me. If I go there, I'll be working for him." Another MCA executive said that if Wasserman had been offered the powerful chair of Secretary of State, he might have accepted. "But who wants to be Secretary of Commerce?" At the end of the day, Wasserman couldn't leave Hollywood, said a studio executive. He preferred building the Democratic National Committee's contributions from the West, handling ever-bigger piles of money. In May 1965 he sent the White House a $200,000 check—30 percent more than he had the previous year. By May 1966, he promised the president he'd bring in $300,000 more. In less than three years, he built a Democratic fundraising machine in California that had zoomed from very little to some $750,000 in contributions—another astonishing feat.

• • •

Wasserman's studio was the busiest in town and he was hailed for reinvigorating Hollywood. Only Wasserman and Walt Disney Studios were weathering the industry recession—the worst ever, according to some. United Artists was standing, but it didn't actually film movies; it incubated independent filmmakers and distributed their work. Lew, however, was changing the business. Gone was the old system of vertical "integration," wherein he had dominated the film agency business, film packaging, and TV production. Gone, too, was the old studio system, whereby the moguls dominated filmmaking, distribution, and exhibition. Instead, Wasserman pushed into new frontiers beyond Hollywood, such as theme parks, and leisure-time businesses such as gift catalogs and magazines. He liked to say that he believed in films—but he didn't count on them to pay the bills. He was trying to offset the steep cost of filmmaking with money from TV series, studio tours, music sound tracks, and savings and loans. As historian Doug Gomery explained: "Wasserman fought the antitrust forces and opened up deregulation. When he bought Universal and Decca Records, he opened up other kinds of diversification in the industry. All the studios copied him after that."

For better or worse, Wasserman's model lured Wall Street to town. The go-go 1960s were luring giant corporations to Hollywood, where they saw easy pickings. The film industry was a natural place for outsiders to cash in on the growing leisure hours in the average American's week. Investment bankers saw undervalued companies out West and, before long, corporations that were expert in mining, insurance, and funeral homes started buying studios. In 1966 Paramount Pictures was purchased by Gulf + Western, whose core business had been oil. That year, Warner Studios was purchased by Seven Arts, which had grown rich selling old Warner and Universal films. In a few years, Warner would be sold again, this time to Kinney National Services—a patchwork of funeral homes, parking lots, and cleaning services. After several box-office hits, United

Artists was sold to Transamerica Corporation in 1967—just as the hit films fell off. Transamerica executives, who were experts in the insurance business, felt as if they'd been gypped; they did not understand that packaging movies is a lot less reliable than calculating the odds on death. Generally, these outsiders were dazzled by what Wasserman had done with the once washed-up, ramshackle studio.

Despite his following, Wasserman was not yet a corporate manager. He was dictatorial, paternalistic, and extremely hands-on. He ran his conglomerate just as he had run his agency—with every man reporting to him. He still wanted to know everything that occurred on his watch, from the latest rewrite to the commissary's lunch sales—even to what the top political consultant thought of this cause or that candidate. Wasserman regularly extracted information from the consultants and organizers who passed through his office, including Joe Cerrell, a former executive with the California Democratic Party, who by now had become a political consultant. The two men began meeting frequently, often at Wasserman's office, where they'd organize political fundraisers and strategize over party politics. At one such meeting, a secretary regularly slipped into Wasserman's office and handed him slips of paper. "I'd see these index cards with numbers scrawled on them—84, 96, 123," Cerrell recalled. After a while, the consultant realized what the numbers signified. "That was how many people were coming through the studio that hour." Wasserman was keeping tabs on every corner of his expanding empire.

To make sure his executives knew what they were doing, Wasserman peppered them constantly with questions, some of them arcane. He once asked a production manager about a film's promotional campaign. "I presume it's taken care of," the man answered.

"Don't ever presume anything!" Wasserman snapped. "When you come into this office, you either know or you don't know." The fellow didn't last long, said Ernie Nims. It took a certain type of personality to work in MCA's culture. "To me, MCA was like family," said Dorskind. "Yeah, sure it was 'I'll kick you in the pants if you don't behave.' " Wasserman yelled and threatened his men, but they loved him for it. "It was a strange, Jewish family psychology that he tapped into," said one insider.

Wasserman balanced his harshness with a sensitivity that bordered on affection. After Nims's young son died from his long battle with polio, Wasserman sent him a note of condolence. "I still have it, thirty years later," said the film editor. When an MCA employee's wife suffered a nervous breakdown, Wasserman made sure Chasen's delivered a hot dinner to her hospital room—just as her husband arrived after work to begin his bedside vigil. "You don't ever forgot something like that," said the man. When TV writer Jo Swerling, Jr., and his wife welcomed a baby boy, Swerling sent nickel cigars to every man, including all the executives. "I never heard a peep from those guys, whom I know were really busy," Swerling said. "But I got a lovely congratulations from Lew. I mean, here's the busiest man of all, who found the time to write me a note, which frankly, I've treasured." But Wasserman never complimented his men on a job well done. "He was afraid we'd turn complacent," said one.

Wasserman's idea of brotherhood stemmed from his own childhood as the youngest of three boys. In 1920 Lou's oldest brother, Max, was fourteen years old, Bill was twelve, and he himself was seven. He looked up to the other two, but young Louis could see that Max was different. His face and hands sometimes jerked, he was sensitive and moody, and he'd fall on the floor unconscious, his limbs shaking uncontrollably. Max and the Wassermans became the butt of neighborhood jokes. As Max grew older, his epileptic convulsions turned so violent he'd bite his tongue and soil himself. These seizures scared the family. At the time, epileptics were seen as dirty or evil, and since the illness was believed to be contagious, their immigrant neighbors shunned the Wassermans.

The family tried to care for Max, but his condition worsened. They sought cures that were often crueler than the illness: Epileptic children were left in the rain for hours, burned with hot irons, or given foul-tasting concoctions that made them sick for days. Max's convulsions became so uncontrollable that, finally, his parents gave up. They enrolled him at the Ohio Hospital for Epileptics, located 200 miles away in Gallipoli. The three-story brick building, which resembled a Gothic orphanage, housed "the weak and feeble-minded." It, too, employed primitive treatments of the day. At fifteen, Max seemed doomed to live with psychotics, the suicidal, and the mentally deficient.

On October 23, 1922—the day before his sixteenth birthday—the young man died from "exhaustion of epilepsy." His family mourned, and the grief marked young nine-year-old Louis, who had watched his big brother suffer unfairly.

Forty years later, Wasserman feared that he, too, might someday fall to the floor in a convulsion. One of the few valuables he kept locked in his personal safe was a textbook on epilepsy. Few people knew this, though Wasserman's associates were keenly aware of his personal obsession to "adopt" a strong male assistant or surrogate son. Perhaps if Wasserman could somehow find a healthy kinsman at MCA, he could resolve his inner conflict and heal his old boyhood wound.

Lew used fraternal love and hate to manage his $218 million corporation. "That's what it was like," agreed Dorskind. "We'd fight among ourselves all the time. But if anyone from the outside of our gang comes in and hurts one of us, watch out!" Wasserman clung tightly to a code of honor that was part brotherly love and part Jewish syndicate. Explained Dorskind: "Lew would die for his word. If I gave him a handshake, I could go to the bank with it. I never knew him to fudge on anything." The chief expected the same from his men. "I remember that when you did a deal with MCA, their word was as good as any memo," said one rival agent.

Wasserman's emphasis on loyalty made any departure by one of his own men seem like treachery, which is what happened in 1965 with Sonny Werblin. For several years, Jennings Lang had been usurping Werblin's power by selling Universal TV shows directly to the networks, said Frank Price. MCA was now a publicly held company, accountable to shareholders and the Securities and Exchange Commission—and that also rankled Werblin. "Everything's lousy," he told Berle Adams. Werblin had thrived in the agency's free-wheeling days, when he could sell talent in New York without having to consider anyone outside of the company. "It's not so much fun anymore. It's no longer a personal business."

Werblin already owned approximately $10 million of MCA stock—as well as a piece of the money-losing New York Titans football team. He had paid $300,000 to assume the team's debt and changed their name to the Jets. "My dad was always sort of a visionary, and he thought that sports would be the next big thing in entertainment," said Tom Werblin. In 1965, after thirty-three years of working for MCA, Werblin quit his job abruptly and turned his energies to the team. Werblin himself "always had good memories of those days," said his son. "But Jules and Lew were very hurt by his resignation, and they all felt betrayed," said Stein's niece, Patsy Miller Krauskopf.

Werblin would go on to make sports history by signing charismatic quarterback Joe Namath to the Jets. "Broadway Joe" brought showbiz pizzazz to a tired team, and Werblin did elevate sports into an enormous entertainment sector. "Sonny went on to become bigger and richer than he had ever been at MCA," said Adams.

A few months later, Wasserman received another blow. Jerry Gershwin was chafing under Lew's rule. As Wasserman's aide-de-camp and secretary, he was living "in the shadow of a great man," said Jackie Gershwin. "He felt like he was suffocating." He lived in Lew's former house, entertained at his old bar, and welcomed former MCA clients as if they were still his own. He had helped develop Wasserman's empire at Universal City and had served as his eyes and ears. Although Gershwin started to assume more control, later he'd say that he could no longer tell "just who I was—myself or a part of

Lew Wasserman." But others claimed that he arrogantly began making decisions on film sets and about the tour business that were not his to make. Edie tried to talk some sense into him, but he refused to listen, said Jackie. "He was bullheaded." One day, however, he went too far. "He stepped over the line and that was it." Gershwin was thrown out of the Tower. He went on to produce films with Elliott Kastner, another former MCA man. But his departure really hurt Wasserman, said Jackie. "Lew was not one to have best friends, and Jerry had been his best friend for years." Worse was Edie's reaction: "She was very upset and felt she'd been deceived." The Gershwins were no longer invited to the Wassermans' house for dinner or parties. After years of spending nearly every day with Edie Wasserman, Jackie no longer saw her surrogate mother. The Gershwin children rarely visited their godparents. "It was awful," said Jackie. "I still saw Jeannie [Martin] and Janet [Leigh], but not Edie. She felt she had to stand by Lew."

Gershwin produced *Harper* (1966), starring Paul Newman, which was written by William Goldman and based on a sophisticated Ross Macdonald book. He then produced *Where Eagles Dare* (1968), a Clint Eastwood feature based on another fine script, this one by Alistair MacLean, from his own best-seller. But then business turned rough, said Jackie. "Jerry lost his humor and started making bad decisions. He realized he had made a mistake by leaving Lew." Four years later, Gershwin called on Wasserman and apologized. He asked for his old job back—any MCA job, really. "But Lew told him it was too late." Gershwin never regained his prized perch in the industry. "He regretted leaving Lew until the day he died," said Jackie.

Despite the betrayals, Wasserman kept up his personal, paternalistic style of management. He cemented his existing relationships with members of the old gang. He instilled in younger men an unusual amount of respect. He amassed a storehouse of goodwill, just in case another confidant might be tempted to leave, as Werblin and Gershwin had. Wasserman thought he was protecting his company by marshaling allegiances. Before long, his own career would depend on them. If he intended to save his professional life— the only life that mattered to him—Wasserman would have to call on this fraternity soon.

TWENTY-ONE

EDIE CELEBRATED HER FIFTIETH BIRTHDAY on November 4, 1965, by inviting hundreds of movers and shakers to gather at Universal's Stage 12. Lew had invited President Johnson and some of his men, but the president sent regrets. "Much joy and enduring happiness," he and Lady Bird wished the doyenne. Yet the most surprising guest was Robert F. Kennedy. Several guests were floored that the former attorney general—Wasserman's old nemesis—had not only been invited but had actually accepted. "Lew was a gambler and knew that at some point he'd need Bobby Kennedy," said Frank Price. Added another invitee: "When you're Lew Wasserman, you may hate your guest. But you're playing for the future."

More shocking was Edie's behavior, said Merrill Park. That evening, Merrill and her husband, Art, were savoring the fact that Art no longer worked MCA's punishing shifts. Instead, he ran his own boutique agency and worked normal hours. "We were dancing to a wonderful orchestra when we saw Robert Kennedy," recalled Merrill. She told Art: "I'm going up to that man right now and give him a kiss. I had no idea what life could be like with my husband around." Art laughed, but stopped abruptly when he saw Edie. She was laughing and posing graciously for photographs with Kennedy. "We couldn't believe it," said Merrill Park. "I mean, she detested Kennedy for what he had done to Lew." But here she was, a scant three years later, smiling at her former tormentor. "It was a very shrewd move on Edie's part."

Those months were full of MCA parties, political fundraisers, and backroom deal-making. During the mid-1960s, the Steins, the Schreibers, and the Wassermans—sometimes all three—hosted events. Yet, when all three couples sponsored an event together, it was as chilly as a Cold War summit. "Doris was the queen bee of Los Angeles and had to be 'It,' " said one studio executive. Before she met Stein, Doris had been a Kansas housewife, married to a mild-mannered insurance agent and raising two sons. "Doris had come a long way," said producer J. B. Lesser. Now, she spoke with an accent so cultivated, she dropped the letter "g" from words that didn't even have it. "Edie liked to be the center of attention, too," said Myrle Wages. She could be brusque and outspoken—much to Doris's disdain. As for Schreiber's wife, Rita, she tried to maintain a smiling but quiet presence amid the dueling divas. She got along well with Doris and steered clear of Edie. "Lew and Jules never spent any time together outside of the business, and their wives most assuredly did not either," said Tanen. Added a publicist: "I was always told to keep those two apart."

That wasn't easy, given that in 1965 MCA and its executives were about to celebrate the golden anniversary of Universal Studios. At dinner parties, the Steins and Schreibers were usually placed at one end of the room, and the Wassermans at another. "There's bad blood there," planners were told. Whatever the reason, the three women apparently nursed their differences more intently than did the men.

As Wasserman promoted the studio's celebration, President Johnson sent him congratulations, noting that the men at MCA/Universal "have been effective spokesmen for the American way of life." Wasserman was so pleased with the letter he asked to print it in MCA's advertising supplement inside the Sunday *New York Times*. A Johnson aide quickly persuaded him that turning the president's personal note into a commercial ad was impolitic. In September, Johnson appointed Wasserman to the National Advisory

Council, which oversaw the Peace Corps. By now, the two were close enough that White House staff felt free to refer budding musicians to Wasserman, who for his part called the White House to arrange VIP tours for Milton Rackmil and his kids. Even Edie had no compunction about contacting aides to complain that signed photographs of the president "did not arrive in perfect condition."

Edie opened her home to a new set of friends, whose influence was felt offscreen. In October 15, 1965, she and her husband cohosted a fundraising dinner for the President's Club of Southern California. Edie invited a select group to her home for a cocktail party beforehand. Her guests were then ferried by limousine to the Beverly Hilton Hotel, where the Wassermans hosted Governor Edmund "Pat" Brown and Democratic supporters. The dinner dance honored the president and first lady of the United States—yet Edie invited neither the Schreibers nor the Steins.

Taft Schreiber had different political goals. He had watched his MCA client George Murphy turn from a tap dancer into a U.S. senator. Schreiber had seen Reagan grow into a skilled speaker and spokesman for a large corporation. So, in 1964, when General Electric asked Schreiber to help select a last-minute keynote speaker for its sales convention, he did not hesitate. Herb Steinberg recalled: "G.E. asked Taft if he thought Reagan would do the job." Schreiber quickly replied, "He'll do as he's told."

To make sure all the right themes were sounded, Schreiber brought in some of Stein's GOP friends, said Steinberg. "Holmes Tuttle, Bloomingdale, all of those guys had a speech written for him." Schreiber helped Reagan rehearse. By the time he faced the crowd, he was a little nervous, said Steinberg. "It was the first time that Reagan had ever faced a live political audience." But he gave a rousing performance and basked in the crowd's applause. Upon his return, he told Schreiber, "I did great. I'd like to do more of those speeches."

ALAMEDA FREE LIBRARY

Meanwhile, Arizona Senator Barry Goldwater was campaigning for the GOP's presidential ticket. Blunt and honest, he promoted conservative themes by calling for an end to Social Security, the elimination of welfare, and the privatization of utilities. Goldwater was known for his funny, profane, and sometimes outrageous statements. The Misty Mountain crowd worried that Goldwater's foot-in-mouth disease might ensure four more years of Democratic leadership. After the Arizona senator won the nomination, Henry Salvatori and Schreiber arranged for Reagan to give another address, said Steinberg. Goldwater let the washed-up actor deliver a televised campaign speech for him on October 24, 1964. "They say the world has become too complex for simple answers," said Reagan. "They are wrong." He voiced the grievances and fears of the right in a way that Goldwater could not. "That speech ultimately led to Reagan's own political career," Steinberg explained.

Some say that Asa Call selected Reagan to run for office. Others say it was Tuttle, a man of lesser influence. Some believe that it was Reagan's own doing. But those who worked in Hollywood claim that Stein and Schreiber had been cultivating Reagan for this role since the mid-1950s. "Reagan didn't know those guys until Stein collected them," said a Universal executive. "He introduced them." Added Henry Denker, who later wrote a roman à clef about it all: "Jules and Doris had these parties with all of the state's power brokers. They were all rock-ribbed Republicans who saw Reagan as a winner with style, if not exactly substance." Like any good actor, Reagan could deliver his lines with passion, conviction, and authority. Without a script, he was worthless, said many sources.

After Goldwater's defeat, California conservatives, including those in Stein's circle, reorganized. Some wanted to finance Reagan's run for the governor's mansion, said Steinberg. "He presented a shining American image. To them, Reagan was the cowboy in the white hat." He was the perfect politician for the TV age, explained Ted Berkman, the screenwriter of Reagan's film *Bedtime*

Henry Beckerman (left, foreground), Edie Wasserman's father, was arrested in New York on Dec. 7, 1933 and was taken to the Tombs by detectives, shown here. He later stood trial for arson in the torching of a warehouse that the Cleveland Syndicate had used as a bootleg factory. (Credit: Corbis/Cleveland Public Library)

above left: Lew Wasserman, seated in his Beverly Hills office in the 1940s, modestly called himself "just a paper pusher," when he was actually Hollywood's first industry chief. (Credit: Cleveland Public Library) **above right:** Jules Stein was the son of a rag store owner and invalid mother, who saw to it that her children learned to play music. Stein put himself through school by playing violin in orchestras and booking bands in speakeasies and beer halls. He co-founded MCA in 1924.(Courtesy Jules Stein Eye Institute)

When Mrs. Doris Stein (nee Jonas) joined her husband Jules in Hollywood in 1937, she melded screen glamour to old California money to help transform an enormous migrant village into the cosmopolitan city of Los Angeles. Doris, with her children Larry and Gerry Oppenheimer, and Jean and Susan Stein (seated below), lived a block from Grauman's Chinese Theater in the late 1930s. (Courtesy Author's Collection)

While Edie entertained MCA clients at her home, Lew (seated, right) would fete stars such as (left to right) William Holden, his wife, actress Brenda Marshall, aka Ardis Anderson, and Jane Wyman, aka Mrs. Ronald Reagan, in this 1951 photo. Bell Captain George Alpert (standing, left) and owner David Chasen (at Lew's shoulder) considered Lew to be among their best customers at the famed Chasen's Restaurant. (Credit: Wanamaker/Bison Archives)

above left: Cheek to cheek, if not exactly eye to eye, Edie and Lew celebrated New Years Eve 1950, in their own distinctive style: She in her sprightly, festive mood, and he on the phone, deep into some serious negotiations. (Courtesy Author's Collection) **above right:** Lynne Wasserman (left), Edie and Lew's only child, inherited her parents' progressive political ideals. She grew up in MCA's circle, and is pictured here in the 1950s with Temme Brenner (center), wife of a top MCA agent, and her mother Edie (right). (Courtesy Author's Collection)

Two years after Lew nearly lost his perch in an MCA palace coup, Lew sits bemusedly upon his throne next to his mentor, MCA chairman Jules Stein. (Courtesy Jules Stein Eye Institute)

In 1966, Taft Schreiber was placing his political bets on Ronald Reagan and Wasserman was funding Governor Pat Brown, while Jules Stein was opening his Eye Institute. At the Stein's home, Misty Mountain, he gathered his family, from left to right: Jerry Oppenheimer; Jean, Doris, Jules, and Susan Stein, and Larry Oppenheimer. Standing: Charles Miller, Mrs. William vanden Heuvel, William vanden Heuvel, Virginia Oppenheimer, James Cogan, Adelaide Stein Miller, David Stein, Ruth Stein Cogan. (Courtesy Author's collection)

The Wassermans shared a warm friendship with Lady Bird and Lyndon Johnson. After LBJ offered Lew a chance to become his Secretary of Commerce, Lew discussed the job with Edie and declined the president's offer. Edie and Lew consoled the couple during the darkest days of LBJ's presidency and visited them a few months before he left office, on Sept. 13, 1968. (Credit: LBJ Library)

Shirley MacLaine, in her early 20s, is pictured with then-husband Steve Parker, who is enthralled with the lace dress worn by the lovely Jeannie Martin (Mrs. Dean Martin), one of Edie's girls. Jeannie would soon appear in The Jack Benny Show, produced by Lew's Revue Studios and sold by Taft Schreiber at MCA. A few years later, MacLaine would moon a busload of Universal City tourists, giving them an unexpectedly intimate view of studio life. (Courtesy Author's Collection)

Alfred Hitchcock and his agent Lew Wasserman were so close, they joked, confided and even carped at each other like blood brothers. Here, circa 1957, Hitch outlines a story idea around a MacGuffin, replete with comedic touches, to the delight of his agent. (Courtesy Author's Collection)

During the 1960s and 1970s, Universal TV ruled the small screen, creating innovative concepts such as The Wheel, which consisted of four revolving mysteries including "McCloud," starring Dennis Weaver, who from 1970–1973 was chief of the Screen Actors Guild, here shaking hands with Lew. (Credit: Wanamaker/Bison)

Standing tall in the Oval Office on May 26, 1983 are the twin pillars of power in Washington, D.C., and Hollywood, former MCA client, President Ronald Reagan, and political kingmaker Lew Wasserman, MCA chairman. While president of the Screen Actors Guild in the 1950s, Reagan reaped the benefits of a secret land deal with MCA, which gained the agency an exclusive waiver permitting them to produce TV shows. (Courtesy Ronald Reagan Library)

Sid Sheinberg grew to become Lew's most trusted and loyal executive, so much so that in the 1990s, wags called MCA "Wasserman & Son." (Credit: Wanamaker/Bison Archives)

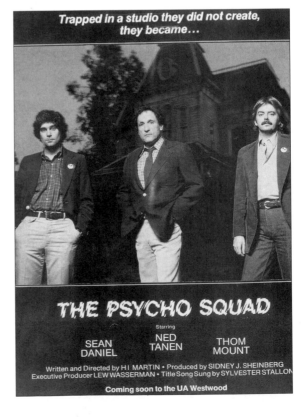

Trapped in a studio they did not create, they became...

THE PSYCHO SQUAD

Starring

SEAN DANIEL   NED TANEN   THOM MOUNT

Written and Directed by H I MARTIN • Produced by SIDNEY J. SHEINBERG
Executive Producer LEW WASSERMAN • Title Song Sung by SYLVESTER STALLON

Coming soon to the UA Westwood

Universal Studios was the first to form a low-budget movie division, drawing novice filmmakers whose anarchic ways often clashed with the tightly regimented studio. Ned Tanen, center, and his assistants, Sean Daniel and Thom Mount, taught free-wheeling auteurs all about Lew's Rule, producing a chaotic, if lively, era. (Courtesy Author's Collection) *for Bonzo.* "He was friendly, and had the well-rehearsed pitchman's aura of sincerity."

But Reagan's ambition was almost ruined by one of his own movies. He had a part in Wasserman's first made-for-TV movie, *The Killers.* In this remake of a 1946 thriller, Reagan played a brutal crime kingpin. Because of its violence, *The Killers* was pulled from the TV roster in 1964 and scheduled for theatrical release. Reagan was worried that his thuggish part—he slapped Angie Dickinson several times—would undermine his good-citizen image just as he was preparing a run for office. He asked Wasserman not to release the film, which irritated the mogul. "Lew didn't like Reagan," said Ronnie Lubin. Added Roy Brewer, who had been one of Reagan's compatriots during the McCarthy era: "Ronnie had a lot of problems with Wasserman."

Wasserman disregarded Reagan's pleas and released the $300,000 film in theaters, where it fizzled. Ironically, some critics say that *The Killers* is Reagan's best screen role ever. But Reagan was hurt by the incident, said Merrill Park.

He evidently put those feelings aside when he published his autobiography—an odd project for a fifty-three-year-old B-actor. *Where's the Rest of Me?* reconstructed his Hollywood history and laid the foundation for his new career. "Art was Reagan's primary agent for years during his acting days," said Merrill Park, though Wasserman negotiated all of MCA's talent deals, including those for Reagan. In his autobiography, Reagan barely mentioned Park while crediting Wasserman for things he didn't do. For example, he wrote that Wasserman negotiated a seven-year studio contract for him in 1942 which was Wasserman's first million-dollar deal.

But that wasn't true. In the late 1930s, Wasserman had gotten a three-year $1 million contract for a popular radio performer, Kay Kyser and his *Kollege of Musical Knowledge.* Wasserman had signed deals for Betty Grable and Betty Davis that were almost as big. In any case, Reagan never fulfilled his contractual obligations, and

Wasserman never collected his commission. Yet, for years, the actor-candidate repeated the story, and Wasserman never publicly corrected him.

Reagan grated on Lew's nerves, and in 1965, several other Universal managers were finding the actor tiresome, as well. "I dealt with Ronnie when he used to be called Ree-gun, rather than Ray-gun," said writer/producer Roy Huggins. The two had worked on an episode for *Kraft Suspense Theater* when Huggins's production assistant told him, "I'm sorry, but Reagan said he won't read any of your propaganda against capital punishment." Huggins chuckled. Reagan was playing a bit part in one episode, and Huggins's scripts were more dramatic than didactic. He reread Reagan's lines and shook his head. "Ronnie was worried about one line that didn't say anything, really." But the actor refused to come out and discuss the matter, "which seemed a little disingenuous," said Huggins. "He'd already signed a contract and agreed to do the piece as is."

Huggins solved the problem by having Reagan purse his lips, jut out his chin, and refuse to speak. "Everyone on the set was relieved, and the scene worked." A few weeks later, Huggins bumped into Reagan at a party and asked, "What happened to you on the set? You know very well that the script had no propaganda."

"Well, Roy," Reagan said, jutting out his chin again. "I haven't really made up my mind how I feel about capital punishment." And he walked away.

Huggins asked his host, "Is Ronnie going to run for office or something? I just talked to him and he sounds a lot like a politician."

Huggins's suspicions were soon confirmed. Schreiber and his fellow Republicans had already formed a group called The Friends of Ronald Reagan. Cy Rubel had lent them an office in his Union Oil Building in downtown Los Angeles. Holmes Tuttle chaired the new group's new Executive Committee, and Schreiber started managing the campaign. By June 1965, the Friends had collected $135,000—a sizable fund for the time.

On January 4, 1966, the fifty-four-year-old actor announced his intention to run against California Governor Pat Brown. "Taft and Jules had been lifting him up to the Republican party for a while," said Huggins. "It was good business." Reagan began campaigning against the "filthy free-speech movement," accompanied by a covey of young "Reagan girls." The attractive women wore costumes designed by Nancy Reagan, who made sure no girl on her husband's revue had a waist thicker than 25 inches. The wholesome, the young women made Reagan look grandfatherly.

Jules Stein must have been pleased with it all. He and Schreiber were creating Republican candidates while Wasserman was advising Democratic leaders. No other Hollywood studio had pulled off such a bipartisan coup. In 1966 MCA had its bases covered, said Huggins. "No matter who got into office, MCA would win."

Politics increasingly became a jousting field for Wasserman and Schreiber. "You had Schreiber on one side, Wasserman on the other, and friction in the executive suite," said Walter Seltzer. Schreiber was a slightly built man of average height with wavy dark hair and bad eyes. He was five years older than Wasserman and had started working for MCA in 1926, a decade before Lew, when MCA was just a six-man band-booking outfit in a two-room office. At the time, the groups were booked willy-nilly, so that one would play a weekend in Illinois, the next in Ohio, and the third in Illinois again. Schreiber's genius was to organize MCA's band circuit using train timetables, Western Union's list of hotel clients, and his own disciplined precision. He mapped out regular circuits whereby MCA orchestras could work every day of the week in separate but adjacent towns.

But neither he nor Stein were known for their musical taste. Schreiber booked MCA's first black musician, Jelly Roll Morton, after hearing him play at an all-night joint on the South Side. Failing to realize just who he had, Schreiber booked the jazz great on a small-town route. He baptized the group, which included Cab Calloway, the Chicago Blew Blowers because Schreiber had already prepared advertising posters under that name. Jelly Roll changed the band's title to include his name. He refused to play the sappy popular tunes Schreiber had chosen, and built his act around his own hot jazz. "People don't come here to see a show, they come to hear old Jelly play the piano," he told Schreiber. MCA quickly dropped Morton, who forever after decried the music agency's tin ear and mercenary focus.

Schreiber kept busy collecting money from Chicago's jazz joints, which were run by Capone's gang. He did business with guys like Blue Steel, a gunman named for the plate in his head that covered a wound. He negotiated with Al Quodbach, who liked to recline in his office chair and shoot the rats that scurried over his basement pipes. Every Christmas, Stein gave an autographed picture of himself to his clients as a present. Quodbach nailed his photo to the wall and used it for target practice whenever Schreiber and the boys came around. "It was pretty well shot up by the spring of '29," recalled MCA publicist Karl Kramer. By the time MCA finally made a substantial profit in 1936—fourteen years after it had started—Schreiber had proven himself every bit as unflappable and formidable as his very scary clients.

By then, Schreiber was running the West Coast office, but the music agents had become a joke in Hollywood. In 1939, shortly after Wasserman made his $1 million deal for Kyser, Stein sent him west to help Schreiber. From the first, the two men clashed. "Wasserman hated to do things by rote or just because it had been done like this before," said one veteran. Yet Schreiber insisted that tasks be done by the book. Wasserman was dazzled by the movie industry; Schreiber considered many of its figures crude and sordid, and most of their movies in need of the restrictive Hays Motion Picture Production Code. Indeed, fifty years later, when I pressed Wasserman to give one example of Schreiber's renowned business skills, the octogenarian replied, "Sure," baring his long porcelain teeth in what was supposed to be a smile. "He welcomed me with open arms when I was sent out here." Wasserman held his rather menacing grin for several seconds longer than seemed natural.

In 1946 MCA veterans were certain that Schreiber was in line to become the next MCA president. But when Stein was to finally appoint his successor, Schreiber's asthma worsened and his allergies made him ill. The setback discouraged him deeply, but his health was at stake and he was forced to retreat from his grueling work schedule. "He didn't actively run to become head of the company because of that," said Schreiber's daughter, Lenore Greenberg.

Stein surprised everyone by naming Wasserman president. "Jules had a much closer relationship with Schreiber," said Frank Price. Schreiber knew more about Stein's secrets than anyone else, and he was the only executive who didn't answer to Wasserman. Added Al Dorskind: "Taft resented Lew for leapfrogging over him. It was probably unfair that Taft didn't get the post." From that point on, the rivalry between the two men intensified. Over the years, the adversaries oscillated between cooperation, distrust, and open hostility. Stein seemed to enjoy the wrangling. "He believed that competition even among his men was good for business," explained Berle Adams. Besides, the two men were different enough in their leadership styles. "I always used Taft as an example in my private life and Lew as the model for my career," Dorskind explained. "Taft had his art, Jules had his antiques, but all Lew had was his work."

Schreiber spent more time with his wife and two children than Wasserman did with his family. "My dad was very much a family man, and didn't want us to grow up in that Hollywood lifestyle," said Greenberg. He socialized with only a handful of his dearest clients—Jack Benny, George Burns, and Gracie Allen. Later, he also handled many of MCA's top film stars, but he seemed most fond of the clean-cut, upstanding types. "That's how Taft was, very straight and moral," said Roy Gerber.

He collected art long before the hobby became de rigueur among stars and agents. Schreiber and his wife, Rita, bought pieces by Jackson Pollock, Joan Miró, and Piet Mondrian before those artists became well known. The Steins encouraged the Schreibers' passion, and the two couples often socialized together, said several executives. By 1966, the Schreibers' art collection was legendary for its scholarship and consistency. The executive became a trustee of the Los Angeles County Art Museum, an overseer of the prestigious Huntington Library in Pasadena, and a member of the International Council of New York's Museum of Modern Art. His tastes and decorum lifted the profile not just of MCA but of California as well. Still, he kept his competitive business edge.

"There was always a bitter battle between Taft and Lew," said Denker. "But Stein was right to pick Lew—he was the killer type."

The California gubernatorial race of 1966 was a critical juncture for MCA's long-running internal rivalry. Wasserman and Schreiber each had his own candidate running. "Wasserman was very big for Pat Brown," said Joe Cerrell. But Wasserman was also known as "Johnson's man," and he felt he should check with the president before committing to work with Brown. Johnson not only approved, he publicly threw his weight behind the incumbent governor, calling him "a true and lifelong friend" whose counsel he often sought. With the president's blessing, Edie and Lew threw themselves into the fray. They hosted a dinner at their house that raised a then-record amount, said Cerrell. "I'd never seen anything like it." Guests paid $5,000 each—at a time when fundraising *tables* went for $1,000 each. "It was the most expensive political dinner of its time." Wasserman then organized an even larger Brown fundraiser that was originally slated to be held at the Palladium. The President's Club sold so many seats that it had to move the event to the Los Angeles Sports Arena. "Lew sold that out in no time, too," Cerrell said.

Edie and Lew worked hard in the weeks leading up to the election, eager to see their candidate win. Wasserman lined up a raft of entertainers who on their own could have headlined in Las Vegas. He secured the Supremes, Dean Martin, Frank Sinatra, and other members of the Rat Pack. Dionne Warwick, Nancy Wilson, Jose Feliciano, and Keely Smith also made appearances. The governor and his men were wowed. "It was more impressive than most of the inaugural events I've been to," said Cerrell. "What Wasserman did is give this event his imprimatur." As soon as a Hollywood executive heard that Lew was organizing the show, he'd sign on or write a check.

Meanwhile, Schreiber worked the other side of the aisle, advising and boosting Reagan during his campaign. When election day finally dawned, there was more at stake than voters realized. Brown lost to Reagan by 100,000 votes. Many Californians were shocked when they woke up to find their governor was going to be the former TV show host. In some circles, it became a joke, said Ronnie Lubin. He attended a party the next night when someone told Kirk Douglas that he should run for president, saying "Hey, Kirk, if Reagan can do it, you can, too."

Ever pragmatic, Wasserman accepted the outcome though he undoubtedly disliked some of the decisions made by the new governor. During his administration, Reagan cut education funds, closed state mental hospitals, and called police down on protesting students. Many of the programs that Johnson had promulgated for his Great Society, Reagan weakened or eliminated. Reagan and Wasserman didn't communicate much during the Sacramento years.

Shortly after the election, the Jules Stein Eye Institute was dedicated. Schreiber, Wasserman, and the Steins helped fete 1,000 guests. "It was orchestrated like a true showbiz extravaganza," said Dr. Bradley Straatsma. Nobel Prize winners, Harvard professors, and radio and movie stars mingled with a few members of royalty. Stein's institute resembled a Renaissance palace. Its entry was flanked by travertine columns, and its floors were paved with beige and pink terrazzo. An enormous Salvador Dalí watercolor, *Emotions on the Recovery from Blindness,* greeted guests, and two bronze busts of Dr. Stein by sculptor Jacques Lipchitz were placed prominently in the foyer and the auditorium.

The National Institutes of Health had given Stein's center its seal of approval with a small—but crucial—construction grant. Now Stein wanted the NIH to set up a National Eye Institute, which could be another source of funding and research grants for his cause. He, his executives, and New York philanthropist Mary Lasker persuaded those on Capitol Hill to create the NEI. "The process wouldn't have gotten very far without Dr. Stein pushing it through," said Dr. Straatsma. Nor without Wasserman's hand. Just as President Johnson was about to leave office, the government finally created NEI, and Stein served on its advisory council.

The elite in Los Angeles feted the Steins' new center. "Lew wanted all the people who had been with MCA from the very beginning to attend the party," said Dorothy Barton. While the Steins entertained society friends at their hilltop manse, the Wassermans hosted a cocktail party at their home. Dorothy's husband, De Arv Barton, manager of MCA's Cleveland office, was one of those invited. Thirty years earlier, he had loaned Wasserman the train fare to his interview in Chicago. As soon as Wasserman saw Barton coming through his door, he rushed to greet his old friend. "Lew was always so good to us," said Dorothy Barton.

After cocktails, the Wasserman party moved to the newly opened Century Plaza Hotel. There the Steins and Schreibers greeted their distinguished guests, while Edie and Lew attended to MCA's former clients and employees. That weekend, Edie squired several visitors to other social events, including a particularly crowded dance. "Edie didn't want to sit in any ordinary place," recalled Barton. "So she asked the maitre d' to set up another table for us, at the very front. I was embarrassed as all get-out but that's the way she was." It may have been Doris Stein's weekend, but Edie was going to remain front and center.

In the turbulent spring of 1967, as national debates raged over black power, free love, and the horror of young Americans dying in Vietnam, Edie helped her husband launch his most elaborate, expensive Democratic gala ever. This was for his friend, the president of the United States. "Wasserman had a very close relationship with Johnson," said Joe Cerrell. Although Wasserman worked with cochairs George Killian and store magnate Cyril Magnin, Lew spearheaded this fundraiser, said Cerrell. For LBJ's anticipated 1968 presidential campaign, Lew invited West Coast burghers to a $1,000-a-plate dinner at the Century Plaza Hotel.

Wasserman had been trying to stop a divisive move within his own party. LBJ's policies on the Vietnam War were so controversial that many Democratic leaders wanted an open primary "so that a new candidate can . . . reunify us and lead us to victory." Wasserman tried to defuse that movement, and that spring resolved to turn his LBJ fundraiser into a successful rally.

He invited all of California's politicos. He booked comedian Jack Benny, Freddy Martin and his Orchestra, and the Supremes. He closed the event to the press, and vetoed the idea of a receiving line. But upon learning of the presidential visit to Los Angeles, the media protested. White House aide Bill Stinson urged Johnson to create a reception line of L.A. dignitaries and some reporters, according to papers at the LBJ Library. Wasserman acquiesced, and handpicked a few reporters to attend.

But Wasserman could not control what happened that day. On June 23, 1967, a crowd of protesters climbed the hill on the Avenue of the Stars and headed to the president's hotel. The Los Angeles Police Department had granted a permit to some antiwar demonstrators, expecting no more than 1,000 people. Earlier that day, a peaceful crowd of primarily middle-class people had heard Muhammad Ali speak against the war. Then, gathering strength and numbers, they marched north toward the hotel, where some 1,300 policemen waited with nightsticks and barricades. Edie and Lew could hear the chants before they saw the crowd: "Hey, hey, LBJ, how many kids did you kill today?" And then it appeared, a massive throng of 10,000 people, pouring toward the hotel. Pandemonium swept through the police ranks.

Edie and Lew tried to shield the president and his daughter Lynda from the onslaught. "It came on us, totally unexpected, and was scary," said Cerrell. He was on the hotel's second floor and frantically summoned an elevator so he could get downstairs and perhaps find Edie and Lew. When an elevator finally arrived, its doors opened and Cerrell's aide stepped out. "His eyes were about to pop out of his head," Cerrell recalled. The young man kept blathering: "I just saw the police beating people with clubs."

Cerrell pushed him back in the elevator, away from members of the press. "Do you realize what you're saying? Calm down!"

But worse was to come. As Lew, LBJ, Edie, and Lynda watched from a hotel room, the police tried to disperse the crowd. Bullhorns ordered the group to move on, but few could even hear the command. Others turned only to find themselves penned in by barricades. The police started beating men and women bloody. "Even I was shocked," said Cerrell. Edie was aghast, her voice rising in alarm. Fifty-one people were arrested and dozens more injured in what became one of the first mainstream antiwar protests.

Inside the ballroom, however, the show went on. Throughout the evening, Edie tried to cheer a rattled Lynda Johnson. They talked about Universal's latest film hit, *Thoroughly Modern Millie* (1967), which Lynda loved. The young woman admired the giant floral displays that Edie had arranged, and the mogul's wife assured her they wouldn't go to waste. Later, Edie sent them to Cedars-Sinai Medical Center, where patients could enjoy them.

That night, Lew squired the president around the room until Jack Benny came onstage at 10:00 P.M. For a few hours, the president and the mogul forgot the riot outside. Guest Berry Gordy believed the ordeal was "the most grueling twenty-four hours ever experienced by a president of the United States." Johnson never campaigned in public again, except at safe spots like military bases. As the country's antiwar sentiment swelled, LBJ finally withdrew from the race— nine months after the debacle in Los Angeles. Wasserman and others tried to talk him out of it, but he was resigned to leaving office.

In April 1968, Wasserman called Cerrell. "I want to see you," he said. The political consultant had spent eleven days working on an event for Wasserman and his President's Club, but it had just been canceled because the president wouldn't be running. Cerrell was owed money. He went to Wasserman's office, sat down, and expected no more than $1,000 for his labor. Wasserman said, "How about we settle this for $5,000?" Cerrell jumped up and shook hands on the spot. "I thought I'd died and gone to heaven," he said.

"It was probably the largest single per-diem fee I've ever known."

TWENTY-TWO

HOLLYWOOD NO LONGER SNICKERED behind Wasserman's back. His purchase of an old studio had more than panned out, and the once-cockamamie idea of making movies for TV had proved to be a bonanza. MCA bought him a new car every year, most recently a white Jaguar XKE coupe. He had added more MCA offices around the world and talked regularly to Paris and London while taking calls from the White House. He reveled in his workaholic lifestyle, admitting, "I'm a strange breed of cat. I don't play golf, and I don't have any hobbies."

The profitable and prestigious television division was his pride and joy. His concept of made-for-TV movies had finally taken off. In his grandiose manner, Jennings Lang had changed the name of Project 120 movies to *World Premieres*—even though they were broadcast only in the United States. By the end of 1966, he and his men had begun working on $150 million worth of *World Premieres* to be produced over the following three years. That huge contract equaled nearly 70 percent of MCA's revenues that year. "With that, MCA began to change the face of TV," said Sidney Sheinberg. Many of these TV movies—*Columbo, Ironside, McCloud*—became TV series, and their entertaining stories remained contemporary enough that they'd be rerun again and again in the forty years after their debut.

For a time, Lang ran the TV division with an ever-changing triumvirate of junior executives. George Henshaw was in charge of casting; Jerry Adler was a production manager; and Sheinberg was in charge of business and contracts. "Unofficially, Jennings was in charge of movies," said Frank Price. "He had no title, and that's how a lot of stuff happened at Universal. People just took power." Wasserman didn't like titles or clearly defined duties, explained Price. "His company had always gotten along by having everyone compete." Men wandered off and found projects or assumed more authority. That's how Sheinberg started making creative decisions. "One day, Jennings felt that I should be in charge of development, and then I became head of production," said Sheinberg. This freestyle management wreaked havoc and internal confusion, but it also created some of the best programming in television history.

One of Sheinberg's first efforts was *Fame Is the Name of the Game*. The film focused on an investigative magazine reporter delving into the murder of a call girl. Directed by Stuart Rosenberg, it starred Tony Franciosa, Jill St. John, and Susan St. James. When the TV movie debuted in November 1966, critics were nonplussed, but one-third of all TV viewers tuned in. With its brightly lit sets, colorful fashions, and high production values, "it was hip to the culture," said critic Brian Fairbanks. It was also prescient. Several years before Bob Woodward and Carl Bernstein became household names, St. James as sexy Peggy Maxwell was introducing investigative reporting as a glamorous line of work. The show's fictional magazine was called *People,* and it, too, appeared several years before its real-life Time, Inc., counterpart. The movie later became a hit in Europe, but the network did not immediately order a series.

Wasserman's men tried again, this time with Price's movie *The Doomsday Flight.* Written by Rod Serling and directed by William Graham, the tale revolved around a bomb on a plane. Unless a ransom was paid, an altitude-sensitive trigger would explode the bomb. Again, critics ridiculed *Doomsday Flight* as a cheap imitation of a real film. But when it aired in December 1966, *half* the nation's TV viewers were glued to the NBC broadcast. "It got a 50-share, which was amazing," said Price. The *Doomsday Flight* helped Universal sign a bigger contract with the network. "The ratings pretty much settled the argument as to whether the public would go for ersatz films," said Price. "They would and did."

Doomsday presented a new dilemma. Price had grown accustomed to making weekly ninety-minute TV episodes for $240,000 in six days. He had produced the two-hour *Doomsday* movie in an astonishing seventeen days, compared to the months it took to film a feature. Moreover, Price had spent only $470,000 on the product for which Wasserman had charged NBC a whopping $800,000. "It embarrassed Lew and Jennings that we had made the movie for practically half of that amount," he explained. Wasserman convinced NBC that it was a fluke and would never happen again. Then he made sure it wouldn't occur twice. He narrowed the margin between cost and sales prices by increasing the overhead fee on all *World Premieres* from 20 percent to 30 percent, and by loading on some new fees. That helped fatten the movie budget, said Price. "From that time on, that's what we charged our clients."

By the end of 1966, Wasserman had completed seven such films and had contracts to produce dozens more. As these movies spun into regular TV shows, the MCA men added a twist. "NBC very much wanted to do something new each year," explained Sheinberg. "They looked to us to come up with some crazy things that they could tell the world about."

He helped turn *Fame Is the Name of the Game* into a series called *The Name of the Game*. Rather than have each character appear every week, it rotated the cast into a "wheel" format. Character Glen Howard, played by Gene Barry, was involved with boardroom battles and political scandals that took him around the world. "It was considered one of the first intelligent shows for TV," said Fairbanks. Dan Farrell, played by Robert Stack, was confronting bad guys with their crimes. Jeff Dillon, played by Anthony Franciosa, was more interested in afflicting the comfortable. But the true star, Peggy Maxwell (St. James), assisted all of these guys in uncovering the truth as she wore short skirts and knee-high orange vinyl boots to the office. In the real world, only barmaids and actresses dressed that way for work, but Universal's TV shows telegraphed cultural fads to the nation. Before long, the style spread and aerospace engineers and accountants were sporting ankle-high boots and flared trousers, just like Stack and Franciosa.

The series won a Golden Globe for Best TV show in 1969 and an Emmy for Outstanding Dramatic Series before its run ended in 1971.

Price produced a TV movie about a paraplegic detective, starring Raymond Burr; it became the first TV series to feature a disabled person. The unusual cop had three assistants, including a policewoman and a black ex-convict—the kind of heroes that never appeared on *Perry Mason. Ironside* debuted in the fall of 1969 with a cool, jazzy Quincy Jones score. The show dealt with civil rights, crooked cops, and women's rights, neatly resolving these knotty issues in one commercial hour.

Next, Price produced a TV movie about a suave burglar who plies his trade for the U.S. government. One of Wasserman's former clients, Robert Wagner, had just played a great villain in *Harper*. Having seen the film, Wasserman called the actor into his penthouse and pointed to a copy of *TV Guide*. "This is where you belong!" Wagner starred in the made-for-TV movie *It Takes a Thief*, which debuted on ABC in January 1968 and revived Wagner's career. Later it, too, became a ninety-minute weekly series. Wagner, portraying the daring thief Alexander Mundy, was hailed as the new Cary Grant. *It Takes a Thief* ran for three years and won numerous awards, including a Golden Globe in 1970 for Wagner as best actor.

Universal TV shows did not introduce new social theories or provoke dissent. But they did touch on controversial issues that most studios—including Universal—didn't touch. "At a time when people considered B theater movies to be dead, Universal was producing them on TV, often better than so-called A movies," said Fairbanks. It styled its shows with mod colors and bright settings, and cast great-looking people moving through action-packed frames. In 1964, when Marshall McLuhan said, "All media exists to invest our lives with artificial perceptions and arbitrary values," he might have been watching a Universal TV episode. *McHale's Navy*, *The Munsters*, and *Dragnet* kept on filling airtime, but the division's reputation now rested on its innovative, high-caliber work.

Lang, Sheinberg, and Price started to build a stable of some of the best writers/producers in town. Lang lured the prolific team of William Link and Richard Levinson to his set. The pair had created the hit series *Mannix* for ABC and didn't want a conventional seven-year contract. They made an under-the-table deal with Lang. "If things didn't work out, we agreed that the deal would be void," said Link. Their first project was a TV movie based on their popular Broadway play, *Prescription: Murder*. Link and Levinson had envisioned an older man to play the detective and sent the script to Bing Crosby. But he didn't want to play a disheveled, fumbling investigator. When thirty-eight-year-old Peter Falk got hold of the script, he telephoned Link: "I'd kill to play that cop."

Falk was signed for the TV movie *Columbo: Prescription for Murder.* Directed by Dick Irving, the film was shot in eighteen days—a clipped pace, but two days longer than Wasserman demanded. Irving was mortified that he had violated "Lew's Law" by going beyond schedule, and Wasserman didn't make him feel better. Yet, when the movie aired in February 1968, it scored a 37 percent rating and ranked as the week's top show. Wasserman took the unusual step of complimenting his director, said Jerry Adler. "Lew told Irving it was the best thing [the director] had ever done." An NBC network executive called Link and Levinson with an offer to make a series. But the writers were put off by the prospect of producing a high-quality show every week for four months. The grueling schedule also posed problems for Falk, who was performing in a Broadway play. "We tried to convince Peter, but he didn't want to do it," said Link. And the writers couldn't imagine how they could set up a murder, develop elaborate clues, and deliver the final mystery-solving "pop" in a one-hour episode. So they passed, which angered NBC executive Herb Schlosser. "How could you creative people turn our money away?" he yelled. "Ah, that's just network-think," Link told him.

With *World Premieres,* Universal TV had solved one of the thorniest problems in TV production: the quick demise of expensive TV series. In 1966 nearly half of all weekly shows were canceled at the cost of millions of dollars—some of them after only a few weeks on the air. But these made-for-TV movies allowed the producers to introduce a character and, through ratings, gauge audience interest. The network—in this case, NBC—paid for the production, found commercial sponsors, and promoted the TV movies in hopes of reaping high ratings. Lang assured NBC that if the movies were hits, his writers would turn them into hot new series. Often, the network would order twenty-six follow-up episodes for about $7 million. The arrangement allowed Universal to gamble on new programming formats and offbeat characters for a fraction of the cost of an untested series. "We not only had an experimental vehicle, but a way to support it financially, which was very important," said Price. On average, the ratings for these movies were an impressive 40 percent.

Even better were the financial rewards for Universal. Once the broadcaster had aired its TV series once or twice (depending on the contract), rights reverted to Universal TV. MCA/Universal would then lease the popular films to independent buyers, collecting anywhere between $300,000 and $500,000 per showing. Sometimes Universal released the films in domestic or foreign theaters; other times the products went straight to nonnetwork TV. Over the decades, Universal would collect hundreds of millions of dollars selling reruns of *Columbo, Ironside,* and its other shows.

The rise of Universal TV had coincided with a growth in expenses. By 1968, a ninety-minute episode of *The Name of the Game,* for example, cost $280,000. A twenty-six-episode series of *The Virginian* cost $7.15 million—or roughly double the figure from eight years earlier. The TV shows of the 1960s ran deficits in their first year. The networks paid for most of the shows' costs, but, increasingly, it wasn't enough to cover Wasserman's high standards. "Lew was always in a mentally schizophrenic mode, because on the one hand, he wanted the shows to be good," said Sheinberg. "He wanted them to have production value and stars, and be shot nicely. On the other hand, he wanted them to be made on budgets that were not always realistic."

As Universal TV hired more writers and producers, the salaries were charged indiscriminately against various TV series. Every month, Jerry Adler would receive an accounting report, and he'd see names of people who had never worked on his shows. At first, he couldn't figure out why this was happening. Worse were the irate telephone calls from Wasserman, who would chew him out for going over budget. "I went through this tragedy—I call it a charade now—when Lew would call me and say, 'What's going on? Keep the damn costs down.' It became a ritual." Adler discovered that

Wasserman himself was shoveling phantom expenses into his TV budgets. "I kept trying to cut costs while Lew kept adding to them. It got to be a joke. Accounting would send me the monthly report, I'd sit in my office and wait, and Lew would call and tear into me," said Adler.

No overrun was too small to trigger the boss's temper. Adler recalled one instance concerning a film directed by Norman Lloyd about ten people in group therapy. The movie was over budget and behind schedule, and Wasserman ordered Adler to replace the director. "That would have created even more havoc," said Adler. The movie was shot in one room, with a close-knit group of actors who couldn't easily switch to a new director overnight. "I tried to explain that to Lew, but he just couldn't understand." A replacement would cost even more time and money, but Wasserman was adamant. "You could disagree with him, but, boy, it was hard." Wasserman finally let Norman Lloyd remain.

Another time, Wasserman learned that Adler had hired a director for a few dollars more than scale. After a screening, the mogul grabbed the producer in the hallway and chewed him out for his extravagance. "After twenty minutes of his screaming, I thought, 'Jesus! What is this?'" Later, Wasserman apologized—but not for screaming. "He told me he should have gone through channels, and reamed my boss, not me."

Meanwhile, Edie and Lew became exacting arbiters of Universal's TV shows, scanning edited versions before they were released. "He'd take home the damn movies and view them with Edie," said Adler. She'd critique the actors, their clothes, and their hairstyles while Lew would analyze holes in the plot. "He was watching them very carefully." The next morning, Adler would arrive at work early and find Wasserman's car already in its stall. "Then it was just a matter of when the phone would ring," said Adler. "When it finally did, my whole life flashed before me." The producer would let the phone ring a few times, then answer. "I'd hear all of their complaints, and, let me tell you, it was not wonderful." Ironically, Wasserman's changes added to the productions' costs.

The triumvirate of TV managers continued to change. For a while, Adler oversaw TV movie budgets, Sheinberg the network program series, and Price produced TV movies. "We were Lang's whipping boys who got chewed out by Lew," said Adler. Then Price ran the TV unit. "I wore two hats for a while," he explained. He was also producing *It Takes a Thief* and *Ironside.* "I was working myself into exhaustion and didn't want to produce anymore." So he tried his hand at movies. In 1968 Sheinberg headed the TV division— then suddenly didn't any longer. In 1969 former NBC executive Grant Tinker was head of Universal TV—and then he left. "Who ultimately had control of this unit evolved over the years," said Sheinberg. "There was still Taft Schreiber, Jules, and Lew [to please]," he explained. "It was a stressful period."

The loose, aggressive management style got out of hand and Lang turned into a figurehead, leaving the others to jockey for position. "You had all of the guys who had worked together for twenty years or more, and they were ready to kill each other," said Ned Tanen. And expenses in Wasserman's most profitable division—TV—ballooned, as did the costs of developing the lot and its real estate. Universal Studios' feature movies were still not returning profits, and they looked increasingly like Universal TV shows. There was talk of containing this sprawling financial mess, and a few insiders started gunning for Wasserman's office.

When Edie and Lew needed to relax, they'd often head north to the Santa Cruz Mountains getaway of Alma and Alfred Hitchcock. When the director was working on a film, he usually stayed in his modest home on the edge of the Bel Air Country Club, but he and his wife preferred spending time at Heart of the Mountains, their Santa Cruz estate. "The Hitchcocks were the only ones that the Wassermans really vacationed with," said one executive.

To get there, the Wassermans had to drive up the coast or fly to San Francisco, where Hitch's chauffeur would whisk them down and across the peninsula. Edie and Lew would meet Alma and Alfred in their rambling Spanish-style home, which had been built in the 1930s on 200 mountaintop acres. There, guests could behold most of Scotts Valley out to Monterey Bay. Hitch's garden displayed a mosaic by Georges Braque, one of the founders of Cubism. Hitch also owned tennis courts and a winery across the highway.

Most evenings, the friends would eat gourmet dinners prepared by Hitch's longtime German cook and drink vintage wine from their host's cellar. The Wassermans stayed in a tower room, with a winding outdoor stairway and a cozy fireplace. Wasserman knew that Hitchcock gathered inspiration from this area. The Bates Motel in *Psycho* was modeled on the dilapidated Hotel McCray not far away, and the house in *Psycho* was a dead ringer for the decaying Bernheim House in Santa Cruz. *The Birds* was born after Hitch read a local news item about birds getting lost in the fog and crashing into Santa Cruz storefronts.

Wasserman loved spending time with Hitch away from Hollywood. "See, there's a picture of us taken close to fifty years ago at his ranch," he told me years later. "There's the man himself in the background." Wasserman pointed to Hitchcock, who was cracking up like a young boy. In the foreground is a younger, tanned Wasserman sprawled carelessly on a chair, laughing long and hard at his friend. "You'll notice there is no gray hair," Wasserman pointed out. "Handsome," I remarked, and the mogul bowed his head slightly in appreciation. But truly, Wasserman did look handsome and happy in that photo with his friend, and the pair were reminiscent of two teenage boys who have ditched school and are up to no good. Why did Wasserman grow so close to Hitch? "I don't know," he said, shrugging. "We just hit if off. He was a superb man."

One key to their friendship was that both had boyhoods that were cut short. Each man disdained constraints. Wasserman like to break rules and replace them with his own; Hitchcock, who had been raised by a stern father, "needed to break rules," Jerry Adler explained. Both Wasserman and Hitchcock shared an acute sense of psychology and how it motivated people. But whereas the director used his insight to create cinematic masterpieces, the mogul used his to influence people and bend them his way. "He knew which buttons to push in you," said Ned Tanen.

Their penchant for psychological, sometimes sadistic, manipulation was notorious inside Universal's gates. Once, on a Friday before the Academy Awards, several Universal TV producers had left work early to attend to jobs preparing the awards show. Hitch complained to Wasserman, who came immediately to the director's bungalow. Adler was summoned, and the mogul roughly demanded an explanation: "If we don't have a producer on Friday afternoon, we'll have to find a new one by Monday." Adler grew flustered—no one should be fired over this, he said, and he tried to convince the two titans that the employees were attending to studio business. Then he noticed Hitch sitting back in his chair, smiling and enjoying the little drama, while Wasserman was frowning and grousing. Finally, the junior executive realized what was going on. "Lew was making a big scene on behalf of Hitch, and the two of them were both playacting. There I was, squirming in the middle." Both men were enjoying the show, said Adler. Hitch's guiding principle about moviemaking—"Always make the audience suffer as much as possible"—applied to the workplace, too.

During his studio meetings, Hitchcock liked to sip his orange juice and vodka. Bob Raines, a marketing executive, recalled the difficulties he had devising an ad campaign for *Torn Curtain* (1966), starring Paul Newman and Julie Andrews. Raines had spent weeks developing different themes for the movie's billboards. He showed each concept to Hitch, but in five meetings held over several weeks, the director rejected each one. The film's advertising costs were climbing, so Raines took his problem to Wasserman.

He showed the studio head all of the ads that Hitch had rejected. "Some of these are excellent," Wasserman commented. He assured Raines that Hitchcock would approve something soon. As a matter of fact, Hitch had already devised his own campaign, Wasserman told Raines. "He showed it to me some time ago."

The marketing man held his tongue. As Wasserman instructed, Raines returned to the director with more ideas—all of which Hitchcock turned down. One morning he called Raines into his office. "I'm sure you'll show me something that I can approve," he said, sipping his screwdriver. "Meanwhile"—he pulled a crumpled napkin from his breast pocket—"take a look at this. Does it have some merit in your opinion?"

It sure did—and ended up on the promotional material. But the accounting department demanded to know why advertising costs were so high. "Because the old man still likes to play games," Raines wanted to say. But he didn't bother. The critics blasted *Torn Curtain* as a flaccid, overburdened thriller, and it did less business than *The Birds*.

At Universal, Hitch did not have the free rein to refine his style and technique that he had enjoyed at Paramount at the peak of his career. When he moved to Universal, that had all changed. Wasserman's studio had the discipline and efficiency of the old studio system combined with the financial rules and commercial focus of the new era—but it lacked creative license. Hitchcock's films weren't matching his earlier successes—and Wasserman needed a hit desperately. Hitch felt the pressure to deliver and, in 1967, began working on an avant garde work.

Influenced by new wave director Michelangelo Antonioni (*Blowup*), Hitch wanted to shoot his next film on the streets of New York, using a cinéma-vérité style—unknown actors, natural light, and real-life settings. He'd use a hand-held camera, which was a radical break from his usual practice. He filmed his new thriller, *Kaleidoscope,* in New York's hippie dens, and in one scene, had his half-naked protagonist remove a pinecone from his posterior. When Wasserman saw the dailies, he thought his friend had gone too far. Other execs were outraged at the grisly work, and Universal pulled the plug. Years later, critic Dan Auiler discovered the old footage and claimed that if Universal had left the director alone, *Kaleidoscope* would have gone on to break film barriers that the violent *Bonnie and Clyde* was about to shatter. "Here was one of cinema's greatest directors (perhaps the greatest) proposing a groundbreaking film that would have eschewed the American studio style for the kind of filmmaking Hitchcock was seeing in France and Italy." But the work never made it to theaters. Wasserman told the director to concentrate on more commercial fare and gave him $4 million—a sizable amount—for his next film, *Topaz,* based on a Leon Uris novel. The mogul believed that he knew better than his own filmmakers—including his dear friend, the master of suspense.

"Lew always wanted to be Irving Thalberg," said Ned Tanen. "But, hell, even Irving wasn't a Thalberg, as his myth was so overblown." Yet, every American director daydreams about receiving the Thalberg Award. Given by the Academy of Motion Picture Arts and Sciences, the special Oscar is given only to those producers whose body of work "reflects a consistently high quality of motion-picture production."

To its shame, the Academy had never honored Hitch with an Oscar for the direction of any of his films—neither his Paramount masterpieces like *North by Northwest* nor his Universal features, such as *The Birds.* Perhaps Wasserman knew that his friend was losing his touch. In the spring of 1968, the mogul made a few phone calls, and the Academy honored Hitchcock with a Thalberg Award. That night, when the rotund director walked onstage to receive the statue, he gave the shortest speech in Oscar history. "Thank you," he said, and shuffled offstage.

TWENTY-THREE

AFTER THE LUNCH RUSH, Ed Muhl walked into the commissary to grab something to eat. He walked to his usual table near the front of the room, where he spied Stein and Wasserman deep in conversation. As Muhl approached, he heard their voices rise and turn harsh. "They were arguing about the quality of Universal's movies," Muhl recalled. Before the studio manager could greet the men, Wasserman got up abruptly and stalked off. The studio manager looked at Stein, who was shaking his head. "He was vexed," Muhl recalled. Over the past year, Muhl and Wasserman had often fought about the same sore subject. Muhl, who empathized with Stein, told the MCA chairman, "I just don't understand the fascination Lew has with TV. Movies just don't work the same way." Stein rose from the table and agreed glumly, saying, "I can't argue with you there."

Stein was upset about delays and expenses. The opening of the Sheraton Universal Hotel had been planned for four years, but instead of opening for Christmas 1968, it wouldn't be ready until the following March. Doris Stein wanted to celebrate the event in grand style, with a party and movie premiere. For the occasion, Wasserman had planned to issue what he thought would be a smash Universal movie called *Sweet Charity*, based on Fellini's *Le Notti di Cabiria*. Wasserman had turned the story into a musical comedy about a dance-hall floozy who wants to be loved, yet winds up with every kind of wrong man. "It was Lew's favorite movie," said Sid Sheinberg. It was scheduled to debut around the Sheraton Hotel's grand opening, but producer Ross Hunter had stormed off the set after fighting with director Bob Fosse. Now the budget was ballooning toward $8 million.

Inside the studio gates, the sixties were turbulent years. "There was a new generation out there, but the studio guys didn't want to know about them," explained Ned Tanen. "I'm not just speaking of MCA—it was everybody. None of the studios understood the changes, and then suddenly, it was hitting them in the face, like a pie," he said. Twentieth Century Fox had deposed Spyros Skouras as company president and installed Darryl Zanuck, who had written "Rin Tin Tin" scripts in the 1920s and produced several films in the 1940s, including *The Grapes of Wrath*. Zanuck got the studio moving again with *The Sound of Music* (1965), but he also approved expensive flops like *The Bible* (1966). By 1969, Fox was on its way to recording a disastrous $100 million loss. MGM posted good and bad years with *How the West Was Won* (1962), *Dr. Zhivago* (1965), and *The Dirty Dozen* (1967). But it was about to be taken over by Las Vegas financier Kirk Kerkorian. Warner Brothers produced *Who's Afraid of Virginia Woolf?* (1966), *Camelot* (1967), and *Bonnie and Clyde* (1967)—its biggest success of the decade—but steady profits were elusive. Paramount, now owned by Gulf + Western and managed by Robert Evans, was regaining its footing with *The Odd Couple* and *Rosemary's Baby* (1968). Despite those hits, Paramount was hemorrhaging $65 million that year. All the studios were taking large write-offs making movies that couldn't hold an audience, said Price. "No one knew what to do."

MCA's Universal had *Thoroughly Modern Millie* (1967) but no other financial success to its name. "If you look at the six years or so after MCA went into the movie business and see what they did, I defy you to find a good movie," said a former MCA agent. Wasserman kept trying to apply the methods of his successful TV division to his motion pictures. "He kept insisting that you could make movies on the TV show schedule," said Muhl. "I'm sure he could have made features films for $1.50," he said sarcastically. "But that wasn't the point. Who would go to the theater and see what basically amounted to a TV show?"

The idea of making films in Europe—embraced by several studios— had produced mixed results. Columbia Studios had enjoyed success with its foreign productions *A Man for All Seasons* (1966) and *To Sir with Love* (1967). United Artists, the undisputed art-house king, scored an Oscar with *Tom Jones* (1963), a million-dollar film that did

$17 million in business. But London had not been good to Wasserman and his deputy Jay Kanter. They had had high expectations for *A Countess from Hong Kong* (1967), with Sophia Loren and Marlon Brando, but critics called it the "insipid swan song" of Charlie Chaplin, who wrote, directed, and scored the piece. The studio reworked Tennessee Williams's play *The Milk Train Doesn't Stop Here Anymore* into an opulent, fuzzy film called *Boom!* (1968), starring Elizabeth Taylor and Richard Burton, but it, too, fell flat. *The Secret Ceremony* (1969) starred Taylor as an aging prostitute, Mia Farrow as a nymphomaniac, and Robert Mitchum as her stepfather. But that violent thriller was so poorly conceived that it was later reshot for TV to clarify and sanitize the story. Perhaps the biggest disappointment was *Isadora* (1969), a biographical tale about dancer Isadora Duncan. Almost three hours long, the opus was directed by Karel Reisz, starred Vanessa Redgrave, and was shot in England, France, Yugoslavia, and Italy. Wasserman was so confident about its success that he had released it on a reserved-seat basis, like a Broadway play. The marketing ploy lent prestige to the film, which only made its abysmal box-office debut that much more humiliating. "It was a disastrous run," said Price. By the end of 1968, MCA's London experiment had cost the corporation $40 million.

That year, Stein insisted that Wasserman shut down Kanter's operation. But Wasserman dragged his feet. He planned to go and personally help Kanter discontinue MCA's contracts. Instead, Stein ordered Berle Adams to do the job and, in early 1969, Kanter resigned. The producer said he'd heard "vague reports of friction" between Wasserman and Stein and didn't want to add to his mentor's problems. But several MCA executives say that Kanter was fired: "He became the patsy for Lew's losses, as Lew had approved every one of his scripts." While Wasserman tried to stem the bleeding, Kanter remained in London, where he formed a new film venture with Alan Ladd, Jr.—and Jerry Gershwin. It was a personal loss for Wasserman, as well as a business defeat.

"Stein disagreed with Wasserman a lot, and you could see the tension," said Muhl. MCA had borrowed steeply over the past five years until its debt had more than doubled from $32 million in 1965 to $67 million in 1967, and higher. The mounting red ink forced Wasserman to delay some of his development plans. The year 1967 had brought a nice 15 percent increase in income—which encouraged Wasserman to increase his slate of films to thirty, his highest number yet. But most of the movies bombed, and 1968 earnings fell a steep 20 percent. "Stein hated to lose money," said Muhl. The gap between Jules and Lew widened to an abyss.

At Stein's urging, Wasserman made some management changes. In March 1968 he promoted three ambitious executives to oversee parts of MCA's sprawling conglomerate, calling them executive vice presidents—the first such posts in the company's history. Al Dorskind headed the company's administration and real estate divisions; Berle Adams was in charge of MCA's television syndication, records, music publishing, and foreign film distribution; and Dan Ritchie became the liaison with the financial community, charged with mergers and acquisitions. Ritchie, a former Lehman Brothers partner and head of MCA's savings and loan, had joined MCA in 1962. "He was a bean counter with grandiose ideas," said Dorskind. This new triumvirate was supposed to free Wasserman for long-range planning. But Wasserman felt threatened by it.

Rather than delegate responsibility and groom a replacement—as Stein had ordered—Wasserman held fast to the reins. The three executives reported directly to Wasserman, who had the final word on their projects. "Lew never wanted to have one person hold too much power," explained Adams. "He was always reluctant to pass on duties to anyone. He was possessive that way."

"Let's face it," said Sheinberg. "The power was with Jules Stein, and these other people were basically working for him behind the scenes."

To further his plan, Stein turned to his longtime consigliere, Taft

Schreiber, who emerged from semiretirement. Suddenly the sixty-year-old executive was on the scene again, energetic, healthy, and ready to assume control over MCA's daily operation. Schreiber started questioning Wasserman's decisions and grilling his men, said Frank Price.

Stein, Schreiber, and Adams began discussing how to solve the studio's growing financial problems. "We had been great agents, but we didn't go after the best talent at that time," said Adams. "At the studio, we tried to negotiate too much. Instead of going for quality, we were looking for bargains. And we weren't giving people a piece of the action. All of the things that we had fought for as agents and sellers, we wouldn't give away as buyers of talent. It was a terrible time."

Wasserman was still a hands-on mogul, making decisions about story, casts, and promotional slogans. At the same time, he had diversified the company. MCA had acquired several record companies, as well as a grab bag of small firms. Gauss Electrophysics made high-speed magnetic recording equipment; Saki Magnetic made magnetic heads for recording devices; Danelectro Corporation made electric guitars and amplifiers; and Spencer Gifts was a retail and catalog company that could sell products connected to Universal films. MCA still made educational and corporate films, operated a thriving theme-park business, ran a few record labels, and oversaw a healthy savings and loan. "What were we doing with all of these businesses?" asked Dorskind. Inside MCA, growth became unwieldy, but Wall Street loved MCA, whose stock had just split and paid regular dividends. The conglomerate looked like an attractive merger or acquisition target, and to Stein and Schreiber, that seemed like the way out of this money-losing movie business.

Stein wanted MCA to merge with a blue-chip corporation, and Schreiber engineered a merger with Westinghouse Electric. The venerated Pittsburgh-based industrial firm made appliances, light-bulbs, and other consumer products; in the summer of 1968, it offered to buy MCA for $365 million. The deal would reduce MCA's debts while supposedly giving it autonomy. The appliance maker also promised to finance an expanded Universal City tour and develop condominiums and malls on the site. Since Westinghouse's revenues and profits were ten times that of MCA, a merger seemed attractive, at least on paper.

Westinghouse liked the marriage because MCA's records, movies, and TV shows could be shown on Westinghouse's radio and TV sets—an early move toward the synergy fever that would sweep Hollywood in the 1990s. Wasserman warmed to the merger because Westinghouse also owned TV stations that could distribute his TV shows. Networks were just beginning to grow more powerful in syndication, an area that MCA had long dominated, and had started taking a higher percent of MCA's syndication revenue. A merged MCA-Westinghouse company would keep all of that money in the family. Westinghouse's cash could also help Wasserman weather the inevitable down cycles of filmmaking.

At Stein's urging, Wasserman invited Westinghouse executives to MCA's commissary. But almost immediately the session turned tedious. "I just couldn't identify with those guys and their uptight mentality with their Brooks Brothers suits," said Ned Tanen. "There was no sense of style or imagination." Yet a successful deal would have the effect of making Stein one of the largest Westinghouse stockholders, earning him approximately $100 million. Wasserman and Schreiber would also collect tens of millions of dollars if the deal went through. As the talks droned on, it was clear that Stein was eager to close the deal and get out of show business. Jennings Lang turned to the Westinghouse CEO and quipped, "Does this mean we get refrigerators wholesale?" It broke the ice, but Schreiber did not laugh.

At one point, Wasserman said he feared that the Justice Department would question the deal: Westinghouse owned TV and radio stations that, combined with MCA's films and records, might violate antitrust law. Wasserman's concern seemed a bit disingenuous, given how close he was to the Johnson administration, and how instrumental Schreiber had become to Richard Nixon's emerging presidential campaign. In October 1968, a few weeks before voters were to choose between Nixon and Hubert Humphrey, MCA stockholders approved the merger. Stein and Schreiber were delighted and relieved.

But Wasserman insisted on securing more ground and autonomy in the deal—so much so that the merger soon unraveled. "I don't believe anybody in my world was particularly looking forward to the Westinghouse deal," said Sheinberg. "It just didn't seem to be that wonderful." Stein and Schreiber, however, had been all but banking on it.

After that, Schreiber grew testy. He questioned progress on the movies. "Jennings Lang was spending money trying to make films with Fellini and [Ingmar] Bergman," said Price. "He was doing things that just didn't work." One day, Schreiber called Lang and ordered him to drop a costly film project. Neither one of these men had ever felt warmly toward each other, said Price. Close in age, they were miles apart in sensibilities. Schreiber had wanted to fire Lang after his scandalous bullet-to-the-groin incident eighteen years earlier. Lang found Schreiber insufferable. "He thought he was pompous," said Price.

So, when Schreiber ordered Lang to drop a project that Lang had been working on for months, Lang yelled profanities at the imperious MCA veteran: "You jerk!" exclaimed Lang. "You don't know what you're talking about. You're out of it—you're a relic from the prehistoric age." Schreiber was outraged. No subordinate had ever talked to him so disrespectfully, he screamed. The shouting match escalated until one man slammed down the receiver. A few hours later, Price heard about the blowup from a mutual friend who had just seen Schreiber. "God, is Taft ever pissed at Jennings! What the hell's going on over there?"

As it turned out, Schreiber and Stein were about to overthrow

Wasserman. The two intended to depose the longtime president and any other executive who supported him. In January 1969 Stein saw to it that Schreiber became a member of the board, joined by Adams, Dorskind, and Ritchie, all of whom were Schreiber supporters. Wasserman's friends were now outnumbered on this new ten-person board—and the MCA directors were about to review the disastrous finances of 1968. MCA's profits had dropped a stunning 82 percent to $2.5 million—a paltry income for a company with $306 million in sales. Wasserman had been forced to write off even higher expenses on nearly all of his films from that year. Because of a recession, rising interest rates, and MCA's dire need for cash, the company's debt was now close to $100 million.

"Lew was very vulnerable," Tanen recalled. Wasserman looked so pale and exhausted that he almost resembled his skeletal Bernard Buffet portrait. "Lew had some mysterious illness," Sheinberg explained. He was afflicted by either a blood malady, a drug allergy, or exhaustion, depending on whom you talked to. The illness turned acute after Wassserman learned of Stein's plan to remove him from the president's seat. Stein called an emergency board meeting for March 31, 1969, said Adams. "But Jules never got a chance to explain this: He wanted Lew to move up to the chairman's seat, with Stein becoming chairman emeritus." All Wasserman heard was that he was being pushed aside in a power struggle. "They always denied this, saying they just wanted Lew to take it easier," said Tanen, who didn't quite believe that Stein had Wasserman's interests at heart. "It all came down to Jules trying to dump Lew."

It was the ultimate betrayal.

At Misty Mountain, Doris Stein was addressing gilt-edged invitations to her socialite friends, Jules's fellow tycoons, MCA's film stars, and six dozen members of European royalty. The Steins were throwing a three-day spree of extravagant parties to mark the opening of the Sheraton Universal Hotel. The "Hotel of the Stars" was considered the crowning achievement of Universal City's expansion, and the Steins were using the occasion to celebrate Doris's sixty-seventh birthday—and to showcase their pride and joy, the Jules Stein Eye Institute.

For months now, Doris had been overseeing details of the Sheraton's construction. It was "Doris's baby," and the white-haired lady was often seen on site, stepping daintily around drop cloths and sawhorses to inspect her project. She found that the bathroom lights made the enameled fixtures glow purple. "They'll never do," she said; they were replaced. The hotel's fire-alarm bells were ugly and had to be removed, she demanded. After a worker sheepishly mentioned that the alarms were required by law, Doris ordered: "Then paint them out." And they were, on all twenty-one floors. She wanted the entrance to be commanding, so the marquee rose from a niggling 20 feet to a stately 60 feet. Construction costs on the hotel soared, too.

The Steins had invited 750 guests—including the top echelon of MCA. The guest list included Governor and Mrs. Reagan, the Salvatoris, and other members of Reagan's Kitchen Cabinet. Jack Warner, UCLA Dean Franklin Murphy, the Oscar de la Rentas, the Jack Bennys, and the Bob Hopes were also expected. The Steins were also flying in nearly 100 of their closest friends from Lisbon, Paris, London, and New York. They had chartered a plane from New York and a Lufthansa flight from Paris. Traveling at MCA's expense were Prince Tassilo von Furstenberg of Italy, Princess Gina Liechtenstein, Count and Countess Bernadotte of Sweden, the Marchese and Marchesa Emilio Pucci, and at least five other princes and princesses, half a dozen dukes and duchesses, and several faux noblemen.

"They brought people in from all over the world," said Gerald Oppenheimer. "They were proud of what they had accomplished and wanted to show it off. They also wanted their friends to see the

Eye Institute and invite them to participate and give money." Staged like a Cecil B. De Mille epic, the weekend bash would start with a small dinner Friday night, hosted by the Alfred Bloomingdales. Then guests would be ushered to the elegant Pantages Theater for a benefit premiere of *Sweet Charity.* After that, guests would be transported to the Universal Hotel's ballroom for a lavish supper buffet. The movie and dinner would cost $100 per couple, and proceeds would benefit the JSEI. Doris had scheduled a VIP tour of Universal Studios, a guided visit to the institute, and trips to Disneyland, the Santa Anita Racetrack, the Music Center (which Wasserman had helped build), and the Los Angeles County Museum of Art. In addition, some of the Steins' friends had agreed to host satellite parties to fill any idle hours in the weekend. One *Los Angeles Times* editor gushed that Doris had worked "the logistics for the whole thing, down to the last cracker and olive."

As the March 28 event approached, the jet-set crowd on both continents was atwitter. In two weeks, "one of the country's longest, biggest and most opulent parties" would start, according to the *New York Times.* By March 31, most guests would be flying home. But after all the celebrations, Stein, Schreiber and Wasserman would be facing off behind closed doors.

When Lew Wasserman's fifty-sixth birthday arrived on the third Saturday in March, Edie and Lew were plotting to outflank their enemies. The date was significant, said Dorskind. "I had tried to arrange the opening of the hotel for Lew's birthday on March 15." But that had been overruled by the Steins. The date was not just the day Wasserman marked his birthday, but the anniversary of the assassination of Julius Caesar. If Edie had her way, this year's Ides of March would see the demise of the plans of Julius Caesar Stein, and she mounted her attack meticulously.

Wasserman had planned to convene a meeting of MCA sales personnel on Monday, March 17. Originally, he had wanted all salesmen from every foreign office to participate in planning for the year and to celebrate the new hotel. But when Wasserman failed to appear Monday morning, his absence fueled rumors. "Everyone in town knew it," said a producer. "Lew was on thin ice and was about to be thrown out of the company."

Edie started spreading tales of Stein's treachery. She talked to allies in the Democratic party, in Los Angeles' civic circle, and to some columnists. Then she tried to drum up sympathy for her husband by declaring that he had suffered a heart attack on his birthday. She called MCA's publicity department and dictated an announcement. She insisted that her missive be typed on company stationery and released immediately to the press. Berle Adams, who was now acting as president, learned about it when an MCA publicist showed him the release sheepishly. "I had to approve everything that went to the press," said Adams. Concerned about Wasserman's health, Adams investigated and learned that "Lew was *not* in the hospital." Nor had he suffered a heart attack. Wasserman was simply at home resting.

"You can't have a publicly held company issuing statements that aren't true," Berle told his staff, visibly upset. But he saved his outrage for Edie, who had gone behind his back. He reported her machinations to Stein, who was home preparing for the March 28 party. Stein conferred with Schreiber and, later, Adams. Schreiber telephoned Edie and confronted her about her false report. It was a terse conversation, said Adams, and she hung up. That's when Stein finally decided that not only would Wasserman be out but that Schreiber would be in charge, with Adams acting as president. Later, Stein met with Schreiber, Adams, Dorskind, Ritchie, and a few others at the Hotel Bel-Air, where the men strategized their next move and carved up Wasserman's duties.

Meanwhile, Lew met with his few remaining supporters. By now he was taking and making dozens of telephone calls at home. "Lew could call anyone at any time, and that's what he did," said Tanen. During the twelve days between Lew's birthday and Doris's birthday, Wasserman summoned stalwarts, both inside and outside of MCA. One of those was Jennings Lang. With Lew's blessing, Lang voluntarily boarded a plane for New York and met with five MCA men, including Louis Friedlander and Stein's brother-in-law, Charles Miller, said Monica Lang, Jennings's wife. "His allegiance to Lew was very strong, and he adored Lew," she explained. "He wasn't about to see him leave without a struggle." Lang also visited a few advertising and network friends to take their temperature on MCA's corporate politics.

Back at Universal City, many executives scrambled to curry favor with Adams, the heir apparent, and Schreiber, the power behind the throne. By the last full week in March, Adams had called into his office most top executives, including some of Wasserman's lieutenants. At one such meeting, he told Sid Sheinberg, "I'm going to be president of the company, and you're going to be working for me from now on," Adams announced.

"Good luck," said Sheinberg. "I quit."

"Now, why would you do that?" Adams asked.

"Because I've observed you, and I can't work for you." Sheinberg felt that Adams was devious and undercut people. He believed that Adams was the real "villain" who had conspired to replace Wasserman. Adams would deny this, insisting that Stein and Schreiber had simply wanted Wasserman to step down. "Jules was reorganizing the company and wanted Lew to stay out of production and the day-to-day business," Adams recalled. "But before he got a chance to sit down with Lew and explain this, Lew got 'sick' and stayed home."

A few days before the Sheraton opening, Tanen called Wasserman's house. Edie answered the phone.

"How's he doing?" Tanen asked.

"He's doing better."

"Can I talk to him?"

"Just a minute. I'll see if he's awake."

Finally Lew came on the line, and Tanen said, "Lew, I've never done this before, and I don't know why I'm doing it now, but if you are leaving the company, I'd like you to give me thirty seconds' notice so I can get out, too." Wasserman thanked Tanen calmly and hung up. Tanen realized that he was not the only one calling and that Edie was writing down the name of another supporter. "And there was Lew, sitting at home, taking calls, and banking his chips," said Tanen. "His loyalty to his men had paid off very well."

By Wednesday, March 26, the Steins' guests started arriving with their valets and trunks. One Palm Beach socialite was upset that she could not get a second free hotel suite for her fluffy white dog. A Portuguese noble was drinking heavily in the bar, while society columnists were slavishly recording it all. Come Monday, they'd heard, the Wassermans would be history. Edie tried leaking items about MCA's "palace revolt," as it would soon be called, and several newspapers printed her plants as the Steins' party day approached. A *Variety* reporter called Jules, who denied the rumors about Lew's firing and called them "absolutely ridiculous." Edie meanwhile located her friend Eugene "Big Gene" Klein, a Democratic fundraiser who had worked closely with the Wassermans. Klein was one of the few men who was actually richer than Stein.

Edie knew that Klein's niece was married to James Bacon, a columnist at the *Los Angeles Herald Examiner*. Edie sketched out the rough details of the MCA coup and asked Klein to help her place the item. He did.

"Everyone knew that Lew was going to get fired," said Bacon. So he wrote about it. On Doris's birthday, Bacon's column landed on her doorstep. "A Guiding Genius May Soon Find Himself Out of an Important Job," the headline blared. The column blasted Stein for planning to fire the one man who had built MCA from a Midwest band-booking agency to a show-business conglomerate. It quoted Stein as explaining that Wasserman was simply ill and at home, to which Bacon added: "If he's ill, it's because of what his associate of more than 30 years is doing to him." In Hollywood, "you're only as good as you last financial statement." The prominent story featured a big photo of Stein and ended with two lines: "Doris Stein is much too social to let her husband spoil her parties with nasty business details." But, the story predicted, Wasserman will be fired.

That night, the Steins' party—and the Wassermans' showdown—began. Lew had slaved over the production of *Sweet Charity*, but was notably absent at its premiere. Many of the sixty-year-old guests considered the brassy, jazzy film déclassé, since it glorified loose morals and "cheap frills."

After the movie, guests were driven over the hill to a black-tie, after-theater supper, mounted in lavish style. The hotel ballroom glowed a soft blue underneath a canopy of chandeliers. Tables were covered in blue cloth and silver netting, topped with bowls of white tulips sprouting above gold epergnes. "Beautiful people stood around and gaped at the stars," said one wag. Ricardo Montalban, George Jessel, Irene Dunne, and Dorothy Lamour mixed with Senator George Murphy, Mark Taper, UCLA's Dr. and Mrs. Franklin Murphy, attorney Paul Ziffren, and Albert and Mary Lasker. Holding court in one corner was Governor Reagan surrounded by his and Stein's friends, attorney William French Smith, the Jorgensens, the Tuttles, and the Salvatoris.

Jules and Doris greeted their guests in a reception line. Dressed in a blue-and-green gown with a white-ruffled cape, Doris laughed gaily. Next to her stood the Schreibers, then Berle and Lucy Adams. The new lines of command were obvious for all to see. As the crowd turned boisterous, Edie Wasserman suddenly arrived arm in arm with Herb Steinberg. As soon as Edie saw the Adamses taking the Wassermans' place in line, she turned steely, said Tanen. "Doris had a conniption," added guest George Christy. And Dorskind noticed the abrupt change in the atmosphere. "I had a whole table full of people I didn't even know, who were talking. Then all of a sudden, the diners left and I was sitting alone at the table." Other tables began to buzz as Edie sat down and promptly ordered a drink.

Edie scanned the room for allies. She saw Sheinberg dancing with a chorus girl from *Sweet Charity*. "I recall that I was quite taken with the girl, but I can't remember her name," he said. Edie saw Lang, Price, and other friends. At one point, she asked Tanen to dance with her. "I always got along with Edie, I don't know why," he said. "But that night, she spoke some pretty crass language, which I won't repeat." Edie swirled amid the royal guests in sashes and tiaras, dancing with several partners to the Bernie Richards Orchestra. Her elbows were unusually sharp as she bumped into dukes and ladies, and she nodded and smiled through gritted teeth while swearing a blue streak. "She was one tough lady that night," said Tanen. Before she left that night, she told him: "You just watch. We're going to piss on all their graves."

PART III

Celebrating the Crown: 1969–1980

Twenty-Four

LEW WASSERMAN DID NOT BELIEVE Jules Stein's benign utterances any more than Stein believed that Wasserman had really suffered a heart attack. In the days leading up to MCA's emergency board meeting, Wasserman was away from work for two weeks. During that time, he contemplated his own dire predicament. Should he start his own production company? Sue Stein and MCA? The fact that his mentor and idol was dropping him shook Wasserman, said Berle Adams. "Jules was a very paternal person, and Lew was his son, I would say." It was awful for Wasserman to realize that his surrogate father was throwing him out of MCA's top position after all that he had done for the company.

"Lew always had the ambition to run a studio," said Adams, and over the years, Wasserman had turned down several opportunities to do so. In 1941, when Wasserman was trying to sign Hollywood clients for Stein, he was summoned by L. B. Mayer, who had asked: "Who's that agent that represents Hattie McDaniel?" McDaniel had just won an Oscar for Best Supporting Actress as Mammy in *Gone With the Wind* (1939)—the first black ever to win an Academy Award. Wasserman rushed over to see Mayer, who curtly outlined a deal. "This is what I'm willing to do. [One] thousand a week, with the ability to buy stock." Wasserman thought, "Wow. This is great." But all he said was, "I like it, and I'll certainly tell my client about the offer."

Mayer was puzzled: "I don't know what you're talking about. Are you ready to start on Monday?" Wasserman realized *he* was the one being wooed. He told this story several times to illustrate the fact that Mayer tried numerous times to lure him to MGM, always offering a fatter salary. Finally, Mayer handed Wasserman a piece of paper and said. "Fill this in with anything you want, and it's yours." Lew declined. "Mayer could not believe that Lew would turn down all that money," said Dan Slusser, a former vice president at MCA.

In the early 1950s, the two lawyers who took over United Artists asked Wasserman to join their team. "Lew is one of the two or three smartest men in the industry," said studio owner Bob Benjamin. "I wish he was president of U.A." And in 1958, after Mayer was ousted from MGM, the chairman, Arthur Lowe, inquired if Wasserman would assume the reins. "But he turned that down, too," said Jay Kanter. That same year, Columbia's chief, Harry Cohn, wanted to hire Lew as his right-hand man. They were scheduled to discuss the post when Cohn died a few days before the meeting, said Tony Curtis. By that time, Wasserman was boasting that, as things stood, he was running all the studios, anyway.

But he'd never leave Stein for another job—not for all the money in the world. "I was very taken with Dr. Stein when we met," he explained to me years later. Stein had hired Wasserman during the worst days of the Depression, and supported him when Lew's own father could not help him. "I guess Dr. Stein had a lot of faith in me," said Wasserman. The young man went on to prove that Stein's confidence had not been misplaced. Even though MCA perfected the art of the Hollywood contract, Stein never bothered to sign one with his own talented protégé. "I never had a contract with him in the forty years we worked together," explained Wasserman. That any corporate chief would work so long without a binding compensation agreement was unusual in American industry. In Hollywood, it was a freak occurrence. As Kanter explained, "Lew had a great deal of respect for Jules, and Jules really respected Lew."

But Lew had ignored Stein's repeated warnings over the past year. The son had aggravated the father, said Adams. "Jules was very disappointed."

Edie was outraged. How dare Stein oust her husband, after all he had accomplished? She and Lew had invested their lives in MCA! That night, after Edie returned from the Sheraton opening, where *Sweet Charity* had raised $125,000 for Stein's eye institute, she gave her husband a blistering report. She railed about the ersatz aristocrats, the freshly minted politicians, and the Philadelphia bluebloods. One phony nobleman had taken a free ride on Stein's jet only to invite his friends to his Sheraton suite for an all-expenses-paid bacchanal, an act of license that Edie would later leak to the *Los Angeles Herald Examiner*'s columnist, in hopes of embarrassing Doris. One drunken socialite had announced to the press that this party was "the most wonderful weekend in mankind." Edie also told Lew about other executives at the party and which way they seemed to be leaning.

The next Monday, Wasserman would face several obstacles in regard to his fate. To begin with, Stein and Schreiber together owned 31 percent of the stock. Wasserman had only 13 percent. At most, Wasserman had the support of two other directors on the ten-man board—not enough to save him. In addition, Schreiber had hired the independent accounting firm of Price Waterhouse to review the financial status of Universal's one- and two-hour TV shows. "Jennings Lang was in charge of those," said Dorskind, and Schreiber was gunning for Lang. When the accountants' report confirmed what Schreiber had suspected—that Lang's shows lost money—he had another log to throw on the pyre. Schreiber himself wanted to show Stein the financial problems in Lang's division, but Dorskind, who was trying to keep a foot in each camp, had already sent the chairman a copy. Schreiber told Dorskind, "I won't forget you did this, Al. And I won't let you forget it, either."

Without a negative topspin from Schreiber, the report wasn't especially damning. "Yeah, we lost money on the first run, but by the second or third run, we were doing very well," Dorskind said. The business had been set up so that the networks owned the first-run programs and usually the first rerun. After the rerun, Universal owned all the rights—and it syndicated the shows to the tune of tens of millions of dollars. But the Price Waterhouse numbers could be construed to place Lang and Wasserman in the worst light. "These people were just cooking up anything to throw at Lew," said Sid Sheinberg.

Wasserman had contributed to the problems. "I always felt that Lew picked the wrong kind of people to surround him, assistants, bodyguards, and sycophants to some degree. They were all wrong—Gershwin, Kanter, and some others," said Ronnie Lubin. And Lew's own worst enemy was his constant need to control everything. "He could be stubborn, which was both his strength and weakness," said Dorskind.

Frank Price was keeping a low profile, although he clearly supported Wasserman. "At some point, Jennings went to Jules and said, 'Look if anything happens to Lew, we'll all resign.' That would have wiped out the company," said Price. Television accounted for 40 percent of the gross revenues of MCA—far more than films (22 percent), records (22 percent), the tour, and other ancillary businesses (16 percent). The executives and their writers and producers had created series that had sold $200 million, waiting to be collected. Without a strong TV department, MCA would crumble, and it wouldn't matter if Adams, Schreiber, or Stein himself became president, Lang told MCA's chairman.

"I learned about all this later," said Price. "I figured that Jennings could afford to resign. But I couldn't." Even so, Price was counted in, along with Sheinberg and a few others from TV; Ned Tanen, who was heading a small but profitable music label; and a few MCA veterans, including Charles Miller, Stein's brother-in-law. "These guys threw in their lot with Lew, which was great support for him," said Price.

When the board finally met on March 31, 1969, in the basement of the Chicago National Trust, the tension was palpable. According to James Bacon, Edie's columnist friend, "Lew went into that meeting and said, 'Look, if I go, I'll take all the guys from NBC with me, some of the advertisers, and all the fellows who do the creative work here.' "

Stein was forced to relent. "To hell with it," he said. Wasserman not only held fast to his position, he received an unusual show of support. The board reelected him as president—three months before its annual stockholder meeting in June. "That quelled the rumors," said Price. The board also voted to keep him as president for another fifteen months; at the subsequent shareholder meeting in June 1970, directors would review his progress. Until then, however, Stein insisted that Wasserman share decision-making power with Schreiber. Wasserman had come so close to losing it all, he had to agree to this most uncomfortable concession.

Even so, Wasserman managed to dash off a shareholder letter that very day, in time for inclusion in MCA's annual report. In it, the MCA president said the outlook for 1969 was brightened "by the early reception of *Sweet Charity* and by what we believe is a significantly improved potential" for Universal's other movies. He and Stein both signed the letter.

Edie's calls, leaks, and lobbying had helped save her husband's job. And her efforts had another desired effect. While Stein's decision was not swayed entirely by an item in the *Examiner*, he and Doris were embarrassed by the publicity, said a few people. After Wasserman's sudden, come-from-behind victory at the board meeting, "Big Gene" Klein called his nephew and said, "Your story saved Lew's job." Bacon quoted his anonymous source in the next day's column.

Sweet Charity did not fare as well as Lew did. By the time the credits rolled at the premiere showing, the audience sat in numbed silence.

"I think Jules was expecting *Lawrence of Arabia*," said one guest. That Oscar-winning epic would have been more appropriate entertainment for Stein's friends than the tale of a prostitute with a heart of gold. From its rendition of "Hey, Big Spender" in one seedy scene, to the psychedelic music numbers, the movie offended viewers such as Henry Salvatori—a man who once called President Kennedy a radical—and his dinner companion, Nancy Reagan.

The public did not embrace *Sweet Charity*, either. It opened on April Fool's Day to dismal business. "Who knows why no one ever came?" said Sheinberg. "It was Lew's favorite picture and a fabulous film. You should see it. But in the movie business," he added, "you never know what will hit." Wasserman's creative instincts and his sense of the public's taste were simply not as strong as he wanted to believe.

He and Stein still had to mend the ugly rift that had separated them. "Lew felt very strongly about Jules, and it was difficult," said Adams. In the weeks following the attempted coup, the two men seemed to walk on eggshells, and many of their discussions were pained. Stein "was embarrassed," said Price—and Wasserman's unwillingness to give up power, along with Stein's and Schreiber's machinations, had divided the Tower. If MCA intended to recover its financial health and regain its creative footing, the warring moguls had to bury their grievances and unify the troops. Schreiber was now a comanager. "Somehow, Taft and Lew worked it out," said Price. "For that year or so, it was basically a power-sharing arrangement."

As part of the truce, however, Wasserman and Schreiber each had to sacrifice at least one man, chosen by the other. Stein oversaw the process.

Jennings Lang was "cut off at the knees," said Price. "He wasn't active in TV after that and lost some management control," at Schreiber's insistence. But Wasserman did give his man a film-production deal that would soon become famous. Schreiber's guy,

Dan Ritchie, was demoted; his duties were cut back to supervising the banking business, and he soon left MCA for Westinghouse Corporation. Stein gave more power to his brother-in-law Charles Miller, who had tried to broker peace among Stein, Wasserman, and Schreiber.

Al Dorskind's fate proved to be a difficult decision. He had initially supported Schreiber in the palace revolt, then had fallen from grace by sending Stein the outside financial review. He was caught between the two camps and knew it. He went into Wasserman's office and offered to resign, but Wasserman declined. He and Schreiber had already agreed to strip Dorskind of his pet real-estate duties, and Schreiber was reviewing candidates to assume the key post. Meanwhile, Dorskind was demoted to administrative duties.

In the midst of all this, Stein fell seriously ill. "That was even more amazing than the coup, as Jules was practically dying," said Adams. In the fall of 1969, Stein suffered intense intestinal pain and wound up in UCLA's Medical Center. Publicly, he was said to have had ventriculitis, an inflammation of the digestive tract. But exploratory surgery revealed that Stein's cancer had reappeared. His rectum and intestines were inflamed by so many malignant tumors that doctors did not expect the seventy-five-year-old to survive. One doctor used an experimental drug that seemed to halt his pain. But then his kidneys shut down. "Every doctor and organ specialist was brought in to monitor his organs and to counteract whatever side effects this new drug produced," said Adams. Stein underwent surgery again in January 1970 and seemed to improve. But a few weeks later, his condition worsened and he underwent a third surgery. By February, he was slipping in and out of comas, barely hanging on to life.

Stein's daughters were called in from New York, and his siblings appeared at his bedside to say good-bye. Doris asked UCLA's Dean Murphy to write Stein's eulogy, and she reviewed her husband's elaborate multipage funeral instructions—the same ones he had prepared in 1957 when he first fell ill. Stein's grave condition presaged more internal turmoil for MCA.

Stein's living will ensured that, if he ever fell ill, Schreiber would be endowed with his voting power. This meant Schreiber now had control of 31 percent of MCA votes. And if Jules died, Doris would hold her husband's shares—25 percent of the outstanding stock. She'd make the key decisions in the company, and everyone knew she was closer to Schreiber than to Wasserman. Adams confirmed: "She'd fulfill Stein's wishes and make me president," with Schreiber as chairman. Wasserman would be expendable; his 13 percent position would never be enough to maintain his rule.

Years earlier, in 1948, after Dore Schary assumed control at MGM, Wasserman had told his client: "Get rid of the whole bunch of executives—if you don't, they'll kill you." Now he took his own advice. While Stein's life hung in the balance, Wasserman called Berle Adams into his office, where attorney Charles Miller was already seated. Wasserman asked Adams to leave MCA. Adams resisted, saying that he had given twenty years to the company and didn't deserve to be fired. "Consider it a resignation," Wasserman suggested. He'd make sure that Adams would receive his pension and benefits and he could remain for a year, until he found something else. He could even write his own press release, announcing his departure from MCA.

In the end, Adams accepted his fate. "After Jules got sick and Lew moved in, it was clear I was going to be out," said Adams. "It was an emotional time." Adams agreed to leave MCA in February 1971. "Lew wanted me to stay a year to finish coordinating changes at the Decca record label."

Then Stein had an amazing comeback, said Wasserman. "Some young doctor had the idea of giving him a shot of magnesium." All Stein needed evidently was an essential trace mineral, which was added to his intravenous drip. Within a week, MCA's chairman was up and reading his stock charts in the *Wall Street Journal.*

From his hospital bed, he called Adams. Stein said he was sorry about what had happened during the revolt, but the chairman didn't offer to reinstate his man. As Stein regained his strength, he was moved to the tenth floor of the hospital. There, he had a new perspective of his precious eye institute. He saw that although the walls of his monument were made of rose-colored marble, the roof was covered with ugly tarpaper. The black swath dominated his view. "He called someone up, and the next day, the top was scraped up and a more modern, better-looking beige top was laid down," said his stepson, Gerald Oppenheimer. Workmen artfully raked marble chips across the rooftop and camouflaged its ugly vents.

"That made him feel better."

TWENTY-FIVE

THE SUMMER OF 1969 brought *Easy Rider,* a film written by Dennis Hopper, Peter Fonda, and Terry Southern, to American theaters. The Columbia Pictures release marked a sea change in Hollywood, said Ned Tanen. "*Easy Rider* hit a nerve and people went nuts trying to ride that wave." It was made under the banner of BBS, run by Bert Schneider, son of a high-ranking studio executive. *Easy Rider* was its first big-screen hit, and the old moguls almost released the movie in drive-in theaters as a low-budget B film, but the young bucks opened it at a theater on New York's Upper East Side. In one week, the $500,000 film made back its entire investment and went on to earn about $60 million.

"There were these bearded wonders who were doing good things, or at least different things, at a time when movies were not working for the studios," said Tanen. "Suddenly, every studio wanted to tap into the youth market." Paramount had its young man, Robert Evans, and Fox was about to release *Butch Cassidy and the Sundance*

Kid. Warner Brothers-Seven Arts Studio had just signed the twenty-nine-year-old Francis Ford Coppola to produce four "youth" pictures. That left Universal the odd player out.

Jules Stein wanted what Columbia Pictures had found. Any film that returned 12,000 percent on a studio investment was one that belonged at his studio. Jules's daughter Jean Stein vanden Heuvel was then separating from her husband, and happened to be dating Dennis Hopper. Through her, Stein arranged a deal in which Hopper would direct, write, and star in his own new movie, financed by MCA.

Now that Stein was back on his feet, Wasserman felt even more pressure. Yet, oddly, he didn't change the studio's management team. Still in place were studio manager Ed Muhl, production chief Melville Tucker, and most of the marketing team, including Bob Raines. "They were a bunch of Okies who didn't have a clue," said Tanen. Under them, Universal was releasing *How to Frame a Figg* (1971), with Don Knotts, and the witless *Cockeyed Cowboys of Calico County* (1970), starring the gentle giant Dan Blocker, who played "Hoss" on *Bonanza.* They didn't have the foggiest notion how to market films by or for a younger generation. Worse, they didn't care, said Tanen.

Schreiber, meanwhile, wanted MCA to hire professional filmmakers with solid track records. "Taft's complaints were that a lot of Universal's bad pictures had been done by people who had never made pictures before," said Price. The studio began making deals with independent producers on a film-by-film basis. Jennings Lang brought in Hal Wallis, a veteran who had produced *Barefoot in the Park* (1967), with Jane Fonda and Robert Redford. Lang hoped that Wallis would add fresh material and prestigious films to Universal's slate. He didn't disappoint.

A few months after striking the deal, around Christmas 1969, Universal released *Anne of the Thousand Days* —just in time for an Oscar consideration. Wallis's classy picture had an excellent cast—

from world-weary Richard Burton to sprightly newcomer Genevieve Bujold. Filmed in England, the picture garnered ten Academy Award nominations and two Oscars: one for costumes and another for cinematography.

Meanwhile, Wasserman cleaned up several messes. Lang and Price had been in the middle of a deal with Lionel Bart, whose film *Oliver!* (1968) had won two Oscars. Bart was hired to write the script and score a new version of *Ruggles of Red Gap,* about a hick from the West who wins an English valet in a poker game. The film had been made several times before, the last in 1935, with Charles Laughton and ZaSu Pitts, but MCA now owned the rights. "I thought it would be a good musical," said Price.

Bart worked only at night, while riding around London in a limousine. "I thought he was eccentric," said Price. "He'd hum into a tape recorder and write. He wrote some pretty good songs that way." Yet after a year there was still no *Ruggles* script. MCA was paying for endless midnight limo rides around the East End, and Price couldn't understand the delays. "What I didn't know is how deeply into cocaine Lionel was," said Price. He flew to London to press Bart about the script, and Bart confessed: "I can write only when I'm taking drugs." Bart left the project to detoxify and Price called upon a fledgling filmmaker, Philip Kaufman, who had done only two films, including the incoherent *Fearless Frank.* But Price saw talent in the man who in 1988 would direct *The Unbearable Lightness of Being.* "We're going to write that script for Bart," Price told Kaufman.

But the movie winds had changed. Despite the success of *The Sound of Music* (1965) and *Thoroughly Modern Millie* (1967), MGM-style musicals were not returning profits in the 1970s. *Paint Your Wagon, Hello Dolly,* and *Sweet Charity* all flopped, said Price. "Suddenly, no one wanted musicals anymore." After spending a few million dollars and the previous year trying to get Bart's musical out, Price was ordered back to Universal City. He'd soon return to Universal TV.

Other films could not be aborted. Richard Burton had signed up for *Raid on Rommel* (1971) and came to rue the day. Most of the film's action scenes were bits of stock footage clipped from *Tobruk* (1967), an earlier Universal bomb. But after Wasserman viewed *Rommel*'s rough cut, he ordered his marketing staff to "go all out" promoting Burton's next film. A publicist asked Burton to narrate radio and TV commercial spots as teasers for the film. Incredulous, Burton replied: "Good God, man! Do you think I'm a double fool? It's bad enough that I made the picture. Why would I want people to see it?" When the film premiered, Burton received the worst reviews of his career.

Meanwhile, problems escalated with *Airport,* a Ross Hunter production. The film was based on the best seller by Arthur Hailey and charted the trials of a planeload of passengers—including a bomb-carrying psychopath. Similar stories had been done before—*The High and the Mighty* (Warner, 1954) was one example—but never with Hunter's polish. *Airport* had a glittering, albeit geriatric, cast of fifteen stars—mostly former MCA clients: Burt Lancaster, Dean Martin, Van Heflin, Maureen Stapleton, and Helen Hayes. Yet, by late 1969, the studio's $8 million investment was spinning out of control. "Lew was wild about cost overruns. He was yelling, 'Get out of the damn thing,' " said Tanen. The studio pressed on, hoping to recoup its investment with foreign runs. By the time the film wrapped, its cost had zoomed to $10 million, an astronomical amount for a studio on the ropes.

Universal released *Airport* in March 1970. Wasserman had booked the film in as many theaters as possible, hoping to collect his money before bad reviews could do much damage. Amazingly, the film worked. As box-office figures streamed in that spring, Wasserman realized that the film was breaking previous records. *Airport* was earning $5 million, $15 million, $20 million. Hunter and his partner, Jacques Mapes, the assistant producer on the film, became the toast of the town. They boasted that their film had saved

Wasserman's job and, in a way, they were right. The film came out three months before MCA's board was due to decide on the renewal of Wasserman's contract. But Hunter's boasts angered Edie, who read about them in film and society columns.

When Hunter's seven-year studio contract expired, the producer expected Wasserman to renew it; from *Pillow Talk* to *Thoroughly Modern Millie,* Hunter had made more box-office hits than any other Universal producer. Instead, Wasserman threw Hunter off the lot unceremoniously. He even took back some artwork he'd given the producer in happier times, said Robert Blees, screenwriter for *The Magnificent Obsession* (1954). "It was a nasty parting," he said. Hunter never regained the success he'd enjoyed at Universal. Out of spite, perhaps, the producer started making TV movies at Paramount, which sold them to NBC—Universal's biggest client.

Wasserman knew he didn't understand the new audience. "Wasserman had gotten slapped on the side of the head" by Stein, said Price. He *had* to surrender creative control. "He didn't know what to do about it, but he had the idea of putting somebody else in the line of fire."

To make his youth films, Wasserman plucked a promising executive and set him on the executive floor of the Tower, in an office next door. Ned Tanen had never made films before, but he had a knack for the "youth market." In late 1966, Wasserman had given Tanen $750,000 to start a new record label. "I called it UNI because I didn't want it associated with MCA," said Tanen. "The corporate name had a lot of attitude left over from its agency days." He didn't want Lew's intimidating style around acts like the Strawberry Alarm Clock. He rented an office on Sunset Boulevard, hired Russ Reagan to find talent, and added six other employees. In 1968 UNI beat out Columbia and Warner Records and signed Neil Diamond to a five-year, eight-album contract for $200,000. The singer appeared on *The Merv Griffin Show* and *The Mike Douglas Show,* singing his UNI hit, "Brother Love's Traveling Salvation Show." In 1971 the label signed Olivia Newton-John, a pretty Australian whose Bob Dylan cover, "If Not for You," topped the U.S. charts. "Then we found Elton John at the bottom of a pile of records," Tanen recalled. "Russ Reagan was a genius, and money was flying out the door."

In early 1969 Tanen had wanted to buy A&M Records, which was owned by Herb Alpert, of the Tijuana Brass fame, and Jerry Moss. The label produced Brasil 66, Joe Cocker, and other new acts, and its sale price was $7 million. "We almost got it, but the palace revolt derailed the deal," said Tanen. "Lew was all for it, but Jules vetoed it at the last minute," he explained. A&M grew into the hottest, richest independent label of its time. "I kept bringing it up to Lew, saying what a shame that deal failed." Wasserman's response was to move the long-haired manager out of records and into movies. Tanen's job was to make hit movies that appealed to this strange new youth market.

"I was the reluctant bride," Tanen said.

Wasserman couldn't figure out why movies such as *Bonnie and Clyde* (1967), *The Graduate* (1968), and *Easy Rider* had done so well. "Nobody else understood this new business, including the people who were getting into it," said Tanen. But at least Wasserman realized that he'd better start riding the wave. True to form, MCA did some research that showed young people didn't care about stars or big names. They wanted movies about real people and real situations, said Tanen. That went against all of Wasserman's long-held beliefs about the moviegoing public. So, too, did the profit deals that the studios were giving the young directors.

Until now, Wasserman had refused to give filmmakers a chunk of the profits—even though he had parlayed that practice into a career highlight. As an agent, Wasserman had always maintained that equity deals were good for the industry. "I don't think there's such a thing as [studios] overpaying talent—as long as they earn it," he said when he bought Universal. But as time went on, he wasn't as sanguine. Wasserman's friend, Jimmy Stewart, had certainly benefited from Lew's equity arrangements, but in 1969, the actor was warning friends: "If you work for Jules and Lew, don't expect any fifty-fifty deals."

Once Columbia started writing equity contracts for young film-makers, however, Wasserman did, too. Universal would produce films for $750,000—certainly no more than $1 million. The talent would be paid scale, but they could get a chunk of profits at the back end—after expenses were deducted. Even better, Universal offered these young talents a final cut—a rare gift.

The first movie Tanen signed was the one Stein had delivered courtesy of his daughter: *The Last Movie.* Dennis Hopper had a rep-utation for being pugnacious, unreliable, and intoxicated. Tanen had asked Stein: "Are you sure you want to do this?" But Stein was adamant, since he believed the world was waiting for the next *Easy Rider.* He told Tanen to "give the kid whatever he wants." Tanen gave Hopper $850,000 and control of his movie. He'd get half of the film's gross receipts—before any expenses or studio overhead was subtracted. In the meantime, though, he had to work for a piddly $500 a week in the jungles of Peru. But Hopper liked working in the world's cocaine capital. Several times during filming he got in trouble with Peruvian authorities, Tanen recalled.

Hopper's film was supposed to be a meditation on the greed and violence of Western movies and, by extension, on the death of America's colonial culture. Instead, it turned out to be a rambling film essay . . . and the death of Hopper's directorial career. Instead of editing his film in the customary span of three months, he took a year. Rather than work in Los Angeles, close to the studio, he insisted on working in Taos, New Mexico. Publicly, Hopper was a sensation, pictured on the cover of *Life* magazine, an auteur about to release a much-awaited film. Privately, Wasserman was leaning on Tanen to get the film finished. So, when Tanen heard that Hopper was in Los Angeles, the executive visited the director to discuss his progress. What he found was an orgy, "boobs and buttocks everywhere and

Dennis stoned out of his bird." Tanen never did learn that day where Hopper was in the editing process, but his visit was not auspicious.

When Universal finally received Hopper's film, Tanen screened the movie with Hopper and Jules Stein at the top of the Black Tower. After its last frame, Tanen and Stein sat in stunned silence. From the projectionist's room above, someone wisecracked: "He sure named this movie right, as it's going to be the last movie this guy ever makes." This was not a disaster film like *Airport,* said Tanen. "It was a catastrophe." Yet the studio gamely conducted press reviews and screenings. Wasserman attended one press showing when the projectionist mixed up the first and last reels. "The end of the film was shown first and the first shown last, but the film was so confusing, it didn't matter," he later said.

Tanen turned to more promising directors. The first movie he produced on his own was the substantial *Diary of a Mad Housewife* (1970). Directed by Frank Perry and starring Carrie Snodgrass, it examined the dying marriage of a materialistic lawyer (Richard Benjamin) and his bullied wife. Scripted by Eleanor Perry, it portrayed strong characters and was the breakthrough role for Snodgrass, who won an Oscar for Best Actress.

Next up was the impressive American debut by a Czech director. "I found Milos Forman in a garret in the East Village," Tanen recalled. He had directed half a dozen films and had a gift for casting an ironic eye on ordinary people. After the Prague Spring, when the Soviets invaded his homeland in August 1968, Forman tried to make films in the United States. Paramount had turned him down, but Universal gave him $400,000 to film *Taking Off* with Buck Henry. Forman applied his European sensibility to the American family, gently mocking middle-class parents who smoked marijuana to understand their "troubled" teenagers. It may sound like a cliché now, but at the time the director was saying something fresh about his adopted home. The film was a critical hit and landed Forman a Grand Prize of the Jury at the Cannes Film Festival.

Hired Hand, said Tanen, was another result of Wasserman's experiment. "Jules Stein got that one for Peter Fonda." Shot in New Mexico, this offbeat western followed a drifter (Fonda) who returns home to the wife he abandoned, only to leave her again. The film alternated between lyricism and pretension, said critics. Fonda directed and starred in the film, which was released in the spring of 1971 to critical success.

Tanen got the multitalented John Cassavetes to direct *Minnie and Moskowitz,* a manic romance about a lonely gentile museum curator who falls for a crazy Jewish parking attendant. Cassavetes is now considered a pioneer of American cinéma vérité, and the independent filmmaker always resented studio interference. Perhaps anticipating that Universal wouldn't promote his film properly, Cassavetes prepared a rough layout of an advertising poster with copy. The studio said it would consider his idea, but used an advertising-agency campaign. Cassavetes blasted the concept and later posted his own sheets on telephone poles along Coldwater, Laurel, and Beverly Canyon roads—where at least his friends would see them.

Some people thought Universal's attempt to make such films was cynical. "They saw these films as a way to make fistfuls of money," said Roger Corman, a low-budget producer at the time. The films cost very little to make, yet studios expected to make piles of cash. But isn't that the dream of every business in America? To its credit, Universal was the only studio to start an in-house picture division where younger filmmakers could try and reach a wider audience.

One of the most promising projects was a film by Monte Hellman. He had made two personal westerns—including *The Shooting*—that by 1970 were underground classics. The films had never been released in the United States; but in Paris, where people lined up for blocks to see them, critics called Hellman an American director of major importance. For Universal, he directed *Two-Lane Blacktop,* a minimalist piece about a road trip starring the singer James Taylor, Warren Oates, and Harry Dean Stanton. A few months before its release, *Esquire's* cover story hailed it as "movie of the year." It even published Rudy Wurlitzer's script. No studio could *buy* that kind of publicity. Universal had such high hopes for the film, it agreed to let Wurlitzer film a movie in India. But after Hopper's Peruvian fiasco, the studio pulled back.

Two-Lane Blacktop was made in seven weeks for $875,000—less than its budget. Hellman's existential metaphor about a road race from the Southwest to Washington, D.C., was a masterpiece and achieved cult status in 2000, when it was rereleased in New York theaters.

But when Universal premiered the film in 1971, it didn't do well. It opened on the Fourth of July, then one of the worst weekends to introduce a movie. "They ran one bland newspaper ad, but otherwise, did not offer much support," said Hellman. He had developed a "great ad campaign" outside of the studio, but it wasn't used. "Some theater owners in Portland and Seattle asked for it and got good showings," he said. But despite his efforts, strong reviews, and unprecedented advance buzz, *Two-Lane Blacktop* died after forty-two days without making much money. "I strongly believe that Wasserman didn't like the picture. He let it die," Hellman told me. "It happened to represent all of the things that he and the industry despised."

Yet, he added, his creative experience with Universal was fair. "Ned gave me freedom in that film, and it's the only one I made that I never had to change."

Next up was a sci-fi environmental film, *Silent Running,* which was filmed in thirty-two days and completed in the winter of 1971. It concerned a botanist in outer space, played by Bruce Dern, who must keep alive earth's last biological specimens. When he's ordered to destroy the plants, he rebels. Released in March 1972, the film was slow and had a downbeat ending. Today it seems dated, with its kitschy robots and Joan Baez songs, but its point about humanity's neglect of our planet has grown only more pressing.

The film gave several people valuable training. Douglas Trumbell learned how to be a director. Michael Cimino (*The Deer Hunter*) helped write the script, as did Steven Bochco (*Hill Street Blues, NYPD*), who was then a Universal TV writer. John Dykstra provided special effects and would later work on *Star Wars,* among other films. The apprentice program that Wasserman had set up in 1963 was now working. Even better, *Silent Running* and Tanen's five other experimental films did not lose money and gained critical notice.

Still, Wasserman wasn't enthralled with the boutique business. "The studio was putting up the money, but it was a reluctant, foot-dragging thing," said Tanen. "And the people who had to sell the movies were certainly not allies of them. The pictures never had the chance to find their audiences. The distribution people had no remote understanding of how to handle these films—whether it was a George Lucas or a François Truffaut," said Tanen.

The young directors weren't helping matters. Some were difficult and recalcitrant. They refused to don suits to go to work; in fact, they defied Lew's rules by wearing jeans, sandals, and ponytails in MCA's commissary. They had as much respect for authority as the Marx Brothers, only without the humor. Yet Wasserman's budgets and schedules gave life to the directors' films, which otherwise might not have been financed. The young talent didn't see it that way, said Tanen. "Everything was so confined at Universal, which was the most structured of the studios." Indeed, no other studio was more corporate than Wasserman's, and that's what the self-styled Hollywood rebels were agitating against. The marketing men "were looking at these movies from the so-called bearded wonders and they weren't sure which they disliked more: the directors or their movies," said Tanen.

At Columbia Pictures, the independent effort was waning, too. Bert Schneider was tired of fighting the status quo and was slipping into drugs. "I wasn't a genius or anything," said Tanen. "Bert Schneider had his thing at Columbia, and I had Lew Wasserman and twenty guys who were waiting to kill me." The surfeit of counterculture values and their lack of box-office success had a deadening effect. Wasserman might have continued this experiment if the films had been less political. But they criticized parents (*Taking Off*), social norms (*Minnie and Moskowitz*), authority (*Silent Running*), and American values (*Two-Lane Blacktop*). "At some point, Wasserman wondered 'How much damage can America do to itself?' " said Tanen. But his decision really came down to money. None of Universal's boutique films scored an *Easy Rider*–like 12,000 percent return on investment. And that, after all, had been the purpose of this experiment.

Elsewhere in the studio, Ed Muhl and his crew pushed Hitchcock's *Frenzy* (1972), the director's fifty-fourth and penultimate film. In this misogynistic movie, the director tracks a violent sexual predator and lingers on shots of openmouthed rape victims. Gratuitous nudity and cold-blooded violence had become commonplace in Hollywood, but Hitch was capitalizing on it. Despite some good reviews and a large marketing campaign, *Frenzy* did not do well at the box office, either.

Jennings Lang had produced *Tell Them Willie Boy Is Here,* a true story about the last Western manhunt for a Native American. Directed by Abraham Polonsky, who had been blacklisted during the McCarthy witch-hunts, and starring Robert Blake, the movie had a deft script about social concerns at a time when political messages were generally overbearing. The work was potent, but not a smash. Lang oversaw several other decent films: *They Might Be Giants* featured Joanne Woodward and George. C. Scott in a sentimental piece about a crazy judge. *Winning,* with Paul Newman, Woodward, and a spectacular seventeen-car pileup, was more about cars than characters. *Sometimes a Great Notion* was a workingman's tale about Northwest loggers, based on the novel by Ken Kesey, a revered figure of the counterculture. Finally, Lang gave former Universal contract actor Clint Eastwood a chance to direct his first film, *Play Misty for Me.* That thriller more than earned back its investment.

CELEBRATING THE CROWN: 1969–1980 263

Only *Airport* was really selling tickets—$30 million and rising. Hunter now bragged that Wasserman and his studio lived off *Airport* for three years—quite true. The film was driven by the suspense of a ticking bomb somewhere onboard, and in its final grand explosion, Wasserman saw the future. Despite the roster of great actors, the real stars in this film were the Boeing 707 and the blizzard-racked Minneapolis airport. *Airport* heralded a new type of movie: the disaster film. At the time, the genre was dismissed as schlock, but thirty years later, it was going strong, throwing off sequels, copycats, and boom-boom epics. *Airport* had an amazing theater run of $45 million—extraordinary for its time.

By 1972, Wasserman wanted more commercial fare. He told Tanen: "I'm putting up the money, I'm distributing the film, and you're going to have to accommodate me." Tanen found a script about kids who drag raced on Saturday nights. The story resonated with the producer, who had grown up in the desert town of Lancaster, eighty miles northeast of Los Angeles. "The town had about a thousand people. It was an awful time for me, but this script reminded me of that place." Tanen went into Lew's office several times with the treatment, telling him he wanted a green light. "Each time, he threw me out. I didn't understand why he wouldn't do it. The whole exercise of trying to get that done was one big slap in the face."

Wasserman refused to approve it until Tanen got a proven name attached to it. He signed Francis Ford Coppola to direct the film by George Lucas. *American Graffiti* was Tanen's last-ditch effort to find his own commercial hit.

TWENTY-SIX

IN THE MONTHS FOLLOWING THE ATTEMPTED COUP, Edie and Lew Wasserman walked on slippery ground. "Can MCA survive after

Wasserman?" Wall Street analysts wondered. "Can Wasserman survive at MCA?" Hollywood insiders whispered. Now that Lyndon Johnson had retired, the Wassermans no longer had a direct line to the White House. And the occupant of the California governor's mansion—which had recently housed a Democratic friend—now counted on Taft and Rita Schreiber for his fundraisers.

"We had been invited to the Reagans' house many times in his Hollywood days," Merrill Park explained. "But after things turned political, Nancy totally turned us away." Art Park, her husband, had been the first in Hollywood to contribute to Reagan's gubernatorial campaign. "He'd write letters to Ronnie, but I don't think Nancy ever gave them to Ron. We never heard from Reagan while he was in office. To Nancy, we were 'B' list people, especially compared to the Schreibers. That hurt Art." During this period, the Wassermans were not close to the Reagans, either.

Reagan and his staff of self-confessed amateurs knew little about the intricacies of state government. He instituted an across-the-board 10 percent budget cut, then raised state taxes by $1 billion. His finance director, Gordon Smith, did not know what he was doing, said Stu Spencer, a well-known Republican consultant who had devised Reagan's campaign. "Reagan's office was in disarray," and Schreiber grew alarmed by the situation. He ordered Spencer to go to Sacramento and "straighten out" the problem by hiring a new finance officer. "I didn't like the assignment," Spencer said. But the MCA executive insisted. "I talked to Nancy and she agrees that you should do the job, too." So the political consultant flew to Sacramento, fired Smith, and hired a new state financial officer. "I made a lot of enemies in the process," he recalled. But the situation improved a bit. "Taft was always doing stuff like that while monitoring Reagan's progress. Taft was very bright, but not as smooth as Wasserman," Spencer added.

Schreiber and Stein maintained frequent contact with the new governor during this time, but not Wasserman. And Doris made a point of telephoning Nancy Reagan. "I heard them talking on the phone a lot," said Spencer.

Reagan did not forget his studio friends. While he was removing some 300,000 poor children and their mothers from state welfare rolls, he delivered a $600 million subsidy to the Hollywood studios in the name of art preservation. Since MCA owned the biggest film library in town by far, it collected the lion's share of funds. "I'm sure he did other things for Hollywood, too, and that Taft lobbied for them," said Spencer.

Schreiber also became MCA's connection to the White House. He had been asked by top Republican fundraiser Maurice Stans to help raise money for Richard Nixon's campaign, and Schreiber turned his MCA office into a Republican finance outpost. He raised so much money for Nixon that the candidate didn't use it to campaign. Instead, Schreiber's $1.1 million in contributions were kept by Stans, who stashed rolls of $100 bills in his desk drawer. This cache would later help underwrite the historic Watergate burglary.

"Taft organized Celebrities for Nixon," said David Brown, a producer at Universal. He invited convoys of former MCA stars to drive down to San Clemente, site of Nixon's Western White House, to show their support. Charlton Heston, Frank Sinatra, John Wayne, and dozens of others congregated inside Nixon's Casa Pacifica, a Spanish-style home on the beach. "Nixon was very relaxed, entertaining Hollywood's conservatives," said Brown. "What he missed most about being in the Eastern White House was not seeing as many movies." So Schreiber regularly sent Nixon gift packs of Universal films to watch in Washington.

Later, Schreiber brought industry leaders and union chiefs to Casa Pacifica to lobby Nixon for more gifts and subsidies. Heston, who was head of SAG, pleaded for the government to bail out his spendthrift studio employers, despite his views as an anti-welfare Republican.

Nixon returned Schreiber's largesse a thousandfold. He helped

Hollywood get loans from the Export-Import Bank to sell its movies abroad—something the credit agency had resisted in the past. That helped reduce MCA's giant debt. Schreiber persuaded Nixon to make sure that Hollywood would receive liberal treatment under new accelerated-depreciation tax laws. The 1971 Revenue Act allowed companies that invested in film and TV shows—primarily Hollywood studios—to write off that income. In its first year, the tax law handed MCA a $3.5 million savings, which allowed MCA to report its most profitable year ever in 1972. Although revenues grew a meager 4 percent to $345 million, net income boomed 25 percent to $21 million—and about 97 percent of that profit stemmed from the new tax rules.

But Nixon's biggest gift to Schreiber's MCA related to TV.

By 1970, the three networks had become TV programmers for the world, handling foreign distributions rights for thousands of TV series. They already reached 95 percent of American households, and advertising revenues were booming. In 1968 networks received syndicated rerun profits from 60 percent of prime-time shows—compared to just 25 percent a decade earlier. Now the networks were producing more of their own TV shows—to the detriment of Universal and other major producers. Wasserman and other producers sued CBS and ABC in civil court, claiming they were violating antitrust laws by acting as both distributors and producers.

"That was quite a feat to sue the networks while you're still trying to sell them product," said Jerry Adler. While Wasserman placated the networks, Schreiber lobbied strenuously for Nixon to move against them. As it was, Nixon detested TV—a medium that showed him in his worst light. He believed that TV correspondents were rude and their bosses were out to get him. In 1970 Nixon's FCC implemented new rules to limit broadcasters' power. One rule prohibited the networks from syndicating shows; the other barred them from taking any financial interest in a show beyond its first run. The "fin-syn" rules protected such TV producers as Doug Cramer, Aaron

Spelling, Norman Lear—and Lew Wasserman, who sold programs to TV. It also unleashed a fountain of fresh, independently produced shows: *All in the Family, Sanford and Son, The Mary Tyler Moore Show, Dynasty, Love Boat, The Rockford Files* and dozens more.

But most important, Nixon's "fin-syn" rule gave Hollywood studios—especially Universal—a future stream of TV income. "It would be hard to trace," said the studio's lobbyist Jack Valenti. "But that rule would be worth $2 billion or more. Remember," he added, "the rules stayed in place for decades."

During Nixon's years in office, Schreiber delivered to Universal City—and the film industry—more valuable federal gifts than Wasserman ever had.

Lew's near-dismissal from MCA had shaken Edie. She had almost lost her standing in show business—the heart of her world—and that fact surely scared her. As Columbia studio head Harry Cohn once said, "Who will talk to me if I don't own a studio?" Who would talk to Edie if she and Lew lost their exalted perch? Edie had already experienced the pain and humiliation of falling from grace. She knew what it was like. "She'd always been coy about her past," said Marge LaRonge. Actually, she'd been trying to keep it secret.

Edie's father, Henry Beckerman, the son of a German rabbi, had immigrated to America when he was only three. By the time he was forty, in 1921, he was a millionaire—a rare achievement in those days. Beckerman had bought land in Cleveland that was soon developed into such communities as Maple Heights and Warrensville. He rode the real estate boom in Boca Raton, Florida, during the Roaring Twenties and, with partners, built an illegal casino and amusement park on Detroit's Belle Isle. By the time Edie was born, her father was practicing law without trying cases, and running Cleveland's City Hall without ever having been elected.

Around 1922, Beckerman and some of his friends embezzled money from the Cuyahoga County treasury, with the help of

Deputy Country Treasurer Alex Bernstein and two other officials. In fact, Beckerman and his cronies were said to have looted public coffers for years. He packed off one son to Harvard, helped another get into the laundry business, and sent his youngest child, Edie, to an elite academy. In 1927 the twelve-year-old attended Miss Anne Hathaway Brown's School for Girls—one of "the most advanced fashionable schools in the country," which boasted 18 acres, tennis courts, and an English garden. Edie studied Latin, math, and literature, and learned how to fence and serve tea.

The following year, however, Cleveland's property market fell apart and many speculators, including Beckerman, couldn't pay their property taxes. In November 1928, Bernstein called his friend Beckerman in a panic. State regulators were coming to examine the county's books in a few days; they'd certainly find out about the missing money. To replace the funds, Beckerman and his mentor, Maurice Maschke, borrowed $200,000 and quickly put it in the county coffers. State auditors blessed the county's books.

Edie Beckerman seemed blissfully ignorant of her father's problems. She drove her own car, collected a huge $185 weekly allowance, equivalent to almost $2,000 in 2003 dollars, and had a closet full of dresses. "She lived a charmed life," said Merle Jacobs. All that was to change. After the stock market crash in October 1929, Beckerman failed to meet a $100,000 margin call; in the fall of 1930, he pulled his daughter out of private school. "The Beckermans were socially prominent until then," said Arlene Rich, a Cleveland native. He enrolled Edie in a public high school in Cleveland Heights, where she struggled to adjust, barely passing classes and failing French. As the Depression deepened, her father lost some of his properties, and Edie began taking business classes. She scored an "A" in typing—her best grade ever.

The Depression squeezed thousands of Cleveland's families, but not all of them found their names splashed across the front pages of newspapers. In 1931 state auditors found $500,000 missing from the county treasury, much of it traced to Beckerman. He had not paid taxes on his real estate holdings for several years and, because of his friends in high places, county officials hadn't bothered to collect from him. In June 1932, Beckerman, Maschke, Bernstein, and City Councilman Herman Finkle were indicted for forgery and embezzlement. "Thirty-year-old Dynasty Totters as GOP Chiefs Face Accusations," the papers blared; the Beckerman indictments signaled a change in the city's political machinery. Day after day, the papers detailed the scandal, and Edie found herself shunned by upper-class acquaintances and ridiculed by public-school classmates. "There was always some question about the Beckermans after that," said LaRonge. The indictments pulled the family down into "a class of people that you didn't want to spend time with."

In July 1932, a grand jury called on Beckerman to explain his role. He claimed he had placed $200,000 into the county funds to help a former partner who couldn't pay his property taxes. But the excuse fell flat; the partner didn't own much property, and he'd been found dead not long before. Prosecutors were outraged that Beckerman would use a dead man as his scapegoat.

In the fall of Edie's senior year, her father stood trial. It was "the most outstanding criminal case in the history of the city," heard as a bench trial. In just twenty minutes, three friendly judges acquitted Beckerman and his friends. The prosecutor vowed to pursue "those responsible for the looting of the public treasury."

The Beckermans never regained their social standing—a fall from grace that left its mark on seventeen-year-old Edie. "Whenever someone made a quip about her father, Edie just turned up her nose," said a Cleveland woman. "She'd just say that her father was a great attorney." Sometimes Edie overcompensated with a bravura that grated. "She was a prima donna," LaRonge sniffed. "She'd say she just had lunch with some well-known person and generally pretend to be better than anybody else," added Dorothy Barton.

In June 1933, Edie graduated high school. She was accepted to

Ohio State University in Columbus but never completed a term. Instead, she found a clerk's job at the May Company and earned $18 a week. She continued living with her parents and spent her leisure time club-hopping in the city's café society. When the spunky brunette met the tall nightclub employee, she cared little that Wasserman hailed from the wrong side of the tracks. "No father would willingly let his daughter associate with anyone from show business," said Kay Thackery, another Midwesterner. But Edie's dad was in no position to object to his daughter's romantic choices. After Beckerman stood trial again in 1936, Edie became Mrs. Louis Wasserman. Six months later, when her husband received a job offer that would move them out of Cleveland, Edie seized her chance, said LaRonge. "The Beckermans had no money or standing, and Edie had to get out of town."

The young woman started over with a new name. She pushed and sacrificed to speed her husband's rise to the top, and her efforts—combined with his abilities—paid off well in the subsequent thirty-five years. Edie had no intention of ever being exiled again.

Edie wiped the slate clean on several fronts. Against Edie's express wishes, her only child, Lynne, had broken up with her husband. "Lynne said she only married Ronnie Lief because her mother had picked him out," said one of Lynne's friends. The überagent's daughter had married the then-MCA agent on her parents' wedding anniversary in 1962 in an effort to please her parents, according to some sources. Yet when Lynne divorced, Edie shunned her daughter for much of the following decade. "They had a falling out over something, as sometimes happens with families," said Janet Leigh. Lynne had a toddler, Carol Anne, and in 1970 was remarried to a stockbroker. In the meantime, Edie adopted other young women as surrogate daughters, ranging from Ronnie Lief's new bride, whom she introduced at parties as "my daughter," to Eve Foreman, wife of screenwriter Carl. "These were Edie's crypto-daughters," said an MCA executive. She no longer had agents' wives to cultivate as protégées and she turned to the spouses of other powerful men—members of the New Hollywood.

In the 1970s, Hollywood had a heightened sense of self-awareness. The old guard was crumbling while superstars were ascending. Paparazzi chased the nouveau riche, and everyone collided during lunch at Le Boite, St. Germain, or a few private clubs. Edie's girls shopped at Giorgio's, Gucci's, Bonwit's, and Amelia Gray's. They ran into each other at periodontists and hair salons. The gambling dens and dinner-dance clubs that had once crowded Sunset and La Cienega had vanished, replaced with topless bars, head shops, and purveyors of aphrodisiacs and hot tubs. The Temple of Oral Gratification now flanked Santa Monica Boulevard, not far from MCA's former colonial manse.

Edie kept abreast of the antiestablishment crowd, while maintaining some choice connections. She increased her activities at Cal Arts, the school founded by Walt Disney to cultivate young creative talent. She sat on the board of Cedars-Sinai Medical Center, where she organized benefits like stage productions. She once persuaded Frank Sinatra and Gene Kelly to perform "Singin' in the Rain" as a duet, which brought even Johnny Carson to his feet. Edie belonged to the Music Center's Amazing Blue Ribbon Club, a prestigious group of four hundred women.

In the mid-1960s, Lew had helped build the $50 million Los Angeles Music Center along with Buffy Chandler, wife of the *Los Angeles Times* publisher, but Edie and her "amazing" group now made sure that the cultural center served all of the city's residents. While Reagan was slashing state education programs, Edie and the ladies formed the Music Center Education Division, an arts outreach program. They bussed inner-city children to the downtown center to show them that live theater was not just for the affluent. Edie's work kept her aligned with the powerful WASP wives from Pasadena and San Marino.

Yet her closest friend was Joyce Haber, a syndicated columnist for the *Los Angeles Times*. "Edie and Joyce were best friends for years," said David Patrick Columbia, a New York society writer. Long before mass media, Hollywood lived in fear of gossip columnists Louella Parsons and Hedda Hopper. When Edie first came to town, she reportedly hired a publicist to plant her name in those two well-read columns, but Doris Stein trumped her every time.

Now Haber was the most powerful gossip in town, and Edie's name landed regularly in her column. Haber was a saucy blonde who wore bubble rings and pale lipstick. She was married to Doug Cramer, a vice president of ABC and later the producer of *Love Boat*. "Doug had quite a lot of clout and influence and, either helpfully or not, he gave her a lot of leads," said Charles Champlin, former *Los Angeles Times* critic. Haber wrote about New Hollywood and coined the phrase "'A' and 'B' lists." "She had great flair and a big following," said Champlin. "Haber was so popular, she had three telephone receptionists working for her," said Columbia. "She got hundreds of calls a day—including two a day from Edie. They used to go out all the time."

The two would sometimes meet at a hot spot run by Jack Hansen, whose store, Jax, had outfitted Edie's girls during the 1950s. Now he owned The Daisy, a discotheque where young stars boogied. At night, it was a private club for members only, "meaning that anyone with a thousand dollars or any hooker could join," Haber wrote. One might see Mia Farrow, Jane Fonda, or Michelle Phillips. "Aaron Spelling met his wife Candy here," said columnist George Christy. By day, The Daisy turned into a sidewalk café that overlooked Rodeo Drive and lured such hot agents as Sue Mengers. "You could slip out in the gardens for a snort or a toke," said Dominick Dunne. The dress code was platform wedgies, sequined hot pants, and turquoise jewelry—not exactly Edie's style, but she liked being au courant, said Christy. "It's where starlets went looking for their big breaks."

Edie and Joyce also saw each other at "A" list parties, usually dinners that took place inside Beverly Hills homes. Hostesses served superb food prepared by their house staffs—except for Edie, who still hired Chasen's. "A"-listers like Edie also rented houseplants so they could be replaced regularly with fresh ones; hired florist David Jones for his stunning orchid displays; and asked Edith Head or Arnold Scaasi to design their special gowns. Edie read several newspapers a day, as well as the trades, and now had two telephone lines in her home, including one with a long cord that allowed her to roam the house during protracted conversations.

Edie sometimes fed her columnist friend tidbits. "Joyce could be vicious," said her editor, James Bellows. Some called her "Joyce Saber." When Julie Andrews learned that the gossipmonger was going to have open-heart surgery, she said that doctors "should go in through her feet." In 1970 Haber unwittingly printed a false item from the FBI, reporting that Jean Seberg was pregnant—not by her husband but by a Black Panther. Seberg grew so upset that she took an overdose of sleeping pills, resulting in a miscarriage of her Caucasian baby. Over the years, it caused so much pain that Seberg tried suicide several times before her death in 1979.

Meanwhile, Doris Stein cultivated her own social standing. "She thought she was related to the queen of France, although that tie must have gone way, way back," said one of her relatives. Like Marie Antoinette, the sixtyish Doris kept her white hair coiffed impeccably, her face powdered and rouged, and her Louis XVI tables so polished, they could blind a visitor. She was named often in George Christy's *Hollywood Reporter* column—"I called her 'the empress,' and she just loved that," he said. Doris's dinner parties were still coveted invitations, but she found it harder to get Jules out of the house. Once Stein asked his wife if they needed a driver for New Year's Eve. After learning that Doris was taking him to six parties, he cried: "Driver? We'll need an ambulance."

Doris now partied with Elton John—"one of Jules's favorite

singers," Wasserman said—and held suppers for "the pretender to the throne of Botswana," Tanen recalled. "Doris drank a lot, but I'm sure you've heard all of those stories," Dunne told me. Once the tipsy woman tottered out of the Beverly Hills Hotel, climbed into her Rolls-Royce, and immediately put it in reverse, running over a bed of geraniums. "Oopsie," she said, before speeding off with a wave. Said Dunne, "Those were the times we lived in, and Doris fit right in." At one of her famed dinner parties, Dunne found himself sitting between the Duchess of Argyle and Mae West. At another party, Doris was seen laughing with Mick Jagger of the Rolling Stones. "She loved people and, as she grew older, didn't care what others thought of her," said famed couturier Luis Estevez.

Privately, she had her own mother-daughter problems. The divorce of her eldest child, Jean, had dashed Doris's hope that the vanden Heuvels would someday become a political power couple. But Doris's role in society embarrassed Jean. "Mother was a very remarkable woman, and she was of great help to my father. But getting into that little social world [wasn't] something I wanted to do," Jean said.

Unwittingly, perhaps, Jean followed in her mother's footsteps, throwing parties that were featured in society columns and glossy magazines. Her social affairs revolved around liberal—not conservative—politics, and were filled with bohemian friends, rather than community pillars. Jean possessed what her friend Alexander Cockburn called a "whim of iron," replete with eclectic tastes and no day job. New Journalist Tom Wolfe detailed in his famous essay, "Radical Chic and Mau-Mauing the Flak Catchers," how Jean and other Park Avenue types courted Black Panthers. Meanwhile, Jules and Doris fumed at their wayward child and threatened to disinherit her.

Their younger daughter, Susan, was even worse. An inveterate party giver, she'd been featured in *Cosmopolitan* magazine, which noted: "She serves drinks in the elevator and dinners around the pool table." Susan lived in New York's stately Dakota co-op apartment building, ran a travel agency funded by her father, and, against his wishes, appeared in a Broadway play. In December 1968 Susan surprised her parents by showing up with Gil Shiva, her tall, dark, Israeli fiancé, and insisted on marrying him right away. "Doris almost had a coronary when Susan married him," said realtor Bruce Nelson. The playboy was not the sort of new son-in-law the Steins had envisioned. Yet Doris hastily planned a little ceremony at "Stein Simeon," as her friends now called her mansion, and she threw a reception. Interior decorator Billy Haines, designer Jimmy Galanos, the Sam Goldwyns, and her bosom buddies, Dolly Green and Anne Ford, attended.

Edie Wasserman and Doris Stein shared similar anxieties. They privately worried about who would inherit their august mantles, and how their daughters would survive in their divorces and new marriages. They clucked over their husbands, who grew preoccupied with MCA's enormous debt and cloudy future. Edie and Doris had played primary roles in the palace revolt, and each had known just how far to go. "Hollywood wives are powerful that way," said Dunne. "They can break up friendships between men." As for Edie, she knew when to stop. Her husband's job depended on his finessing the delicate new relationships with Schreiber and Stein. If Edie intended to keep her perch, she'd have to bide her time. Edie and Doris began maintaining an uneasy détente.

TWENTY-SEVEN

THANKS TO HIS CONTRETEMPS WITH SCHREIBER, Jennings Lang was no longer heading television at Universal. But he couldn't resist annoying his nemesis. One Friday afternoon, after arguing with Schreiber, Lang arranged for some studio craftsmen, painters, and plasterers to come in over the weekend and seal Schreiber's office door. "I mean, he removed the door, as well as any trace of a door, to his rival's office," said Sean Daniel, a production assistant. When Taft arrived for work Monday morning, he found a blank wall where his office door used to be and couldn't figure out what had happened.

Even with new management in place, the TV division remained a manic place, said Frank Price. "All of these guys were very vocal. You're not dealing with subtle chess players here." Ned Tanen added: "They are in-your-face screamers." Lang would yell at Sheinberg, who would "say some not very kind thing to him," he admitted. Price and Sheinberg jostled for position, and the junior executives were left to decipher the power plays. "I think that part of Lew's modus operandi was to set up what appeared to be a balance of powers," said Price. "But that wasn't always a happy situation."

Wasserman and Lang often had shouting matches that could be heard a few floors below. "Lew supported Lang, but Jennings could be a strong critic of Lew and felt a competitiveness towards him," said Sheinberg. "On occasion, Lew was not as deferential as he should have been to Jennings," who was two years older than Lew. "It became a complex relationship."

After one especially nasty quarrel with Wasserman, Lang stewed for a few days. Then, after a few drinks, he climbed into his private plane and headed for the Black Tower. "In his relaxed condition, he flew his plane around the Tower several times," said Daniel. Lang wanted to see if Wasserman was shaking his fist from his window—until it dawned on him. "It was the weekend and no one was in the office," Daniel explained.

Wasserman actually owed a great deal to Jennings and his creative crew. In 1971 MCA's revenues were flat, but its profits had zoomed 26 percent. Wasserman cut costs in many areas of his company—but not Universal TV, which was on its way to producing the largest number of series in its history. The division now accounted for 37 percent of the company's gross revenue—or $130 million. Thanks in large part to TV, Wasserman had managed to whittle MCA's debt from $100 million to approximately $70 million in about two years. Lang reminded Wasserman who had helped him achieve that.

"He's the one who really got the last batch of guys, including me, some stock," said Tanen. Until then, only forty-five MCA veterans had been given stock in MCA—all in the 1950s. Lang told Wasserman that his creative crew—Sheinberg, Price, Tanen, and a few others—had lined up for him during his dark hour. "You'd better give these people, including me, some stock or we're going to leave you. It's been long enough." Wasserman agreed.

For the first time in MCA's history, it tried selling TV programs to all three networks—no easy feat. CBS was very resistant to any overtures from MCA, said Price. "There were some very hard-nosed attitudes against MCA." The bad blood went back to Schreiber who, in the 1940s, had helped raid the radio network's stable of stars. "They still hated us for that," said Price. And ABC was still behind in the TV movie business, as its then-chief-executive Leonard Goldenson later publicly admitted. ABC eventually signed a deal with MCA, although Wasserman himself scuttled an early opportunity.

Roy Huggins had told Wasserman about one of his new concepts: shorter films for TV. He had directed a 77-minute movie for Columbia Pictures in 1952 called *Hangman's Knot* and wanted to do the same for the small screen. He told Wasserman that he wanted to film a 90-minute movie—something different from Universal's two-hour *World Premieres*.

Huggins dubbed his idea *Movie of the Week*, borrowing the title from *Life* magazine's regular film column. But Wasserman believed it would compete against NBC's *World Premieres* and declined. Huggins, who was free to take his idea elsewhere, tried CBS, but was turned away. Then he visited his friends at the third-place network.

"ABC loved Roy because of all he had done for them," said Price. Huggins had created the network's best series—*Maverick, The Fugitive,* and *77 Sunset Strip*. But in the late 1960s, the network was ranked third out of three. Huggins met with ABC executive Leonard Goldberg and his assistant, Barry Diller, and laid out his idea: He'd produce a 90-minute movie for $400,000, if ABC would buy twenty-six of them per season. The executives looked at each other. "I thought that this could actually work," Diller reportedly said. He told Huggins he'd get back to him. But, according to Huggins, ABC executives went behind his back and met with MCA executives. The network wanted to hire Universal TV to produce weekly movies for ABC. "But Wasserman had a problem," said Price. He was charging NBC a fat $800,000 to produce two-hour movies. For a 90-minute movie, the price should be about $600,000. Agreeing to ABC's $400,000 deal would put Wasserman in the awkward position of producing an ABC movie that ran 75 percent as long as the NBC program time—but at half the price. "Lew knew that NBC would either want a price cut or demand to know why it was being over-charged," said Price. Even if he could find a way around the dilemma, he wouldn't make much money with ABC. "Lew had to wrestle with that for a while."

Wasserman tried to negotiate a higher price, but ABC would not budge. During the talks, Sheinberg and Diller started arguing. According to Diller's reported account, Sheinberg insisted that if Universal did this deal for ABC, it would have to produce all of ABC's TV shows. (Sheinberg denied this.) The twenty-five-year-old Diller tried to bluff and got up from the table. Instead, Wasserman walked out, telling the young man, "Don't ever make an offer unless you're willing to walk away from it." Diller's response was to start shopping around the *Movie of the Week* concept. Many other pro-ducers wanted the ABC order, worth an estimated $11 million. But only Universal had the well-oiled TV factory to actually produce it.

Wasserman then tried to revive the deal. He said Universal would agree to ABC's original terms of $400,000 per show. And although Diller had discovered that independent producers would create movies for as little as $350,000, his ABC boss wanted to hire Uni-versal as the exclusive producer. They asked Wasserman for an addi-tional price break, but he wouldn't budge from $400,000. So ABC chief Goldenson convinced the network's board to invest $14 million to form its own production company. It signed deals with such producers as Aaron Spelling and Merv Adelson's Lorimar—which got its start from this deal.

Huggins was furious. Diller had not only stolen his idea, he had cut him out of the action. "Roy thought about suing ABC, but decided against it," said Price. Later, ABC offered Huggins a chance to produce some of those movies, but Huggins was so insulted that he refused. When ABC's weekly movie debuted in the fall of 1969, it drew big ratings. *Movie of the Week* became a seminal hit, and many executives—including Diller—boosted their careers by claiming credit for it. Wasserman later admitted to Sheinberg that it was a mistake to try to inflate the price of those ABC films. Universal could have owned the entire ABC franchise.

But Price saw the failure as an opportunity. "I know all the guys at ABC well," he said. "Yet we don't do any business with them." He went to Wasserman and said, "Let me see what I can do." Wasserman promoted him to executive vice president and told him to sell ABC a series.

Price and his crew developed *Marcus Welby* for them. While ABC's *Movie of the Week* scored fine ratings, the network couldn't keep an audience on Saturday nights. "So I sold them their first *Suspense Movie*," said Price. Then he sold them the idea of having a regular series—twenty-two mystery movies in a season. Once again, Diller refused to give Universal an exclusive agreement, said Price. "But I made a deal where we would do thirteen, and the rest [eleven] would be filled by others." The compromise allowed Price to bring in a $5 million contract—Universal's first big sale to ABC.

Price received a call from Wasserman an hour later. Uncharacteristically, the mogul congratulated him. "Lew had a full plate at the time, with the movies, the tours, and all the development," said Price. "But from then on, every time I sold ABC something, he'd call me."

Universal TV became such a formidable sales engine that other studio chiefs wanted to hire away its TV executives. But none dared do so without Lew's blessing. When Paramount Studios' chairman needed a seasoned executive to manage his TV division, "Charlie Bluhdorn talked to his good friend Lew," said Price.

"Look," Bluhdorn said, "you have a lot of executives with depth and strength in your TV department, and I don't. We're buddies, goddammit, so why don't you let Frank Price come over with me? It's only one guy I'm taking."

Wasserman said, "Forget about it."

Another time, William Paley of CBS wanted Price to run its Cinema Center Films. Paley flew out to Universal Studios to discuss Price over lunch with Lew. "I saw them go into the fancy dining room behind the commissary and thought: 'What's going on?' It turned out they were talking about me," said Price. Paley explained that he needed a veteran producer, so why not let Price go? Wasserman said no. "He didn't like Paley tampering with his contract people," said Jerry Adler. Most of Universal TV's executives heard about the meeting a few hours later, said Adler. "I'm not sure how sincere Frank was about keeping his position at Universal, but it was a great opportunity for him to enhance his position."

CBS eventually contracted with independent producers for their prime-time fare. By 1973, the network would rule Saturday nights with five classic shows: *All in the Family*, created by Norman Lear; *M*A*S*H*, by Larry Gelbart; *The Mary Tyler Moore Show*, by Grant Tinker; *The Bob Newhart Show*, also by Tinker, and *The Carol Burnett Show*, which was her own production. CBS programming chief Fred Silverman once said that his Saturday lineup was "probably the best single night in the history of TV."

Price himself used the idea of 90-minute movies to launch some new series for ABC. In 1973 he developed several films that became the basis for *The Six Million Dollar Man*, starring Lee Majors, which ran until 1978; *The Bionic Woman*, starring Lindsay Wagner; *The Incredible Hulk*, starring Lou Ferrigno, and *Battlestar Galactica*. "Suddenly we went from having nothing on at ABC, to having one hour, to being their biggest supplier with five hours of prime-time TV a week," said Price. Universal was now programming 25 percent of ABC's programs.

With Jennings Lang now producing movies full time, Sidney Sheinberg became head of Universal TV in 1970, and soon developed a close relationship with NBC's Herb Schlosser, who had replaced Bob Kintner. Sheinberg's favored producers, Link and Levinson, had written another Columbo movie, *Ransom for a Dead Man* (1971). "Again we were the number-one show that week," said Link. "So, now, NBC is salivating for a weekly series." The same problem surfaced: Falk, Link, and Levinson feared the grueling production schedule. But this time, Wasserman wasn't about to let a sale slip by. He and Lang devised a new programming concept. They'd create four different series and rotate each one into a two-hour prime-time slot on Sunday evenings. They called it "The Wheel," and, under Sheinberg's hand, this concept broke new ground. One spoke of the wheel would come from Link and Levinson; Sheinberg asked them to write and produce a *Columbo* series. But instead of producing twenty-four weekly shows, they'd create six dramas. The writers resisted, said Link. "We didn't think we could do it, but Sid insisted." Sheinberg added, "I just tried to inspire them to do the work that the rest of the world didn't think they could do." Sid told Link and Levinson they could easily write and produce six ninety-minute dramas in five months. After a marathon meeting in Sid's office, the duo agreed. "We walked out of his office feeling very light-headed."

Sheinberg turned his heat on another writer-producer, Leonard Stern, who created the second spoke of the wheel with *MacMillan and Wife*. It became so popular that the movie spawned its own twenty-six-week series. For the third spoke, Adler hoped to use a script about a New Mexican cop who goes to New York to solve crimes. It became known as *Coogan's Bluff*. "I was going to produce it for a TV movie, but Jennings cherry-picked the script and stole it," Adler said. It became the first film produced by Clint Eastwood on Universal's lot.

Adler found something else to fill the third slot: *McCloud.* Starring Dennis Weaver, it grew into a long-running series that, in 2000, was still being syndicated. "*Columbo* was by far the most popular," said Link. "We never did find a successful fourth spoke."

The Wheel concept turned into *NBC Mystery Movie,* in which a different detective entertained viewers for two hours every Sunday night. "We started developing a better reputation," said Sheinberg. "And I'll take a lot of credit, because no one will give it to me. We did slick, heavy-production-value, pseudo-star shows, and, believe me, it was a trying time. Revue Studios was probably more profitable in the 1950s. But we basically put MCA [TV] on the quality map."

The Wheel was a clever stroke for producers because big stars were more attracted to a movie project than a TV series. They had to commit to only six shows—not twenty-six—in a season, and so could be free of the small screen's hectic pace. And many of the movies spun off long-running series. "It was good for us, good for Universal, and great for NBC," said Link.

During the 1960s, Universal TV had established itself as the wizard of TV programming, consistently creating new formats. "Lang encouraged you to stretch and was very open-minded. In fact, he'd rather hear a wild idea than a traditional concept," Price said. Now, in the 1970s, the division was selling these formats to all three networks, giving each of them shows that attracted high ratings. "Every year we would come up with something theatrical and different," said Sheinberg. In 1969 he had helped create *The Bold Ones,* another revolving series that won awards. It included *The New Doctors, The Lawyers,* and *The Senator.* "No one thought people would sit still for rotating characters in rotating formats," said Sheinberg. "But they did. We only made a few of them, but they were quite good." For the first time, Universal TV's shows received awards and rave reviews regularly. Best of all, the division collected an astounding $305 million in programming contracts and fees.

In 1971 Sheinberg and NBC programmer Mort Viner made the

first two-part series for television. The network invested more than $2 million to produce a four-hour movie shown on two nights. *Vanished* was based on a best seller by Fletcher Knebel, and starred Robert Young and Richard Widmark. It told the tale of a presidential adviser who had disappeared. When it debuted in March 1971, it made TV history.

Pretty soon young talent flocked to Wasserman's lot. "Today television is all twenty-five-year-olds, but back then it was different," said Jerry Freedman. "It used to be very hard for young guys to get into the directing business." If an aspiring director, a Martin Scorsese or Woody Allen, couldn't find an independent way to finance his film, he might apprentice at Universal for a spell. "They didn't pay you any money, but they promised that if you were a good writer, you could write or produce a TV show." Soon, twenty-something kids arrived, sporting sideburns and wearing jeans. "A lot of guys came from blue-collar families, hungry to work at a studio," said Ross Johnson, a former editor at the *Hollywood Reporter*. They learned how to produce a TV show as a crash course. Before a TV producer received a green light to film a show at Universal, Wasserman gave him two weeks to obtain a script, props, actors, and equipment—on a minuscule budget. Once that was in place, Universal gave a producer sixteen days to shoot his show, said Adler. "That was Lew's Rule, and God help you if you broke it."

Price capitalized on this influx of new young talent. He started a farm-club system in which he'd pair up-and-coming writers and directors with seasoned producers. "I always emphasized the writer-producer. That's the key talent in television." Without a good script and an experienced producer, Price couldn't sell a network show. He paired Huggins with newcomer Stephen J. Cannell, who worked on *Ironside* and grew into one of Universal's most successful writer-producers. Price paired producer David Victor (*Marcus Welby*) with Steve Bochco, who cocreated the first surfer detective series, *Richie Brockelman*, and left to create the acclaimed *Hill Street Blues* and *NYPD Blue*. Such veterans as Bill Sackheim and Jack Laird helped young directors, including Sydney Pollack (*Out of Africa*), John Badham (*Saturday Night Fever*), David Lowell Rich (*Airport '79*), and Michael Ritchie (*Downhill Racer*). "After a year or two with more experienced people, the young writers could produce their own shows," said Price. Universal was seeding the next generation of hot TV talent.

But gaining entrée was not easy. "There was a lot of resentment at the time about young guys coming onto the lot, and a lot of sub-terfuge against them," said Freedman. The older guys had sweated during TV's dark days, and now these young bucks wanted to shove them aside. "A lot of guys came in with an attitude and would snarl and disrespect the veterans," said Freedman. They didn't last long. "You had to cooperate and show you were willing to learn," added Cannell. Then you'd get a chance.

One guy who understood the system was Steven Spielberg, who had made friends with old-timer Chuck Silver, head of Universal's film stock. Spielberg had shown Silver his twenty-six-minute film, *Amblin,* which had been released in 1968, and Silver showed it to Sheinberg, who liked it so much that Sheinberg asked to meet "this scrawny twenty-year-old."

"What do you see yourself doing?" Sheinberg asked Spielberg.

"I see myself as a writer, director, and filmmaker, Mr. Sheinberg. But I just have one request. In my heart, I want to direct something before I'm twenty-one."

Sheinberg didn't promise anything but signed him to a seven-year contract. Spielberg's first job was directing the second of a three-part pilot for Rod Serling's *Night Gallery.* Originally, the show was sup-posed to star Bette Davis, but the diva refused to work with a twenty-one-year-old. When Joan Crawford was selected, she refused to be seen publicly with Spielberg; she felt uneasy about his ability to direct. She dialed Wasserman, her former agent-turned-studio-chief, and said this young director couldn't direct traffic. "Can't you find another director?" she asked. "Joan," Wasserman told her, "if you're unhappy with him, don't complain. Because if you do, they'll fire you." So the actress held her tongue and soldiered on. She was playing an older, rich woman obsessed about losing her sight. "Spielberg is very visual," said Price. "And this was an interior show with an old-time star who could be difficult under any circumstances. Some kid directing her was not likely to get her best effort."

The show aired in November 1969 and flopped. "In all of the years we were in business with NBC, I never received any phone calls from them objecting to the work of a director," said Sheinberg. "But this piece was so bad, NBC asked that Spielberg never do anything again." Spielberg admitted it was a mistake, saying he would have done better financing his own films, rather than directing television for Universal. "I was a pariah in Hollywood after that," he said, and didn't work for eighteen months.

Still, Sheinberg always kept Spielberg in mind. Sometime later, in the commissary, Sheinberg saw Epstein and Dick Irving, "who looked as though their best friend had just died." Sheinberg learned they were about to shoot a show but had no director. "I suggested Steven, but they immediately got nervous," said Sheinberg. "Then I really leaned on them. 'For God's sake, he's a talented guy, he's not my brother-in-law, and he'd be great for this.' " Spielberg eventually directed an episode of *The Name of the Game*. "But it was a forgettable effort," said critic Brian Fairbanks. Nevertheless, it started a relationship with Epstein, who over the years helped Spielberg finally overcome a series of failures. Said Freedman, "Steven had an old guy's sensibility in a young man's body, and he fit in well with the pros at Universal TV."

TWENTY-EIGHT

THE GLAMORTRAM PULLED UP TO A BUNGALOW on the back lot in the early 1970s. The tour guide recited the curriculum vitae of its occupant: Edith Head, Hollywood's greatest costume designer, has created costumes for more than 400 films. She's been nominated for an Academy Award thirty-four times and won seven Oscars (soon to be eight), or more than Billy Wilder. "Let's see if she's available," the guide said. At that, the bus driver honked his horn, and a birdlike lady appeared, her face framed by dark bangs and shaded by tinted spectacles. The tourists were awed, recalled a guide. "She'd come out with a pencil in her bun and some sketches in her hand, as though she were working hard." Head would graciously sign autographs and wave good-bye, just like a star.

Like the sets of *Adam-12* or *Ironside*, Edith Head was a Universal Studio Tour attraction. Prior to joining the studio, she had spent forty-four years at Paramount Pictures. She had dressed hundreds of glamorous women and given Carole Lombard, Barbara Stanwyck, and Audrey Hepburn some of their on-screen flair. A clever self-promoter, Head had also designed dresses for Edie Wasserman, Hollywood's real-life leading lady. So when Edie Wasserman heard that the new owners of Paramount had fired the famed costumer, she immediately called her husband. Universal hired Head in 1967, but didn't give the seventy-year-old the salary or esteem that she had once enjoyed at Paramount. Even so, she had a steady job. Instead of working on forty films a year, she was now making five pictures—including *Airport* and *The Sting*—while giving a little thrill to the sightseers on the Universal Tour.

In 1972 some 1.5 million people peeked inside the studio's gates. That year, the tour business really took off and brought in some $4 million a year, according to Harrison "Buzz" Price, who had advised Wasserman on this venture. The consultant had helped Walt Disney build Disneyland in 1953, had set up a few World's Fairs, and was an expert on resorts and parks. "Wasserman knew I was heavy into Disney and he liked that," said Price. Wasserman had hired Price as early as 1961 to explore the potential of what Lew called Revue

Village. "Lew knew he had a great piece of property at Universal, and he played around with the idea of an attraction."

The mogul's acreage was "a marvelous location in the center of town," Price explained. "It had a great show-business history and thematic context." It could exhibit its TV stages, show period sets of a French villa, or demonstrate filmmaking techniques. Price told Wasserman he could make an immediate profit by charging admission and selling souvenirs, food, and drink. But Wasserman didn't jump at the opportunity, Price recalled. "He was a real pragmatist. I've worked for a lot of tigers over the years and Lew had a lot of wisdom and sly intelligence. He was like Walt [Disney] in that he was beyond ego, or at least he was in my dealings with him."

Wasserman continued to review Buzz Price's proposals, even after the mogul officially started his studio tour in 1964. A couple of years later, the studio chief looked into the idea of building a theme park. Throughout it all, Wasserman patrolled his tour operations like a general on duty. "I remember him coming out for inspection or escorting some VIPs and being very stern and frowning," said Laura Meyers, a tour guide in the 1970s. Wasserman regularly inspected his guides, who were students. "It was really a waste of his time, but in those days, we were all in fear of him," Meyers said. The students referred to the fourteen-story executive building as the "Tower of Fear." Wasserman forbade nepotism in his executive ranks, but the platoon of tour guides were the offspring of executives, stars, and directors.

Once an old lady presented a 1915 Universal token bought during the studio's tour in Carl Laemmle's day. She insisted her token was good and refused to pay the $6 admission. "We had to let her in," groused Jay Stein (no relation to Jules), manager of the tour operations. By this time, the actors had gotten used to tourists appearing on sets and accepted them as fans. John Wayne, Kirk Douglas, Gregory Peck, and Charlton Heston posed for photos. "They saw that it was good public relations," Stein said.

Wasserman kept looking for ways to squeeze more money from his sprawling operations. One brilliant idea came from an unlikely source, recalled publicist Herb Steinberg. One of the most popular attractions was Universal's stunt shows, which were held in an outdoor arena. "A young kid on the tour, Danny Bramson, said to me, 'Why don't we try to set up concert here?' " Steinberg said. "We have three thousand seats and room for another two thousand people to sit on those stone steps."

On Labor Day weekend in 1968, the studio booked the Peanut, Popcorn and Coca-Cola Film Festival, where it showed some of its old Paramount and Universal films, such as those starring Mae West and Boris Karloff. The response was "unbelievable!" said the publicist. "We had a [backup] on the freeway every night because of the traffic." The gimmick was this: For $1.50, viewers got free parking, old movies, popcorn, and peanuts. "But you had to buy the Coke, as Coca-Cola had paid for the advertising," said Steinberg. One night, the studio played a Marx Brothers' movie, he said. Wasserman, Schreiber, and a few other executives watched as a new generation discovered the delightful antics of MCA's former agency clients. "Taft called his old friends Harpo and Groucho and said, 'You've got to come down here and see this. These kids love your movies.' " Clearly, Universal could attract paying customers to its lot in the evenings, too.

In 1972 Wasserman brought Harrison Price back for another study, this time to expand the tour. The concert idea was applauded, and Jay Stein began building an amphitheater. "Ned [Tanen] was helpful because of his connections to the music business," said Stein. He helped line up acts and sound experts to ensure its success. "We couldn't have done it without Ned," Stein explained. For the amphitheater's opening, Stein planned a special ceremony and commissioned a seven-foot-high bronzed statue of

Tanen. "We had trained a pigeon to come and crap on Ned's statue. And it did, right on cue, while Sid and Lew watched." The new generation of executives were creating new forms of hazing in the MCA tradition.

The first act to appear at the Universal Amphitheater was the Grateful Dead. As Wasserman drove off the lot, he passed a procession of hippies walking up the hill. From the other direction, a swarm of long-haired kids in tie-dyed T-shirts approached carrying bongs and pipes. "There is a huge line of people waiting to see Jerry Garcia, and Wasserman turns right around and heads back," said Tanen. He rode the elevator to the penthouse floor, and found Tanen. "What in the hell are you trying to do to my company?" Wasserman bellowed.

Don't worry, Tanen explained. They're just Deadheads—3,500 or so theater patrons. Wasserman scowled. "The Grateful Dead is not quite what I had in mind for the amphitheater," he said.

Universal Amphitheater concerts triggered a 30 percent jump in tour attendance that year, making it the fastest-growing outdoor attraction in Southern California. For the balance of that summer, though, it booked less-flamboyant acts like The Carpenters, John Denver, and artists on MCA Records. It also drew 250,000 people to the stage presentation of *Jesus Christ Superstar,* the Andrew Lloyd Webber/Tim Rice rock opera—a year before MCA released its low-budget, high-grossing film of the same name.

By 1973, Wasserman's Universal Studios had evolved into a multifaceted marketing machine. "We kept getting involved in these weird projects, and a lot of them turned out to be quite successful," said Tanen. "And most of them didn't cost anything." Wasserman kept adding "gimmicks," such as a Junior Stunt School for children; a simulated view of a hurricane from the storm's eye, and the parting of the Red Sea. Indeed, he liked the tour business so much that he expanded it to Washington D.C., where he bought a tour operation that squired people around Arlington National Cemetery and the National Mall. He began exploring the idea of a Universal Studio theme park in Orlando, Florida, twelve years before actually breaking ground. But every move had to be studied and plotted by his own executives, then verified by outside consultants. "You had to be logical with Lew and present a plan, step-by-step," said Jay Stein. "He'd wait for you to slip up just once in your presentation; then he'd zoom in and exploit it. He wasn't doing it maliciously. But you had to be sure of your facts. If you didn't have all of the evidence on your side at that moment, it could be torture.

"You didn't wing it with Lew."

Meanwhile, Taft Schreiber was pursuing his own projects. He had not given up on the idea of merging MCA with a blue-chip firm. After the failed Westinghouse bid, Schreiber discussed a merger with his friend, Leonard Firestone, head of Firestone Tire and Rubber Company. The two Republicans both supported Reagan and shared many views, but their companies didn't have much in common. The $2 billion rubber conglomerate didn't even own a TV or radio station. Firestone offered to buy MCA's eight million shares—nearly three-quarters of which were held by MCA executives—for $325 million. He promised to give MCA complete autonomy, but Wasserman didn't like the prospective arrangement, and it soon died.

Schreiber and Al Dorskind set up merger talks with Xerox Corporation. "They were in the communication business, with their paper copiers, and I thought we should be in communications, too," said Dorskind. He proposed inviting Xerox executives to dinner at Schreiber's house, but Schreiber balked. "Let's use your house," he said. Dorskind had recently moved into his place and didn't have much furniture. Schreiber told him to get the studio's prop department to outfit his new home. "I came home from work one day, and the place looked great," said Dorksind. He had new carpets, chairs, and tasteful pictures on the wall. The catered dinner that night was delicious, but the talks didn't proceed any further. The next day, the props department moved out the lovely furnishings.

Meanwhile, Wasserman kept trying to parse expenses and lift MCA's star even higher. In 1970 he and his friend Charles Bluhdorn of Paramount Pictures formed Cinema International Corporation to distribute motion pictures abroad. Other studios had formed partnerships on a country-by-country basis to sell films in foreign markets, but CIC was its own entity. The offshore tax shelter would save both studios billions of dollars over the next thirty years.

Income from MCA's savings and loan business tripled in 1971 to a historic high of $2 million and assets had grown 800 percent, thanks to a healthy real estate market. "Every big outfit worth its salt has a real estate arm that plays around," said Harrison Price. During the 1970s, Chrysler, Alcoa, Ford Motors, and others invested in property, and MCA was no different. Al Dorksind headed MCA's development unit, which became a hedge for Universal, said Price. "In case their movies were lousy, they could still make some money," even if it was only $2 million—a few weeks of box-office receipts from a hit film.

By now, Schreiber's federal and state lobbying efforts, along with Wasserman's improving management skills and tax dodges, started turning MCA's losses into profits. But Lew still had to fulfill one key duty. "Find a successor," Stein had been nagging him since the late 1960s. "MCA never really built people," said Frank Price. Wasserman had spent years grooming Jay Kanter and Jerry Gershwin, but after both men left, he hadn't replaced them. To rise through the ranks, an executive had to seize power or fight among his peers. "I wasn't going to get into that," said Price.

Jennings Lang kept pushing some of the younger bucks, especially Sheinberg. "In a sense, a lot of us were protégés of Jennings," said Price. Tanen agreed: "Jennings could be riotously funny and disgustingly vulgar, but in retrospect, I think he was the only one who was having fun." Still, Wasserman took his time.

There were only a few candidates, and Tanen was one of them. "Lew and I talked about it for, like, a minute. But there was no way in the world I would do it," said Tanen. Dark, moody, and mercurial, Tanen was not the best manager of people, he himself granted. Dominick Dunne recalled an experience he had with Tanen, producing Universal's film *Play It As It Lays* (1972), based on the novel by Joan Didion, the wife of John Gregory Dunne, Dominick's brother. At their first meeting, Tanen told Dunne, "This is a piece of crap." Dunne recalled, "He never once said anything nice about the project, and I got into a huge fight with him at the end."

Frank Price might have been a candidate. But after he had contemplated leaving MCA for Paramount or CBS, he was knocked out of the running. "I was on the traitors' list because I had tried to leave," he said.

That left Sheinberg, whom Lang had championed all along. "Jennings kept shoving Sid in Lew's face and bringing him along," said Tanen. Once, after Wasserman, Sheinberg, and the others screened a movie on the fifteenth floor, Wasserman stopped Jerry Adler to chew him out. The chief began yelling so loudly that Sheinberg walked away. "I don't want to be a witness to this," he said. Wasserman froze. "That was a turning point in Sid's career," said Adler. "After that, Lew saw Sid in a whole different light."

Later, Wasserman approached Sheinberg in the deep-carpeted hallway and slipped his arm over his shoulders. "What are you doing to bring young people into the division?"

"Gee," said the thirty-something. "I thought *I* was young."

"Well, you always have to bring in younger people to the business." Then Wasserman walked off. "That shook me up," said Sheinberg.

The lawyer had been at Universal for nearly fifteen years—most of that time at Universal TV. The unit was healthy, Sheinberg was loyal, and he told Wasserman everything that was going on in his division. Even better, Sheinberg stood up to Wasserman. "I'm very direct, and so is Lew," said Sheinberg.

In 1972 Wasserman raised the issue of succession with him. The younger man said he didn't want to be president. He liked working in TV with writers and producers. He didn't believe he was up to the responsibility of heading the company; he'd never even taken an accounting course. "The idea of being responsible for the profit and loss of the company was scary," he explained. "And besides, who was kidding whom? To even try and step into Lew Wasserman's shoes was scary at the time." He resisted.

Over a tuna sandwich in the commissary, Wasserman ordered Sheinberg to accept the presidency. "At the next board meeting, I'm nominating you for the presidency. I'm recommending you at the next shareholders' meeting, and I'm ordering you to replace yourself in TV."

"That's when I really got scared," said Sheinberg. The die was cast. After twenty-seven years, Stein was retiring, Wasserman was becoming chairman, and MCA had a new president. The new chief, who was raised in a middle-class home in Texas, was an attorney who knew contracts and clauses. He would alter MCA's corporate culture considerably and help shape a new era in Hollywood.

Sheinberg's first challenge was to earn respect from his former peers. "I had to relate to people I had never worked with and learn from them," he said. Division chiefs in the music, film, theme park, and other units were supposed to report to him. "All of these people wanted to continue reporting to Wasserman," not some thirty-eight-year-old. "It wasn't as if Lew went away. It was a period of time before I could fight my way into the job." Sheinberg's real job was to free Lew from day-to-day responsibilities so he could look at the big picture. There was plenty to think about. The other studios were selling off real estate, MGM was auctioning Dorothy's slippers from *The Wizard of Oz,* and the film industry had debts and inventories that amounted to more than $600 million.

The industry could not live on fin-syn and IRS rules alone. It needed new products and fresh ideas to lure more customers and expand its markets. Did Wasserman, who had just turned sixty, still have the vision to see the next new trend? Could Lew lead MCA into a new future for Hollywood?

TWENTY-NINE

EARLY ONE MORNING IN MAY 1973, Lew Wasserman approached the Rexall Drug Building on the corner of La Cienega and Beverly Boulevard—about ten blocks east of his old office. Through the window, he could see its early-twentieth-century marble counters, ornamental mirrors, and vestiges of a soda fountain. The place had been remodeled and the upstairs was now home to the Association of Motion Picture and Television Producers. This labor-relations arm of the monolithic Motion Pictures Association comprised all of the studios, and Lew was its head. Through it, he negotiated dozens of union contracts for Columbia, Paramount, Twentieth Century Fox, Universal, and Warners. "Lew would take complete control in the negotiations," said Berle Adams. "He was the only guy who was willing to put himself on the front lines and to fight for things. He'd fight for things that the studio heads didn't want to deal with. He was always there."

That day, Wasserman was the first in his group to arrive for tough contract negotiations with the Writers Guild of America (WGA). Michael Franklin, the WGA president, saw him ambling down the hall, carrying a large box of doughnuts. The two ostensible adversaries greeted each other amiably. Wasserman walked into the caucus room toward a long sideboard and set down the nibbles. Franklin had already brewed a pot of coffee—one of several that would be consumed that day—and the opponents stood in front of a large picture window overlooking the busy intersection, waiting for the rest of the bargaining teams to arrive.

That year, the studios and the writers were again fighting over terms of a contract. The WGA had been on strike since March 6, paralyzing most of the town's TV and motion-picture productions. At least two independent producers had settled with the WGA already: the pioneering Quinn Martin, producer of *The Streets of San Francisco*, and Grant Tinker's MTM, producer of *The Mary Tyler Moore Show*. "The smaller guys felt they couldn't afford a strike and wanted to keep working," recalled Del Reisman, then a WGA officer. But the big network and studio bosses were holding out.

It wasn't as if Wasserman could afford a strike, either. He had spent the last four years turning around MCA, the industry's biggest producer. Eight weeks into the strike, work on his lot had screeched to a halt. Without scripts, there could be no shows.

Compounding the problem was the WGA's feisty mood. This union was unlike any other. The Directors Guild of America had never in its thirty-seven years struck the studios, except once, for about fifteen minutes. SAG's relationship to management had been more cozy than confrontational in recent years. And WGA, unlike the blue-collar unions, had managed to fend off any whiff of mob control. "The WGA has always been the most militant of the town's unions," said Franklin. Its members felt they were routinely under-valued in the filmmaking process. Indeed, despite the importance of the script, moguls had denigrated writers since film's early days. As MGM's Irving Thalberg once groused, "What's all this business of being a writer? It's just putting one word after another."

Studios had long ago usurped the screenwriter's prerogatives. Although playwrights hold the copyrights of their work, Hollywood screenwriters never had. The studios have always owned the script and, according to their contract boilerplate, actually write them, too: "The studio, hereafter referred to as the author . . ." is the legal phrase found in most screenplay deals. "It was brilliant of the studios to arrange that way back when," mused one writer. By doing so, the studios turned the writer into a worker-for-hire, with few rights and little power. The underlying assumption was that anyone in Hollywood can tell a story, and the studios own them all. This Marxist-style quirk explains many of the industry's idiosyncrasies, as well as its power struggles.

In May 1973 many WGA members resented the studios, and Wasserman in particular. They remembered his "Wasserman formula," which, among other things, paid writers 4 percent of the sales of their movies to TV. But the formula kicked in only after the third rerun. In 1960 the WGA had thought it a good deal and seized on it to settle its five-month-long strike. But since then the deal hadn't worked out very well. Networks rarely showed movies more than twice. "We were only getting about 11 cents a check," said Reisman.

So there was plenty of bitterness over that deal when contract negotiations had rolled around again in 1966. Some writers unleashed their ire on Wasserman, who barely flinched. "This marked the start of Wasserman's major period of participation in negotiations," said Franklin. "He really immersed himself in the issues and never showed any great anger." After a while, union members noticed that the studio chief actually listened to their grievances. He moved around the large wooden table, which seated twenty people. Sometimes he sat in the back and listened to heated debates. Other times he sat at the front and took charge. "There were lots of people on either side, and everybody had to make a speech," said Franklin. But Wasserman moved discussions along.

In 1966 the guild had opted out of the Wasserman formula and negotiated a flat, capped fee. "We got more money in a quicker fashion," said one writer. But years later, the guild regretted leaving Wasserman's plan. "If we had stayed with it, the payouts would have been tremendous because of the growth of reruns and the foreign market," Franklin admitted.

That year, another contentious issue had reared its head, the possessory credit—the one that reads "A Film by Allen Smithee," as though Smithee alone created the film. Three years earlier, in 1963, the studios and writers had agreed that no such credit could be given to anyone but a writer. "It could be a writer/director such as Billy Wilder, but it had to go to a writer," Franklin said. When Wasserman led the 1966 negotiations, he agreed to extend the limit as part of the WGA contract. "The directors got into an uproar over that," said Reisman. Though the DGA sued the WGA, it couldn't change the contract. Newly minted auteurs were inflamed that the writers held such power over the vanity credit. It all boiled down to power—and who would wield it: the writer or the director. The directors held many meetings to "get the writers to quit this nonsense," said one director, and generally made life miserable for the studios and for Wasserman.

Lew finally agreed that directors could negotiate individually with studios for a possessory credit. This violated the earlier WGA contract and undid ten years of WGA progress. When the WGA discovered the DGA's deal, its members were livid, said Franklin, especially because of Wasserman's much-vaunted reputation for upholding his agreements. Even so, in 1970 Lew asked the WGA to drop the possessory credit from the contract. He promised that the studios would never make it part of any blanket bargaining agreement. "It's got to be negotiated individually," he said. "But we can assure you that those credits will not proliferate. They'll be limited." Finally, the guild agreed, securing a huge pay increase in the bargain.

But Wasserman *had* reneged on his deal. "There was no way around that fact, and it would come back to haunt him," said Franklin. By 1973, Lew was trying to make good with the WGA for this transgression—and a few others.

Wasserman and Jules Stein had each played roles in the vitriolic, violent history of Hollywood unions. When Stein first arrived in Los Angeles in 1932, his friends, members of Chicago's underworld, were already there, expanding their gambling, extortion, and labor-racketeering businesses in the West. The first Hollywood union that had clout was the International Alliance of Theatrical Stage Employees (IATSE), which represented the projectionists. They could level the movie industry by refusing to run their machines in the nation's theaters. "They were very powerful," said Roy Brewer, an IATSE official. The mob traditionally infiltrated legitimate business through labor unions, and Hollywood was no exception. With the help of the Chicago syndicate, George Bioff, and his partner George Browne, gained control of the projectionists' union, and in 1934, Browne became IATSE president.

The mob planned to use Bioff to take over the Hollywood film industry and extort as much as half of its profits. Several legitimate labor groups were vying for studio recognition, but Bioff used muscle to beat them back. Then he threatened the studios with a national strike unless they made a deal with IATSE. The studios acquiesced, and some 3,000 employees were forced to join the union. Workers grumbled about a vague 2 percent "assessment charge" confiscating their money, not realizing that Bioff and the outfit were collecting $1.5 million for themselves.

To oversee Bioff and the extortion business, Sidney Korshak traveled west to California. The Chicago attorney represented many shady and legitimate men, including members of Capone's gang. A federal agent once described Korshak as "a finesse-type guy, who dressed very, very well." He was also an old Stein acquaintance. Korshak started negotiating contracts for the Teamsters, who "were allowed to come on the set, but had to stay out of the studios," said Berle Adams. "They were all Korshak's bunch, and, boy, were they a tough group." The mob then went after the actors' guild—but SAG fought back. "They tried to take over the Writers Guild, but that didn't work, either," said Ray Evans, an Oscar-winning lyricist for the song "Que Sera, Sera" from the Hitchcock film *The Man Who Knew Too Much*. Bioff then tried a new tack. If studio chiefs would pay him, he'd maintain labor peace. And so the Chicago gang collected another $2 million. "The studios preferred paying tribute to the mob rather than dealing with its workers," said Evans.

Legitimate craft unions rebelled at being locked out of the studio. In 1937 a group of electricians and carpenters struck the studios. Bioff called in some Chicago hoods who had easily obtained gun permits from the friendly Los Angeles Police Department, and bloody labor battles ensued. Yet the studios and the agents— including Stein and, later, Wasserman—looked the other way. "Did Lew participate in the IATSE scandal?" asked historian Doug Gomery. "Yes. Did every other studio boss? Yes. But that deflects the issue of Wasserman's greatness."

Part of Lew's greatness was knowing when to remain silent. "I'm sure that Lew met Sidney in Chicago, when Stein introduced them," said Berle Adams. When Wasserman arrived in Hollywood in 1939, Korshak introduced him to all of the studio chiefs, Adams explained. "Do business with this guy," Korshak told the moguls. Indeed, as soon as Wasserman had some clients to sell, they transacted plenty of business with the lanky agent. MCA's men were not about to meddle in any arrangement that their friend Korshak might have in Hollywood.

In 1940 the California State Assembly began investigating the town's labor violence and discovered that the studios were paying Bioff and his Chicago-controlled union to keep production running smoothly. Bioff and Browne were indicted for extortion, along with several Chicago mobsters—the men whom Stein had done business with in the 1920s. In 1943 Bioff and Browne were sentenced to prison.

Still, conditions for studio workers did not improve. When the Conference of Studio Unions tried to organize story analysts, publicists, electricians, and office assistants, many workers applauded. "The CSU was the kind of union I supported," said Evans. It was more honest than IATSE and boasted a large number of World War II veterans, said Bob Goldfarb, a story analyst and, later, William

Morris agent. But CSU members were growing angry at the studios' stonewalling. Events turned nasty after Roy Brewer—and SAG member Reagan—falsely accused the CSU of being Communist. "That was ridiculous," said Evans. There was an attitude among management that labor organizations were part of a Communist plot, Goldfarb explained. "It was not only untrue but slightly ludicrous."

But the accusations drew another government investigation—this time from the House Un-American Activities Committee. In 1944 HUAC started questioning labor activists and guild writers—not mobsters or studio moguls. "And Wasserman stood by," said WGA member and author John Sanford, husband of Marguerite Roberts, the blacklisted screenwriter of *Ivanhoe* and other films. In the fall of 1946, tensions came to a boil after CSU picketed the studios. New IATSE chief Roy Brewer was determined to beat down the rival "Commie" union and met with several leaders, including Wasserman. He said, "I've always had a good relationship with him."

Brewer and his men confronted the CSU picketers and triggered the ugliest labor melee in studio history. "There were riots and blockades," recalled Evans. "It was awful, but the studios loved IATSE because they kept a lid on legitimate organizers." A few miles away at MCA Square, Wasserman collected reports of escalating violence from his agents. As president of MCA, he and Stein could have at least cautioned restraint, but again Wasserman stood by as Brewer, Ronald Reagan, SAG director Jack Dales, and others smeared the labor activists unfairly. "It was silly, really," said Dales. "Looking back on it, I've always been a bit ashamed of it. Some very active union people were hurt." At the time, though, it seemed like the right thing to do, he explained. Evans disagreed sharply: "The mob, the studio, and their stooges killed the CSU."

HUAC then went after screenwriters who either belonged to the Communist Party or were deemed un-American. Though it was perfectly legal for U.S. citizens to hold any political, religious, or personal belief, the committee prosecuted those people it considered suspect. "The Hollywood Ten were mostly our clients," said Sam Jaffe, a top agent at the time. "I fought the blacklist because it was destructive, and the people on the list weren't harmful." He defended his clients and continued submitting their work to studios, eventually using pseudonyms to place their work. "I never dropped a client," he recalled. But his income plummeted 50 percent. After the studios announced that they would not employ anyone on HUAC's list, Jaffe was incredulous. He thought surely someone from William Morris or MCA would object. "But neither Wasserman nor Stein ever spoke up," he said. "Jules didn't want to touch that," Adams explained. "It wasn't good politics." MCA was in the business of getting people jobs—just not certain people.

Wasserman and Stein worked with Brewer, who became the arbiter of who was red and who was true-blue. "I helped a lot of MCA clients get off the blacklist," Brewer explained. Sterling Hayden was pressured by his MCA agents to give false testimony, though he later recanted in print. Screenwriter Ned Young, who wrote the interracial drama *The Defiant Ones,* starring Tony Curtis, Sidney Poitier, and Theodore Bikel, was called in front of HUAC and, the next day, was dropped by his MCA agent. Playwright Arthur Miller refused to point fingers at HUAC's behest and from then on couldn't find a job, either. "Wasserman didn't even offer his material to the studios after that," said MCA agent Malcolm Stuart.

Gene Kelly had protested the HUAC hearings publicly, which got him in trouble. Wasserman asked Brewer to talk to his client, and Brewer did. "Kelly decided he had made a mistake and changed his views," the IATSE chief explained. The American Legion threatened to picket *Moulin Rouge,* starring MCA client Jose Ferrer, who was supposedly a Communist for having supported antifascist forces in the Spanish Civil War. Wasserman again called Brewer, who advised the MCA client to criticize the great singer, actor, and civil-rights activist Paul Robeson, who had just received the Stalin Peace Prize. Ferrer blasted Robeson, harming the black man's singular career but saving his own. *Moulin Rouge* went on to box-office success and Oscars.

For nearly two decades, Wasserman participated in the horrible charade, without ever raising his hand. "Lew never took a stand, and maybe that's part of his genius," said MCA agent Ronnie Lubin. "Wasserman was no liberal when it came to unions," added John Sanford. "He was a powerful guy and could have stopped that blacklist if he'd decided to. But he didn't have the interests of the downtrodden at heart."

By 1973 Hollywood had finally changed. Former blacklisted writers were selling scripts under their own names, and Wasserman was negotiating labor peace with legitimate unions. Some activists believe that the studio mogul was motivated by guilt. "After all," said Jeff Corey, a blacklisted actor, "Lew allowed the artistic community to be turned over to these yahoos in Washington. I think he was probably pretty unhappy about his role because, essentially, he was a good man."

In July, Wasserman completed contract negotiations with the WGA. He agreed that studios would pay residuals for movies that ran on supplemental markets like satellite and pay TV. Time Inc. had just started HBO, adding pay cable TV networks to the media horizon. The studios also agreed to pay extra money to writer-producers, which elevated the status of TV scribes. And they seeded a WGA health plan. Wasserman had settled another union strike.

That year, he also negotiated new contracts with SAG, the American Federation of Musicians, and IATSE, which now embraced craft workers and projectionists. He started overseeing about fifty labor agreements in Hollywood, said Dan Slusser, an MCA executive. "He was on top of every union contract, administration problems, and grievances. Couple that with the fact that there were three or four strikes a year at the time, and you get an idea of what Lew was dealing with." In the summer of 1975, he turned to contract talks with IATSE, which would be his last labor negotiation.

The union was still a powerful force, since 65 percent of Hollywood's production costs were "below the line," related to the crafts industries. The key issue that year was pay. IATSE business agent Jack Coffey insisted that the new contract include cost-of-living increases over the next three years. He argued that the union members had not had any significant increase in a long time, due to Hollywood's faltering economy. Now that the studios were enjoying good times again, it was time to reward laborers. Plus, inflation was eroding their salaries further. "Many workers earn less than enough to care for their families," he told Wasserman. Coffey wanted a 15 percent increase in the first year, a 12 percent increase in the second, followed by 12 percent. At the time, increases were usually in the 5 to 8 percent range. "But the studios were offering us 6, 6, and 6," said Coffey.

Wasserman argued that the studios couldn't afford to give the bigger cost-of-living protections. That upset many union leaders, who knew that MCA and other studios were posting strong earnings. Wasserman himself had just gotten a big raise to $250,000 at a time when the average household income was $17,000—about the same as that of an IATSE member. In a front-page *Hollywood Reporter* story, Coffey criticized Wasserman for "poor-mouthing." Coffey recalled that "Lew got mad at me for revealing his salary." The mogul met with IATSE leaders at the Roosevelt Hotel.

There, he, Sheinberg, Coffey, and a few other union men sat at a table.

"What does it take to make this deal?" Wasserman asked.

Coffey repeated the 15, 12, and 12 percent increases.

"Okay. What else? "

"No more talk about eliminating a third man," on the customary three-men production crews. Wasserman agreed, and the union had a deal.

But Columbia, Warners, and the others refused to honor it, believing the pay increases were too rich. "What do you want me to do?" Wasserman asked.

"Renege," the executives replied.

"That word is not in my vocabulary," Wasserman said, and he walked out.

He arranged for Universal and Paramount to break away from the AMPTP and form their own group, The Alliance. "From then on, there were two studio bargaining groups," said John McLean, head of WGA. An IATSE official asked Wasserman if he would like the union to strike against the dissenting studios, but Wasserman said no. "Work it out. We don't want to hurt the industry like that."

But those talks marked a turning point for Wasserman. After eight years as head of the AMPTP, he stepped down. He handed the reins to younger men, including Sheinberg. He had paid his debt. In years to come, he'd return to labor talks only as a last resort, but he would be sorely missed. "There's not a CEO in town who came close to what Lew did for labor," said McLean. Adams agreed: "Lew did a great job for the industry. I remember when he had proxy power for Paramount, Columbia, and Warner Brothers. He would speak for all three of them at one time. And they all trusted him."

THIRTY

ERNIE NIMS WAS COMPLETING *The Day of the Jackal*—his last Universal film before retiring—and the sadness of the occasion made him contemplative. His tight pre-editing skills had saved Universal a lot of money, but had insulted some people in the process. Director Fred Zinnemann had refused to cut a single page from his film, but Wasserman's rule meant that Zinnemann couldn't get his film budget until Ernie edited the script. The director had been forced to relent and, after seeing Nims's skillful cuts, told studio executives, "Hey, this guy Ernie really knows what's he doing."

Towards the end of production, Wasserman came up to Nims and said, "I hear you're filming your last big hit." The two had worked together for nearly fifteen years; now they shook hands and said good-bye. Nims had helped create several Universal successes, including *Pete 'n' Tillie* (1972) and *Jesus Christ Superstar* (1973). Soon *The Day of the Jackal* would be hailed as a "terrifically paced movie," and it *would* become a hit. Nims left Wasserman with three winning films in fourteen months, lifting Universal's reputation.

By then, most of the studio's old guard had departed along with Nims. Milton Rackmil, Ed Muhl, and marketing manager Melville Tucker were all gone. Though they had once groused about Wasserman's parsimonious approach to filmmaking, they had been won over gradually by his dedication to Universal. "If Wasserman had all the money in the world, he couldn't have done a better job," said Muhl. "He never gave me a problem in his life. Throwing away those old studio papers like that burned me up," he added, "but Lew was alright."

At MCA's board meeting in June 1973, a formal changing of the guard occurred, as anticipated. Dr. Stein, as he now called himself, resigned as chairman of MCA and gave Wasserman the title of chairman of the board and chief executive officer. Sid Sheinberg became president, and Wasserman elevated a few other young bloods, including Jay Stein and Ned Tanen.

Universal now had successful producers on the lot, including partners Richard Zanuck and David Brown, whose résumé listed *Butch Cassidy and the Sundance Kid.* The two had been fired from Twentieth Century Fox after a political contretemps with Richard's father, Darryl Zanuck, the sixty-year-old who still ran the studio. "Lew was the first one to make us an offer," said Brown. But they

declined it and instead took jobs at Warner Brothers. That arrangement soured quickly. "We had to quit, and I wasn't sure that
Wasserman would hire us," said Brown. But their agent was former
MCA man Herman Citron. He called every studio to find new jobs
for Zanuck and Brown, but only Wasserman made an offer—albeit
not a very attractive one. "We called him Wassuh, as in 'Get Wassuh
to give us a better deal,' " said Brown. But Citron couldn't get his
former boss to offer as much as another dollar.

The producers held out until, finally, Wasserman groused to
Citron, "You tell those boys that if they're not interested to just say
so." By then, Wasserman's was the only offer the producers had.

But before signing on, Zanuck and Brown went to visit Edie and
Lew. "We wanted to run a few projects by him," said Brown. Citron
objected. "Are you crazy? They may not like your ideas, and then it'll
be all over." The two went to Wasserman's home, anyway, and outlined some concepts for the couple. Edie and Lew were fascinated
by one story about two gamblers who slyly fix a game. "There'd been
a dark chapter in Lew's life when he was a gambler," said Brown.

In the 1930s and 1940s, when Sunset Strip was a wild, unincor-
porated part of Los Angeles County, the area crackled with juice
joints and high-rolling gambling dens. Edie and Lew Wasserman
loved to frequent those hot spots. They were patrons of The Clover
and several other illegal dens, said George Riff, a dealer who later
became an executive at The Stardust. "Lew loved to gamble and
shoot craps. But he was a mediocre bettor," and didn't often win.
Twice, Wasserman allegedly lost his home on Sierra Drive—yet
managed to win it back each time. "He gambled a lot in Las Vegas,"
said Berle Adams. Once, he lost about $100,000, and Stein was
forced to bail him out. The last thing MCA needed was trouble with
the Chicago, Cleveland, or Detroit underworld. "Jules told Lew that
he had a year to clean up his habit, or else he was out," said producer
William Link. After that, Wasserman stayed away from the tables.

So, when Lew read Brown's script, written by David S. Ward

(*Steelyard Blues, Sleepless in Seattle*) and produced by the young trio of Michael and Julia Phillips and Tony Bill, he recognized the characters immediately. "Lew didn't like to read scripts, but he read *The Sting* and loved it," said Brown. The story was set in 1930s Chicago, where two confidence men take revenge on a mob boss by snaring him in the biggest con game ever.

The script helped clinch the deal, and Zanuck and Brown signed on at Universal. When they discovered that Bill and the Phillipses had already shopped *The Sting* to MGM, the partners feared they'd lose the project and offered the trio everything they wanted—including 50 percent of the net.

Wasserman kept urging Brown to move ahead on *The Sting*. "Go ahead, fellas. Make that movie," he said. He gave them a $5.5 million budget and, when the film was finished, another $15 million to distribute and promote it. But Tony Bill never warmed to the studio, calling it the coldest and most impersonal place in town. The coproducer never even attended the party for the movie's completion because of Universal's rule forbidding children at such events.

Meanwhile, Ned Tanen was hoping he had a small-budget hit with *American Graffiti*, the George Lucas script directed by Francis Ford Coppola. The nostalgic coming-of-age tale about four teenagers in the early 1960s who spend Saturday nights cruising in hot rods had started shooting in the summer of 1972 with some then-unknown actors: Richard Dreyfuss, Harrison Ford, Ron Howard, and Cindy Williams.

From the start, the movie had been plagued with problems. It had a budget of about $700,000, and a twenty-nine-day schedule. The day before filming was to start, a crew member was arrested for growing marijuana. The first night of shooting, it took so long for the crew to mount cameras on the cars that actual filming didn't start until 2:00 A.M. The project was half a day behind schedule before they'd even begun. Outdoor footage was supposed to be shot on a blocked-off street in San Rafael. But a local bar complained about losing so much business that the city revoked the crew's film permits. Lucas and his crew moved to Petaluma, twenty miles away, where a cameraman was run over, an actor was rushed to the hospital with an allergic reaction, and Dreyfuss gashed his forehead the night before his close-ups. During the film's drag race, one car's axle broke. On the second try, the other axle broke. On the next try, the car failed to veer off the road as planned and barely missed two cameramen. For this, Lucas was getting $20,000 and 25 percentage points of whatever profit the movie might earn.

As Wasserman was shutting down the youth film division and bringing in older, more experienced producers, Tanen was also feeling the heat. When Tanen finally tested *American Graffiti,* it was shown to a young audience in Northpoint Theater in San Francisco. In a story that is now legendary in Hollywood, the film received a great audience response. But Tanen saw only an amateurish work that moved slowly to its rock-'n'-roll sound track. He called the film "unreleasable." As an exhausted Lucas looked on, a furious Coppola offered to buy the film from Universal. Tanen and the director finally worked out a compromise, though Universal's "suggested" modifications to the film made Lucas very unhappy.

With the changes in place, Tanen then had to battle his studio. "Universal didn't like the movie at all," he said. "They weren't even going to release it." Wasserman's concern was heightened by a generally sluggish turnout at theaters that year. And the marketing men didn't know what to do with the film. In an ugly recollection, Tanen explained, "They thought *American Graffiti* was a bunch of niggers painting railway cars. That's exactly what they said." The best tagline the studio could muster was "Where were you in '62?"

Wasserman wanted to preview the film at the Acme Theater on Melrose in Los Angeles. "I had to get kids there," said Tanen. "So I called Wolfman Jack [who played a DJ in the film] and said, 'You've got to help me. I'm dying.'" Wolfman hosted the evening, and 100 kids showed up. Each time the studio screened it, the DJ reeled in more teenagers. "Then they booked it at the Cinerama Dome, which didn't have the right type of screen," Tanen recalled. "I was up at the front of the movie, waving my arms in the dark because it was distorted. It looked like a Bromo Seltzer ad." But Wasserman saw the crowd's enthusiastic reaction.

American Graffiti was released in the summer of 1973 and became a huge success. It posted a record on its nonholiday opening in August, and by fall was grossing $10 million. In December *The Sting* was released. It clicked immediately and eventually took in $78 million in theatrical rentals—an astounding sum for the time. The movie sound track that featured Scott Joplin ragtime music sold a record-breaking 2 million albums. Suddenly, for the first time, Wasserman had a surfeit of Universal movie hits.

American Graffiti became the first financial success from Tanen's youth division. Its sound track of doo-wop and early rock 'n' roll also went platinum, selling more than 1 million copies. Ironically, it was also the last film to be released under Universal's low-budget film experiment. Wasserman had already shut down that operation.

On April 2, 1974, Edie and Lew sat in the audience at the Dorothy Chandler Pavilion, fidgeting with anxiety. Two of Universal's pictures, *The Sting* and *American Graffiti*, had been nominated for Best Picture. One win would break the forty-three-year-old losing streak for Universal, for the last time the studio had won such an Oscar was in 1931 for *All Quiet on the Western Front.* The suspense was excruciating, said David Brown. "Lew hated to be surprised. He never wanted to be caught without information that other people had. That was certain death."

Wasserman was also nervous because he was about to receive the town's top honor: the Jean Hersholt Humanitarian Award. The twenty-year-old distinction was given to those whose efforts had brought credit to the entire motion-picture industry, and it had been handed out only twelve times before that night. But

Wasserman seemed frightened rather than pleased. "He was terrified to get up onstage," said Patsy Krauskopf, Stein's niece. "He hated speaking publicly."

The 46th Academy Awards would later be remembered as one of Hollywood's greatest shows, replete with controversy, final appearances, and frontal nudity—all live on national TV. A hoary-looking John Huston boldly admonished the town's "jeremiahs," those rebels who had boycotted the awards for being frivolous in the midst of so much political upheaval. The elegant, three-time Academy Award winner Katharine Hepburn made her first Oscar appearance. She received a standing ovation for presenting the Irving Thalberg Award to her old friend Lawrence Weingarten, producer of *Adam's Rib* (1949) and *Pat and Mike* (1952). Comedian Groucho Marx appeared for the last time onstage, looking frail as he accepted an honorary award. Wasserman was away from his seat during the evening's most outrageous spectacle. A streaker ran in front of the camera as David Niven introduced the next presenter. The nude man paused in front of cameras, flashed a "peace" sign above his family jewels, and took off. The urbane Niven then delivered one of the greatest ad-lib lines in TV history: "It's fascinating to think that the only laugh that man will ever get is by stripping off his clothes and showing his shortcomings."

Niven presented Diana Ross, who spoke briefly about the importance of the Hersholt Humanitarian Award. But as Ross tried to introduce the next speaker, Wasserman suddenly walked onstage, striding forth like a sovereign crackling with energy. He approached Ross from behind as she said, "Here's a man whose film career dealt with emotionally charged words." The camera picked up Wasserman, who looked confused and stopped abruptly. The audience saw him and burst out laughing, confusing Ross, who was unaware of anyone standing behind her. Gamely, she smiled into the camera and continued: "*Suspicion, Notorious, Psycho.*" Wasserman's face fell—would anyone really describe him like that onstage? Then he seemed to realize his mistake. Ross was not introducing Wasserman, but his rotund English friend. The studio chief beat a hasty retreat into the wings as Ross announced the presenter of the next award. "Ladies and gentleman, the distinguished director, Alfred Hitchcock."

Wasserman was mortified as he stood in the wings. He waited as the next scene played out like one of Hitchcock teasers. The orchestra struck up the theme song from *Alfred Hitchcock Presents.* The camera found Hitch's profile silhouetted in the dark against a guillotine-like prop. The lights went up, Hitch faced the audience and, dressed in a black tuxedo, hooked his thumbs on his trouser pockets, hung his egg-shaped head, and shuffled forward. He looked like a junior-high kid who had just won the science award. It was a long walk to center stage and, when he finally reached the podium, Hitch looked into the camera and drawled, "Good evening." He waited until the laughter died down.

Then Hitchcock turned serious. "The Jean Hersholt Award is given not just for what you have done, but for who you are." He seemed to be talking to his friend in the wings. "It is not merely presented for achievement, but for the manner in which these achievements were made." Over the years, Hitch explained, this man had given of his time, his efforts, and his intelligence "to the betterment of the lot of his fellow man in philanthropic endeavors, in culture . . ." in business and in nearly every other humanitarian sphere. Of the three special Oscars, the Jean Hersholt Award was the most coveted in this town. It honored not just the recipient, but reflected magnanimously on the entire motion-picture industry. It marked a builder, a giver, a person who loved show business so much that he went beyond the call of duty to further its fortunes. "That's why we are proud to honor him tonight, secure in the knowledge that this award will forever be in the good hands of Lew Wasserman."

The orchestra started, and this time Wasserman waited for his cue. A silver oblong prop rose to reveal the tall, reed-thin figure in a tapered-waist tuxedo and snappy bow tie. He restrained himself as the spotlight lingered on his elegant presence. Then he walked slowly toward his old friend, his patent-leather shoes gleaming in the klieg lights. Midway across the stage, he sped up. Wasserman had just turned sixty, and looked virile and strong. His thick mane of silver hair was combed back in soft, wavy tufts. His big smile showed off a dazzling set of capped teeth. Only his darting eyes betrayed his nervousness.

When Wasserman reached the podium, Hitchcock dramatically laid the bronze statue prostrate in Lew's outstretched hand. He bowed slowly and low, as though he were about to kiss Wasserman's ring. Startled, the mogul laughed at the mock deference, but Hitch continued his playacting. This time, the audience didn't laugh. The stars, directors, writers, and producers understood the gesture completely. Lew was king of the town, and Hitch his court jester—the only Hollywood character who would dare pantomime the true relationship between the legendary leader and the Hollywood talent he employed.

For the second time in Wasserman's career, he had managed to rise above the crowd. Once he had ruled the town as agent, representing most of the top stars and dictating film projects to the studios. At the end of that era, he believed he could segue smoothly into the new role of studio boss. "But he found it wasn't so easy," said one of his agents. Indeed, Wasserman had all but failed. Four years later, however, he had come back from the brink, once again.

As chairman of MCA Inc., he ruled over the biggest and most profitable film studio in the world. The newspapers called 1973 the "Universal Year." *The Sting* with Paul Newman and Robert Redford, had been nominated for nine Oscars, besides the one for Best Picture. According to the trades, Wasserman was a big reason why Hollywood was enjoying its best box-office year after a seven-year drought. He had just ended a sixteen-week WGA strike that had paralyzed the town's TV productions. He was the driving force behind a new SAG contract, as well as the new DGA agreement. He had helped build the Dorothy Chandler Pavilion, home of the evening's Oscar ceremonies, by bringing the West Side Jews to the civic bench with Los Angeles's Protestants. The MCA chief had helped forge political ties that were enriching the film industry beyond measure. Wasserman had been the first agent to take control of a studio, and the first to build a back lot into an entertainment conglomerate. No one came close to matching Wasserman's longevity, ability, or clout. Not in 1974, and not for the balance of the twentieth century.

Of course, Wasserman managed more than just a film studio. His sprawling operation created TV series and hit music records. In 1974 MCA Records pressed eight gold records and eleven gold albums that had sold 19 million copies. Wasserman's labels included titles by Cher, The Who, Neil Diamond, Elton John, and Olivia Newton-John. He had just combined half a dozen of his firm's labels under one MCA name, using brand recognition to sell more records worldwide. Wasserman was also Hollywood's first real estate developer, erecting hotels, commercial high-rises, and restaurants. He had also orchestrated the growth of a business that had boomed from a couple of tour buses to a monster $21 million theme park.

Wasserman was also developing technologies that would advance the entertainment industry tremendously. In 1974 he was marketing a new theater sound system called "Sensurround," an effect so real that a movie patron would feel as if he or she were *inside* the film. Universal would win a scientific Oscar for its Sensurround technology in *Earthquake*. And, for better or worse, its wizardry would kick off a host of movies that relied more on box-office special effects than character and plot.

However, Wasserman's most brilliant technological development was DiscoVision, the first home-entertainment device. Years before VCR and Betamax machines, Lew's device could replay movies on a home TV. He was as excited about DiscoVision as he had been about television thirty-five years earlier. "I think its potential is mind-boggling," he said. The mogul couldn't wait to introduce the world's first disc player to the American consumer.

At a time when "synergy" was still a relatively unfamiliar word, Wasserman demonstrated the logic of owning as many parts of the entertainment whole as was legally possible. Even better, he actually made it work for several years. In 1974 MCA reported a 161 percent jump in pretax profits to $102 million, making it the most profitable year in MCA's fifty-year history—and converting MCA/Universal into the richest of studios. There was no longer any question of who was in charge. "Lew was the architect, the choreographer, the soul and sparkle of MCA," said producer Walter Seltzer. "It was Wasserman more than Stein who built the company. Lew had the passion, fortitude, and guts to see it all through."

That night, as Edie watched her husband onstage, she beamed. "She was so proud of him, she was practically jumping on her seat," said Krauskopf. Edie had her own connection to Jean Hersholt, the Danish immigrant actor who had founded the Motion Picture and Television Fund. That charity—and the country house and hospital it ran—helped old, sick, and down-on-their-luck Hollywood workers. When Hersholt died in 1956, the Academy had named the town's first humanitarian award after him, hoping to inspire a raft of Hollywood philanthropists. But some years, the Hersholt Humanitarian Award just sat on the shelf, bereft of even one worthy honoree.

Edie had adopted Hersholt's MPTF as one of her causes; she had suggested to Lew that they give a large donation to the fund, and were now regular donors. Edie sat on the MPTF board and had turned the charity into her own zealous mission. "These people made us rich!" she'd say, and thereby wring a donation from another Hollywood power. Wasserman's bronzed Oscar that night belonged to Edie, too.

Not everyone in the Oscar crowd knew this as they continued applauding Wasserman. The tall mogul approached the podium.

Hitchcock started to back away, but Lew whispered for him to stay. The lion-maned chief towered over his short, bald friend as he gave a memorized speech. He thanked Hitch and the board of governors of the Academy. As he spoke, he rocked toward and away from the microphone, forcing the cameraman to move back and forth, and aggravating the soundman. Wasserman said:

"I would also like to thank my wife, Edie, Jules Stein, and all of my associates at MCA for permitting me to devote time to the work that the Academy thought was worthy of this deeply appreciated honor." His lisp came through, but he stumbled only once. Then he added with a smile: "Good night, Carol," naming his seven-year-old granddaughter, who was watching at home.

The crowd gave him a standing ovation. Somehow it was fitting that there were more stars in that night's audience than at any previous Oscar ceremony. Later that evening, *The Sting* would take home an impressive seven Academy Awards, including those for Best picture, director, producer, and screenplay. The film would become one of the top-grossing films of its day, selling $100 million in tickets. And Wasserman and his studio had finally broken their forty-three-year-old Oscar losing streak.

Universal's *American Graffiti* earned an Oscar for best editing. It, too, would bring in buckets of money—$190 million total. The $700,000 project would hold the record for highest profit margin of any film ever made. Its record would stand for three decades until 2000, when the $35,000 digital film *Blair Witch Project* would make over $200 million and shatter *Graffiti*'s record. Wasserman would bask in the afterglow from this night's Oscar ceremony for years to come.

Jules Stein never thought he'd live to see this day. In August 1974 his beloved MCA turned fifty years old. At seventy-eight, Stein had survived the '29 crash, the depths of the Great Depression, two world wars, and one cold war. He had outlived Capone, McCarthy, two Kennedys, two other MCA cofounders, and several bouts of cancer. Stein had lived to see MCA's half-century birthday—no small feat.

Yet something still remained to be accomplished. Stein wanted to write his autobiography. Several of his friends had penned their life stories, but most of their efforts had fallen flat. Their books didn't convey the entrepreneurial zeal or dastardly decisions that had driven their careers. Their books sat in cartons, unsold inventory in their own or their publishers' warehouses.

Stein, in his inimitable style, wanted a best seller. He had hired several writers to craft his life story and encouraged his erstwhile publicist, Karl Kramer, to give it a try. But none of the results pleased Stein, said Murray Schumach, a *New York Times* reporter. "He was frustrated because people would do a draft, and it wouldn't work." Somehow, MCA's story never sounded as august as Julius Caesar Stein had imagined it would. "I mean, come on, who was he fooling?" said one source. To convey the history of his blue-chip corporation accurately, he'd have to tell the whole truth, beginning with his early days. "Wasserman was against the whole idea because he hated publicity," Schumach explained. "He wanted to have absolute control of what other people knew. And once a story is in a book, you no longer have control."

Stein dismissed Wasserman's concerns and commissioned Schumach, who covered Hollywood for the *Times*. Schumach was such a friendly reporter that Billy Wilder once compared him to a stenographer who took dictation from his sources. Schumach spent months on the MCA project and delivered it to Stein, who read it by his pool. But in the end, it, too, was mothballed. Stein had sanitized his own story so much that the result was a dry and tedious opus. He didn't believe it would sell.

His published acknowledgment of MCA's fiftieth anniversary was confined to the company's annual report. Its first line read: "Dr. Stein founded MCA in 1924." He never mentioned the company's two cofounders, including his late brother Billy. Nor did he fill in the lines of his fifty-year run in American show business. In the end, the entire truth was too villainous, shocking, and spectacular for the captain of what was now a $640 million entertainment colossus. Besides, Stein's rule was over, although he wasn't quite ready to depart.

Wasserman waited, amazed at how long Stein had lasted. "He'd been ill a couple of times and had a few death scares," he told me years later. But every time the older man approached death's door, luck or fortune intervened "through the magic of some young doctor," Wasserman said. Once, when Stein was lying in a hospital bed, he told Lew: "When you're rich, they won't let you die." Stein had negotiated for—and received—several years of a wildly colorful and entertaining life, but even Dr. Julius Caesar Stein couldn't stave off death forever.

THIRTY-ONE

DESPITE SWEEPING THE OSCARS, Universal did not suddenly become a magnet for film directors. "It wasn't considered a talent-friendly place," said Michael Phillips. He and his wife, Julia, and Tony Bill had to fight for credit on the *The Sting*'s advertisements, and for the percentage points they had been promised in their contract. "I don't think that emanated from Wasserman," said Phillips. "It came from business affairs or the old guard. But it was very unpleasant."

In the mid-1970s, Universal's executives still wore dark suits and ties. "It was a stern and forbidding place," explained Phillips. "Universal was not as creative as their counterparts were, with the exception of Ned Tanen. Its lot felt suppressed and fearful. It's ironic, because Universal didn't have tremendous turnover, and the others did. But you could feel the fear and heavy atmosphere on that lot. And fear constrains creativity."

Universal was making a slew of catastrophe films, following the pattern it had kicked off with *Airport.* Inspired by Stanley Kubrick's *2001: A Space Odyssey* (1968), Jennings Lang had snapped up the rights to a Michael Crichton best seller, *The Andromeda Strain.* He tapped the California Institute of Technology, the Jet Propulsion Lab, and others to ensure realism in the story about a virus from outer space. The film had been released in March 1971 and boosted the careers of both Crichton and Lang.

In the fall of 1974, Lang produced *Airport 1975,* one of the first movie sequels. This script had originally been submitted to the TV department, but the film producer snapped it up. The $3 million movie featured a 747 jumbo jet that collides with a plane in midair. This time, the airline's vice president (George Kennedy) and ace pilot (Charlton Heston) coach the stewardess (Karen Black) on how to land the plane. The rest of the cast included Myrna Loy, Gloria Swanson, Sid Caesar, and Jerry Stiller. It didn't match *Airport* in many ways, but it did make $25 million.

Lang followed that with *Earthquake* (1974), which included a seven-minute sequence detailing the destruction of Los Angeles. Low-frequency sound waves were added to the sound track during the dubbing process, producing a rumble. Theater owners had to rent special speakers and an amplifier—at $500 a pop—to get the added effect. Producer/director Mark Robson heightened the audio experience even more by creating other innovative effects. The $7 million movie was more of an experience than a film, and it received an Oscar for best sound and another for special achievement. Best of all, it went on to collect $40 million in theaters and about $60 million more in foreign distribution sales. In time, the movie would earn even more money from videocassette sales, but that sector was still about five years away from becoming an established market.

Next up was *The Hindenburg* (1975). Director Robert Wise ransacked film archives to find footage of the German zeppelin's 1937 crash in New Jersey, but ruined the rest of the tale with silly characters. Still, it won an Oscar for special achievement and cinematography. As for Lang, he continued scouting for blockbusters. One summer, he got hold of galleys of *Jaws,* a book by Peter Benchley. "Jennings got it a year before it was published and loved it," said his wife Monica.

It was a tale of horror on the beach, centering around a small New England town, a few sharks, and a big ocean. The twenty-nine-year-old Steven Spielberg got hold of the galleys and asked Lang if he could direct it. By then the project had fallen under the aegis of Zanuck and Brown. The group brought in a series of writers, but after six months there was still no script, and Spielberg wanted out. But Zanuck and Brown told him this was his big opportunity. "Don't blow it," they warned. Spielberg was given $3.5 million, a two-month shooting deadline, and was sent to Martha's Vineyard in September 1974.

Trouble dogged him from the start. The script was still a mess, so the actors Roy Scheider, Robert Shaw, and Richard Dreyfuss improvised. The mechanical sharks kept breaking down. Wasserman, Sid Sheinberg, Ned Tanen, and others back at Universal City were viewing the dailies, wondering: What is this? Film editor Verna Fields, known as Mother Cutter for her skillful edits, was calling Spielberg regularly, asking, "Where is the action?" He had unwatchable scenes of sunsets and ocean. As the budget crept higher and the project fell farther behind schedule, Wasserman grew testier. Lew, Sheinberg, and Tanen were considering replacing Spielberg with a pro. In addition, the director was having anxiety attacks during the day, clutching his pillow at night, and praying for a miracle.

Zanuck and Brown had already told Spielberg that the studio was about to replace him. "They said Universal was going to shut down the movie or raise ticket prices on the tour to get their money back from *Jaws,*" Spielberg told me. Then the president of MCA flew out to the Vineyard to have a heart-to-heart talk with him. Spielberg was terrified: "I thought the other shoe was going to drop." Instead, Sheinberg sat down with Spielberg on a porch overlooking the Altantic Ocean. "Look," he said. "We'll either send everyone home and somehow recoup our losses, or you can finish the picture. Just tell me if you can finish this damn thing." Spielberg knew that after so many false starts and failures at Universal, *Jaws* represented his last best chance. If he backed out now, after spending $7 million of Wasserman's money, he'd be ostracized by Hollywood.

"I think I can finish the picture," Spielberg said tentatively. "I want to stay."

"Fine," Sheinberg told him. "Everybody will stay off your back."

Sheinberg ran down a list of problems and encouraged Spielberg to wrap it up. "He rallied my spirits," said the director.

By the time Spielberg returned to Universal City, he had spent $10 million and nearly six months to deliver a film that was still a mess. Mother Cutter went to work, and excised much of the shark footage, focusing instead on the actors' emotional reactions to the man-eating creatures. The difference was thrilling. Finally, the movie was ready to release.

Wasserman was eager to make back his money and decided to break a few rules of film marketing and promotion. He had learned a thing or two about boosting public interest in scary movies, beginning with his early job as a theater usher in Cleveland. When Universal released *Dracula* with Bela Lugosi (1931), Wasserman was working at The Palace in Cleveland. Business was flagging during the Depression, and Wasserman had an idea about how to attract audiences. Although he was only an usher, the manager let Wasserman try his gimmick, said fellow usher Al Setnik. Since *Dracula* was about bloodthirsty vampires who preyed upon unsuspecting women, Wasserman hired two nurses to stand near the theater doors with stethoscopes around their necks. Their presence signaled that *Dracula* was so scary, theater patrons were fainting from fright and would need swift medical attention.

"Before long, people were stacked inside the theater like sardines," said Setnik.

Wasserman needed a more clever scheme to recoup his money from *this* scary movie. He decided to bypass critics, who would probably pan the film anyway. Instead, he ordered a large purchase of national TV advertising spots so Universal could barrage viewers over a weekend. "We were on every channel from Thursday to Sunday night in prime time," he said. He spent $700,000—the equivalent of some films' shooting budgets—and that helped distinguish *Jaws* from other summer fare. "It was a natural development," he explained to me later. "We knew we'd get more money faster. If you get it on television, everybody will know that you've got a picture."

Then he broke a distribution rule. Instead of opening in New York and Los Angeles and saturating the market slowly before moving on to other cities, Wasserman distributed widely, to hundreds of theaters around the country. Such an approach was usually reserved for bad movies. The tactic allowed studios to "hit" the audience quickly so it could recoup expenses before negative reviews spread. Paramount had tried this ploy before, but Wasserman took it further.

He released *Jaws* in early summer, just as school vacations began. That way, the film would have a chance of riding its wave the entire season. He also treated the campy B feature like a prestige film. "We were asking for terms that were rather high for the industry," he said. "We didn't get it into all of the theaters we wanted." But he was able to open in 409 venues. "There were lines around the town, not around the block," he recalled. "The following Monday, we got the movie into all of the theaters we wanted."

During the next few weeks, Wasserman kept close track of the receipts. On a flight from New York to Los Angeles, Wasserman sat with a calculator on his lap and a list of national box-office numbers at his side. By the time the plane landed, he had figured the gross total of the film. He told his flight companion, Robert Evans of

Paramount Studios, that he'd be within 5 percent, and he was. *Jaws* beat *Airport*, rapidly racking up $129 million in ticket sales—then an all-time high. "The marketing was certainly to Wasserman's credit," said film critic David Thomson. The movie became the first orchestrated summer blockbuster, supported by prime-time TV ads and a wide, fast opening. *Jaws* didn't receive many good reviews, as Wasserman had suspected. But by then, it didn't matter.

It carried filmmaking—and film marketing and promotion—to a new arena. "MCA learned that critics no longer mattered as they had before," said Douglas Gomery. *Jaws* showed that cinematic effects, tight film editing, and tension-building scenes still thrilled movie audiences.

From then on, B-style movies would dominate American screens. Disaster films, science-fiction fantasies, and violent action films— no matter how melodramatic and kitschy—would be hyped, promoted, and marketed into blockbusters. Political films and social-message movies were dying, and character studies endangered. The financial agenda was clear and *Jaws* gave birth to a studio megahit mentality. "Now it's so much a part of our world that we don't even know when it started," Gomery said.

Years later, when Wasserman reflected on that summer, he did not recall his anger at *Jaws*'s bloated budget or the director's string of missed deadlines. All he remembered was that he had helped save the film. "I not only had a lot of faith in the way we advertised the movie *Jaws*, but I had approved the making of it. So my faith went all the way back to the beginning of its history."

Meanwhile, Doris and Jules Stein were delighted with the movie's effect on the price of MCA stock. They placed a warning sign on their pool gate: "Beware Guard Dogs and Sharks."

In the spring of 1974, as MCA was testing its film *Earthquake* in theaters, several executives were previewing the film in Atlanta, Georgia. Wasserman was staying at the governor's mansion, while

Sheinberg and the others were at a hotel. Wasserman called Sid and asked, "Will you come over to the governor's place for dinner tonight?"

"I didn't even bring a necktie. I can't."

"It doesn't matter. It's very casual here."

Sheinberg and Clark Ramsey, head of Universal marketing, arrived later that night and found Jimmy Carter in the kitchen, moving between the refrigerator and the chopping board, helping prepare food for his nine guests.

Most of the MCA men were fighting about *Earthquake.* "That's usually what previews are all about," Sheinberg explained. "Arguing."

Carter just listened to the bickering executives. "These guys weren't paying a lot of attention to the governor," said Sheinberg. "You know, Hollywood types—to them, he was just another Southern politician."

But Edie Wasserman had already seen something in Carter that the MCA marketers missed. After supper, the governor walked Wasserman and his men to the door and said good night. Once outside, Sheinberg told Wasserman, "I'm very taken with this guy. You ought to back him."

"It's funny you should say that," said Wasserman. "That's what Edie said."

She had met Carter at a Democratic fundraiser and reportedly told her husband, "I've just met the next president of the United States." She was excited about his prospects, and her husband trusted her judgment. In Carter, Edie and Lew saw a "true-blue American image that could be very attractive to the populace," explained Sheinberg. Carter was eleven years younger than Wasserman and, although he had been raised in a comfortable home, he had grown up in the Depression, surrounded by neighbors who lived in abject poverty. The men shared many beliefs, said political consultant Bill Carrick. "Wasserman was a New Deal Democrat, and so was Carter."

While the Wassermans started working with Carter, Taft Schreiber maintained his Republican ties. Although Nixon had resigned in disgrace in the summer of 1974, Schreiber was a trustee of the Richard M. Nixon Foundation, which would build his presidential library. He was also friendly with the new president, Gerald Ford, who named Schreiber to the National Heart and Lung Advisory Council of the National Institutes of Health. Reagan was no longer governor, but a rich man in Pacific Palisades. The ranch that MCA had given him in 1951—and the inflated price on its sale that Schreiber had arranged in 1966—had made Reagan worth about $2 million—equal to about $11 million in 2003. Reagan spent his days contemplating his next political move.

The Wassermans made their own conservative associations.

In January 1975, Edie and Lew hosted a dinner party at their Foothill Road home for Henry Kissinger, who was now Ford's secretary of state. Edie and her friend columnist Joyce Haber had met Kissinger years earlier, when the politician was single and enamored with starlets. "I remember seeing Henry at Joyce's house late one night, with Jill St. John sitting on his lap as he told his stories," said Jim Bellows, Haber's editor. In those days, Edie and Haber had often invited the Washington star to Beverly Hills parties and introduced him to actresses and players. Now he was more circumspect, newly married to a Washington socialite. That winter, when the Kissingers pulled up to the Hollywood mogul's house, they were surprised to see their host waiting at the foot of the driveway, standing near the guardhouse. "Lew always made his events very personal," which surprised visiting dignitaries, said Joe Cerrell. "They were used to bigger egos than Lew ever displayed."

Once inside the Wasserman home, the Kissingers were greeted warmly by Edie, who introduced them to her guests: Alfred Hitchcock, Mr. and Mrs. Gregory Peck, Mr. and Mrs. Kirk Douglas, Sid Sheinberg, labor attorney Paul Ziffren, and columnist Joyce Haber.

Edie's home was warm and inviting; its large floor-to-ceiling windows looked out on acres of green lawn. Her florist, David Jones, had filled the rooms with large exotic plants and yellow and white flowers. Every lady had a spring flower on her napkin at dinner, which started with a baked potato topped by Iranian caviar and ended with Dom Perignon champagne. That night, Kissinger noted the many mutual interests shared by Hollywood actors and Washington diplomats—the only difference being that "politicians play only one role and have a shorter life."

Schreiber was focused on seeing that Kissinger's boss, Ford, stayed in office. But then Reagan surprised him by saying that he wanted to run for president in 1976. "Taft didn't think he would win it," said Stu Spencer. "A lot of us didn't think that Reagan could win." The governor had had a tough time in office during his last few years and had left without a base of regional support. "You need a few states to carry, and Reagan didn't have a base," Spencer explained. That year, Schreiber told Reagan that he wasn't going to support his campaign. "Ronnie understood," said Spencer. But Nancy was less sanguine. Schreiber had always thought her astrological consultations were silly and could be harmful to Reagan's image. The couple's reliance on these forecasts wouldn't surface publicly for a few years, but Schreiber had never forgotten the governor's inauguration, held after midnight on January 1, 1967, to coincide with the best planetary aspects. "It was a little strange, but I'd already had too much to drink by then and wasn't [fazed]," Spener admitted. However, Schreiber was appalled and went so far as to warn Reagan's potential presidential backers about Nancy's stargazing habits.

In contrast to Reagan, Carter had a significant base of supporters, at least in the South, as Wasserman learned from *his* consultants. Lew and Edie set about helping the candidate add some West Coast support. Earlier in the campaign season, Edie and Lew had thrown a big event at their home to raise money for the Democratic leaders of both the House and the Senate. Guests noticed a man wandering around the periphery of the party. "No one was paying much attention to him," said Sheinberg. People were asking, "Who is that guy?"

It was Carter, and as he left the event, escorted by Wasserman to the door, he turned to Lew's houseman. "The next time you see me, I'm going to be the nominee." Sure enough, Carter became the Democratic nominee in July 1976, and by then all Hollywood knew about him. "When I decided to run, Mr. Wasserman was one of the first out-of-state people I told," Carter told a reporter. "People respected his judgment in political affairs. When he let his friends know he had confidence in me, it was extremely helpful."

After Carter's victory at the convention, Edie and Lew feted the nominee. Again, Edie filled her home with flowers and fed her guests the usual Chasen's-catered buffet. When Carter left this time, he thanked Edie and made another prophecy to her houseman: "The next time I see you I'm going to be the president."

Taft Schreiber started to work even harder for the Republicans. He became cochair of the finance committee for Ford's campaign, taking with him former Reagan supporters Henry Salvatori, Dr. William Banowsky, and even his own strategist, Stu Spencer. That hurt Reagan politically and personally, said Spencer. "Taft didn't do a lot of work for Ford, not like he did for Nixon." But he did raise plenty of money for the presidential candidate. "Taft was pragmatic about it. He knew that Reagan couldn't win. Taft wanted to go with a winner." Stein was also upset over Schreiber's decision.

In June 1976, Schreiber took time out to attend to a medical problem, scheduling a routine operation for a urinary tract problem. He checked into UCLA's Medical Center and underwent surgery on June 3. But during recovery, doctors noticed something seriously wrong with Schreiber's vital signs. Someone had given Schreiber the wrong blood type for his transfusions. Though the mistake was corrected, Schreiber now had dangerous blood clots in his body. Some two weeks after entering the hospital, Schreiber died.

"It was a shock to everybody," said his daughter, Lenore Greenberg. "It's not something you ever come to grips with easily." Schreiber's wife Rita was devastated by her husband's death, and bizarre rumors about Taft's demise ricocheted around town. "Taft was always the power behind the throne," said Jane Rosenbaum, an MCA secretary. "He helped get Reagan into the governor's mansion and Nixon into the White House. He was instrumental in doing many things for Stein, most of them beneath the radar." Even jaded politicos were thunderstruck. "When Taft died, I was shocked," said Spencer. "It was unbelievable. How could something like that happen?"

Two days later, the front page of the *Los Angeles Times* reported the death of the MCA executive as the result of blood-transfusion error. Stein thought the story dishonored Schreiber's memory and complained to the publisher. "I thought you would instruct your people to do a momentous obituary on my associate of fifty years," Stein said. But Stein himself did not choose to mention Schreiber's passing in MCA's 1976 annual shareholder letter. He mentioned the passing of Charles Miller, Stein's brother-in-law, in that annual report. But neither Stein nor Wasserman publicly acknowledged Schreiber's death, let alone his years of unstinting service. His name was simply dropped from the list of MCA's directors and never mentioned again.

Those inside the Tower noticed the glaring omission. Schreiber had always been a mystery among his own in Hollywood. "All I can say is that Taft's death was very strange," said Walter Seltzer. Now several MCA employees suspected foul play. Rosenbaum had the nerve to mention this to Schreiber's niece. "How can you be sure it's not murder?"

"No one's sure."

One thing *was* certain. For the first time in his career, Wasserman was free of his nemesis. He was the sole emperor of MCA. Now the only visible threat to Lew lay somewhere beyond his studio gates.

• • •

Wasserman believed he held the key to entertainment's next big wonder. In 1971 he realized that MCA owned the technology to create the first videodisc system. "We stumbled into that one when we bought a small electronics company," in 1967, he said in one of our interviews. As soon as Wasserman realized his good fortune, he felt the excitement of discovery—the same adrenaline rush he'd felt in 1939, when he peered into his one-inch, mirror-reflected "vaudeo" box and saw the future. Now he was witnessing a new technological wonder, and envisioned the day when an optical videodisc system would be available to everyone in the comfort of their home. All they had to do was hook a machine to their TV set, pop in a disc, and watch a new MCA movie, an old Universal TV show, or one of the 11,000 old films from MCA's mammoth library.

"I consider it the most advanced concept for home entertainment today," Wasserman said. He was certain it would rank up there with the invention of radio or TV, and he would be right—eventually. This was Wasserman at his best: innovative, forward-looking, and eager to lead the culture into the next big craze. At sixty, Wasserman still had his keen foresight, and his passion for the next big thing. He felt invigorated knowing that he was contributing a scientific invention to global entertainment.

From 1970 to 1973, Wasserman poured about $10 million into developing the technology. He called it DiscoVision—an apt name for the disco-crazed 1970s—and it would pack all the color and sound of a theater onto a twelve-inch-diameter plastic disc, like a vinyl record. Wasserman intended DiscoVision to have full stereo sound, which would make it the first home stereo unit with a video program. MCA was developing the product's hardware as well as its software. It was tapping its library and making inexpensive prerecorded programs. In 1972 Wasserman unveiled his product to the public, and the trades buzzed about his breakthrough.

Even the CIA heard about Lew's system, and paid him a visit. The agency wanted to store and retrieve volumes of covert data on Disco-Vision's system. One CIA official, a James Bond aficionado, confessed that he'd love to impress cabinet members by flipping a thin disc into a machine, pressing a button, and flashing mounds of classified material on a screen. Wasserman endeavored to provide the government with a DiscoVision Industrial Player, spending another $10 million on that. In 1974 he struck a deal with Philips Electronics to manufacture and distribute a videodisc player.

Then the Japanese upset Lew's plans. In 1975 Sony presented a *video recorder* that was inferior to MCA's laser device. About the only thing that Sony's Betamax system could do was copy existing movies or shows off TV—including MCA films and Universal TV shows. Indeed, when Sony launched its U.S. advertising campaign in 1976 it touted the new machine as capable of recording *Columbo* and *Kojak*—two of the highest-rated TV shows owned by MCA.

Sid Sheinberg was outraged. "I wasn't going to let them sell products that would essentially rip us off." In 1976 MCA sued its Japanese competitors for copyright infringement, arguing that the Betamax would allow consumers to record MCA's shows off the air without paying for them. Considering the mother lode of movies and TV shows that MCA owned, Sheinberg figured that MCA could potentially lose billions of dollars. VCRs are "tools of piracy," he argued, because they make unauthorized copies of copyrighted movies and TV programs. Sheinberg invited Disney to join the case.

They were in for a long battle.

Meanwhile, Wasserman worried about his now-$30 million investment, as well as his cherished dream. He was certain that his disc system was superior to the video recorders. Trying doggedly to perfect DiscoVision, he increased his stake and went to Congress to seek industry protection from Sony. He sent Jack Valenti, the head of the Motion Picture Association of America, to testify before lawmakers. Valenti gave a rousing performance, declaring that "the

VCR is to the American film public what the Boston Strangler is to the woman alone."

The lawsuit moved forward.

MCA's opponent was no babe in the woods about American business. Since 1960 Sony had tried hard to blend into the culture of U.S. commerce and had worked diligently to understand its legal system. Sony chairman Akio Morita once remarked, "If you don't know your way around the law, it is impossible to do business in the United States."

The Betamax case would be Sony's first test, and Morita was determined to defend his position to the end. At stake were Sony's future and its share of the global electronics business. As his lone weapon, Morita invented the legal concept of "time-shift," which would become accepted in American jurisprudence. In the Betamax case, the phrase meant that a person didn't have to watch a TV show at its programmed time; he could tape the show and watch it later. Led by Morita, Sony lawyers argued that since the American TV airwaves are owned by the public, at least in theory, the VCR does not infringe on anyone's copyright. It merely allows people to watch free information at a time that suits them. Sony's argument were logically brilliant.

Nonetheless, the litigation kept Betamax from really entering the marketplace. In 1977 JVC, a company owned by Japan's Matsushita Electric Industrial, was selling video-recording machines for its VHS systems. The machines were expensive, but to Sheinberg their appearance signaled yet another enemy advancing on MCA's turf. "Sid would salivate every time you mentioned Betamax," said Ned Tanen. He was furious at the encroachment on his company and the insult to his chief and boss.

After three years in office, Sheinberg was becoming accustomed to his role as MCA president. By this time, however, MCA's financial health was slipping. After four years of record-breaking profits, the conglomerate reported decreased earnings in 1976—to $802 million. Sheinberg set about expanding Wasserman's conglomerate and learned a few hard lessons.

The first business he purchased was Yosemite Park and Curry Company, the concessionaire that had served the national park for a century. "I always thought that MCA should be in recreational services, where we could grow," he explained. "I loved Yosemite because it was one of a kind." Set aside in 1890, the national park was located in the spectacular heart of the Sierra Nevada Mountains, with craggy mountains and groves of giant sequoias. "Disney could not build another Yosemite," said Sheinberg. To him, that was part of the acquisition's appeal.

In 1973 MCA paid about $13 million to take over the conservatively run firm and its four hotels, four camping areas, food services, and ski area. Revenues from MCA's recreational services division immediately jumped 90 percent to $21 million, and Sheinberg worked aggressively to increase park business. MCA announced it would build a chairlift to carry visitors up to Glacier Point, a granite rock towering 3,245 feet above the valley; it would refurbish the elegantly simple Wawona Hotel and dress the staff in nineteenth-century costumes. Sheinberg's plans were unrolled just as the environmental movement swept California, and the idea of promoting business in this mountain retreat outraged many people. "We don't want anyone making amusement parks out of our national parks," said a Sierra Club leader.

The next year, MCA printed brochures describing the park as "nature's eloquent answer to a convention city." The corporation intended to construct hotels, upscale restaurants, and a conference center. The resulting uproar swelled even louder. Sheinberg said his concept was misunderstood and withdrew the brochure quickly. But he was called to testify before a Senate committee about MCA's plans for commercialization. "We are good citizens, or certainly try to be," Sheinberg assured the senators. He assuaged legislators' fears—until some prankster faked a drawing of a giant escalator bursting out of Tuolumne Meadows. The counterfeiter sent the sketch to the Sierra Club, which alerted the media and lawmakers. Ned Tanen recalled, "Next thing you know, Sid's back in Washington, explaining, 'No, no. We're not building a Mr. Toad Tour Ride.' MCA was always being accused of trying to deflower Yosemite."

Once Universal TV tried to shoot a show featuring John Denver inside the park. Producers lifted a large rock and moved it five feet, out of camera range. "What are you doing?" shrieked a ranger. "You can't move rocks around like that." The production was shut down for a few hours, which cost money. As one wag noted, "MCA thought they owned the whole park." After 1978, when the U.S. Department of the Interior restricted development in all national parks, the specter of Glam Trams scaling Yosemite Peak faded. Looking back on this period, Sheinberg sighed, "Sure we made some mistakes, but that was the first business I acquired."

His next purchase went more smoothly. "Universal always wanted to get into publishing," said Fred Klein, former executive at Bantam Books. MCA had enjoyed great success turning novels into films, like *The Andromeda Strain* and *Jaws,* and Sheinberg's urge to acquire a publishing arm grew stronger. He discussed this with his recent hire Stan Newman, who was developing ideas for licensing. "That's how we stumbled into publishing. We began to see it as a business that was related to ours," said Sheinberg.

MCA pursued one of the biggest firms in the industry, Simon and Schuster—just as Charlie Bluhdorn of Paramount started wooing that firm, too. So MCA in December 1975 bought G. P. Putnam's Sons, which years earlier had published Vladimir Nabokov's famous *Lolita.* MCA paid only $9 million for Putnam, which had a massive list of 250 hardcover titles but brought in only $10 million in annual revenue. "It wasn't much, but we thought we could build up the paperback part of the business," said Sheinberg.

A year later, Putnam hired Phyllis Grann as editor in chief, and she set out to raise its low annual revenues of $23 million. Every year, Wasserman would call together the heads of his divisions to review and forecast. Grann would tell Wasserman how much money Putnam was going to make and how. "In the absence of earthquakes or floods, you knew that she was going to deliver that amount or a little more," said Sheinberg. "She always kept her books in a slightly strange way, burying little nuts for winter so that if something went wrong, she'd have a surprise."

Newman helped work out a marketing strategy for Putnam. He wanted to publish fewer authors and focus on those with bigger names. It was rather like Wasserman's filmmaking concept of producing fewer movies, but with bigger names. Putnam set about publishing star writers in both hardcover and paperback, using a coordinated team.

When Universal released *The Promise* (1979), directed by Gil Cates, it marked a turning point in publishing. "Here was a romance that could be novelized," Sheinberg said. It was a love story about two college students, a rich boy and poor girl who are injured in a car wreck as they try to elope. The young woman's face is so disfigured that the rich kid's mother offers to pay for her plastic surgery if she leaves her fiancé. Universal promoted it as "a haunting story of love and betrayal," Putnam found a woman to novelize the movie, and there was born a new, successful venture—and a career for Danielle Steel, the author of the novelization.

"Universal became the first to novelize movies," said Klein. "It was a smart way for them to capitalize on them." Under Wasserman's management, Grann and Putnam also began to create brand identities with their best-selling authors.

On the movie side, the indefatigable Jennings Lang spun out increasingly chaotic films about potential Armageddons. *Airport 1975* came out in late 1974; *Airport '77* arrived in late 1976, and *The Concorde—Airport '79* in August 1979. Each successive version of the air-disaster movie suffered from diminishing returns. In other corners of the lot, Walter Mirisch tried his hand at *Midway* (1976), which was a big-budget disappointment, followed by *Gray Lady Down* (1978), a smaller military-disaster film. Mirisch then resurrected one of Wasserman's old favorites, *Dracula* (1979), directed by former Universal TV writer John Badham. But none of these films matched the success of *Airport* or *Jaws*. By now, only blockbusters could feed the monster conglomerate that Wasserman had built.

THIRTY-TWO

THE THIRTY-FIVE-YEAR-OLD PRODUCER stood behind a gold-braided rope inside the Universal Studios commissary, waiting to be seated for lunch. The commissary was a large rectangular room, and the lunch rush was its busiest time. At ten minutes before noon, young men in denim began to jostle behind the rope in hopes of getting a good table.

The seating arrangement was jealously hierarchical. All seats radiated from the power center: Lew Wasserman. "It was like a court, and the closer you sat to Lew's end of the room, the more important you were," said Stephen J. Cannell, the producer in question. A wide aisle led to the MCA chairman's table, which occupied the prominent spot and sat against the front wall. On either side of the aisle, tables were arranged like spokes from a hub. "Wasserman always sat facing the rest of the room," David Brown recalled. At the tables closest to the tycoon were his top producers: Jennings Lang, Frank Price, Roy Huggins, Alfred Hitchcock, and others. Sometimes these tables included foreign guests. Other times, they displayed promising directors or the studio pet du jour. The young men behind the rope all itched to sit as close to the king as possible.

Hostess Kathy Donahue would consult her organization chart, which listed the hall's reserved and numbered tables, then lead a group to an empty table close to the window. Sometimes a young man would complain, "Hey, come on! Is that the best you can do?" He'd try and slip her $20 and beg for a spot closer to the front. It took all of her patience to maintain her composure, she said.

Cannell never understood the jockeying for lunchtime position. When he was an unknown writer with no track record, he once asked a friend about the hullabaloo. "What difference does it make where we sit?"

"It's the pecking order, man, and it counts," his friend insisted. "If an executive sees you against the window, he knows you're nothing. *Everybody* knows you're nothing."

Lunchtime at Universal's commissary was more about ceremony than nutrition, as was obvious most days around five minutes past noon. That's when Wasserman would appear in the doorway.

"When Lew finally walked into the commissary, it was like King Arthur coming into the hall," Cannell recalled. The room would fall silent as the silver-haired figure made his way up the aisle, stopping along the way to greet his men. "How are you, Jack? The show looks great," he'd say. He'd take a step and turn his head, nodding to another gentleman. "Congratulations on the ratings," he'd say, and so on. He'd move slowly up the aisle, shaking hands, touching shoulders, and sprinkling encouragement over the assembly like a cardinal with holy water. Then he'd sit down, usually with Sid Sheinberg, and wait for his order of tuna on white bread. The hall's lunchtime chatter would resume.

Wasserman had become a living legend to a new generation. He no longer simply walked into a room, he commanded it. He wasn't tall, he was a giant. He was no longer taciturn. "He was a theatrical personality," said Del Reisman, a Universal TV writer. Stories grew about his photographic memory, his habit of sleeping just four hours a night and working for twenty, and his obsession with hygiene and numbers. Taft Schreiber's death had actually frightened the mogul, and he now feared hospitals, said one attorney. Wasserman's secretaries swabbed his telephone receiver with alcohol several times a day, so the chairman wouldn't catch a virus and fall ill.

When it came to decisions, Wasserman was still hands-on. Outside consultants who did business with Universal were often surprised to see how tightly Wasserman held the reins. Buzz Price came in from time to time to discuss Universal's theme park. "Universal wasn't like Ford or General Motors, where there were echelons of freestanding managerial responsibility," Price said. "Lew was a very dominant and intelligent personage. He was the leader of the band."

That band was mostly male and quite talented. Steve Bochco had written stories for the award-winning series *The Bold Ones* (1971). He and Cannell wrote a TV movie about a surfing detective, *Richie Brockleman* (1976). "We hung together a lot," said Cannell. Bochco also worked on several *Columbo* features in the 1970s, while David Chase worked on *Kolchak: The Night Stalker* (1974–1975). That series was about a newspaper reporter investigating the supernatural—a precursor of *The X-Files*. Later, Chase wrote the hit series *Northern Exposure* (1990–1995) for Universal TV, before leaving to produce *The Sopranos* (1999–present) for HBO. Glen Larson was producing *Six Million Dollar Man* TV movies (1974) and *Quincy* (1976–1983). Donald Bellisario worked on *Baa Baa Black Sheep* before producing *JAG,* his own hit series. On the basis of their Universal TV successes, these young men became known as auteur producers, that rare Hollywood writer who actually runs the show.

Frank Price and Sheinberg attracted talent, said Cannell. "Sid absolutely loved the people who worked for him," while Price believed fiercely in his writers. Actors changed with different shows, and directors were itinerants; the only other variable in the TV business was the writer. Given the enormous amount of money at stake, Wasserman wanted every show to be high quality, and that began with the script. "Universal took the position that writers were the assets, who could protect scripts and get the job done," said Cannell. "The result of all that was that the TV writers at Universal became stars."

The writing team of Richard Levinson and William Link created controversial stories under Price. *That Certain Summer* (1972), with Martin Sheen and Hal Holbrook, became the first TV movie to address teenage homosexuality and won an Emmy. "We tried to use TV as a vehicle where we could deal with social issues in a dramatic form," said Price. Edie Wasserman was quite taken with *A Case of Rape* (1974), in which Elizabeth Montgomery offered a raw, uncompromising look at a woman who is raped, then mistreated by the system. Educators used *Sarah T: Portrait of a Teenage Alcoholic* (1975), starring Linda Blair, to discuss how ordinary teen angst can turn to despair when coupled with drink.

Link and Levinson produced *The Execution of Private Slovik*— their favorite movie at the time, and Edie's and Lew's as well. Starring Sheen, the film was based on the true story of the only American solider to be executed for desertion since the Civil War. Eddie Slovik followed his conscience rather than kill, and in 1945 that was a crime. The piece won an Emmy for the writers, as well as other honors.

Cannell had gotten his start by writing *Adam-12* shows, proving so industrious that Sheinberg noticed his work and assigned him to work on a new Jack Webb series. That led to his working for his idol, Roy Huggins, where he received his real breakthrough. After the long WGA strike of 1973, Universal TV was hungry for scripts. It needed to fill eight hours of stories a week for *Marcus Welby, Adam-12, Kojak, Lucas Tanner, The Night Stalker, Ironside,* and the *NBC Mystery Movie.* With many productions behind schedule, Huggins decided to produce a new series quickly. He called Cannell into his office and opened MCA's telephone directory. "Okay," Huggins said, flipping through the pages. He pointed to the name Rockford. "Our new character is Tom Rockford, and he handles only murder cases that were closed but should have remained open." Within a few minutes, Huggins had figured out a simple story for Cannell to write. But instead of developing the traditional, no-nonsense detective, Cannell created an ex-con who'd rather fish than fight. His hero was a man who was perennially broke and scared of getting shot.

Huggins read the script. "This is funny. You've written *Maverick* as a private eye." He showed it to James Garner, who also loved it, and the character became Jim Rockford. ABC, however, hated the irreverent script.

So Frank Price called NBC and offered to make a ninety-minute movie-of-the-week starring James Garner. The network wanted to see the script first, but Price refused. "You have until five o'clock to say yes, or we'll send it elsewhere," he said. The NBC executive agreed, but after reading the material, he turned nervous. "This guy Rockford is a coward. We can't air this show, we'll embarrass ourselves. Change the script." Garner gave NBC an ultimatum: "I agreed to do this show based on the script. If you change a word, I'll walk."

NBC acquiesced, and the tale came to include a beautiful woman (Lindsay Wagner) who pays Rockford to reopen the case of her homeless father's murder. When it aired in 1974, *The Rockford Files* was a huge hit. "It scored a big 35 share, numbers you don't even hear about now," said Cannell. It turned into a TV series that ran until 1980, and it put Cannell on Wasserman's radar. The young man went on to write 50 of the 123 episodes and won an Emmy in 1978. The show would give plenty of work to other writers, too. But it took Cannell to a new level.

"That was the best time of my career," he said. The hits kept rolling off the lot, and before long talent started negotiating for a slice of the profits.

On a warm day, Huggins rode the elevator to the top of the Tower, where the air was always cool. He passed the desks of Wasserman's three secretaries, and waited to be announced. Once inside Lew's office, he started discussing Roy Huggins/Public Arts Production.

Huggins had a joint-venture arrangement with Universal, in which he was supposed to receive part of his shows' profits. His production center was arguably the most prolific on the lot: Huggins had produced three hundred stories for the studio, many of them written under his pseudonym, "John Thomas James." He had registered his pen name with the WGA and received benefits for his alter ego, including a studio parking space. He got more fan mail than most of the other producers, but he was too busy to read it all. Huggins was also producing several made-for-TV movies and supervising a number of shows and hit series, including *Alias Smith and Jones, The Rockford Files, Run for Your Life, Toma, Cool Million,* and *City of Angels.*

He had been working for Lew since 1961, when Wasserman had asked him to save a Revue show. Wasserman had been so impressed that he made Huggins a corporate vice president and gave him stock. But Wasserman warned: "I must tell you that I think our stock at $38 is badly overpriced." Huggins had thought: "My God, I'm dealing with an honest man." He happily signed on with MCA, despite Lew's stock warning.

Huggins worked at night, after his family was asleep. He'd write, rewrite, and tighten the scripts of his protégés. He'd turn in around 6:00 A.M. and arrive in his executive office at 2:00 P.M. After a while, he realized he didn't belong in the Tower and returned to creating TV fiction full-time. But before he changed roles, he and Wasserman agreed that Huggins would get his own production company. "I had a contract that clearly stated I'd receive 50 percent of the profits."

For fourteen years, he worked under that deal, believing those terms were solid. Now he wasn't so sure. "My original deal was for 50 percent of the profits," he told Wasserman. But Huggins hadn't received a dime from any of his TV movies. The mogul suggested he talk to the head of finance and straighten it out.

When Huggins discussed the problem with those in finance, he learned that his ownership had shrunk to 25 percent of the profits. "That had nothing to do with my original deal," he objected. Worse, he learned that all of his movies were losing money, even though several of them had been aired on foreign and domestic TV stations repeatedly for *the past eight years*. Huggins asked to see the documentation, but was told the studio didn't have those reports.

Dazed, Huggins took the elevator down to the ground level, where he could think clearly. He recalled his handshake deal with Wasserman. Lew had a quirky way of shaking hands. He didn't extend his arm. He kept it close to his side, at pocket level, with his palm turned up, as though he expected you to drop a few coins into his open hand. To complete the customary grip, a man had to reach into Wasserman's space. Somehow, Huggins realized, he had given Wasserman and MCA all of his participation profits—without being aware of how that had occurred.

Huggins wasn't alone. Several other writers, producers, and even musicians were questioning the studio's books. "Universal ran a pretty tight ship, and they didn't give anything away," said David Brown. He and his partner, Richard Zanuck, had signed a profit deal, too. But the profits that were due from *The Sting* had been diverted to a so-so film, so that the hit transmuted into a flop. In a practice called cross-collateralization, the diversion robbed the men of compensation from a successful film. "All the studios liked to do it," but Universal was worse than the other studios, said Brown. "That became our big issue."

By 1977, Universal was charging so many expenses against productions that its net profit deals became the town joke, said Cannell. "It was the Universal definition of net profit—everyone in the universe gets something before you do."

The studio subtracted 30 percent of gross receipts to distribute the film domestically, 40 percent to mail those film canisters overseas, and out-of-state travel expenses for executives who attended annual sales conventions. It charged industry membership dues and sundry costs of political lobbying. It charged all advertising costs against profits, plus an arbitrary 10 percent advertising overhead fee; all production costs, plus an arbitrary 15 percent production overhead, and so on.

In addition, strange new accounting terms, written in red ink, floated down from the executive floors. Risk factors, float penalty, house nut—the terms sounded comical to those who worked in the real world. But when subtracted from movie profits, they became fighting words to such writers as Mario Puzo, who wrote the script for *Earthquake* and the film adaptation of his own book, *The Godfather.* He believed that Wasserman had cheated on his net-profit deals and took revenge by skewering the mogul in his book *The Last Don.* Producer Don Devlin once asked Wasserman point-blank if he kept two sets of books. Even Wasserman's friend Tony Curtis joked about how Lew charged producers $700 for one lightbulb. Hollywood money is unreal, Dorothy Parker once said: "It's congealed snow; it melts in your hand."

There were "rolling grosses" or "rolling break-even" points, which meant that studios loaded extra charges to the cost of a film *while the film played in theaters.* As the box office receipts grew, so did the break-even point, which kept rolling away from profit participants. "It's like a moving target," said Huggins. "It's a bookkeeping jungle," added Cannell.

Huggins, Brown, Zanuck, and others began to catch on. Huggins received his money from non-Universal shows, such as *The Fugitive, Maverick, 77 Sunset Strip,* and *Cheyenne.* "I always got my profit checks from the other studios—but not from MCA." It dawned on Huggins that he was a witness to one of the town's best-kept secrets. "I honestly believe that Lew Wasserman came up with the creative accounting that Hollywood is known for."

In the late 1940s, as fledgling Revue struggled for profits, MCA agents started loading costs onto the carts of its corporate sponsors, which underwrote the MCA programs. The practice flourished in the Golden Age of television, until the quiz-show scandals changed the industry's economics. After Wasserman and MCA could no longer count on deep-pocket sponsors, they relied on networks to sell commercial time. In 1962, however, networks weren't about to hand over all of their profits to MCA. They would pay no more than 20 percent or so in "overhead" charges. So the only place Wasserman could continue making big money on his TV operation was in rerun syndication. By 1974, he wasn't inclined to share profits with his partners unless he had to, Huggins said.

That explained the bookkeeping riddle whereby hit shows like *Rockford* would play for years in TV markets around the world, yet suffer enormous losses. "After Universal started doing it, so did all the other major studios," said Huggins.

But it would take years for the profit participants to realize the extent of this sleight of hand. James Garner, for one, owned a percentage of profits for his role in *The Rockford Files*. In 1977 the series was in its third year and going strong. At some point, the network would cancel the show and sell its reruns. Garner, Huggins, and others believed they'd start collecting millions of dollars. "Jim felt his ownership position in that show was going to be his annuity." He was soon disabused of that notion.

Under Frank Price, Universal TV continued breaking barriers. He looked for new terrain to conquer, partly for personal stimulation. "I got interested in the concept of novelization," he explained. "Since the time of the Greeks, you couldn't really do long-form mass entertainment." People wouldn't sit still to watch six hours of dramatic theater, but they might tune in if those hours were broken into ninety-minute movies. That way, one could film an entire book.

Universal bought the rights to an Irwin Shaw novel about two very different brothers and their trials and triumphs. *Rich Man, Poor Man* became TV's first miniseries, and the biggest project ever done on TV. ABC bought all 720 minutes and aired it in eight weekly parts, each 90 minutes long. Released in February 1976—and helped by inclement weather across much of the country—the show became a winner. "We got a huge rating on the first night, Monday," Price recalled. "Had it aired on consecutive nights, the audience numbers would have been bigger." Instead, it was broadcast on consecutive Monday nights and became the year's second-highest-rated show. It won several Emmy awards, conferred fame on Nick Nolte, and spawned a series that ran for two years.

"One of the good things about this era is that there was always something new next year," said Price. "We always had to top ourselves, whether it was with increased audience, higher expectations, or some new form. And that all came from Lew."

But now Universal TV had plenty of competition. In 1977 ABC aired its own miniseries, *Roots,* produced by David Wolper and Warner Brothers. The show was originally scheduled to run as a four-hour presentation on two nights, but it turned into a twelve-hour piece shown over six consecutive nights—another TV first. Based on Alex Haley's harrowing tale of several generations in an African-American family, it, too, aired during a stormy week. The miniseries became the most watched TV show in its time.

Wasserman pushed Price to top that record.

Since American viewers were captivated by tales of space creatures, Universal capitalized shamelessly on their fascination with a made-for-TV movie, *Battlestar Galatica* (1978). Written and produced by Glen Larson, the movie was about a race of robots that had colonized earth millions of years earlier and returned to destroy it.

George Lucas believed the series was a blatant rip-off of his movie *Star Wars,* and filed suit against Larson and Universal. Sid Sheinberg promptly countersued, accusing Lucas of "borrowing" from Universal's own *Buck Rogers* serial (1939), and its *Silent Running* (1971). Lucas had once said that his picture was inspired by the *Buck Rogers* cartoons he had watched as a child. "At least Lucas played his distillations with a sense of humor and a conscious mythological resonance, whereas *Galactica*'s copies are so deadening and one-dimensional, it's excruciating," said critic Richard Scheib.

The irony was thick enough to cut both ways. Wasserman had once told Stanley Kubrick that science-fiction films should not exceed $1 million in budget. Kubrick went on to make *2001: A Space Odyssey* for $10 million and collect $190 million in total receipts. Nine years later, Wasserman approved a $20 million budget for *Galactica,* making it the most expensive TV show of its time. Even so, it made a huge profit for ABC and MCA.

By now, the studio produced fourteen hours of weekly prime-time TV. "We had a lock on dramatic television," said Price. Universal TV was not only the world's largest TV producer, it finally had panache and prestige, said Cannell. "I thought it had some soul." The camaraderie among the dramatists was similar to that found in boot camp, where men work under pressure for long periods of time. The production schedule gave a crew six days to prepare for a TV episode and six days to shoot it. The Tower expected perfection, and the staff delivered. "Guys would be working until three in the morning to get stuff out of the door," said Cannell. "It was pretty exciting."

Occasionally, screen legends were drawn to Lew's shop. The great screenwriter Carl Foreman arrived after spending two decades in exile as a victim of the blacklist. He had written such classics as *The Bridge on the River Kwai, High Noon,* and *Born Free.* But after being called in front of HUAC in 1950 and refusing to name friends, he became a pariah. In 1977 he returned to work at Wasserman's place, where he lunched with prolific writer Stirling Silliphant (*In the Heat of the Night, Route 66,* and fifty books), veteran comedy writer I. A. L. "Izzy" Diamond (*Love in the Afternoon, Some Like It Hot*), and Diamond's writing partner, director Billy Wilder. When the great Swedish director Ingmar Bergman arrived in Hollywood for the first time, his first official stop was Universal Studios, where he was treated like royalty.

Wasserman presided over them all, the chief amid the world's most successful filmmakers who assembled in his grand hall. But outside, one could hear the rumblings of discontent.

During company events and dinners, Price began to find himself seated next to Edie Wasserman, and his wife, Katherine, was next to Lew. The third or fourth time that Price found himself beside the boss's wife, he realized the arrangement was deliberate. "Edie would lecture me a good part of the evening on the number of MCA executives who had jumped out of the plane, left the company, and had failed," Price recalled. Her message was clear: "No one leaves MCA and does well. Don't make that mistake."

By the late 1970s, Price's work had lifted Universal TV higher than ever. The studio now supplied eighteen hours of weekly prime-time programming—an incredible amount. "We had about three hours on CBS, five hours on ABC, and nine hours on NBC."

But he felt stymied. Networks were going behind his back and offering deals to top Universal TV producers. Price had spent fifteen years cultivating Universal's stable of talent, and he couldn't afford to lose his stars. He discussed the problem with Sid Sheinberg. "We've got to find a way to hold on to these guys," Price said. "We can't do it through money, or a title, or even a show," said Price. The networks could give them all that, too. What many of the top TV producers wanted was a chance to make their own feature film. "If I hold that prize out to these guys, they'll stay. They want a deal in low-budget pictures."

Sheinberg turned down the idea flat. He feared that the TV guys would lose money for MCA making movies for the film division, said Price.

Priced then tried to lure comedy writers to his shop. Other studios were doing well with TV comedy producers. Norman Lear enjoyed great success with *All in the Family* (1971–1979) and *The Jeffersons* (1975–1985); Carl Reiner was producing *The New Dick*

Van Dyke Show (1971–1974); Sherwood Schwartz had *The Brady Bunch* (1969–1977) and *M*A*S*H*. Most of these shows topped the charts.

Price met with some comic producers but could not entice them to move. "Universal isn't a very funny place," one writer told him. Those who set foot inside Wasserman's lot felt a chill. "Writers felt that Lew would be looking down on them the whole time." During one executive meeting, Price suggested that "we wrap the Tower in red candy stripes to make it more friendly." Only Jennings Lang laughed.

Price talked with Ed Weinberger (*Taxi*) and James Brooks (*Rhoda, Lou Grant*) and learned that Brooks might sign on. Price told Sheinberg: "This could be our breakthrough hire. But we need to give him something." Price wanted to offer Brooks a chance to make a $5 million movie.

"We can't do that," said Sheinberg. He didn't explain why.

"If we don't offer him this deal, Barry Diller at Paramount will make it."

"Barry wouldn't do that," Sheinberg said. The discussion ended.

The next day, Sheinberg told Price: "See? I was right." He had called Diller, explained Brooks's proposition, and received Diller's assurance that he and Paramount wouldn't lure the hot writer by promising him a feature film, either.

"Sid!" Price objected. "I'd been trying to keep my negotiations secret." But it was too late. Sheinberg was adamant that MCA would not move a TV guy into a film director's job.

The following week, Brooks signed on with Diller at Paramount. He produced his first movie, *Starting Over* (1978), and then wrote, directed, and produced *Terms of Endearment* (1980), a mid-budget film that made $50 million and received five Oscars.

"I knew that soon the other producers would leave," said Price, who grew demoralized. True, his division was a great success financially; TV revenues had jumped an astounding 42 percent during the last two years of the decade, and now amounted to $410 million—one-third of MCA's total revenue of $1.2 billion. But he felt stuck. He'd been supervising the company's television unit for twenty years, since the days when Wasserman critiqued Price's *Virginian* script inside one of the last remaining bungalows. The two had come a long way since then. Surely, Wasserman wouldn't let his TV chief leave now—not when MCA needed TV revenues more than ever.

THIRTY-THREE

EDIE TRIED HARD TO KEEP LEW'S MEN TOGETHER, while shielding the women in her circle, including Beatrice Korshak, Sidney's wife. "Edie was very close to Bea," said Wendy Goldberg.

Edie and Lew had met Korshak back in Chicago, when Korshak worked for Chicago's nightclub owners and Wasserman handled the bands. Korshak was a boxer and graduate of DePaul University's law school, who had started his practice by representing two-bit hoods, prominent flappers, and shakedown artists. When Chicago's underworld bosses flourished in the 1920s and 1930s, Korshak started representing them, too. Even Jules Stein hired Korshak to settle disagreements with the syndicate, said Berle Adams.

Korshak came to Hollywood to oversee the Chicago mob's racketeering enterprise, which skimmed money from the International Alliance of Theatrical Stage Employees and bribed studio heads. He represented the Teamsters in Hollywood, the Culinary Workers Union, and the American Federation of Musicians. "He didn't believe in breaking unions, and his word was good as gold," said Max Herman, head of the American Federation of Musicians. Korshak used to tell the producers, "Don't be greedy" in their labor contracts, and Wasserman took that to heart. He and Sidney also had similar tastes in women. Like Edie, Bea was short, spunky, and loquacious. "She was gorgeous," said one admirer. In 1975 both women were married to the town's most powerful men—Korshak was the highest-paid lawyer in America, and Wasserman was the country's biggest studio chief.

Yet Korshak had no law office, briefcase, or yellow legal pad. He kept office hours at The Bistro, a Beverly Hills restaurant, which he co-owned. Seated at his corner table, flanked by two telephones, he'd greet executives, producers, and patrons such as Edie, who'd stop by to chat. For more serious discussions, Korshak would move outdoors to a small bench on the sidewalk, where he couldn't be taped or overhead.

Other times, he did business inside the Beverly Hills office of Associated Booking Corporation (ABC), an agency that Korshak co-owned. "He worked behind an unmarked door, with no visible files, off Rodeo Drive," said Bill Gardner. Every Friday, a parade of beautiful women would ride the elevator up to ABC's office. Sidney would be slouched behind the desk, where he'd give each woman a packet of money, said producer Jerry Tokofsky. "That embarrassed me, since I knew about two-thirds of them," he said. Tokofsky realized that these starlets were actually hookers, living on stipends from Korshak.

When Tokofsky had a problem with the Teamsters, he'd go to Korshak. Once, he told the attorney: "I can't afford to hire twelve or fourteen drivers on this picture." Korshak picked up the phone and talked to his union man right then. "Hold on," he said, and, cupping the receiver, asked Tokofsky, "How many drivers do you want?

"I'll take three."

"Don't be a pig," he said, scowling. "Take six."

Tokofsky took six.

While their husbands did business, Edie and Bea supported each other in their own way. "Bea enjoyed needlepoint," said one friend. When Edie's daughter, Lynne, and her friend opened The Haystack, a needlepoint shop in Beverly Hills, Bea brought all her friends there. "Everybody bought pillows and purses," said Virginia Korshak, Bea's former daughter-in-law. The crafts business thrived until Lynne Wasserman and her business partner, Julie Payne, ended their association abruptly. "Lynne was the daughter of the most powerful man in town, so it was a tense situation," said Payne. Several high-powered entertainment attorneys were hired to negotiate the business dissolution, treating the crafts boutique like a corporate leviathan.

After Bea's son Harry eloped with Virginia, Bea and Sidney gave them a home a few blocks from their house as a wedding present, The Korshaks paid for a housekeeper and a driver, who spied on the newlyweds and reported back to Bea and Sidney. "Sidney was not happy when we eloped," said Virginia. Even so, the Korshaks' friends rallied around them. Debbie Reynolds and her husband, shoe magnate Harry Karl, gave the newlyweds a lavish reception at their Beverly Hills home. Karl was shocked at the younger crowd's informal dress code and asked: "What, no shoes?" As Virginia explained, "We were all hippies who went barefoot." Nonetheless, Edie gave Harry and Ginny an expensive wedding present.

When Harry and Virginia had a child, the grandparents were ecstatic. Bea decorated and furnished the baby's nursery—then duplicated the room in her own home. "Bea and Sidney felt free to stop by the house anytime to play with the baby," said one source. Some nights their limousine would crawl up to the house, and out would bound Bea. She'd run up to the nursery, check on the baby, then climb back into the orca-sized limo, which would slink into the night.

"Bea and Sid were very controlling people," said David Debbin, a friend of Virginia's. He recalled dropping acid and smoking pot in that house. "Between the overweening grandparents and the druggies, Virginia's house became a little crazy." Eventually, Harry split from Ginny, who started dating other men. Before long, she decided to move to Marin County with her then-paramour, Debbin.

Bea was so upset, she called Edie in tears. Later that week, Sidney dropped by Virginia's house and said, "I don't want you to move away. I don't want you to take the baby and leave us. It's best if you stay."

Shaken, Virginia relayed this to her lover. "So what?" Debbin asked.

"You don't understand. When Sidney tells you to do something, you *have* to do it."

The suitor didn't last, and Virginia fell in with Ned Tanen. Now it was Edie's turn to cry. "Edie and Lew really tuned me out socially after I started seeing Virginia Korshak," said Tanen. Bea was possessive of her granddaughter, and "that little girl was the apple of Sidney's eye," said Debbin. The Chicago fixer hated the idea of another man playing with his only grandchild, and several people picked up on his strong feelings.

"Sidney was not thrilled about my dating Virginia," Tanen admitted. But Tanen was smitten with Virginia. "She was this vivacious pixie—an adorably wacky California blonde," he said. Tanen soon moved in with Virginia and even let her use his new MCA car, a blue Ferrari Dino.

One day Tanen was in his penthouse office facing his enormous floor-to-ceiling window. He rarely noticed the view, or the way the Valley sparkled like a miniature world with highways, trees, and rooftops laid out neatly. He had just received an angry call from Virginia, who, before hanging up, had ordered: "Look outside your window in about five minutes." Now Tanen was waiting, his nose up against the glass, his hands clasped behind his back, trying to enjoy the panorama.

Just then, Wasserman opened the door to Tanen's office. He walked up and stood beside Tanen at the window. For a minute, the MCA chairman and studio president waited in companionable silence. Then Lew asked, "What are we looking at?"

"I'm not sure," said Tanen, his eyes scanning the roads.

Wasserman squinted, too.

In the distance, they saw a small blue dot whipping in and out of traffic. The dot grew larger. "We were both staring as this car went through a red light." It sped along Lankershim Boulevard, and jerked across several lanes, passing several vehicles. At the bottom of the entrance road, the blue Ferrari screeched around the corner.

"Oh, Christ!" said Tanen.

The men watched the sports car zip up the road toward them and accelerate. "She purposely rammed the car, head-on, into a telephone pole. The car had smoke and flames coming out of the engine." Virginia, wearing a miniskirt, got out of the smoking wreck, and faced skyward. "She looked up at the window where Lew and I were standing and flipped us the bird."

"Is that Virginia?" Wasserman asked.

"Yup. Yup," said Tanen.

"Is that your car?"

"Actually, Lew, it's *your* car."

Wasserman shook his head, and walked out of Tanen's office.

It was a romantic breakup, Hollywood style. "Virginia was as wacky as a jaybird. I think we stopped seeing each other about that time." Virginia claimed she didn't hurt his car, Tanen said he paid for the wreckage, and Edie reinstated the now-unattached executive on her "A" guest list. "She was so pleased we broke up," said Tanen. So were the Korshaks.

After *The Godfather* elevated the Mafia into esteemed status, it became tougher for the government to prosecute labor racketeers. Law-enforcement agencies in Los Angeles kept tabs on friends and associates of East Coast mobsters, but rarely arrested them. "Sidney Korshak just got lucky, that's all," said H. E. "Hal" Yarnell, Jr., a captain in the Los Angeles Police Department. Organized crime chic was proliferating on the screen, and the public now rooted for dons of all stripes. There was *Godfather II* (1974), the *The Black Godfather* (1974), *Godfather's Fury* (1978), and *Disco Godfather* (1979). Korshak, however, was a sort of fairy godfather, who granted wishes and protected friends. As Tokofsky explained, "Whenever I had a problem with some guy from the union, I'd call Sidney." For his services, Korshak billed anywhere from $30,000 to $1 million. "I never saw a check," said Virginia. "Everything was paid in cash, or with Picasso art, or a new Mercedes."

It got so that an invitation from Korshak was authentication of one's lofty status. Every Christmas, Korshak would fly to Chicago to pay his respects to his mob bosses, but he'd return home in time to host his New Year's Eve celebration. Most years, Bea and Sidney hosted the party at their home, where as many as 300 people drank French champagne and ate beluga caviar. Edie and Lew were always invited, and in the 1970s, the crowd became a mix of old and new Hollywood. "Edie was very cold and calculating," said Virginia. "She was jealous of anybody who was the least bit attractive and talking to Lew." If Edie felt threatened by another woman, she'd cling to her husband like a barnacle and steer him to another group. By now, some of the older men felt no compunction about taking their wives *and* inviting their mistresses to the Korshaks' parties. Once, casino owner Beldon Katleman dressed his spouse and mistress in a similar aqua Scaasi gown. When Mrs. Katleman ran into the younger woman, she turned white and ran out of the party, sobbing. "Beldon was a sadist," said Payne. Edie and Bea tried to comfort the humiliated wife.

In 1976 Korshak called Wasserman in an attempt to broker peace between the mogul and producer Dino De Laurentiis. Universal had been planning to remake the original 1933 *King Kong* movie, to be titled *The Legend of King Kong*. At the same time, De Laurentiis announced his own modern version of the film. Lawsuits flew between Universal and the independent filmmaker until a desperate De Laurentiis called Korshak for help. "The only way to get through to Lew is to talk to Sidney," he explained.

The three men met at Sidney's home on Chalon Road, amid his Baccarat crystal, Chagall art, and Italian bodyguards. Wasserman listened as De Laurentiis explained. Finally, détente was reached: De Laurentiis could proceed with his *King Kong*; in return, he'd make a film for Universal. Paramount distributed De Laurentiis's $24 million *King Kong* in Christmas 1976, but it was panned by critics and made only $37 million. De Laurentiis nevertheless paid Korshak $30,000 for mediating the conflict.

A year or so later, De Laurentiis repaid Wasserman by making Universal's *The Brink's Job* (1978). Based on a true story, it featured a small-time criminal (Peter Falk) who discovers a weakness in Brink's security system and sets up the famed 1950 heist. The film quickly ran into problems, said Tanen.

The crew was shooting in the North End of Boston, which at the time was dominated by Italians and Irish. The neighborhood was perfect for the late 1940s setting—except that every rooftop now sprouted a TV antenna. A unit man canvassed the neighborhood, asking people to take down their antennas for a few hours. The most courteous reply was a door slammed in his face. "These people were abusive," said Tanen. The crew couldn't shoot the scene without removing the evidence of 1970s life.

Tanen walked into Lew's office. "I have this really stupid problem," and he laid it out.

Lew nodded. "I'll take care of it."

Wasserman called Korshak, and two hours later, Tanen received a call from the unit producer. "You want to see something funny?" he said ecstatically. "You ought to see these 280-pound Italian women climbing up on their roofs, tromping around in their black skirts and work boots, ripping out their TV aerials." The crewman was happy, Tanen was impressed, and the film finished on time. Released in 1978, it even won an Oscar for set decoration—a tacit nod to Sidney's handiwork.

"Now, there's nothing dishonest about that," said Tanen. "But Lew had called his good friend Sidney, and they had got it done."

A federal grand jury in Boston, however, did see something dishonest about that and other phone calls. The jury found that the Universal production had paid Ralph Lamatina and Joseph "Joe Shoes" Cammoratta for their help in persuading North End residents to "cooperate" with a crew of *The Brink's Job*. And De Laurentiis claimed that he had been forced to hire twice as many Teamsters drivers as he had needed, which added more than $1 million to the cost of the Universal film. The affair made the national news, including *NBC Evening News* and the *Los Angeles Times*.

For some time now, Korshak had been an unwilling cause célèbre. The Internal Revenue Service had hounded him for failing to pay back taxes, and questioned his large write-offs for meals at The Bistro. He managed to avoid fraud charges by settling the tax claim—for 15 cents on the dollar. In the summer of 1976, the *New York Times* had run a four-part series on Korshak that was read widely but contained little that was new. But Bea was very upset. A few days later, Edie and Lew welcomed the Korshaks to their fortieth wedding anniversary party. Lew embraced Sid and squired around to greet his 300 guests, while Edie took Bea aside and whispered, "How are you doing, honey?" The two commiserated about the awful story as Edie tried to soothe her friend. As Wendy Goldberg explained, "Edie will go to any length to protect her friends. She will fight for you to the end."

Soon a real Hollywood scandal overshadowed Korshak's front-page attention. Edie and Lew had known the courtly David Begelman since 1948, when the smooth-talking agent began to work for MCA. Now Begelman was head of Columbia Pictures, where he had produced a string of hits, including *The Way We Were* (1973) and *Shampoo* (1975). In September 1976, Begelman was accused of forging the endorsement on a $10,000 check that Columbia had issued to actor Cliff Robertson. When Robertson received an IRS letter demanding taxes on the income, he called the police. Now the Los Angeles District Attorney was investigating. "We couldn't believe David was guilty," said Goldberg.

If true, his embezzlement scam could be more destructive to Hollywood that any of Korshak's deals, and the town somehow needed to meet. As it happened, Begelman's wife, Gladyce, had coauthored a book, *New York on $1,000 a Day Before Lunch,* and wanted a publication party. Edie didn't dare host such a controversial event, but flamboyant producer Allan Carr was happy to throw one. The entire town, including Edie and Lew, showed up for the event. "No one talked about the book because we were all gossiping about Begelman," Dominick Dunne recalled. That night, furious arguments raged about what Begelman's troubles meant for Hollywood's image, and how best to deal with him. Edie, who advocated rallying the forces, pressed her point with several people, including Fran Stark, wife of producer Ray Stark. "It was then that I realized that this town would protect one of their own," said Dunne.

Edie and Lew had known for years that Begelman had a deep-seated problem, he explained. "David had stolen money from [ex-MCA client] Judy Garland far beyond what anyone else had stolen from her." But Lew never spoke out. In fact, "all of them would keep silent about Begelman," said Dunne. That night, "Edie and Lew closed the wagons around the town's own." Begelman was allowed to resign from Columbia; he eventually received a mild sentence—three years' probation for grand larceny and a $5,000 fine. A few years later, the convicted felon returned to the executive suite as head of MGM. About twenty years later, he committed suicide in the Century Plaza Hotel. As Lew told Dunne, "I knew David when he was a crook, and he stayed a crook till the day he died." Dunne explained, "All of the studio heads had agreed to stand behind David, and I can't help but think that was because of Lew."

But Begelman's whistle-blower, Cliff Robertson, was unable to find a job for four years. He and his wife, heiress Dina Merrill, were dropped from the town's "A"-list parties.

By the late 1970s, tales of Hollywood fraud, embezzlement, and "connections" were spreading beyond the movie colony, which upset Edie. What if the *New York Times* investigated the *wives'* connections? What would that do to their men and the studios? Hollywood depended on the public's goodwill, and Edie worried that someday the mudslinging might stick to Lew—and to her.

In 1977 the Los Angeles District Attorney formed a committee to investigate the ties between the mob and show business. Pornographic films financed by laundered mob money, for example, were increasing. A year later, the California Organized Crime Control Commission, which included Edwin Meese III, identified Korshak as "the most important link between organized crime and legitimate business." The report angered Korshak a great deal and upset Bea even more. As for Edie, it was too much! She urged Lew to speak out.

Wasserman talked to a reporter at the *Los Angeles Herald Examiner* and decried "the crescendo of ambiguity." He'd become troubled by scattershot attacks on Hollywood that unfairly tarred thousands of movie workers. "Why is it," he said rhetorically, "[that] when something adverse occurs it's 'the industry' that's in trouble? There are some sixty thousand people who work here, but somehow, the press had equated fifteen or twenty individuals with the entire film industry." I'm more concerned that some guy in Kansas City thinks that Hollywood is full of crooks. It's just not true."

For her part, Edie took to polishing the town's tarnished star. In 1979 she joined all three boards of the Motion Picture and Television Fund and doubled her efforts to build Hollywood's flagship charity. It had been neglected for years—at a time when aging workers from the studio-system days needed help. Edie collected donations from executives and stars, cajoling, wheedling, and bullying when necessary. When one producer heard that Edie

Wasserman was waiting to see him, he cried out: "God, not her again!" He wrote a big check hastily, gave it to his secretary, and left his office for the afternoon, citing "an emergency meeting." Edie did not spare her own husband; she got him to suggest that every studio contribute an annual gift to the MPTV. She was relentless in building the Hollywood charity, whose motto she shared: "We take care of our own."

THIRTY-FOUR

IN THE LATE 1970S, Wasserman was still deeply involved in film-making. He took a special interest in *MacArthur*, starring his friend Gregory Peck. He approved *House Calls* with Walter Matthau, and the melodramatic *The Sentinel*, with Ava Gardner. If Wasserman insisted on giving the green light to *The Last Remake of Beau Geste*, a comedy with a great cast including Terry Thomas that barely got reviewed, he also okayed *Smokey and the Bandit*, which delighted audiences. The year 1978 marked an all-time high for MCA film revenue and income: $462 million.

His pet project was an all-black version of *The Wizard of Oz*. At sixty-five, Wasserman was still enamored of musicals, and he set out to bring a Broadway version of *Oz* back to the screen. As he envisioned it, *The Wiz* (1978) was going to be a contemporary piece that would ride the era's blaxploitation wave. Universal convinced Motown Records' Berry Gordy to offer financial support, signed Diana Ross and Michael Jackson, and found a nice little script written by newcomer Joel Schumacher. "Lew loved *The Wiz*," said Ned Tanen. "He was convinced it would be a hit."

But then the vision expanded. The script transplanted the tale of Dorothy from Kansas City to Manhattan and substituted jive for English. What was supposed to be an offbeat black production became overblown. Quincy Jones handled music, Sidney Lumet directed a huge cast—and somehow Berry Gordy didn't come through with his funding, said Tanen. Nevertheless, Wasserman was excited after watching the dailies. "He kept thinking we had a hit," and pulled out the stops.

The budget doubled to $24 million—a huge amount for a Wasserman film. By the time it premiered, MCA executives were seating Gordy and his entourage alongside fashion designers Bill Blass, Norma Kamali, and Calvin Klein, who had helped outfit some 300 dancers. As Tanen watched the film, he slouched deeper into his seat, thinking: "Can't we please go back to the Munchkins?"

Critics panned the film, calling it "garish spectacle and a lot of din." *The Wiz* was too scary for children, and too silly for adults. Yet Wasserman maintained his faith in it until a week after the film's opening, when his venerated box-office numbers foretold the future. The movie collected only $13 million and lost millions more. "*The Wiz* got derailed by its own steam and hype," Tanen said.

Wasserman and Tanen then made the mistake of turning down one of the richest franchises in the history of film. After George Lucas had finished Universal's *American Graffiti,* he brought Tanen a second project he wanted to direct: a science-fiction tale with characters named R2D2 and Obi-Wan Kenobi. Tanen wanted Universal to produce the inexpensive film and left the script with his boss. "Lew had read the script, but he just didn't get it," said Tanen. "He pointed out that science-fiction films don't do well, and besides, Lucas's characters weren't likable, let alone human." Universal had thirty days in which to respond to Lucas. "I kept going into Lew's office with this script that cost only $25,000, and saying, 'Why don't we do this? We can't lose.'" Finally Tanen threw up his hands and returned the script to Lucas.

One of the sticking points in the deal was that Lucas wanted profit participation. He had watched *American Graffiti* build its audience week after week, and for his second film, he wanted a piece of the action. But Wasserman wasn't about to give up control, let alone profits.

Wasserman turned Lucas down. A week later, Twentieth Century Fox paid Lucas $160,000 to write and direct *Star Wars*. Passing up an additional $500,000, Lucas negotiated 60 percent of the merchandising and sequel rights to the film for a period of two years. After that, the filmmaker would own all of those rights without having to share a dime. Fox executives didn't believe they were giving away anything of value, since the studio had tried merchandising the characters in *Doctor Dolittle,* with no success. And, in the 1970s, sequels routinely earned only one-third of the original movie's income.

But if *Star Wars* became successful, Lucas would be richer than Lew.

In May 1977—nearly four years after Universal had turned down the project—Tanen and his wife, Kitty Hawk, sat in the Chinese Theater for the film's premiere. As the lights went down in the theater, Tanen watched the introductory credits roll by as the title *Star Wars* unfurled like a flag. Excited, Tanen whispered to his wife, "This is the biggest hit ever made." She turned and asked, "How do you know? You haven't even seen it yet."

Tanen just knew: "Lucas had captured the eternal comic strip, that seminal stuff."

Tanen dreaded returning to the Tower on Monday. "Lew had heard the buzz about the movie and knew I had seen it." He arrived early to avoid sharing an elevator with Wasserman. Tanen walked straight to his office and closed the door quietly. Within a few minutes, Wasserman walked into his office and asked nonchalantly, "Well, how was it?"

Tanen looked up. "Do you really want to know?"

Wasserman scowled. "Of course I do."

Tanen sighed. "It was great, Lew. It's a big hit."

Wasserman gave Tanen his cold mogul glare and slammed the

door. "All those ridiculous English prints fell off the wall, as they occasionally did," Tanen recalled. A few seconds later, Wasserman opened Tanen's office door again, his face flushed with denial and anger. He roared, *"You* put that film in turnaround, didn't you?" meaning Tanen had killed the deal.

Wasserman slammed the door again, this time rattling pictures on other peoples' walls.

Star Wars became one of the industry's all-time greatest hits. Its budget had tripled during development but was still only $11 million. In three months, the film generated more than $100 million at the box office. Six months later, it had raked in $200 million, besting Universal's *Jaws.*

Fox had no premonition that the film would shatter all records. After screening *Star Wars,* the studio considered selling the film quickly and taking a tax loss. Someone said the studio could recycle it as a TV show. Yet *Star Wars* went on to collect $779 million worldwide in theatrical rentals alone, with most of the money going to Lucas.

And Tanen became known as the man who turned down *Star Wars.* "I've been tainted with that legacy ever since," he said. However, he and Wasserman paid attention to the merchandising phenomenon *Star Wars* kicked off— one that still has not abated. In 1979 the movie spun off T-shirts, socks, Halloween masks, plastic tableware, lunch boxes, greeting cards, and dozens of other products. By 2002, the gewgaws would pull in at least $4 billion, said Tom Pollock, who was then Lucas's attorney.

The other result of *Star Wars* was its threat to the studios' hegemony. The film became the first blockbuster franchise that left little of its spoils in Hollywood. After battling Tanen and Wasserman, Lucas grew to disdain show business's culture, epitomized by Universal. He later told a reporter: "We are the guys who dig out the gold. The man in the executive tower cannot do that. The studios are corporations now, and the men who run them are bureaucrats."

But to Hollywood, the ultimate insult was Lucas' expatriation of his movie profits out of town. All of the income from the sequels *The Empire Strikes Back* (1980), *The Return of the Jedi* (1983), *The Phantom Menace* (1999), and others flowed north to San Rafael, enabling Lucas to buy Skywalker Ranch and build his own studio, Industrial Light & Magic.

Sid Sheinberg faulted Tanen for not pushing Wasserman hard enough for *Star Wars*. But Wasserman had turned into the town's Abominable "No" Man. When bandleader Artie Shaw once asked Wasserman why he turned down so many scripts, the mogul replied, "If I say no to a script, that makes me right 99 percent of the time." Wasserman's litmus test for film approval was to measure the advocate's commitment. "Lew made it so that if his guys really, really believed in something, they could do it," said Pollock. "But boy, if you screwed up, it was your head on the line. Lew figured if they were passionate about something, they'd see it through." Then he'd approve the project. MCA executives summoned numbers, logic, reports from consultants, and surveillance on competitors— anything to get a yes.

The approach worked well in developing theme-park shops, where an executive could calculate retail sales dollars per square foot. But moviemaking was a chimerical thing, with no comparables or equations. "Lew never understood that," said Tanen. As a result, Tanen grew frustrated with Universal's film-development process.

"Those were Ned's angry years," said Pollock. "I think you can see why." On one side, Tanen and his staff fought "the Mill Valley Mafia"; on the other side he tried to manage the executive suits. "The studio guys drove me crazy—you couldn't do anything right with those guys," said Tanen. Wasserman and other MCA board directors couldn't understand some of the executive producer's film choices: "They thought I smoked pot all the time."

Few of Tanen's projects gave Wasserman as many headaches as the National Lampoon projects. Tanen had wanted to buy the

National Lampoon magazine so he could tap its rich vein of gifted gag writers. One day, Tanen brought Wasserman to a *Lampoon* story meeting. The two sat quietly as the young men tried to outgross one another with sexually graphic, obscenity-laden story ideas. The sixty-seven-year-old Wasserman was disgusted. "It was only a twenty-minute meeting and the kids were throwing out bon mots and one-liners, most of which were bad," said Tanen. "But Lew acted like 'Keep these bearded kids away from me.'" But out of these sessions came a few solid ideas from unproven writers, such as Harold Ramis and Douglas Kenney.

One of the concepts was built on a character from *Saturday Night Live,* a hit TV show. Sean Daniel, an assistant to Tanen, championed what would become *Animal House.* "But Lew didn't want any movie to move ahead without a big name attached to it," said Daniel.

The *Lampoon* writers suggested John Belushi, whose toga-clad Bluto was all the rage. After some wrangling, Universal signed Belushi as an actor for $35,000, which at the time was high, given that Belushi had no film experience. Wasserman approved a $2.7 million budget, and Tanen appointed Daniel to oversee the film. In October 1977, John Landis started directing by shouting obscene orders, throwing food at actors, and generally triggering sophomoric antics.

During the filming, Wasserman, Jennings Lang, and Tanen screened the dailies secretly. Wasserman complained about the scene in which Belushi spied bare-breasted coeds pillow-fighting. The chief also hated the horse manure and projectile vomiting. Lang criticized the screenplay, written by Kenney, Ramis, and Chris Miller, and Tanen grew despondent over his seemingly impossible position.

Editing spilled from the normal three-month process into six months. Finally, in the spring of 1978, Tanen previewed the film in Denver, where it received a standing ovation. Daniel was relieved and Belushi was ecstatic. But after the film premiered in New York, Tanen fell into one of his dark, depressed moods. "That night, he told me to decide which building to jump from tomorrow," said Daniel. Confirming Tanen's fears, New York critics greeted Belushi's film debut coolly. Nevertheless, over the next few weeks, *Animal House* racked up $60 million from hundreds of other theaters around the nation. *Newsweek* called it a "panty raid on respectability," and yet it grossed $170 million.

Wasserman didn't like *Animal House,* with its disrespectful references to Jackie Kennedy and the Vietnam War. But on a visceral level, he began to realize that he didn't understand the era's moviegoing public. After *Animal House,* Wasserman gave Tanen, Daniel, and the rest of his "baby moguls" more latitude, which was his way of cheering them on. "With Lew, encouragement meant that he didn't hit us over the head with a pole and yell at us to stop."

Wasserman worried that Alfred Hitchcock was slowing down. When Wasserman visited his friend on the set of *Family Plot* (1976), he noticed that Hitch's face looked whiter and fleshier, and his jowls hung ever lower. But the movie was a lighthearted suspense story about a phony psychic (Barbara Harris) and an investigator (Bruce Dern) who encounter two kidnappers (William Devane and Karen Black). Hitch seemed to be enjoying himself for the first time in a while.

Wasserman knew Hitch better than he knew his own brother, according to several accounts. At one time, the two had behaved like frat boys themselves, sharing locker-room pranks and dirty jokes. Hitch once threw a Halloween party on Lew's lot and surprised everyone by dressing in drag, with lipstick and all.

But the director's behavior turned increasingly bizarre. Before he finished filming *Family Plot,* he French-kissed actress Karen Black on the set. His wife suffered a stroke, and the director was so worried about her he remained by her side and off the lot for several weeks. After she recovered, he returned to work on his next film, *The Short Night,* but progress was slow. "Hitch had arthritis and needed help all of the time," said Herb Steinberg. The eighty-year-old director was still drinking several screwdrivers during the day, and had resumed his old cigar-smoking habit.

Wasserman once suggested that he retire. "What would I do?" he responded. "Sit in a corner and read a book?" The two never discussed the topic again.

Meanwhile, the movie business was flagging again. United Artists was wobbly, and Walt Disney's studio subsisted on sheer inertia, thirteen years after its founder's death. Columbia was struggling to recover from the Begelman scandal, and MGM was at a nadir. Steve Ross was working on reviving Warners, and Twentieth Century Fox was looking for another *Star Wars.* Only Universal seemed to own the present and the future. Its film *The Deer Hunter* had just won the Best Picture Oscar, and the film's director, Michael Cimino, had nabbed the Academy's Best Director award.

But in 1979, even MCA needed increased earnings to shore itself up. Wasserman grew worried about troubles outside of the movie division. The bugs in his cherished DiscoVision system were still plaguing him, and MCA Records had just lost $10 million that year, a result of disco music's waning popularity. Wasserman started looking for a new chief to restore the music division's profits, and sharks were now circling the corporate waters, although MCA was considered less of a target than vulnerable Disney Studios or even Paramount, both of which would soon be acquired.

Not about to take a chance, Wasserman and Sheinberg devised anti-takeover measures for the directors to approve at MCA's next meeting. It would be nice if Wasserman could walk into that room and hand Jules and his company directors a hit like *Star Wars.* Wasserman leaned heavily on his own executives to deliver some magic.

• • •

Wasserman had been expecting Hitchcock's death for years, but that didn't make his friend's decline any easier. "He knew that my father was dying," said Patrick Hitchcock O'Connell. Although Hitch was absent from the lot for long periods, Wasserman never touched his personal bungalow, which included a sitting room, a screening room, and a full bar. He could have seized the prime piece of real estate, said O'Connell. "Everyone on the lot wanted that office, but Lew let my father keep it until the end. He knew he was never going to make another picture."

In 1978 Wasserman arranged for Hitch to receive the American Film Institute Life Achievement Award. The following year, Queen Elizabeth knighted the director, and Wasserman asked two of Hitch's stars to accompany the honoree to England. Cary Grant and Janet Leigh escorted Hitchcock to his native land for what would be his last visit.

A few months later, in April 1980, Hitch died in his sleep. At his memorial service, musicians played Hitchcock's theme, Charles Gounod's "Funeral March for a Marionette," just as musicians had played it that Oscar night in 1974, when Hitch had bowed low onstage to give Lew his honorary award. Wasserman choked up as he gave the eulogy at Hitchcock's funeral. Later, he asked his chauffeur to drive around the streets aimlessly for a while.

Right after Wasserman said farewell to Hitchcock, Jules Stein landed at UCLA Medical Center again—this time under an oxygen tent. Eventually Stein returned home, but he looked wizened, frail, and unhappy. Stein asked Wasserman to promise that no matter what happened, he would never break up MCA. He wanted the company to remain intact. American business was about to begin a long binge of merging and acquiring companies. In fact, at the moment that Stein uttered his last wish, Los Angeles financier Michael Milken was fine-tuning another dark art: that of "leveraging" buyouts and company breakups. However,

Wasserman had given his pledge, and now he was honor-bound. As Al Dorskind told me, "I never knew Lew to break his word, ever." In the advent of the new gilded age, Wasserman and his word would be sorely tested.

PART IV
Safeguarding the Legacy: 1981–2002

THIRTY-FIVE

UNDER A SUNNY CALIFORNIA SKY, on May 3, 1981, a solemn Henry Mancini led his twenty-member orchestra in "Tangerine," the wistful 1942 tune by Jimmy Dorsey—one of Jules Stein's long-time clients. Five days earlier, the eighty-five-year-old Stein had finally died. Thousands of MCA stars mingled that Sunday afternoon on a patio of the Jules Stein Eye Institute at UCLA, and the dappled sunlight fell through the whispering eucalyptus trees. Angie Dickinson smiled behind oversize sunglasses, and Charlton Heston moved royally through the crowd, wearing gold chains. The orchestra played thirty-three of Stein's favorite songs for the farewell that one columnist called "an Event in the tradition of Show Biz."

Stein had not wanted this memorial service to resemble a funeral. "It was a celebration of life," said *Hollywood Reporter* columnist George Christy. "And that's how Jules's friends and family treated it." Chanteuse Helen O'Connell sang one of her hits, "Green Eyes," mindful that her own sight had been saved by Stein's institute. George Burns gently cracked a few jokes, aware that Doris was still a grieving widow. Gene Kelly looked elegant in a formal suit. When he had first heard the news of Stein's death, he had rushed up to Misty Mountain to console the widow, just as she had gathered the family around her formal dinner table. Dinner was hot dogs and canned beans served from sterling silver dishes, Doris's comfort food and a rare link to her humble Kansas City origins. When Kelly had appeared that evening, the grande dame turned him away because he was not wearing a tie and jacket. Now, in the May sunlight, she allowed her old friend to kiss her cheek.

Stein had requested that his 1,200 guests leave their mourning attire at home but, please, no casual sport coats. He had left behind dozens of other instructions in a thorough, six-page burial briefing that he had given to Wasserman before he died. The MCA chief had attended to every jot and squiggle in his boss's last commandments— and then some. Hours before the memorial, Wasserman was rearranging the folding chairs so guests wouldn't face the late-afternoon sun. "He didn't want the guests to squint from the bright light," said Dr. Bradley Straatsma.

Stein, who had finally succumbed to a heart attack, was laid out in a custom-cut Italian wool suit inside an exquisite mahogany casket of eighteenth-century English design. His staged affair cost $100,000 and Stein himself had selected the seventy-six honorary pallbearers, who held ropes of gold braid tethered to Stein's casket. They encompassed California's crème de la crème: burgermeisters Norton Simon, Samuel Colt, and Frank Kilroe; and political king-pins Earle Jorgenson, Alfred Bloomingdale, and James C. Petrillo, president of the American Federation of Musicians. Actors Cary Grant, Jimmy Stewart, and Fred Astaire marched alongside agents George Chasin, Herman Citron, and Arthur Park. Directors such as Henry Hathaway, William Wyler, and Mervyn LeRoy walked in sync with producers Sam Goldwyn, Jr., Hal Wallis, and Fred Brisson (Mr. Rosalind Russell). For once, MCA old-timers Sonny Werblin, Maurice Lipsey, and Mickey Rockford marched in lock-step with the company's young bloods Ned Tanen, Jay Stein, and Sidney Sheinberg. The lineup also included medical doctors, including those from the institute. And the entire procession had been choreographed and rehearsed like a Busby Berkeley movie musical.

The only pallbearer who could not attend sent his condolences from the White House and Wasserman read the telegram from Ronnie Reagan. Many mourners believed that Reagan's occupancy of 1600 Pennsylvania Avenue ranked as Stein's most outstanding achievement. The U.S. president expressed his regrets at Stein's death, and insisted that "memories do grow warmer through the years."

The most human moments occurred when Stein's relatives addressed the crowd. Katrina vanden Huevel, Jean Stein's daughter, joked about her grandfather's parsimony. "You might guess that all of us who have flown here from the East for this weekend arrived in economy class." For once, Wasserman was at a loss for words, admitting that his mentor's death "leaves me bereft of a member of my family, in ways that defy the power of language to express." As Jean Stein later explained, "The relationship between Lew and Jules was incredible. They were not exactly sentimental men, yet they were very close." At the podium, Wasserman recounted the official history of MCA, before his voice broke with emotion and he left the stage hastily.

For Edie, this afternoon had been a long time coming. She had often joked about that moment in 1936 when her groom told her he was taking a job with MCA. What was so appealing about a position that meant leaving Cleveland and taking a hefty $40-a-week pay cut? She asked, "Why do you want that job?"

"Because," Lew told her, "Jules is an old man." The twenty-three-year-old Wasserman had figured that his forty-year-old boss would die pretty soon and leave him the agency. Now, forty-five years later, his strategy had finally paid off. When Edie arrived at the service, she sat down and said, "Well, it's about time!"

Doris inherited MCA's voting shares, which irked Edie. Together with the widow, Wasserman executed the rest of Stein's meticulous will. He made just one request: "When Dr. Stein passed on, I asked

Doris if I could take some of his furnishings." She gave him several of Stein's favorite pieces. "I'm the only one in the company who still has them," he told me proudly, twenty years later.

Stein, who spent his leisure hours looking for ways to save money, had divided his estate into three pieces: one for his widow, one for his family, and the third for his vision center. Newspapers had estimated his worth at about $10 million. Imagine the buzz when, a week after the funeral, Hollywood learned that Stein had left behind $200 million in assets—about $500 million in today's dollars. His sister Ruth had managed his investments for years and was known for her eccentric, squirrellike bookkeeping. Said Wasserman, "She was brilliant."

As for Stein's MCA, it was worth $1.2 billion. Concerned that his death would leave its future in jeopardy, Stein didn't want his company to become the spoils of hostile raiders. But his death did indeed fuel speculation about takeover bids, and on the morning he died, the New York Stock Exchange temporarily halted trading of MCA stock. One of the potential bidders was Seagram Co. Ltd., headed by Samuel Bronfman, Jr., the son of a Canadian rumrunner who had once done business with Cleveland's Moe Dalitz and Chicago's Al Capone. Now, decades later, Seagram was a blue-chip Toronto firm, Dalitz was a Nevada philanthropist, and the late Capone was one of America's most romanticized outlaws. As for MCA, it boasted a compound annual growth rate of 27 percent— an awesome figure that Wasserman often quoted. Few companies came close to matching that.

But if Wasserman expected to protect his firm from the vulgarians at his gate, Lew knew that he and Sheinberg had better safeguard its assets. And, at that very moment, several of his most valued producers were fleeing the lot.

The talent drain had begun a few years earlier, with Frank Price. One morning, an MCA car had arrived to drive him to work, as it did most mornings. He climbed in next to Sid Sheinberg, who was reading the morning paper. Price once again told Sheinberg that he wanted to move beyond managing TV and that he needed a new challenge.

Price saw warning signals ahead. At NBC, Price's biggest customer, Fred Silverman, had taken over the presidency. Price knew him from his previous work at ABC, where Silverman had lifted the network's ratings with his "jiggle TV"—programs about scantily clad women. The mercurial programmer was also credited with doing more to lower TV standards than any other figure and, to top it off, he was notoriously difficult to work with. For example, Silverman thought nothing of changing the sound track of a TV movie the night before it aired. "He'd make my life miserable, as he didn't understand the particular problems of production," said Price.

Price was also running into static from the other networks. "We got so good at TV that one year, we were turning down orders," he said. "We got very arrogant, and it scared the networks. They started turning away from us." At the same time, "Cable was coming in, and our audience was getting more fragmented, making it harder for us to get the ratings." Wasserman *said* he was committed to being in cable, but so far, MCA's participation in that new medium had been limited to its 20 percent interest in the ill-fated Premiere Channel venture, and its 50 percent of the start-up USA Network and Sci-Fi Channel. Lew's moves were not as bold as those of his competitors, and Price wanted out of the company.

That morning, in the car with Sheinberg, Price asked him point-blank: "When am I going to get into producing motion pictures?"

"Not until I get out."

"In other words, never," Price thought.

Despite Edie Wasserman's many exhortations, Price left Universal Studios in 1978 and signed on as president of Columbia Pictures, where he worked on such successes as *Kramer vs. Kramer, Gandhi,* and *Tootsie.*

"A lot of guys left TV after that," said Marvin Antonowsky, a senior vice president at Universal TV. "A lot of them wanted the opportunity to make films, but Universal had closed the door on that idea. Ned Tanen didn't want that." Nor did Sheinberg.

By the late 1970s, Stephen Cannell was in a quandary about his future at MCA. The writer/producer had several Universal shows on the air, including *The Rockford Files, Dr. Scorpion, Baretta,* and *The Duke.* "I was making a pretty good living," he said, "although I wasn't earning the money that a big executive-producer got." He was also writing a few hours a week in order to qualify for WGA benefits and residuals. When it came time for Universal to renew Cannell's contract, Sheinberg offered him a deal that would give him an executive-producer credit on all of his shows. That meant a substantial amount of money, but it would remove some of the benefits that Cannell now received as a writer/producer. "Essentially, I'd lose money if I took the promotion."

Sheinberg offered to fix the problem if Cannell signed a multiyear contract. Initially, Cannell declined. "I didn't want to lock myself in like that." But Sheinberg sweetened his offer. "I got a $1 million-a-year deal, which was unheard of for a writer-producer," recalled Cannell. Despite the money, he sensed that the studio's glory days were fading. "One thing I constantly preached to my guys was that it's got to be fun to work." And whatever fun remained at Universal was quickly being leached out of the lot. While Cannell's million-dollar contract was being negotiated, a junior executive called him into his office one day. He started yelling at the veteran producer about *Baretta*'s high budget. Some suspected that the abusive tantrum was meant to score points with his boss, but if so, it backfired. "If there was ever a chance of Steve staying after that, they blew it," said one witness. The deal fell apart.

For Cannell, the point was fairness. "I looked at what Universal was making on my programs and what I was making and I didn't like it." After his contract expired, he left Universal and formed

Stephen J. Cannell Productions. "I'm sure the guys at MCA expected me to fall on my face," he said. But he had learned well at Wasserman's school. He used many of the budget standards and management techniques he had learned at Universal. When Stephen J. Cannell Productions introduced *The A-Team* in 1983, the producer was on his way to selling six hours of weekly prime-time programming. For the next fifteen years, he'd capture business from Universal's network clients and produce $1 billion in TV fare, becoming the third-largest supplier of TV shows.

Soon Cannell's mentor, Roy Huggins, began questioning his place at MCA, too. Huggins had created some of Universal's most unconventional heroes: misfits in *Rockford* and *Toma*, the alienated in *The Outsider* and *The Virginian*, loners and outlaws in *Run for Your Life* and *Alias Smith and Jones*. Yet his characters never whined or wept, and they collectively lifted TV beyond its usual mediocre fare. Indeed, his stories were among the best in twentieth-century TV.

Huggins never complained about his own situation, either. When his contract came up for renewal, he scanned the new agreement and placed it in a drawer. Then he returned to his hectic schedule and ruminated over the terms of his deal. In all of his agreements, Wasserman and Sheinberg had assured Huggins that he'd receive a piece of the profits. "I had done about twenty Movies of the Week in which Sid had told me I'd make at least $25,000 apiece," he said. "But I hadn't seen a nickel." By his tally, he'd made Universal some $500 million.

One day, Huggins discussed the issue with Sheinberg. "Sid denied that the [earlier] conversation took place," said Huggins. Aware that two other people had witnessed their conversation seven years earlier, Huggins "went to one fellow who said he recalled the discussion very well, and that $25,000 had been a conservative estimate." Jo Swerling, Jr., also was in the room.

Huggins returned to his office to wrestle with his decision.

Should he sign the contract and remain at Universal? Or should he fight to enforce the terms of his previous deals? "I had done most of my dealings with MCA directly with Wasserman. I'm not a lawyer, and I didn't have one myself." But he couldn't shake the feeling that he had been "terribly mauled."

He reviewed his old talks with Wasserman through the prism of his now-empty profit deals. "Wasserman was always quiet, never showing his hand. It was like he was playing the role of an executive or playing a game," Huggins recalled. Wasserman would sit at his desk, endlessly turning his gold letter opener, which resembled a sword, or tapping it sharply on his unnaturally clean desk. He'd listen to you describe the problem. After you left his office, he'd consult with others, gather his numbers, and make a decision "out of sight," said Huggins. That was typical of many CEOs. "But Wasserman was calculating," said Huggins. "He was guarded and you never saw him clearly. Watching him was like looking through a glass darkly."

Meanwhile, Sheinberg learned that Huggins had consulted witnesses of the last round of contract negotiations. "Sid went ballistic," said Huggins. "I got a call from someone in legal who told me that MCA was withdrawing its offer."

In 1980 Huggins quit. A short time later, he joined Swerling and several other former Universal employees at Stephen J. Cannell Productions. By then, other Universal executives had quit to work with Price at Columbia Pictures, or some other studio executive. Still others started independent production houses.

In the end, it wasn't a disgruntled producer or writer who uncovered the true meaning of "Universal net profit." It was a character from a Huggins series, the easygoing investigator Jim Rockford—or, rather, his real-life counterpart, actor Jim Garner.

In 1980 *The Rockford Files* finished its first five-year network run and began syndication, from which Garner and Huggins were supposed to receive a percentage of net profits. *The Rockford Files* played morning, noon, and night someplace in the world, and it proved to be one of the most lucrative TV shows ever. Garner had contracted to receive a 37.5 percent share. In return, he had agreed to take less than his usual fee: just $30,000 to $60,000 per episode. "I could have gotten a lot more," he said. But he'd opted for the infamous "Universal net profit" deal and waited. And waited.

MCA statements showed the series had earned $52 million during its five-year run. Yet now it was bleeding $9 million. In the weeks between its network and syndication runs, the show had mysteriously acquired millions of dollars of debt. Some expenses were outrageous. In one episode, Rockford needed a car to drive into a lake. Universal charged the show for a car, and the producers had to repair the vehicle before returning it to the studio. A few episodes later, a *Rockford* script called for an auto crash—and the show had to buy the same car again from Universal—and again pay for its repair—at marked-up values. "We bought that car from the studio four times," Garner said.

To distribute each *Rockford* episode, Wasserman charged $50,000, which paid for a few Teamsters to drive the film five miles from Universal City to NBC Studios. At twenty-two episodes a year, for five years, that was $5 million. The studio had built in its own profit. But there was no such guarantee for its partners. As Cannell explained, "Jim Garner was never going to see a cent."

Garner blamed Huggins, not realizing that Huggins wasn't getting his share, either. In 1981, the actor threatened to sue MCA and Universal, unless they made good on their contract. Meanwhile, several other people were filing complaints, including Fess Parker, star of NBC's *Daniel Boone* series (1964–1970), and Aaron Spelling, creator of ABC's *Charlie's Angels* (1976–1981). The Los Angeles District Attorney looked at Spelling's case and remarked that, although there was insufficient evidence of criminal conduct, the movie industry sure was plagued by "shoddy business practices."

A slew of "creative accounting" cases and broken contract claims began to proliferate in Los Angeles Superior Court, leading to one of the most-watched, off-network shows in years. If even one case made it to trial, Wasserman's reputation and MCA's future could be damaged. Did anyone have the chutzpah, cash, and legions of lawyers necessary to best the town's wiliest dealmaker?

In 1981 the Writers Guild of America and studios began negotiating a new contract. In the past, these discussions had led to disillusionment. In 1966 the WGA had gained the possessory credit, only to be persuaded three years later to give it up in return for a pledge about bargaining agreements that was never fulfilled. In 1973—the year of the last strike—the guild members had believed that pay-TV, or cable, and satellite TV were going to become the next new market. "So we had worked on an equation for those residuals," said Del Reisman. But the new market became videocassettes, and writers were left behind again. "That led to a great deal of anger."

The WGA felt as though it had been deceived by the Association of Motion Picture and Television Producers, whose chairman was now Sid Sheinberg. "Lew felt that it was part of my job," he said. Sheinberg believed he had an affinity with writers, going back to his heyday at Universal TV in the 1960s. "These were people I knew and had worked with, and some were close friends." He tried to adopt Wasserman's smooth style, but found that the new technologies created unwieldy obstacles to bargaining. "It's always contentious because the [talent] believes that if they don't establish a precedent, they'll never get paid. And the corporate side believes that they may be giving away the store. So there's a great deal of fear on both sides."

When the issue hinged on the writers' getting their share of video sales from their movies, the talks faltered. Their contract expired and, in April 1981, the WGA struck, shutting down the production of TV and movies. SAG members had just returned from a strike over the same issue, and the studios were still paying for that work stoppage. The directors and musicians were also in contract talks. Hollywood was like a powder keg, waiting for a match. "That was one of the toughest times in the business," said John McLean, head of the WGA, the locus of the most incendiary arguments.

"Then, in the sixth week of the writers' strike, in walks Wasserman, as if to say, 'Okay folks. Daddy is here,' " Del Reisman recalled. Wasserman stood at the head of the table, his senatorial voice as calming as a sedative. He said, "We are going to negotiate this thing until it's settled."

It was not so easy. By now, old movies like *Casablanca* and *From Here to Eternity* were reaping tens of millions for the studios. "Older guys like Julius Epstein and Daniel Taradash had no idea their features would sell so well," said Reisman. Worse, the studios didn't offer to pay the old-timers even a nominal fee, which would have gone a long way to healing the wounds.

Similarly, TV writers who had created fabulously popular series such as *I Love Lucy* or *Leave It to Beaver* blinked in disbelief as their episodes continued to play, for the thirty-fifth year in a row, in obscure corners of the globe and major media markets alike. "Yet [Lucy's writers] Bob Caroll, Jr., and Madelyn Pugh Davis never got a dime of residuals," said Reisman. The issue surfaced increasingly during strikes and negotiations as "the money the writers were asking for was nothing compared to the extraordinary amount the studios were collecting. It's amazing, really, that the studios after all this time wouldn't give them something," said Reisman. According to one executive, it would have cost each studio about $1 million to satisfy the writers' demands. Such a pittance, split among hundreds of writers, would not be enough to buy each one a new home, but it just might help a retiree keep the lights on and the furnace running.

Wasserman reacted to the people at the bargaining table like long-lost companions. As it always did, the AMPTP laid out a luncheon buffet. "We'd line up, and Lew would work the line, going up to everyone and shaking their hands," said Reisman. He'd say, "I haven't seen you in a while. What are you up to? How's it going?" Wasserman listened as each man described his current project.

Reisman recalled the bonhomie of the noon hour: "He was very genial and friendly. Then we'd go back to the negotiating table, and his personality would change. He became a tiger, or would turn cold as ice. It was all part of his negotiating tactic, of course."

If a guild member proposed a residual rate, Wasserman would nod. "Okay. How much will that cost?"

"Of course, we didn't know, as we hadn't figured it out," said Reisman. Over the following six weeks, the two sides nailed down a higher rate of residuals for reruns on free TV and basic cable. They also set a minimum residual for made-for-video works and pay TV. On July 14, 1981, the strike ended.

"It was taxing for Lew," McLean remembered. Wasserman was sixty-eight years old. His shoulders were drooping, his once-tall frame had shrunk a bit, and the years of beating off younger alpha males showed on his face. "That was the last time he was at the bargaining table for any length of time," said McLean. But in years to come, Wasserman would still keep his hand in the table, seizing as many rights and residuals for Hollywood conglomerates as he could.

THIRTY-SIX

AFTER NEARLY A DECADE OF BEING ESTRANGED from her only child, Edie finally reconciled with her daughter, Lynne. In 1982 Lynne had pleased her mother by divorcing Jack Meyers, her second husband. Now Edie had her entire family together, including sixteen-year-old granddaughter Carol Anne Lief and eight-year-old Casey Meyers—who became like Lew's son. Several MCA insiders saw the youngster as a reflection of the mogul. "I'm so glad Lynne finally gave Lew the son he always wanted," said

Jackie Gershwin. Wasserman fairly beamed now that he had his own male descendant. "Casey has been the greatest thing to happen to Lew," said Tom Pollock. The men in the Black Tower referred to Lynne's son as Wasserman's greatest achievement, forgetting that the boy *did* have a father and a mother. Some went so far as to speculate that if Casey had been ten or fifteen years older, Lew might have given him the company. But that notion presumed that MCA was Wasserman's private property, rather than a publicly held enterprise. Certainly, Edie's reconciliation with Lynne was a redemptive moment for Lew, who could now enfold all the members of his small family. And the new closeness was a boon to Casey, who could invite friends to his grandpa's Universal Studio Tour— for free.

Edie's family became her newest project. In her late sixties, the dowager was still powerful and, although her days of cuckolding her husband were long over, she was still attractive. Her skin was creamy, her eyes sparkled, and she styled her hair in a classic pageboy that showed off her heart-shaped face. "Edie was always very well put together," said one of her male friends. However, she had undergone several of her own surgeries, including a hysterectomy. She also had her own bout with cancer and had suffered through a traumatic mastectomy. "It was horrible, but at least she survived," said one friend.

Edie also shed some of her friends. Joyce Haber, whose *Los Angeles Times* column Edie had used to settle scores and gain favors, was one. "Joyce got information from Edie sometimes, although Joyce wasn't always 100 percent accurate," said her former editor, Jim Bellows. Haber had made several enemies in town, had divorced TV producer Douglas Cramer, and was popping pills to keep up with her hectic nightlife and newspaper deadlines. "She was a fall-down drunk," said one society type, who echoed many other sources.

Haber had received a large book advance to write a Hollywood roman à clef. At a party with Doris's friends, Haber told department-store heir Prentis Hale, Jr., and his wife, Denise (the former Mrs. Vincent Minnelli), that she planned to mention their names in her book. "Prentis almost attacked her," said couturier Luis Estevez. Hale roared at Haber, forbidding her to use his name and threatening to destroy her career if she did. "I was like, 'Calm down, kiddos,' " said Estevez. "Prentis was a mean man." Indeed, he later called his friend Dorothy Chandler and said that unless Haber was fired, Hale would withdraw all of his stores' advertising from her husband's newspaper. "The *Times* dropped her like a hot potato," said Estevez.

And then so did Edie. After eight years of almost daily contact and intimate confidences, Edie no longer returned phone calls from her best friend. "It was as if Edie had said, 'I love you, honey, but the show's closed now. Good-bye,' " said society columnist David Patrick Columbia. "Edie never again talked to Joyce after she lost her high-profile job." Haber grew embittered, but her book *The Users* was published in 1976, and became a biting, best-selling look at Hollywood. Two years later, Dominick Dunne turned Haber's book into a TV movie with the same name. But his own Hollywood career was in a downward spiral, too.

Dunne became an alcoholic, started using cocaine, and was even arrested for marijuana possession in front of his two children. "I was a jerk," he told me. "I was self-destructing from a 'B' level to a 'C,' " the lowest social rung on Hollywood's ladder. But Haber saved Dunne inadvertently. By 1980, she had received a second, fat advance but was too inebriated to finish the book. Dunne was asked to complete the tawdry story, *The Winners*. Though it flopped, he was thrilled to be panned by the *New York Times*. "It was the best thing that ever happened to me. I found a new career." Edie and Lew had rarely taken note of Dunne when he was producing low-rated movies. "They operated at a much higher level than I did at the time," he explained. But after 1984, when Dunne started to write

Vanity Fair articles about the rich and infamous, Edie began inviting him to dinner and parties.

Edie had already lost her public ardor for another old friend. As President Jimmy Carter grappled with high oil prices, inflation, and the Iran hostage crisis, the Wassermans' enthusiasm for him faded. They supported his 1980 bid for reelection, but only tepidly. Hollywood and the rest of the country's voters preferred a former Hollywood actor, and they elected Ronald Reagan. Fortunately, Edie had maintained her contacts with both of Reagan's wives. She had been close to Jane Wyman, the first Mrs. Reagan, since 1939, when MCA acquired several Hollywood talent agencies—including the one that represented Wyman and Reagan. "Between them, I think they were getting about $350 a week at Warner Brothers Studios," Wasserman told me. "Wyman was earning $250 a week while Ronnie was getting $100." But the two names didn't really register on Wasserman's radar, said Jay Kanter. Lew was busy attending to the agency's big clients such as Bette Davis, Errol Flynn, and bandleader-turned-movie-actor Kay Kyser.

World War II drew Edie and Jane together, said Janet Leigh. Ronald Reagan served the war effort by making training films at Hal Roach Studios in Culver City—Fort Roach—where he virtually lived. Lew worked constantly, too. Both women were raising baby girls; two-year-old Maureen Reagan was three months younger than Lynne "Lyndie" Wasserman. Maureen called her little pal "De-de," while Lyndie referred to her buddy as "Mermie"—a nickname that stuck throughout Maureen's life. During those years, the two mothers and their babies kept frequent company, said Leigh.

When Wyman told Edie that she was frustrated with her inferior roles, Edie helped her convince Lew that she was ready to play a supporting role in Billy Wilder's 1944 film, *The Lost Weekend.* The picture made her a star. Reagan returned home in mid-1945, his career moribund but his political and union activities on the rise. The new focus strained his marriage, which ended in 1949.

Edie remained loyal to Wyman, and when Reagan remarried in March 1952, Edie did not embrace his new B-film actress wife, who put on airs. "Nancy was not really welcomed into MCA's circles," said Merrill Park. Park's husband, Art, and other agents said that Nancy couldn't "act her way out of a paper bag." Yet when Reagan was elected governor, Edie paid attention to Nancy. The mogul's wife was pragmatic about her relationships, Wendy Goldberg explained. "There were certain people that Edie didn't like, but she believed that you had to play that game." Edie stayed in touch with Nancy Reagan during the gubernatorial years—even though Lew did not. MCA's Taft Schreiber kept abreast of Reagan's progress and Stu Spencer recalled hearing Nancy and Edie talking on the phone from the governor's home.

In January 1981, Edie's years of assiduous networking paid off. She and Lew, as well as Merrill and Park, Jimmy and Gloria Stewart, and Bob and Dolores Hope, as well as other Hollywood Brahmins, were invited to Reagan's inauguration. It was the most expensive in history, a $16 million extravaganza, with fireworks and symphonies and eight white-tie balls. The Misty Mountain crowd—the Annenbergs, Darts, Tuttles, Jorgensens, and Bloomingdales—all had front-row seats to the inauguration in Washington. Edie and Lew sat farther back. Nancy dressed like her heiress friends, too, in diamond-and-pearl drop earrings and a $10,000 Galanos gown. The first lady would help kick off the decade's display of extravangant wealth and blatant excess.

Edie and Lew were thrilled to be as close to the action as they were. It was a reunion, of sorts—even though Lew and Ron had not been especially friendly during MCA's agency years. "It was only later, after Reagan left Hollywood, that they were close," said Dunne. By then, each man could help the other, and there were no hard feelings between them. "Wasserman was so skilled in politics, he managed to keep a strong relationship with Reagan even while he was supporting Democrats," said Douglas Gomery. But it was actually Edie's widespread net, combined with Lew's lofty position, that had gotten them into the White House that night. It also helped that Reagan was not one to hold grudges, said Spencer. "Ronnie [was] the most affable guy, it's hard to see how anyone could not like him."

In Washington, D.C., as in Hollywood, reconstructed history often burgeons into accepted fact. At the inauguration ball that night, Nancy and Ronnie embraced the movie contingent and introduced the Wassermans and the Jimmy Stewarts to a few uniformed generals. Although Art Park and Taft Schreiber had represented Reagan in his acting days, "Nancy kept repeating that Lew was Ronnie's agent, and always had been," said Merrill Park. "Of course, Ronnie went along with it. He was always happy with everybody." From then on, the Parks accepted this bit of Nancy's fiction. "That's how most of Hollywood is, anyway," she explained. "Those at the top want to be associated with others at the top, even though most people started somewhere at the bottom. Oh, well." And she laughed.

By now, Wasserman had all but abandoned his dream of personally shaping movies, à la Irving Thalberg. Hollywood cinema was entering an era in which the screen was dominated by male teenage comedies, and Lew did not have that raunchy sensibility. After *Animal House,* Thom Mount, another of Tanen's protégés, persuaded John Belushi to sign a three-picture contract for $1.8 million. One of those films became *The Blues Brothers.*

From the onset, however, the movie was ill conceived. The story grew out of a stunt Belushi and his partner, Dan Aykroyd, had developed. They sometimes warmed up audiences by masquerading as blues musicians, and they wanted to turn that act into a full-length movie. They pitched the idea to Sean Daniel, who checked with Tanen, who checked with Wasserman, who gave his blessing. While *Animal House* was racking up its millions, *The Blues Brother* deal was done—over the phone and without a script. Budgeted at

Tanen's usual low figure, Aykroyd started writing the musical comedy.

Wasserman considered the comedians' antics juvenile. One skit in *The Blues Brothers* mocked the *Peter Gunn* theme song, written by Lew's friend Henry Mancini. He feared that the scene with the legendary Cab Calloway singing about Minnie the Moocher would fail to stir a young audience. "Lew claimed there was an inordinate amount of automobile crashes in the film, which was true," said Daniel. But Wasserman's complaints paled compared to the film's destructive undertow.

Drug use on the set was out of control. Dozens of musicians and crew members smoked pot, snorted cocaine, and shot heroin openly. Director John Landis tried to hold things together, but it became obvious that Belushi had an incorrigible problem. Many times, the crew was kept waiting while Aykroyd tried to prop his stoned partner up in front of the camera. Other times, Belushi would disappear in search of a dealer who could inject him with enough speed to keep him dancing. Daniel received a phone call nearly every day. "Once, John passed out, and paramedics took him to the hospital. His lips had turned purple, and we thought he was dead," he said. Tanen was frequently screaming on the telephone. "I loved John," Tanen explained. "But a lot of the time we were trying to get the needle out of his arm long enough to shoot the next scene.

"Lew knew about the problems, too, but he didn't want to know the details, if you know what I mean," Tanen explained. Wasserman had dealt with drug and alcohol dependents—Judy Garland, Oscar Levant, Marilyn Monroe, and many others. But this generation could be flagrant and self-destructive in its drug use. Instead of learning his lines, Belushi sat in his trailer, drenched in urine, drinking Courvoisier, a pile of coke on the table. Wasserman, who drank a rare vodka tonic, could not fathom why a talented actor would jeopardize his career for a "high," said Daniel. "He talked about the waste and tragedy of it and how it got in the way of people's best work."

On top of that, *The Blues Brothers* became mired in financial problems. "Lew was absolutely hysterical that we were over budget on this one, too," said Tanen. "On any given day, something would go wrong." The script now numbered 320 pages—three times the standard length. "That movie was cursed to remain in some kind of hellish, hallucinogenic state," recalled Daniel. He, Tanen, and junior producer Ivan Reitman struggled to keep the beast under control, but costs climbed from $18 million to $22 million and more.

One day, Wasserman barged into Tanen's office during a meeting. He screamed, "I'm telling you, I want you to shut this down, RIGHT NOW! Do you hear me! SHUT IT DOWN." Tanen didn't say anything. The film project was too insane to continue, but too far gone to shut down.

When *The Blues Brothers* was finally in the can, the studio threw its traditional wrap party. Belushi and Aykroyd appeared in their Blues Brothers porkpie hats, Ray-Ban shades, and dark suits. Belushi was obviously stoned, yet he climbed onstage and performed. At one point, he gave a little speech and remembered to thank Daniel, Mount, and Reitman. Then Belushi told Tanen to come up on the stage. He did, and Belushi put his arm around the president of the studio, and said, "The only reason this movie got made is because of this man." The applause was minimal, but Tanen was smiling: "John Belushi was the only person who ever talked to me like that at Universal. It was really neat."

As some members of the crew snorted cocaine around the sound stages, the party continued. A now-manic Belushi was grabbing food from the caterer's plates and wisecracking at the big suits. Wasserman watched from the sidelines; he failed to see the comic's star quality, but maybe *The Blues Brothers* would make some money after all. Lew returned to the fourteenth floor.

When the party broke up, the two comedians roamed Universal's lot. Suddenly Belushi spied an armored military truck, emblazoned with bold swastikas on its side—a studio prop—just begging him to take it for a ride. Aykroyd and Belushi jumped into the tanklike vehicle and drove off. They rolled right through the studio gate as the security guard tried frantically to stop them. They rumbled down Universal Way and up the ramp of a busy Hollywood freeway.

Wasserman was talking on the phone and gazing out the window, when he saw Nazis rolling down the highway. "He called me in a panic," said Tanen. Wasserman had figured out that the two comedians had stolen MCA property, and he was enraged. "What the hell are you trying to do to my company?" he shrieked at Tanen. "Get those goddamed guys off the road!" He slammed down the receiver.

Tanen barked some orders to his staff, then shook his head. "God bless those guys," he thought. Come June, the $28 million movie *Blues Brothers* would receive mixed reviews and make $32 million. Tanen had to admire the actors' anarchy in the face of MCA's rigidity.

Wasserman may have felt alienated from his own movies, but the energy of *The Blues Brother* and others like it clicked with a crass, mostly male audience. *Animal House,* which had cost about $3 million, went into video that year, and sales climbed past $170 million. The stoner culture appreciated many of Universal's products, from the "Cheech and Chong" films to *Smokey and the Bandit.* "By now, a lot of these things were starting to work," said Tanen. Video rentals on the low-budget films soared. "I know they weren't exactly award winners. But they made money." And that *did* please Wasserman.

The mogul had an opportunity to make George Lucas's next blockbuster. The director brought him his script about snakes, Nazis, and the Ark of the Convenant. He wanted a 50-50 deal, which "drove Lew and Sid crazy," said Tom Pollock. To Lucas, it was only right that he get a percent of the gross, since he created, wrote, and would produce this film. But Wasserman said he was demanding "unheard-of percentages" in ownership—an irony that wasn't lost on anyone. Angry at being pushed into a corner, Wasserman threw Lucas's science-fiction script on the floor and passed on the *Raiders of the Lost Ark* (1981).

Steven Spielberg had returned to Universal, only to bomb with his movie *1941*. He really wanted to direct *Raiders,* but since Wasserman didn't want to produce the film, Spielberg wanted out of his seven-year contract at Universal. "I had a meeting with Sid and Lew, and George came with me," said Spielberg. "On my behalf, George said, 'Please let Steven out of his contract. Suspend and extend the contract, if you will, but let him do the *Raiders* project for me at Paramount. ' " They agreed.

"Sid believed that if there was something I was dying to do, I should do it," Spielberg told me.

Raiders of the Lost Ark cost a hefty $20 million to make, then raked in $116 million in theatrical rentals—and far more in supplemental markets. It went on to earn $400 million worldwide, boosting Paramount's bottom line. This time, Wasserman had no one but himself to blame for losing what could have been at least $200 million.

Just as troubling was that Paramount's *Raiders* had kept Spielberg away from Universal. The *Jaws* director had made hits at Columbia, Paramount, and was now ensconced at Warner Brothers. "The projects were better outside of Universal, and I'd just gone to where the projects were," he explained. Wasserman and Sheinberg began discussing ways to lure the director back to Universal, where he had gotten his start. That goal took on an urgency as Wasserman's top producers, Darryl Zanuck and David Brown, grew more unhappy. The talented men had become disenchanted with Universal's bookkeeping—especially its way of moving profits from one hit movie to the losses of a so-so film so that the producers couldn't collect on their net profit deals. "We eventually left over the cross-collateralization issue," Brown explained.

Still, Universal had some adult hits, such as *Coal Miner's Daughter,* based on Loretta Lynn's autobiography. Directed by Michael Apted, it starred Sissy Spacek, who actually sang the country star's songs while avoiding the clichés inherent in a rag-to-riches tale. Wasserman knew the film would do well in Memphis—it did—but he wasn't so sure about Boston. MCA executives took the film to a small theater there. After the film's last scene, people just sat still. "They didn't applaud or move," Tanen said. He asked the manager for his reaction.

"I think they'd like to see it again," he said.

They replayed the film and, sure enough, the audience stayed to the end a second time.

"People came out of there, saying, 'Good movie. Fine acting,' " Tanen recalled. "It was very gratifying, and I knew we had a hit. It was one of our first real serious movies," at least on Tanen's watch.

The film opened in 1980, grossed $80 million, and took seven Oscar nominations—including Best Picture, Best Screenplay, and Best Actress, which Spacek won.

Throughout the hits and misses, Edie hovered in the background. "Edie and Lew ran every movie the studio ever made, right there in their house," said Sean Daniel. "Edie's friends used to come to the screenings," Tanen recalled. "We had a lot of Monday-morning feedback about what David May [of the May Company store chain] thought of your movie, after Edie and Lew screened it for him on Saturday night."

In 1982 two radically different films established the path that Universal would travel in the years to come.

One was *Missing*, directed and written by Constantin Costa-Gavras. The drama was based on the true story of young American journalist Charles Horman, who disappeared in Chile after Salvador Allende was killed in a CIA-engineered coup. The Universal film production could not film in Chile because the script criticized the regime of General Augusto Pinochet, the U.S.-installed leader of that country.

In the movie, the young man's conservative father (Jack Lemmon) joins his skeptical daughter-in-law (Sissy Spacek) to try and find their loved one. As the pair become trapped in a Kafkaesque puzzle, the father comes to realize that his own government cooperated with Chile's fascist dictatorship to torture and kill his son. (Nearly twenty years later State Department memos from August 25, 1976, that were declassified on October 8, 1999, verified this conclusion.)

But where to film the coup? Sean Daniel recalled scouring the globe for places that resembled Santiago. "We were trying to decide between Mexico City and Barcelona." The young producer showed Wasserman the script, knowing that the mogul had connections in the Reagan White House. "I thought it would be valuable to get his opinion." Wasserman placed a call and, a few days later, told his junior executive to shoot in Mexico City. "Do *not* go to Spain," he warned.

Not long after that, Daniel picked up the paper and read that paramilitary civil guards had rushed into the Spanish parliament and attempted to overthrow the country's elected leaders. It was an eerie case of life imitating art imitating life; Wasserman had saved his film crew from experiencing a coup while making a film about one. Daniel was impressed: "Lew's contacts within the State Department gave him sound information."

A sensation at the Cannes Film Festival, *Missing* won the Golden Palm and went on to nab numerous other awards, including Best Screenplay and another Best Actress for Spacek. Yet, in Washington, D.C., *Missing* was seen as a shameful affront to the U.S. government.

"I was sued by all of the people you could imagine," said Tanen. "The State Department and foreign service were very upset because it touched on Allende. The movie didn't make our government or the CIA look too good. Lew got some heat, too," he said. Secretary of State Alexander Haig, former Secretary of State Henry Kissinger, and Nancy and Ronald Reagan all registered strong disapproval. Sheinberg recalled the brouhaha. "Reagan was very upset. But Lew didn't say anything like 'Why did you guys make this movie?' He just kept fielding the telephone calls."

"It was the only movie that was attacked and roundly criticized at an official State Department briefing," said Daniel. At Universal City, producers took note. The movie did modest business, but nothing approaching the ticket sales of *Star Wars*—a film whose name Reagan borrowed for his big-budget defense program. Tanen explained, "In the beginning of developing *Missing,* Lew was a liberal because it was the time of Carter. But when Reagan and Bush came along, he swung just to the right of center. His politics just depended on who was in office."

The film that followed *Missing* offended no friends or neighbors, unless they were bicycling in outer space. *E.T. the Extra-Terrestrial* blended science fiction with a heartwarming story about a boy dealing with his parents' divorce. Director Steven Spielberg returned to Universal to make this film, lured by a deal that gave him merchandising rights and a percent of the profits—but no rights to any sequels. Written by Melissa Mathison (then Mrs. Harrison Ford), and filmed in the San Fernando Valley's middle-class suburbs, the movie made stars of child actors Henry Thomas and Drew Barrymore.

Wasserman not only attended the previews, he went as far as to rent a corporate jet. "Now, Lew had been to a lot of movie previews in his life," said Daniel. "He had sat in the back of many theaters and watched lots of films take hold of the audience." But during *E.T.*'s preview, the executives were all caught up in the audience's reaction: "At times, it almost levitated us," said Daniel. When the lights finally went up, and the audience burst into applause, Daniel looked over to Wasserman, whose eyes were shining. "His face had this look of complete and utter delight." Wasserman turned to Daniel and Tanen and said, "Never seen a preview like that one."

Added Tanen: "It was a religious experience for Lew." It was also a profound financial success. The $10 million film collected $12 million on its opening weekend, and Wasserman started casting his runic numbers until he was satisfied with their prophecy. Every

morning, he dialed Spielberg's office to give him the day's predic-
tion. But *E.T.* defied even the chairman's forecast, earning $228 mil-
lion in theatrical rentals and $700 million worldwide. In marked
contrast to the director of *Missing*, Spielberg was invited to personally screen his film at the White House for Nancy and Ronald
Reagan.

In 1982 Universal set a new industry box-office record, thanks
not just to *E.T.* but also to *Best Little Whorehouse in Texas* and *On
Golden Pond*—three radically different hits. From then on,
Wasserman and the studio made a sharp right turn toward producing safe, inoffensive—and, some might say, mediocre—fare. As
Costa-Gavras lamented twenty years later, Hollywood no longer
took risks by making films like *Missing*. "The role of art is to be
ahead of the times, to try to criticize and be very aggressive against
the injustices in our societies," he said. "But more and more, art is
in the hands of the political and economic powers." Few directors
epitomized that shift better than Spielberg.

By the time Universal released his blockbuster, Spielberg had been
away from the lot for about five years. "After *E.T.* came out, I wanted
to come home," he said. He called a meeting to tell Sid and Lew: "I'm
here to tell you that I miss you guys and I want to return." He thanked
them for allowing him to produce films at other studios. "Now I'd just
like to pick out a bungalow or office and move in."

Lew immediately rose from his chair. "Let's go bungalow shopping," he said.

Wasserman, Sheinberg, and Spielberg climbed into a golf cart
and toured the back lot. "The first one that Lew showed me was
Hitchcock's old office," Spielberg said. Ever since the master of
suspense had died, Wasserman had been waiting to hand off
Hitchcock's space to some other worthy talent. But Spielberg
objected: "I can't move into the great man's shoes. He'd haunt the
office, and I'd be afraid of letting Hitch down. I'd never get any
work done."

The trio continued cruising, past the gigantic sound stages and posh buildings. Finally Wasserman stopped the cart. "Look, I've got an idea," he said. "Why don't we build you a place?"

"Are you kidding?" Spielberg asked. "That's going to cost a lot of money."

"We'll spend as much money as *E. T.* makes in Paraguay."

They retraced their path and started looking for locations. "I found a street that I've always loved," Spielberg said. It was small and crowded with sets as old as some of Revue's greatest hits. "It had the house for *Leave It to Beaver,* and Robert Young's set from *Father Knows Best,* and the Munsters' house and the Addams Family's home."

Spielberg looked around, remembering the 1960s, when he was trying to get a break in the business. This is where he'd take walks and contemplate his future. Now he turned to Wasserman. "If I had my druthers, I'd put the office building right here," and he pointed to the foot of the street.

"Fine," said Wasserman. "We'll just move the street up."

And so they built the headquarters for Amblin, Spielberg's independent production company at Universal. Wasserman spent $3.2 million constructing the director's dreamworld, which he decorated in a southwestern motif and surrounded with cacti. It opened in 1983.

"And I haven't left since," he said.

Wasserman finally came around to the idea of sharing profits. He gave Spielberg 2 percent of gross ticket sales from Universal's future theme-parks—in return for the director's advice on the projects. It was an unprecedented arrangement, one that could easily pay him $500 million by 2000, and continue in perpetuity.

But who would have believed that little *E. T.* would be dragged into a scandal? As soon as the film slipped into video, its name became linked to the fortunes of an East Coast family whose gestalt was more New Jersey industrial than Northridge suburbia.

Thirty-Seven

FBI AGENTS ROLLED THEIR CAR UP TO A WAREHOUSE in Clinton, New Jersey. To their surprise, they found a quiet, empty space with no workers or trucks. They checked the address again; this was allegedly where the videocassettes of MCA's hit movie, *E.T.*, were being boxed along with videos of other MCA properties. But where were the workers and why was the site abandoned? "The agents couldn't figure it out," said one government prosecutor. There were several elements to what seemed like a phantom operation. First of all, MCA made its videocassettes in Newberry Park, California. Second, the corporation's records showed that MCA was shipping millions of the cassettes 3,000 miles east to this address, where Northstar Graphics was printing cardboard sleeves and packing them with MCA videos. This was not the only firm in the country producing videocassette cases, yet MCA trucked its inventory here to be boxed, wrapped, and shipped back to the San Fernando Valley—an expensive exercise.

On top of that, MCA paid almost double the going rate for this service—34 cents a case versus eighteen cents charged by Southern California vendors. And MCA paid a $500,000 premium for the pleasure of being overcharged by Northstar Graphics, with whom MCA Home Entertainment had just signed a $5 million long-term contract. Given Wasserman's notoriously tight fist, this deal made no sense.

The mystery deepened after FBI agents learned that the warehouse business was actually a mob front. Northstar Graphics was owned by Ed "The Conductor" Sciandra, who in 1981 was convicted in New York for tax evasion. Prosecutors had been trying for years to get Sciandra, a known member of the Bufalino mob family in Pennsylvania.

Yet MCA in 1983 and for several years thereafter continued to do business with Sciandra's company. According to Richard Stavin, an

Organized Crime Strike Force attorney, MCA had to have known this was a mob-controlled business; the news was in court documents and all over the newspapers. Why did the blue-chip corporation maintain this connection? One reason, Stavin learned eventually, was that the president of MCA Home Video was related to Sciandra. "We didn't know whether Sciandra was the blood uncle of MCA's Gene Giaquinto or not," Stavin explained. But Giaquinto called him "uncle" in at least one FBI wiretap, which was later made public.

Giaquinto, a heavyset man with a thick neck, dark hair, and a horsey smile, had started working for MCA in New York during the 1970s, handling 16-mm film rights and other ancillary businesses. "He was a nickel-and-dime salesman from Queens," said one MCA executive. But after videocassettes boomed from a side business to a major unit, MCA Home Video moved to Universal City, changed its name to MCA Home Entertainment, and kept Giaquinto in charge.

Stavin and FBI agents soon realized that Giaquinto was working with the Bufalinos through the New Jersey packing house. It was a dangerous liaison, one that could undermine all of Wasserman's hard work. In a few more years, the relationship would nearly ruin his carefully laid plans.

Music represented the soul of MCA—the trade that launched the careers of both Jules Stein and Lew Wasserman—Jules in the mob-owned speakeasies in Chicago, and Lew in the illegal gambling clubs of Cleveland. In 1927, when singer Joe E. Lewis left Al Capone's nightclub to take a higher-paying job at a rival club, Capone punished the singer by having his throat slit. Although most club owners did not go so far to control the talent, it's safe to say that impresarios in those days used other unconscionable means—ranging from onerous long-term contracts to exorbitant fees. From the liquor and linen suppliers to the music and stage owners, nearly every corner of early American show business was shaped or controlled by organized crime. The business aberrations in that demimonde were eventually adopted by even legitimate operations, so that by the twenty-first century gangsterlike financial ploys in the music industry seemed like generally accepted accounting principles.

Wasserman had briefly managed a band—and had felt the lash of MCA's mobbed-up practices even before he met Jules Stein. In 1933 Wasserman was working in Cleveland when he met the leader of an exciting new orchestra. The band had just been signed by MCA, but had lost its manager. Wasserman eagerly signed on, quit his theater job, and bid his family good-bye. "The orchestra went to the West Coast, and that's the last time I saw Lew," said Paul Beck.

But Wasserman and the band fell on hard times in Los Angeles and were abandoned by their own agents. Stranded, Wasserman spent his days gambling at a "sawdust joint" where patrons were frisked for guns, said George Riff, a dealer at the club. "He was a mediocre bettor, but friendly enough." Wasserman fell seriously ill with jaundice, yet managed to return to Cleveland. In 1934, when Seymour Heller ran into his friend there, Wasserman's skin was yellow and his face gaunt. "I was really surprised at how weak and frail he looked," Heller said. The disastrous band tour had embittered Wasserman, who ranted against MCA even in front of its agents.

"He told me that MCA robbed and cheated its clients by overcharging them," said Merle Jacobs, then an MCA agent. Wasserman claimed the agency strangled its clients by charging them for travel, advertising, telegrams, and so-called "overhead expenses." How could musicians make a living in servitude? MCA had a reputation for taking as much as 50 percent of a client's earnings. "Lew threatened to expose us to James Petrillo, head of the American Federation of Musicians union [AFM]," not realizing that Petrillo had given his childhood chum Stein an exclusive sweetheart deal. "Lew really tore into me and MCA," said Jacobs. "By the time I left, I thought he was a smart-alecky, cocky kid—the snootiest guy I'd ever known. But you know something?" he added. "He was right." Benny Goodman, Tommy Dorsey, and other big bandleaders felt the same way.

Stein's underhanded ways grew so notorious that in 1938 the government began reviewing allegations that MCA had forced its contracts on hotel owners and bandleaders. In 1940 the Department of Justice looked into the deal with Petrillo's AFM. In fact, over the course of the twentieth century, the government would scrutinize MCA at least a dozen times for allegations ranging from antitrust violations to labor racketeering. Stein and Wasserman, meanwhile, built a multibillion-dollar corporation by fine-tuning the mob model that had made its vice dens so profitable. Today's recording industry remains notorious for its seven-year contracts, its practice of charging artists for recording, promoting, and shrink-wrapping music CDs, and its penchant for keeping murky ledgers so that even top acts can't obtain a true and complete royalty statement. As noted music attorney Don Engel said, "Record companies today get away with murder."

In 1983, however, MCA's music division had been overshadowed by its film and TV business. MCA Records had languished for so long that it was jokingly called the Music Cemetery of America. It had some country-and-western names, a few well-known pop artists, and a handful of rock 'n' roll stars, like Tom Petty—but not enough talent to support a national distribution system. Wasserman wanted to revive the business and bring it back to its glory days.

That spring, Wasserman and Sheinberg met with well-known recording executive Irving Azoff. Short, mercurial, and competitive, Azoff was known as the "Poison Dwarf." MCA was well acquainted with the executive's venomous side. Years earlier, Jimmy Buffett, one of Azoff's management acts, had recorded on MCA Records, and Azoff sued the label over money. "I alleged they were so inept that they didn't legally constitute a record company at all," he said. But Azoff had also helped MCA assemble one of the first rock sound tracks for the Universal film *FM* in 1978. "That caught everybody's attention," said Grammy Award–winning music producer Bones Howe. "It was a hugely successful sound track that opened up a whole new venue for musicians." Howe and some of Azoff's clients, such as The Doobie Brothers and Steely Dan, called Azoff "The Little King" because of his ego and genius. "But we never said that to his face, as he could turn nasty," said Howe.

Wasserman felt it was better to have Azoff inside his tent than outside. Universal Studios and Universal TV employed hundreds of musicians, composers, and arrangers who created the audio portion of the visual product. It also had several labels under its umbrella, and all of them had contracts with singers and bands. "MCA was one of the few conglomerates that had both a film music department *and* a record label," Howe explained. The potential for one division to work synergistically with the other and enrich MCA was enormous; Azoff was just the sort of empire builder who might pull it all together.

Wasserman was unfazed by the reputation of the Poison Dwarf; he had grown up alongside shady guys with malevolent nicknames. In April he hired Azoff to turn MCA Records around.

Soon after joining the corporation, Azoff signed an agreement to distribute Motown Records in the United States and brought in his own team of managers. One of the many new faces was Sal Pisello, also known as Sal the Swindler. Law-enforcement agencies on both coasts knew him as a soldier in a crime family, a guy who smuggled drugs in lobster tanks. Tall, garrulous, and in his sixties, Pisello had allegedly defrauded Los Angeles investors in a series of restaurant and nightclub deals in the 1970s. Now Pisello was working for MCA selling, among other things, millions of out-of-date records, which the industry called "cut-outs." Most days, he arrived at his MCA office wearing open-necked shirts and gold chains around his neck. Pisello would eventually negotiate $3 million in MCA deals— none of which would ever made money—but which would net him more than $600,000. MCA Records' arrangement with Picello would one day cause Wasserman a great deal of trouble.

Wasserman had just turned seventy. His hairline had receded slightly, his nose was thick and bulbous, and his trademark big glasses had grown conspicuously dramatic. Michael Caine, Cary Grant, and Irving "Swifty" Lazar, a former MCA agent who threw très chic parties on Oscar night, all wore similar black frames. But only Wasserman was associated with the bold, oversized eyewear, which became an expression of style—or a symbol of two giant movie screens, depending on one's perspective.

Lew was now blazing two trails into virgin territories—video copyright law and music technology. Even now, after decades of work and acclaim, he was determined to deliver at least one more major achievement to his industry.

In December 1978, MCA had finally introduced DiscoVision, calling it a unique product in a new marketplace. The videodisc and its accompanying machine allowed average viewers to watch movies in the privacy of their own home—then a novel idea. MCA had acquired an experienced partner, Philips NV, to help manufacture the machines while MCA developed the software and the 12-inch discs. The two were also creating an infrastructure to license programming and distribute it to the consumer. "Everything was invented as we went along," Wasserman said, and the electronics industry eagerly anticipated his invention.

But Wasserman's dream project was plagued from the start. In its Amsterdam plant, the Philips-made machines inexplicably overheated and "cooked" the discs. At the disc-processing plant in Carson, California, MCA was turning out one defective disc for every three it made. As Wasserman later recalled: "We had to have an absolutely clean room for DiscoVision." But how clean was clean? Even tiny dust particles made quality control impossible.

Meanwhile, MCA had already printed a large DiscoVision catalog, filled with hundreds of movie titles that were supposed to be available. The manufacturing problems, however, had stalled the shipment of discs. People who had received a DiscoVision player for Christmas 1978 returned several times to stores to buy discs for their system—only to find the same meager selection.

By 1978, when the costs of DiscoVision had mounted to $50 million, MCA fell out with its Dutch partner, leaving Wasserman with a big investment but no product. In September 1979, he accepted the fact that he was in the business of entertainment—not electronics—and formed DiscoVision Associates, a 50-50 venture with IBM. The electronics giant took over manufacturing, research, and development. On the sidelines was Universal Pioneer Corporation, a joint venture between MCA and Pioneer Electronics, which developed laser disc players for industrial clients like the CIA.

Despite its problems, DiscoVision marked a phenomenal advance in engineering, and its creator, Wasserman, became a minor deity in the pantheon of scientists. Around 1980, a Greek physicist from MIT made a pilgrimage from Cambridge, Massachusetts, to Universal City specifically to meet the great Wasserman. "The man was very well respected and really wanted to meet Lew," said Ned Tanen. "He believed that Lew was a genius for inventing it." Tanen escorted the distinguished gentleman to Wasserman's office, and the two men shook hands.

Wasserman had just learned about the latest bout of disc problems, and he was trying to decide if he should pump even more money into his dream. The MIT professor did not realize this and, in a heavy accent, told Wasserman, "I want to congratulate you for bringing us into the twenty-first century with this invention. It's really stunning, and shows a tremendous amount of foresight and vision."

Wasserman's faced turned red. He began to scream at the professor.

"You have the guts to come in here and talk to me like that?" he yelled, standing up. "How dare you!" And he threw the scientist out of his office.

Visibly shaken, the man looked at Tanen, aghast. "My God! What happened?"

"Mr. Wasserman doesn't take rejection very well," Tanen said. "MCA is having a few problems with DiscoVision, and he thinks you're mocking him."

MCA and Sony were still slugging it out in court over Betamax. In October 1979, the Los Angeles District Court accepted Sony's arguments and rejected MCA's case. "They were wrong," said Sid Sheinberg, and he took his case to the U.S. Court of Appeals. Two years later, the appeals court overturned the lower court's decision and handed a victory to MCA, ruling that the Betamax machine's copying of TV shows did indeed infringe on Universal TV's copyright. Sheinberg was elated. However, the fight was far from over.

By now, the ground had shifted. MCA was not only distributing its movies on its videodisc system, it was also manufacturing videocassettes to play on a Japanese system—the VHS machine. MCA was aggressively acquiring video rights for independent films, and its videocassette division was collecting $46 million a year.

Still, Wasserman pressed ahead stubbornly with his DiscoVision, envisioning the day when his superior product would rule the home-entertainment sector. Armed with all the information that MCA and Philips had amassed throughout the years, Pioneer was able to quickly pinpoint the source of the recurring problems. Wasserman wrote another large check, and Pioneer began producing superior machines. In 1980 it opened a disc-pressing plant in Kofu, Japan, with a superclean room. The disc runs had only a fraction of the defects found at MCA's Carson plant and, over the next sixteen months, DiscoVision made enormous progress.

But so did VCRs. As the price of these machines dropped, it became clear that America's choice for home-recording equipment was going to be the VCR—at least for the moment. As for disc players, "Lew was hooked," said Tanen. "He just couldn't give it up."

His manufacturing partner had no such qualms. DiscoVision was still not perfect, and IBM wanted out of the disc manufacturing business. Wasserman had spent far more money than he had intended. "He tried to practically give away DiscoVision to IBM. But that didn't work," said one executive. Instead, Wasserman shed the Carson plant and turned all of his disc production over to Pioneer.

In 1981 Sony's appeal of the Betamax decision was heard in the U.S. Supreme Court. Reporters were following the case closely, questioning the appellate decision that had outlawed Sony's machine. One editorial cartoonist depicted MCA's partner, Disney, as Mickey Mouse slapping handcuffs on a hapless VCR user. It was time for Wasserman to make decisions on two fronts—and in both cases his judgment would falter. First, he poured more money into the Supreme Court battle, vowing to fight the video technology. Incredibly, the court wanted both sides to reargue their case, which increased the already-substantial legal expense.

Sheinberg believed the machines were piracy tools that ripped off studios. Yet by the time the high court heard this argument, it rang hollow. Japanese technology had not hurt MCA; it had enriched it. In 1981 MCA's video sales had doubled to $81 million and would double again. In 1984 the Supreme Court rejected Sheinberg's arguments and sided with Sony. It ruled that because VCRs primarily enabled noninfringing uses—such as shifting the time when a consumer watches a free program—the devices were lawful under copyright laws. Ironically, this was also a victory for MCA—and the other studios. Not only did the sales of VCRs boom, but a whole stream of new revenue began to flood into town. After this ruling, videocassette sales figures climbed higher than box-office receipts, eventually accounting for most of a film's total profit.

As for DiscoVision, Wasserman shut it down reluctantly in 1982. He stopped manufacturing laser-optical discs, and allowed Pioneer to take over Universal Pioneer Corporation. He had spent ten years and $100 million trying to pull off a technological tour de force, and twenty years later he still felt the disappointment. "We sure tried hard enough on that one," he told me, shaking his head in displeasure.

Three years after Wasserman gave up on his innovation, the videodisc suddenly came into its own, but MCA was no longer in the game. In 1985 Pioneer took DiscoVision and turned it into the LaserDisc. The product would hold the title of the best home-theater system for nearly twenty years. Its Optical Disc technology would lead to further refinements, including the compact disc—and the latest incarnation, the DVD.

Wasserman had started it all, beginning in 1971, when no one knew how to make a laser disc. As George Jones, the vice president of DiscoVision, later explained, "Taking that into consideration, it's pretty amazing DiscoVision went as well as it did."

Wasserman had come close to cinching yet another triumph at the age of seventy. "They finally developed the product," he told me years later. "And lo and behold, now others things surpassed it, like DVD." Few people realized how much the mogul had contributed to that music technology, but for Wasserman himself, it was enough to know that he had been there first.

THIRTY-EIGHT

A RINGING BELL ROUSED THE YOUNG WOMAN from her sleep. Given the heat and light inside the shuttered room, she realized it was probably late morning. The phone was ringing, and she picked up the receiver.

"Hello?"

"Is Lucy there?" a man inquired.

"No, she's not," the woman said, still drowsy.

"Well, can you do this favor for me? A guy is coming over, and he wants to visit. Be nice to him." The caller hung up.

Awake now, the young woman felt confused. She attended UCLA, studied music, and worked part-time. She was subletting the house while her friend Lucy was vacationing in Italy for a few weeks. The residence sat on a quiet street east of Cedars-Sinai Medical Center, in an old neighborhood just south of Beverly Hills.

The woman showered and dressed, then called a friend. "If I'm not over at your place in a few hours, come and get me." She was nervous.

A few minutes later, Lew Wasserman showed up on the doorstep. What he saw was a pretty, meek blond student. "She was a very fat girl with large breasts and a beautiful face—she was blond and blue-eyed," said her teacher, songwriter Molly Ann Leiken. "She had a gorgeous voice, too, although I don't think that Lew ever knew that."

According to the young woman, Wasserman kissed her, and one thing led to another. "We started screwing around. He said he wanted to set me up and do this regularly. He was married and committed, but he said that he'd like this on the side."

For the next week or so, Wasserman showed up around the same time. His driver waited for him in the limousine outside. The young woman was certain that her visitor was Lew Wasserman, head of Universal Studios. "I was trying to get into the music business at the time, and I'd seen him at industry functions. I know it was him; he was very old." After their tryst, the young woman came to understand how her friend, a low-level employee at Lorimar Telepictures, always seemed to be flush with cash. Lucy was earning money sleeping with men on the side, she said.

Wasserman and the blonde enjoyed another rendezvous or two. "But after the third time, I told him I didn't want to do this anymore," she said. "I didn't feel right about it."

The mogul refused to hear it. He came around a few days later and knocked on her door. "I'd keep my blinds closed, but he wouldn't take no for an answer."

She grew frightened enough to tell her music teacher about her indiscretion. "Lew used to chase her around from room to room, and I don't think it was a sexual game. She was scared of him," said Leiken. "He'd lock her in the house and wouldn't let her go."

Leiken had worked at A&M Records for years. She had written a number of hit songs for Cher, Tina Turner, and Anne Murray, as well as the theme for the TV show *Eight Is Enough* (1977). By the time her student confided in her, Leiken had grown accustomed to hearing such tales from young women. "All the guys in town screwed around," she explained.

"But this was very scary for her, especially because she knew who he was. He wasn't just a producer," said Leiken. "He was head of an enormous studio."

Wasserman kept his philandering a tightly held secret for decades. Few producers knew he fooled around. "I always thought of Lew as asexual," David Brown said. But several women knew otherwise. "He indulged in anything that gave him pleasure, whether it was sex or money," said Adele Huggins, a former dancer in Xavier Cugat's band. As an MCA client, she had heard stories about Wasserman's affairs over the years and figured that extramarital sex was the prerogative of a Hollywood producer. Wasserman was simply enjoying the perks of his job.

In 1980 there was a clear double standard. While the town often clucked about Edie's past flagrant affairs, they overlooked her husband's. Yet the husband's infidelities often explain those of the wife, as one producer noted. "Usually, when a woman cheats on her husband, it's a way of getting even with him and his cheating." As a young agent, Wasserman had traveled with MCA bands from town to town, coming into contact with eager young women. Wasserman was very close to his client Bette Davis. Later in life, he often told stories about being propositioned by Davis, whom Lew admired greatly, and who was generous with her affections. He was also smitten with his client Barbara Stanwyck—as were several other Hollywood men. Henry Fonda was so crazy about his costar in *The Lady Eve* that he often talked about Stanwyck with his friends and agent, Lew. Whenever Edie found Lew daydreaming around the house, she'd say "Barbara Stanwyck," and he'd snap to attention.

Yet when Stanwyck, witty and attractive at fifty-four, came to Wasserman and asked for a Universal TV show, he said no. In 1965 he didn't believe that an older female star who didn't color her graying hair would attract enough viewers to justify her own series. Stanwyck proved him—and several other executives—wrong. She landed a starring role in *The Big Valley,* which became a hit ABC series (1965–1969). It won numerous awards, including three years of Emmys for Stanwyck and her "outstanding performance."

Wasserman's sexual attitudes were in tune with the times. During MCA's agency days, he and his men indulged in office affairs, which were tolerated as long as the amours remained quiet and didn't pair a boss with his own secretary, according to several sources. For years, Wasserman kept an MCA secretary as his mistress. The woman worked for another executive, spoke with a charming foreign accent, and behaved very properly at work. "He bought her a place and paid her expenses for years," said one producer. Wasserman kept his mistress even after he moved to Universal Studios, as did several other MCA executives.

"Wasserman wanted to have beautiful girls around the office," said Myrle Wages, an attractive woman herself, who hired many of the agency's secretaries. "Maybe this is shallow," she said, "but we hired girls for their looks. They were rich little Beverly Hills girls—mostly Jewish—who lived at home with mom and dad and didn't need a salary." Wages advised them on manners, protocol, and dress. They all shopped at Jax in Beverly Hills and bought expensive clothes designed by the owner, his wife, or hot designers like Rudy

Gernreich. They got their hair curled and teased by Gene Shacove, the hairdresser upon whom the movie *Shampoo* was based. There was no written dress code, but MCA's secretaries routinely wore provocative dresses, tight sweaters, and form-fitting jerseys. "The girls were so beautiful and rich. They had nothing to do with their money but shop for clothes and go the beauty salon," said Wages.

In those days, everyone at MCA flirted. "That was part of the fun of working there," said Wages. "You'd feel put out if no one hit on you. I had a million flirtations and never once took offense," she explained. "You threw all these beautiful people together in a glamorous setting, and all of kinds of things happened."

While at the agency, Wasserman rented swank Ciro's nightclub for MCA's annual employees-only Christmas party. "There was wine, champagne, dancing—and no wives," Wages emphasized. "Everyone threw all caution to the wind. It was wild." Agents grabbed young women and danced through the night, sometimes waltzing them right out the door and into a hotel room. "The next day, everyone would return to work as though nothing had ever happened, saying, 'Good morning, Miss X.' 'How are you, Mr. Y?'" said Wages. MCA's no-fraternizing policy was elastic: Some employees were fired after being discovered in flagrante delicto, while others were allowed to carry on. The only firm rule was that employees could not marry and expect that both partners could continue working at MCA.

MCA Square was the scene of many mad crushes and sexual overtures. Paul Newman, Gregory Peck, Tyrone Power, and Marlon Brando topped the girls' list of idols. Clark Gable wanted to date the twenty-one-year-old receptionist Jane Rosenbaum, but Wasserman advised against it, she said. George Montgomery frequently came up behind her and placed his hands on her breasts. "George! You're married," Rosenbaum would giggle. Actresses like Zsa Zsa Gabor and Judy Garland might dress down or disguise themselves as they walked through MCA's door. But Wasserman demanded that his agency's secretaries be walking advertisements for screen glamour and sex appeal. "People used to say that our secretaries looked so good, it was hard to tell the difference between them and the stars," said Wages.

Edie certainly knew of her husband's indiscretions and, after a while, acted as though it took nothing away from her marriage. She had come of age watching strong, sexual women onscreen, before the Production Code of 1934 squashed such figures and whitewashed any depiction or sex, drugs, or female sensuality. There were actresses like Ruth Chatterton, who as a boss lady in *Female* (1933), has a love nest with a buzzer system and stud service, and Norma Shearer, aka Mrs. Irving Thalberg, who flirts and vamps her way through *The Divorcee*. As a teenager, Edie went to see a motion picture almost every week, said Merle Jacobs, who sometimes accompanied her. Like her cinematic role models, Edie grew into a woman who was the equal of any man, enjoying the same powers and erotic perks. She was aggressively sexual with men, "who were scared to turn her down, given her position," said one woman. But as she grew older, she chafed under Hollywood's double standard, which grew stronger.

Male chauvinism permeated MCA in several ways. "Lew and Jules had a terrible attitude toward women," said Al Dorskind. "Jules said he didn't trust them with money because all they'll do is spend it. And Lew, he was always looking for a boy," a surrogate son.

That attitude governed talent, too, said Jack Rael, an agent for GAC. "They were never interested in girl singers," he said. "They stumbled into some," like Betty Grable and Judy Garland—but both of them landed inside MCA only after Stein purchased other Hollywood agencies in the 1930s. Grable was originally so disgusted with MCA's representation that she left the agency. After World War II helped turn her into the highest-paid performer of her day, Stein and Wasserman wooed her back, showering her with gifts and pledges of an even higher salary. Monica Lewis, who later married

Jennings Lang, worked for years as a chanteuse in small clubs. She left MCA because "they didn't take me seriously. I wanted to branch out and do other things," she explained. "They didn't give much attention to women or female clients."

When Wasserman took over Universal Studios, he assumed control of a studio that historically had championed women. "Carl Laemmle was great for women," said Kay Thackery, who in 1924 supervised scripts for Universal. The mogul rarely paid top salaries, but female directors and producers were used to working for less money, and Laemmle's studio became an incubator for them. "At Universal, women had more of an opportunity to do well than at any other studio," Thackery said. Shortly after it opened in 1914, Universal had a dozen female directors, many of them giant talents. Lule Warrenton had her own production company, known for the 1917 hit *A Bit o' Heaven.* Ruth Stonehouse wrote, directed, and produced her own movies. Cleo Madison directed so well that crewmen considered her the best of the lot. Ida May Park shot twelve features in eleven months, producing pictures on time and under budget— which would have made her a Wasserman favorite. The greatest artist of them all was Lois Weber, whom Laemmle called "The Mayor" of Universal City, and whose many assistants included John Ford and Henry Hathaway.

Today, most of the films made by these women no longer exist. Did Wasserman throw out the works of Madison, Park, and Weber when he seized the studio and dumped its archives? Details about them are rare, too. In any case, once the capital-intensive talkies took over, Universal's female directors became a thing of the past, and not even the forward-thinking Wasserman would bring them back. Most of the star directors ended up like Weber, who was reduced to supporting herself by managing apartments in Fullerton, California, until her death.

Wasserman's studio had only a few token women. Alma Reville

was the astute and indispensable adviser, screenwriter, and editor on many of the films made by her husband, Alfred Hitchcock, said the couple's daughter, Patricia Hitchcock O'Connell. "My father didn't make a movie without my mother's involvement." Hitchcock also relied heavily on Joan Harrison, whom he considered a valuable "idea woman." She was actually a screenwriter who fed him story ideas, wrote, and cowrote some of his best films: *Suspicion, Saboteur, Foreign Correspondent,* and *Rebecca.* She left Hitchcock to produce her own films at Universal, such as *Ride the Pink Horse* (1947), which Wasserman's men recycled for one of their made-for-TV movies. At one time, Harrison was one of only three female producers working under any studio contract. She had always wanted to do a film made entirely by women—a radical idea then, as it still is now. But Hitch lured her back, and she produced *Alfred Hitchcock Presents* until 1965. As Jerry Adler recalled: "She was the only woman producer we had on the Universal lot."

Since women continued to work for less money than men, it's odd that Wasserman didn't exploit that fact. In the seventies, he prized well-educated employees. Nevertheless, a blue-collar man could get into the TV director's chair faster than a female film-school graduate. "There were hardly any women on the lot outside of actresses," said Stephen Cannell. "Monique James was head of talent, and that was about it. There were almost no women producers, no women directors, and no women executives that you could spot in any really important roles." Few women worked in the less-visible film-editing room, either. One who flourished was Vera Fields, the patron saint of fledgling male directors, aka "Mother Cutter." She won an Oscar for improving George Lucas's *American Graffiti* and rescued a flailing Steven Spielberg by infusing his movie *Jaws* with enough dramatic pacing to overcome its flaws. Not until 1982, when Amy Heckerling landed on the lot, did Universal have another female motion-picture director. Ned Tanen gave her $4 million to make *Fast Times at Ridgemont High* (1982), a funny portrait of suburban teenagers that featured a gallery of new performers: Sean Penn, Jennifer Jason Leigh, Judge Reinhold, Phoebe Cates, Forest Whitaker, Eric Stoltz, and Nicolas Cage, under his real name, Nicholas Coppola. *Fast Times* went on to earn $80 million—not bad for a low-budget film. But Heckerling was the exception in 1981—and was still in 2001. "Hollywood is sexist," said screenwriter William Goldman. Even though women in 2001 made up half of America's labor force and half of its movie audience, they accounted for only 6 percent of all working directors in Hollywood.

One woman whom Wasserman clearly admired was Phyllis Grann, head of MCA's book publisher, Putnam. By 1982, she was building the house into a juggernaut that at decade's end would ring up over $300 million in annual sales. "Lew Wasserman taught me that you're only as good as the talent you have under contract," she told a reporter. Grann built several writers into brand names, including Dick Francis, Robert Ludlum, and Tom Clancy. Through the 1980's, she produced annual growth rates of 14 percent, well above book publishing's norm.

But with Putnam's success came new, unforseen challenges. "This solid small business became more and more difficult, given the amounts of money demanded by star writers," said Sid Sheinberg. And the publishing business now competed with cable channels and videocassettes plus blockbuster movies, all of which were included among MCA subsidiaries. "Later, other forms of entertainment began to prove a challenge," said Sheinberg. "Readers got distracted."

Although Wasserman rarely used the word "synergy" himself, he had pioneered the idea of acquiring entertainment-related companies under a single umbrella, with the idea that each part would complement the others, and lift the whole. But that philosophy didn't always translate neatly into annual earnings. In the 1980s, it became clear that Universal's subsidiaries could also cannibalize one another, and that book sales, for example, could shortchange the movie kiosk. This phenomenon was the natural—albeit dark—consequence of corporate synergy, and it posed a problem.

In addition, some of MCA's subsidiaries were awkward fits. MCA had bought *The Runner,* an athletic magazine published by "guys who looked like they were shot out of cannons," said one director. No one on the company's board was a running enthusiast, and even as the fad swept the country, the magazine soon folded.

MCA also bought Spencer Gifts, but that purchase made little sense, said Dorskind. MCA knew little about the gift-catalog business. "How are we going to put our 'expertise' into this division, when expertise has nothing to do with the business?" another director asked. These conversations didn't always filter up to the fourteenth floor. As one man explained: "I always got the feeling that those MCA guys were bottom-feeders. They were looking for tchotchkes, some great deal like the Paramount library. Instead, they ended up selling whoopee cushions through a mail-order service." It seemed to be beneath the corporation that Lew had created.

By the early 1980s, Wasserman and Sheinberg were growing disenchanted with several MCA divisions: the slow-growth book publisher, the straggling gift-catalog business, the politically hot Yosemite Park concessionaire, and a savings-and-loan division that was starting to bleed money. "We did diversify, but we did not do very well in anything," Dorskind said.

Wasserman's desire to expand his realm fought constantly with his fear of overextending it. In 1976 Jay Stein, one of Wasserman's young lieutenants, had urged him to buy Sea World, a run-down, 166-acre marine zoological park in San Diego. The attraction was home to dolphins, sharks, penguins, polar bears, manatees, otters, and other sea creatures, and housed a marine-life rescue and research program.

"I wanted to do all kinds of hotels and parks and more theme-parks," Stein said, and he believed that Sea World was a great way to begin that. Its stock was trading at $2 a share, and Wasserman agreed to pursue a deal. But as he studied it further, he feared that Shamu, the killer whale, would be too unpredictable for his staid corporation. "We had two concerns," explained Sheinberg. "One was that the entire business would be wiped out by some animal illness. The second was that the animal-rights activists could put the kibosh on the business. We always looked at it as scary."

Even so, Wasserman offered $35 million for Sea World. "It was a bargain," said Buzz Price, who sat on Sea World's board. But the marine park's directors thought Wasserman was pretty scary himself, said Price. "They were afraid of MCA. Its reputation was tough, heavy-handed, and hands-on." Wasserman could have smooth-talked his way into a deal, but his fears about the animals, along with his aversion to paying more than necessary, prevailed. "At some subconscious level, those fears made us more conservative than even we were inclined to be," Sheinberg admitted.

Wary of Wasserman, Sea World directors accepted a higher bid— only $1 million more—from Harcourt Brace Jovanovich, which ended up with the park at a bargain price. Said Sheinberg, "With the wisdom of hindsight, we should have been more aggressive in trying to buy it."

Harcourt Brace practically ignored its new acquisition. By the early 1980s, the marine park had deteriorated so much, "it would have been better for Sea World if MCA had bought them," said Price. Yet real estate along California's coastline was appreciating faster than a treasure chest full of Spanish doubloons. Once again, Wasserman had an opportunity to swoop in. In 1989 he offered about $900 million for the run-down park and its coastal land. Instead, Harcourt Brace sold Sea World to Busch Entertainment for an astounding $1.1 billion, making a 3,000 percent return on its investment, said Price.

In 1977 Wasserman had decided to buy Coca-Coca Bottling Company of Los Angeles. The purchase made sense: The beverage was sold at Universal's parks and at its movie showings. But when

Wasserman called the chairman, Arthur D. MacDonald, and coldly informed him that MCA was about to take over his company, the soda pop chief thought Wasserman rude. When the mogul offered a chintzy $140 million for his operation, MacDonald thought him arrogant, too. The bottling executive was so insulted by Wasserman's attitude that he encouraged competitive bids and fought MCA with paid newspaper advertisements and a federal lawsuit. "That was a frustrating deal; I don't deny it," said Sheinberg. Wasserman's stunning lack of charm allowed white knight Northwest Industries to snap up the bottling company for a respectable $200 million.

Four years later, in 1981, Northwest sold it for $600 million—tripling its investment. By then, Wall Street analysts were telling these stories to underscore how Wasserman's regal style and "bottom-feeding" terms were strangling MCA's growth. Said Sheinberg, "Lew was tough. There were things that we could have done and should have done that would have strengthened us for the future. But it had to be a hell of a deal for it to pass muster with Lew. Opportunities like buying Universal's lot for $11 million didn't come along very often anymore."

Lew's men continued pitching deals to their boss, hoping that he'd run with one. Jay Stein would spend weeks studying a potential acquisition. He'd commission studies, prepare charts, and assemble numbers in a multimedia presentation, aiming to sell Wasserman and a roomful of executives on the beauty of his proposal. On presentation day, Stein would stand at the head of the room, in front of a polished conference table, trying not to perspire. Wasserman would sit in his high-backed chair, head to one side, and scrutinize the executive and his data. "He would wait for you to slip up just once during your presentation," Stein recalled. "Then he'd come in and pounce." As a roomful of Armani suits looked on, Wasserman would quiz Stein ruthlessly about his numbers and assumptions. "He wouldn't do it maliciously," Stein explained. "But you had to be sure of your facts and have all the evidence on your side. Otherwise, it was torture. You could not make a presentation to Lew and Sid without it turning into a free-for-all."

Stein began to bring in reinforcements. He had junior executives study arcane corners of a proposal so they could field Lew's penetrating questions. "But then, they'd get intimidated by Lew or Sid. They'd choke up or stutter." The squeamish would wither under Wasserman's barrage; later, they'd be reamed out vehemently by Stein for failing the test. "I don't suffer fools easily," Stein said, acknowledging his own reputation for ranting and raving.

Wasserman didn't have to play the heavy, but if he perceived any weakness during these agonizing presentations, he'd kill the deal. If he couldn't find any holes, he'd mull it over. Savvy presenters soon realized that in order to convince Lew, they had to enlist Sheinberg, too. "Sid could be a terrific supporter," Stein explained. If he liked something, he would work on Wasserman. "I kept talking so much to Lew and Sid, Lew and Sid, that it became Sue and Lid, Sue and Lid."

By 1981, the relationship between Wasserman and Sheinberg mirrored the one that had existed earlier between Jules Stein and Wasserman. In both cases, the two men were rarely more than a few feet or a phone call away. Lew had always kept Jules informed, and now Sid kept Lew informed and "made him a player," said Stein. "There was never a lock on the door, and Lew would sometimes interrupt our meetings. That used to drive me crazy, because Sid and I would be talking about how to convince Lew to do something." Then Wasserman would wander in, plop down in a chair next to Stein, and start pelting him with questions. "What do you mean, you want to do this? Why? When?" Without his ammunition of charts and numbers, Stein would have to ad-lib his case.

Wasserman hated to be out of the loop on anything—especially discussions about himself or MCA. When Jules had been alive, he had sometimes invited young bloods like Jay Stein to lunch in the commissary. "We had nothing in common, we weren't the same age, and I don't know what he saw in me," said Jay. But the old man felt isolated from the business he had built and talking with young men kept him abreast of the culture. Yet Wasserman hated to let his mentor meet alone with protégés—he had not forgotten the attempted 1969 palace coup. So Wasserman invited himself to the Stein-on-Stein luncheons to make sure that he too was kept in the loop. "Lew wasn't intimidated by me, but he didn't want anyone else to brief Jules," said Stein. Sometimes the older Stein would put the younger one on the spot by asking about a project that Wasserman hadn't even heard of yet.

The younger Stein would stall, saying, "Well, I haven't discussed that with Lew yet."

Jules would turn testy. "Go ahead and tell me," he'd order. The younger man would have to divulge new information about Universal's theme-park business as Wasserman listened. His boss would not say a word, but the tension was there.

The other studios were following the path blazed by Lew twenty years earlier. Wasserman had built the town's first entertainment empire by melding TV production, record labels, real estate, movies, banking, tourism, retail, and electronics into a single Hollywood-based conglomerate. He had moved horizontally across industry sectors, geographically across time zones, and politically over party lines. In the 1960s Wasserman had made it look easy, attracting insurers like Transamerica and undertakers like Kinney National Services to scoop up studios for the first time. Now some of these outsiders were bailing out, leaving Wasserman as the undisputed king. In their stead, however, came newly minted financiers, profiteers, and corporate chiefs with no experience in—nor passion for—making movies. Would Wasserman outlast this second wave, too?

Transamerica Corporation, for example, grew disenchanted with United Artists, and in 1981 sold it to Kirk Kerkorian, a Las Vegas–based financier who already owned the decimated MGM Studios. He formed MGM/UA Entertainment Companies. That same year, the rotund oilman Marvin Davis of Colorado purchased Twentieth Century Fox and eventually moved to Los Angeles. MCA alumnus Frank Price had replaced the scandalous David Begelman at Columbia Studios, but by 1982, Price was reporting to the studio's new owner—the Coca-Cola Company. Paramount Studios was run by the foul-mouthed head of Gulf & Western Industries, Charlie Bluhdorn, until he died abruptly in 1983. Then Martin S. Davis, the new head of Gulf & Western, stepped in. Although Barry Diller and Michael Eisner had helped resuscitate the flagging studio, they couldn't continue posting the big profits Davis wanted. Paramount lost several top executives.

In his seventies, Wasserman turned even more cautious—and increasingly vulnerable to attack. Beyond the studio gates, young Turks ambitious to run their own glamorous movie studio believed that the old gray wolf had lost his fangs and fire. Junk-bond dealer Mike Milken had made a practice of helping his Drexel Burnham clients mount hostile takeovers, and one of them was Steve Wynn, the son of a bingo-parlor owner. Wynn had acquired the shabby Golden Nugget Casino in Las Vegas and quickly renovated it into a top property. With Milken's help, Wynn had built a second Golden Nugget in Atlantic City, and in 1983 Wynn was worth $100 million and itching to expand. He again turned to Milken.

Wasserman learned that someone was acquiring blocks of MCA stock. It turned out that Milken was helping Wynn amass 2 million MCA shares—or 4 percent of its outstanding stock. Wasserman took swift action. He hired private investigators to scour Las Vegas, Atlantic City, and New York for every detail about Wynn's past. "Anyone who was in that situation would have done the same," said Sheinberg.

Wynn soon discovered that Wasserman wasn't so vulnerable after all. The wily mogul himself owned 7.1 percent of MCA shares, and was the controlling executor of Stein's family trusts, which held about 11 percent of stock. The MCA profit-sharing trust was held by MCA employees loyal to Wasserman; that added another 3.5 percent. All in all, Wasserman controlled more than 21 percent of MCA stock, and he'd recently presented to the board a bylaw that would protect him and his job. He could be ousted only if holders of three-quarters of MCA's stock voted for a change in management. Wasserman could easily thwart a raider just by gaining support of only 5 percent of the stock from outside shareholders. That would be enough to prevent Milken from obtaining votes from those who held 75 percent of the stock, which was necessary to boot Wasserman out. A raid would be nearly impossible.

But just in case, Wasserman raised his bank credit limit to $1 billion and instituted other antitakeover measures. Then, to make sure that Wynn got the message, Wasserman sent an emissary to Las Vegas. The messenger told Wynn that if he bought more than 5 percent of MCA stock—a SEC ownership benchmark—Lew would consider him an unfriendly buyer. "He got his butt kicked," said Joe Delaney, a columnist for the *Las Vegas Sun* and former casino worker. "Someone was sent to tell Steve: 'Hey, kid, you've gone too far. Don't go any further.' "

To reinforce the warning, Wasserman personally called Wynn, said Dan Slusser, then an MCA vice president. Nonchalantly, Wasserman told him it wasn't a good idea to buy MCA stock for any other reason but passive investment. Wynn not only backed off, he sold his holdings quickly. The gray wolf still had fangs.

For years, Wasserman watched as other studios leaped in to develop sectors of the entertainment business. Warner Communications had bought Atari and rode the video-game boom from a $200,000 unit to a $65 million annual business in 1980. It bought a cable TV system, too. Another company, Time Inc., had started cable system Home Box Office (HBO) in 1972, but MCA waited to see how the new business would fare. Once HBO started to surge, Wasserman entered the fray, albeit gingerly. He joined three other studios and

Getty Oil to create an all-movie pay-TV service called Premiere. Then, just before its debut in 1980, a federal judge blocked the cable venture on antitrust grounds. In 1981 Premiere's launch was still pending—much to Wasserman's annoyance.

With raiders and rustlers moving outside his tower, Wasserman looked for other ways to protect his kingdom. In 1983 he approached NBC about a merger, but that fell through. The next year, the TV network was purchased by electronics giant RCA. In 1984 Lew approached his old friend Thornton Bradshaw, chairman of RCA, with the idea of merging MCA and Bradshaw's conglomerate. At first, the two companies were far apart on money: RCA offered $90 a share; Wasserman wanted $120. The merger talks ended, only to start up again. As negotiations progressed, the two began to meet halfway, and what a deal it was to be! Universal TV would have its own TV network, and the MCA/RCA merger would be the first marriage of a big TV broadcaster and a big TV producer. "We didn't acknowledge it publicly at the time, but we were very close to doing the RCA deal," said Sheinberg.

Wasserman was supposed to be chairman of the executive committee that oversaw the merged companies. He would reign supreme, and Sheinberg would still report to him. "Thornton was very anxious to have this deal happen," said Sheinberg. "But at one of the last meetings, a guy from RCA came up with a whole other organizational structure." Sheinberg would not be reporting to Wasserman but would have to answer to Bradshaw. "That screwed it all up." Once Wasserman saw the new design, he put his arm around Sid and led him away from the table. "You're not going to like this," he told Sid.

"We both agreed it wasn't going to happen."

For a second time, the deal collapsed. A few months later, Bradshaw's RCA was folded into General Electric; the 1985 purchase was the biggest non-oil-company merger of its time. For the former band booker Wasserman, it was also a sad footnote. The Radio

Corporation of America in 1924 had inspired Jules Stein to name his agency the Music Corporation of America, and both RCA and MCA had grown during the twentieth century to command their respective fields. Now RCA no longer existed: Unless Wasserman moved quickly, MCA could disappear, too, despite the safeguards and phone calls.

The mega-merger that swallowed RCA was a harbinger of more to come. Many of these deals made little sense. As early as 1985, a study by the management-consulting firm McKinsey & Company criticized the merger movement, finding that most combined companies resulted in poorer, not better, overall performances. But Wasserman had helped trigger the merger trend, at least in Hollywood. Over twenty years, MCA's appetite for consecutively higher annual earnings combined with its relentless grab for even more ancillary avenues had created a monster that threatened to turn on Wasserman. Unless he could expand MCA even more—without blowing it up—his company would soon attract someone else who could. And that would lead to Wasserman's becoming irrelevant in his own industry. Given the voracious appetite of the Wall Street mob, Wasserman had little choice. He had to boost MCA higher into new gravity-defying heights, even if that jeopardized his company's stability.

Edie Wasserman's mother, Tillie Beckerman, was ailing. Edie and Lew had bought the widow a home in Beverly Hills, not far from theirs, and Edie had staffed it with round-the-clock caretakers. "Edie was very devoted to her mother," said Wendy Goldberg. In 1983, when her mother passed away at 102, Edie had a tough time. She buried Tillie at Hillside Memorial Park, alongside Tillie's husband, Henry, and not far from her in-laws, Isaac and Minnie Wasserman. The longtime Cleveland residents were now at rest in this Jewish cemetery that was the burial site of Al Jolson, George Jessel, and MCA star Jack Benny.

Edie's longtime nemesis, Doris Stein, was still going strong, although by now she was known for falling asleep at parties. She often embarrassed herself by drooling at dress fittings or spilling her drink at fashion shows. Her faux Bryn Mawr accent had slipped away, too, and none of these developments surprised Edie; she had always thought that Doris would someday turn into a doddering old woman. But Doris's niece, Patsy Krauskopf, grew concerned with her aunt's odd behavior and consulted a doctor. He diagnosed the widow as having Parkinson's disease. "Aunt Doris refused to be confined to a wheelchair," said Krauskopf. After a hospital stay, nurses and doctors tried to wheel the dowager outside to her driver, but the feisty woman fought them at every corner. "She was screaming mad." Doris insisted on leaving by her own two feet.

Back at home, Doris managed to keep up with her girlfriends and their exhaustive round of lunches, cocktails, and dinners. She also remained the driving force behind the Jules Stein Eye Institute. But a few weeks after her eighty-second birthday, Doris was sent to the UCLA Medical Center. She died on Saturday night, April 7, 1984.

The family held a memorial celebration for her at the institute, just as they had for Jules, inviting some 300 people to the ceremony. "We made it a big cocktail party with drinks and food because my mother loved cocktail parties," said Gerald Oppenheimer. He set up television screens so friends could circulate throughout the institute yet catch the speeches he and his brother, Harold Oppenheimer, made and the tributes from friends. There weren't many of Doris's confidantes left, said columnist George Christy: only Connie Wald, widow of producer Jerry Wald; Jean Howard, the Ziegfeld girl-turned-Hollywood-starlet; fashion diva Diana Vreeland; and *Vogue* editor Eleanor Phillips, among others. Edie showed up, too. Said one insider, "People can say what they want about Edie, but she always paid her last respects."

Several of Doris's friends were certain they'd be remembered in the doyenne's will. "For years, Doris had gone to their homes for postprandial drinks or intimate suppers," said Christy. Her friends had supported the institute, contributed to Jules's favored GOP candidates, and accompanied Doris on her wild jaunts and excursions. "Her friends were thinking that they'd get a bauble or something to remember her by," said Christy.

That was not to be. Everything went to Doris's surviving daughter, Jean Stein, her grandchildren, or the institute. "Several of her longtime friends were quite surprised," said the columnist. Two years later, her property was auctioned off. Christie's sold $1 million worth of Doris's necklaces, rings, bracelets, and brooches—three dozen in all. There were diamonds, emeralds, sapphires, rubies, and pearls—including a giant 28-carat rectangular-cut diamond ring of rare quality. Doris owned more than five hundred antique chairs and tapestries, among them an exquisite fourteen-piece George III suite from Upton House, Essex, England and several rare Chinese works.

"I'd say her greatest contribution was to the world of fashion," Wasserman said. True to her spirit, Doris left to the Los Angeles County Museum of Art her enormous collection of hats—some 130 pieces, including those by Beverly Hills designer Mr. John. "Some of her hats had bird's nests in them, others had geometric designs," said her son. Doris also endowed the museum with enough money to store her hats and fund the Doris Stein Costume and Textiles Research and Design Center. The center housed rare pieces of clothing, a library, and a collection of designers' sketches, drawings, and fashion plates. In time, it acquired rare books and manuscripts from as early as the sixteenth century, all related to textiles and dress. And it maintained important archives of individual designers, including those of James Galanos.

To Edie, Doris bequeathed her place as queen of the realm. The two women had really never gotten along. For half a century, theirs had been an intense, even nasty rivalry, full of schemes and snubs. But in the end, Edie gave Doris grudging respect. "Doris had always been supportive of Lew," Goldberg explained. And as the years had rolled by, Edie came to appreciate those who valued and deferred to her husband. Since Jules's death, Doris had increasingly leaned on Lew for advice with the institute and trusts. "He was good in helping the family make tough decisions," said Gerald Oppenheimer.

"Doris had been the grande dame of Hollywood," Goldberg noted. When Doris died, so, too, did the idea of the Hollywood woman of leisure—that charming hostess whose giddy, stylish guests led conga lines straight to the pool. "In those days, Hollywood parties weren't about the business," said Rex Reed. Added Christy, "The town used to be quite social, with people inviting their friends over just to have fun." Doris and her socialite friends would dress in jewels, take their Rolls-Royces out to Santa Anita Racetrack, and bet the ranch on the ponies. They'd drink too much, laugh too long, and treat every outing like a jolly good adventure. "After Doris died, that carefree energy and cosmopolitan style started to fade from Hollywood," Christy explained.

As for Edie, she had never been a slave to fashion. Unlike Doris, she was not vain about her looks. "She had no cosmetic surgery that I knew of, which is unusual [in Hollywood]," said Goldberg. Edie didn't color her gray hair, wear too much makeup, or even shave a few years off her birthdate. "She used to laugh at me when I'd turn sensitive about my age," said Goldberg; Edie was proud of her age and even though she, too, had a safe full of gems, given to her by Lew, she always wore them sparingly and never to attract attention. "She was not ostentatious, like some people we know," said Goldberg. "She always did things in good taste."

In 1984 the town became a little more like Edie—less carefree and more practical. She and Lew no longer invited film stars, MCA executives, and chummy-chums for Sunday-afternoon barbecues. "There were no more small dinner parties at home anywhere in town, certainly not like before," said Dominick Dunne. Instead,

Edie invited guests to soirees and suppers with definite agendas that weren't always obvious, even to the most jaded attendee. She gathered intelligence on a more sophisticated level now. She knew which producer was undergoing rehab for what sort of addiction, whose son was no longer speaking to his family, and which screenwriter was pitching which studio on a particular idea.

Around 1982, the sixty-seven-year-old Edie met several times with screenwriter Terrence McDonnel and his partner. Over lunch at Café Moustache in Westwood, the trio discussed a film project about the nuclear Manhattan Project in the 1940s. "Edie was very interested in our story, which took place in Chicago," said McDonnel. She met with the writers over a span of several months until, suddenly, her interest dried up. "I don't know what happened. Maybe she wasn't going to bring it to Universal Studios after all."

As surely as Lew struggled to lead MCA and Hollywood into the next era, Edie did, too. She pushed her pet causes, working as a trustee for CalArts, and giving $1 million so that fifty students could study art. She and Lew funded four-year scholarships for dozens of middle-class students at CalTech as well as at Brandeis, New York, Georgetown, and Texas universities. She increased her efforts at the Motion Picture & Television Fund, and now sat on all three of its governing boards. She began spearheading a $50 million fundraising campaign to build a hospital and residential wing for filmdom's senior citizens. "It took many years to raise the money, but Edie was a driving force," said Walter Seltzer. "She became the heart and soul of that place," added board member Irma Kalish.

By the mid-1980s, there was a waiting list of down-on-their-luck retired studio employees who required medical care—thanks largely to a recession and Reagan's cuts in social programs. Edmond O'Brien, one of Edie's longtime friends, had Alzheimer's disease and needed help. She tried to get him a room, but the home couldn't accommodate an Alzheimer's patient. When a special wing at the

MPTF home finally opened in May 1985, Edie called the old actor at the Veterans Hospital, but O'Brien had just died. "It broke my heart because Eddie had been a very close friend," Edie said.

A few weeks later, the MPTF gave Edie its Silver Medallion Award of Honor. At the June 1985 luncheon at Chasen's, she made a rare public speech. It had been seven years since she had first joined the board, hoping to polish Hollywood's image. But now the MPTF had become her mission. "It's her life," said Lew. Yet, despite her relentless fundraising, Edie had a hard time getting charitable contributions. She'd hit up her friends—Roddy McDowall, Anne and Kirk Doulgas, and Fran and Ray Stark—for money, but it was tougher to reach the younger generation of moguls and stars. She called on executives in their offices and brought along powerful men for support, including producer Howard Koch. She once made an appointment with Michael Landon, former "Little Joe" Cartwright of *Bonanza* fame, and now the producer of TV's *Highway to Heaven*. The MPTF's fund was so inclusive—"even your secretary of twenty years can live at the home," she told Landon. The producer promised to give the home $50,000 for every year his show was in production, which delighted Edie.

But he was the exception in the 1980s. The Gordon Gekko character in *Wall Street* was declaring that "greed is good," and the town's New Establishment seemed to agree with him. Actress Jane Fonda was making a fortune selling exercise tapes, and Madonna, the Material Girl, was looking for fellows with "hard, cold cash." Edie was not completely old-fashioned—she worked out with her own personal trainer. But the eighties zeitgeist, with its ostentatious displays of wealth, was anathema to her. Building one's body and one's portfolio ranked miles ahead of charitable works.

Edie simply redoubled her efforts.

Lew Wasserman's First 50 Years with MCA

In 1986, Hollywood toasted the town's monarchs, Edie and Lew Wassserman, with parties that marked the Golden Anniversary of the couple's marriage as well as their enduring MCA reign. No other partnership in town lasted as long, not before or since. The celebratory scrapbook given to all guests at one anniversary gala included pictures of Edie and Lew with luminaries from show biz and politics. (Courtesy Author's Collection, from gala scrapbook)

Program

DOC SEVERINSEN and the Tonight Show Orchestra
Overture

SID SHEINBERG — President, MCA INC.
Welcome

JOHNNY CARSON

FRANK SINATRA
"The Gentleman is a Champ"

GLADYS KNIGHT & THE PIPS

"THE FIRST FIFTY YEARS"

PRESENTATION

RAY ANTHONY and his Orchestra
Dancing in the Mayfair Casino

MCA gratefully acknowledges the contributions of the following: Special Lyrics by SAMMY CAH.
"THE FIRST FIFTY YEARS" Executive Producer DAVID L. WOLPER · Producer/ Direc
Research VICKI CRAWFORD · Assistant Direc.

The fete included an opulent menu and entertainment with Frank Sinatra, narration from Johnny Carson, and production by David L. Wolper. (Courtesy Author's Collection, from gala scrapbook)

SALAD VARIÉ
Boston Bibb, Radicchio, Limestone
and Arugula Lettuce
Vinaigrette "Maison"

CHAPPELLET CHARDONNAY 1983

ROASTED MEDALLION OF WISCONSIN VEAL
Sauce Marsala
BABY VEGETABLES AU BEURRE
in Squash Basket
TIMBALE OF PECAN WILD RICE

CHAPPELLET CABERNET SAUVIGNON 1981

CHOCOLATE AND VANILLA ICE CREAM
AND BERRY SHERBET
with Chocolate and Raspberry Sauces
Florentine Wafer
AFTER DINNER MINTS AND COFFEE

"CHAMPAGNE TOAST"
Shramsberg Blanc de Noirs 1981

man is a Champ" Music and Original Lyrics by RICHARD ROGERS and LAWRENCE HART.
RWIN ROSTEN · Photography BERTRAM VAN MUNSTER · Editor JAMES KENNING
NE DANIEL · Narrated by JOHNNY CARSON

The anniversary booklet also contained a special 45 rpm recording of Frank Sinatra singing lyrics of Sammy Cahn, who reworked Rodgers & Hart's "The Lady is a Tramp" into "The Gentleman is a Champ" for the occasion. (Courtesy Author's Collection, from gala scrapbook)

Edie and Lew supported Rosalynn and Jimmy Carter's Habitat for Humanity project and applauded Carter's global mediation efforts. The Wassermans believed that Carter never realized his presidential potential due to "bad luck." (Courtesy Author's Collection, from gala scrapbook)

Edie befriended Jimmy Stewart six years before the easy-going actor became Lew's client and, later, dear friend. MCA landed Stewart and other stars after buying the Leland Hayward-Nat Deverich agency. (Courtesy Author's Collection, from gala scrapbook)

In 1916, when the top picture was taken, Universal Studios had just released a Lois Weber hit. The ranch-turned-studio was only two years old, Lew Wasserman was barely three, and the silent film era was in full swing.

Forty years later, Universal Studios had expanded considerably. It was producing "B" movies featuring Ma and Pa Kettle, Francis the Talking Mule, and the Creature from the Black Lagoon, in the Gill-man's final dive out of the deep, while signing two-picture contracts with Lew's MCA clients Charlton Heston, Joan Crawford, Gregory Peck, Dana Andrews, and Donna Reed. At the same time, in, 1956, Lew was using Universal's sound stages to churn out his lucrative Revue TV shows, like *Dragnet* and *The Adventures of Ozzie and Harriett.*

By 1986, Wasserman had developed the 410-acre studio lot into a bona fide city, with its own mayor, zip code, and cadre of lobbyists. The Black Tower, in the foreground, may have been the shortest high-rise in the Valley, but it was the most feared spot in Hollywood. (Courtesy Author's Collection, from gala scrapbook)

Edie Wasserman became a tireless advocate for old and forgotten studio workers. She turned the decrepit Motion Picture & Television Fund home into a top health care facility. By 1999, she and Lew had given more than $12 million to Hollywood's flagship charity. (Courtesy Jules Stein Institute)

LEW WASSERMAN: 1913-2002

One of Edie's—and Los Angeles'—favorite editorial cartoonists was three-time Pultizer-Prize winner Paul Conrad, whose masterful obituary cartoon of Lew's visual signature so delighted the widow that she asked Conrad for a copy. (Courtesy Paul Conrad and Tribune Media Group)

THIRTY-NINE

IN THE SPRING OF 1983, Wasserman flew to Washington to visit his erstwhile client Ronald Reagan. Lew and Ronnie, as the mogul called him, had met in the Oval Office several times by then. At eighty-one, Reagan was eleven years older than Wasserman, yet Reagan dyed his hair in an unsuccessful attempt to appear younger. His eyes were obscured by droopy eyelids, while Wasserman's orbs sparkled. The white-haired studio chief was clearly happy to be close to the seat of national power, ready to make another stunning deal.

Wasserman had already set the president "straight" about pay-TV, he said. Although a federal judge had ruled that MCA's Premiere pay-TV movie service violated antitrust laws, Wasserman envisioned a time when cable service could link with MCA's savings and loan, or its gift catalog, so viewers could bank and shop electronically. His vision was years ahead of the market; services like the Home Shopping Network wouldn't catch on for several more years. Still, the old man hadn't lost his prescience, and Reagan's administration would come around to his way of seeing and allow studios to partner on cable ventures.

Lew was not alone that day; he and other members of the Motion Picture Association of America (MPAA) were there to explain their business needs. The former actor seemed to want to talk more about his Hollywood days than his current duties. "He loved the movie industry," said Stu Spencer, and joked about returning to the set.

Reagan and Wasserman were similar, yet different. "Wasserman [was] certainly no conservative when it [came] to politics," said Sid Sheinberg. Wasserman had long championed social welfare, public education, minority assistance programs, free speech, and low deficits—everything that the Reagan administration was knocking down. The president had already narrowed the Freedom of Information Act to keep public information out of view. His FBI was spying on more than one hundred domestic groups that opposed his foreign policy. The Star Wars defense buildup, combined with his tax cuts to the rich and incorporated, was about to triple the national debt to $300 billion—a record high. But Reagan and Wasserman both knew that it took many pulleys and levers to obtain and retain a seat of power. "I think you can get pretty much anything you want," Wasserman once told me. The trick was learning how to compromise. "That's the secret, really." Wasserman was always willing to consider a compromise if it meant obtaining his goal.

Now he dearly needed a favor: He wanted to hang on to a lucrative government regulation that ran counter to Reagan's pro-business philosophy. "There was a push to get government off the backs of the people," said Douglas Gomery. Reagan deregulated businesses by dismantling decades of laws that had protected consumers and restrained companies in the banking, communications, retail, and broadcast industries. Among those measures was fin-syn, the FCC financial syndication rule that had forbidden networks from producing TV shows.

Because of it, MCA for years had managed to keep most TV syndication money for itself. In the late 1960s, foreign and domestic TV stations paid producers millions of dollars to run episodes of *Dragnet* and *Leave It to Beaver,* MCA shows that the networks had popularized. The networks had wanted more of that revenue, but the 1971 Financial Interest and Syndication Rule had prevented that. In the thirteen years since, Wasserman's company had collected at least $1.3 billion in revenue, according to MCA's annual reports. But Reagan's deregulation would end the bonanza and devastate Wasserman's company financially.

The networks, which were facing increased competition from cable TV and independent stations, had been lobbying the FCC for months, arguing that the fin-syn rules were outdated. Their audiences and profits were starting to shrink, yet they couldn't produce their own shows. FCC chairman Mark Fowler agreed to revisit the issue, and before long, his staff, along with those at the departments of commerce and justice, all agreed that fin-syn should be killed.

The studios were frantic. Wasserman called back MPAA head Jack Valenti, who was vacationing in Hawaii. "It became Valenti's job to keep those rules in place," said Gomery. As Valenti recalled, "I held meetings three times a week with my people on this." He met with any lawmaker he could, collaring FCC staff members, the president's counsel, Edwin Meese III, and U.S. Attorney General William French Smith. Valenti had to, he said: "The networks brought a full-scale attack against us." But he wasn't getting anywhere.

"Reagan was kind of torn about this issue," said Gomery. On one hand, the president wanted to appease his GOP supporters; on the other, he wanted to help his Hollywood friends. Just as the FCC was about to overturn the rule, Wasserman paid Reagan a friendly visit. The two men lunched and walked through the Rose Garden. Meanwhile, in another federal building, an FCC official was writing his testimony about why the rule should be abolished. He was to deliver his findings to Congress the next day, "when he was told that the rule had to stay," said Gomery. When Valenti was asked about Wasserman's visit to the president, he said only: "I don't know. I don't ask. And I don't tell."

It was reminiscent of the old days, circa 1952, when Wasserman had requested and received an unethical favor—a union waiver—from Reagan, then head of SAG. Decades had passed. Reagan no longer ran a union, but a country, and the FCC was supposed to answer to Congress, not to the executive branch. But in this case, it obeyed the White House, said Gomery. "The reversal was strange, because it went against Reagan's deregulation credo." The network executives considered it outrageous. "I'm all but certain that Wasserman personally got [to] Reagan," ABC attorney Ev Erlick said at the time.

In fact, Wasserman kept the networks out of the rich fin-syn pie for another fifteen years—through three more presidents, both Democrat and Republican. MCA would go on to collect at least $2 billion more in revenues. "Maybe more," said Valenti. The silver-maned mogul had negotiated another fantastic deal, not just for Universal but for all of the studios. "Lew had called in his chips," said Gomery.

He became a little cocky after that. Wasserman approached ABC chief Leonard Goldenson several times, proposing that the two companies merge. "Now, why on earth would I do that?" Goldenson asked. He knew that FCC's fin-syn rules prohibited networks and producers from forming any partnership, including a merger. "There is only one reason I can think of that might have prompted Lew to seek a merger with ABC," Goldenson told one writer. "His pal Ronald Reagan . . ."

Reagan also got cocky. He and CIA director William Casey had been financing a paramilitary "contra" group to overthrow the elected Nicaraguan government. In 1983 Congress unanimously outlawed the use of public money to support the Contras. Despite that, in what would become one of the more deceptive foreign ventures in U.S. history, the Reagan White House defied Congress and approved a secret war that used other, illicit channels to fund the group, sell weapons, and launder money. Before too long, MCA would be enlisted in Reagan's pet project.

For a time, Sid Sheinberg had tried keeping up with Wasserman's herculean schedule, but he eventually gave up. "Only a fool would try and step into Lew's shoes," he explained. Still, Sheinberg had adopted some of his boss's habits, such as rising before dawn, reading four newspapers, and studying the business sections intently. "I was afraid that Lew Wasserman was going to examine me and that I might fail."

Wasserman had grown into such an icon that even he knew he was slipping into self-parody. One day Wasserman was striding across the studio lot, surrounded by a phalanx of black-suited acolytes. He noticed a man dressed in a white suit, with white hat and shoes—the antithesis of MCA's dress code. A few years before, Wasserman might have reprimanded the dandy. That day, he asked, "Who died?" As Laird Koenig recalled, "Everyone snickered but Lew."

Wasserman was certainly not amused at the declining level of Universal's product. The company's once-vaunted reputation in TV drama was sliding, and its movies were suffering, too. "I hated to go to work each day, it was so oppressive," said Robert Lewis, who had directed several Universal TV movies. By 1980, Lew's Rules for TV productions were tighter than a balled fist. "We had only ten days to make a two-hour movie, which made it very stressful," Lewis explained. "When we went over budget, we got decimated." Once, the director was behind schedule on a ninety-minute movie and arrived at the set early on the eleventh day, aware that he had thirty more scenes to shoot. Someone handed him a note from Wasserman: "You are finished shooting at 7:00 tonight. What you shoot today will be in the movie. What you don't shoot is out." The director finished his movie, but was not pleased with the result.

The divide between the executives and creators had grown wider. "The executives never came onto the back lot. If you shot more than three takes of a scene, you had to call the production department and explain," Lewis recalled. Universal's TV editors were considered third-rate, primarily because they were given so little time to finish their work.

The TV syndication arm, however, posted ever-higher returns. "They had the best overseas salesmen who would sell your shows two, three, and four times," said Lewis. Yet even they ran into problems. The IRS investigated the rumor that Wasserman kept two sets of TV books. Federal auditors did discover several problems with MCA's accounting system, and the company agreed to alter its procedures, said Lewis. But changes did not come soon enough for those who held net profit deals, which comedian Eddie Murphy mockingly called "monkey points."

There were plenty of claimants. James Garner sued MCA in 1983 to force the studio to pay his *Rockford Files* net profits. Though the TV series had grossed $125 million for MCA, Garner hadn't received any of his contractual 37 percent. Harve Bennett, the writer/producer of *The Bionic Woman,* sued MCA to get his profit points from that series, as well as those from *The Six Million Dollar Man.* Talent often had to sue Universal to force it to uphold other clauses in their contracts. Veteran music composer Gil Mellé (*The Andromeda Strain*) had scored the music for the movie pilot of *The Six Million Dollar Man* and had contracted to write all of the music for the following episodes. "Universal did one hundred shows, over five years, and I kept waiting for them to make good on the contract." Mellé idolized Wasserman and was reluctant to sue MCA. "I loved the studio because that's where I got my start," he explained. Finally, just before the seven-year statute of limitations ran its course on his case in 1980, Mellé filed his suit.

MCA attorneys did not settle quickly. "It was their policy to drag out cases as long as they could," said Lewis. Garner's net-profit case continued for five years until he finally settled in 1988 for about $14 million. Harve Bennett was walking up the courthouse steps, about to go to trial, when the MCA attorneys offered to pay his net profits on *Six Million Dollar Man.* Even Mellé settled his case eventually. "I got as much money as I would have had I done the scoring that MCA had promised me," he explained. But after that, Mellé couldn't find a job. "I was a pariah or something." He didn't score a studio project for several more years. And Roy Huggins fought MCA until it finally settled with him in the early 1990s, ten years before he died.

Contracts, deals, and preemptive rights seemed more important than creative shows or packages. "MCA is not an entertainment company—it's a law firm," said AJ Cervantes, who sold his record company to MCA, sued to collect money, and lost. But there was truth behind his jest. Sheinberg was trained as a lawyer. "Lew thought like a lawyer," said Sheinberg. And MCA's legal department had grown so large, it filled three executive floors. "I once said that I looked at the law department as a profit center and, to this day, I don't know what's wrong with that philosophy," said Sheinberg. Surely, if someone violates copyright law or steals property, litigation is well and good. But just as often, critics said, MCA lawyers were weaving loopholes into boilerplate contracts designed to ensnare talent. This was true of most Hollywood studios, but Wasserman's handiwork stood out. "Universal was deceptive and duplicitous," said Lewis.

Industry legend portrayed Wasserman as an honorable man, a prince among thieves. "Lew inculcated in me that your word is your bond," said Jay Stein. "No matter what you say, you must honor your agreements," he told his men. "Sid was the same way." But at the end of the day, when a man drove off the lot and glanced back at the Black Tower, he could see a pattern of broken promises and crooked claims.

FORTY

NED TANEN WALKED INTO WASSERMAN'S OFFICE one day and said he wanted to leave Universal Pictures. "After twenty-eight years of working at MCA, I just didn't want to do it anymore," Tanen explained.

His boss scolded him. "Now, Ned," Lew said, swiveling in his chair. "You're on the board of directors of MCA. You make movies and turn out hits. You have MCA stock and a great salary. Why leave? People would sell their children to be where you are right now."

Tanen was going through a second divorce and was raising two teens. "I can't do this anymore," he repeated.

Wasserman froze.

"The minute he heard that, the screen went blank," Tanen recalled. "I was history. I was no longer in the company, or in their lives."

But Lew wasn't about to let his top movie executive completely out of his contract. If he did, Tanen might move to another studio. "I'm not going to turn around and have you bite me in the ass," Wasserman told the younger man. So Tanen became an independent producer, giving Universal first look at his projects. After twelve years of shepherding Universal movies that made approximately $1.5 billion, Tanen left the fourteenth floor. Then he honed in on the suburban teenager's mind, producing three hits in eighteen months: *Sixteen Candles* (Universal, 1984), *St. Elmo's Fire* (Columbia, 1985), and *The Breakfast Club* (Universal, 1985).

One day Tanen received a call from Paramount Studios executives Barry Diller and Michael Eisner. They needed some movie successes, and Eisner told Tanen, "We want to talk to you about coming over."

"I can't talk to you now," Tanen said, referring to his agreement with Lew.

"It's okay, it's okay," Eisner assured him. "We've already asked Lew if we could approach you."

"What did he say?"

"He gave us the go-ahead. He said that you'd never take our offer." Wasserman believed his loyal executive would never compete against him. But the assurance backfired. Angry at Wasserman's attempt to control him, Tanen said, "I'll come."

"Wait," said Eisner. "We haven't even talked money or anything."

"I don't care. You just sold me. I'm leaving." And he did.

During his long run at Universal, Tanen had helped Joel Schumacher, John Hughes, Matty Simmons, and several other writers and directors. The movie executive got paid well for what he did, and the entire arrangement had made Wasserman happy. But as soon as Tanen left, he was branded as a betrayer. He never heard from Edie or Lew again.

"At MCA, if you died in the line of fire, they'd treat you like a hero," Tanen explained. "They'd pay for your funeral and put your kids through college. But if you left of your own volition, you were exiled," he said. "No. It was worse than that. They didn't hate you. You no longer existed. It was like 'Ned? Ned who?' They'd never heard of you."

At Paramount, Tanen went on to make several hits, giving Wasserman stiff competition. Wasserman hired Robert Reehme to head the studio. "But he was overmatched by Lew and Sid," said Tanen. "They made it too difficult for him," and Rehme left after a year. Wasserman became so desperate that he broke his own rule and rehired a deserter. He asked Frank Price, who had just left Columbia, to return to the fold.

Price arrived at Universal just as the studio was about to release *Streets of Fire,* a movie built around Bruce Springsteen's songs. "The film was nearly finished, but no one had received permission to use Springsteen songs," said Price. The original musical idea was scuttled and replaced with music by such MCA acts as Tom Petty.

Wasserman's passion for the ephemeral business of film did not curry favor on Wall Street. MCA Inc. earned 85 percent of its profits from TV and movies—too much, according to some analysts. In 1983 MCA's operating income fell 26 percent due primarily to its poor run of films. In 1984 its income dropped even more steeply— nearly 50 percent—to $96 million. Wasserman had promised Stein that he would keep MCA intact, but he was growing old, and time was working against him. Pressured by the markets, Wasserman began to lessen his conglomerate's dependency on its core asset: film. Perhaps that would save MCA from the predators pacing outside his gate.

Universal Studio's theme park was now MCA's crown jewel. In 1981 MCA listed the 420-acre asset on its books at only $6 million—just over half of its original $11 million purchase price. "We put a low value on the land because of taxes," said Al Dorksind. The property's market value was closer to $1.2 *billion*, which represented a 1,320 percent return over twenty years. Wasserman had put a $12 million roof on the expanded amphitheater, which now did business year-round. Universal's tour and concert business generated $52 million, and the theme park lured 4 million guests a year—not as many as the 10 million who visited Disneyland, but Universal had more room than the Magic Kingdom, and Wasserman made it grow.

He moved bulldozers and pile drivers onto the lot for another expansion phase. Office space was so scarce in Los Angeles that Wasserman started building a $100 million commercial structure, half of which he had already leased to Getty Oil. He erected a second hotel for $65 million and turned some of his lot into a wilderness area so that Universal could save money on film locations.

He began planning a park in Orlando, Florida, a city projected to become America's top tourist spot by 1985. MCA had already spent $173 million buying 423 acres of land a few miles north of Disney World. Now Wasserman intended to build a film facility and a tour that would differentiate his park from the competitors. He increased MCA's credit line to $375 million and visited Mike Milken to discuss venture capital. But he later thought better of working with Milken, and turned to other studios for financing. "Lew thought we needed to do it with a partner," said Jay Stein, who didn't like the idea. But Sheinberg explained the reasoning: "We aren't greedy pigs. We can share the bounty," he told Stein. "But in case the project turns out to be a disaster, we'll be able to spread the risk."

However, disaster stalked the venture. MCA approached Paramount Studios about joining forces on a Florida theme park, and Wasserman and Sheinberg met with Paramount's president, Michael Eisner. The two sides spent hours in meetings and worked out plans for a $170 million attraction that would open in 1984. They had got as far as producing aerial drawings and designs when, toward the end of negotiations, Eisner left Paramount to become CEO of Disney. He dropped the deal with MCA and brought in MGM to help build a Disney studio tour in Florida, said Sheinberg. "That went down very hard."

Sheinberg blustered, cursed, and threatened to sue. Wasserman was outraged. "I've never seen him angrier," said Stein. "He didn't yell and scream." Lew burned like a flame, blue and constant. "It was very nasty," agreed Sheinberg. At one point, Wasserman picked up the phone and called Sid Bass, who held a large stake in Disney. "Your guys are operating underhandedly," he told the Texas investor. "Rein in your boys." Stein recalled, "Lew left the implication that if something wasn't done pronto, he was going to be very unhappy."

Ultimately, Eisner went ahead anyway. He announced that Disney would soon unveil a movie-theme-park in Orlando to augment Disney's Epcot Center and Magic Kingdom. The Disney-MGM Studio tour was nearly identical to the one that Eisner and Sheinberg had agreed to build. "They did everything that we were going to do, except use our name," said Stein. The Disney-MGM deal was outrageous, but Wasserman was helpless. "The standards of business behavior that Lew taught me—and that I think characterize our company—are in my opinion different from those of Michael Eisner," said Sheinberg, who to this day dislikes the Disney boss. The reversal delayed Universal's theme park in Florida by half a decade, and cost MCA hundreds of millions of dollars extra. Even worse was Eisner's overt disrespect for Wasserman. Not every player in the new establishment esteemed or even feared the aging lion, but it would take a while for him to realize this.

Like many other companies, Disney had been "in play" months before Eisner joined the studio. The irony was that Wasserman could have bought the studio a few months earlier and thus managed to curb Eisner. As it happened, Saul Steinberg, the king of Wall Street greenmail, had enlisted Milken to help him launch an unfriendly takeover of the studio. In April 1984, Sheinberg called Walt Disney's son-in-law, Ron Miller, who was also the company's president, and commiserated with him. "It'd be a shame to have Disney acquired for such a low price, since it's one of the great institutions in our business," said Sheinberg.

He and Wasserman met with Miller and Disney chairman Ray Watson and explained how MCA could help. Wasserman didn't even hint that he had also called shareholder Roy Disney and attorney Stanley Gold—who were acting as white knights to rescue the studio from Steinberg—to see if MCA could "help" them, too.

Wasserman wanted to buy Disney outright. "At the time, they had no movie-market share, a small theme park, and a film library that hadn't been used for years," said Tom Pollock. But the studio's fifty-year-old cartoons still sparkled with Snow White, Mickey Mouse, and The Three Little Pigs; its animation stock was second to none; and although its Anaheim attraction was smaller than Universal's, it was a children's park that could complement MCA's adult studio tour at the opposite end of Greater Los Angeles.

Wasserman and Sheinberg discussed the possibilities. MCA could open Disney's vaults and sell cartoons in TV syndication. They could make new movies with the old characters, expand their theme-park businesses, and grow big together. "It would have given us a great division," said Sheinberg. "And the company wasn't that expensive at the time." They could have bought Disney for as little as $1.5 billion. "It was a hell of a bargain," said one man.

But Wasserman ultimately decided against the deal. "Lew didn't want to do it for reasons I don't think were valid," said Sheinberg. Pollock added, "The price was a little too rich for Lew's blood."

Wasserman was also concerned about arousing antitrust attention. He told his men that the Justice Department "would never allow the deal." As one MCA executive explained, "Lew was always more spooked by the specter of antitrust attorneys than anybody else was. But then, he was the only one who had been burned by them."

By September 1984, Saul Steinberg had gone away, after forcing Disney to pay a $60 million premium for his shares in greenmail, a form of corporate bribery. But Disney shareholders were so mad about that, they sued Steinberg, his company, and his investment bankers at Drexel Burnham, who repaid shareholders $45 million.

That fall, Wasserman's chance to buy the flagging company disappeared, too. "It was a mistake not to buy Disney," said Sheinberg. But what could he do? "For such a nice, meek man, Lew could be quite stubborn in those days."

Wasserman's cherished theme park began to take on a menacing edge. In 1984 Universal Studios Tour opened the Conan the Barbarian show, a frightening spectacle. The next year, it introduced a drive-through King Kong ride, which gave visitors a violent shaking. The rides initiated a new era in theme-park design, in which attendees were shaken, whirred, or scared. "When you pitched an idea to Jay Stein, you had to include the number of 'Jay Bangs' you had," said one theme-park consultant. "Jay Bangs" were code for big, special effects that were designed to disorient or frighten visitors. "This was widely taken to be some kind of latent hostility or contempt that Jay had for park guests."

Stein was growing frustrated with efforts to expand Universal's theme-park business. He had proposed opening a Universal park in Las Vegas, where kids' attractions were suddenly in demand. "Lew loved the idea and got real excited," he said. Wasserman told Stein to call Kirk Kerkorian, who owned the MGM Grand Hotel, let him win a game of tennis, and talk about a partnership. Those conversations spurred Universal to contact other potential partners in Nevada, too. "We were in talks with half a dozen people," Stein recalled. "I kept wanting to go there with a hotel and theme park and rides."

But then Wasserman's zeal for a Las Vegas project turned tepid. As Tanen recalled, "We were futzing around in Florida for years and poor Jay Stein was always bringing [Lew] money and partners."

Stein grew so frustrated that he finally confronted his boss and asked, "Why did I go talk to Kerkorian and these other people if we weren't serious about doing business?"

Wasserman had thought better of the idea, he told Stein. Corporations now owned many Las Vegas casinos, but the town was still influenced by organized crime. Wasserman worried that MCA would be forced to do business with shady characters if it owned a Vegas property. "Once you get in there, you can't avoid those guys, no matter how legitimate it looks," he told Stein. The younger man disagreed but he sensed Lew's misgivings. "It was the crooked noses," he said later, referring to the underworld denizens. "I'm sure that Jules and Lew were associated with them at one time. Why else would they be so sensitive about the mob?"

What most of MCA executives did not realize is that Edie's lineage to the mob were stronger than that of her husband's. She loved Las Vegas, the men who had built it, and their showplaces and dance floors. Sometimes, for Edie's birthday, Lew would take her to a nightclub in Las Vegas, flying a planeload of friends to Sin City for the weekend. "Lew would give all the girls purses filled with chips and money," said Wendy Goldberg. He'd give each man a roll of bills, and he'd treat them all to front-row seats of a show featuring Steve Lawrence and Eydie Gorme, one of Edie's favorite acts. Later that night, the party might go dancing, or watch a comedy act. "Then we'd either stay the night or fly home. Edie loved Lew's present. He was so thoughtful."

Edie got the Las Vegas royal treatment, and her links to the casino bosses preceded her birth. "She always said that her father was an important attorney," said Dorothy Barton. "But she never said much." In fact, Edie's father, Henry Beckerman, was the political protégé of Maurice Maschke, who led Ohio Republicans for thirty years and was a front man for the mob. Beckerman had started as an inspector of county elections in 1915 and helped elect William

Howard Taft to the presidency. "He was a big figure in politics and was one of the few men who controlled the Republican platform in Ohio," said Merle Jacobs. He was part of the machine that had placed Warren Harding and his Ohio Gang in the White House, where they drank Moe Dalitz's liquor and stole the Teapot Dome oil reserves.

Beckerman also controlled Cleveland's city hall, a notoriously crooked place in the 1920s and 1930s. "Even the greenest of precinct captains knows that Henry and his silent partners are powerful factors in running the town," said one report. He had an interest in the mob's Thistledown Race Track, his realty company was listed on the deed and liquor license of Moe Dalitz's Mayfair Casino, where Lew had worked for nearly two years. And Edie's father bought and sold other property for the syndicate as he grew increasingly rich—and brazen.

After 1926, when Beckerman's sweetheart road-paving deal with the city was made public, "Edie's father was often in the papers," said Marge LaRonge. Beckerman owned the land beneath the city's new police station, and the warehouse where Dalitz distilled illegal whiskey. "He was almost as well known in New York City as he was in Cleveland, and had myriad friends in Florida and Chicago, including Nicky Arnstein," one reporter noted.

But few people in Hollywood had ever heard of him. "Didn't Edie's father end up in the slammer or something?" Tony Curtis asked me. After Henry Beckerman passed away in 1949, the only men who remembered him were his former clients: Dalitz and the other founding members of the Cleveland syndicate. Edie's father had helped them create shell companies and daisy-chain deals, enabling them to launder their ill-gotten money.

So whenever Edie Beckerman visited Las Vegas, "Uncle Moe" was delighted to see her. He'd fete and pamper her. She often arrived without Lew, in the company of male and female friends. Her mother used to play cards with Dalitz; her daughter used to bounce on his knee. "Edie loved to gamble," said Roy Gerber. She knew most of the casino owners by their first names and could call them in a pinch. In 1955 she helped organize the wedding of Jerry Gershwin to Jackie Joslin, who sang on the *Dinah Shore Show*. Lew stood in for Jackie's father and gave away the bride. For the ceremony, Edie chose The Sands and "invited every star you could think of, including big names who weren't MCA acts," said Jackie. Some two hundred stars showed up, but two hours before the wedding was to take place, reporters descended. Gershwin was angry; his bride started crying. Lew slipped away to the telephone, while Edie made new arrangements.

Within an hour, Beldon Katleman of El Rancho had raised a platform amid his crap tables and set up a buffet by the slot machines. "Edie had all of our stuff packed, and we moved like one gypsy caravan," said Curtis. Soon Janet Leigh took her place as matron of honor, and Curtis as best man. The Harry James orchestra struck up the wedding march, but Jackie froze. As everyone watched, Wasserman squeezed the bride's arm and whispered, "Come on, honey, start with your left foot." Then he deliberately stuck out his right foot, which made Jackie giggle. "Lew made me relax during the most nerve-racking day in my life," she said.

That night, Hollywood stars mixed with Vegas gangsters. "It was hysterical to see all of these people," said Curtis. Sammy Davis, Jr., and Lena Horne sang a duet; Martin and Lewis performed a skit; Chicago bagman Johnny Rosselli brought a present; and Jack Entratter came over from The Sands. "Moe Dalitz was running around, smiling at everybody," Curtis recalled. "We loved it. It was the Jewish mafia, and everyone intermingled."

The orchestra stopped just before dawn. Edie ushered the newlyweds into a white limousine that she had filled with red roses, and the couple sped back to MCA's headquarters in Los Angeles. After that, El Rancho moved to the top of Hollywood's tryst list, said Muriel Stevens, whose husband worked in the casinos.

"Every star who came to Vegas to get married had to do it at Beldon's place."

To Edie and many women in Las Vegas, the crooked noses were good fellows. They raised their families, and built schools and temples for both Reform and Orthodox Jews. Dalitz also helped build a Catholic church with a sacrilegious name: Our Lady of Las Vegas. Every Sunday, the Italian counters would drop their skimmings into the collection basket. "We tried to lead very normal lives in a most abnormal time," said Stevens. Dalitz and his gang civilized Las Vegas, founded charities, and built the Sunrise Hospital, Boulevard Mall, Wintercourt Golf course, the Las Vegas Convention Center, and the University of Nevada at Las Vegas. "The gangsters were good for this town," insisted Barbara Greenspun, who raised her family here. "Their kids could go to school and, for the first time, they could say what their father did. 'He owned a casino.' It gave them respectability, which they had never had before."

The casino owners always gave Edie the red-carpet treatment— and she grew accustomed to the perks and deference. So, in September 1984, when Edie heard that a TV producer was finishing a national story that might link her husband to Dalitz, she made some inquiries. It was true: The New York–based *60 Minutes* was working on a piece that would link President Reagan to what producers called a mob figure. The story concerned Moe Dalitz, Nevada Senator Paul Laxalt, who was then a Reagan intimate, and Lew Wasserman. "The show was to open the [TV] season," said producer Lowell Bergman. He had spent three months working on the exposé, which was to air six weeks before the 1984 presidential election.

The piece centered on Laxalt, who was heading Reagan's reelection campaign. The senator had long been a target of FBI veteran Joe Yablonsky, who had learned that Laxalt's political career had been funded by Dalitz and other mob figures. "I had Yablonsky on the record saying that Laxalt was a mob politician," said Bergman.

The story also examined how Laxalt and his friend, newspaper publisher Hank Greenspun, were trying to ruin Yablonsky. Greenspun's editorials blasted the FBI man for giving Las Vegas a black eye with his numerous investigations of casino owners. Laxalt had already asked Reagan to make FBI agents in Nevada more accountable to state officials. The story would also mention Wasserman as a longtime friend of Dalitz and Reagan, Bergman said. It was to be narrated by Mike Wallace, another Reagan friend, and it started generating buzz. *Sixty Minutes* executive producer Don Hewitt even discussed the story on the *Phil Donahue Show*. Wallace claimed that the episode could alter the course of the upcoming presidential election.

"I stayed in the edit room on Monday night, working," Bergman recalled. He wanted to show Hewitt a finished version by the Tuesday morning before the Sunday broadcast. But as the producer labored over his piece, Hewitt dined with Lew and Edie.

Hewitt had grown close to the mogul's wife. "He stayed with the Wassermans every time he went to Hollywood," said Bergman. Still, CBS had a policy about not discussing stories outside of the newsroom, except for fact checking. "You certainly don't talk to sources who might be affected by the story," Bergman explained. But over cocktails and dinner that night, Hewitt told Edie and Lew about the upcoming episode. Edie and Lew had spent years trying to avoid public attention about their ties to Dalitz, and now they feared that Hewitt's national TV show might undo their efforts.

What the *60 Minutes* staff did not realize is how far back the connection stretched. During Prohibition, Edie's father had fronted Dalitz with a huge warehouse, which the mobster had used to house his distillery and bootleg liquor business. The six-story building covered an entire city block in the notoriously venal Woodland District, Lew Wasserman's childhood neighborhood. City councilmen, beat cops, and even judges had been bribed to ignore the distillery, which supplied much of the Midwest with whiskey.

By 1931, the business had grown so large that Dalitz and his mob moved it to Elizabeth, New Jersey. There he joined forces with Eastern gangs to expand the bootleg operation, in what became the first venture of the national crime syndicate. The move left Edie's dad with a vacant building and a $300,000 mortgage. Henry Beckerman became desperate. In the early morning of November 30, 1931, smoke curled out of his six-story building. Firemen rushed to the scene and, in the basement, found a platform that held twenty-four oil drums filled with seven hundred gallons of gasoline—enough to blow up the entire neighborhood. The gasoline drums were surrounded by mountains of flammable wood shavings and connected to dozens of electric irons and toasters. The firemen unplugged the smoldering appliances—and saved the city from an inferno.

So began the biggest arson investigation in Cleveland's history. Had Beckerman's building gone up in flames, he would have collected about $1 million in insurance. Instead, he was facing jail time. Beckerman accused his hapless building supervisor of starting the fire, and the super was convicted. But due to an error in jury instructions, the super had to stand trial a second time. This time, he implicated Edie's dad. In 1933 a grand jury indicted Beckerman for arson. Two days after the end of Prohibition—December 5, 1933—marshals found him in a New York hotel, where he'd been trying to settle his and the mob's far-flung bootleg operations. The police found documents listing a network of syndicate breweries, stills, and liquor interests—all of which became front-page news in Cleveland.

Beckerman claimed he was being framed, which may have been true. Nevertheless, in May 1934, Beckerman stood trial for arson. After a friend approached two female jurors with bribes, the judge declared a mistrial for jury tampering. At a second trial two years later, Beckerman claimed he was destitute. "Today, Beckerman painted himself as a man absolutely without assets and facing possible eviction from his pretentious home," said one editorial. Yet he

wore "an expensive smile, paid for by taxpayers and bank deposi-
tors." The county prosecutor produced several checks that Beckerman had written to three known arsonists. Yet neither the torch
man from Chicago nor the two hired guards from Detroit were ever
extradited to Cleveland. On June 30, 1936, Beckerman was
acquitted.

A week later, Edie's father threw a big party celebrating his
freedom and his daughter's marriage to the publicist for Dalitz's Mayfair Casino—Louis Wasserman. About one hundred people attended
the garden reception on July 5. Edie and her groom greeted politicians and mobsters, including Dalitz, said Seymour Heller, who was
there. "A lot of us were still talking about Henry's trial." A few
months later, the newlyweds left Cleveland, but they never lost touch
with Dalitz. MCA always gave the casino owner a special holiday gift,
and Edie and Lew kept him on their personal Christmas card list
until the mobster died in 1989 at the age of eighty-nine.

Now, in the Manhattan supper club with Don Hewitt, the
Wassermans tried to convince the *60 Minutes* producer that Dalitz
was a good guy. "He hasn't done anything illegal since Prohibition," Wasserman said. "He's a wonderful man," Edie added. To
her, Dalitz was "Uncle Moe."

The next morning, Bergman had just finished his piece when
Hewitt walked in and told him: "I talked to Edie and Lew last night
about Moe Dalitz." He repeated what the Wassermans had said.

Bergman was incredulous. "Here we are working on a story that
might include Wasserman, and you're telling him all about it?"
Bergman started yelling and accused his boss of a huge breach of
ethical conduct. Over the next forty-eight hours, Bergman learned
that Hewitt had also talked to Nancy Reagan about the story. "He'd
call her regularly and read her jokes. He was quite proud of that."
And Hewitt discussed the story with Pete Peterson, an investment
banker and large GOP fundraiser. "Subsequently, there were discussions with other friends of Hewitt," said Bergman.

Reagan had already been tainted with mob connections: He had named Cleveland Teamster official Jackie Presser as an adviser to his 1981 transition team—as the FBI was investigating Presser for fraud. The signal Hewitt was receiving was that one more story about yet another shady character within Reagan's circle could harm his re-election efforts. "At the time, Reagan was deregulating the broadcast industry," Bergman explained. "The story might boomerang on the CBS network. Why would they drop a turd on the carpet?"

Sixty Minutes wasn't the only media outlet pursuing the story: *Mother Jones,* ABC, and others were interviewing some of Bergman's sources. Yet if Hewitt ran this piece, his relationships with a few powerful people might suffer; certainly, Edie and Hollywood would ostracize him. A few days before the story was scheduled to air, Hewitt pulled it, said Bergman. "It was the first episode in my career in which I became aware of self-censorship."

FORTY-ONE

WHEN UNIVERSAL TV'S *Miami Vice* DEBUTED in September 1984, Edie and Lew watched it in their private projection room. Created by Michael Mann Productions, the hit series would run through the decade and would introduce America to a new capital of vice and drugs: Miami. The series revolved around detective Sonny Crockett (Don Johnson) and his partner, Rico Tubbs (Philip Michael Thomas). Pastel suits, streamlined decor, Jan Hammer's pulsating music—the TV show's style was irresistible and its edits cocaine-quick. Rock stars Glen Frey of The Eagles and Iggy Pop made guest appearances, and *Miami Vice* was packaged with rhythm, flash, and moral ambiguity.

Wasserman called the show a "megahit," and in 1985, *Miami Vice* won several Emmys. It quickly became the most expensive network series, costing $1 million per episode. All that cash brought with it labor problems and Wasserman asked self-styled labor fixer Marty Bacow to intervene and handle Teamster demands on the *Miami Vice* set.

By now, the federal Organized Crime Strike Force was looking at Bacow as part of a larger investigation of the mob's influence in Hollywood. Richard Stavin, an attorney on the force, knew of Bacow's long-standing ties to gangsters; FBI files listed him as an arbitrator in disputes between the Teamsters, IATSE, and the studios—a possible conflict of interest, if not an outright violation of labor laws. "We believed he was taking care of labor peace in the industry. He wasn't on the level of Korshak," said Stavin. "But he boasted to others about his association with Teamsters officials. He also bragged that he could get Edie or Lew on the phone anytime."

The strike force had collected these tidbits from wiretaps and various other sources. "One of the first names that came up was the chief of MCA's video division, Gene Giaquinto," said Stavin. The MCA executive talked often with Bacow, and at first, the federal attorneys couldn't believe their ears. Giaquinto kept referring to the Gambino family boss John Gotti and other known crime figures. "During our investigation, it became abundantly clear that the MCA executive had significant ties to the mob," said Stavin. For one thing, there was his "uncle" Ed Sciandra, the mobster whose Northstar Graphics company in New Jersey packed MCA videocassettes at extortionate prices. And now the references to Giotti the "G-man." Stavin told his supervisors in Washington, D.C., about his findings, and a federal judge approved a request to expand the wiretaps.

But instead of finding a clear answer to the mysteries, Stavin stumbled into more intrigue. Giaquinto was now talking to Robert Booth Nichols, a CIA character who skulked around the airfields of Miami. "FBI files listed him as being tied to the Gambinos, a guy involved in narcotics and money laundering," said Stavin. Nichols and Giaquinto discussed a joint venture in which Nichols would travel the globe to stamp out bootleg copies of Universal shows—like *Miami Vice*—and thus protect MCA's copyrighted works. Nichols would be able to use dozens of MCA offices around the world.

What Stavin didn't realize was that Nichols was already working with General Richard Secord, then Deputy Assistant Secretary of Defense, and a point man for the Iran-Contra effort. Reagan officials were illegally selling weapons to Iran, Pakistan, and other rogue nations, and using the proceeds to fund the Contras' overthrow of Nicaragua's elected government. Congress had passed the Boland Amendment to outlaw the U.S. government's meddling in the affairs of that Central American country. But the work continued covertly.

One of Secord's agents, retired U.S. Navy Lieutenant Commander Al Martin, recalled meeting Nichols in Miami: "Nichols had eight different social security numbers and four different dates of birth." Martin said he helped launder money through friendly American corporations. That's how Martin met Nichols, a dapper spook who looked like Clark Gable and moved like James Bond. According to Martin, Nichols was laundering money, too, but strike-force investigators didn't know this for certain. "Nichols was in the government, but not exactly in the government," said Stavin.

When government investigators heard that MCA wanted to hire Nichols to stamp out pirated works, Stavin realized that the job could be a cover for a clandestine operation. "It was our feeling that we might have stumbled onto another Iran-Contra," said Stavin. "MCA could pay for Nichols to travel, visit certain countries, and act as a bagman to deliver money to foreign nations. We did not know that for a fact," he stressed. "But that possibility became one of our working suppositions."

As for MCA's association with Northstar Graphics, Stavin and his Justice Department supervisors theorized that it might be a similar cover. "Perhaps MCA was funneling money into the video-box business, through Nichols, to get to where the money needed to go abroad." Such a scenario was no more preposterous than the gun-running plot currently being produced by the White House, and it was one of several possibilities that the strike force considered.

One thing was certain: The mob was inside MCA through its business dealings with the New Jersey video packager. Stavin and his superiors wanted to know how deep the penetration went. This could be the biggest prosecution of Stavin's career, and his strike-force team began to build a case.

Inside the Black Tower, a long-simmering rivalry was about to blow up. During the 1970s, Frank Price and Sid Sheinberg had coman-aged Universal TV. But by the time Price returned to take over faltering Universal Studios, Sheinberg was president of MCA. "They had always respected each other, but it was very competitive," said Marvin Antonowsky, vice president of marketing under Price. Wasserman had always believed that such internal competition sharpened MCA's edge; unchecked, however, the rivalry could turn destructive.

Price brought a film project with him to MCA. He gave the script to Sheinberg, who read it and said, "I don't know why you want to make this picture. I don't even know what it's about."

"It's very simple," Price responded. "It's a love story directed by Sidney Pollack and starring Robert Redford. Women will flock to see it." Sheinberg disagreed, but Price went ahead and made the film, *Out of Africa,* for $30 million. It earned $90 million in theaters and $50 million more in video—and its success only intensified their rivalry.

The two clashed more often, said Tom Pollock. "Frank by nature does not share information, and Sid does. Sid resented that Frank kept him in the dark about certain things." In addition, Price was slow to make movies, and the studio needed lots of product to cover its overhead. But the most damaging element in the feud was that

Sheinberg's protégé, director Steven Spielberg, detested Price, according to several people. "That's not a good thing, when your single biggest film asset hates the head of the studio," said Pollock. Added another man: "Sid fueled the fire between Steven and Frank. Steve was Sid's kid, and he wanted to keep it that way." Price refused to have anything to do with Spielberg, who reported directly to Sheinberg.

"The animosity was so strong that two camps formed," said Pollock. In 1985 Spielberg was co-producing the Robert Zemeckis film *Back to the Future*, while Price and his men were making *Out of Africa*. By the time the Academy Awards rolled around, both films were up for nominations. *Out of Africa* won for Best Picture, while *Back to the Future* nabbed a lesser Academy Award for Special Effects. The resentment spread beyond Frank and Sid to their men.

George Lucas—who had returned to Universal to make a film based on a comic strip about a sarcastic duck—contributed to the strained atmosphere. "Sidney lobbied very hard for *Howard the Duck*," said Antonowsky. Wasserman and Sheinberg felt they had missed the boat with Lucas's earlier films, and they weren't about to repeat that mistake. "George Lucas swore up and down that he would help us with the script and film, but he never did." The production grew unwieldy, and when the movie was released in the summer of 1986, it was an embarrassment to all. Both Price and Sheinberg distanced themselves from the film, but Price got blamed for it. Some wags believed that George Lucas was paying back Hollywood and Universal, in particular. The *Hollywood Reporter* smelled blood and published a story headlined "Duck Cooks Price's Goose."

By now, the Tower was a pressure cooker. Some days, Sheinberg would open his office door, lift up his head, and howl like a wolf, sending shivers down the secretaries' spines. Other times, Jay Stein would yell at an assistant. Wasserman no longer had to work himself into his infamous tyrannical tantrums, for now his executives did that for him. They fell into one of the more primitive traditions of MCA—and Hollywood—by demonstrating loud and boorish behavior.

The tension in the Black Tower finally exploded. One day, a fist-fight broke out on the fourteenth floor as Price and Sheinberg threw punches at each other. The newspapers reported the story, which some executives later disputed. "But the underlying point of the story was absolutely correct," said one man. Goaded by Sheinberg, Price left Universal again without leaving much behind from his brief two-year stint. *Howard the Duck* was just one of several box-office bombs. In 1982 MCA had made a record $176.2 million on revenues of only $1.59 billion. Now, four years later, it had earned $155.2 million on $2.44 billion—less profit on 40 percent more revenue. During that time, its movie income had dropped nearly 50 percent. Meanwhile, TV, video, and music sales had risen. For the first time in Hollywood history, motion-pictures represented a shrinking portion of studio-based business. The industry was changing radically and, in 1986, Wasserman hired entertainment attorney Tom Pollock as motion-picture chief. Lawyers and busi-ness-school graduates—not writers or agents—began to dominate MCA's executive suite.

In 1985 the government sentenced Sal Pisello for evading income taxes from 1980 to 1983, right before he had joined MCA. Before he went to prison, Pisello had been representing MCA, appearing at national record-industry conventions, selling about five million of its out-of-date records, and allegedly distributing counterfeit record-ings of MCA's top artists. Grand juries in Los Angeles, New York, and Newark, New Jersey, were now investigating the cut-out busi-ness, yet news was rather slow until the spring of 1985. John LaM-onte, a budget record distributor in Philadelphia, had bought a shipment of old MCA records from Pisello, only to find that the best titles had been skimmed off. He had refused to pay Pisello, who was connected with organized crime, and a New Jersey mafioso had beat in LaMonte's face. Photos of the beaten man, who suffered broken bones, eventually ran with stories linking MCA and the mob.

During Pisello's two-year-stint at MCA, the company had paid him cash through his companies, such as Consultants for World Records, which "was created solely to receive money," said Marvin Rudnick. The Organized Crime Strike Force prosecutor had convicted Pisello for tax evasion, and now Rudnick grew convinced that Pisello's ties to MCA were deep. Wasserman called the media coverage the "worst publicity this company has had in fifty years."

MCA's board called for an internal audit.

The audit committee included Wasserman, Sheinberg, and another executive. They issued a six-page report on the incident but recommended no action. In fact, the audit raised more questions than answers, and several board members were upset at its conclusions. Directors Howard Baker, the former Senate Majority Whip, and investment banker Felix Rohatyn argued that several MCA Records executives should be fired for working with Pisello. But Wasserman, supported by Sheinberg, believed nothing should be done. "They thought the controversy would blow over," said one source. Ultimately, the board supported Wasserman, and no one was fired.

But the brouhaha did not die down. In February 1986, prosecutor Rudnick served MCA Records with a subpoena; Wasserman and his men were ordered to turn over all company records about Pisello. Edwin Meese had just become Attorney General, head of the U.S. Department of Justice and overseer of its investigations. For the first time in decades, Wasserman could feel the government agents' breath on his neck.

Edie concentrated on passing the torch to her "surrogate daughters," including Wendy Goldberg, wife of independent TV producer

Leonard Goldberg. "She taught me so much," said Goldberg. Edie brought the younger woman into her circle, teaching her how to throw parties, where to rent plants, and which caterer was appropriate for A-list hostesses. In 1986 Goldberg was ready to host her first big event—a last-minute wedding reception for Merv Adelson, head of Lorimar Telepictures, and newswoman Barbara Walters. "By then, I had graduated from Edie's class," said Goldberg. In three days, Edie's protégée put together a sit-down dinner for the newlyweds and one hundred guests. Edie encouraged her from the sidelines, but when the rabbi didn't show up as scheduled, she clucked, "What are we going to do with all of these people? We have to keep things moving on schedule." As it was, the rabbi was simply late, and the candlelight dinner was a success.

Meanwhile, the grande dame was working on a party of her own, one that would make obvious her extraordinary reach. It would also celebrate the Wassermans' fiftieth wedding anniversary.

"Edie had gone to the studio to scout out a location," said Goldberg. Unlike other power couples, Edie and Lew didn't leave planning to others. "They had a good support system, but were very hands-on." They decided to throw the party in the back lot's town square—where *To Kill a Mockingbird* had been shot in 1962 and where *Back to the Future* had been set. Only this time, the sets and props would make the scene look like Cleveland in 1936. Edie spent months planning the July 14 party.

That Saturday night, guests were driven up the hill in zippy little golf carts. Women wore long gowns, men wore tuxedos, and most were delighted by the movie-set scene. "It was spectacular," said Goldberg. There was the May Company store where Edie had worked as a clerk in 1934; the Hippodrome theater where Lew had ushered in 1931; and the Mayfair Casino—the mob club where Edie and Lew had met in 1935. Edie glowed like a bride that night, and she circulated among the tables to thank most of her seven hundred friends, including Lucille Ball, Bob Hope, Carol

Burnett, and Audrey Hepburn. Edie greeted Henry Kissinger, a few former U.S. ambassadors, and California's two U.S. senators, Alan Cranston and Pete Wilson. Edie hugged Lady Bird Johnson, now a widow, as well as a few childhood friends from her Cleveland Heights days.

In attendance were MCA directors Bob Strauss, a Democrat, and Howard Baker, a Republican; Northrop chairman Tom Jones; investment banker Felix Rohatyn; *Charlie's Angels* producer Leonard Goldberg, and his wife, Wendy; *Murder, She Wrote* star Angela Lansbury, and her producer husband, Peter Shaw; as well as CBS lion Bill Paley. That night, Lew shook hands with the men and draped studio crew jackets around the bare shoulders of the women. "Here, honey, it's cool," he told one producer's wife, kissing her cheek before disappearing into the crowd. At seventy-one, Edie looked stunning in a red sequined Givenchy gown. "That was unusual for Edie because it wasn't her color," said George Christy, a columnist from the *Hollywood Reporter*. He had not been invited because he had once been close to Edie's nemesis, the late, great Doris Stein.

A month or so later, the Wassermans began preparing for another big event—their fiftieth anniversary with MCA. They did not want a tribute, but MCA's board of directors insisted upon it. The golden anniversary party, on December 12, 1986, marked the exact day when Lew Wasserman had joined MCA.

Once again, Edie oversaw most of the party details, only this time the movie set resembled Prohibition-era Chicago, with gold sidewalks and velvet-lined violin cases. Edie mounted a mini-production and timed the entertainment to make sure the show wasn't too long. Every detail had been meticulously arranged, so that before the first guest arrived, parking valets were standing at attention in white coats and bow ties, and waiters were assembled for last-minute instructions. "Everything ran like clockwork that night," said Goldberg. Edie had put together an elaborate program book whose cover featured an attractive photo of her with her husband. Inside were pictures of Lew with Hitchcock, Lew with Jimmy Stewart, Lew with Jules Stein and Sidney Sheinberg. Below a gray Depression-era photo of her husband as a teenager, Edie recounted the old story about why Lew took the job: because Jules was old at forty, and Lew at twenty-three believed he'd have a chance to take over soon. "That began our first fifty years," Edie said. "I'm sure that our next fifty years will be just as exciting."

None of the 1,300 guests dared to question the pleasant fantasy. Instead, they fostered the illusion, drinking Chappellet Carbernet Sauvignon with their roasted veal medallions and baby vegetables, and capping it off with berry sherbet. At one point, the ladies and gentlemen stood for a champagne toast, raising their glasses to the town's king and queen, honoring them as *sui generis*. "Nothing quite like this celebration has ever occurred in the history of Hollywood," *Variety* proclaimed.

The program's emcee was Johnny Carson, host of *The Tonight Show*, who brought along Doc Severinsen and his orchestra. On behalf of MCA's board, Sheinberg went onstage to thank Lew for the "first fifty years of outstanding corporate leadership." The directors saluted Wasserman "for his commitment to the entire entertainment industry, devotion to public affairs, and tireless and generous philanthropy." The crowd gave Wasserman a standing ovation, and he bowed gallantly. As Edie and Lew held hands, Carson narrated a mini-movie that detailed the highlights of Wasserman's half-century career.

Frank Sinatra, who had left MCA forty years earlier after arguing bitterly with Wasserman, offered a glowing tribute to Lew, singing "The Gentleman Is a Champ" to the well-known Cole Porter song, "The Lady Is a Tramp." Gladys Knight and the Pips serenaded the crowd and, once again, Nancy and Ronnie sent congratulations from the White House, this time with an embarrassingly obsequious message: On videotape, Nancy explained that since the president would soon be out of work, she wondered if Lew could fix him up with a job. In fact, at that moment, Reagan was under fire from the Tower Commission and other committees investigating the Iran-Contra scandal. "It was all over the papers, and some of us were talking about nothing else," said one guest.

For the rest of the night, Ray Anthony and his orchestra played big-band music. On that mild December evening, the dim lights softened wrinkles, the brassy trumpets melted away the years, and anything seemed possible. Maybe the seventy-three-year-old Lew and his seventy-one-year-old bride *would* go on to rule another fifty years. If anyone could pull it off, Edie and Lew could. They had climbed so many other peaks. Only a handful of other power couples had scaled these heights: Irving Thalberg and Norma Shearer, Bill Goetz and Edie (Mayer) Goetz, and perhaps Clark Gable and Carole Lombard. But none of them had lasted so long, not even Jules and Doris. Half a century was an eternity in Hollywood. At a time when aging American executives were acquiring trophy brides like stock tips, Edie and Lew were still together.

In the moonlight, surrounded by make-believe sets in their own fanciful "city," the couple stood at the summit. Lew called his wife "madame," a term that acknowledged her authority and bestowed respect. "She had been a great force in his life and was really always on the mark with her advice to Lew," said Goldberg. Edie had been so involved in Lew's work and MCA's business, some were certain she even read scripts before Universal turned them into movies. Her legend began to grow and match that of her husband's.

To Edie, Universal was "Lew's studio," 430 acres of Wasserland. That night, on the old Campo de Cahuenga, the couple resolved to keep going for many more years, and to continue building their empire. The globalization of MCA and of Hollywood was just beginning; it would boom beyond anything Edie and Lew could conjure, let alone imagine—but it would not last another fifty years.

As it was, the Wassermans were pressing their good fortune. In

December 1986 the federal investigators were circling, and Edie, Lew, and MCA were about to find themselves enmeshed in national scandal.

FORTY-TWO

WASSERMAN AND U.S. ATTORNEY GENERAL Edwin Meese would soon begin working together to raise money for Reagan's presidential library. That winter, the two began sharing responsibilities as cochairmen of the $60 million campaign, and they talked regularly about donors and logistics. Wasserman had already pledged $517,969—the largest individual donation to what would be the biggest presidential library yet—and had enlisted other donors. Meanwhile, in early December, his colleague Robert Strauss was asked to visit the Reagans to help them contain the erupting Iran-Contra scandal. Strauss had sat on MCA's board since 1982, and his friendship with Wasserman stretched back to the 1960s, when they were raising millions for Democratic leaders. Wasserman admired Strauss, who moved easily between the smoke-filled clubrooms of Democrats and Republicans, a trick that Wasserman himself had learned. But, unlike the mogul, Strauss freely admitted to working both sides of the aisle—and enjoying it. Strauss's politics were ecumenical, which is why the Democrat had been asked to advise the Republican president.

Reagan was insisting that he had never traded arms for hostages, nor had he sold weapons to Iran to bankroll the CIA mission in Nicaragua. But officials within his own administration were contradicting him, so that now even former allies were scoffing at his denials. "Reagan had to know," Barry Goldwater said, and the public's trust in its leader plummeted. Strauss visited Reagan and his wife and explained in blunt terms how his illegal operation was damaging his credibility. He recommended that he "make a fresh start" by changing members of his administration, especially his chief of staff. Strauss named several possibilities, including Howard H. Baker, Jr.

A few months later, in February 1987, Baker left his board position at MCA and took a new job in Washington as Reagan's chief of staff. Baker would return someday, but for now he needed to help the president control his scandal. The Iran-Contra mess had grown bigger than Strauss had predicted, and the Tower Commission was talking about charging Reagan with perjury and maybe even impeachment. But Baker had been through similar rough seas before. The former Republican senator from Tennessee had been a close adviser to President Nixon, and during the Watergate hearings he had made history by repeating: "What did the president know and when did he know it?" This shibboleth was about to resurface in an entirely new set of hearings.

While Reagan was under fire, Wasserman and the MCA attorneys were fencing with U.S. Justice Department prosecutors on three investigative fronts. The first was a payola investigation that threatened the status quo not just at MCA Records but at all major record labels. The industry often paid record promoters to give radio station managers gifts like drugs, women, or money in return for playing certain records. During the 1980s, promoters spent $80 million a year to push big labels' releases onto the Top 40 playlist. "Everybody denied practicing payola, but by the 1980s, it was roaring," said record producer Bones Howe, winner of several Grammy Awards. "Money and drugs flowed freely in both directions."

MCA Records chief Irving Azoff was spending 400 percent more promotional money than the company had spent before his arrival—a sign of payola. Investigators also believed that MCA and other labels hired mob figures to deliver illegal gifts to radio outlets.

Azoff's MCA Records had worked with a few of the members of the so-called Network.

Azoff had certainly transformed MCA's music division. Its sales had more than doubled since he'd taken over. Adding Patti LaBelle, Boston, and others to the roster, he had turned the Music Cemetery of America into a producer of eleven gold albums (500,000 copies or more) and eight platinum (1 million or more). "Universal was one of the few successful conglomerates that put out great records," said Howe. "They were hugely successful." Wasserman was delighted with the turn in fortunes, and he and Sheinberg rewarded Azoff handsomely.

In May 1986, MCA bought three management companies from Azoff for $30 million in stock. The deal gave Azoff a huge bonus without a tax bite. It also gave MCA, a major record producer, a management agency of such musicians as Boz Scaggs, Don Henley, and Jimmy Buffett. It was like the old days—before the 1962 federal antitrust case—when MCA, a major TV producer, owned an agency of talent and performers. Only this time, Meese's Department of Justice had approved MCA's agency purchase. "It's shocking," said competing producer David Geffen, of Geffen Records. But Wasserman's purchase simply demonstrated how much the business had changed.

By 1986, the industry's payola practices were being scrutinized by half a dozen grand juries around the country. The developments that year topped NBC's *Nightly News,* which aired a report that showed independent promoters hobnobbing with mob figures at a record-industry dinner. Cameras had caught MCA's Azoff, prompting his daughter to remark, "Daddy was on the news again with those Mafia guys." MCA defended its record impresario, who quickly severed his tie to at least one independent promoter, but not to others. Eleven other major label chiefs cut their ties to some independent promoters, too.

However, MCA stood out because of its second problem: Sal

Pisello. Before Marvin Rudnick had sent Pisello to jail, he had found that Pisello had evaded more taxes from his MCA income. Another tax-evasion case was not as interesting as why MCA would hire a cheat and Mafia associate like Pisello. Rudnick began serving subpoenas on MCA executives. "I wanted to understand why MCA would deal with a guy like Pisello," he explained. In 1986 he called six MCA record executives to testify in front of a grand jury. Five of them refused to incriminate themselves unless they were granted immunity.

Meanwhile, a third federal case against MCA gained momentum. The FBI now had several wiretaps within Hollywood, and some of the subjects talked often with Gene Giaquinto. By now, Giaquinto had been promoted to vice president and corporate officer as the head of MCA Home Entertainment. As such, he was part of MCA's inner sanctum. "We started hearing all sorts of things," said Richard Stavin, and his strike-force team of FBI agents began to follow new leads.

One trail led to a possible violation of insider-trading laws. But a second, more disturbing development involved a growing power struggle between Giaquinto and Azoff. Each man seemed to have his own ties to a different crime family—Giaquinto with the Gambinos and Azoff with the Genoveses, the federal government believed. MCA's corporate squabbles could very well burgeon into a bitter takeover battle on the streets of Philadelphia, New Jersey, and New York.

Wasserman had little faith in Wall Street's obsession with corporate acquisitions. He believed that American business was merely succumbing to the latest fad, and he would be proven right. Companies acquired others as a way to grow annual earnings—a management technique that left a lot to be desired. "There is logical diversification, and there is conglomerate diversification," Wasserman liked to say, and he preferred erring on the side of logic. But deregulation was changing the old rules. In 1981 a court had declared that Columbia Pictures could purchase part of the Walter Reade theater chain; later Warner and Paramount became partners in the Mann and Festival theater chains. In 1986 Wasserman bought a 50 percent interest in Cineplex Odeon theaters, a national chain headed by Garth Drabinksy, whose "Rolls-Royce" operation offered yuppie comforts like tea served in fine china. Forty years earlier, the U.S. Supreme Court had prohibited studios from owning theaters. The ruling had sounded the death knell for the old studio system and emboldened the then-thirty-five-year-old Wasserman to make his move. He seized control of the talent that the financially struggling studios had let out of long term contracts, using them to build his agency business and produce shows for the experimental new media, television.

Now eighties-style deregulation was tossing aside the antitrust rules that had served Lew—and the consumer—so well. An older Wasserman feared the no-holds-barred environment, believing that the resulting bloated companies were in danger of toppling. Indeed, the ambitious Drabinsky would build so many multiplexes so quickly that by the end of the 1980s he'd wind up with $580 million in debt—half of which would belong to Lew.

Even so, Wasserman joined forces with Drabinsky to build his Florida theme park—much to Jay Stein's horror. "Garth Drabinksy is a big character with a lot of chutzpah and a bass voice," Stein said. The deal was to be financial only, but Drabinsky brought in his own accountants, builders, and theme-park people. "These guys didn't know anything about the business," said Stein. "Drabinsky had Sid so buffaloed that he started to take control." The $700 million theme park became a $1 billion headache, behind schedule and over budget. As Drabinsky headed toward bankruptcy, Wasserman turned to another partner, Rank Industries, to help finish the project. But the younger MCA executives balked at sharing control.

"If there's one thing I regret at MCA, it's that we had to work with partners," said Stein. Whenever Stein pitched a potential partner about MCA's surefire project, the other man would ask, "If this is such a damn good deal, why aren't you doing it by yourself?" Stein would look the guy in the eye and retort, "If it were up to me, we *would* do it alone." MCA had plenty of money to develop these projects on its own, but at seventy-three, Wasserman felt more comfortable spreading his risks. He was no longer the nimble agent, looking for a way to lunge headlong into some wild, new territory.

In the spring of 1987 Congress heard testimony from several Iran-Contra players, including former National Security Adviser Robert "Bud" McFarlane, who called Reagan "a hands-on boss." Oliver North described shredding parties that destroyed documents related to illegal weapons sales and laundering operations. More than one hundred officials in Reagan's administration stood charged with illegal and unethical activities. Even the U.S. Attorney General was under a cloud, as an independent counsel began investigating Edwin Meese and his role in influence-peddling. Wasserman and Meese temporarily set aside their fundraising work for Reagan's presidential library.

Then Wasserman's health took a bleak turn, too. His doctors found polyps in his colon. Lew was on the verge of developing intestinal cancer—just as Jules Stein had. As Wasserman prepared to undergo surgery to remove the growths, he was keenly aware of Wall Street poachers. He publicly declared support for Sheinberg, noting that he—Wasserman—still controlled 13.4 percent of MCA's stock. If anything should happen to him during his hospital stay, Sheinberg would inherit control of his 5.2 million shares. To further repel the circling sharks, the mogul set out a poison pill that would allow MCA to issue preferred stock, which would raise the cost of any takeover bid.

Satisfied that his MCA was safe, on June 24, 1987, Wasserman checked into Cedars-Sinai Medical Center, where Edie was a trustee. Surgery was successful, and he was wheeled into the post-op to recover. A nurse checked his vital signs and placed a thermometer in his mouth. Wasserman was still groggy with anesthesia, and his workaday musings turned into hallucinatory nightmares. He had plenty on his mind: MCA's troubled acquisitions, its plagued partnerships, its payola scandal, the trial of Pisello, the Poison Dwarf, Iran-Contra; the Bufalinos, Gambinos, and Genoveses. As he lay on the gurney, Wasserman clenched his teeth and shattered the glass in the thermometer. He started swallowing the shards and mercury. When a nurse walked by, she saw blood on Lew's lips and cried for help. "Fortunately, Rex Kennamer was there," said Wendy Goldberg. Wasserman's longtime physician realized what had happened and flew into action.

A team of emergency doctors wheeled Wasserman back into surgery as Edie paced in the waiting room. Initially, she lashed out at the staff. "You shouldn't have given him a glass thermometer." After everything she and her husband had built, Edie feared losing Lew. Memories of her own frightening surgeries surfaced, as did the recollection of Taft Schreiber's tragedy, a reminder of how routine procedures can snowball into fatalities. Once MCA veterans learned of Lew's accident, they could not get over the eerie parallels between the mogul's freak accident and that of his nemesis. "It was the repeat of a bad dream," said one man.

Doctors rushed to save the mogul's life, opening Wasserman's throat and lungs to retrieve the glass. By now, his vocal chords were sheared, and he was bleeding internally. "For ten or twelve hours, it was a question of life or death," said Patsy Miller Krauskopf. After doctors had completed their work, no one was certain how much of the deadly mercury had seeped into the elderly man's bloodstream. Edie began her deathwatch.

For several days, she barely slept. Her only child, Lynne, joined Edie in her vigil. "I think it was a great blessing that Edie had finally reunited with her only child by then," said Krauskopf. Edie began to fully appreciate the strength that family can provide and she clung tightly to that comfort. She began protecting her own forty-seven-year-old, twice-divorced daughter, her twenty-one-year-old granddaughter, Carol Anne, and her thirteen-year-old grandson, Casey, with the same ferocity and passion and that she had once reserved for stars and wives.

Wasserman's other family—the corporate one—was less than forthcoming about the chief's condition. An MCA press release said that the chairman had recovered nicely from minor surgery. But he was in intensive care, hanging on to life. Word of Wasserman's near-fatal accident spread up and down his chain of command. At least one division manager was heard on a wiretap telephone, relaying bad news from inside the Black Tower to those far beyond it. Within hours, word of Wasserman's imminent death passed among a handful of FBI agents and strike-force attorneys. Word ricocheted to the East and a few underworld clans, then pinged down to Wall Street, where it echoed in tips and speculation. Factions began to marshal their forces, hinting at hostile raids and internal skirmishes. It was everything that Wasserman had feared before his surgery: MCA was now in play.

The specter of Lew's death excited Ron Perelman, chief of Revlon and another Michael Milken client. He'd been bitten by the showbiz bug and was eager to become head of Universal. So, too, were Nelson Peltz, head of Triangle Industries, the world's largest packaging company; the men at Coniston Partners, an investment group who had broken up Allegis, the parent of United Airlines; Denver oilman Marvin Davis, who had once owned Twentieth Century Fox; Michael Eisner of Disney; and General Electric, owner of RCA. Several self-proclaimed Masters of the Universe hovered ghoulishly over MCA, waiting to seize a dead man's empire.

MCA was a solid company with several recognized brand names. It had a library of three thousand movies, prime land on both coasts, a line of best-selling books, and experienced management. It was flush with cash and carried very little debt.

But Wall Street did not value MCA's stock because it had no

immediate payoff. Wasserman's prudent management style was not in fashion in the go-go 1980s, but rather was viewed as a detriment. Potential buyers could carve his company into pieces and sell each one, squeezing at least 30 percent more money from the parts than it could get for the whole. Then the owners of the pieces might take them public again, or reacquire them and put MCA back together. Or they might engineer some paper transactions that would churn more brokerage fees and produce great wealth for a few individuals.

Sheinberg tried to buy more company shares and seek greater control, but the stock speculators beat him. In the two weeks after Wasserman entered the hospital, MCA's stock price jumped from $48 to $52. The longer the chief was away, the higher the stock climbed—and the more bizarre became the plots.

FBI agents and their supervisors heard ear-popping conversations, said Richard Stavin and others. Giaquinto was discussing taking over MCA with the aid of outsiders. "It's a run for the roses," one shady character assured him. The insider told callers about the stock moves of Sheinberg, Perelman, Davis, and others. "Giaquinto was supposedly maneuvering to align himself with people to take control," said Stavin. He was allegedly passing insider information to outsiders who wanted to seize the helm of MCA.

In another corner of the Black Tower, Azoff was planning *his* takeover. He had tried to expand his division by acquiring MCA's video unit, which would have placed Giaquinto under his command. "It's warfare," Giaquinto was warned. But Azoff's ability to take control might be stymied since "the government had him" in their ongoing payola and Pisello cases. "The two executives were each jockeying for position as to who would become the bigger division," said Stavin. The outcome of this race would have several repercussions. There was the question of how the fight in MCA's suite might alter the balance on East Coast streets. Stavin had evidence of prosecutable crimes, ranging from racketeering to stock fraud, but how to proceed? There was also the issue of MCA's already-precarious position. "Everybody [at the FBI] was concerned about what would happen if word got out about Giaquinto, Azoff, and the mob," Stavin explained. "That would have caused a major, major hit on MCA's stock value." As it was, on July 15, the stock had closed at $60. As Giaquinto told a friend, "It's going crazy!"

Then came a strange, slightly ludicrous twist right out of a pulp spy novel. Giaquinto met Robert Booth Nichols for lunch at Le Dome in Hollywood, and while the video chief and the spook nibbled, FBI agents ran the license plates of Nichols's car. They traced the plates to Harold Okimoto, a leader in a Hawaiian syndicate that owned casinos around the world. FBI agents also learned that Okimoto had worked with Frank Carlucci, a former deputy director of the CIA, who in November 1987 would become Secretary of Defense. Stavin and his chiefs were floored. "Nichols and his work had the look of a covert operation."

Further investigation revealed that Nichols was president of Meridian Arms, a subsidiary of Meridian International Logistics. The firm had both CIA and organized crime connections, according to Lieutenant Commander Al Martin, a Secord associate whom Nichols knew from the Iran-Contra operation. Meridian sold U.S.-made biowarfare products to the Middle East, Afghanistan, and other political hot spots. "Hold on," thought Stavin. "This is way beyond our purview."

However, some of these findings were relevant. Nichols and Giaquinto discussed taking over MCA and swapped information about the corporation. Stavin and other federal officers wondered if MCA was helping the government move money and resources around the world. Years later, Martin claimed that it was, although he had no documentation to prove it.

At the time, Stavin simply relayed these new details to his superiors.

On July 16, Wasserman had recuperated enough to be sent home—some twenty-one days after entering the hospital. One of the first things he did was contact his broker. MCA share prices had reached an all-time high of $62, and on July 17, Wasserman sold part of his holdings—23,950 shares. Not only had the grizzled mogul rejoined the land of the living, he'd made a tidy $312,000 profit on his near-death experience. *Variety* had already prepared an obituary for the man "whose shrewdness and toughness was second to none," and Wasserman got a copy of the laudatory piece and kept it. There wasn't much time for Wasserman to sit on his laurels and count his winnings, however. Wall Street was already pricing his corporate empire at $5 billion to $5.5 billion, and that didn't include a passion premium—what an outsider might pay to land the feature role of the next Lew R. Wasserman.

On August 1, 1987, the mogul returned to work. Giaquinto, Azoff, and most of Hollywood burned up the telephone lines; a few conversations were intercepted by wiretaps. Everyone from over-the-counter traders to underground raiders swapped gossip about Wasserman's pale complexion, his hoarse voice, and MCA's uncertain future. But if Wasserman was anxious, he didn't show it. He ordered MCA to swallow its poison pill, which allowed MCA employees—from the secretaries to the suits—to buy additional shares at low option prices. That nearly doubled the number of outstanding shares, making it all but impossible for outsiders to acquire a controlling interest. The speculators' rush expired, and MCA's stock price settled down to $50.

A few MCA executives kicked themselves for not cashing in on the stock run-up when they had the chance. "Don't worry, boys," Wasserman joked, "If the stock gets too low, just park an ambulance in front of my house."

FORTY-THREE

ONE DAY, AS WASSERMAN HUDDLED WITH HIS STAFF, a Pacific Bell Telephone Company van pulled up to the Universal Studios gates. The uniformed repairman showed his work order to the guard, who waved him through. The Pac Bell worker parked his van and entered the basement of an MCA building that housed Azoff's MCA Records and Giaquinto's Home Entertainment unit. He opened a telephone box and began fiddling with the wires to install an FBI wiretap. As he worked, an MCA security guard swooped down on him. The phone man flashed his work order again, but it didn't mollify the guard—a former member of the LAPD—who knew that MCA had an exclusive contract with AT&T. The burly guard unceremoniously escorted the repairman off MCA's premises.

"That never happens," said Stavin, who had ordered the wiretap. He suspected that either MCA had been tipped off by someone inside the federal justice system, or that MCA's security man was extremely good. By September 1987, Stavin had collected enough evidence to believe that MCA was "playing with the mob," he said. "I wanted to open an investigation and look at MCA under RICO," the Racketeering Influence and Corrupt Organization Act. More wiretaps would help him make his case, but he had just been thwarted.

Stavin's counterpart, Marvin Rudnick, was making headway in his case. While Wasserman was in the hospital, the prosecutor had charged Pisello again, this time for evading taxes on MCA's largesse. It was Pisello's second indictment in three years, and Rudnick had filed them while Pisello was finishing his two-year prison sentence for his 1985 conviction. Pisello would do anything to avoid returning to prison, even if it meant turning against the men in the Black Tower. "One of the mysteries was how far up MCA Pisello's relationship went," Rudnick said. Pisello no longer worked for MCA, but several supervisors and executives who oversaw his deals were still ensconced at the firm. Rudnick wanted to put a few of these MCA executives on the stand and ask: "What did you do about the Pisello problem?" He believed that MCA brass knowingly paid mobsters, and he wanted to develop that theory at Pisello's next trial, scheduled for early 1988.

When Wasserman learned about the telephone repairman and his foiled wiretap, he became irate. He and his attorneys were certain that Rudnick had ordered the wiretap; they were evidently unaware of the second federal investigation against Giaquinto and MCA's Home Entertainment. Targeting Rudnick, Wasserman called upon all of his political muscle to ambush the unsuspecting prosecutor.

Edie and a recovered Lew returned to the party circuit in the third week of September. Pope John Paul II was about to make a two-day visit to Los Angeles, and the Wassermans had lobbied Cardinal Roger Mahoney to allow them to host the pontiff. The Vatican agreed, which elevated Wasserman's profile in the midst of MCA's three federal investigations. It was a coup for Edie and Lew, and they created a Hollywood jubilee for what was the pope's second coming.

Pope John Paul II had traveled to the United States once before in 1979—the first time a pope had set foot on American soil. Wasserman had tried to capitalize on that visit, too. An MCA label had released *John Paul II,* a record album by the pope, sung in his native Polish. The company had shipped one million copies of the album, which sold like hotcakes in the Polish neighborhoods of Milwaukee, Detroit, and Chicago, but virtually nowhere else. After the pope left North America, three-quarters of the albums were returned to Universal City, costing Lew a bundle. This time, there would be no record deal for the pope—just a studio tour, a lavish reception, and priceless media coverage of the spiritual leader blessing Universal City.

It was the biggest event the couple had ever held. During the weeks leading up to it, stars and executives had inundated Edie and Lew with calls, begging for invitations. The pontiff's visit to Wasserman's studio became the social event of the year. At the same time, MCA's lawyer, Allen Susman, called Marvin Rudnick to express his displeasure with him over the attempted wiretapping. "We want you to know that we're not happy with the way you're handling the [Pisello] case," he had told the federal prosecutor. "Really," Rudnick replied, surprised at the attorney's arrogance. "That's right," the MCA lawyer continued, "We have friends in the courthouse, too. We can make life very difficult for you."

To Rudnick, the call indicated that MCA was nervous about Pisello, whose testimony could lead up to MCA's executive suite. "I was going to ask him who at MCA let him do these money-losing deals," Rudnick explained. Pisello had said he'd do anything to avoid prison, even if it meant "having witnesses intimidated or even killed." After hearing from MCA's attorney, Rudnick felt confident that the issue went deeper than a simple case of tax evasion. "Lew had to have known what was going on with Pisello," he told me years later. "The way Wasserman runs his company, he must have known."

That week, the pope arrived in Los Angeles and celebrated mass at Dodger Stadium. He was resplendent in gold and white robes, and his voice carried to the bleachers. Later, he motored through the streets of Los Angeles in his bubble-topped Popemobile, waving to the crowds and vendors selling pope-on-a-rope soap. The next day, September 16, 1987, he was welcomed at Universal City by Edie and Lew, who proudly showed off their hilltop realm. They gave the pope a VIP tour of the back lot and escorted His Holiness to the amphitheater, where he held what Wasserman described as "a dialogue with young people."

The Wassermans then brought the pope to an elite reception at the Registry Hotel in Universal City. Edie and Lew had handpicked 1,500 of Hollywood's most prominent leaders in media and entertainment. They had allowed every network, local TV station, and major newspaper reporter inside to document the pope's visit to Wasserland. Assembled was the baroque court of Rodeo Drive, a crowd of movie millionaires and demi-billionaires. Barbara Walters, Merv Adelson, Bob Hope, and Charlton Heston attended, along with Michael Eisner of Disney Studios, David Puttnam, president of Columbia Studios, Sid Sheinberg, and MCA's feuding warlords, Irving Azoff and Gene Giaquinto. The pope told this enormously wealthy crowd that they could act as forces of great good or evil; he urged them to concentrate on "noble" acts.

Lew then led John Paul around the room to shake hands with the show-business people, many of whom seemed starstruck. Cameras captured the pair as they moved through the glittering crowd, and the industry rabbi towered over the pontiff. Wasserman's throat had healed since his near-fatal accident, though his words now dropped like gravel falling down a pipe.

A few days later, Marvin Rudnick appeared in front of a judge, alongside attorneys for Pisello and those for MCA executives. Pisello's lawyers had requested a list of witnesses that the government intended to use at his trial. But Rudnick didn't have such a list. He told the judge that several MCA executives had taken the Fifth Amendment during the grand-jury probe and that they would testify only if they were given immunity. But Rudnick couldn't grant immunity yet. "Until I can be sure of what [they are] going to say, I can't represent to this court that they'll be witnesses." The judge ruled that the witness list didn't have to be revealed until two weeks before trial. Reporters rushed out of the courtroom to file what had just become a hot story.

The following day, *Variety* blared: "Pisello Case Drops Bombshell on MCA." Another paper announced: "MCA Executives Take the Fifth in Grand Jury Probe." It looked as though MCA and its executives had something to hide—and the allegations angered Wasserman and Sheinberg. They believed that Rudnick was turning a tax case into a smear campaign against MCA and tying it unfairly to the mob.

"That's when Wasserman brought in the heavy artillery," said

Rudnick. Rather than address the government's concerns, MCA went on the offensive. Lew sent six lawyers to the U.S. Attorney's office downtown. They accused Rudnick of unfair behavior, stating that he shouldn't have mentioned in open court that MCA executives had taken the Fifth—though the judge had allowed it and that was what the executives had essentially done. MCA lawyers also accused Rudnick of lying about their clients' uncooperative stance, despite evidence to the contrary. Then the lawyers, mistaking Rudnick for Stavin, falsely blamed Rudnick for trying to place wiretaps inside MCA. Rudnick's boss thanked the corporate attorneys for their visit, and they departed.

A few days later, Rudnick found himself working for a new supervisor, John Newcomer. All of a sudden, the new boss limited Rudnick's prosecution to Pisello's tax case—nothing more—and monitored Rudnick closely from his Los Angeles office. Meanwhile, Wasserman added to his legal arsenal a top gun from Akin, Gump, Strauss, Hauer & Feld, where Bob Strauss was a partner. This was not just any lawman, but William Hundley, an old government nemesis of Wasserman's. In 1958, when the talent agent was buying studio land, Hundley had been chief of the new Organized Crime and Racketeering Section. In 1962, when U.S. Attorney Robert F. Kennedy had filed his antitrust against MCA, Hundley had been Kennedy's special assistant. Hundley not only knew MCA intimately, he was the grandfather of the strike force that was now bearing down on Wasserman.

In September 1987, Hundley, now a corporate attorney working for MCA, lunched with the strike-force chiefs in Washington, D.C. He complained about Rudnick, who a few weeks later was placed under investigation for his performance in the MCA case. "You're embarrassing MCA," Newcomer told Rudnick, "Stop looking for mob ties to Irvin Azoff or any other MCA executive."

"Lew brought it on, I'm sure, although he didn't have to be so heavy-handed," said Rudnick. "I was just a flea, and he knocked me down with a bazooka."

Wasserman had reason to come on strong: He was trying to sell his company before it got snatched from him by a raider or speculator. The investigations and sensational news stories tying MCA to the mob cast him and the company in the worst possible light. Rudnick noted that none of MCA's representatives ever flatly denied that the company was involved with mobsters, and no one refuted that Wasserman was exercising his formidable clout. But not even Lew could control what happened next.

On "Black Monday," October 19, 1987, the stock market crashed. The Dow Jones Industrial Average fell from 2,600 to 1,700, or 35 percent—a drop steeper than the one that had triggered the Great Depression. Wasserman felt the crash more acutely than perhaps any other mogul. As MCA's stock fell to $30 a share, market gurus predicted steeper drops ahead. After the 1929 crash, it had taken the Dow Jones Industrial Average twenty-five years to regain its pre-crash level; Wasserman didn't have twenty-five years and he needed a deep-pocket partner. Now.

Meanwhile, Rudnick continued to prepare for the Pisello trial. That December, David Margolis, the head of the Organized Crime Strike Force, ordered Rudnick to fly from Los Angeles and appear at headquarters immediately; it was rare for the chief to summon a deputy attorney to Washington, and Rudnick was anxious. His meeting took place on a wet and rainy morning, he recalled. "I was waiting in this huge, cold room inside the federal building." He noted the wainscoting, the federal seal, and the whiff of damp, rotting wood. One wall featured an organization chart of the strike force. Another held three enormous portraits in somber colors.

Margolis finally arrived and sat down.

The chief gestured to the three oil paintings on the wall behind him. "You see those guys?" Rudnick looked up at President Ronald Reagan, Attorney General Edwin Meese, and William Hundley, who had founded the strike force. "When one of these guys starts complaining about you, Marvin, we have a problem."

His message was pointed. Try the tax case; we'll discuss your career later. Rudnick flew home to Los Angeles that afternoon and went back to work. He wasn't allowed to subpoena MCA executives, obtain their testimony, or call other music-industry witnesses. "Why is the Justice Department playing favorites with Lew Wasserman?" Rudnick kept asking colleagues.

On New Year's Eve, the Reagans returned to California to celebrate with their friends in Palm Springs. Among their visitors were the Bloomingdales, the Annenbergs, and the Wassermans, who all lent support to a president besieged by scandals. Howard Baker was fielding the attacks on the administration, and in a few months, the Iran-Contra scandal would spin off criminal indictments of Oliver North, John Poindexter, and Richard Secord. It was shaping up to be quite a drama, more riveting than Reagan's last Universal movie, *Law and Order,* and more widely distributed than his final Universal TV production, *The Killers.* It all reached a crescendo in March 1988, just as Ed Meese emerged as a significant player in Iran-Contra.

Several high-ranking Justice Department attorneys grew disgusted with their boss. The attorney general was still under investigation for using his post to help others and enrich himself, and his mounting problems became a liability for several top officials, including Deputy Attorney General Arnold Burns and Assistant Attorney General William Weld. They worried not only about the fate of their boss, but also about the integrity of the department and their own careers. Burns, Weld, and others complained about their boss to Howard Baker, the president's chief of staff. Weld said that his superiors often asked if he couldn't close pending investigations of Meese's friends: "Hasn't that [case] been hanging around a long time? Can't that be closed out? It's really hurting [the person or company under investigation]." In more than one case, the subjects of those investigations were in California, Weld said later. He and Burns were growing frustrated at being undermined and sidestepped in Meese's office.

Nevertheless, Baker urged the two well-respected lawyers to remain on staff. They did, briefly. But the situation worsened, and, a week later, on March 30, 1988, Burns, Weld, and four top aides resigned from the Justice Department. It was an unprecedented mass exit, the signal of a complete loss of faith in the U.S. Justice Department. The Justice Department was now seen as so corrupt that Senator Robert C. Byrd (D.-W. Va.) called Ed Meese the "crown jewel of Reagan's sleaze factor," and demanded his resignation. Even so, the exodus left Meese unbowed and still in charge.

Back in Los Angeles, Richard Stavin was preparing his indictment against Gene Giaquinto. He was unaware of Rudnick's problems, and did not know the details about the mass resignations in the Justice Department. He was following a dozen FBI divisions around the country that were discovering Mafia influence in business, ranging from padded payrolls for Hollywood Teamsters to rampant fraud in health and pension funds. In the past ten years, mobsters had become financiers and distributors in the film industry, funding hard-core pornographic films such as *Wet Rainbow,* or financing B movies such as *Screwball Hotel.* In 1981 the California Attorney General had reported a large influx of members of East Coast crime families into Southern California. These men managed "to have deeply ingratiated themselves into many aspects of the [entertainment] industry," the report stated, from money laundering, film distribution, supplying narcotics on the set, and controlling labor relations.

However, actually proving these things in court would be a breakthrough. "There was a lot of interest in having indictments come out of our Los Angeles case," said Stavin. He received authorization to prosecute three men for obstructing justice, including MCA's Giaquinto. But because his agents were so close to documenting other, more serious counts, Stavin delayed prosecution. He requested the assistance of another attorney who would bring in more FBI agents and investigators to help mount labor racketeering and RICO charges.

One of these sources was initially on the record. I had talked to this source a few times over the years, and spent hours reviewing the case material. By then, the story was nearly twenty years old, and some of the players had died. Even so, in the final stages of this book's production, I checked a few facts with this source, who suddenly refused to be named in the account below. By then, it was 2003, and MCA no longer existed as a corporate entity, but evidently, its long-standing reputation for skulduggery and ruthless vengeance was alive and well. It made me wonder what my source feared.

In May 1988, Giaquinto learned about the government investigation of him. "He went ballistic," said my source. MCA's executive Giaquinto had had enough. "I'm calling Meese and getting this thing stopped right now," he said.

Sure enough, after Giaquinto dropped Meese's name, the three cases against MCA—the payola, videocassettes, and record investigations—began to lose steam. Rudnick wound up his tax case against Pisello, and a jury sent Sal to prison again. But in July 1988, Rudnick was fired for no official reason, he said. Years later, he told me: "This is a cover-up that goes all the way to the top." In August 1988 Irvin Azoff resigned from MCA Records, and in December MCA placed Giaquinto on a paid leave of absence; he was replaced quietly. As for Stavin, he quit the strike force, fearing that he'd soon be set up as Rudnick had been. The video case was eventually dropped.

The sound of strings being pulled resonated throughout the legal community, and the entire score landed in the pages of legal journals and magazines. William Dwyer II, who represented three fired MCA executives who had cooperated with Rudnick, suspected foul play. "There was [talk] about how Ed Meese wanted certain actions taken because Nancy Reagan had a friend in high places in the entertainment industry," he told me. Indeed, other investigators and attorneys believed that Wasserman and Meese had covered up a larger case of mob infiltration and CIA influence at MCA. "It's just not happenstance that two of MCA's presidents of two of their major divisions are doing business with the mob," said Stavin. "Especially taking into account the history of MCA and how it started in Chicago."

In March 1992, Stavin, Rudnick, FBI agent Thomas Gates, and others were called to testify before a House Judiciary Committee about these and other matters. The committee, headed by Representative Jack Brooks of Texas, collected depositions from Rudnick and Stavin, who separately detailed their strike-force findings. Rudnick reviewed his findings about Pisello, Azoff, and the mob, as well as the government's abrupt closure of his case. Stavin discussed the ties between Gene Giaquinto and Robert Booth Nichols. Stavin believed that MCA was helping the government by offering the cover of its offices around the world. Later, to the surprise of both Stavin and Rudnick, the committee did not discount that. "They indicated that we were closer than we initially believed," said Stavin. "They felt that there were other Iran-Contras out there, besides Ollie North's deal." Added Rudnick: "Gianquinto was on the board of a company that dealt with the CIA, which is part of what the judiciary committee was investigating."

In July 1988, Howard Baker left the White House job. He had considered running for president, but when George H. Bush became the GOP candidate, Baker returned to MCA's board. It was March 1989, just in time to help Wasserman celebrate his seventy-sixth birthday. It had been a close call, but MCA had survived yet another government investigation—its tenth federal case in sixty years. But other less predictable forces were about to lay siege.

FORTY-FOUR

BY 1989, THE JAPANESE HAD LANDED ON AMERICAN SHORES, buying landmarks such as the Hotel Bel-Air in Beverly Hills and Rockefeller Center in Manhattan. Japanese investment in the United States jumped from a few billion dollars in 1980 to $55 billion in 1988. The yen flooded onto the West Coast and tied it closer to Asia, forming the Pacific Rim, a new financial frontier.

Lew Wasserman had already begun looking to Asia to expand his holdings. In February 1989, he was trying to decide whether to build his next theme park in Osaka or Tokyo. (He'd choose Osaka.) He was realistic about which sectors of show business held the most promise for the future. Despite all the noise about box-office hits, and even though the U.S. population had surged some 25 percent in two decades, movie attendance had not risen much at all. However, studio advertising costs had risen so high that half of a movie's cost was now allotted to marketing and promotion. Those costs were expected to rise, along with the globalization of the market. Wasserman knew that movies were a shrinking part of the new entertainment conglomerates. Television networks, cable stations, theme parks, music labels, and technology were the divisions that would propel studio-based giants in the next millennium.

The giants were turning into behemoths. In 1985 Capital Cities bought ABC for $3.5 billion. That same year, Australian Rupert Murdoch and his News Corporation bought Twentieth Century-Fox and Metromedia's TV stations, making the first instance of foreign ownership of American studios and broadcasters. In 1986 General Electric bought RCA and its property, NBC; Loews Corporation bought a controlling stake in CBS. Now Giancarlo Parretti, head of Pathé Communications, was the latest mogul-in-waiting; he'd soon buy MGM for $1.3 billion. By the time Time Inc. merged with Warner Communications in 1989, all Wasserman could do was size up his hefty competitors:

"We're a 200-pound gorilla in a game with 1,000-pound gorillas," he told shareholders that year.

At seventy-six, Wasserman was throwing up his hands. "I don't think he had the energy to keep up with the fight," said Ned Tanen. "Lew realized that, whatever he was doing, MCA was sliding down a hill of sand." Nor he did think that Sidney Sheinberg alone could lead the company into the future. However, Wasserman wanted to make sure his aide-de-camp was taken care of. The two men had created one of the longest-running executive partnerships in the history of Hollywood. They had grown so close that people jokingly called the company "Wasserman & Son." The pair continued scouring the horizon for bargain acquisitions, sensing that only five to seven major media companies would survive into the next century. Unless MCA managed to wangle a killer deal soon, it would not be able to compete. As Sheinberg explained, "The issue became financing."

Michael Ovitz had become the town's biggest talent broker. He had grown his own agency, Creative Artists Agency (CAA), by using several of Lew's tricks—from selling packages that bundled CAA directors, writers, and actors to offering take-it-or-leave-it deals to cowed studios. He was as feared, reviled, and admired as Wasserman had been in his agency heyday. But after two decades of representing individual star talent, Ovitz hungered for corporate clients, with quarterly earnings and long shelf lives. As Japan's star rose, Ovitz became smitten by the country's philosophy and culture. He studied the martial art of aikido, and memorized Sun Tzu's *The Art of War,* an ancient military treatise. He also began to act as Hollywood's ambassador to Japan.

Sony had already advanced into Hollywood in 1987 by buying CBS Records for $2 billion, becoming the first major Japanese partner of a U.S. company. Ovitz was asked to help Sony find a studio. During Wasserman's illness, Ovitz had watched the gyrations of MCA's stock and had later recommended that Sony buy MCA. Wasserman understood very well the commercial potential between entertainment-hardware companies like Sony and software-content providers like MCA. Indeed, the Japanese had turned the VHS technology into a global juggernaut partly because it sold VCRs with compatible videotaped movies. Imagine how much larger Sony could become by linking up with an American entertainment storehouse to supply products for its other electronic toys, such as high-definition TV! As for MCA, it could withstand the long, bumpy road of moviemaking if it had a deep-pocket parent behind it. As usual, Wasserman wanted too much money for his gem—reportedly $100 a share, or $9 billion, plus full control of his company, and a guaranteed contract for Sheinberg. The deal was too rich for Sony and, in September 1989, it bought Columbia Pictures instead for about $4.7 billion—a stunning deal.

Wasserman was shaken by his missed opportunity, and he approached Paramount Studios' Martin Davis about a merger. But during those talks, he insisted that Sheinberg and Davis co-manage any merged studio entity; not surprisingly, Davis refused. Lew then approached Philips, Nippon Steel, and other potential buyers, with little success. "In many ways, they were trying to find a partner but they didn't quite want to," said one executive. "It's hard to describe, but I really think that Lew believed he was going to merge with another company [and] he would be running the show. Someone else might be buying MCA, but there was this attitude that, of course, we're going to be in charge." Naturally, when the issue of control came up, the bigger party would have to say, "No, no, no. You don't understand. *We are buying you.*"

Added Tanen, "It was a bit of arrogance, but it was more about two different worlds. Lew really understood the entertainment business. And [outsiders] really have no comprehension of the entertainment business."

In late 1989, Matsushita Electric Industrial Company decided to buy a studio, too. The Osaka-based firm contacted Ovitz, who was eager to repeat his success with Sony. In many ways, Matsushita was like MCA. The company had been founded in 1918 by Konosuke Matsushita, who had invented an electrical socket and attachment plug. Like Jules Stein, Matsushita grew his company steadily, producing fans, refrigerators, vacuum cleaners, washing machines, and other modern conveniences to feed Japan's postwar prosperity. Eventually, it was making semiconductors, stereos, and TVs. The founder anointed his son, Masaharu Matsushita, as head of the company, just as Stein had appointed Lew Wasserman.

The firm attracted several rising stars—Akio Tanii, a brilliant engineer who made the VHS video format a technological standard—and Masahiko Hirata, a financial manager who racked up huge sales. As Wasserman had done with Sid Sheinberg and Frank Price, Matsushita elevated Tanii and Hirata into the executive suite. Also like MCA, Matsushita had become revered in its own country as one of the most stable, conservatively run, prestigious corporations. The Japanese giant had little debt and was flush with cash—$15 billion at the ready, plus another $12 billion in securities. Matsushita and MCA could be a match made in Zen heaven.

In November 1989, Matsushita executives asked to meet with Ovitz in Honolulu. "I had worked with the Japanese before, and knew how long they could take making a decision," said Jay Stein. Japanese businessmen generally send lower-level executives to initial meetings, where they gauge the prospects and report back to the chief. When Ovitz learned that he'd be meeting with Matsushita's executive vice president, Masahiko Hirata—the top aide to president Akio Tanii—he realized they were serious. Then, just as the groom was about to meet the bride's broker, MCA's dirty laundry was aired.

Once again, *60 Minutes* was preparing a show involving Wasserman and the mob. Unlike its 1984 piece, which had been killed, this episode would focus on the investigations into MCA's music and video businesses. Once again, Lowell Bergman was the producer. "We identified Wasserman and MCA with this mob guy from the record industry," said Bergman. The producers intended to show a photograph of Lew sitting at a banquet table with Sid Sheinberg to his left and Gene Giaquinto to his right.

"I decided to do the story and push the Wasserman connection to the mob," said Bergman. CBS lawyers reviewed and vetted his work, and Don Hewitt watched the piece. Hewitt struggled with one sequence in which the camera panned the faces of MCA board directors: Wasserman; Sheinberg; former senator Howard Baker; Mary Gardiner Jones of Consumer Interest Research Institute; Howard P. Allen, CEO of Southern California Edison; Thomas Jones of Northrop; Tom Pollock; Felix Rohatyn; Robert Strauss; and MCA executive Thomas Wertheimer.

Hewitt turned to Bergman and said: "I don't care about Lew and Edie. But I care about Felix Rohatyn. I have lunch with him, and he's a really good man. Can you do me a favor? Can you take out his picture?" Bergman knew that dropping Rohtayn's face from the film clip would not eliminate him from the board, or change his responsibilities. But rather than argue with Hewitt, Bergman acquiesced, he told me. "I figured it was a small price to pay to get the story on the air."

Meanwhile, Edie found out about the piece. She urged Lew to talk Hewitt out of it. "Lew tried to get it killed, or at least balanced," by telling his side of the story, said Tom Pollock. "Hewitt received a call from Lew," said Bergman, "and from Edie, who screamed at him over the phone." Edie, in particular, was incensed and warned Hewitt, "You will never stay at our house again."

The story, "Hollywood and the Mob," aired on November 19, 1989. The government's two investigations that had been killed eighteen months earlier, resurfaced like a bad dream. Both Stavin and Rudnick appeared on camera, voicing their suspicions about MCA, the mob, and the government's role in shutting down their cases. *Sixty Minutes* reporters asked MCA executives or their attorneys to appear on camera, but they declined. Instead, they wrote a letter denying the allegations, claiming that prosecutors had "unfairly damaged the company."

The story infuriated Wasserman and Sheinberg, who years later recalled the episode in horror. "The thought that somehow this was reflective of some massive Mafia infusion is just silly," Sheinberg said. "I mean, really. Do I look like some kind of mafioso?" he asked, spreading his arms wide. "This guy Rudnick was on a mission or something."

That week, Edie visited friends in New York City. "I took Edie to '21' and right next to us was Don Hewitt," said Dominick Dunne. Hewitt stood up to embrace his old friend, and said, "Edie, how good to see you!" But Edie froze him out. "It was more than a snub. She cut him off so cruelly, she was unforgiving." Over dinner, Edie explained why, said Dunne. "Hewitt had supposedly promised Edie that something wouldn't be revealed—or at least she had believed so."

The next night, Dunne and Hewitt ran into each other at a party, and the *60 Minutes* producer was inconsolable. "He was so upset, he couldn't understand it," said Dunne. "But from that point on, Don was on the outs with Edie." He'd never regain his intimacy with the Wassermans. "It ended a very long and happy relationship," said Pollock. "Lew felt it had been a hatchet job, a metafiction. Just because Lew knew all the people in organized-crime circles didn't mean he was controlled by them."

If the *60 Minutes* incident was a barometer of Lew and Edie's waning power, it also tarnished MCA's image and upset Wasserman's plans at a delicate juncture. Matsushita was taking a keen interest in MCA, and the Japanese firm represented what appeared to be Wasserman's last great hope.

Despite the bad media coverage, the trans-Pacific talks turned serious over the next few months. In the fall of 1990, Wasserman invited Masahiko Hirata and another Matsushita executive to a meeting at his Foothill Road home. The elegant but relatively modest house was a perfect meeting site that showed off the simple, exquisite style of the mogul and his wife. The living room's large windows overlooked a still blue pool. The home's decor glowed with soft colors of gold, red and black, and Edie had a few bonsai trees and many pieces of Asian art—including an antique eight-paneled Chinese screen that she had purchased decades earlier, and a stunning horse sculpture from the Tang dynasty. Most rooms had huge windows that opened to acres of manicured yard planted with ferns, ivy, orchids, and palms. "Lew loved his garden and spent a lot of time out there," said Wendy Goldberg. Edie had lured from retirement the noted landscape architect Philip Shipley, and he had designed a serene park with a fishpond and viewing platform. In the early 1980s, Wasserman had stocked his pond with an exotic species of Japanese carp called koi; he was especially taken with an enormous white specimen that had cost some $100,000. "Lew loved feeding those fish," said Goldberg. He'd stare at the water and watch his fish swim, eat, and breed. In time, they would multiply so much that the outdoor aquarium would be worth several million dollars, making it perhaps the richest water hole in Beverly Hills. By then, Lew had so many fish, he'd give his precious koi away as gifts to friends like Aaron Spelling, Leonard Goldberg, and even Edie's personal trainer.

In such a setting, the Japanese must have felt at home. By all accounts, Hirata and Wasserman hit it off as they exchanged stories about movies and stars. Edie had set out refreshments of crudités, smoked salmon, California wine, and green tea. Papers reported that a possible agreement would include a per-share price of between $80 and $90. That translated into a potential sales price of $7.5 billion deal—a huge deal. Reports of MCA's worth began climbing to $8.7 billion.

Ovitz had a team of 125 people to carry out the negotiations, including five CAA staffers, an entire public-relations company, and a law firm. Sheinberg told MCA's board about the pending sale, and somehow the news leaked out. When the takeover story was printed, MCA's stock jumped from $34 to about $54—a whopping amount. This upset the Japanese, who believed that MCA executives had fed the story to the press as a way to pump up MCA's stock price and extract a richer price; they said as much to Japanese reporters. Now it was Wasserman's turn to act insulted; he hadn't spoken to the press. Though the two sides were scheduled to meet around Thanksgiving, chiefs at both companies were hot under the collar. "Problems in the discussions are being resolved and no other suitors for MCA have emerged," said one report. But Wasserman knew that he could not afford to walk away from this opportunity. Through his various ambassadors, he calmed the waters, and soon the meeting was on again.

Edie celebrated her seventy-fifth birthday on November 4 at an intimate gathering at a Sutton Place apartment in New York. Their host was Wasserman's old friend Abraham Ribicoff, the son of poor Polish immigrants who had risen to become congressman, governor, and senator. The Connecticut Democrat, his wife Casey, Dominick Dunne, and others all toasted the guest of honor. Composer Sammy Cahn serenaded the birthday girl, just as he had done at her parties in the 1950s, when Cahn, Dean Martin, and Rita Hayworth had commandeered a piano, a mike, and a set of drums for an impromptu performance. This time, Cahn played the ivory keys and sang a few songs, including his 1945 hit, "It's Been a Long, Long Time."

For this occasion, Cahn changed the lyrics:

We must applaud this small-town broad,
Who's gone as far as she could go.
It's been a long, long time.

That night it seemed neither Edie nor Lew had felt like this in a long time. Certainly, the Cleveland sweethearts had come a long way from their clerk-and-usher days. Did they ever in their wildest dreams imagine that someday they'd sell their firm to a Japanese outfit for several billion dollars? Lew was in rare form that night, and he joked, "I never thought I'd be sleeping with a seventy-five-year-old woman." The table erupted into laughter and Cahn tickled the keys and sang one of his swing hits, "It's Magic," substituting his witty ad-libs for his original clever lyrics.

Days later, a final round of talks began in earnest. In New York, Wasserman and Sheinberg meet with Kirata and Keiya Toyonaga, another Matsushita executive. Ovitz and Felix Rohatyn were present along with Bob Strauss, who was both a paid adviser to Matsushita and a paid MCA director. A few days later, they all met again, in Sheinberg's apartment in Trump Tower, to nail down the details: Wasserman would have a life-time position at MCA. The company's current chiefs could run the company with absolute authority, as long as they remained within the Japanese parent's budget. Sheinberg secured a guar-antee that he would succeed Wasserman once he retired. The only element not in place was the sales price—which Lew was always a stickler about.

Wasserman had told his men that MCA would fetch $90 a share, said Daniel Welkes. "That was his sale price." But given the pre-vailing global recession, Wasserman had figured that $75 was fair, and Ovitz had pointed to that number, too, in earlier discussions. But outside factors now intervened. George Bush was moving troops to the Persian Gulf, and in a few weeks the Gulf War would begin. Hirata told Ovitz that because of the threat of war, the global recession, and Matsushita's falling stock price, he could offer only $60 a share for MCA.

Wasserman said the deal was dead. But he was bluffing, and the Japanese called his bluff. They stuck by their offer. MCA's stock was now at about $64. Wasserman surmised that if the deal fell through, it could fall as low as $40. Then where would he be? It wasn't likely that Lew could turn around and sell MCA for $7 billion or even $6 billion, which is what the Japanese were offering right now. The next deal—if there was one—might be closer to $4 billion. Wasserman could not back out without facing his stockholders' ire, and he could not leave the table without risking a tragic ending to an incredible career.

That Thanksgiving eve, Strauss and his wife had dinner with Edie and Lew. The grizzled mogul indicated that if Matsushita could throw in another $2 or $3 to the stock price, he'd sign. The ambassadors and Ovitz scurried to relay this message to those across the Pacific. On Monday, the deal was sweetened by two dollars, and Matsushita bought the firm for $6.13 billion—or $66 a share.

Wasserman had topped even himself. The sale was the biggest buyout ever of an American firm by a Japanese investor. Now four of the seven major studios were owned by foreign entities: Columbia was owned by Sony, MGM was owned by Giancarlo Parretti and his French bankers, Twentieth Century Fox was owned by Australian Rupert Murdoch, and the oldest and biggest studio of them all—MCA/Universal—was in the hands of Matsushita. Lew's sale was "a personal triumph," *Variety* declared. It was a storybook ending for Edie, and heralded the end of an era in Hollywood.

FORTY-FIVE

WASSERMAN WAS ECSTATIC AT WHAT HE THOUGHT was the capstone of his career. The American capitalist had always displayed a gift for getting others to see things his way, and Japanese businessmen were no different from the greenest movie star. In the twelve months following MCA's sale, the two companies enjoyed their honeymoon. Wasserman relaxed, Matsushita installed executive Atsuro Uede on Universal's lot, and the parent corporation remained upbeat about its latest acquisition. President Akio Tanii and vice president Masahiko Hirata believed that MCA's intellectual property of some 50,000 copyrighted works—from records to TV shows—would play exceptionally well on Matsushita's products, which included National Panasonic, Technics, and Quasar brands.

But then the global recession chilled the air. All studios in Hollywood cut expenses but only MCA froze the salaries of three hundred managers. In March 1992, Matsushita's finance subsidiary suddenly lost about 50 billion yen—$380 million—because of the poor judgment of Nui Onoue. The comely investment consultant had used séances to gain stock-market tips from spirit guides. But the lady had failed to pick up any warnings about the future bear market. Onoue and her clients had therefore lost hundreds of millions, and could not repay an enormous loan from Matsushita's bank. The scandal snowballed into a huge flap in Japan and forced the staid corporation to post a 40 percent drop in profits. To atone for the problems, the chairman and president of Matsushita accepted a 50 percent pay cut for three months.

Meanwhile, Wasserman and Sheinberg sought ways to expand MCA—which had been Wasserman's intent in what he still called "the merger." In 1992 he leaped at the opportunity to buy Britain's Virgin Records, offering to spend $750 million of Matsushita's money. The Japanese said no, and the label was snapped up quickly by Britain's Thorn EMI for $973 million. Wasserman decided it was time to build the Osaka theme park he'd been considering for several years, but he had to seek the parent company's approval to begin his $1.5 billion construction project. He made his request, then waited . . . and waited . . . in vain.

"We had two problems with the Japanese," said Sheinberg. "Number one, we weren't smart enough to figure out that the bubble economy was going to burst as it did. Plus, we didn't know that the consumer-electronics industry was entering a stagnant period, with no new products. Then," he added, "there were some scandals." In addition to lending large sums of money to a psychic medium, Matsushita was now forced to recall some faulty compressors and other products. "It was a frustrating time for us," said Sheinberg.

Meanwhile, Edie maintained political connections and key friendships. When Reagan left the White House, he took an office in Century City and called Lew for lunch. Later, the men's wives arranged to meet for dinner at Chasen's. Always a stickler for punctuality, Edie fumed while she and Lew were publicly kept waiting at a prime table set for four. Twenty minutes later, their guests breezed in with apologies and air kisses. Lew excused them, but Edie complained about their tardiness.

For Reagan's birthday in 1991, Edie and Lew attended a birthday party at Chasen's, even though Ronnie was absent. "It was all Republicans," said Dominick Dunne, who was also a guest. Edie groused bitterly about the lack of liberals, asking loudly and repeatedly, "I can't believe this! Where are all of the Democrats?" It got so bad that Nancy shot her friend a plaintive look, which Edie ignored. "That's Edie," said Dunne. "Loyal, outspoken, and not afraid of anybody."

The Wassermans still threw political fundraisers, but it was apparent that MCA's younger guard did not share their interest. "Lew would have a party for two hundred people, and he'd go from table to table, shaking hands and checking in with guests," said Jay Stein. Meanwhile, Edie would notice the MCA executives bunched like folding chairs in a corner. "Lew would get frustrated with us because we'd be against the wall instead of circulating among the guests," Stein admitted. And Edie would swoop down on them, wagging her red-nailed forefinger and uttering admonishments.

Republican Pete Wilson, Democrat Michael Dukakis, and nearly every other politician stopped by the Wassermans' place, seeking alms and benediction. But these pilgrimages grew too hypocritical for even jaded Hollywood veterans. Ned Tanen once recalled hearing about a right-wing politician holding forth on Foothill Road. "What do I care about Representative Weaseltere from Georgia?" he asked, using a fictitious name. "The guy will make one of those gratuitous ten-minute speeches, Lew will load up the drinks, and Edie will serve Chasen's chili." However, to Edie and Lew, the political backslapping and dark-horse trading became one of the more meaningful parts of their lives. MCA/Universal was in a holding pattern, behind virtually all of the other studios. But here, just a block above Sunset Boulevard, the statesmen mingled with the stagemen, and the Wassermans directed it all. Edie would ask her guests, "Have you had your picture taken with the senator yet? No? Well, come on, let me take you there." And she'd lead her guest to the camera. As Wendy Goldberg said, "A lot of us were shy and didn't want to intrude, but Edie wouldn't listen. She'd say, 'That won't do,' and take us in hand."

Edie loved having the inside track on political races, while Lew relished political gossip. As much money and effort as they threw into industry issues, each one also believed fervently in supporting progressive causes, according to several friends. "Edie would never support a candidate who wasn't pro-choice, and she was big on supporting judges for the Supreme Court," said Goldberg. "She didn't want people in Congress who would overtax the common man," and as the 1990s wore on, Lew believed that issue loomed large, as he indicated in our discussions.

Indeed, he was genuinely worried about the growing divide between the upper and lower classes. "We should be doing more for the middle class and young people," he once told me. "The young are our future leaders." He had listened to Jerry Brown, Ralph Nader, and others decry the growing commercialization of democracy, the process whereby the one with the fattest campaign contribution wins the juiciest government subsidies. But however the game was rigged, Wasserman had to play. "I've been doing it for sixty years, so I must think it's important to keep in touch," he told me. "Washington is the hub of the country, isn't it? It's where everything happens with laws and restrictions. I've got a lot of friends back there because I've been doing it for so long."

In 1993 Wasserman learned that Hollywood would soon lose finsyn, its financial syndication benefit—the gift that Taft Schreiber had secured in 1970 and the one that Wasserman had rescued in 1983. The FCC would allow the old rules to lapse by 1996. By now, syndication money was depositing some $3 billion a year into producers' coffers, most of that in Universal City. Though the windfall would drop a bit, the FCC was giving Wasserman and the studio moguls another gift. Deregulation would soon allow them to buy their own TV networks. Disney would soon buy Capital Cities/ABC, while Wasserman looked at CBS. He wanted Matsushita to spend a few billion yen to let him buy the network in partnership with ITT Corporation.

This time, he planned for success. On September 17, 1994, Wasserman and Sheinberg flew to Osaka with their proposal. Their old allies, Tanii and Hirata, had left Matsushita. The new president, Yoichi Morishita, was consumed by larger problems that impacted the Japanese company's integrity, finances, and future. For some reason, Morishita kept the two Americans waiting outside his office for two hours. Exhausted by his trip, the eighty-one-year-old Wasserman was humiliated by the rude treatment, which also angered the sixty-two-year-old Sheinberg. Sid later wrote a stinging letter to Chairman Masaharu Matsushita, complaining about their reception. The Japanese were shocked by Sid's insulting letter.

"Lew felt that because he was Lew Wasserman, they would allow him to run the company," said Sheinberg. Wasserman believed—

erroneously—that the Japanese would follow his recommendations. "After a while, they retreated and didn't return phone calls," said Sheinberg. Now it was Wasserman's turn to be stunned; no one had treated him with such disrespect since 1950, when Jack Warner, upset at Lew's escalating financial demands, finally barred the cocky agent from his lot. Later, Wasserman bought his own studio and threw a few producers off his lot, too. Or course, Wasserman understood how different the circumstances were: The Japanese owned MCA/Universal Studios—Wasserman & Son—and that fact lay at the core of Lew's problems.

He arranged for a showdown, and prepared one last proposal to present to MCA's foreign owners. To force the issue, he, Edie, and Sheinberg turned to the press, which for the first time publicly aired the mogul's grievances. On October 18, 1994, Matsushita President Morishita greeted the two MCA chiefs in San Francisco and expressed his discomfort with the negative stories. The meeting disintegrated quickly into a five-and-a-half-hour confrontation. Sheinberg had a hard time controlling his temper, he later admitted, while Wasserman coolly summoned all of the leverage he could muster. He issued his ultimatum: He wanted to buy back controlling interest of his company. Otherwise, he'd resign from the company when his contract expired in 1995. He would take with him Steven Spielberg, who had formed DreamWorks SKG with the idea of distributing his popular films through Matsushita's Universal. Lew had shot the moon, but he had grossly miscalculated. "The Japanese don't respond well to threats," said Jay Stein.

Each camp returned to its side of the Pacific. Wasserman anticipated more discussions, but the Japanese rebuffed the idea of selling anything back to the American mogul. "That totally demoralized us," said Sheinberg.

But what more did the old lion expect? Look how much he had achieved: Wasserman had sold MCA to an owner who had kept the company intact. He had wrung forth some $30 million in annual stock dividends, as well as a $3 million salary per annum, guaranteed for five years. He had also managed to extract a secret $350 million cash payout for his MCA shares, a tax-free gift that saved him $100 million. This was a premium stock price that had not been offered to MCA's other shareholders—a violation of a federal securities rule. But Wasserman believed that Matsushita would never sell MCA—certainly not in his lifetime—and that his illegal stock package would therefore not surface for years. In the meantime, Wasserman was still chairman of his realm, the Zeus on his personal Mount Olympus.

But that autumn, Wasserman was dissatisfied. For years, the mogul had grown accustomed to hearing his own voice echoing around Hollywood. But Japanese executives did not revere his pronouncements automatically and were not keen on sharing the risks for another one of his pioneering deals. Matsushita was struggling to rescue its own finances and chart a brighter future. Besides, MCA's revenues represented about 10 percent of its parent's sales. Wasserman was only a bit player to this global giant, and that must have gone down hard. Worse, Wasserman had no political allies he could tap—he had not funded the campaign of any Japanese parliament member, had no friends in the prime minister's office, and had not a single backer in his parent company. "If the Japanese aren't going to be helpful to us in terms of capital, then who needs them?" he told Sheinberg.

Wasserman couldn't believe he had been so betrayed by his corporate parents—and his own judgment. "It came at a time when it would have been good for us to do dramatic things," said Sheinberg. But that time had passed. "The question became: How do we get out of this mess?" Sheinberg recalled. Wasserman and Sheinberg resolved to buy back all of MCA. "I'm sure Edie pushed Lew to do that," said Goldberg. She hated to see her husband beg for permission to lead MCA into the new century. "She saw the sale as a mistake, too." Wasserman lined up financial backers, while Sheinberg huddled with the town's creative vanguard. However, thanks to the Wassermans' use of the press, rival executives now knew all about MCA's rift with its Japanese owner. Tele-Communications, Inc. chairman John C. Malone, QVC chairman Barry Diller, and others began inquiring about MCA, just as Chairman Matsushita called on Michael Ovitz to see if there was any way to salvage the strained situation.

But then along came Edgar Bronfman, Jr., the Seagram heir. In March 1995, he flew to Osaka to speak with the Japanese chairman and a month later announced an agreement: On April 7, 1995, Seagram Corp. would buy 80 percent of MCA for $5.7 billion. Bronfman's father, sixty-five-year-old Edgar M. Bronfman, Sr., called his old friend Wasserman to inform him of the done deal. Wasserman was polite, but he and Edie were outraged at being shut out of the loop. "It was awful that MCA was sold right out from under him," said Welkes. But Wasserman had done the same thing several times in his day, most recently with his surprise 1990 sale of MCA to foreigners, which he had kept from his own employees.

A few months later, Edgar, Jr., paid homage to Edie and Lew by throwing a party for them at Universal, on the stage of the 1925 movie *Phantom of the Opera.* That night Bronfman announced he was renaming the Black Tower the Lew Wasserman Building. Bronfman gave Edie a magnificent orchid plant with an envelope in its branches that contained a $100,000 check made out to her prized Motion Picture & Television Fund, along with a pledge to give $100,000 in each of the following nine years, for a total of $1 million. Gradually, the Wassermans recovered from their shock and hurt feelings over MCA's sale. They held out hope that, this time, they'd be treated better, given that their connections went way, way back. The rum-running Bronfmans had made their fortune smuggling whiskey from Canada into the United States, trading with Edie's father and Lew's bosses in Prohibition-era Cleveland. As Ned Tanen explained, "They thought Bronfman was going to be great."

Then the forty-year-old chief fired all of MCA's managers, including its veteran labor negotiators. Bronfman struggled in his new role and criticized Hollywood in general and Wasserman and Sheinberg in particular for poor management. The neophyte said that movies should be marketed like bottles of juice, priced according to their budget. A ticket for a $60 million hit like *Apollo 13* would therefore cost less than one for a $180 million fiasco like *Waterworld.* His proposal set off howls across town. When Bronfman sold off Universal's rich TV division—one of Lew's most enduring legacies—and scaled back Wasserman's ambitious theme-park plans, his personal stock fell even lower. He never even bothered to move to California, and shuttled between Universal City and his five-story town house on Manhattan's Upper East Side. "We see him in the office about twice a week," said one MCA executive assistant.

"I never knew there were so many ways to waste money," she added.

Then came other betrayals. Bronfman stripped the sterling MCA name from its buildings and mastheads and replaced it with "Universal," effectively burying Jules Stein's imprint. I asked Wasserman if that had saddened him, and he looked down at his enormous hands, and inspected his manicured nails. "I imagine it does," he said in a detached manner. "But the era had already passed after MCA's executives disappeared to death, resignation, or retirement," he explained. It was a wooden but media-savvy reply meant to deflect attention from the pretender to Lew's throne. Ever the gentleman, Wasserman would not stoop to criticize Bronfman publicly. Facts said it all. By 1998, Bronfman had spent three years and $100 million trying to reengineer the studio, using spreadsheets to quantify box-office potential. He had sold MCA's book-publishing arm, allowed the theme-park plans from Lew's regime to languish, and grossly overpaid—by 30 percent—for Polygram Music, forcing the layoffs of 500 employees and 250 recording artists.

"What happened to Lew under Bronfman was even worse than what occurred with the Japanese," said Tanen. "There was a colder reality to it." MCA was now owned by a newcomer who had no idea what he was doing. Sheinberg was furious. "This is not what Lew envisioned when he sold the company," he said. Bronfman then ushered Wasserman off MCA's board and secretly planned to demolish the Lew Wasserman Building after the old man died. Wasserman learned of the plans and reportedly felt confused. As one MCA executive explained, "Lew would never lower himself to speak out." Said another: "Lew's manner comes off as graciousness, and you know what? In this world, that's more than enough."

Meanwhile, Edie and Lew turned their private home into Hollywood, D.C., raising money for governors from faraway states. To some, their tented, catered, and valeted affairs seemed as absurd as a Fellini circus. Tanen kept wondering, "Why do these politicians keep coming out to Hollywood when they bum-rap our movies? Because this is where the big Jew money is," he said. "I'd look at some of these politicians and realize that this guy would throw us all into the oven if he could get away with it. Why are we giving him money? He doesn't care about California, or where we work." But to Edie and Lew, every challenger and incumbent represented a coupon they could redeem at a later date.

So it was exhilarating when, at this stage in their lives, Edie and Lew finally found their best man. Lew fell head over heels for Governor Bill Clinton, whom the couple had first met in the 1980s, when Clinton was governor of Arkansas, trying to lure producers to make films in his rural state. "Edie and Lew could smell power, whether it was in Hollywood, Washington, or Arkansas," Dominick Dunne explained. So when Clinton wanted to run for president, they helped and encouraged him. Hollywood's royal couple was also taken with Hillary Clinton, a strong, independent woman who over the years had remained loyal to her wandering husband, just as Edie had with Lew. No doubt the Wassermans also resonated with the sentiment that Clinton expressed when he referred to his wife in a campaign speech: "When you vote for me, you get two for the price of one."

The Wassermans and Clintons spent hours discussing the nation's ills and potential solutions. "Health care is a political football," Lew told me, with obvious disgust. "Everyone in this country should have the opportunity to get an education, a job, and medical care." That encapsulated much of Clinton's platform, and Edie and Lew supported it eagerly. They eventually attended the inauguration ball and, after a decade of Republican presidents, were optimistic about the country's new direction. But when President Clinton tried to pass a bill for universal health care, not even Hollywood's most griz-zled legislative strategists could have anticipated the fierce corporate opposition. Nor the intense investigations that followed the disclo-sure of Clinton's sexual scandal. All the while, Lew maintained fre-quent contact with Clinton, lending counsel, moral support, and raising funds for his $11 million legal defense. "Lew helped me become president, and he helped me stay president," Clinton said later. "He helped me become a better president, and never asked me for anything."

By the end of the 1990s, however, the world was crashing around Edie and Lew. Despite Seagram's fortune and his family's indomitable genes, Edgar Bronfman, Jr., could not master Lew's conglomerate. After barely five years, in May 2000, he sold Uni-versal to a bigger fool—a French water-utility company run by an exuberant Americanophile named Jean-Marie Messier. Just when Wasserman thought his company's prospects could not sink any lower, Messier went on a shopping binge, buying back what Bronfman had shed and then some: He repurchased Universal TV for $10 billion, Houghton Mifflin Publishers for $2 billion, and online music portal MP3.com for $372 million. The stock market rose to surreal heights. Company profits no longer mattered, said financial analysts. The hybrid called Vivendi/Universal began to swell with pretense and $34 billion in debt. It all became too ridiculous to recount, and Wasserman knew exactly how it would end. "I don't feel we're headed for a crash. I *know* we are," he told me, his eyes flashing. "It's just a question of when."

His industry was showing signs of discord. The availability of free music on the Internet, the jostling over new copyright laws, the marketing of R-rated movies to teenagers—these important issues were pitting studio conglomerates against each other. Not a chief among them could unify the group, not as Wasserman had done when he headed the Motion Picture Association of America. At the same time, Hollywood's unions kept hoping for a studio executive to step into Lew's shoes. Instead, the industry suffered a few contentious strikes—including an actors' walkout in 2000 and a writers' impasse in 2001. "It was so senseless," said one union official. Worse was that no one seemed willing to bring the skills and respect that Wasserman had always carried to the bargaining table. Rather, the new guard scoffed at the idea of working smoothly with unions, said Max Herman, former chief of the musicians' union. "I told some Park Avenue attorneys that when Lew Wasserman was around, we shook hands on an agreement and went back to work the next day. They laughed at me." He sounded hurt. "They said it takes months to get a contract and that unless everything is written down, it's no good. They said I was just an old man who was lying."

They also say that power is never seized or claimed, but proven over time, under duress, and in jubilation. Edie and Lew certainly possessed real power. Furthermore, they had the discipline to refrain from using it indiscriminately. And that characteristic—perhaps more than any other—marked them as true leaders in an industry that wasn't likely to see such a pair anytime soon.

EPILOGUE

In the final years of his life, Wasserman continued working most mornings at his fourteenth-floor office inside the Lew Wasserman Building, taking calls and greeting visitors. "He once said he didn't want to become just another rich Jew," said one of his marketing executives, and that fear kept him busy in politics, philanthropy, and new technology: He kept a laptop at his side, surfed the net and, at eighty-seven, sat on the board of a dot.com. Friends and former executives met Wasserman for lunch at the commissary, and they'd talk about the past and the future. But the present seemed too painful a subject. "I'm not going to comment on the industry today," he once snapped at me, and I understood. It had become too outlandish for words. The latest chief of Universal had, at the ripe age of forty-four, written his autobiography, *Jean-Marie Messier: Myself, Master of the World.* Worse, Messier was on his way to merrily losing $12 billion of Universal's money—another strike against the Frenchman. One got the sense that if Wasserman got started on the topic of the New Conglomerators, he'd break into a volcanic tantrum or a mournful silence. All of the studio owners were behaving like drunken sailors on a twenty-four-hour shore leave. Far better that Wasserman simply gather close his friends around himself, and recount old chestnuts and spin new tales until his Corleone voice grew hoarse.

About the only people who didn't visit Lew were the Vivendi/Universal executives who worked right below Lew's office. They didn't ask him about the company he had built, or the industry he had led for most of a century, and that mystified Wasserman's intimates. "Why didn't they just sit down and, you know, pick his brain?" Tony Curtis asked me. "That's where Lew lives, in his brain. Imagine to be able to exchange ideas with this giant figure."

Several veteran MCA executives also believed it was a mistake for the arrivistes to ignore the emperor. It seemed especially foolish given the intoxicating dangers of the so-called New Economy. Wasserman had seen many a boom and bust in his time, and if anyone had asked, he would have warned them to slow down. He could describe nearly every peak and pitfall that awaited a media pioneer. In 1949 he had sold one of the first big TV production packages, *The Adventures of Kit Carson,* and started writing production contracts that quickly became the standard among the networks. In 1950 he signed up corporate sponsors to pay for the TV programs made by Revue Productions. Wasserman knew the dangers that lurked behind wildly popular game shows like *Twenty-One,* and by 2000, you couldn't help but notice that his stories were not so much history lessons as directions for the future.

By then, deregulation had allowed about six studio-based entertainment giants to control most of the 500-odd TV channels. Yet, with few exceptions, the same sort of programs appeared on most channels. New programming concepts became riskier; show profits grew slimmer, and TV contracts began to change as audiences shrunk. As new technology like TiVo allowed consumers to skip TV commercials, corporate sponsors started to insert themselves directly into TV programs. It was déjà vu all over again. Just as General Electric once sponsored Revue's dramatic anthology series, Kellogg and Coca-Cola were signing deals to sponsor *The Sopranos* and *American Idol.*

As for game shows, they had been resurrected and, for the first time in forty years, were sweeping the ratings with *Who Wants to Be a Millionaire* and *Survivor.* Charges of collusion, fraud, and even poor taste dogged these productions, too, just as they had done in Lew's era. "The industry is going through a great deal of change today—in television, in movies, with the Internet and technology developments," Wasserman told me. "In my day, things weren't as complicated."

In February 1939, when Wasserman took over MCA's fledgling Hollywood operations, the business was rudimentary and far less acquisitive. And therein lies one of Lew's many secrets. By his own admission, MCA didn't become a Hollywood power until seven years later, after a long run of taking over the competition. In 1945 Wasserman bought the most prestigious agency, co-owned by Broadway producer Leland Hayward. Hayward's top clients— Jimmy Stewart, Clark Gable, and Henry Fonda—all returned to movie sets in 1946, after World War II, and Wasserman recalled: "That's when we really took off."

By then, he and his men had come to know the studio chiefs— and their weaknesses. "We couldn't believe how dumb these guys were business-wise," said Al Dorskind, chuckling. The MCA guys snickered about the rubes and pants pressers who didn't understand the tax implications of a percentage deal, or the benefits of talent corporations. Columbia's Harry Cohn had been a pool hustler; Jack Warner had operated nickelodeons; Paramount's Adolph Zukor had worked in the fur business. None of these men had studied finance, law, or tax codes as diligently as Lew Wasserman had. "The studio guys were crass and used four-letter words all the time," Dorskind explained. "They didn't know a thing about the professional way of doing business. That's why we had such a good time in the agency business. It didn't take much to do better than those guys."

Before Wasserman bought studio land in 1958, he was already running the town, dictating the studios' movie slates and casting films with his talent packages. But, like Edgar Bronfman or Jean-Marie

Messier, Wasserman did not truly appreciate the vagaries of manufacturing and selling aesthetic creations until he himself was an official mogul. In 1962 antitrust laws forbade Wasserman from owning too much of any one entertainment sector—unlike forty years later, when five media giants control about 90 percent of what we watch on TV and in movie theaters. By 2003, the landscape had fallen under the sway of an "oligopoly," said Barry Diller—"a handful of companies that are in charge of everything, both vertically and horizontally . . ."

And therein lies another of Wasserman's secrets. The old antitrust policies had left room in the market so that someone of Wasserman's ingenuity could join the competition. Regulation had confined him for a time, forcing him to concentrate and build his assets—instead of acquiring them willy-nilly. The old, moderate regulations actually counteracted the naturally rapacious appetites of big business. That balance, combined with Wasserman's immigrant work ethic and his unabashed love of the show, helped hone his ability to manage and lead.

That doesn't mean his path was marked with sunshine and roses. "Has there ever been an easy time in Hollywood?" he once asked me. In 1962, right before he became Universal Studios chief, he had been forced to dissolve his cozy arrangement with his agents and to compete for talent on the open market. He was angry and thrown off guard by the last-minute change in plans. But the resulting tension, conflict, and insecurities became catalysts for some of MCA's most brilliant creations. When Revue desperately needed TV sales in 1962, Wasserman and his men devised the first ninety-minute weekly series. When the company needed more TV sales to support its straggling studio, MCA inaugurated the first made-for-TV movies, and used the two-hour pilots to launch more new series. In 1968 one of Lew's favorite writers developed the idea of a ninety-minute made-for-TV movie, which landed MCA—and others—even more production business.

Universal Studios, once known for campy horror films, created bigger ways to lure dollars from audiences, beginning in 1970 with a string of disaster films. When that novelty wore off, Wasserman bent marketing rules to turn a "B" horror film into a blockbuster. He advertised *Jaws* on TV, released it wide and fast to a summer audience, and demonstrated the power of a promotional blitz. Movies would never be the same. His Universal Studios launched the commercial debuts of dozens of American filmmakers, from George Lucas to Amy Heckerling, and gave voice to such serious directors as Milos Forman and Constantin Costa-Gavras. And where would Hollywood be if Wasserman's studio had not nurtured überproducer Steven Spielberg, whose *Jurassic Park* made nearly $1 billion in 1993?

Lew's Rule set strict standards for budgets and schedules for the efficient production of weekly TV programs. The Wasserman Formula was used time and again in labor negotiations to give the creators of Hollywood's product—the writers—a sliver of the growing pie. But his idea of profit sharing was the Universal Deal—whereby everyone in the universe gets money before you, baby. Wasserman applied Moe Dalitz's habit of keeping two books to his own ledgers, and managed to turn it into an accepted standard. More than any man, Wasserman is responsible for spreading the funny-money accounting practices through the modern studio system and, arguably, beyond. Late-twentieth-century business barons like Ken Lay of Enron and Bernard Ebbers of WorldCom borrowed it for their own headline performances.

Wasserman was the first man to turn a studio into an entertainment conglomerate, replete with a TV production subsidiary, books and magazines, theme parks, music labels, banks, magnetic tape firms, R&D technology divisions, hotels, theaters, and even whoopee cushions. Edie called it "Wasserland," and over the decades her husband had built it all so patiently and deliberately that, for decades, he knew exactly how to run it. His grace and elegance made

Wasserland look like the birthright of every mogul. By the new millennium, though, other, far less capable men would jerry-build prefab constructions, cobbled together with overweening debt and mindless growth.

By 2002, Warner Studios was part of AOL/Time Warner, the world's largest media company, with Warner Music, Warner Brothers Studios, WB Network, CNN, HBO, TBS, and Time Inc. But the $38 billion asset firm was so obese that, some two years after its birth, the company's limbs were being sawed off to salvage its core.

Walt Disney Company was a $24 billion conglomerate with a studio, theme-park business, ABC network, and several cable channels, among other units. The sixty-one-year-old Michael Eisner has been chief for twenty years, collecting about $1 billion in salary, options, and bonuses during that time. By 2002, he was struggling to grow the company while trying to achieve his oft-repeated goal of "synergy." The carrot-topped octogenarian Sumner Redstone managed his $23 billion Viacom, which included Paramount Studios, MTV, CBS, and Simon & Schuster, well, but he seemed to enjoy public fights with his own executives. The aging Australian Rupert Murdoch owned his $14 billion News Corporation, including English and American tabloids, Twentieth Century Fox studio, and the right-wing, in-your-face Fox TV network. Murdoch wanted a global network of direct-broadcast satellites to beam his politically biased "news" shows all over the world—further narrowing the range of views. The former Columbia Studios, now called Sony, was a $9 billion fiefdom that includes Sony Pictures, Sony Music, Play Station, and TV shows, all part of a much-bigger Tokyo-based corporation.

None of these entities matched the breadth and longevity of Wasserland, yet all of these chiefs have borrowed Lew's model. In their effort to best Wasserman and his empire, a few actually brought down their studio-based conglomerates. None of the dismantlings was more painful to watch than the implosion of the $25 billion Universal/Vivendi. For thirteen years, Wasserman had tried to keep MCA intact as it was sold and resold. But neither the Japanese, nor the Canadians, nor the French could maintain—let alone grow—a corporation built by a high-school graduate. Wasserman had created a giant only he could control. Without him, Universal/Vivendi would soon be forced to sell its assets.

Meanwhile, Edie continued with her charitable and political work. One morning, as Wasserman was about to leave for the studio, he noticed a stranger slinking in his backyard bushes. "Who's that?" he asked the butler. "That's a Secret Service man, sir." Lew inquired: "What is he doing here?" The butler replied, "The President is coming to visit, sir." Wasserman realized that Bill Clinton was dropping by to cheer up his girl Edie, who had not been feeling well. "Oh, that's nice," Wasserman said, and walked out the front door. He knew his wife would be tickled by her visitor, and didn't want to spoil the surprise.

Edie had long been Wasserman's secret weapon and double agent, the fluctuating moon to his brilliant, constant sun. When she arrived in town in 1939, Edie had been shunned as the wife of a flesh peddler, and a new one at that. It took years for her to regain the high ground she had once held as the daughter of a prominent Cleveland attorney. Fortunately, she loved night lights and velvet ropes, and she danced for hours inside the swank clubs Ciro's, Mocombo, and the Trocadero. In the 1940s, she threw herself into the war effort, emerging as one of the town's most avid volunteers. She spent just as many hours with stars and directors as Lew did, and played muse and patroness to big-screen talents. And Lew's MCA agents never could have worked such inhuman hours without the support of their wives; Edie taught them how to cope and thrive in what became an arid, misogynistic town. With her piercing eyes, and passionate, sometimes acerbic, personality, she moved deftly, and far beyond most men's expectations.

As much as anyone, she had encouraged her husband to stay out of the limelight. Edie Beckerman knew from bitter experience the dangers of appearing in print, and she excelled at using the press, rather than allowing reporters to use her. "Nice people in those days didn't attract attention to themselves," said Judy Balaban Kanter. "It was unseemly and crude." But in the modern age of instant celebrities, Edie's reluctance to be courted in the press elevated her into a classy exception.

Her Hollywood Wives Club was the original, and its members cared more for one another's well being and company than they bothered with private gain or status. "We didn't connive against each other, not like the backstabbing that goes on today," said one of Edie's girls. After Edie moved on, the term "Hollywood wives" took on a pejorative meaning—as in vacuous, self-involved, and plastic. But Polly Bergen, Rosemary Clooney, Judy Balaban Kanter, and Edie "were the real thing," said Rex Reed.

By the time Lew became a mogul, Edie had refined her role. After the government had hounded Lew in 1962, Edie vowed never to suffer that indignity again. A descendant of a member of the Ohio gang, a prodigy of an old-style elections inspector, Edie took to national politics like a natural. She instinctively knew how to spot "winners," how to flatter and push, and when to support whose campaign for what reason. As the goddaughter of the Silent Syndicate, Edie had moxie and daring. She feared no one and nothing, said her friend Dominick Dunne. Her network of interlocking yet disparate pieces had served her well over the decades. She could shape social columns and stop broadcast-media stories. She had connections in many state capitols, legislative houses, and the West Wing. She had more pork-barrel sense than her own husband, managing to keep in touch with the Reagans long before "Ronnie" became chief of state, and plucking from obscurity Jimmy Carter, who became president, a world statesman, and Nobel Peace Prize winner.

By the year 2002, Edie's pet charity was being overshadowed by the expensive fundraising balls of the new Hollywood Wives. The widow of network chief Brandon Tartikoff, Lilly, had started the Fire and Ice Ball to raise money for an excellent cause, breast cancer. Marvin Davis's wife, Barbara, had her Carousel of Hope Ball, which benefited juvenile diabetes research. The number of lavish galas had multiplied exponentially since Edie had started her work in 1978. But unlike Edie's MPTF fundraising, these soirees sold tables for $100,000 and required dozens of big-name stars to show up. "Some stars will only come if their names are emblazoned somewhere on the wall," groused one gossip columnist. Added film producer Douglas Cramer: "I've been chagrined that not enough people in the entertainment business contribute [to causes] as I believe they should." Edie herself grew discouraged that so many younger talents ignored the town's flagship charity.

By then, the stock-market bubble had burst, the dot-com economy was imploding, and shamefaced CEOs began parading across the evening news. The last time I saw Wasserman was on September 29, 2001, and he looked shrunken and frail, unable to move without a cane. Even so, he stood above the crowd. Enron's Kenneth Lay and several of his executives were about to be ousted after snookering California's electricity customers. Tyco, Qwest Communications, Arthur Anderson, WorldCom, and dozens of other firms collapsed into bankruptcy, the victims of phony accounting and greed. These corporate leaders, malefactors with great wealth, had squeezed employees, cheated shareholders, and robbed working families of their savings and retirement. Wasserman knew most of these men, including Global Crossing's CEO Gary Winnick. Winnick had long admired Wasserman and had recently purchased MCA's illustrious old headquarters in Beverly Hills, with its Georgian columns and marble fountains. Endeavoring to catapult his company beyond MCA's starry heights, Winnick had named a conference room after Wasserman and invited Edie and Lew to its grand opening.

The couple dropped the poseur immediately after he looted $734 million from his publicly traded company and retired to his $94 million mansion. By then, celebrity CEOs had turned an entire class of men into apes and jackals, cruder than the foul-mouthed pants pressers who had built Hollywood a century earlier. For Wasserman, this was a distressing turn of events. "It was like that in 1930, when I was in high school," he told me glumly. "All you needed was a Depression."

The end came on June 3, 2002, when Lew died. Weeks earlier, he had suffered a heart attack and was placed on life support. Edie had braced herself and was ready when he finally passed on. She didn't want an L. B. Mayer-like funeral or a Frank Sinatra-size tribute. The industry was no longer a town, but it still needed to mourn the passing of its patriarch. On July 15 Edie allowed a memorial service to take place inside the Universal Amphitheater. Former President Bill Clinton, House Minority Leader Richard Gephardt, Governor Gray Davis, a passel of Kennedys, several senators and two former first ladies—Nancy Reagan and Lady Bird Johnson—attended, alongside Jodie Foster, Sharon Stone, Warren Beatty, Ron Howard, and some 4,000 other stars and leaders. There were a few speakers, but one man stood out.

Wasserman had been a wizard of one of the last mysterious arts and over the years he had practiced his unique brand of alchemy in both darkness and in light. But compared to the black-hearted four-flushers of the new millennium, he really had behaved like a prince among thieves. "I would fly anywhere to be part of anything associated with Lew Wasserman," said John Sweeney, head of the AFL-CIO. "Most of the CEOs today have made their money by stepping on people on their climb up. But not Lew. He started out at the bottom and never forgot what that had felt like."

Endnotes

I conducted more than 450 interviews for this book. All quoted passages are from those interviews (as noted below by A.I., for "Author Interview") unless otherwise noted. Many sources sat for multiple interviews. I tried to avoid anonymous sources as well as as those who declined to be named. But in the few instances where unnamed sources are noted, the dates of the interview are given.

Prologue
p. x: "On their first . . . have a chance." Pleshette, at Lew Wasserman's memorial service, July 15, 2002.
p. xii: "I'm sure he . . . told me." A.I. Goldberg, May 8, 2003.
p. xiii: "I can't think . . . own," he said." Valenti, at the MPTF home, Oct. 31, 1998.
p. xiv: "Women in this town . . . turn mean." A.I. Muhl, May 5, 1997.
p. xiv: "As Lew himself . . . for granted," A.I. Wasserman, Nov. 3, 1999.
p. xiv: "Jimmy lived at . . . cheer him up." A.I. Leigh, Feb. 5, 1998.
p. xiv: "Three years later . . . 'my favorite friend.'" Wasserman as quoted in "He was the Real Thing," by Leonard Klady, *Variety*, July 3, 1997.
p. xv: "She was a driving . . . .front lines." A.I. Payne, June 12, 2002.
p. xv: "Edie was the . . . longtime reporter." A.I. Alec Ben Block, July 15, 2002.
p. xv: "Today, the so-called . . . .affect our times." A.I. Reed, Jan. 30, 2002.
p. xvi: "That night, I was . . . to imply." A.I. Wasserman, June 10, 1999.
p. xvii: "I had never seen . . . better and faster.'" A.I. Wasserman, June 22, 1999.
p. xvii: "He loved talking . . . clay and abuse." A.I. June 10, 1999.
p. xvii: "Lew was the . . . I ever met." A.I. Merle Jacobs, Feb. 1, 1997.
p. xvii:. "For example . . . to get in." A.I. Herb Steinberg, Aug. 4, 1998.
p. xvii: "We didn't have . . . second day." A.I. June 22, 1999.
p. xvii: "Think . . . a subject." A.I. Nov. 3, 1999.
p. xviii: "Yet, when . . . We did not." A.I. June 22, 1999.
p. xviii: "By the way . . . class acts." A.I. Nov. 3, 1999.
p. xviii–xix: "The studio-based conglomerates . . . immeasureable harm." Taken from

the Economic Report of April 22, 2002, published by the International Intellectual Property Alliance, a group composed primarily of entertainment corporations and their subsidiaries.

p. xix: Federal revenue . . . in annual revenues." The $135 billion figure equals the 2001 revenues of all six studio-based conglomerates gleaned from each of their annual reports.

Part I

Chapter 1

p. 3: Descriptions in this scene were culled from interviews with Ed Muhl, May 5, 1997, and Sept. 18, 1997; Al Dorskind, Feb. 26, 1997, April 1, 1997, and Aug. 4, 1998; one undisclosed source; several 1950s photographs of Universal Studios.

p. 3: "The studio hadn't won . . . $2 million a year in 1958." A.I. Bernard Dick, June 22, 1996.

p. 4: A.I. Ed Muhl, May 5, 1997; Sept 18, 1997.

p. 4: A.I. Wasserman, June 22, 1999.

p. 4: "He looked like the type . . ." From Karl Kramer's personal papers; MCA history from "Star-Spangled Ocotopus," David Wittles, *Saturday Evening Post* Aug. 10, 1946.

p. 5: "When big stars had no pensions . . . " Clinton, Anderson, *Beverly Hills Is My Beat* (Prentice-Hall, 1960), p. 10.

p. 5: A.I. Berle Adams, March 31, 1997.

p. 5: "We didn't need to . . . blood," A.I. unnamed, April 14, 1998.

p. 5: A.I. Sam Jaffee, April 21, 1998.

p. 5: "If necessary . . . he did it twenty times," A.I. unnamed, Feb. 4, 1997.

p. 6: A.I. Ronnie Lubin, Feb. 18, 1998.

p. 6: "Few people left . . . $13 million in today's dollars." Deals include Ronald Reagan's $3,500 a week for 42 weeks for 7 years as detailed in *The Agency*, by Frank Rose, p. 81, to the package for "The Young Lions," July 1960 issue of *Fortune*, p. 115; today's value computed using the government's Consumer Price Index figures.

p. 6: "By 1958 . . . Mayer." Dates of deaths of moguls from *The Film Encyclopedia*, Ephraim and Klein.

p. 6: A.I. Frank Price, Aug. 5, 1998.

p. 6: A.I. Bernard Dick, June 22, 1996.

p. 6: A.I. Price, Feb. 18, 1998.

p. 7: "'No interviews. No panels . . . suit.'" Lubin; A.I. Roy Gerber, March 27, 1998.

p. 7: A.I. John Weber, Aug. 7, 1998.

p. 7: A.I. Al Dorskind, Feb. 26, 1997.

p. 7: "Stein had started his plan . . . 1940s." London Sunday *Times*, June 17, 1983.

p. 7–8: "On Halloween, 1951, . . . $1 per share." *Variety* story, Oct. 31, 1951.

p. 8: A.I. Joe Delaney, "'Stein made a deal . . . two companies.'" April 10, 1998; Also *City of Dreams*, by Bernard Dick, discusses stock deal in pp. 157-159. A.I. Dick June 26, 1996.

p. 8: "Vice president Taft Schreiber . . . consigliere." Karl Kramer's papers.

p. 8: A.I. unnamed source, March 20, 1997.

p. 9: "Wasserman greeted Nate Blumberg . . ." *New York Times*, July 25, 1960 obit.

p. 9: "The deal . . . said a studio executive." A.I. March 20, 1997.

p. 9: "All Hollywood studios . . . could barely post a profit." Joel Finler. *The Holly-wood Story* (Crown Publishers, 1988), under each studio listing.

p. 10: Selznick quote: Gabler, Neal, *An Empire of Their Own* (Doubleday, 1988), p. 425.

p. 10: "The biggest studio . . . independent filmmakers." A.I. Muhl, Sept. 18, 1997.

p. 11: A.I. Wasserman, June 22, 1999.

p. 11: "Between 1954..some $50 million a year." *Fortune*, "No Business Like MCA's Business," July 1960, p. 115; also MCA's first annual report, dated 1959, p. 3.

p. 12: "Rackmil faced Dorskind . . . business in a dying industry." A.I. Dorskind, Feb. 26, 1997.

p. 13: "The MCA men then walked out . . . historical ground." Pictures from Universal's archives, *Universal City-History* (1960 file).

p. 13: "This was the site of . . . Sherman Oaks, and Encino." A.I. Jim Gulbranson of the San Fernando Valley Historical Society, March 17, 1999; also materials from special collection in the Los Angeles Public Library.

p. 13: "And here is where 'uncle' . . . East Coast bullies." John Drinkwater, *The Life and Adventures of Carl Laemmle*, 1931.

p. 14 "At the end of the century . . . most European nations." From International Intellectual Property Alliance, "Copyright Industries in the U.S. Economy" report; also iipa.com, copyright and trade issues.

p. 14: "Wasserman and the men . . . on the ten-year note." A.I. Dorskind, Feb. 26, 1997.

p. 14: "It was a hell of a deal." A.I. J.B. Lesser, Oct. 2, 1996.

p. 15: "Wasserman's deal . . . and equipment." A.I. B. R., March 20, 1997.

p. 15: "The Internal . . . agents hooted." A.I. Dorskind, April 1, 1997.

p. 15: "As one Decca . . . Rackmil.'" Joe Delaney, April 10, 1998.

Chapter 2

p. 15–16: "The wizards . . . discreet brass plate." Taken from MCA's property sale pamphlet, "America's Most Distinguished Office Building," author's collection; also *Paul R. Williams, Architect, A Legacy of Style*, by Karen E. Hudson, pp. 24-25; 91-95.

p. 16: "Lew Wasserman . . . done yesterday.'" A.I. Kory, Aug. 7, 1998.

p. 16: "There were the usual . . . arranged for her." A.I. Welkes, March 28, 1998.

p. 16: "Joan Crawford . . . hotel room." A.I. Mrs. Art Park, April 16, 1998.

p. 16: "Charles Bronson . . . for another agency." Frederick Kohner, *The Magician of Sunset Boulevard*, (Morgan Press, 1977) p. 129.

p. 16: "Then there were . . . phenobarbital." Clinton Anderson, *Beverly Hills iI My Beat* (Prentice Hall, 1960), p. 8; *Vanity Fair*, "The Neighborhood," April 1999.

p. 16: "The chief . . . or its stars." Anderson, p. 8.

p. 16–17: "According to several ex-officers . . . and clients." A.I. Hal Yarnell, March 26, 1998; Roger Otis, July 1, 1998; R. Johnson, Sept. 20, 1996; Charles Reese, Feb. 13, 1998.

p. 17: "The captain debriefed . . . clients." Yarnell, and off-record from MCA executive.

p. 17: "Stein had . . . contracts and ledgers." A.I. Adams, March 31, 1997.

p. 17: "In 1948, the wife of MCA . . . counteroffer to the comedians." A.I. Jim Murray, Roy Gerber, March 27, 1998.

p. 17: A.I. Greshler Feldmann; May 20, 1998; lawsuit mentioned in *Daily News*, August 29, 1950; *Variety*, Nov. 23, 1949; A.I. Arthur Kalish, Oct. 26, 1996.

p. 17: "Lew had maybe 250 agents . . . knows it." A.I. Fields, Feb. 26, 1997.

p. 18: "Yet Wasserman . . . production facilities.'" A.I. Henry Miller, July 15, 1997

p. 18: "'Work hard . . . last very long.'" A.I. Wasserman interview, Nov. 3, 1999.

p. 18: "Wasserman's wood-paneled . . . loved it.'" A.I. Myrle Wages, March 27, 1998.

p. 18: "MCA's offices . . . first hires." From Karl Kramer's private papers.

p. 19: "Studio chiefs braced . . . after that." *Fortune* article, July 1960.

p. 19: "They were expected . . . said one agent." A.I. Adams, March 31, 1997.

p. 20: "Fagin meetings . . . quit now, he bellowed. " A.I. Ned Tanen, July 7, 1998.

p. 20: "After these . . . drink or dinner." George Chasen quoted "Lew & Edie Wasserman," by Marshall Berges, *Los Angeles Times Home Magazine*, Dec. 2, 1973.

p. 20: Herman Citron; A.I. Wages, March 27, 1998.

p. 20: Arthur Park: A.I. Mrs. Park, April 17, 1998.

p. 20: "As one producer . . . demanding." A.I. D. L., Feb. 4, 1997.

p. 20: "One time . . . get rid of him." A.I. Gerber, March 27, 1998.

p. 21: "Wasserman recessed . . . to sell." A.I. Murray, March 27, 1998.

p. 22: "There were . . . junior agent." A.I. A.B., Nov. 11, 1996.

p. 22: "One was William . . . action going." A.I. Goldfarb, Feb. 18, 1998.

p. 22: "Another critic . . . Siegel of GAC." A.I. Gerber, who worked for Siegel and Murray, July 1, 1998.

p. 22: "Federal investigators . . . repeated the same allegations." *Dark Victory*, by Dan Moldea, p. 133; A.I. Miller July 15, 1997; Goldfarb Feb. 18, 1998 and Weber, Aug. 11, 1998.

Chapter 3

p. 22–23: "At five o'clock . . . hair down." A.I. Jackie Gershwin, June 23, 1998.

p. 23: "Respected and feared . . . at Edie's house." A.I. Janet Leigh, June 19, 1998.

p. 23: "According to . . . her for advice." A.I. Kanter, Jan. 23, 1996.

p. 23: "Petite and vivacious . . . could be a flirt." A.I. Jacobs, Feb. 1, 1997.

p. 23: "While Lew . . . Cleveland Heights, Ohio." Descriptions of both houses verified by author viewing; Thank you to Cleveland realtor Donna Onda, at Chagrin Valley Realty Co., for interview and materials about Edie's childhood home, sent Dec. 11, 1997, and to Sharon Coyle, then-owner of Edie's home, for the photos and interview Dec. 19, 1997.

p. 24: "The home featured . . . Estevez." A.I. Luis Estevez, Dec. 5, 2000.

p. 24: "Occasionally, Edie . . . Cock 'n' Bull." A.I. Leigh, Feb. 5, 1997.

p. 24: "Though the granddaughter . . . 'too negative.'" A.I. A.B., Nov. 11, 1998; Also, Eddie Fisher, *Been There, Done That*, p. 90.

p. 27: "In late afternoon . . . her gossip." A.I. Leigh, Feb. 5, 1998; A.I. Gershwin, Sept. 15, 1998; "No one understood . . . MCA executive." Rosenthal as quoted in "Lew," Susan Deutsch, Calfiornia, March 1985.

p. 25: "The first . . . she explained." A.I. Gershwin, June 23, 1998.

p. 25: "Another member . . . up to MCA's door." A.I. secretary Jane Rosenbaum, July 9, 1998, and June 19, 1998

p. 25–26: "Janet Leigh . . . undying loyalty." A.I. Feb. 5, 1998.

p. 26: "Sometimes . . . on his behalf." A.I. Jackie Gershwin, June 23, 1998. Details of Martin's acting career, "Tales of Dear Old Dad," Jan. 23, 2002, in *Los Angeles Times;* also from *Dino*, by Nick Tosches (Doubleday).

p. 26: "Then there was . . . and TV performer." A.I. Gershwin, Feb. 23, 1998.

p. 26–27: "Rounding out . . . through me." A.I. Judy Balaban Kanter, March 19, 2001

p. 27: "Her husband . . . network specials." A.I. Miller and Thompson, *Fortune*, July 1960.

p. 28: "I know that Janet . . . to juggle." A.I. Tony Curtis, Feb. 17, 2000.

p. 29: "It became Edie's . . . ice sculpture of a stork." A.I. Gershwin; also described in *Girl Singer*, by Rosemary Clooney (Doubleday, 1999), p. 150.

p. 29: "MCA syndicated . . . not including rerun income." *Fortune* piece; estimates based on interviews with MCA agents Jim Murray and Roy Gerber.

p. 29: "Clooney's private life . . . sleeping pills." Clooney's book; A.I. Balaban, March 19, 2001; A.I. Leigh Feb. 5, 1998.

Chapter 4

Much of this chapter based on several interviews over a year's time with Twenty-One producers and executives Fred Stettner, Al Freedman and Howard Felscher. Some of the material, but not all, is also recounted in the fine book by former Assistant District Attorney Joseph Stone, Prime-Time and Misdemeanors: Investigating the 1950s TV Quiz Scandal, (Rutgers University Press, New Jersey, 1992). Former federal investigator Richard Goodwin also relates some of this in one chapter of his book, Remembering America, which was the basis of the 1994 movie *Quiz Show*. But his version differs with the one provided herein. He did not respond to an interview request, Herb Stempel declined to be interviewed and Charles Van Doren did not respond to several interview requests.

p. 30: "Park Avenue . . . gold bullion." Frank B. Schwengel, story in *New York Times*, Dec. 5, 1958.

p. 30: "The Wassermans . . . in town that week." A.I. Adams, March 31, 1997.

p. 30: "Edie . . . eldeset daughter." From "Jules Stein daughter Will Wed Easterner," by Louella Parsons, Sept. 5, 1958, *Los Angeles Herald Examiner;* also *Variety*, Dec. 8, 1958.

p. 30–31: "With MCA's . . . and nineteenth floors." A.I. with Stettner, Oct. 10, 2002.

p. 31: "The scandal . . . twenty-two quiz shows on network TV." A.I. Freedman, Nov. 3, 2001; also *Prime-Time and Misdemeanors*, Stone, p. 213.

p. 31: "New York prosecutors . . . depositions." Stone, pp 121-135.

p. 31: "Si, in December, . . . was the man." A.I Welkes, March 25, 1998.

p. 32: "Werblin . . . West Coast office." From Kramer's papers.

p. 32: "Upon becoming president . . . suit well-pressed." A.I. Charlton Heston, July 28, 1998.

p. 32–33: "Wasserman needed Werblin . . . guys who aired them." Kramer's papers; A.I. Tom Werblin, Oct. 28, 2002.

p. 33: "Now, seven years later . . . .way to limit the damage." A.I. Al Freedman, April 2, 2000.

p. 33: "On Friday . . . corporate captains." From story *Variety*, Dec. 10, 1958; also Parsons, *Herald Examiner*, Sept. 5, 1958.

p. 34: "To Jean's girlfriends . . . .take my eyes off him." A.I. Patsy Miller Krauskopf, Aug. 2, 1998.

p. 34: "It was odd . . . parties." A.I. Balaban Kanter, March 19, 2001.

p. 34. "She denigrated her . . . Marion." A.I. Phillips, Feb. 7, 1997.

p. 34–35: "[The wedding] . . . Moore and Trubin in New York . . . " item in *Hollywood Reporter*, Dec. 8, 1958.

p. 35: "Everyone was talking . . . program irregularities." A.I. Stettner; Stone, p. 268.

p. 35–36: "Quiz shows . . . Revlon." Stone, p. 213.

p. 36: "After that hit . . . MCA." A.I. Stettner, Oct. 10, 2002.

p. 36: "We were . . . he or she would answer." A.I. Freedman, Dec. 6, 1999.

p. 36: "Since neither . . . de rigueur." Stone, p. 321.

p. 36–37: "When CBS's show . . . with a plan." A.I. Stettner, Aug. 11, 2000; A.I. Freedman. April 2, 2000.

p. 37: "At the time . . . programming chief." *The General: David Sarnoff*, Kenneth Bilby (Harper & Row, 1986), p. 40.

p. 37: "In October 1956 . . . make this work.' " A.I. Stettner Aug. 11, 2000; Oct. 10, 2002; A.I. Freedman Dec. 6, 1999; Aug. 5, 2002; A.I. Felscher, Aug. 1, 2002.

p. 38: "The show gave away . . . in today's dollars." A.I. Freedman; CPI index numbers, Bureau of Labor Statistics.

p. 38: "In November . . . the Jewish character." A.I. Freedman, April 2, 2000.

p. 38: "Charles Van Doren . . . moral theater." *Time* magazine, Feb. 11, 1957.

p. 39: "On December 5 . . . missed a question deliberately." Stone, p. 118.

p. 39: "Wasserman watched the show," A.I. Gershwin, Dec. 15, 1999.

p. 39: "The next year, . . . total revenue," Stone, p. 36; 178-182.

p. 39: "When the courtly . . . costs for *Twenty-One*." Stone p. 167; 181.

p. 39: "In early 1957 . . . their attorneys." Stone, pp. 180-182; A.I. Stettner Oct. 10, 2002.

p. 39–40: "The only glitch was . . . Enright sought advice." A.I. Stettner Oct. 10, 2002. Parts of this recounted by Stone's book.

p. 40: "Lew knew what was going on with the show." A.I. Freedman, Aug. 5, 2002; A.I. Stettner, Aug. 11, 2002; A.I. Felscher, Sept. 11, 2002.

p. 41: "On May 2, 1957 . . . sale price was $2.22 million." Stone, p. 181; A.I. Stettner, Aug. 11, 2000.

p. 41–42: "But that didn't . . . . .to a twenty-year-contract." *New York Times*, "Rainer and Wife," Dec. 5, 1958; Dec. 8, 1958.

p. 42: "It was a sentimental . . . one guest." A.I. Eleanor Phillips, Feb. 7, 1997

p. 42: "Mrs. Stein was . . . " A.I. Wages, March 27, 1998.

p. 42 "I saw Edie later . . ." A.I. unnamed source, March 5, 1998.

p. 42: *Variety*, Dec. 10, 1958.

Chapter 5

p. 43: A.I. Balaban Kanter, March 19, 2001.

p. 43–44: "Indeed, MCA had a long . . . said one old-time agent." Karl Kramer manuscript, Chapter IV, p. 4.

p. 44: "Stein and . . . New York Stock Exchange . . ." *Fortune*, March 1937.

p. 44–45: "Balaban and the moguls . . . feudal system." Douglas Gomery, *Shared Pleasures*, p. 231, 248, 249.

p. 45: "Without a guaranteed . . . not the studio chiefs." A.I. Douglas Gomery, Feb. 6, 1997.

p. 45: "Before the . . . KTLA." *Variety*, Oct. 26, 1949; A.I. Dorskind; Klaus Landsberg Biography, KTLA (1959).

p. 45: "Wasserman . . . package of vocalists." Story in *Variety*, March 16, 1949, "American Tobacco's announced . . ."

p. 45: "In September . . . *Kit Carson.*" A.I. archivist Ronnie James, June 26, 1998.

p. 45–46: "Wasserman scrambled to . . . union members." A.I. Roy Brewer, April 17, 1998.

p. 46: "Continental Studio," From Gene Kelly biography, p. 111.

p. 46: "In 1958, Jules . . . $2.2 million." A.I. Dick, June 22, 1996; *Fortune*, July 1960, p. 165

p. 46: "Those metal canisters . . . *Wizard of Oz.*" Gomery, *Shared Pleasures*, pp. 248-9.

p. 46–47: "In late 1957, . . . MCA's counteroffer." A.I. Adams, Feb. 20, 1998; also papers from Justice Department filings, spring 1958; Moldea, *Dark Victory*, p. 125.

p. 47: "Wasserman offered . . . could sell." MCA annual report, 1960; A.I. Dorskind, April 1, 1997.

p. 47: "But Wasserman knew . . . time." *Fortune*, p. 165.

p. 47: "Before the ink had dried . . . at least initially." A.I. Adams, Feb. 20, 1998.

p. 48: "Independent stations . . . networks paid." Jules Stein, current biography, 1967 edition, p. 401.

p. 48: "MCA was making so . . . few years." MCA Annual Report, 1961, note 3.

p. 48: "Wasserman's deal earned . . . authorities." J.A. Trachtenberg, "A rare look at the most powerful," *W*, Oct. 8-15, 1982; Adams and Justice Department filings, spring 1958.

p. 48: "Assistant Attorney . . . pertaining to the Paramount sale." Moldea, *Dark Victory* p 58.

p. 48–49: "He knew that Werblin . . . a drink?" A.I. Adams, Feb. 5, 1998. Moldea, *Dark Victory*, p. 128.

Chapter 6

p. 49–50: "In the spring of 1959 . . . homey touches . . ." Muhl, Sept. 18, 1997; also *Variety*, May 21, 1959.

p. 50: "After a day of shooting . . . thin-lipped suits." A.I. Curtis Feb. 17, 2000.

p. 50: "Universal Studios was making . . . Spartacus . . . " Hirschhorn, *The Universal Story*, pp. 253-255.

p. 50: "On the same grounds . . . *Frontier Circus.*" *Variety*, Sept. 29, 1959; A.I. Adams Feb. 20, 1998.

p. 50: "Not every Revue . . . only eleven films in 1959." A.I. Muhl, May 5, 1997.

p. 50: "Revue was churning out . . . mediocre." *Variety*, Sept. 29, 1959. Also, $33 million figure.

p. 50–51: "Despite the load . . . me years later." A.I. Wasserman, Nov. 3, 1999.

p. 51: "At one point . . . endangered list." A.I. Jo Swerling, Jr., Feb. 22, 2000.

p. 51: *Thriller* details from Internet Movie Data Base; *Thriller* lasted for two years.

p. 51–52: Conversation between Swerling and Wasserman, A.I. Swerling Feb.22, 2000.

p. 52: "Wasserman . . . Bing Crosby." A.I. Jay Kanter, Jan. 23, 1998.

p. 53: "That way . . . and back again." Adams, A.I. Feb. 20, 1998.

p. 53: "When he arrived in Los angeles . . . he boasted to me." Wasserman, June 22, 1999.

p. 54: "Actually, it had been . . . .cooking lessons." KTLA, Tech-Notes, TV, 1959.

p. 54: "The older music . . . he recalled." A.I. Wasserman, A.I. June 22, 1999.

p. 54: "Lew turned . . . corporate programming." A.I. Ronnie James, June 26, 1998.

p. 54: "Before long . . . General Electric Theater." Museum of Radio and TV archives.

p. 54–55: "Kraft Foods . . . like Ronald Reagan." A.I. James, A.I. June 26, 1998; archivist Original Filmvideo Library; also Museum of Radio TV archives.

p. 55: "You have to . . . for a G.E. show host." A.I. Adams, Feb. 2, 1998.

p. 55: "In 1953 . . . each episode." Anne Edwards, *The Early Years,* pp. 424-434.

p. 55. "The program ended . . . .in the ratings." Screen Source, on-line listing of top TV shows per decade.

p. 55: "Reagan's role . . . than him." A.I. Laird Koening, Aug. 20, 26, 1998.

p. 55: "Reagan made $125,000 . . . years of movie acting." *Dark Victory,* pp. 183-189; Anne Edwards, *Early Reagan,* p. 435.

p. 55: "And each year . . . behind the scenes." A.I. Park, April 16, 1998.

p. 55–56: "Reagan's Pacific . . . all for free." A.I. Park, Ibid; Kitty Kelly, *Nancy Reagan* (Pocket Books), p. 97.

p. 56: "Reagan gained . . . Actors Guild." Reagan's biographical listing, Presidential Library.

p. 56: "In 1955 Schreiber . . . not prestige." *Early Reagan,* p. 441; SAG archives.

p. 56: "Although SAG . . . should not have." SAG archives, A.I. Valerie Yaro, Nov. 25, 2002.

p. 56: "In February 1959 . . . old movies sold to TV." A.I. Berle Adams, Feb. 20 1998; A.I. Yaro; A.I. James.

p. 56–57: "The Stein manse . . . .colony summered." Description from eye witness account, Oct. 3, 1997.

p. 57: "On party nights . . . of the door." A.I. Estevez, Dec. 5, 2000.

p. 57: "Doris adored . . . like her husband." A.I. Philips Jan. 27, 1997; Philips verified list of guests and their occupations.

p. 57: "She invited . . . Insurance Company." Call and the others would soon join the "millionaires group" that would propel Ronald Reagan into the governorship; Oppenheimer also verified list of Stein's guests and their ventures.

p. 57 "Mother organized . . . in a party mood." A.I. Oppenheimer, Aug. 12, 1997.

p. 58: "Dr. Stein . . . miraculously recovered." A.I. Wasserman, A.I., June 22,1999.

p. 58: "Several times . . . two butlers." A.I. Luis Estevez, Dec. 5, 2000.

p. 58: "Between the parties . . . which grated on Wasserman." A.I. Adams, Feb. 5, 1998.

p. 58: "But he was..throne." A.I. Rosenbaum, June 26, 1998.

p. 59: "Lew was . . . whom it represented." A.I. Gerber, Feb. 5, 1998.

p. 59: "Schreiber disagreed . . . secretive Wasserman." A.I. Oppenheimer, Aug. 12, 1997.

p. 59: ". . . gross revenues..to $48 million." MCA's annual report, 1959.

p. 59: "Without planning . . . the problem." Thompson, *Fortune,* July 1960, p 117.

p. 59: ". . . buildings that house . . . to his own company." Ibid.

p. 59: "Stair & Co . . . .imports." A.I. Adams; A.I. Krauskopf, March 7, 2001.

p. 60: "When necessary . . . in the room." A.I. Artie Shaw, June 13, 1995.

p. 60: "Most of the time . . . absent." A.I. PhilipsJan. 27, 1997; A.I. Estevez, Dec. 5, 2000; A.I. Shaw, Ibid.

p. 60–61: List of guests: A.I. Oppenheimer Aug. 12, 1997; Esteves and Philips Ibid.

p. 61: "In 1959 . . . .worth about $12.5 million; *Fortune*, July 1960.

Chapter 7

p. 62: "Lew looked . . . come home and collapse." A.I.. Gershwin, July, 3, 1998.

p. 62: ". . . sofa in the den . . . IATSE." A.I. Roy Brewer, April 17, 1998.

p. 62: ". . . One weekend . . . .Sunday afternoon." A.I. Tony Curtis, Feb. 17, 2000; A.I. Janet Leigh.

p. 64: "Marlon Brando . . . .advisor." "Brando" by Richard Schinkel (St. Martin's) p. 82.

p. 64: "Marilyn Monroe..on him." A.I. Rosenbaum, June 26, 1998.

p. 64: "Former client Grace . . . from the industry." Some of this chapter comes from *Bridesmaids*, by Judy Balaban Quine, (Weidenfield & Nicholson, 1989).

p. 64: "Sometimes the Martins . . . and Anne Douglas." A.I. Gershwin, June 23, 1998.

p. 65: "At 34, Curtis . . . *Winchester 73*." Curtis' biography, p. 115.

p. 66: "Both studios and . . . regular salaries." A.I. Curtis. Feb. 17, 2000.

p. 66: "It would be . . . *Great Love Teams*." Janet Leighs' studio bio.

p. 67: "Wasserman pulled . . . *The Young Lions*," A.I. D.L, Feb. 5, 1997; *Fortune*, July 1960.

p. 67 "*Variety* called . . . saved his career." *Variety*, March 17, 1958.

p. 67: "Martin shrugged off . . . truth in his words." Tosches, *Dino*, p. 331.

Chapter 8

p. 69: "In the summer of 1959 . . . plenty about MCA . . ." A.I. Adams, Feb. 5, 1998; Welkes, March 28, 1998; Park, April 16, 1998.

p. 69: "Stien had bought . . . Oval Office." From a brochure about the history of "Global Crossing Plaza." Thank you to Gary Winnick's office.

p. 69: "To the FBI . . . can touch us." Based on DOJ memos, sections of Moldea, *Dark Victory*, and clippings in Universal Studio archives; also A.I. Malcolm MacArthur Aug. 31, 1998.

p. 69–70: "The Justice Department . . . smaller agencies." A.I. Miller; July 15, 1997; A.I. Adams, Feb. 5, 1998; also, John Cones, "Politics, Movies and the Role of Government," on-line MCA's anti-trust sins.

p. 70: "Now Wasserman . . . MCA's ploys." A.I. MacArthur, Aug. 31, 1998; A.I. Adams, Feb. 29, 1998.

p. 70: "Arthur Park . . . intimidated you." A.I. Mrs. Park, April 16, 1998.

p. 70: "Among them were . . . agency profits." Eddie Fisher, *My Lives, My Loves*, (1988) pp. 136, 138.

p. 70–71: "Sonny Werblin . . . later told investigators." Ibid.

p. 71: "Tensions . . . the boss really is." DOJ memo that Fisher said he saw (Ibid).

p. 71 "Fisher was furious." Ibid.

p. 72: "Cary Grant . . . tailor-made for him." Nancy Nelson, *Evenings with Cary Grant* (William Morrow and Co., 1991) p. 157.

p. 72: "But Wasserman . . . .50-year-old Stewart." A.I. Maureen Donaldson (Grant's ex-girlfriend) A.I. April 5, 1999; John J. Puccio, DVD Town.com.

p. 72: "The following year . . . *Vertigo*." imdb.com for *Vertigo*.

p. 72: "The film . . . ended the meeting." A.I. unnamed source, A.B. July 29, 1997; A.I. Curtis, Feb. 17, 2000; DOJ documents.

p. 73: "Producer Walter . . . first choice." A.I. Seltzer, July 15, 1997.

p. 73: "Stars like . . . is inside." From *SHOW* magazine, Feb. 1962, courtesy of SAG.

p. 73: "More damaging . . . all-inclusive contracts." I.A. Adams, Feb. 29, 1998.

p. 74: "The Andy Williams . . . financial success." Archives at IDB.com

p. 74: "GAC's top agent . . . for the GAC client." A.I. Henry Miller, March 5, 1998.

p. 74–75: "Soon even big . . . too big." A.I. Steve Allen, March 6, 1997

p. 75: ". . . the FBI . . . a few months earlier." FBI report, Sept. 16, 1962.

p. 75: "I had so many . . . of the month." A.I. Welkes, March 28, 1998.

p. 75: "The rigid code of . . . aggression." A.I. Ned Tanen, July 7, 1998.

p. 75: "Like Mafiosi . . . ethnic groups." Robert Warshaw, *The Gangster as Tragic Hero*, article from 1948; published in book form (Atheneum, 1975).

p. 75: "They didn't . . . Fusco to Murray." A.I. Murray, July 1, 1998.

p. 75: ". . . norms (that) . . . passed up to the chief." Alan Abner Block, "Lepke, Kid Twist and The Combination," UCLA dissertation, 1975.

p. 76: "As Swifty Lazar....at MCA." *Swifty, My Life and Good Times*, p. 92. (Swifty quit MCA in 1947.)

p. 76: "What really . . . like a criminal syndicate." From Daniel Bell's essay, "Crime as an American Way of Life;" and from Block's UCLA dissertation.

p. 76: "The secrecy . . . said Posner." *Dark Victory*, p. 147.

p. 76: "He told his . . . or were lost en route." Ibid.

p. 76: "In MCA's first . . . do exist." Notes 9 to financial statement of 1959.

p. 76–77: "However, too many government . . . live properties." *Prime-Time Crimes and Misdemeanors*, p. 210; also Justice Dept. memo, July 28, 1959;

p. 77: "Now Wasserman . . . such as Revue." WGA archives.

p. 77: "At the same . . . director of SAG." A.I. Jack Dales, April 16, 1998.

p. 77: "Wasserman's problem . . . Lew Wasserman." A.I. Howard Keel, Sept. 13, 2001.

Chapter 9

p. 77: "Howard Keel . . . Dore Schary." A.I. Keel, Sept. 13, 2001.

p. 78: "After Schary had . . . in 1944." *Heyday*, by Dore Schary, (Little, Brown & Co. 1979), pp. 132-4.

p. 78: "Schary . . . by 1951 headed MGM." Ephraim Katz *Film Encyclopedia*, Fourth Edition, (Harper Resource, 2001).

p. 78: "The suspended actor . . . never trusted him." A.I. Keel, Sept. 13, 2001.

p. 78: "SAG's contract . . . now playing on TV." A.I. Dales, April 16, 1998.

p. 78–79: "Television had boomed . . . 15,000 old films in circulation." WGA archives; also "Writers Demands Heard," May 17, 2000, *Los Angeles Times*.

p. 79: "The possibility . . . March 31, 1960." SAG archives; A.I. Dales, April 16, 1998.

p. 79: "SAG needed a . . . said Dales." A.I. Dales, Ibid.

p. 79: "So was Ronald Reagan . . . producer, too." *Early Reagan*, p. 467.

p 79–80: "Indeed, in 1952 . . . secret deal." Robb, David, "New Info on Reagan, MCA Waiver Probe," *Variety*, April 18, 1984.

p. 80: "It gave MCA—a blatant conflict of interest." SAG archives letters; A.I. MacArthur, Aug. 31, 1998.

p. 80: "In 1954, Wasserman . . . extended until 1960." Robb, April 18, 1984; A.I. SAG historian Yaros, Sept. 17, 1999.

p. 80: "Ronnie . . . Denker." A.I. Denker, Aug. 20, 1998.

p. 80: "No one ever expected . . . on MCA." A.I. Chet Migdon, July 7, 1999.

p. 80: "The town believed . . . favorable treatment." A.I. Seltzer, July 15, 1997.

p. 80: "Wasserman called . . . nonsense." Robert Marich and Alex Ben Block, "Wasserman Ascension Marks the End of an Era," July 12, 1995, *Hollywood Reporter.*

p. 81: "Dales...he was to Lew." A.I. Dales, April 16, 1998.

p. 81: "After being . . . Schreiber and Wasserman." A.I. Adams Feb. 20, 1998; Dales, April 16, 1998.

p. 81: " . . Reagan again assumed . . . SAG post." SAG archives, A.I. Yaros, Sept. 17, 1999.

p. 81: "But, as he later . . . at Revue." The Feb. 5, 1962, transcript is reproduced in *Dark Victory,* by Dan Moldea, pp.167-201.

p. 81: "The guild's . . . as the AMPP's spokesman." From the November 1959, *Screen Actor,* SAG's newsletter.

p. 81: "Reagan told . . . at one meeting." A.I. Dales, April 16, 1998.

p. 82: Spyros Skouras background from Katz's Film Encyclopedia; and from Finley's *The Story of Hollywood.*

p. 82: "Skouras detailed . . . It's non-negotiable." A.I. Dales, April 16, 1998; also *Early Reagan,* p. 468.

p. 82: "After a few exchanges . . . several minor ones." SAG archives; A.I. Val Yaros, Aug. 20, 2002; also U.S. Department of Labor Work Stoppage report, April 27, 1960.

p. 82: "Soon Wasserman . . . set was dark." A.I. Park, April 16, 1998; *Variety* March 7, 1960.

p. 82: "According to Ed Muhl . . . the film business." A.I. Muhl, Sept. 18, 1997.

p. 82–83: "Rackmil was . . . at Wasserman's urging . . ." A.I. Delaney, April 10, 1998.

p. 83: "Rackmil offered . . . from 1948 to 1960." SAG archives, A.I. Yaros, Aug. 20, 2002.

p. 83: "After Universal's pact . . . same deal, too." A.I. Yaros Ibid.

p. 83: "It got so that Richard . . . got SAG." From item in *Variety,* March 7, 1960.

p. 83: "So many craft workers . . . Reagan." A.I. Denker, Aug. 20, 1998; Bob Hope's quote from *First Father, First Daughter Maureen Reagan,* (Little Brown, 1989) p. 89.

p. 83: "But the movie producers . . . two camps formed." A.I. Yaros, Aug. 20, 2002.

p. 83: "One side called . . . for residuals." *Early Reagan,* p. 470;

p. 83–84: "That night, SAG..of the original $4 million offer." A.I. Yaros Sept. 17, 1999; Dales, April 18, 1998; Keel, Sept. 13, 2001.

p. 84: "Reagan sold us . . . said Gene Kelly." Kitty Kelly, *Nancy Reagan,* P. 108.

p. 84: "There was much . . . Great Giveaway." A.I. Robert Mitchum, Jan. 27, 1993.

p. 84: "Compounded . . . $100 million in residuals." Margaret Cone, of WGA, May 17, 2000.

p. 84: "At SAG's next . . . as a producer." SAG files, Minutes from June 15, 1960.

p. 84: "He remained on the . . . Reagan resigned as a SAG officer. . ." Ibid.

p. 84: " . . . upset at growing . . . from the East." Reagan as interviewed by Charles Denton, "Headman's Headaches," *Los Angeles Examiner,* May 1960 (reprinted in SAG's newsletter).

p. 85: "But Schreiber lessened . . . fallen considerably." Reagan's bio and A.I. James, archivist, June 26, 1998.

p. 85: "Meanwhile, Wasserman . . . said Franklin . . ." A.I. Michael Franklin, Oct. 23, 1998.

p. 85: "That prompted other . . . post 1960-work." WGA archives.

p. 85–86: "Separately, the . . . and the Internet." *Cone*, May 17, 2000; A.I. Del Reisman, April 2, 2003.

p. 86: "But he never . . . for $20 a piece." WGA archives, and Amazon.com.

p. 86: "Once WGA gave up . . . $300,000." WGA archives; A.I. Reisman, April 2, 2003.

p. 86: "In 1960 . . . to any other market." *Variety*, Oct. 19, 1998; *Cone*, May 17, 2000.

Chapter 10

p. 86–87: "Then Washington lawmakers . . . federal government.' " Stone, p. 210.

p. 87 Note: Rep. Harris also used his subcommittee to highlight the recording industry's payola practices, which destroyed D.J. Alan Freedman's career but did little to eradicate the practice. Indeed, some fifty years later, it appears to be going strong.

p. 87: "Quislings.." is Art Buchwald's term.

p. 87: " . . . much to the horror . . . to their agent." A.I. Stettner, Aug. 11, 2000.

p. 87: "Harris's investigation . . . in the station." Stone, p. 213.

p. 87: "Harris's . . . on a voluntary basis." Stone, p. 211-212.

p. 87: "But according to . . . signed by Harris." *Prime-Time Crimes and Misdeameanors.* pp. 211-214

p. 87: "Goodwin tracked down . . . said the producer." A.I. Al Freedman, Oct. 10, 2002.

p. 87–88: "By then, reporters . . . in Washington." Stone, p. 219.

p. 88: "It became like . . . Communists." A.I. Stettner, Oct. 10, 2002.

p. 88: "When Harris finally . . . three-ring circus." Stone, p. 219

p. 88–89: "But they focused . . . to hear about that fraud." A.I. Felscher, Aug. 2, 2002

p. 89–90: "Even worse was how . . . signed a deal." Stone, p. 241.

p. 90: "Contestants paid talent . . . in his account." Stone, p. 240-1; 280-1.

p. 90: "MCA and its . . . knew about it." A.I. Freedman, April 2, 2000; August 5, 2002.

p. 90: "Instead, the cameras . . . five-minute spot." Stone, p. 258.

p. 90: "Van Doren was so popular . . . business career." A.I. Stettner, Oct. 10, 2002.

p. 90: "On Nov. 2, 1959 . . . last three years." Stone, pp. 247-8.

p. 91: "Now, it was networks . . . become president of NBC." Stone, 265.

p. 91: "After Kintner's promotion . . . my very good friend." *Fortune*, July 1960.

p. 91: "Now the NBC executive . . . said Felsher." A.I. Felsher, Aug. 1, 2002; Stone, p. 265.

p. 91: "Lawmakers took turns . . . for his testimony." Stone, p. 267-8.

p. 91: "NBC, however, . . . canceling the $2.2 million.." Stone, p. 215.

p. 91–92: "In July 1960, the New York . . . with perjury." Stone, p. 289.

p. 92: "About eighteen *Twenty-One* . . . charges dismissed." *One Nation Under TV*, p. 139.

p. 92: "However, he would never . . . said Freedman." A.I. Freedman Aug. 5, 2002; He later produced shows in England and abroad and later went to work for Bob Guccione, publisher of *Penthouse.*

p. 92: "It appeared as if lawmakers . . . on quiz shows." Stone, p. 303.

p. 92: "But, the hearings . . . like Revue." Stone, pp. 318-329.

p. 93: "This was an uneasy time . . . his clause rigorously." A.I. Curtis Feb. 17, 2000.

p. 94: "Meanwhile . . . A real star." A.I. Gershwin, June 23, 1998.

p. 94: "Meanwhile, the wives turned aggressive . . . destroyed relationships." A.I. Balaban. Portions of this is also described in her fine book, *Bridesmaids.*

p. 95: "Dean and Jeanne . . . explained Gershwin." A.I. Gershwin, June 23, 1998.

p. 95: "Though Lew had just . . . living together." Ibib. Also Tosches, *Dino*, p. 255; 311.

p. 95: "Cary Grant . . . .Hartman." Lee, Guthrie, *The Life and Loves of Cary Grant*, (Drake Publishers).

p. 95: Hartman's office: description from A.I. Balaban March 19, 2001.

p. 95: "Grant was thrilled . . . being." *The Life and Loves of Cary Grant*, (Drake Publishers).

p. 95: "Williams . . . psychoanalyst." Esther Williams, *The Million-Dollar Mermaid*, (Simon & Schuster, 1999), Chapter 1.

p. 95: Jay and . . . warning bells clanged." A.I. Judy Balaban, March 19, 2001; "Movie Mob," *Bridesmaids*, p. 254.

p. 96: "Whenever a chum . . . sipped champagne." A.I. Curtis, Feb. 17, 2000.

p. 96: "Gable was one of . . . her house rule." A.I. Curtis Ibid.

p. 96: "At one party . . . never cornered him here." A.I. Gershwin, June 23, 1998.

p. 96–97: "You heard such . . . raconteur himself." A.I. Heston, July 20, 1998.

p. 97: "One party night . . . and walked off." A.I. Curtis, Feb. 17, 2000.

p. 97: "Rosemary Clooney . . . marriage was crumbling." *Girl Singer* p. 206.

p. 97: "Shelley Winters . . . it was a welcome respite." A.I. Balaban, March 19, 2001; Clooney, p. 23.

Chapter 11

p. 97: "Wasserman had been . . . Richard Nixon." Ronald Brownstein, "Rebitrh of Hollywood's Political Clout," *Los Angeles Times*, Dec. 9, 1990.

p. 97: "Instead, Lew and Johnson campaign . . ." Memos from LBJ Library.

p. 98: "Getting involved . . . Of course!" A.I. Leigh Feb. 5, 1998, and Curtis Feb. 17, 2000.

p. 98: "Rosemary Clooney sang at . . . Bobby Darin." A.I. Leigh Ibid.

p. 98: "As for the Hollywood . . . felt inspired to act." A.I. Balaban, March 19, 2001.

p. 98: "There was something . . . about politics, she said." A.I. Leigh, Feb. 5, 1998.

p. 98: "Wasserman had been . . . including JFK's father." A.I. Wasserman, Nov. 3, 1999.

p. 98: "Joseph Kennedy . . . early employer." A.I. Joe Delaney, April 10, 1998, *Las Vegas Sun* columnist and historian.

p. 98: "When Lew joined . . . Wasserman explained." A.I. Wasserman, June 22, 1999.

p. 98: "Later, whenever Jules . . . explained Berle Adams. " A.I. Adams, Feb. 5, 1998.

p. 98–99: "Wasserman's first step . . . he remarked." A.I. Wasserman, June 22, 1999.

p. 99: "John F. Kennedy . . . 1960 presidential campaign." From Ronald Kessler's *Sins of the Father*, as detailed at Kessler's website.

p. 99: "Studio moguls ran tour . . . than the city's nightclubs." Patrick Goldstein, "The Birth of Cool Politics," *Los Angeles Times*, Aug. 13, 2000; A.I. Muhl, May 5, 1997.

p. 99: "When Kennedy was nominated . . . starlet Marion Davies . . ." A.I. Herb Steinberg, Aug. 3, 1998.

p. 99: "In January 1961 . . . said Jay Kanter." A.I. Jay Kanter, Jan. 23, 1998.

p. 100: "After Kennedy's . . . the FCC discovered." FCC Program Inquiry, 1960; Frank Rose, *The Agency*, pp. 234-6.

p. 100: "One witness . . . six-foot, two-inch boss." A.I. Bill Gardner, Oct. 27, 1999.

p. 100: "As Berle Adams . . . possible." A.I. Adams, March 31, 1997

p. 101: "It is well-known . . . in 1960." *Variety*, Dec. 9, 1962; Motion Picture Exhibition, Nov. 17, 1962.

p. 101: "The FCC . . . packaged, or sold." FCC Program Inquiry, 1960.

p. 101: "They had stressed, repeatedly . . . 10 percent." *The Agency*, p. 228.

p. 101: "Whereas William Morris . . . $10 million . . ." Ibid.

p. 101: ". . . MCA had taken in $82 million." 1961 MCA annual report.

p. 101: "And while Morris . . . foreign distribution." DOJ memo, Sept. 27, 1961; *Dark Victory*, p.124; *Fortune* July 1960.

p. 101–102: "The commission subpoenaed . . . out of the hearing room." FCC Program Inquiry, 1960.

p. 102: "Schreiber's arrogance . . . focused on MCA." A.I. MacArthur, Aug. 31, 1998; A.I. Welkes, March 28, 1998.

p. 102: "Meanwhile . . . to step up his investigation." A.I. Gunther Schiff, Feb. 5, 1998; *Variety*, "MCA Dissolves Entire Agency," July 24, 1962.

p. 102: "MCA's clients . . . check in." A.I. Myrle Wages, March 31, 1998.

p. 102–103: "Judy Garland . . . performances." A.I. Welkes, March 28, 1998.

p. 103: "The Pulitzer Prize . . . without his MCA agent." A.I. Curtis, Feb. 17, 2000; A.I. Abe Polonsky, April 3, 1998.

p. 103: "Congress cited . . . clearing his name." Note: A court reversed the House in 1958, which cleared Arthur Miller.

p. 103: "MCA had recently sold . . . worked on the set." Susan King, "The Misfits Finally Get Some Respect," Oct. 1, 2002, *Los Angeles Times*; also "Great Performances: The Making of the Misfits," KCET, Oct. 3, 2002.

p. 103: "The project was so messy . . . massive heart attack." A.I. Robert Mitchum, Jan. 27, 1993.

p. 103: "Edie and Lew . . . troubled Monroe as well." A.I. Kanter, Jan. 23, 1998.

p. 103–104: "Wasserman was now forty-eight years . . . loving care." A.I. Wasserman, Nov. 3, 1999.

p. 104: "Wasserman knew . . . .obvious connection." A.I. MacArthur, Aug. 31, 1998.

p. 104: "Before the sale . . . were MCA's packages." A.I. Dick, June 22, 1996.

p. 104: "Now, Wasserman . . . the lot." Thompson, *Fortune*, July 1960; p. 195.

p. 104–105: "In 1950, he and Jimmy . . . star performance." A.I. Muhl, May 5, 1997.

p. 105: "For example..his previous salary." *Early Reagan*, Edwards p. 408.

p. 105: "When one of MCA's . . . *In My Arms*." A.I. Dick, June 22, 1996.

p. 105: "It got so that . . . by Milton Rackmil." Axel Madsen, *Stanwyck*, p. 260.

p. 105: "The Russian . . . over the years." "How Can a Banker Help? Serge Semenko," *Newsweek*, Dec. 23, 1963, pp. 62-4.

p. 105: "He told Stein . . . Decca and Universal." A.I. Delaney, April 10, 1998; also A.I. Dick; *City of Dreams* pp. 157-159.

p. 105: "Semenko helped Stein . . . in 1946 . . ." London Sunday *Times*, June 17, 1983; "and [stock] in Universal in 1951:" item in *Variety* Oct. 31, 1951.

p. 105–106: "Rackmil presided . . . following year." Finler, Joel. *The Hollywood Story* (Crown Publishers, 1988). P. 229; 231.

p. 106: "We thought..Decca Records." A.I. B.R., March 20, 1997.

p. 106: "That set up . . . the Decca/Universal asset." A.I. Dick, June 23, 1996.

p. 106: "All I remember . . . mob-controlled." A.I. Adams, March 31, 1997.

Chapter 12
This chapter owes a debt to Hank Messick and his work, specifically, *The Silent Syndicate* (Macmillan Co., 1967).

p. 106: "A black, familiar face." A.I. Mr. and Mrs. Paul Beck, April 17, 1998.

p. 106: "The rose-colored among equals." A.I. George Riff, July 7, 1997.

p. 106–107: "Dalitz . . . armed and dangerous." Foia.fbi.gov/dalitz.

p. 107: "Wasserman's . . . 'Pinky' Miller." A.I. Adams, March 31, 1997.

p. 107: "A woman watched . . . looked the part." A.I. Mrs. Paul Beck, April 17, 1998.

p. 107: "The Wassermans . . . in Las Vegas." A.I. Gerber, Feb. 5, 1998.

p. 107: "During the Great . . . Cleveland." A.I. Merle Jacobs, Nov. 22, 1996.

p. 134: "The syndicate..crowded the bar." *Cleveland Plain Dealer*, Oct. 23, 1935, "Top Hats and Silks Crowd New Casino," by William F. McDermott; also Norman Siegel, "New Night Life is Born Tonight at the Mayfair," Oct. 23, 1935.

p. 107: "Part of Mayfair's . . . about it." A.I. LaRonge, Dec. 5, 1996.

p. 108: "The Mayfair . . . in the Midwest." A.I. Hank Messick, May 10, 1997.

p. 108: ". . . Elliott Ness . . . Dalitz and His Gang." *Cleveland Plain Dealer,* March 31, 1935, "Raiders Find Bootleg Sold in 300 Spots."

p. 108: "Dalitz claimed . . . he often said." *Las Vegas Sun*, "One Hundred People Who Shaped Las Vegas" (online).

p. 108: "He was sly...didn't always work." A.I. Jacobs, Nov. 22, 1996; Hank Messick, *The Silent Syndicate*, p. 42.

p. 108: "But payoffs . . . were numbered." A.I. Daniel Kerr, historian, Jan. 6, 1997; *Cleveland Plain Dealer*, May 23, 1981, George Condon "47 Years as MCA's Man in Cleveland," Ohio House Bill No. 855, from 92nd General Assembly, Third Special Session, 1937-1938.

p. 108: "Dalitz prepared . . . Shapiro." "Casino to Purchase Mayfair," *Cleveland Plain Dealer*, Nov. 12, 1936.

p. 108–109: "The two men were . . . .national syndicate." A.I. Messick, March 10, 1997; and *Silent Syndicate*, p. 52;. "Sale completed in December." French Casino to Buy Mayfair Here," Nov. 12, 1936, Cleveland Plain Dealer; also Dec. 15, 1956, *Mayfair Casino Sale.*

p. 109: "In the mid-1940s . . . *Las Vegas Sun*." A.I. Greenspun, April 14, 1998.

p. 109: "Wasserman sent his client . . . sit in the audience." A.I. Delaney, April 10, 1998.

p. 109: "William Morris . . . and chorus girls." A.I. Gerber, March 27, 1998.

p. 110: "The people who . . . talk to Lew." A.I. Wasserman, Nov. 3, 1999.

p. 110: "And Wasserman . . . The Sands." A.I. Murray, March 23, 1998.

p. 110: "They never stayed . . . 1947 murder." A.I. Heller, Nov. 14, 1997.

p. 110: "Many believed . . . one of Dalitz's old flames." A.I. Merle Jacobs, Feb. 1, 1997; A.I. Riff July 7, 1997.

p. 110–111: "He continued to do . . . Lew's boys." A.I. Gerber and Murray, March 27, 1998.

p. 111: "Still, Wasserman . . . sensitive about that." A.I. Jay Stein, July 28, 1998.

p. 111: "The FBI suspected . . . Greenbaum." "Jake the Barber," by John Tuohy, *American Mafia* magazine, March 2001.

p. 111: "The bureau also . . . poisoning." Foia.fb i.gov/dalitz.

p. 111: "Before becoming . . . indicted anyone." "Organized Crime and Disorganized Cops," Ronald W. May, *The Nation*, June 27, 1959.

p. 111–112: "So when his staff . . . project or two." *Variety*, "MCA Dissolves Entire Agency," July 24, 1962.

p. 112: "Kennedy and his . . . by 80 percent." MCA Annual Reports: 1959, 1960, 1961.

p. 112: "FCC chief Newton..and offending." Stone, p. 324.

p. 112: "A few days later . . . America's TV screens." Rose, p. 236; JFK Library archives.

p. 112: "Kennedy . . . and other unions." A.I. Malcolm MacArthur, Aug. 31, 1998.

p. 112: "That anyone . . . federal investigation." A.I. Oppenheimer, Aug. 12, 1997; A.I. Phillips, Feb. 7, 1997.

p. 112: "The Steins were . . . her collection." A.I. Phillips Feb. 7, 1997; A.I. Krauskopf, March 4, 1998.

p. 113: "Suddenly . . . slid to 33." A.I. Murray, March 27, 1998; also *Variety*, July 24, 1962

p. 113: "We heard . . . soon enough." A.I. Welkes, March 25, 1998.

p. 113: "In New York . . . general was told." DOJ memos, Nov. 5, 1960; *Dark Victory*, p. 152; A.I. MacArthur, Aug. 30, 1998.

p. 113–114: "From the sidelines . . . get any waivers." A.I. Chet Migden, July 1, 1998.

p. 114: "On Oct. 10, 1961 . . . to exist. "SAG's newsletter, *Screen Actor*, Oct.–Nov. 1961.

p. 114: "The news shocked . . . he said. " A.I. Dales, April 16, 1998.

p. 114: "Even so . . . to Sept. 30, 1962." SAG Press Release, Oct. 25, 1961; A.I. Dales, Ibid.

Chapter 13

p. 115: "Back at MCA Square . . . in due course." A.I. Welkes, March 25, 1998; Dales, April 16, 1998.

p. 115–116: "When Dales . . . over the issue." A.I. Dales, April 16, 1998.

p. 116: "He, Stein . . . Labor Commission." *Wall Street Journal*, July 19, 1962

p. 116: "In the fall . . . and labor leaders." *Variety*, Oct. 24, 1962;

p. 116: "One day . . . dishonest." DOJ transcripts reprinted in *Dark Victory, Nancy Reagan*, p. 114.

p. 116: "The antitrust . . . Migden and others." A.I. Migden, July 7, 1998; A.I. Gunther Schiff, Feb. 5, 1998.

p. 116: "General Electric . . . or Revue." A.I. James, June 26, 1998; also Television and Radio Museum archives, Reagan.

p. 117: "His agent . . .did he expect?" A.I. Mrs. Park, April 16, 1998.

p. 117: "In 1951 Reagan . . . and *Kings Row*). *Early Reagan*, pp. 424, 436, 440; also archives at Reagan Presidential Library; Lou Canon, *Reagan: Role of a Lifetime*, pps. 353-56 and 464.

p. 117: "But where did Reagan . . . a TV writer." A.I. *Link*, July 12, 2002; Also Bob Raines, Oct. 9, 1998 and July 24, 2003.

p. 117: "In the 1903s . . . off the loan." Kramer's papers, IV, p. 15.

p. 117–118: "In 1943 . . . and never repaid the loan." Whittels, *Star-Spangled Octopus,* *Saturday Evening Post,* Aug. 31, 1946, p. 69.

p. 118: "MCA offered Jayne . . . " A.I. Roy Gerber, July 29, 1997.

p. 118: ". . . and Rock Hudson . . . with MCA." Dennis McDougal, *The Last Mogul,* pp. 245.

p. 118: "The Antitrust Division . . . Malibu property." Edwards, *Early Reagan,* p. 478.

p. 118: "In December 1966 . . . 290 acres." *Dark Victory,* p. 240. Note: The ranch sale occurred one month after Reagan won the California governor's race and a few weeks before he took office in January.

p. 118: "The land would . . . California governor." *Dark Victory,* p. 240-1

p. 118: "As Reagan himself . . . the ranch." Lou Canon, *Washington Post,* May 31, 1982.

p. 118: "We had the best . . . ecstatic." A.I. Welkes, March 25, 1998.

p. 118–119: "In April 1962 . . . Universal Studios." *Variety,* April 12, 1962; *The Agency,* p. 245.

p. 119: "He invited reporters . . . SAG franchise." A.I. Welkes, March 25, 1998.

p. 119: "On July 13, 1962 . . . Antimerger Act." *Variety,* "Dept. of Justice Eyes films and TV at MCA," Oct. 24, 1962.

p. 119–120: "Kennedy then delivered . . . new talent agency." A.I. Welkes March 25, 1998; A.I. MacArthur, Aug. 31,1998.

p. 120: "Wasserman was stymied . . . act." J.A. Trachtenberg, "Most Powerful Man in Hollywood," W, Oct. 8-15, 1982.

p. 120: "Three days later . . . SAG's waiver expiration . . . " *Variety,* "MCA Dissolves Entire Agency," July 24, 1962.

p. 120: ". . . Wasserman called . . . good name." A.I. Welkes, March 25, 1998; A.I. Gerber, Feb. 5, 1998.

p. 120–121: "After the meeting . . . ponder the future." A.I. Wages, March 27, 1998.

p. 121. "A few composed . . . very exciting." A.I. Miller, March 5, 1998.

p. 121: "The firm . . . breakdown." A.I. Jim Murray; Roy Gerber, July 29, 1997.

p. 121: "On July 23 . . . and Universal." MCA Dissolves Entire Agency," *Variety,* July 24, 1962; also "MCA Pact May End U.S. Trust Suit," *Los Angeles Times,* Sept. 29, 1962.

p. 121: "By then . . . Kelly." A.I. Wages, March 31, 1998.

p. 121: "Brando . . . become hysterical." A.I. Murray, July 29, 1998.

p. 121: "I want my . . . ever known." A.I. Leigh, Feb. 5, 1998.

p. 122: "Sources chortled . . . a seller." *New York Times* piece, Murray Schumach, Sept. 23, 1962.

p. 122: "On one of Wasserman's . . . hurt Wasserman." A.I. Murray and Gerber, July 29, 1997.

p. 122: "But he vowed . . . ancient Egypt." Wasserman quoted in Deutsch, p. 121.

PART II
Chapter 14

p. 125: "On Sept. 19. . . . It'd better." A.P. Bob Thomas, Dec. 9, 1962; "Hollywood Prospect," Murray Schumach, *New York Times,* Sept. 23, 1962.

p. 125: "The trade papers . . . film production." *Time* magazine, May 25, 1962; Universal archives.

p. 125: "I hadn't been . . . companies had." Robert Marich and Alex Ben Block, "Wasserman Ascension," *Hollywood Reporter* July 12, 1995.

p. 125: "Initially, he would . . . a few buildings." "Bestriding the World," by Fritz Goodwin, *T.V Guide,* July 25, 1964.

p. 126: "But Wasserman still . . . film library." A.I. MacArthur, Aug. 31, 1998.

p. 126 "Seven Arts . . . Semenko." Hank Messick, *Beauties and the Beast,* p. 211–4; also "How Can A Banker Help?, *Newsweek,* Dec. 23, 1963, p. 62.

p. 126: "The deal . . . millions more." MCA Annual Reports 1962, 1963.

p. 126: "The battle . . . recent memory." A.I. Schiff, Jan. 20, 2002.

p. 126: "It was the . . . TV producer." A.I. Ray, Jan. 16, 1998.

p. 126: "MCA never admitted . . . really after." "MCA Pact May End U.S. Trust Suit," *Los Angeles Times,* Sept. 19, 1962.

p. 126: "The Justice . . . worked with." *Variety,* "Dept. of Justice Eyes Films & TV," Oct. 24, 1962.

p. 126–127: "Around Halloween . . . his offices . . ." A.I. MacArthur, Aug. 31, 1998.

p. 127: "The case . . . his 49 years." A.I. Shirley Kory, Aug. 7, 1998.

p. 127: "His smile . . . few pleasures." A.I. Jackie Gershwin, June 23, 1998.

p. 127: "He now drove . . . a serious guy." A.I. Ray , Jan. 16. 1998.

p. 127–128: "At the time . . . raise cash." Marich and Ben Block, "Wasserman Ascension," *Hollywood Reporter* July 12, 1995.

p. 128: "Yet . . . hit movie." A.I. Dorskind Feb. 26, 197.

p. 128: "His new market . . . and backgrounds." U.S. Population, 1960, U.S. Census Bureau.

p. 128: "Wasserman had been . . . up to 55th Street." His address was 2542 25th St., according to U.S. Census document from 1910; later the family moved to 45th Street in the same district, according to the 1920 Census count.

p. 128: "In 1913 . . . care was scarce." Lloyd Gartner, *Jews of Cleveland,* (Cleveland; Western Reserve, 1987), pp.110–127; p. 269.

p. 128–129: "Lew's father . . . he could never keep." U.S. Declaration of Intention, Department of Commerce and Labor, March 31, 1919; Petition for Naturalization, Nov. 1, 1913; Census Records of 1910; 1920; Cleveland City Directory, 1924–1936.

p. 129: "He always dressed . . . Paul Beck." A.I. Beck, Nov. 13, 1996.

p. 129: "Lew's mother . . . pay off the debt." A.I. Lewis Ratener, Oct. 3, 1996; also Beck.

p. 129: "Louis . . . city limits." Census Records 1920; city directories; records from Patrick Henry Junior High.

p. 129: "Everybody . . . skinny Louis had." A.I. Merle Jacobs, Feb. 1, 1997.

p. 129: At the time . . . Dalitz's Jewish syndicate." The Italian toughs would later become the Mayfield Road Gang or Cleveland's Italian Mafia. Hank Messick, *Silent Syndicate* (MacMillan Co. 1967), pp. 5–11; also A.I. Edward Muggins, historian Dec. 15, 1997.

p. 129: "Louis landed a . . . whorehouses." A.I. Setnik. Oct. 27, 1997.

p. 129: "At the theater . . . probably *The Star.*" A.I. Ronald Brown, Nov. 14, 1996.

p. 129–130: "At intermission . . . around midnight . . ." A.I. Jacobs, Nov. 22, 1996.

p. 130: " . . . whereupon Wasserman . . . all over again." Wasserman, 1991 Current Biography Yearbook, p. 603.

p. 130: "Between his job . . . savings it had." 1926 Cleveland City Directory; 1920 U.S. Census; Wasserman as quoted in *Los Angeles Times,* Nov. 18, 1984.

p. 130: "The 44–year-old . . . Great Depression." A.I. Beck, Setnik, Ratener, Oct. 3, 1996.

p. 130: "Wasserman would late r. . . like a hawk." A.I. Dorksind, Feb. 26, 1997

p. 131: "The year . . . he reported." Annual Report, 1962.

p. 131: "Jerry Gershwin . . . MCA as beneficiary." A.I. Gershwin, June 23, 1998.

p. 131: "But to some agents . . . Ned Tanen." A.I. Tanen, July 8, 1998.

p. 131: "The younger man . . . be grass." A.I. Gershwin, June 23, 1998.

p. 132: "Wasserman left only one stage . . . fate." A.I. R.P, March 20, 1997.

p. 132: "To keep the grass . . . one executive." Bob Raines, July 28, 1998.

p. 132: "To level miles . . . Dorskind grinned." A.I. Dorskind, March 20, 1997.

p. 132: "When Jules . . . 450 contiguous acres." A.I. Raines, July 28, 1998; also Dorskind, March 20, 1997.

p. 132: "For some people . . . Ernie Nims." A.I. July 2, 1997.

p. 132–133: "Before MCA acquired . . . stuck to budget." A.I. Dorskind.

p. 133–134: "But the chief's . . . than I deserved." A.I. Sam Carson, Nov. 12, 1999.

p. 134: "Jules hated the tower . . . free rein." A.I. Raines, July 28, 1998.

p. 134–135: "Lew was the . . . modern black tower." A.I. Seltzer, July 15, 1997.

p. 135: "Most weekends . . . watched,' Carson said." A.I. Carson, Nov. 12, 1999.

p. 135–136: "By 1963 . . . and empty space." A.I. Raines, July 28, 1998.

p. 136: "It's carpet . . . screenwriter Gavin Lambert." A.I. Feb. 22, 2001.

p. 136: "The interior decor . . . squirm or leave." A.I. Lambert, Feb. 20, 2001; Carson, Nov. 12, 1999.

p. 136: "If so, Wasserman . . . intimidated visitors." A.I. Paul Lazurus, Columbia vice president, Feb. 5, 1997.

p. 136: "Stein, however, refused . . . He hated it." A.I. Oppenheimer, July 29, 1998.

Chapter 15

p. 137: "She had become. . . .about $24 million." MCA annual report 1959–1962.

p. 137: "The anti-trust . . . by 1963." A.I. Welkes, March 25, 1998.

p. 137: "Two years . . . was not for sale." Marshall Berges, "Lew & Edie Wasserman," *Los Angeles Times*, Home section, Dec. 2, 1973.

p. 137: "When it suddenly . . . for a bargain." A.I. Realtors Bruce Nelson, July 20, 1998; Cecelia Washley, July 25, 1998.

p. 137: "In 1961 . . . floor-to-ceiling glass." A.I Nelson, July 20, 1998.

p. 137: "Wasserman slept . . . on the West Coast." *Broadcasting Magazine*, Profile, April 30, 1973. p. 73.

p. 137: "As Edie entered . . . an arrangement." A.I. Artie Shaw, June 13, 1995.

p. 138: "She always . . . real kicks." A.I. Lambert, Feb. 22, 2001.

p. 138: "She was the wife . . . Ed Muhl." A.I. Muhl, Sept. 18, 1997.

p. 138: "Edie had weathered . . . later confided. A.I. Dunne, Oct. 25, 2002; also Dunne, "The Last Emperor," *Vanity Fair*, April 1996.

p. 138: "But her indiscretions. . . . behind her back." A.I. Wages, March 27, 1998; Raines, March 5, 1998; Shaw, June 13, 1995; and many others.

p. 138: "The fact . . . voice trailing off." A.I. Curtis, Feb. 17, 2000.

p. 138: "Like Lew . . . older boys." Cleveland Census records, 1920.

p. 138–139: "In 1935 . . . loved to dance." A.I. Merle Jacobs, Feb. 1, 1997.

p. 139: "Edie was a . . . going to notice." A.I. Barton. Oct. 3, 1997.

p. 139: "During one late night . . . impressed by him, too." A.I. Heller, April 15, 1997. Also Jacobs, eb. 1, 1997.

p. 139: "So, when Wasserman . . . she later joked." Marshall Berges, "Lew & Edie Wasserman," *Los Angeles Times* Dec. 2, 1973.

p. 139–140: "He came from poor Russian . . . well-known attorney." *Cleveland and Its Environs.* Volume II, Biography (The Lewis Publishing Co., 1918), pp. 373–374.

p. 140: "Edie lived with her . . . entirely different world." Cleveland City Directory listing, 1936.

p. 140: "A year after they . . . including Dorothy Barton." A.I. Barton, Oct. 3, 1997; Jacobs.

p. 140: "Wasserman moved . . . twlweve-room house." Cleveland City Directory listing for 1936.

p. 140: "It had polished wood . . . private bathroom." A.I. Donna Onda, at Chagrin Valley Realty Co., for materials about Edie's childhood home, sent Dec. 11, 1997, and to Sharon Coyle, who owned the home at the time of our interview Dec. 19, 1997 and sent photos.

p. 140: "His bride . . . $18 a week." From "Making a Home for Hollywood," by Barbara Thomas, *Los Angeles Times,* Nov. 3, 1998."

p. 140: "He supported his . . . down only $38." A.I. Jacobs on Mayfair salary; Manhattan Inc. p. 74, profile on Lew lists MCA salary at $60 a week; Bureau of Labor Statistics, annual earnings for jobs in 1934 for comparable salaries.

p. 140: "Later that year . . . Midwest's biggest city." A.I. Barton, Oct. 3, 1997.

p. 140: "In Chicago . . . Murphy bed." Berges, *Los Angeles Times,* Dec. 2, 1973.

p. 141: "Several months later . . . her husband west." A.I. Dorskind, March 20, 1997.

p. 141: "Edie was vivacious . . . picking up men,' he said." A.I. D.F., Feb. 5, 1997.

p. 141: "Errol Flynn . . . conquests." A.I. Raines, March 5, 1998; Wages, March 27, 1998.

p. 141: "Edie was . . . Virginia Korshak." A.I. Korshak, June 20, 2003.

p. 141: "Marnie Sachs. . . ." A. I. Krauskopf, March 4, 1998.

p. 141: "She went. . . ." A. I. Raines, Oct. 9, 1998.

p. 141: "Robert Stack . . . I made." A.I. Mitchum, Jan. 27, 1993.

p. 141: "One of Edie's . . . cared for her." A.I. Lambert, Feb. 22, 2001.

p. 141–142: "The script . . . loved the title." *Nicolas Ray,* by Bernard Eiscenschitz (Faber and Faber, London, 1990) pp. 231–2.

p. 142: "At the time . . . teenager problems." A.I. Dorskind, April 1, 1997.

p. 142–143: "His 1955 film . . . He knew the score." Lambert, Feb. 22, 2001.

p. 143: "Instead . . . before dying in 1979." imdb.com.

p. 143: "Meanwhile, Edie . . . Jack Dales." A.I. Dales, April 18, 1998.

p. 143: "At Edie's urging . . . Veronique." A.I. Gershwin, June 23, 1998.

p. 143: "Bob Wagner . . . party guests." Eisenschitz, Nicholas Ray; Also "Natalie Wood's Fatal Voyage," by Sam Kashner, *Vanity Fair,* March 2000.

p. 143: "Everyone seemed to be . . . said Leigh." A.I. Leigh, Feb. 5, 1998.

p. 143: "My marriage . . . said Curtis." A.I. Curtis, Feb. 17, 2000.

p. 143: "Within a year . . . their godchildren." A.I. Gershwin, June 23, 1998.

p. 143: "Every Christmas . . . Lee Curtis said." Comments at a fundraiser at the Motion Picture and TV Fund home, Oct. 31, 1988.

p. 144: "But the circle . . . disloyalty." A.I. Balaban Kanter, March 19, 2001.

p. 144: "At her husband's . . . from Universal." Berges, Dec. 2, 1973.

p. 144: "When she . . . town took note." A.I. Carson, Nov. 12, 1999.

p. 144–145: "Meanwhile. . . .a little eerie." A.I. Gershwin, June 23, 1998.

p. 145: "With few exceptions . . . off-screen lives." A.I. Rex Reed, Jan. 30, 2002.

p. 145: "To maintain . . . Billy Wilder." Berges, Dec. 2, 1973.

p. 145: "Years later . . . Foothill Drive." A.I. Raines, March 5, 1998.

p. 145: "Edie's circle . . . anger still exists." A.I. Seltzer, July 15, 1997.

p. 145: "John Kennedy . . . Angie and Kennedy." A.I. Frank Price, Aug. 5, 1998. Note: The Rat Pack officially consisted of Frank Sinatra, Dean Martin, Sammy Davis, Jr., Joey Bishop, Peter Lawford.

p. 146: "By early 1963 . . . Kennedy that night." A.I. Carson, Nov. 12, 1998.

p. 146: "An administration . . . a Universal executive." A.I. Herb Steinberg, Aug. 3, 1998.

Chapter 16

p. 147: "When . . . film editor." A.I. Ernie Nims, July 2, 1997.

p. 147: "Wasserman fired . . . advent of talkies." A.I. Muhl, Sept. 18, 1997.

p. 147: "During the 1950s . . . *Imitation of Life.*" *The Universal Story*, by Clive Hirschhorn, pp. 156–8.

p. 148: "A third executive insired . . . abrupt deal surprising." A.I. B.R., March 20, 1997.

p. 149: "In fact . . . conventional B movie." A.I. Nims; Welles correspondence courtesy of Nims files.

p. 149: "His movie . . . director's instructions." Todd McCarthy, "Rehabbed 'Touch of Evil' Gains Clarity," *Variety*, Sept. 4, 1998.

p. 149: "Universal also lost . . . by fire for Kubrick." A.I. Ronnie Lubin, Feb. 18, 1998.

p. 149: "At one point . . . his own crew." Michael Herr, "Kubrick," *Vanity Fair*, August 1999.

p. 149: "In 1961 . . . for Kubrick." imdb.com; British Oscar is conferred by British Academy of Film and Television Arts (BAFTA).

p. 149–150: "But Kubrick . . . par excellence." A.I. Nims; Kubrick's obituary of March 8, 1999, *Los Angeles Times.*

p. 150: "Douglas stayed on . . . studio's marketing." A.I. Lubin, Feb. 18, 1998; also Kirk Douglas, *The Ragman's Son* (Simon & Schuster, 1988) pp. 341–3.

p. 150: "By then . . . at that time." "Universal Second and Trying Hard," by Charles Champlin, *Los Angeles Times*, Nov. 16, 1965; A.I. Muhl, Sept. 18, 1997.

p. 150–151: "Lew's penny-pinching . . . back." A.I. Nims, July 2, 1997.

p. 151: "He gave away . . . groused Muhl." A.I. Muhl, Sept. 18, 1997.

p. 151: "Carl Laemmle . . . the Sherman Antitrust Act." Culled from John Drinkwater, *The Life and Adventures of Carl Laemmle*, Putnam, 1931.

p. 151–152: "Laemmle always . . . Stanely Bergerman." A.I. Bergerman, Dec. 16, 1996.

p. 152–153: "From then on . . . in the land." *City of Dreams*, Bernard Dick, p. 21.

p. 153: "In the golden days . . . a hospital." A.I. Bergerman; Universal employee Kay Thackery, A.I. Sept. 20, 1997; also A.I. Dick, June 22, 1998.

p. 153: "His property was . . . size and income." MCA 1965 Annual Report.

p. 153: "Wasserman constructed . . . entertainment industry." MCA 1964 Annual Report.

p. 153: "Wasserman then . . . recording conglomerate." MCA 1965 annual report; Seagram's Annual Report 2000.

p. 153: "The commissary . . . to Carson." A.I. Carson, Nov. 12, 1999.

p. 154: "That weekend . . . and so did Wasserman." A.I. Dorskind, April 1, 1997.

p. 154: "We can't take . . . movie sets." A.I. Wasserman, June 22, 1999; also *The Universal Story*, Clive Hirschhorn (Octopus Books, 1983), p. 8–9; also old photos from Universal archives.

p. 154: "Still, he knew . . . finally made money." A.I. Steinberg, Aug. 4, 1998.

p. 155: "That first year . . . so bad." A.I. Wasserman, June 22, 1999.

p. 155–156: "He knew that safeguarding . . . overnight." A.I. Bill Burch, July 7, 1997.

p. 156: "The Wassermans . . . President Kennedy." A.I. Steinberg, Aug. 3, 1998.

p. 156: "In May 1962 . . . published accounts." Ronald Brownstein, *The Power and The Glitter*, (Pantheon Press, 1991).

p. 156: "To raise even . . . June 7,1963." Steinberg, Aug. 3, 1998.

p. 156: "We had to . . . micromanged it." A.I. Joe Cerrell, Aug. 3, 1998.

p. 156: "He and Edie . . . other political fund-raisers." A.I. Steinberg, Aug. 3, 1998.

p. 157: "The dinner raised . . . from the President." From John F. Kennedy Library archives.

p. 157: "That night . . . White House." A.I. off-record source, March 27, 1997.

Chapter 17:

This chapter relied on *The Genius of the System,* by Tom Schwartz, for some details on Hitchcock's work.

p. 157: "The 26–year-old . . . another word about it." A.I. Frank Price, Dec. 2, 1999.

p. 159–160: Details about *Red Channels* from Larry Ceplair and Steven Englund in, *Inquisition in Hollywood Politics* (University of California Press, 1988), p. 386.

p. 160: "Wasserman . . . nor well done." Fred Allen quote from Museum of Television and Radio archives.

p. 160: "Sidney Sheinberg. . . .quality of its shows." A.I. Sid Sheinberg March 27, 1997.

p. 160: "By 1963, Wasserman . . . grim reality." A.I. Dorskind; Story April 1, 1977.

P. 160: "Dragnet's tales were . . . and investigators." A.I. Ed Davis, March 3, 1998.

p. 160: "Off-duty officers . . . well for stories." A.I. Reese, Feb. 16,1998.

p. 161: "Young writers . . . in the afternoon." A.I. Stephen Cannell, Aug. 18, 2000; description of the bungalow from A. I. Cannell and Reese, Feb. 16, 1998.

p. 161: "Wasserman so valued . . . for a day." A.I. Dorksind, April 1, 1997.

p. 161: "The English filmmaker . . . very definitely." A.I. Patricia O'Connell, May 14, 1998.

p. 162: "But years later . . . did," he said. A.I. Wasserman, Nov. 3, 1999.

p. 162. "Once Hitch . . . had listed to Lew." A.I. O'Connell, May 14, 1998.

p. 162 "It was the only show. . . .said Adler." A.I. Adler, Dec. 15, 1999.

p. 162–163: "Wasserman also . . . him down." A.I. William Link, Dec. 8, 1999.

p. 163: "Don Siegel was . . . on the phone." A.I. Price, Aug. 5, 1998.

p. 163–164: "Then there was . . . to boast about." A. I. Price, details about *The Virginian* from Internet Movie Database.

p. 164: "Pitching shows . . . Werblin's annoyance." A.I. Price, Aug. 5, 1998; A.I. Tanen, June 2, 1998.

p. 164: "In 1951 . . . Lang lost one testicle." Lang's obituary, *Los Angeles Times*, May 31, 1996.

p. 164: "That never effected . . . said Lang's wife." A.I. Lewis-Lang, July 31, 1997.

p. 165: "But Lang's transgression . . .'one-ball wonder.' " A.I. Dorskind, Feb. 26, 1997, and Tanen, June 2, 1998.

p. 165: "Jennings could sell . . . MCA writer." A.I. Freedman, Dec. 6, 1999.

p. 165–166: "This happened often . . . learned to translate." A.I. Sheinberg, April 28, 1998.

p. 166: "Huggins and Price . . . huge hit." A.I. Price, Aug. 5, 1998.

p. 166: "In 1963, while Jules . . . high-quality show." A.I. Adler, Dec. 15, 1999 and Raines.

p. 166–167: "The studios had now. . . .Oscar-winning films." Douglas Gomery, *Shared Pleasures,*(University of Wisconsin, 1992) p. 249; also A.I. Gomery, Aug. 6, 1996.

p. 167: "Reveue was already . . . NBC signed up." A.I. Price, Nov. 5, 1998, and Sheinberg, May 19, 1998.

p. 167–168: "The first project . . . without even knowing." A.I. Adler, Dec. 15, 1999.

p. 168: "The critics, however . . . took umbrage." A.I. Sheinberg, April 28, 1998.

p. 168: "One major executive . . . he later told a reporter." *Hollywood Reporter*, "Wasserman ascension." *Ben Block* by Marich, Dec. 12, 1995.

p. 168: "Six weeks later. . . .(all former MCA clients.)" A.I. Sheinberg, March 25, 1998; IMDB.com.

p. 168: "By 1965, Universal . . . said Price." A.I. Price, Aug. 5, 1998; Also MCA annual report of 1968.

p. 168: "By this time . . . continued brining in revenues." MCA annual report 1965; *Time Magazine*, Jan. 1, 1965. "A New Kind of King." p. 50.

p. 169: "Not one of these . . . TV shows." A.I. Price, Aug. 5, 1998; Adler, Dec. 15, 1999.

Chapter 18

p. 169: "Stein thought . . . eventually happened." A.I. Lubin, Feb. 18, 1998.

p. 169–170: "MCA's two-party policy . . . published novelist." A.I. Denker, Aug. 26, 1998.

p. 170: "One Universal publicist . . . two ward bosses." A.I. Raines, March 5, 1998.

p. 170: "Stein had watched . . . National Convention." Biographies of Dart, Call and Tuttle as recounted in *Who's Who in America*. Henry Salvatori bio from *Society of Exploration Geophysicists*; also information from *Political Graveyard* on line.

p. 170: "Stein . . . pro-business agenda." A.I. Oppenheimer; A.I. Raines, July 28, 1998; A.I. Lubin, Feb. 18, 1998.

p. 170: "In 1952. . . . and relaxed." *Robert Montgomery Presents*, Museum of Television and Radio archives; A.I. Lubin, Feb. 18, 1998.

p. 170: "George Murphy. . . . the U.S. senate." A.I. Raines, July 28, 1998; also Murphy's biography as *The Political Graveyard*; IMDB.com; A.I. Denker, Aug. 20, 1998.

p. 170–171: "In 1964 . . . answer to Lew." A.I. Cerrell, Aug. 3, 1998.

p. 171: "When the gamesmanship . . . duke it out." A.I. Adams, Feb. 20, 1998.

p. 171: "It was smart business . . . things to come." A.I. B.R., March 20, 1997.

p. 171: "You were never . . . the last word." A.I. Raines, July 28, 1998.

p. 172: "The relationship . . . Steinberg." A.I. Steinberg, Aug. 3, 1998.

p. 172: "Later, the story . . . ever after." Deutsch, "Lew," *California* magazine, March 1985.

p. 172: "When Wasserman . . . Edie and Lew." A.I. Steinberg, Aug. 4, 1998.

p. 172 "Before Kennedy's death . . . enough to build the facility." March 15, 1964 memo to LBJ, courtesy of Johnson Library.

p. 172–173: "In June 1964. . . .Hollywood was still jittery." A.I. Steinberg, Aug. 3, 1998; A. I. Cerrell, Aug. 3, 1998.

p. 173: "Wasserman. . . .only to New York." Brownstein, Ronald, "Rebirth of Hollywood's Clout," *Los Angeles Times,* Dec. 2, 1990.

p. 173: "And the Wasserman's . . . nationally." A.I. Steinberg, Aug. 3, 1998.

p. 173: "Edie and Lew . . . that be." A.I. Gomery, Feb. 6, 1997.

p. 173: "He also wanted . . . Pat Caddell." A.I. Cadell, March 5, 1996.

p. 173–174: "Johnson noticed . . . with Lew." A.I. Steinberg, Aug. 3, 1998.

p. 174. "Johnson admired . . . and Lady Bird." A. I. Jack Valenti, June 5, 1997.

p. 174: "Jules had. . . .a change." A.I. Dr. Bradley Straatsma, July 30, 1997; also, "Vision For the Future, Jules Stein Eye Institute," by Willam Campbell Felch, (University of California, Los Angeles, 1992), pp. 3–27.

p. 174: "Stein graduated . . . age 16 . . ." A.I. Debbie Stone, spokeswoman for West Virginia University, Feb. 14, 1998.

p. 174: " . . . earned a degree . . . at age 19 . . ." A.I. Jay Banasko, spokeswoman for the University of Chicago, Jan. 15, 1998.

p. 174: ". . . and applied to. . . .Rush College." Ibid; also A.I. Oppenheimer, Aug. 12, 1997.

p. 174–175: "But he . . . booking bands in clubs . . . " Karl Kramer papers; "The Octopus," *Time* April 23, 1945.

p. 175: " . . . pocketing 20 or even 50 percent commission." A.I. Rudy Horn, MCA client, Sept. 2, 1997.

p. 175: "When Prohibition . . . who ran the clubs." A.I. Berle Adams, Feb. 20, 1998; A. I. Oppenheimer, Aug. 12, 1997.

p. 175: "At night . . . his studies." Karl Kramer papers.

p. 175: "In June 1922, Stein . . . in January 1923." 1924 *Chicago Medical Blue Book*; papers at Jules Stein Eye Institute.

p. 175: "By that time, . . . band-booking business . . . " A.I. Henry Miller, July 15, 1997; A.I. Patsy Krauskopf, Aug. 2, 1998.

p. 175: "Stein too . . . medicinal drugs." Listing in 1924 Chicago Medical Blue Book.

p. 175: "According to a few sources . . . Capone's nightclubs . . . " A.I. Mitchum, Jan. 27, 1993.

p. 175: " . . . supplying drugs to . . . that the mob operated." A.I. Chuck Binder, historian at the University of Chicago, May 13, 1997.

p. 175: "As MCA's first. . . .get caught." Karl Kramer papers.

p. 175: "Around 1923 . . . standards of 1924." A.I. Oppenheimer, Aug. 12, 1997.

p. 176: "Down the hall. . . .America." A.I. Miller, July 15, 1994; A.I. Horn, Sept. 2, 1997.

p. 176: "A year later . . . lady's slipper." A.I. Horn; also Taft Schreiber as quoted by Joyce Haber "Jules Stein," May 26, 1974, *Los Angeles Times.*

p. 176: "His agency struck . . . Stein was rich and famous." A.I. Miller, July 15, 1997; A. I. Adams, March 31, 1997; A. I. Oppenheimer, Aug. 12, 1997.

p. 176: "Everyone knew . . . very unusual." A.I. Wasserman, June 10, 1999.

p. 176: "But Stein . . . eponymous foundations." A.I. Phillips. Feb. 7, 1997.

p. 176: "He paid for . . . a Stein associate." A.I. Straatsma, July 30, 1997.

p. 176: "In 1960, Stein . . . Prevent Blindness." RPB history fact sheet.

p. 176–177: "In April 1961. . . .said Wasserman." A.I., June 22, 1999.

p. 177: "Stein matched . . . to prominence." RPB history fact sheet. Note: James S. Adams, Mary Laskey, Robert E. McCormick, William Vanden Huevel and Lew Wasserman are mentioned as associates of the RPB by the group's fact sheet.

p. 177." Now, he wanted. . . .decision," said Straatsma." A.I. Straatsma, July 30, 1997.

p. 177: "Jules buttonholed his friends. . . .than $15 million." A.I. Oppenheimer, Aug. 12, 1997; Jules Stein Eye Institute papers.

p. 177:"When the Steins . . . new production." "Break Ground for Stein Institute," *Los Angeles Times*, Sept. 23, 1964.

p. 177: "As Gerald . . . major philanthropist." A.I. Oppenheimer, Aug. 12, 1997.

Chapter 19

p. 178: "When Lew took over. . . .who was boss." As quoted by Bog Gottlieb, "How Lew Wasserman Foiled the Wicked . . ." *Los Angeles Magazine;* January 1979, also A.I. Jackie Gershwin, June 23, 1998.

p. 178: " Lew was . . . said Ned Tanen." A.I., July 7, 1998.

p. 178: "When he was 14 . . . co-workers." A.I. Setnik Oct. 27, 1997.

p. 178: "The theater . . . velvet seats." "Keith's East 105th St. Theater," *The Encyclopedia of Cleveland History.*

p. 179: "It was the place . . . the youngsters." A.I. Judah Rubenstein, an archivist at the Cleveland Jewish Community Federation, Nov. 23, 1997.

p. 179: "He got the job . . . his early career." A.I. Beck, Oct. 3, 1997.

p. 179: "Wasserman loved . . . was coming next." A.I. Setnik, Oct. 27, 1997.

p. 179: "He gave patrons . . . through his doors." George E. Condon, "47 years as MCA's man," *Cleveland Plain Dealer*, May 26, 1981.

p. 179: " *The Jazz Singer* . . . new American scene." Collected from Wasserman's background and the movie plot, as outlined in Internet Movie Data Base.

p. 179: "After *The Jazz* . . . were mysterious." A.I. Ratener, Nov. 19, 1996.

p. 179: "But to Wasserman . . . work schedules." A.I. Stenik, Oct. 27, 1997; A.I. Beck, Oct. 3, 1997.

p. 180: "When I was a boy . . . to that now." Bob Thomas, "MCA's Wasserman," Associated Press, Dec. 9, 1962.

p. 180: "He borrowed a page . . . . James Brolin." "Facts About Universal" press release, March 15, 1965, from Universal Studio archives.

p. 180: "Wasserman backed . . . community theaters." Schumach, "MCA Will Finance Plays," *New York Times*, Oct. 24, 1962.

p. 180: "the mogul doubled . . . in the business." A.I. Muhl, Sept. 18, 1997; STORY.

p. 180: "Universal . . . and Cary Grant." Hirschhorn, *The Universal Story*, pp.256–270.

p. 180: "Ross was. . . .that way." A.I. Muhl, Sept. 18, 1997.

p. 180: "Hunter had a knack . . . seven-year contract." W. Ward Marsh, "Plans Completed for Hunter Theaters," *Cleveland Plain Dealer,* June 25, 1965.

p. 180: "For Universal . . . suspicious niece." imdb.com.

p. 180: " . . . and Hitchcock often said . . . low $800,000 cost." A.I. O'Connell, May 14, 1998.

p. 181: "For Wasserman's Universal . . . of San Francisco." imdb.com.

p. 181: "The director . . . said Jerry Adler." A.I. Adler, Dec. 15, 1999.

p. 181: "By midway . . . through intemediaries." A.I. Freedman, Dec. 6, 1999.

p. 181–182: "Every movie . . . could improve them." A.I. Dorskind, April 1, 1997.

p. 182: "One day, Louise . . . the right formula." A.I. Latham, April 27, 1998.

p. 182: "In 1962, Hitch traded . . . in a studio." A.I. O'Connell, May 14, 1998.

p. 182: "Hitch also gave . . . large and opaque." Details of Bernard Buffet from *Current Biography*, 1982; A.I. Melodie Johnson-Howe, Feb. 6, 2003.

p. 182–183: "Lew had made a . . . greet guests." A.I. Tanen, July 7, 1998.

p. 183: "Stewart agreed . . . film debut." IMDB.

p. 183: "It was a strong . . . worked with him." A.I. Muhl, Sept. 18, 1997; A.I. Nims, July 2, 1997.

p. 183: "*The War Lord* . . . by the studio's dictates." A.I. Seltzer, July 15, 1997.

p. 183–184: "Other producers on the . . . was just dreadful." A.I. unnamed source, Dec. 2, 1999.

p. 184: "But critics . . . the box office." *Hollywood Close-Up.*, "Upheaval Due at MCA," April 14, 1966.

p. 184: "By then, Seltzer . . . my own thing." A.I. Seltzer, July 15, 1997.

p. 184: "I don't think . . . one producer." A.I. D.L., Feb. 5, 1997.

p. 184: "Universal turned out . . . sweeping the country." *The Universal Story*, pp. 261–299; also interview with Prof. C. Wolfe, Chair, Dept. of Film, UCSB, April 17, 1997.

p. 184: "A lot of the . . . Roy Gerber." A.I. Gerber, July 29, 1997.

p. 184: "They used the same . . . same formula?" A.I. Jim Murray, March 27, 1998.

p. 184: "The studio . . . from the other studios." A.I. Ned Tanen, July 7, 1998.

p. 184: "As one producer said . . . at the screen. A.I. D.L., Feb. 2, 1997

p. 185. "By 1964 . . . $14.8 million." MCA annual report, 1984.

p. 185: "I plead guilty . . . movie making." Wasserman quoted *Time*, Jan. 1, 1965.

p. 185: "*Time* magazine . . . manufactures movies." *Time,* Jan. 1, 1965.

p. 185: "They copied . . . much of his movies." A.I. Gerber, July 29, 1997.

p. 185: "If brokers insisted . . . who represented them." A.I. Frank Price, Aug. 5, 1998.

p. 185. "Many agents started . . . . Management Associates." A.I. Gerber and Murray, March 27, 1998.

p. 185: "MCA agents . . . his agency's name." Ibid and A. I. Alan Bregnan, July 29, 1998.

p. 186: "one of the government . . . he said." A.I. Malcolm MacArthur, Aug. 31, 1998.

p. 186: "Tanen agreed . . . who believes that." A.I. Tanen, July 7, 1998.

p. 186: "Unconsciously . . . class act." A.I. Migden, July 7, 1998.

p. 187: "When Wasserman . . . Stanely Bergerman." A.I. Bergerman, Dec. 16, 1996.

p. 187: "That was the period . . . Clint Eastwood." A.I. Jay Kanter, Jan. 23, 1998; also IMDB.

p. 188: "Lew was always . . . Al Dorskind." A.I. Dorskind, April 1, 1997.

p. 188: "Gershwin was . . . right position." A.I. Gershwin, June 23, 1998.

p. 188: "Kanter told . . . Hunter's heavy hand."A.I. Kanter Jan. 23, 1998; *The Universal Story*, pp. 196.

p. 188: "Lew thought. . . .that got made." A.I. Tanen, June 2, 1998.

Chapter 20:

p. 188–189: "Universal Studios . . . tight production schedules." MCA annual report 1965 and 1966.

p. 189: "Cranes, dollies . . . a triumph by any measure." Universal Studio press releases and photos from its archives.

p. 189: "Wasserman was reaching . . . props to *The Munsters.*" *Time,* Jan. 1, 1965.

p. 189: "And somewhere . . . in several TV series." A.I. Carson, Nov. 12, 1999.

p. 189: "Al Dorskind's experiment . . . *don't lose money.*" A.I. Steinberg, Aug. 3, 1998.

p. 189–190: "Wasserman expected . . . Stein disappeared." A.I. Raines, July 28, 1998.

p. 190. "Actors and directors . . . tourists." A.I. Jay Stein, April 6, 1998.

p. 190: "The most amazing thing . . . even made money." A.I. Steinberg, Aug. 3, 1998.

p. 191: "Visitors got to . . . T-shirts." Universal City facts sheet circa 1966.

p. 191: "Wasserman . . . a lot of it." MCA annual reports 1965, 1966; A.I. Dorskind, April 1, 1997.

p. 191: "Wasserman's political clout . . . display of affection." Staff memos from LBJ library.

p. 191: "He was content . . . Jack Valenti." A.I. Valenti, June 5, 1997.

p. 191–192: "Edie and I . . . he would do it." A.I. Steinberg, Aug. 3, 1998; Valenti confirms that Wasserman was offered a Cabinet post, June 5, 1997.

p. 192: "Lew was a political . . . for him." A.I. Dorskind, Aug. 1, 1998.

p. 192: "Another MCA . . . piles of money." A.I. unnamed source, Sept. 19, 1996.

p. 192: "In May 1965, . . . astonishing feat." Details from May 6, 1966 White House staff memo.

p. 193: "Only Wasserman . . . and exhibition." Finler, *The Hollywood Story,* pp. 208.

p. 193: "As historian . . . him after that." A.I. Gomery, Feb. 6, 1997.

p. 193: "In 1966 . . . cleaning services." Finler, *The Hollywood Story,* pp. 143, 188, 231.

p. 193–194: "After several . . . odds on death." Steven Bach, *Final Cut* (William Morris, 1985), pp. 3–12.

p. 194: "Wasserman regularly . . . through his office . . ." A.I. Harrison Price, Sept. 17, 1998.

p. 194: " . . . including Joe Cerrell. . . . expanding empire." A.I. Cerrell, Aug. 3, 1998.

p. 194: "He once asked a . . . MCA's culture." A.I. Nims, July 2, 1997.

p. 194–195: "To me . . . loved him for it." A.I. Dorskind, April 1, 1998.

p. 195: "It was a strange . . . one insider." A.I. PT. Sept. 19, 1996.

p. 195: "After Nims' young son . . . film editor." A.I. Nims, July 2, 1997.

p. 195: "When an MCA . . . said the man." A.I. unnamed, July 28, 1998.

p. 195: "When TV writer . . . I've treasured." A.I. Swerling, Feb. 22, 2000.

p. 195: "But Wasserman never . . . said one." A.I. Tanen, July 7, 1998.

p. 195: "In 1920 . . . himself was seven." 1920 Census Bureau records from Cleveland.

p. 195: "His face and hands . . . soil himself." Typical symptoms as described in *Encyclopedia of Medical History* (New York: McGraw Hill Book Co., 1986) edited by Roderick E. McGrew, pp. 111–114.

p. 195: "These seizures . . . shunned the Wassermans." Owsei Temkin *The Falling Sickness, A History of Epilepsy,* (The Johns Hopkins Press, 1945); pp.115–16; 251–259.

p. 195–196: "They sought cures . . . his parents gave up." Ibid; A.I. with Dr. Robert Harbaugh, an expert in epilepsy, Feb. 14, 1998.

p. 196 "They enrolled him . . . exhaustion of epilepsy." Death Certificate of Max Wasserman.

p. 196: "Forty years . . . . on epilsepsy." Dennis McDougal, *The Last Mogul,* pp. 384–385.

p. 196: "Lew used . . . fudge on anything." A.I. Dorskind, Aug. 1, 1998

p. 196: "I remember. . . .one rival agent." A.I. Alan Bregnan, July 29, 1997.

p. 196–197: "For several years . . . personal business." A.I. Adams, Feb. 20, 1998.

p. 197: "Werblin . . . to the Jets." Robert Thomas Jr., "Sonny Werblin, an Impressario." *New York Times,* Nov. 23, 1991.

p. 197: "My dad was . . . Tom Werblin." A.I. Werblin, Oct. 28, 2002.

p. 197: "But Jules . . . Miller Krauskopf." A.I. Krauskopf, Aug. 2, 1998.

p. 197: "Werblin . . . said Adams." A.I. Adams, Feb. 20, 1998.

p. 197: "As Wasserman . . . eyes and ears." A.I. Gershwin, Sept. 15, 1998.

p. 197–198: ": "Although Gershwin . . . Lew Wasserman." Gottlieb, "Lew Wasserman . . ." *Los Angeles Magazine,* January 1979, p. 205.

p. 198: "But others claimed . . . to make." A.I. Curtis, Feb. 17, 2000; A. I. Tanen, Oct. 27, 1998.

p. 198: "Edie tried . . . died, said Jackie." A.I. Gershwin, Sept. 15, 1998.

Chapter 21

p. 199: Edie celebrated . . . wished the doyenne." Letter from LBJ Library, dated Jan. 5, 1965.

p. 199: "Several guests . . . said Price." A.I. Price, Aug. 5, 1998.

p. 199: "Added another . . . for the future." A.I. C.S., Sept. 3, 1998.

p. 199: "More shocking . . . Edie's part." A.I. Park, Oct. 27, 1998.

p. 200: "During the mid-1960s . . . one studio executive." A.I. Raines, July 28, 1998.

p. 200: "Before she met . . . two sons." A.I. Oppenheimer, Aug. 12, 1997.

p. 200: "Doris had . . . J.B. Lessor." A.I. Lesser, Oct. 2, 1996.

p. 200: "Edie liked to be . . . clear of Edie." A.I. Wages, March 27, 1998.

p. 200: "Lew and Jules . . . said Tanen." A.I. Tanen, July 7, 1998.

p. 200: "Added a publicist . . . two apart." A.I. B.R. March 20, 1997.

p. 200: " . . . given that in . . . Univesal Studios." MCA annual report 1965.

p. 200: "As Wasserman . . . way of life." LBJ letter from LBJ library, Jan. 5, 1965.

p. 200: "Wasserman . . . was impolitic." Jan. 5, 1965 letter from Valenti to Wasserman.

p. 200–201: "In September . . . and his kids." LBJ Library papers: May 19, 1966 letters to and from W. Marvin Watson and Lew Wasserman.

p. 201: "Even Edie . . . perfect condition." Aug. 11, 1965 letter to Edie from Jack Valenti.

p. 201: "Edie opened . . . nor the Steins." LBJ library papers, memos, and guest list.

p. 201: "He had watched . . . of those speeches." A.I. Steinberg, Aug. 4, 1998.

p. 202: "Meanwhile, Arizona . . . outrageous statements." Barry Goldwater obituary; Christopher Caldwell, "Goldwater the Refusenik," *New York Observer,* March 19, 2001, Rick Perlstein, *Before the Storm: Barry Goldwater and Unmaking of the Ameican Consensus,* (Hill and Wang, 2001).

p. 202: "The Misty Mountain . . . said Steinberg." A.I., Aug. 4, 1998.

p. 202: "Goldwater let . . . they are wrong." Speech from records at the Hoover Institute, former site of Reagan's gubernatorial records.

p. 202: "That speech . . . Steinberg explained." A.I., Aug. 3, 1998.

p. 202: "Others say . . . lesser influence." A.I. Lou Canon, Sept. 9, 2002; Bob Colacello, "Ronnie and Nancy," *Vanity Fair,* July 1998.

p. 202: "But those . . . introduced them." A.I. Raines; Oppenheimer, Aug. 12, 1997.

p. 202: "Added Henry Denker . . . he was worthless." A.I. Denker, Aug. 26, 1998.

p. 202: "Some wanted to . . . white hat." A.I. Sheinberg, Aug. 3, 1998.

p. 202: "He was the . . . of sincerity." A.I. Ted Berkman, April 27, 1998.

p. 202–203: "He had a bit . . . run for office." IMDB; A.I. Sid Sheinberg, April 21, 1998.

p. 203: "He asked Wasserman . . . irritated the mogul." A.I. Park, Oct. 27, 1998.

p. 203: "Lew didn't like . . . Lubin." A.I. Lubin, Feb. 18, 1998.

p. 203: "Added Roy . . . with Wasserman." A.I. Brewer, April 17, 1998.

p. 203: "Wasserman . . . best screen role ever." IMDB; *Early Reagan.*

p. 203: "But Reagan was . . . he didn't do." A.I. Park, *Where's The Rest of Me* (Karz Publications, 1965), *Richard Hubler with Reagan.*

p. 203: "In the late 1930s . . . Kollege of *Musical Knowledge.*" A.I. Harry Babbit, member of the group, March 3, 1998; A.I. Steven Beasley, historian, Jan. 23, 1998.

p. 203: "Wasserman had signed . . . as big." Bette Grables $800,000 1941 annual deal from AMPS files as reported in *AMC Magazine*, Nov. 1994; Bette Davis $900,000 annual 1940 salary from *The Lonely Life, An Autobiography*, (GP Putnam's Sons), p. 209.

p. 203–204: "In any case . . . collected his commission." Memo in Rose's, *The Agency*, p. 81; Memos from Warner Brothers Studios on file at University of Southern California between Reagan and studio executives; Canon, *Reagan*, p. 67.

p. 204: "Reagan grated . . . like a politician." A.I. Huggins, Feb. 17, 2000.

p. 204: "Huggins suspicions . . . Gov. Pat Brown." Edwards, *Early Reagan*, pp. 487–491.

p. 205: "Reagan began . . . look grandfatherly." Photos from files of Hoover Institute, former site of Reagan gubernatorial papers; also "Golden State, Golden Youth," *Kirse Granat May* (University of North Carolina 2002).

p. 205: "You had Schreiber . . . Seltzer." A.I. Seltzer, July 15, 1997.

p. 205: "Schreiber was . . . but adjacent towns." A.I. Adams, Feb. 20, 1998; Kramer's papers.

p. 205–206: "But neither . . . he told Schreiber." Kramer's papers, Kramer story on doctorjazz.com.

p. 206: "Schreiber kept busy . . . very scary clients." A.I. Adams, Feb. 20, 1998; Kramer's papers.

p. 206: "By then, Schreiber . . . to help Schreiber." A.I. Adams; A.I. Bergerman, Dec. 16, 1996. *Variety*, "Taft Schreiber," Feb. 6, 1990; A.I. Greenberg, Feb. 6, 1998.

p. 206: "Wasserman hated . . . one veteran." A.I. Raines, March 5, 1998.

p. 206: "Yet, Schreiber insisted . . . Hays Motion Picture Production Code." A.I. Adams, Feb. 20, 1997; A. I. Gerber, Feb. 5, 1997; and A. I. Freddie Fields, Feb. 26, 1997.

p. 206–207: "Indeed, 50 years later . . . seemed natural." A.I. Wasserman, June 22, 1999.

p. 207: "In 1946, MCA . . . Lenore Greenberg." A.I. Greenberg, Feb. 6, 1998.

p. 207: "Stein surprised . . . to Wasserman." A.I. Price, Nov. 5, 1998.

p. 207: "Added Al Dorskind . . . open hostility." A.I. Dorskind, April 1, 1997; A. I. Raines, July 28, 1998; A. I. Sheinberg, April 21, 1998.

p. 207: "Stein seemed . . . leadership styles." A.I. Adams, Feb. 20, 1998.

p. 207: "I always used . . . his work." A.I. Dorskind, April 1, 1997.

p. 207–208: "Schreiber spent . . . became well known." A.I. Greenberg, Feb. 6, 1998.

p. 208: "The Steins encouraged . . . executives." A.I. Wages, March 27, 1998; A.I. Adams, Feb. 20; 1998; A.I. Price, Nov. 5, 1998; A.I. Tanen, June 2, 1998.

p. 208: "By 1966. . . .of Modern Art." William Wilson, "MOCA Given Art Donation of $60 Million," *Los Angeles Times,* May 10, 1989; Richard West, "Possible Blood Error in Schreiber's Death Probed," *Los Angeles Times,* June 16, 1976.

p. 208: "Still, he kept . . . killer type." A.I. Denker, Aug. 20, 1998.

p. 208: "Wasserman was very . . . Joe Cerrell." Aug. 3, 1998.

p. 208: "But Johnson . . . work with Brown." A.I. Valenti, June 5, 1997.

p. 208: "Johnson not only approved . . . he often sought." March 1, 1966 letter to Wasserman from LBJ from archives of Johnson Library.

p. 208–209: "They hosted . . . write a check." A.I. Cerrell and Steinberg, Aug. 3, 1998.

p. 209: "Meanwhile . . . TV show host." Materials on file at the Hoover Institute— site of Reagan's gubernatorial records for a time.

p. 209: "In some circles . . . you can too." A.I. Lubin, Feb. 18, 1998.

p. 209: "During his administration . . . or eliminated." Based on records from Reagan's gubernatorial collection, then housed at the Hoover Institute.

p. 209: "Reagan . . . Sacramento years." A.I. Stu Spencer, March 26, 2003.

p. 209–210: "Shortly after . . . and auditorium." A.I. Jill Stuart, JSEI spokeswoman, July 30, 1997; A.I. Straatsma, July 30, 1997.

p. 210: "The National Institute . . . advisory council." A.I. Straatsma, July 30, 1997.

p. 210–211: "Lew wanted . . . front and center." A.I. Barton, Oct. 3, 1997.

p. 211: "In the turbulent spring . . . Century Plaza Hotel." Series of memos between Waserman and White House, including those from May 5, 8, 10 and June 20, 1967, from LBJ library papers.

p. 211: "Wasserman . . . few reporters to attend." A.I. Steinberg, Aug. 4, 1998; also papers from LBJ Library.

p. 211–212: "But Wasserman . . . mainstream anti-war protests." Kenneth Reich, "The Bloody March That Shook L.A.," *Los Angeles Times,* June 23, 1997; A.I. Steinberg Aug. 4, 1998; A.I. Cerrell Aug. 3, 1998.

p. 212–213: "Inside the ballroom . . . riot outside." A.I. Raines, March 5, 1998; A.I. Cerrell Aug. 3, 1998.

p. 213: "Guest Barry Gordy . . . United States." June 29, 1967 letter from Gordy to Johnson, courtesy of LBJ Library.

p. 213 "Johnson never . . . in Los Angeles." Reich, June 23, 1997.

p. 213: "Wasserman . . . to leaving office." A.I. Steinberg, Aug. 3, 1998.

p. 213: "In April 1968 . . . I've ever known." A.I. Cerrell, Aug. 3, 1998.

Chapter 22:

p. 213: "MCA bought him . . . Jaguar coupe." A.I. Raines, March 5, 1998.

p. 213: "He added more . . . the world." MCA annual reports 1966, 1967, 1968.

p. 213: "He reveled in his . . . any hobbies." Earl C. Gottschalk, Jr. "Show Biz Super-star," *Cleveland Plain Dealer* , July 27, 1973.

p. 214: "In his grandiose . . . that year." A.I. Price, Dec. 2, 1998; MCA 1966 annual report.

p. 214: "With that, MCA . . . their debut." A.I. Sheinberg, March 25, 1998.

p. 214: "For a time . . . in television history." A.I. Price, Aug. 5, 1998; A.I. Adler, Dec. 15, 1998; A.I. Sheinberg Mrach 25, 1998.

p. 214: "One of Sheinberg's . . . viewers turned in." A.I. Sheinberg, March 25, 1998.

p. 214: "With its brightly lit . . . prescient." A.I. Fairbanks, Jan. 7, 1998.

p. 215: "It was also . . . counterpart." Details from IMDB.

p. 215: "Wasserman's men . . . charged our clients." A.I. Price, Dec. 2, 1999.

p. 215–216: "By the end . . . into a 'wheel' format." A.I. Sheinberg, April 21, 1998.

p. 216: "Character Glen Howard . . . ended in 1971." IMDB; A.I. Fairbanks, Jan. 7, 1998.

p. 216: "Price produced . . . the U.S. government." A.I. Price, Aug. 5, 1998.

p. 216–217: "One of Wasserman's . . . you belong." Kasher, "Natalie Wood's Fatal Voyage," *Vanity Fair,* March 2000, p. 256.

p. 217: "Wagner . . . best actor." IMDB.

p. 217: "Universal TV . . . action-packed frames." A.I. Fairbanks, Jan. 7, 1998.

p. 217–218 : "Lang lured . . . Wasserman demanded." A.I. Link, Dec. 8, 1999.

p. 218: "Irving was mortified . . . had ever done." A.I. Adler, Dec. 15, 1998.

p. 218: "An NBC network . . . Link told him." A.I. Link, July 12, 2002; A.I. Schlosser, Oct. 8, 2002.

p. 218: "With *World Premieres* . . . and its other shows." A.I. Price, Dec. 2, 1999.

p. 219: "The rise of Universal TV . . . from eight years earlier." McDonald, *One Nation Under Television,* p. 368

p. 219: "The TV shows . . . always realistic." A.I. Dorskind, Aug. 1, 1998; A.I Sheinberg, May 19, 1998.

p. 219: "As Universal hired . . . to the productions' cost." Adler, Dec. 15, 1998.

p. 221 "The triumvirate . . . hand at movies." A.I. Price, Dec. 2, 1998.

p. 221 "In 1968, Sheinberg . . . any longer." A.I. Sheinberg, March 25, 1998.

p. 221 "In 1969, former NBC . . . then he left." Grant Tinker biography, from Musuem of TV and Radio. (Tinker did not respond to an interview request.)

p. 221 "Who ulimately . . . out of hand." A.I. Sheinberg, April 21, 1998.

p. 221: "Lang turned into a . . . said Ned Tanen." A.I. Tanen, July 7, 1998.

p. 221: "When Edie . . . Santa Cruz estate." A.I. Wasserman, June 22, 1999.

p. 221: "The Hitchcocks . . . one executive." A.I. Tanen, July 7, 1998; A.I. Raines, July 28, 1998.

p. 222: "To get there . . . across the highway." Description of house and site from articles: Ross Eric Gibson, "Hitchcock had link to Santa Cruz, *San Jose Mercury News,* Nov. 29, 1994; Marion Dale Pokriots, "Alfred Hitchcock found contentment in Scotts Valley," *Scotts Valley Banner,* July 24, 1996.

p. 222: "Most evenings . . . from this area." A.I. O'Connell, May 14, 1998.

p. 222: "The Bates Motel . . . House in Santa Cruz." Susan King, "Hitchcock's Haunts," *Los Angeles Times,* Jan. 23, 2003.

p. 222: "The Birds was born . . . Cruz storefronts." "Alfred Hitchcock Using Sentinel's Seabird Story, *Santa Cruz Sentinel,* Aug. 21, 1961.

p. 222: "Wasserman loved . . . a superb man." Nov. 3, 1999.

p. 223: "Hitchcock, who had been . . . Adler explained." A.I. Adler Dec. 15, 1998.

p. 223: "Whereas the director . . . said Ned Tanen." A.I. Tanen, July 7, 1998.

p. 223: "Their penchant for . . . to the workplace, too." A.I. Adler, Dec. 15, 1998.

p. 224: "During his studio . . . he didn't bother." A.I. Raines July 28, 1998; also Raines, *Beneath the Tinsel* (Three Lions Publications, Danville, Ill.) p. 132.

p. 224: "The critics . . . business than *The Birds.*" IMDB.

p. 224–225: "Hitch felt the . . . in France and Italy." As described by Aulier in *Hitchcock's Notebooks* (Avon Books); also Jacmes Wolcott, "Death and The Master," *Vanity Fair,* April 1999, p. 153.

p. 225: "But the work . . . master of suspense." *The Universal Story,* p. 302.

p. 225: "Lew always . . . Thalberg Away." A.I. Tanen, June 2, 1998.

p. 225: "Given by the Academy . . . picture production," from Academy of Motion Pcitures Arts and Sciences website.

p. 225: "To its shame . . . Thalberg Award." Academy records; A.I. Adler, Dec. 15, 1998.

p. 225: "That night . . . shuffled off stage." A.I. O'Connell, May 14, 1998.

Chapter 23:

p. 226: "After the lunch . . . expenses." A.I. Muhl, Sept. 17, 1997.

p. 226: "The opening of . . . following March." MCA annual reports, 1966, 1967, 1968.

p. 226: "Doris Stein . . . said Sheinberg." A.I. Sheinberg, March 25, 1998; April 21, 1998.

p. 226: " . . . but producer Ross . . . toward $8 million." A.I. Robert Bleese, July 1, 1997; IMDB.

p. 226–227: "inside the studio . . . he said. A.I. Tanen, July 7, 1998.

p. 227: "Twentieth Century . . . Rosemary's Baby . . ." From Finler, *Hollywood Story* under each studio section.

p. 227 ". . . which Rosemary Clooney . . . domestic life." Clooney, *Girl Singer,* p. 175.

p. 227: "All the studios . . . to its name." A.I. Price, Aug. 5, 1998.

p. 227: "If you look at . . . a former MCA agent." A.I. Alan Brigman, July 29, 1997.

p. 227–228: "Wasserman kept . . . deputy Jay Kanter." A.I. Muhl, Sept. 17, 1997; A.I. Kanter, Jan. 23, 1998.

p. 228: Details about these movies collected from IMDB; Hirschhorn, *The Universal Story;* Leonard Maltin's 2001 *Movie and Video Guide* (Penguin Putnam).

p. 228: "Wasserman was so confident . . . more humiliating." From MCA annual report 1968; 1969.

p. 228: "It was a disastrous. . . .$40 milloin." A.I. Price, Aug. 5, 1998; MCA annual report 1968.

p. 228: "That year, Stein . . . Kanter resigned." A.I. Adams, Feb. 20, 1998; A.I. Kanter, Jan. 23, 1998.

p. 228: "He became the patsy . . . of his scripts." A.I. Raines, March 5, 1998; A.I. Tanen, June 2, 1998.

p. 229: "Stein disagreed with . . . an abyss." A.I. Muhl, Sept. 18, 1997; A.I. Adams, Feb. 20, 1998.

p. 229: "At Stein's urging . . . possessive that way." A.I. Dorksind, Arpil 1, 1997; A.I. Adams, March 31, 1997.

p. 229–230: "To further . . . a terrible time." A.I. Price, Aug. 5, 1998; A.I. Adams, March 31, 1997, A.I. Muhl, Sept. 18, 1997.

p. 230: "At the same . . . savings and loan." MCA annual reports from the 1960s.

p. 230: "Inside MCA, . . . regular dividends." MCA 1968 and 1969 annual reports.

p. 230: "Stein wanted . . . consumer products." A.I. Adams, March 31, 1997; Gottlieb, "Lew Wasserman . . . " p. 124, *Los Angeles Magazine,* January 1979.

p. 231: "The appliance maker . . . cycles of filmmaking." A.I. Dorskind, June 30, 1998; A.I. Price, Aug. 5, 1998.

p. 231: "At Stein's urging . . . but Schrieber did not laugh." A.I. Tanen, June 2, 1998.

p. 231–232: "At one point . . . anti-trust law." Gotlieb, p. 124.

p. 232: "In October 1968 . . . relieved." A.I. Adams, March 31, 1997.

p. 232: "But Wasserman . . . soon unraveled." A.I. Price, Aug. 5, 1998.

p. 232: "I don't believe . . . that wonderful." A.I. Sheinberg, April 21, 1998.

p. 233: "After that . . . supported him." A.I. Price, Nov. 5, 1998.

p. 233: "In January . . . close to $100 million." MCA annual report of 1968; A.I. Price Ibid.

p. 233: "Lew was . . . Tanen recalled." A.I. Tanen, June 2, 1998.

p. 233: "By now . . . to sources." A.I. anonymous JP, June 24, 2003: also McDougal, *The Last Mogul*, pp. 360–1;

p. 233: "Lew had . . . you talked to." A.I. Sheinberg, April 21, 1998.

p. 233: "The illness . . . power struggle." A.I. Adams, March 31, 1997; A.I. Price, Nov. 5, 1998.

p. 233: "They always denied . . . dump Lew." A.I. Tanen, June 2, 1998.

p. 233–234: "At Misty . . . Eye Institute." Joyce Haber, "Universal Planning A Festive Weekend," *Los Angeles Times,* March 10, 1969.

p. 234: "For months now . . . hotel soared, too." Maggie Savory, "A Film Party on a De Mille Scale," *Los Angeles Times,* Jan. 30. 1969.

p. 234–235: "The Steins . . . give money." Haber, March 10, 1969; Univesal's Global Guests, March 31, 1969, *Hollywood Citizen News*; also A.I. Oppenheimer, Aug. 12, 1997.

p. 235: "Staged like a . . . weekend." Ibid Haber; *Hollywood Citizen News.*

p. 235: "One *Los Angeles* . . . and olive." Savoy, Jan. 30, 1969.

p. 235: "In two weeks . . . *New York Times.*" Editorial, March 31, 1969.

p. 235: "When Lew . . . by the Steins." A.I. Dorskind, April 1, 1997.

p. 235–236: "Waserman . . . of the company." A.I. D.L., Feb. 5, 1997.

p. 236: "Edie started . . . on his birthday." A.I. Raines, March 5, 1998; A.I. James Bacon, July 9, 1997.

p. 236: "She called MCA's . . . Waserman's duties." A.I. Adams March 31, 1997; A.I. Tanen, June 2, 1998.

p. 236–237: "Lew meanwhile . . . outside of MCA." A.I. Tanen, June 2, 1998; A.I. Raines, July 28, 1998; A.I. Price, Nov. 5, 1998.

p. 237: "One of those . . . corporate politics." A.I. Lewis-Lang, July 30, 1997.

p. 237: "At one such meeting . . . replace Wasserman." A.I. Sheinberg, April 21, 1998.

p. 237: "Adams would . . . stayed home." A.I. Adams, March 31, 1997.

p. 237–238: "A few days . . . off very well." A.I. Tanen, June 2, 1998.

p. 238: "By Wednesday . . . recording it all." A.I. Hugh Milkinson, June 10, 1999.

p. 238: "Edie tried leaking . . . said Bacon.' A.I. Bacon, July 9, 1997.

p. 238–239: "So he wrote . . . will be fired." Bacon, "A Guiding Genius May Soon find Himself Out of An Important Job," *LA Herald Examiner,* March 28, 1969.

p. 239: "That night . . . 'cheap frills." A.I. Eleanor Phillips, Jan. 27, 1997.

p. 239: "After the movie . . . in a reception line." Joan Kaiser, "et Set and Stars Collide," *Los Angeles Herald Examiner,* April 1, 1969.

p. 239: "Dressed . . . for all to see." Photographs from *Hollywood Citizen News,* March 31, 1969; and Anne Thompson Smith, "Glamour Puts on a Show," *Los Angeles Herald Examiner,* March 31, 1969.

p. 239: "As the crowd . . . George Christy." A.I. Christy, May 8, 2002.

p. 239: "And Dorskind . . . ordered a drink." A.I. Dorskind, Steinberg, Aug. 3, 1998.

p. 240: "I recall . . . other friends." A.I. Sheinberg, April 21, 1998.

p. 240: "I always got along . . . their graves." A.I. Tanen, June 2, 1998.

PART III

Chapter 24

p. 243: During that time . . . Stein and MCA?" A.I. anonymous, Aug. 29, 1996.

p. 243: "Jules was a. . . . over the years to do so." A.I. Adams, March 31, 1997.

p. 243: "In 1941, when . . . vice president at MCA." A.I. Curtis, Feb. 17, 2000; A.I. Dan Slusser, May 8, 1998..

p. 244: "In the early 1950s, . . . he was president of U.A." Brownstein, *Power and the Glitter.*

p. 244: "And in 1958 . . . said Jay Kanter." A.I. Kanter, Jan. 23, 1998.

p. 244: "That same year,. . . said Tony Curtis." A.I. Curtis, Feb. 17, 2000.

p. 244: "By that time . . . the studios anyway." *Current Biography,* 1982 edition.

p. 244: " 'I was very taken . . . explained Wasserman." A.I. June 22, 1999.

p. 244: "As Kanter . . . repsected Lew." A.I. Kaner, Jan. 23, 1998.

p. 245: "Edie was outraged . . . a blistering report." A.I. Steinberg, Aug. 3, 1998; A.I. Tanen, June 2, 1998; A.I. Bacon, July 9, 1997.

p. 245: ". . . where *Sweet Charity* . . . for eye institute." "Eye Clinic Nets $125,000," *Los Angeles Herald Examiner,* April 1, 1969.

p. 245: "One phony nobelman . . . embarrassing Doris." A.I. Bacon, July 9, 1997; A.I. Tanen, June 2, 1998; Bacon, columns, March 30, 1969, *Los Angeles Herald Examiner,* April 4, 1969.

p. 245: "One drunken . . . in mankind." Suzy Knickerbocker, "Suzy Comes to the Stein Party," *Los Angeles Herald Examiner,* March 31, 1969. Also, "Jet Set and Stars Collide," *Los Angeles Herald Examiner,* April 1, 1969.

p. 245–246: "To begin with . . . in the worst light." A.I. Dorskind, April 1, 1997; stock figures "Top Tier MCA Exec Realigned," *Variety,* Feb. 13, 1970.

p. 246: "These people . . . Sheinberg." A.I. Sheinberg, March 25, 1998.

p. 246: "I was always . . . Ronnie Lubin." A.I. Lubin, Feb. 18, 1998.

p. 246: "He could be . . . said Dorskind." A.I. Dorskind, April 1, 1997.

p. 246: "Frank Price . . . said Price." A.I. Price, Aug. 5, 1998.

p. 246: "Television accounted . . . to be collected." MCA annual report, 1969.

p. 246: "Without a strong . . . said Price." A.I. Price, Aug. 5, 1998; also A.I. Lewis-Lang, July 30, 1997.

p. 247: "When the board . . . Chicago National Trust . . . " A.I Tanen, June 2, 1998.

p. 247: "According to James . . . show of support." A.I. Bacon, July 9, 1997.

p. 247: "The board relected . . . uncomfortable concession." A.I. Price, Aug. 5, 1998; A.I. Tanen, June 2, 1998; and A.I. Bacon, July 9, 1997.

p. 247: "Even so, Wasserman . . . signed the letter." MCA annual report, 1969.

p. 247: "Edie's call, leaks . . . next day's column." Bacon, "Susanne Benton And All That Padding," *Los Angeles Herald Examiner,* April 1, 1969.

p. 247: "*Sweet Charity,* however . . . numbed silence." Jet Set and Stars Collide," *Los Angeles Herald Examiner,* April 1, 1969.

p. 248: "I think Jules . . . *Lawrence of Arabia.*" A.I. D.L., Feb. 5, 1996.

p. 248: "From its rendition . . . offended viewers . . . " A.I. Oppenheimer, Aug. 12, 1997; also Joan Kaiser, "Jet Set and Stars Collide," *Los Angeles Herald Examiner,* April 1, 1969.

p. 248: ". . . Henry Salvatori—a man . . . a radical . . ." from the Society of Exploration and Geophysicists Museum.

p. 248: "'The public did not . . . to dismal business." IMDB.

p. 248: "Who knows . . . what will hit.' " A.I. Sheinberg, April 21, 1998.

p. 248: "He and Stein . . . were pained." A.I. Adams, Feb. 20, 1998.

p. 248: "Stein 'was embarrassed' . . . at Schreiber's insistence." A.I. Price, Nov. 5, 1998.

p. 248: "But Wasserman . . . and Schreiber." From "Top Tier MCA Exec Realigned," *Variety,* Feb. 13, 1970.

p. 249: "Al Dorksind's . . . administrative duties." Ibid; A.I. Dorskind, April 1, 1997.

p. 249: "In the midsdt . . . of the digestive tract." A.I. Adams, Feb. 20, 1998.

p. 249–250: "But exploratory surgery . . . turmoil for MCA." Andrew Tobias, "The Hidden Fight that Finally Made MCA the Greatest," April 26, 1976, *New West.* pp. 100–102. Also, A.I. Patsy Krauskopf, March 5, 1998.

p. 250: "Stein's living will . . . maintain his rule." A.I. Adams, Feb. 20, 1997.

p. 250: "years earlier, in 1948 . . . they'll kill you." Eisenstadt, *Nicolas Ray,* p. 196.

p. 250: "While Stein's life . . . Decca record label."A.I. Adams, March 31, 1997, Feb. 20, 1998.

p. 250: "Then, Stein. . . . *Wall Street Journal.*" A.I. Wasserman, June 22, 1999.

p. 251: "From his hospital bed . . . reinstate the man." A.I. Adams, Feb. 20, 1998.

p. 251: "As Stein regained . . . him feel better.' " Army Archerd, April 28, 1970; *Variety,* A.I. Oppenheimer, Aug. 12, 1997.

Chapter 25:

This chapter owes a debt to Peter Biskind, *Easy Rider, Raging Bull* (Simon & Schuster, 1998) and to Seth Cagin & Philip Dray, *Hollywood Films of the Seventies: Sex, Drugs, Violence, Rock `n Roll & Politics* (Harper & Row Publishers. 1984).

p. 251: "The summer of 1969 . . . studio executive." A.I. Tanen, July 28, 1998.

p. 251: "In one week, the $500,000 film." Dray Dagin, *Hollywood Films of the Seventies,* pp. xiii.

p. 251: "There were . . . youth market." A.I. Tanen, July 28, 1998.

p. 252: "Jules daughter, Jean . . . financed by MCA." A.I. Tanen, July 28, 1998.

p. 252: Now that Stein . . . said Tanen." A.I. Ibid.

p. 252: "Schreiber, meanwhile . . . He didn't disappoint." A.I. Price, Nov. 2, 1998; also item in *Los Angeles Times,* April 4, 1969,

p. 252–253: "A few months . . . cinematography." IMDB.

p. 253: "Meanwhile, Wasserman . . . " A.I. Price, Nov. 2, 1998; IMDB.

p. 254: "Other films could . . . reviews of his career." A.I. Raines, March 5, 1998; also Raines, *Beneath the Tinsel,* pp. 142.

p. 254: "Meanwhile, problems . . . spinning out of control." Hirschhorn, *The Universal Story,* pp. 315; IMDB; A.I. Robert Bleese, July 1, 1997.

p. 254: "Lew was wild . . . do much damage." A.I. Tanen, July 28, 1998; A.I. Raines, March 5, 1998.

p. 254–255: "Hunter and his partner . . . nasty parting,' he said." A.I. Bleese, July 1, 1997; A.I. Raines, March 5, 1998.

p. 255: Hunter never . . . Universal's biggest client." Biography on Ross Hunter, Katz, *Film Encylopedia,* and IMBD.

p. 255: "Wasserman didn't . . . in the line of fire." A.I. Price, Nov. 2, 1998.

p. 255–256: "To make his . . . bride, Tanen said." A.I. Tanen, July 28, 1998; also web-sites of Neil Diamond, Elton John, UNI Records (history), A&M Records.

p. 256: "Wasserman couldn't . . . young directors." A.I. Tanen, July 28, 1998.

p. 256: "As an agent, Wasserman . . . the industry." A.I. Kantner, Jan. 23, 1998.

p. 256: "I don't think . . . bought Universal." A.I. Bob Thomas, Dec. 9, 1962.

p. 256–257: "But as time went . . . any 50–50 deals." Bacon, July 9, 1997; also Kaiser Apreil 1, 1962.

p. 257: "Once Columbia . . . Tanen recalled." A.I. Tanen, June 2, 1998, July 7, 1998.

p. 257: "Hopper's film . . . much-anticipated film." Biskind, *Easy Rider, Raging Bull,* p. 134.

p. 257–258: "Privately, Wasserman . . . a catastrophe." A.I. Tanen, July 2, 1998.

p. 258: "From the projectionists' . . . ever makes." A.I. Raines, March 5, 1998.

p. 258: "Wasserman attended . . . he later said." Marshall Berges, "Lew & Edie Wasserman," *Los Angeles Times Home Magazine,* Dec. 2, 1973.

p. 258: "The first movie . . . for Best Actress." Hirschhorn, *The Universal Story,* p. 308.

p. 258: "Next up . . . Buck Henry." A.I. Tanen, July 2, 1998.

p. 258: "Forman applied . . . Film Festival." Hirschhorn, p. 310; also IMDB.

p. 259: "Hired Hand . . . critical success." A.I. Tanen, June 2, 1998; Hirschhorn, p. 312.

p. 259: "Tanen got the . . . interference." A.I. Tanen, June 2, 1998.

p. 259: "Perhaps anticipating . . . would see them." A.I. Raines March 5, 1998.

p. 259: "Some people . . . piles of cash." Corman as interviewed by BBC *Out of the Blue and Into the Black* (Paul Joyce Productions, 1987), tape courtesy of Monte Hellman.

p. 259: "He had made two . . . major importance." Michael Goodwin, *Rolling Stone,* Oct. 15, 1970.

p. 259: "For Universal, he . . . Dean Stanton." A.I. Hellman, Dec. 14, 1998;

p. 259–260: "A few months . . . in India." *Esquire,* April 1970.

p. 260: "But after Hopper's . . . pulled back." A.I. Tanen, July 7, 1008.

p. 260: "*Two-Lane Blacktop* . . . had to change." A.I. Hellman, Dec. 14, 1998.

p. 260: "Next up . . . more pressing." Hirschhorn, p. 315.

p. 260–261: "The film gave . . . was now working." Film biographies from IMDB and KATZ or *Film Encyclopedia.*

p. 261: Still, Wasserman . . . said Tanen." A.I., June 2, 1998, July 7, 1998.

p. 261: Bert Schneider was . . . into drugs." Biskind, pp. 131; 299.

p. 261–262: "Bert Schneider . . . return on investment.' A.I. Tanen, July 7, 1998.

p. 262: "Elsewhere in the studio . . . either." Hirschhorn, p. 314; IMBD.

p. 262: "Jennings Lang . . . not a smash." A.I. Polonsky, April 3, 1998.

p. 262: "Lang oversaw . . . back its investment." A.I. Lewis-Lang, July 30, 1997; also IMDB.

p. 263: "Only *Airport* was . . . extraordinary for its time." A.I. Raines, March 5, 1998; Hirschhorn, p. 306.

p. 263: "By 1972, Wasserman . . . his own hit." A.I. Tanen, July 7, 1998.

Chapter 26

p. 263–264: "In the months . . . Hollywood insiders whispered." Gottlieb, *Los Angeles Magazine*, January 1979, p. 207.

p. 264: "We'd been invited . . . Reagans, either." A.I. Park, Oct. 27, 1998; also a review of Reagan's gubernatorial papers then located at the Hoover Institute.

p. 264: "Reagan and his . . . $1 billion." Ibid.

p. 264: "His finance director . . . said Spencer." A.I. Spencer, March 25, 2003.

p. 265: "Reagan did not forget . . . art preservation." From Reagan's gubernatorial papers. Aug. 1, 1968 memo; A.I. Bob Lagomarsino, April 6, 1999; *Current Biography* 1991.

p. 265: "I'm sure . . . them, said Spencer." A.I. Spencer, March 26, 2003.

p. 265: "Schreiber also . . . Republican outpost." A.I. Raines, March 5, 1998; A.I. Price, Dec. 2, 1999.

p. 265: "He raised so much . . . historic burglary." Schreiber's effort was one of several that raised $60 million for the Committee to Re-elect the President—more than needed. "Watergate 25," *Washington Post* (on-line); Stans obituary, *Washington Post*, April 15, 1998; Stans Museum, Scott County Historical Society, A.I. Raines, March 5, 1998.

p. 265: "Taft organized Celebrities . . . anti-welfare Republican." A.I. Brown, March 10, 1978.

p. 266: "Schreiber persuaded Nixon . . . depreciation laws." A.I. Adams, Feb. 20, 1998; A.I. Spencer, March 25, 2003.

p. 266: "The 1971 Revenue . . . off that income." David Putnam, *The Undeclared War*, p. 267.

p. 266: "In its first year . . . ever in 1972." Wasserman's letter to shareholders, MCA annual report, 1972.

p. 266: "Although revenues grew . . . new tax rules." MCA earnings story, *Variety*, March 29, 1972.

p. 266: "By 1970, the three . . . other major producers." William and Denise Bielby, profesors of sociology, UCSB, "Controlling Prime-Time: Organizational Concentration and Network TV Programming Strategies."

p. 266: "Wasserman and other . . . said Jerry Adler." A.I. Adler, Dec. 15, 1998.

p. 266: " . . . Schreiber lobbied . . . against them." A.I. Adams, Feb. 20, 1998.

p. 266: "In 1970, Nixon's FCC . . . a future stream of income." Museum of TV and Radio archives, "The Financial Interest and Syndication Rules"; A.I. Price, Aug. 5, 1998.

p. 267: "It would be hard . . . for decades." A.I. Valenti, June 5, 1997.

p. 267: "As Columbia studio . . . own a studio." A.I. Paul Lauzrus, former vice president of Columbia, Dec. 6, 1996.

p. 267: "She'd always been . . . Marge LaRonge." A.I. LaRonge, Dec. 5, 1996.

p. 267: "Edie's father Henry . . . and Warrensville. Beckerman's profile, *Cleveland Press*, Aug. 24, 1936; "Henry Beckerman," *This Cleveland of Ours*, Volume II, (S.J. Clarke Publishing Co., 1933), p. 565–567.

p. 267: "He rode the . . . having been elected." Garland Ashcraft, "Maschke Reign Dealt Big Blow." *Cleveland Press*, July 25, 1932.

p. 267–268: "Around 1922, Beckerman . . . for years." Several newspaper stories including Ralph J. Donaldson, "Beckerman and G.O.P. Boss Say Finkle Laid Shortage to Dead Man,": *Cleveland Press,* July 31, 1932.

p. 268: "He packed off one son . . . elite academy." "Opens Attack on Beckerman," April 27, 1934 *Cleveland Press.*

p. 268: In 1927, the 12–year . . . serve tea." Miss Anne Hathaway School, *The First Hundred Years,* 1977; also records from Miss Anne Hathaway School.

p. 268: "The following year . . . blessed the county's books." "Rubber Checks in U.S. Court," *Cleveland Press,* June 3, 1932.

p. 268: "Edie Beckerman . . . full of dresses." Barbara Thomas, "Making a Home For Hollywood," *Los Angeles Times,* Nov. 3, 1998.

p. 268: "She lived a . . . private school." A.I. Jacobs, Feb. 1, 1997.

p. 268: "The Beckermans . . . Cleveland native." A.I. Arlene Rich, Sept. 29, 1997.

p. 268: "He enrolled her . . . best grade ever." Records from Cleveland Heights High School.

p. 268–269: "In 1931, . . . collect from him." From "Tax Checks in $96,000 Show-down Today," *Cleveland Plain Dealer,* Aug. 3, 1932; and "New Juggling of Taxes Found," *Cleveland Plain Dealer,* Aug. 4, 1932.

p. 269: "In June 1932, Beckerman, . . . political machinery." As reported in the *Cleveland Press* in June 22, 1932; quote is from *Cleveland Press* story, July 25, 1932.

p. 269: "There was always . . . to spend time with." A.I. LaRonge, Dec. 5, 1996.

p. 269: "In July 1932, . . . as his scapegoat." Several articles, including Maschek Snaps Denial," *Cleveland Press,* July 31, 1932.

p. 269: "In the fall of Edie's . . . public treasury." Harold E. Hatch, "Issue For Judges Their Ruling Declares," *Cleveland Plain Dealer,* Oct. 20, 1932.

p. 269: "Whenever someone . . . great attorney." A.I. Mrs. Al Setnik, Nov. 20,1997.

p. 269: "She was a prima . . . sniffed LaRonge." A.I. LaRonge, April 14, 1996.

p. 269: "She'd say she . . . added Dorothy Barton." A.I. Barton, Oct. 31, 1997.

p. 270: "In June 1933, Edie . . . completed a term." Records from Cleveland Heights High School and from Ohio State University.

p. 270: "Instead, she . . . city café society." Marshall Berges, "Edie & Lew Wasserman, *Los Angeles Times Home Magazine,* Dec. 2, 1973.

p. 270: "No father . . . romantic choices." A.I. Thackery, Sept. 20, 1997.

p. 270: "After Beckerman stood . . . Mrs. Louis Wasserman." A.I. Jacobs, Feb. 1, 1997; A.I. Barton, Oct. 31, 1997.

p. 270: "Six months later . . . out of town." A.I. LaRonge, April 14, 1996.

p. 270: "Lynne said . . . Lynne's." Anonymous source, June 12, 2002.

p. 270: "The uberagent's . . . some sources." A.I. Krauskopf, Aug. 2, 1998.

p. 270: "They had a . . . to a stockbroker." A.I. Leigh, Feb. 5, 1998.

p. 270–271: "In the meantime . . . said an MCA executive." Anonymous, Aug. 29, 1996.

p. 271: "In the 1970s,. . . former colonial manse." Based on a reading of Joyce Haber's gossip columns in the *Los Angeles Times,* 1972–1974.

p. 271: "She increased . . . like stage productions." A.I. Harrison "Buzz" Price, Sept. 17, 1998.

p. 271: "She once persuaded . . . to his feet." Haber, *The Users*, (The Delacorte Press, 1976), p. 408.

p. 271: "In the mid-1960s . . . and San Marino." A.I. Sandy Rathke, June 15, 1997; Jeannine Stein, "The Reins of Power," *Los Angeles Times*, June 2, 1996.

p. 272: "Yet her closest friend . . . society writer." A.I. Columbia, Oct. 9, 2002.

p. 272: "When Edie first . . . her every time." A.I. Eleanor Phillips, Feb. 7, 1997.

p. 272: "Haber was a . . . producer of *Love Boat*." Photos of Haber and her obituary, *Variety*, Aug. 4, 1993.

p. 272: "Doug had . . . said Champlin." A.I., May 12, 2002.

p. 272: "Haber was so . . . during the 1950s." A.I. Columbia, Oct. 9, 2002.

p. 272: "Now, he owned . . . Haber wrote." *The Users*, p. 166.

p. 272: "One might see . . . such as Sue Mengers." A.I. Christy, May 8, 2003.

p. 272: "You could . . . Dunne." A.I. Dunne, Oct. 25, 2002.

p. 273: "Edie and Joyce . . . with a long chord." A.I. Columbia, Oct. 9, 2002; anonymous, June 12, 2002; A.I. Gershwin, Sept. 15, 1998.

p. 273: "Edie sometimes . . . Joyce Saber." A.I. Bellows, May 9, 2003.

p. 273: "When Julie Andrews . . . through her feet." A.I. Curtis, Feb. 17, 2000.

p. 273: "In 1970, Haber . . . death in 1979." A.I. Bellows, May 9, 2003.

p. 273: "Doris Stein . . . her relatives." A.I. Krauskopf, Aug. 2, 1998.

p. 273: "She was named . . . need an ambulance." A.I. Christy, June 2002.

p. 273–274: "Doris now partied . . . Wasserman said . . . ' " A.I. June 10, 1999.

p. 274. " . . . held suppers for . . . Tanen recalled." A.I. June 2, 1998.

p. 274: "Doris drank a . . . Mae West." A.I. Dunne, Oct. 25, 2002.

p. 274: "At another . . . Luis Estevez." A.I., Dec. 5, 2000.

p. 274: "Privately, she . . . Jean said." A.I. Stein, Oct. 9, 2002.

p. 274: "Her social affairs . . . no day job." A.I. Cockburn, April 11, 1997.

p. 274: "New Journalist Tom . . . the Flak Catchers." Wolfe, *Radical Chic and Mau-Mauring the Flack Catchers* (Bantam, 1971).

p. 274: "Their younger daughter . . . around the pool table." Michele Wood, "Hostess of the Month," *Cosmopolitan*, April 1965.

p. 275: "In December, 1968 . . . right away." "Susan Stein Married to Israeli," *New York Times,* Dec. 3, 1938, .

p. 275: "Doris almost . . . had envisioned. A.I. Nelson, July 20, 1998.

p. 275: "Interior decorator Billy . . . Ford, attended." Maggie Savoy, "Spur-of-Moment Party Toasts Justwed Shivas," *Los Angeles Times*, Dec. 4, 1968.

p. 275: "Hollywood wives . . . between men." A.I. Dunne, Oct. 25, 2002.

Chapter 27:
p. 275: "Jennings Lang . . . Schreiber's office door." A.I. Tanen, June 2, 1998.

p. 275–276: "I mean, he . . . what had happened." A.I. Daniel, Oct. 27, 1998.

p. 276: "Even with new . . . said Frank Price." A.I. Price. Aug. 5, 1998.

p. 276: "Ned Tanen . . . screamers." A.I. Tanen, June 2, 1998.

p. 276: "Lang would yell . . . complex relationship." A.I. Sheinberg, April 21, 1998.

p. 276–277: "In 1971, MCA's revenues . . . in about two years." MCA annual report, 1971.

p. 277: "He's the one . . . Wasserman agreed." A.I. Tanen, June 2, 1998.

p. 277: "For the first time . . . for that, said Price." A.I. Price, Dec. 2, 1999.

p. 277: "And ABC was still, publicly admitted." Marvin Wolf, *Beating the Odds*, p. 333.

p. 277: "Roy Huggins . . . at the third-place network." A.I. Huggins, Feb. 24, 2000. Also, details that follow are recounted in Huggins' unpublished story, "False Start: An Examination of Barry Diller's Marvelous Marathon."

p. 277–278: "ABC loved . . . get back to him." Wolf, *Beating the Odds*, p. 329–335.

p. 278: "The network wanted . . . started arguing." A.I. Price, Aug. 5, 1998, Nov. 5, 1998.

p. 278: "According to Diller's . . . ABC's TV shows." Wolf, p. 333–335.

p. 278: "The twenty-five–year-old . . . away from it." Diller in his remarks at Wasserman's memorial service, July 15, 2002.

p. 278–279: "Diller's response . . . from this deal." Wolf, p. 333–335.

p. 279 "Huggins was furious . . . out of the action." Huggins, Feb. 24, 2000.

p. 279: "Roy thought . . . including Diller?" A.I. Price, Nov. 5, 1998; also A.I. Huggins, Feb. 24, 2000.

p. 279: "Wasserman later . . . of those ABC films." A.I. Sheinberg, April 21, 1998.

p. 279: "But Price saw . . . not let Price go?" A.I. Price, Aug. 5, 1998; Nov. 5, 1998.

p. 280: "He didn't like . . . his position." A.I. Adler, Dec. 15, 1998.

p. 280: CBS eventually . . . night in the histroy of TV." Michael Schneider, "Back in 73," *Variety*, Sept. 1, 2000.

p. 280–281: "Price himself . . . of ABC's programs." A.I. Price, Aug. 5, 1998.

p. 281: "With Jennings . . . *A Dead Man*." A.I. Sheinberg, April 21, 1998.

p. 281: "Again, we were the . . . production schedule." A.I. Link, Dec. 8, 1999.

p. 281: "But this time . . . they'd create six dramas." A.I. Price, Aug. 5, 1998; A.I. Sheinberg, April 21, 1998. (Herb Schlosser also contributed to this idea, said Link.)

p. 281: "The writers resisted . . . very light-headed." A.I. Link, Dec. 8, 1999.

p. 281: "Sheinberg turned . . . its own twenty-six–week series." A.I. Sheinberg, April 21, 1998.

p. 281–282: "For the third spoke . . . was still being syndicated." A.I. Adler, Dec. 15, 1998.

p. 282: "The Wheel concept . . . said Link." A.I. Link, Dec. 8, 1999.

p. 282–283: "During the 1960s . . . it made TV history." A.I. Sheinberg, March 28, 1998, April 21, 1998.

p. 283: "Pretty soon, young . . . produce a TV show." A.I. J. Freedman, Dec. 6, 1999.

p. 283: "Soon, twenty-somethings . . . on a crash basis." A.I. Johnson, May 7, 1998.

p. 283: "Before a TV producer . . . if you broke it." A.I. Adler, Dec. 15, 1998.

p. 283–284: "Price capitalized . . . hot TV talent.' A.I. Price, Nov. 5, 1998.

p. 284: "But gaining entrée . . . said Freedman." A.I. J. Freedman, Dec. 6, 1998.

p. 284: "One guy who understood . . . *Night Gallery*." A.I. Sheinberg, April 21, 1998.

p. 285: "When Joan Crawford . . . you," he said. A.I. Spielberg, Oct. 8, 1998, July 15, 2002.

p. 285: "Spielberg is . . . her best effort." A.I. Price, April 21, 1998.

p. 285: "The show aired . . . do anything again." A.I. Sheinberg, Arpil 21, 1998.

p. 285: "Spielberg admitted . . . for eighteen months." A.I. Spielberg, Oct. 8, 1998.

Chapter 28

p. 286: "The Glamor Tram . . . just like a star." A.I. Laura Meyers, April 12, 1998; A&E *Biography of Head*, aired Oct.28, 2000; A.I. Johnson, May 7, 1998.

p. 286: "Like the sets . . . on the Universal Tour." Edith Head biography, IMDB; *Reel Women*, p. 275–277.

p. 286–287: "In 1972 . . . of building a theme park." A.I. Buzz Price, Sept. 17, 1998; also two studios performed by Price for Revue Studios, July 1961 and July 26, 1961.

p. 287: "Throughout it all . . . stars, and directors." A.I. Meyers, April 12, 1998.

p. 287–288: "Once an old lady . . . relations, Stein said." A.I. Jay Stein, April 6, 1998.

p. 288: "Wasserman kept looking . . . in the evenings, too." A.I. Steinberg, Aug. 3, 1998.

p. 288: "In 1972, Wasserman . . . an amphitheater." A.I. Buzz Price, Sept. 17, 1998.

p. 288–289: "Ned {Tanen} . . . and Lew watched." A.I. Jay Stein, July 28, 1998.

p. 289: "As Wasserman drove . . . the Amphitheater, he said." A.I. Tanen, June 2, 1998.

p. 289: "Universal Amphitehater concerts . . . of the same name." MCA annual report, 1972.

p. 289–290: "By 1973 . . . wing it with Lew." A.I. Tanen, June 2, 1998; A.I. Jay Stein, July 28, 1998; MCA annual reports 1970–1973.

p. 290: "Meanwhile, Taft . . . and it soon died." A.I. Sheinberg, April 21, 1998; A.I. Tanen, June 2, 1998.

p. 290–291: "Schreiber and Al . . . the lovely furnishings." A.I. Dorskind, Arpil 1, 1997.

p. 291 ". . . Wasserman motion pictures abroad." MCA annual report, 1970.

p. 291: "Other studios . . . the next 30 years." A.I. Valenti, June 5, 1997.

p. 291: "Income from . . . from a hit film." A.I. Buzz Price, Sept. 17, 1998.

p. 291: "Find a successor . . . Jennings, said Price." A.I., Aug. 5, 1998.

p. 292: "Tanen agreed . . . people, he granted." A.I. Tanen, July 7, 1998.

p. 292: "Domick Dunne . . . at the end." A.I. Dunne, Oct. 25, 2002.

p. 292: "Frank Price . . . leave, he said." A.I. Price. Aug. 5, 1998.

p. 292: "Once after Wasserman . . . whole different light." A.I. Adler, Dec. 15, 1998.

p. 292–293: "Later Wasserman . . . big picture." A.I. Sheinberg, April 21, 1998, May 19, 1998.

p. 293: "The other studios . . . than $600 million," David Lewin, "The State of Hollywood," *Today's Cinema*, July 24, 1970.

Chapter 29

p. 294: "Early one morning . . . Lew was its head." A.I. Michael Franklin, Oct. 23, 1998.

p. 294: "Lew would take . . . always there." A.I. Adams, Feb. 20, 1998.

p. 294: "That day, Wasseerman . . . terms of a contract." A.I. Franklin, Oct. 23, 1998, April 3, 2003.

p. 295: "The WGA had been . . . unlike any other." A.I. Del Reisman, April 2, 2003.

p. 295: "The Directors Guild . . . about fifteen minutes." DIG fact sheet.

p. 295: "And WGA, unlike . . . filmmaking process." A.I. Franklin, Oct. 23, 1998.

p. 295: "As MGM's . . . screenplay deals." A.I. Reisman, April 2, 2003.

p. 295: "It was brilliant . . . mused one writer." Milliard Kaufman, quoted in *Los Angeles Times Magazine*, March 25, 2001

p. 296: "In May 1973, . . . again in 1966." A.I. Reisman, April 2, 2003.

p. 296: Some writers unleashed . . . of the WGA contract." A.I. Franklin, Oct. 28, 1998.

p. 297: "The diectors . . . studios and Wasserman." A.I. Reisman, April 2, 2003.

p. 297: "Lew finally agreed . . . haunt him," said Franklin." A.I. Franklin, Oct. 28, 1998.

p. 297: "When Stein first arrived in Los Angeles in 1932 . . ." Los Angeles City Directories: MCA and Jules Stein listed in March 1930; Jules Stein apartment listing of August, 1932; larger residential listing in May 1933, and onward.

p. 297: "his friends . . . business in the West." A.I. Lambert, Feb. 22, 2001; A.I. Messick, March 10, 1997; also Messick *The Beauties and The Beasts*, (David McKay Co. Inc., 1973.)

p. 298: "The first Hollywood . . . no different." A.I. Roy Brewer, April 14, 1998; Larry Ceplair, *The Inquisition in Hollywood*, (University of California Press, 1979) was an excellent source.

p. 298: "With the help . . . $1.5 million for themselves." A.I. Messick; Messick, *Beauties and The Beasts*, pp. 103–109. Cecilia Rasmussen, *Mobsters Muscled Into Film Industry*, Jan. 2, 2000.

p. 298: "To oversee Bioff . . . of Capone's gang." A.I. Brewer, April 14, 1998; A.I. Adams, Feb. 20, 1998.

p. 298: "A federal agent . . . very, very well." A.I. Bill Roemer, Feb. 2, 1996.

p. 298: "He was also. . . . a tough group." A.I. Adams, March 31, 1997, Feb. 20, 1998.

p. 298–299: "They tried . . . bloody labor battles ensued." A.I. Ray Evans, Nov. 12, 1996; also Stephen Vaughn, *Ronald Reagan in Hollywood*, (Cambridge University Press), pp. 133–144; also A.I. J.J. Johnson, IATSE member, Sept. 3, 1997.

p. 299: "Yet, the studios . . . the other way." A.I. John Weber, Aug. 11, 1998; A.I. Evans, Nov. 12, 1996.

p. 299: "Did Lew participate . . . Wasserman's greatness." A.I. Gomery, Feb. 6, 1997.

p. 299: "I'm sure that . . . the lanky agent." A.I. Adams, March 31, 1997.

p. 299: "In 1940 . . . sentenced to prison." A.I. Rasmussen, Jan. 2, 2000.

p. 299: "Still conditions for . . . said Evans." A.I. Evans, Nov. 12, 1996.

p. 299–300: "It was more . . . of being Communist." A.I. Bob Goldfarb, Feb. 18, 1996.

p. 300: "In 1944, HUAC . . . CSU picketed the studios." A.I. John Sanford, Dec. 23, 1997.

p. 300: "New IATSE chief . . . studio history." A.I. Brewer, April 14, 1998.

p. 300: "There were riots . . . legitimate organizers." A.I. Evans, Nov. 12, 1996.

p. 300: "A few miles away . . . his agents." A.I. Adams, March 31, 1997; A.I. Kanter, Jan. 23, 1998.

p. 300: "It was silly, . . . he explained." A.I. Dales, April 16, 1998.

p. 300: "Evans sharply . . . killed the CSU." A.I. Evans, Nov. 12, 1996.

p. 300–301: "Though it was perfectly . . . spoke up, he said." A.I. Sam Jaffee, April 21, 1998.

p. 301: "Jules didn't want . . . good politics." A.I. Adams, March 31, 1997.

p. 301: "Wasserman . . . in print." A.I. Brewer, April 14, 1998.

p. 301: "Screenwriter Ned Young . . . by his MCA agent." A.I. Jaffee, April 21, 1998.

p. 301: "Playwright Arthur Miller . . . MCA agent Malcolm Stuart." A.I., July 30, 1998.

p. 301–302: "Gene Kelly . . . and Oscar nominations." A.I. Brewer, April 12, 1998; also "Garfield, Ferrer Investigate Selves," *Variety*, April 11, 1951.

p. 302: "For nearly . . . MCA agent Ronnie Lubin." A.I. Lubin, Feb. 18, 1998.

p. 302: "Wasserman was no . . . downtrodden at heart." A.I. Sanford, Dec. 23, 1997.

p. 302: "Former blacklisted . . . a good man." A.I. Corey, July 16, 1998.

p. 302: "In July . . . another union strike." A.I. Franklin, April 3, 2003; A.I. Reisman, April 2, 2003.

p. 302–303: "That year, . . . dealing with." A.I. Dan Slusser, May 8, 1998.

p. 303–304: "The union was . . . union had a deal." A.I. Jack Coffey, May 2, 2003; also review of *Daily Variety* articles, from March 16, 1972 to Nov. 12, 1976 about IATSE labor talks.

p. 304: "But Columbia . . . Lew did for Labor, said McLean." A.I. McLean, Feb. 13, 2003.

p. 304. "Adams agreed . . . trusted him." A.I., Feb. 20, 1998.

Chapter 30

p. 304–305: "Ernie Nims . . . lifting Universal's reputation." A.I. Nims, July 2, 1997.

p. 305: "By then, . . . but Lew was alright." A.I. Muhl, Sept. 18, 1997.

p. 305: "At MCA's board meeting . . . and Ned Tanen." Thomas Pryor, "Jules Stein Gives Up MCA Chair June 4," *Variety,* May 23, 1973; also MCA annual report 1973, 1974.

p. 305–306: "The two had been . . . gambler, said Brown." A.I. Brown, March 10, 2001.

p. 306: "In the 1930s . . . didn't win often." A.I. Riff, July 7, 1997.

p. 306: "Twice, Wasserman . . . back each time." A.I. Huggins, Feb. 24, 2000; A.I. Adams, Feb. 20, 1998.

p. 306: "Once he lost . . . away from the tables." A.I. Link, July 12, 2002; A.I. Gerber, July 5, 1998.

p. 306–307: "So, when . . . and promote it." A.I. Brown, March 10, 2001.

p. 307: "But Tony Bill . . . such events." A.I. Bill, Oct. 4, 1996.

p. 307: "Meanwhile, Ned Tanen . . . movie might earn." A.I. Tanen, July 7, 1998; also IMDB on *American Graffitti*; A.I. anonymous, Aug. 29, 1996.

p. 308: "When Tanen finally . . . Lucas very unhappy." A.I. Tanen, July 7, 1998; story is also recounted in Biskind's *Easy Rider, Raging Bull,* pp. 243–244; A.I. Tom Pollock, Sept. 19, 1996.

p. 309: "With the changes in . . . grossing $10 million." A.I. Tanen, July 7 1998; also IMDB.

p. 309: "In December . . . Universal movie hits." MCA annual reports, 1973, 1974.

p. 309: "*American Graffiti* . . . down that operation." A.I. Tanen, July 7, 1998.

p. 309: "On April 2, . . . fidgeting with anxiety." A.I. Patsy Krauskopf, Aug. 2, 1998.

p. 309: "The suspense . . . certain death." A.I. Brown, March 10, 2001.

p. 309: "Wasserman. . . . that night." Records from the Margaret Herrick Library, Academy of Motion Pictures Arts and Sciences.

p. 310: "But Wasserman . . . speaking publicly." A.I. Krauskopf, Aug. 2, 1998.

p. 310: "The 46th Academy . . . shortcomings." Ted Thackrey, Jr. "Glenda Jackson, Lemmon Win Ocars; Sting is Best Picture," *Los Angeles Times*, April 3, 1974, Addison Verrill, "Bit-By-Bit Rundown of Oscar Awards Night," *Variety,* April 10, 1974.

p. 310: "Niven presented Diana Ross . . . talent he employed." Based on several viewings of the Academy Awards show, April 2, 1974, courtesy of the archivists at the Margaret Herrick Library.

p. 312: "At the end . . . said one of his agents." A.I. Murray July 29, 1997.

p. 312: "As chairman. . . .the 'Universal Year.'" A.D. Murphy, "Universal is Laughing to the Bank," *Variety,* Aug. 22, 1973; Murphy, "Biz is Whammo 1974 Getaway," April 10, 1974.; also "Payroll, Production High," *Variety,* July 23, 1975.

p. 312: "*The Sting* . . . one for Best Picture." Universal archives; also IMDB.

p. 312: "Wasserman . . . to the trades." A.I. Murphy, Aug. 22, 1973.

p. 312–313: "He had just ended . . . new DGA agreement." MCA Annual Report 1973; interviews with SAG leader Chet Migdon, Oct. 3, 1998; A.I. Slusser, May 8, 1998.

p. 313: "He had helped build . . . Los Angeles' Protestants." A.I. Slusser, May 8, 1998; A.I. Tanen, June 2, 1998.

p. 313: "His spawling operation . . . Olivia Newtown-John." MCA annual report 1973–1974.

p. 313: "He had just combined . . . a monster $21 million." MCA annual report 1973–1974; A.I. Dorskind, April 1, 1997.

p. 313: "In 1974, he was marketing . . . Earthquake." MCA annual reports 1974; archives at Margaret Herrick Library.

p. 313–314: "Years before VCR . . . the American consumer." A.I. Wasserman, Nov. 3, 1999; also Wasserman quoted in *Fortune*, Nov. 1976.

p. 314: "Even better . . . richest of studios." MCA annual report 1974.

p. 314: "Lew was the architect . . . it all through." A.I. Seltzer, July 15, 1997.

p. 314: "That night, as . . . said Krauskopf." A.I. Aug. 2, 1998.

p. 314: "Edie had her . . . worthy honoree." Materials from the MPTF; A.I. Irma Kalish, board member, Oct. 9, 1997.

p. 314: "Edie had adopted . . . hand in Hollywood." A.I., Seltzer, July 17, 1998; A.I. Kalish, Oct. 9, 1997.

p. 315: "The tall mogul . . . standing ovation." Based on several viewings of the Academy Awards show, April 2, 1974, video record from the Margaret Herrick Library.

p. 315: "Later that evening . . . screenplay." Thackrey, Jr. "Glenda Jackson, Lemmon Win Oscars;" *Los Angeles Times*, April 3, 1974.

p. 315: "The film would become . . . selling $100 million." Murphy, "Universal is Laughing to the Bank," *Variety*, Aug. 22, 1973, IMDB.

p. 315: "Universal's *American*. . . . shatter *Graffiti's* record." IMDB.

p. 316: "Stein wanted to . . . a best seller." A.I. Murray Schumach, May 15, 1998.

p. 316: "He had hired . . . give it a try." A.I. Louise Kramer Mills, May 7, 1998; Kramer's unpublished papers.

p. 316: "But none of the . . . was mothballed." A.I. Schumach, May 15, 1998.

p. 316–317: "His published . . . to depart." MCA annual report, 1974.

p. 317: "Wasserman waited . . . you die." A.I. Wasserman, June 10, 1999; June 22, 1999.

Chapter 31

p. 317: "Despite . . . constrains creativity." A.I. Phillips, Oct. 31, 1998.

p. 318: "Universal . . . Critchton and Lang." A.I. Lewis-Lang, July 30, 1997; IMDB.

p. 318: "In the fall . . . said his wife, Monica." Ibid; also Hirschhorn, *The Universal Story*, pp. 323–326.

p. 319 "One summer . . . he could direct it." A.I. Lewis-Lang, July 30, 1997.

p. 319: "By then, the . . . September 1974." A.I. Brown, March 10, 2001,

p. 319: "The mechanical sharks . . . praying for a miracle." A.I. Sheinberg, April 21, 1998; also A.I. Price, Dec. 2, 1999.

p. 319–320: "Zanuck and Brown . . . said the director." A.I. Spielberg, Dec. 8, 1998; A.I. Brown, March 10, 2001.

p. 320: "By the time . . . ready to release." A.I. Sheinberg, April 21, 1998.

p. 320–321: "He had learned a . . . said Setnik." A.I. Setnik, Oct. 27, 1997.

p. 321: "He decided . . . got a picture.' A.I. Wasserman, Nov. 3, 1999.

p. 321: "Then, he broke . . . we wanted." Ibid.

p. 321–322: "On a flight from . . . and he was." J.A. Trachtenberg, "A rare look at the most powerful," *W,* Oct. 8, 1982.

p. 322: "*Jaws* rapidly . . . high then." IMDB.

p. 322: "The marketing . . . wide, fast opening." A.I. Thomson, June 6, 1999.

p. 322: "MCA learned . . . thrilled movie audiences." A.I. Gomery, Feb. 6, 1997.

p. 322: "From then on . . . mega-hit mentality." David Thomson wrote an infamous essay about on this, "How Hollywood Invented Summer," in *Esquire,* Aug. 1977.

p. 322: "Years later . . . of its history." A.I. Wasserman, Nov. 3, 1999.

p. 322: "Doris and Jules . . . Dogs and Sharks." A.I. Luis Estevez, April 30, 2001.

p. 322–323: "In the spring . . . explained Sheinberg." A.I. Sheinberg, March 25, 1998.

p. 323: "Carter was in . . . abject poverty." Material from Carter Presidential Library; also Jimmy Carter, *An Hour Before Daylight* (Simon & Schuster, 2001).

p. 323–324: "The men shared . . . so was Carter." A.I. Carrick, Sept. 9, 2002.

p. 324: "Although Nixon . . . National Insitute of Health." A.I. Spencer, March 26, 2003; also "Taft Schreiber Aided Ford Drive," *New York Times,* June 15, 1976.

p. 324: "Reagan was no. . . .next political move." Ibid; and *Dark Victory,* p. 240–1.

p. 324: "In January 1975. . . .enamored with starlets." Haber's column, *Los Angeles Times,* Jan. 27, 1975, .

p. 324: That winter . . . ever displayed." A.I. Cerrell, Aug. 3, 1998.

p. 324–325: "Once inside . . . have a shorter life." Haber, Jan. 27, 1975.

p. 325: "Schreiber was . . . star-gazing habits." A.I. Spencer, March 26, 2003; also A.I. Steinberg, Aug. 4, 1998.

p. 325–326: "In contrast to . . . knew about him." A.I. Sheinberg, March 25, 1998.

p. 326: "When I decided . . . Carter told a reporter." Trachtenberg, "A rare look at the most powerful . . ." *W,* Oct. 8–15, 1982.

p. 326: "After Carter's . . . the President." A.I. Sheinberg, March 25, 1998.

p. 326: "Taft Schreiber . . . over Schreiber's decision." A.I. Spencer, March 26, 2003.

p. 326: "In June 1976 . . . Schreiber died." Richard West, "Possible Blood Error in Schreiber's Death Probed," *Los Angeles Times,* June 16, 1976.

p. 327: "It was a shock . . . around town." A.I. Greenberg, Feb. 6, 1998.

p. 327: "Taft was . . . beneath the radar." A.I. Rosenbaum, June 26, 1998.

p. 327: "When Taft died . . . like that happen?" A.I. Spencer, March 26, 2003.

p. 327: "Two days later . . . to the publisher." A.I. Greenberg, Feb. 6, 1998; West, June 16, 1976.

p. 327: "But Stein . . . never mentioned again." MCA annual report 1976.

p. 327: "All I can say . . . Seltzer." A.I. Seltzer, July 15, 1997.

p. 327: "Now, several . . . 'No one's sure.' " A.I. Rosenbaum, June 26, 1998.

p. 328: In 1971, he . . . from MCA's mammoth library." A.I. Wasserman, June 22, 1999.

p. 328: "I consider it . . . Wasserman said." Gottleib, *Los Angeles Magazine,* January 1979.

p. 328: "From 1970 . . . buzzed about his breakthrough." From MCA DisoVision History (Universal archives); David Lachenbruch, "The Videodiscs Are Coming," *TV Guide*, Nov. 25, 1978.

p. 329: "Even the CIA. . . .another $10 million on that." Gottleib, January 1979.

p. 329: "In 1974 . . . a videodisc player." MCA annual report 1974, 1975.

p. 329: "Then came . . . they were in for a long battle." A.I. Sheinberg, April 21, 1998, May 19, 1998; also Sony History, Betamax Case, Sony Corp. (on-line source).

p. 329–330: "Doggedly . . . moved forward." A.I. Valenti, June 5, 1997.

p. 330: "Since 1960 . . . its VHS system." A.I. Sheinberg, April 21, 1998; "Bring on the Video Boom," Feb. 15, 1981; Financial World; Sony History; and "The Betamax Case," and "In Defense of Time-Shift," from Sony Corp.

p. 330: "The machines . . . chief and boss." A.I. Tanen, June 2, 1998.

p. 330–331: "After four years of . . . to $802 million." MCA annual reports, 1972–1976.

p. 331: "The first business. . . . in 19th century costumes." A.I. Sheinberg, March 25, 1998 April 21, 1998; A.I. Jay Stein, April 4, 1998.

p. 331: "Sheinberg's plans . . . a Sierra Club leader." "MCA's plan for Yosemite," *Business Week*, May 11, 1974.

p. 331: "The next year . . . even louder." Papers from Universal Studio archives.

p. 331–332: "But he was . . . Tulomne Meadows." A.I. Sheinberg, March 25, 1998.

p. 332: "Ned Tanen recalled . . . deflower Yosemite." A.I. Tanen, June 2, 1998.

p. 332: "Producers . . . owned the whole park." A.I. D.C., Feb. 5, 19997.

p. 332: "After 1978 . . . business I acquired." A.I. Sheinberg, March 25, 1998.

p. 332: "Universal always . . . *Strain*, and *Jaws*." A.I. Klein, May 22, 1998.

p. 333: "Sheinberg's urge . . . Danielle Steele." A.I. Sheinberg, March 25, 1998, April 21, 1998; also Marion Mancker, "Now for the Grann Finale," *New York Magazine*, Jan. 21, 2002; IMDB for *The Promise*.

p. 333: "Universal . . . their best-selling authors." A.I. Klein, May 22, 1998.

p. 333–334: "On the movie side . . . *Airport* or *Jaws*." Hirschhorn, pp. 322–342.

Chapter 32
p. 334: "The thirty-five . . . the king as possible." A.I. Cannell, Jan. 18, 2000.

p. 335: "The hostess, Kathy . . . she said." A.I. Donahue, Feb. 20, 2000.

p. 335: "Cannell never . . . would resume." A.I. Cannell, Jan. 18, 2000.

p. 335–336: "He was a theatrical . . . hygiene and numbers." A.I. Reisman, April 2, 2003.

p. 336: "Taft Schreiber's . . . and fall ill." A.I. PT, Aug. 29, 1996.

p. 336: "Outside consultants . . . of the band." A.I. Buzz Price, Sept. 17, 1998.

p. 336–337: "The band was . . . Universal became stars.' A.I. Cannell; Sept. 20, 1999, Jan. 18, 2000.

p. 337: "The writing . . . said Price. "A.I. Link, Dec. 8, 1999; A.I. Price, Nov. 5, 1998.

p. 337: "Edie Wasserman . . . Edie's and Lew's as well." A.I. Link, Dec. 8, 1999, July 12, 2002; A.I. Sheinberg, April 21, 1998.

p. 337: "Starring Sheen . . . as other honors." IMBD.

p. 337–338: "Meanwhile . . . the irreverent script." A.I. Cannell, Jan. 18, 2000; A.I. Huggins, Feb. 17, 2000.

p. 338: "So, Frank Price . . . I'll walk.' " A.I. Price, Nov. 5, 1998.

p. 338: "NBC acquiesced . . . of the profits." A.I. Cannell, Jan. 18, 2000.

p. 338–339: "On a warm day . . . that had occurred." A.I. Hugins, Feb. 17, 2000.

p. 340: "Universal ran . . . our big issue." A.I. Brown, March 10, 2001.

p. 340: "By 1977, Universal . . . before you do." A.I. Cannell, Jan. 18, 2000.

p. 340–341: "The studio . . . and so on." Case No. BC 139282, "Estate of Jim Garison vs. Warner, Universal, Columbia, Paramount, Fox and Disney."

p. 341: "In addition . . . *The Last Don.*" A.I. Bob Lewis; Tom Pollock, Sept. 28, 1997.

p. 341: "Producer Don Devlin . . . sets of books." Biskind, *Easy Rider*, p. 434.

p. 341 "Even Wasserman's friend . . . one light bulb." A.I. Curtis, Feb. 17, 2000.

p. 341: "Hollywood money . . . in your hand.' " Will Martin, "Dorothy Parker Says Goodbye to Flippancy," AP, August 1943.

p. 341: "There were rolling grosses . . . from profit participants." A.I. Lewis, March 31, 2001.

p. 341: "Huggins received . . . Hollywood is known for." A.I. Huggins, Feb. 17, 2000.

p. 342: "That explained . . . millions of dollars." A.I. Huggins; also story aired on CBS, *Sixty Minutes*, Dec. 7, 1980.

p. 342: "Under Frank Price . . . plenty of competition." A.I. Price, Dec. 2, 1999.

p. 343: "In 1977, ABC . . . a stormy week." Sander Vanocur, *Plain Dealer* (wire) "MCA's Wasserman rated top brain," March 6, 1977.

p. 343: ". . . Universal shamelessly . . . as a child." A.I. Sheinberg, April 21, 1998.

p. 343: "At least Lucas . . . critic Richard Scheib. roogulartor.esmartweb.com/sf/galatica.

p. 344: "Wasserman once . . . in total receipts." A.I. Raines, Oct. 9, 1998; IMDB.

p. 344: "Nine years later . . . said Price" A.I., Dec. 2, 1999.

p. 344: "Universal TV . . . pretty exciting." A.I. Cannell, Jan. 18, 2000.

p. 344: "Occassionally, screen . . . director Billy Wilder." David Kinghorn, "Written By," Feb. 2002.

p. 344: "When the great . . . like royalty." Paul Kohner, *Magician on Sunset Boulevard*, p. 176.

p. 345–346: "During company . . . grew demoralized." A.I. Price, Nov. 5, 1998, Dec. 2, 1999.

p. 346–347: "True, his division . . . of $1.2 billion." MCA annual reports, 1977–1979.

Chapter 33

p. 347: "Edie tried . . . Wendy Goldberg." A.I. Goldberg, May 9, 2003

p. 347: "Edie and Lew . . . bribed studio heads." A.I. Adams, Feb. 20, 1998.

p. 347: "He represented . . . Federation of Musicians." A.I. Herman, July 21, 1998; A.I. Herman "Backie" Levitt, Nov. 28, 1997.

p. 347: "Korshak used to . . . that to heart." A.I. Jerry Tokofsky, Aug. 12, 1997.

p. 348: "Yet, Korhsak had no . . . taped or overheard." A.I. Ovid De Maris, March 29, 1997. Also De Maris, *The Last Mafioso*, (Times Books,) p. 316

p. 348: "Other times, he did . . . Gardner." A.I. Gardner, Nov. 8, 1996.

p. 348–349: "When Edie's daughter . . . daughter in-law." A.I. Viriginia Korshak, June 20, June 22, 2003.

p. 349: "The crafts busines . . . corporate leviathan." A.I. Payne, June 12, 2003.

p. 349: "After Bea's son . . . Bea and Sidney." A.I. David Debbin, Aug. 21, 1996.

p. 349: "Sidney was not . . . wedding present." A.I. Virginia Korshak, June 20, 2003.

p. 349–350: "When Harry and . . . have to do it." A.I. Debbin, Aug. 21, 1996.

p. 350–351: "The suitor didn't last . . . were the Korshaks." A.I. Tanen, June 2, 1998; also A.I. Virigina Korshak, June 22, 2003.

p. 351–352: "Law enforcement agencies . . . stripes." A.I. Yarnell, March 26, 1998.

p. 352: "As Tokofsky explained . . . call Sidney." A.I. Tokofsky, Aug. 12, 1997.

p. 352: "For his services . . . to another group." A.I. Virginia Korshak, June 20, 2003.

p. 352: "By now, some . . . humliated wife." A.I. Payne, June 12, 2003.

p. 352–353: "In 1976, Korshak, . . . to Sidney, he explained." Jim Hawrood, "Wasserman, Korshak Figure in NBC H'Wood Crime Report; Dino Cries Foul, *Variety*, Dec. 17, 1978, Brian Ross, *Mobsters and Filmmaking*, NBC, Dec. 13, 14, 1978 (transcripts).

p. 353: "Based on a true story . . . security system." IMDB.

p. 353–354: "The crew was . . . had got it done." A.I. Tanen, June 2, 1978, July 7, 1998.

p. 354: "A federal grand jury . . . *Los Angeles Times*." *NBC-TV News Report*; Harwood, Dec. 15, 1978; "The Brink's Job: U.S. Probing Alleged Mob Link with Movie;" Associated Press, *Los Agneles Times*, Dec. 14, 1978.

p. 354: "For some time . . . 15 cents on the dollar." Dennis D. Fisher, "Korshak's Tax bill Settled . . ." *Chicago Sun Times*, Oct. 1, 1974.

p. 354: "In the summer of 1976 . . . that was new." Seymour M. Hersh, "Korshak's Power Rooted in Ties to Labor Leaders," et al, *New York Times*, June 27–30, 1976.

p. 354: "Bea was . . . soothe her friend." A.I. Virginia Korshak, June 22, 2003; A.I. Julie Payne, June 12, 2003.

p. 354: "As Wendy Goldberg . . . to the end." A.I. Goldberg, May 9, 2003.

p. 354: "Soon, a real Hollywood . . . and *Shampoo*." Begelman biography, Katz, *Film Encyclopedia*.

p. 354–355: "In September 1976 . . . called the police." Background from David McClintock, *Indecent Exposure*, (Random House, 1985).

p. 355: "Now, the Los . . . investigating." *Los Angeles Herald Examiner*, Feb. 15, 1978.

p. 355: "We couldn't believe . . . happy to throw one." A.I. Goldberg, May 9, 2003.

p. 355–356: "No one talked about . . . 'A' list parties." A.I. Dunne, Oct. 25, 2002.

p. 356: "By the late 1970s . . . upset Edie." Lowell Bergman, Jeff Gerth, "La Costa— the Hundred Milion-Dollar Resort with Criminal Clientele," *Penthouse*, March 1975; Bill Hazlett and William Farr, 'Terrifying Power' of Alleged Crime Figure Told,' *Los Angeles Times*, Sept. 3, 1975; Peter Bonventre, "FBI Under Cover," *Newsweek*, Oct. 12, 1978.

p. 356: "In 1977, the Los . . . and legitimate business." Bill Hazlett, "Organized Crime Probe Supported by Van De Kamp," *Los Angeles Times*, Oct. 25, 1979; David Robb, "Mob Ties Told," *Variety*, March 13, 1986.

p. 356: "The report angered . . . even more." A.I. Virginia Korshak, June 20, 2003.

p. 356: "As for Edie . . . speak out." A.I. M.A., Feb. 5, 1999.

p. 356: "Wasserman talked . . . not true." "Wasserman Speaks Up," *Los Angeles Herald Examiner*, Feb. 15, 1978; also "Reports of Showbiz Crime Exaggerated, Says Valenti," *Variety*, June 19, 1979.

p. 356: "In 1979 . . . when necessary." Media Relations, MPTF, March 19, 2001.

p. 356–357: "When one producer . . . emergency meeting." A.I. M.A., Feb. 5, 1999.

p. 357: "Edie did not spare . . . care of our own.' " A.I. Kalish, Sept. 9, 1997.

Chapter 34

p. 357: "He took a special . . . which delighted audiences." A.I. Tanen, June 2, 1998.

p. 357: "The year 1978 . . . $462 million." MCA annual report 1978.

p. 357: "His pet project . . . hype,' Tanen said." A.I. Tanen, July 7, 1998; also IMDB.

p. 357–358: "Wasserman and Tanen . . . Lucas down." A.I. Tanen, July 7, 1998.

p. 359: "A week later . . . movie's income." A.I. Tom Pollock, June 5, 2002.

p. 359: "In May 1977 . . . other peoples' walls." A.I. Tanen, July 7, 1998.

p. 360: "*Star Wars* became . . . Lucas' attorney." A.I. Pollock, June 5, 2002.

p. 360–361: "The other result . . . Light and Magic." A.I.

p. 361: "Sid Sheinberg . . . for *Star Wars*." A.I. April 21, 1998.

p. 361: "When band leader Artie . . . the advocate's commitment." A.I. Shaw, March 13, 1998.

p. 361: "Lew made it . . . see it through." A.I. Pollock, June 5, 2002.

p. 361–361: "One one side . . . Douglas Kenney." A.I. Tanen, July 7, 1998.

p. 361–362: "One of the . . . screened the dailies." A.I. Daniel , Oct. 27, 1998.

p. 362: "Waserman . . . waiting to kill me." A.I. Tanen July 7, 1998.

p. 362: "Editing spilled from . . . film debut cooly." A.I. Daniel Oct. 27, 1998.

p. 362–363: "Nevertheless, over the . . . grossed $170 million." IMDB;

p. 363: "After *Animal House* . . . at us to stop." A.I. Tanen, July 7, 1998.

p. 363: "Wasserman worried . . . in a while." A.I. O'Connell, May 14, 1998.

p. 363: "Hitch once threw a . . . lipstick and all." A.I. Adler, Dec. 15, 1998; Swerling, Feb. 22, 2000.

p. 363–364: "But the director's behaivor . . . topic again." A.I. Steinberg, Aug. 3, 1998.

p. 364: "Meanwhile, the movie . . . Best Director Award." Finley, *The Hollywood Story*.

p. 364: "But in 1979 . . . soon be acquired." MCA annual reports 1978, 1979.

p. 364–365: "Wasserman had been . . . Hitchcock's funeral." A.I. O'Connell, May 14, 1998.

p. 365: "Later he asked . . . for a while." A.I. Krauskopf, July 29, 1998.

p. 365: "Right after Wasserman . . . company buyouts." Bacon, "Dr. Jules Stein dies at 85," *Los Angeles Herald Examiner,* April 30, 1981, ; A.I. David Weitzner, March 26, 1998; A.I. Dorskind, April 1, 1998; A.I. Oppenheimer, Aug. 12, 1997.

PART IV

Chapter 35

p. 369: "Under a sunny . . . Show Biz." Jerry Belcher, "Jules Stein, Philanthropist, Doctor, Film Mogul, Dies." *Los Angeles Times,* April 30, 1981, George Christy, "The Great Life," *Hollywood Reporter,* May 7, 1981, *Variety,* May 1, 1981.

p. 369: "Stein had . . . a grieving widow." A.I. Christy, March 27, 2002;

p. 369–370: "Gene Kelly . . . to kiss her cheek." A.I. Krauskopf, March 5, 1998.

p. 370: "Stein had requested . . . Dr. Bradley Straatsma." A.I. Straatsma, July 30, 1997.

p. 370: "Stein, who had finally . . . movie musical." Bacon, "Dr. Jules Stein Dies at

85, *Los Angeles Herald Examiner,* May 1, 1981, Note: One of the pallbearers included author's uncle, Dr. Sherman Mellinkoff, then dean of the UCLA Medical School.

p. 370–371: "The only pallbearer . . . through the years." "Memorial Service Held," *Variety,* May 5, 1981, ; Aljean Harmetz, "$100,000 Memorial" Celebration," *New York Times,* May 5, 1981.

p. 371: "The most human . . . language to express." Ibid; A.I. Krauskopf, March 5, 1998.

p. 371: "As Jean . . . were very close." A.I. Jean Stein, Oct. 9, 2002.

p. 371: "For Edie . . . leave the agency." A.I. Goldberg, May 9, 2003.

p. 371: "When Edie arrived . . . about time!" A.I. Christy, March 27, 2002.

p. 371–372: "Together with the widow . . . twenty years later." A.I. Wasserman, June 22, 1999.

p. 372: "Stein, who spent . . . $10 million." "Family, UCLA to Share Stein Estate." *Los Angeles Times,* May 2, 1981.

p. 372: "Imagine the buzz . . . $450 million in today's dollars." "Jules Stein Leaves Estate . . ." *Variety,* May 6, 1981.

p. 372: "His sister . . . was brilliant." A.I. Wasserman, June 22, 1999.

p. 372: "As for Stein's MCA . . . $1.2 billion." MCA annual report 1981.

p. 372: "But his death . . . Chicago's Al Capone." UPI item, May 4, 1981; also item in *Herald Examiner,* April 30, 1981.

p. 372–373: "The talent drain . . . and *Tootsie.*" A.I. Price, Aug. 5, 1998.

p. 374: "A lot of guys . . . Nor did Sheinberg." A.I. Marvin Antonowsky, Oct. 21, 1998.

p. 374: "By the late . . . out of the lot." A.I. Cannell, Jan. 18, 2000.

p. 374: "While Cannell's $1 million . . . fell apart." A.I. Cannell, Jan. 18, 200; also the *New York Times,* Oct. 1985.

p. 374–375: "For Cannell . . . supplier of TV shows." A.I. Cannell, Sept. 20, 1999; Jan. 18, 2000.

p. 375–376: "Soon, Cannell's mentor . . . withdrawing its offer." A.I. Huggins, Feb. 17, 2000; Feb. 24, 2000.

p. 376: "In 1980, Huggins . . . production houses." A.I. Swerling, Feb. 22, 2000; Freedman, Dec. 1999; Antonowksy, Oct. 21, 1998.

p. 376–377: "In the end . . . its own profit." From *Sixty Minutes,* Dec. 7, 1980.

p. 377: "At twenty-two episodes a . . . to see a cent." A.I. Cannell, Jan. 18, 2000.

p. 377: "Garner . . . on their contract." A.I. Huggins, Feb. 24, 2000.

p. 377–378: "Meanwhile, several . . . shows in years." A.I. Fess Parker, Oct. 23, 1996; *60 Minutes,* Dec. 7, 1980.

p. 378: "In 1981 . . . deal of anger." A.I. Reisman, April 2, 2003.

p. 378: "The WGA . . . on both sides." A.I. Sheinberg, May 19, 1998.

p. 378–379: "When the issue . . . incendiary arguments." A.I. McLean, Feb. 13, 2003.

p. 379: "Then, in the sixth . . . said Reisman." A.I. Reisman, April 2, 2003; A.I. anonymous Aug. 29, 1996; also *Los Angles Times* story.

p. 379–380: "Wasserman reacted to . . . the strike ended." A.I. Reisman, April 2, 2003; WGA files.

p. 380: "It was taxing . . . said McLean." A.I. McLean, Feb. 13, 2003.

Chapter 36:

p. 380: "After nearly a decade . . . Jackie Gershwin." A.I. Gershwin, Sept. 15, 1998.

p. 380: "Casey has been . . . him the company." A.I. Pollock, July 28, 1997.

p. 381: "Edie's family became . . . her male friends." Anonymous STL, June 10, 1999.

p. 381: "Yet, she had undergone . . . one friend." Anonymous PM, March 7, 2001.

p. 381: "Edie had not so. . . . editor, Jim Bellows." A.I. Bellows, May 9, 2002.

p. 381: "She was a fall-down . . . other sources. A.I. Payne, June 12, 2002; also Haber died July 30, 1993 of liver and kidney failure, according to *Variety*, Aug. 4, 1993.

p. 381–382: "Haber had . . . said Estevez." A.I. Estevez, Aug. 5, 2001.

p. 382: "And then so did . . . look at Hollywood." A.I. DP, Columbia, Oct. 9, 2002.

p. 382–383: "Dunne became an . . . dinner and parties." A.I. Dunne, Oct. 25, 2002.

p. 383: "Edie had already . . . elected Ronald Ronald." A.I. Cerrick, Sept. 7, 2002.

p. 383: "She had been close to . . . Wyman and Reagan." A.I. Steinberg, Aug. 4, 1998.

p. 383: "Between them . . . Wasserman told me." A.I. Wasserman, Nov. 3, 1999.

p. 383: "But the two . . . Kay Kyser." A.I. Kanter, Jan. 23, 1998.

p. 383: "World War II drew . . . 'Lyndie Wasserman.' " A.I Janet Leigh, Feb. 5, 1998.

p. 383: "Maureen . . . Maureen's life." Maureen Reagan, autobiography.

p. 383: "When Wyman . . . ended in 1949." A.I. Leigh, Feb. 5, 1998; also Edwards, *Early Reagan*, p. 280.

p. 384: "Edie remained loyal . . . attention to Nancy." A.I. Park, Oct. 27, 1998.

p. 384: "The mogul's wife . . . play that game." A.I. Goldberg, May 9, 2003.

p. 384: "Edie stayed . . . the governor's home." A.I. Stu Spencer, March 26, 2003; also documents at the former gubernatorial library in Hoover Institute verify this.

p. 384: "In January 1981, . . . $10,000 Galanos gown." A.I. Park, Oct. 27, 1988; Steinberg, Aug. 4, 1998; and *Calacello* "Ronnie and Nancy," *Vanity Fair*, July 1998.

p. 384: "Edie and Lew were . . . said Dunne." A.I. Dunne, Oct. 25, 2002.

p. 384: "Wasserman was . . . said Douglas Gomery." A.I. Gomery, Feb. 6, 1997.

p. 385: "It also helped . . . a uniformed guests." A.I. Spencer, May 9, 2003; A.I. Park, Oct. 27, 1998.

p. 385: "Although Art Park . . . she said, laughing." A.I. Park, ibid.

p. 385: "By now . . . sensibility." A.I. Marvin Antonoksky, Oct. 21, 1998.

p. 386: "After *Animal House* . . . destructive undertow." A.I. Daniel.

p. 386: "Director John Landis . . . Tanen explained." A.I. Tanen, July 7, 1998. Also, described by Bob Woodward in *Wired*, (Simon & Schuster, 1984), about Belushi.

p. 386: "Wasserman had dealt . . . its drug use." Gerald Frank, "Drugs and Hollywood," produced and distributed by Screen Actors Guild.

p. 386: "Wasserman who . . . people's best work." A.I. Daniel, Oct. 27, 1998.

p. 387: "Lew was absolutely . . . MCA's rigidity." A.I. Tanen, July 7, 1998; also IMDB.

p. 387–388: "The mogul had an . . . the *Lost Arc*." A.I. Tanen, ibid; A.I. Pollock, May 10, 2001.

p. 389: "Steven Spielberg . . . had gotten his start." A.I. Spielberg, Oct. 8, 1998.

p. 389: "That goal . . . he explained." A.I. David Brown, March 10, 2001.

p. 390: "Still, Universal . . . Saturday night." A.I. Tanen, July 7, 1998.

p. 390: "One was *Missing*. . . . (verified this conclusion.)" IMDB; also Bill Vann,

"Washington and The Pinochet coup in Chile," Oct. 26, 1999, reprinted by *World Socialist Magazine* (online).

p. 391: "But where to film . . . U.S. government." A.I. Daniel, Oct. 27, 1998.

p. 391: "I was sued . . . the telephone calls." A.I. Tanen, July 7, 1998; Sheinberg, April 21, 1998.

p. 392: "It was the . . . defense program." A.I. Daniel, Oct. 27, 1998.

p. 392: "The film that followed . . . Nancy and Ronald Reagan." A.I. Daniel, Oct. 27, 1998; A.I. Tanen, July 7, 1998; A.I. Spielberg Oct. 8, 1998.

p. 393: "In 1982, . . . radically different hits." MCA annual report 1982, 1983.

p. 393: "As Costa-Gavras . . . economic powers." As quoted in an essay by Dimitra Kessenides, "The Role of Art," Jan. 24, 2003. Salon.com.

p. 393: "By the time Universal . . . left since." A.I. Spielberg, Oct. 8, 1998.

p. 394: "Waserman finally came . . . in perpetuity." James Bates, "Universal Theme Parks Come with A Twist: Spielberg Rider," *Los Angeles Times,* June 24, 2003.

Chapter 37

p. 395: "FBI agents rolled . . . made no sense." A.I. Richard Stavin, Feb. 14, 1998, May 16, 2003; "MCA Official Suspected of Funneling Funds to the Mafia," *Los Angeles Times,* Dec. 15, 1989.

p. 395: "The mystery deepened . . . family in Pennsylvania." William Knoedelseder, *Stiffed,* (Harper Collins, 1993), pp. 434–5.

p. 395–396: "Yet, MCA in 1983 . . . later made public." A.I. Stavin, Feb. 14, 1998; May 16, 2003.

p. 396: "Giaquinto . . . one MCA executive." A.I. PT, Aug. 29, 1996.

p. 396–397: MCA represented . . . accounting principles." Based partly on Leo Walker, *Great Dance Bands,* (Da Capo Press, New York); p. 244; Kramer papers.

p. 397: "Wasserman had, briefly . . . said Paul Beck." A.I. Beck, Oct. 3, 1997.

p. 397: "But Wasesrman . . . their own agents." A.I. Heller, April 15, 1997.

p. 397: "Stranded, Wasserman . . . friendly enough." A.I. Riff, July 7, 1997.

p. 397: "Wasserman fell seriously . . . of its agents." A.I. Heller, April. 15, 1997.

p. 397: "He told me . . . he was right." A.I. Merle Jacobs, Feb. 1, 1997.

p. 398: "Benny Goodman, Tommy . . . the same way." Walker, *Great Dance Bands,* p. 244.

p. 39: "Stein's underhanded . . . labor racketeering." A.I. Moldea, *Dark Victory,* p. 50; also John Cones, "Politics, Movies & The Role of Government," from The Film Industry Reform Movement (on-line).

p. 398: "Stein and Wasserman . . . get away with murder." A.I. Don Engle, June 7, 2001.

p. 398: "In 1983, however . . . at all, he said." Fredric Dannen, *Hit Men,* (Random House, New York, 1990), p. 187.

p. 398–399: "But Azoff had . . . said Howe." A.I. Bones Howe, May 15, 2003; also Hirschhorn, *The Universal Story,* p. 334. MCA annual report, 1979–1980.

p. 399: "Wasserman felt . . . to tunr around MCA Records." A.I. Sheinberg, March 25, 1998; MCA annual reports in 1983.

p. 399: "Soon after joining . . . in the 1970s." Knoedelseder, *Stiffed,* pp. 115–6.

p. 399: "Tall, garrulous . . . deal of trouble." A.I. Marvin Rudnick, July 28, 1997; also Knoedelseder, "Salvatore Pisello: A Shadowy Figure," *Los Angeles Times,* May 4, 1986.

p. 400: " . . . a symbol of two giant movie screens . . ." is how Speilberg described Wasserman's glasses in his eulogy, July 15, 2002.

p. 400: "In December 1978 . . . the consumer." Gottleib, "DiscoVision," *Los Angeles Magazine,* January 1979; MCA DiscoVision history, Blam Entertainment, oz.net; A.I. Wasserman, June 22, 1999.

p. 400: "But Wasserman's dream . . . research and development." A.I. Wasserman, June 22, 1999; ibid.

p. 401: "On the sidelines . . . like the CIA." MCA annual report, 1979–1982; also Gottleib, *Discovision,* p. 209.

p. 401–402: "Despite its problems . . . you're mocking him." A.I. Tanen, June 2, 1998.

p. 402: "MCA and Sony . . . $46 million a year." A.I. Sheinberg, April 21, 1998; MCA annual report 1984, which mentions the 1980 sales figure.

p. 402–403: "Still Wasserman . . . over to pioneer." A.I. anonymous, Aug. 29, 1996; MCA annual reports 1980–81; and MCA DiscoVision History.

p. 403: "In 1981, Sony's appeal . . ." A.I. Sheinberg, April 21, 1998; "Bring on the Video boom," Feb. 15, 1981; Financial World; Sony History; "The Betamax Case," Sony Corp. on-line site.

p. 403: "MCA's video sales . . . would double again." The 1981 figure is mentioned in MCA annual report, 1984; also A.I. Wasserman, Nov. 3, 1999.

p. 404: "As George Jones . . . as well as it did." MCA history of DiscoVision, online.

p. 404: "Wasserman had come . . . been there first." A.I. Wasserman, Nov. 3, 1999.

Chapter 38:

p. 404: The name of the young woman has not been used at her request. Interview took place Aug. 13–14, 2002.

p. 405: "She was a very fat . . . ever knew that." A.I. Molly Anne Leiken, May 12, 2002, Aug. 14, 2002.

p. 406: "Leiken had worked . . . from young women." Leiken's biography on IMDB; Leiber, Ibid.

p. 406: "I was always . . . Brown said." A.I., March 10, 2001.

p. 406: "He indulged in anything . . . of his job." A.I. Adele Huggins, Feb. 24, 2000.

p. 406: "Usually, when a . . . his cheating." A.I. anonymous, Aug. 29, 1996.

p. 406: " . . . coming into contact . . . client Bette Davis." Memos from Warner Brothers Studios archives, collected in Cork Millner's "Hollywood Be Thy Name" (Warner Sisters Productions) indicate affection and pranks among Davis and Wasserman against studio executives and directors.

p. 407: "He was also smitten . . . and agent, Lew." Axel Madsen, *Stanwyck* (Harper Collins, 1994), p. 159.

p. 407: "Whenever Edie found . . . he'd snap to attention." Berges, "Edie and Lew," *Los Angeles Times Home Magazine,* Dec. 2, 1973.

p. 407: "Yet, when Stanwyck . . . outstanding performance." Book, A.I. Huggins, Feb. 24, 2000; IMDB.

p. 407: "Wasserman's sexual attitudes . . . to several sources." A.I. Rosenbaum, June 26, 1998; A.I. Wages, March 27, 1998.

p. 407: "For years, Wasserman . . . several other executives." A.I. Huggins, Feb. 24, 2000; A.I Link, July 12, 2002.

p. 407: "Wasserman wanted to . . . working at MCA." A.I. Wages, March 27, 1998, March 31, 1998.

p. 408: "Burton Square . . . through MCA's doors." A.I. Rosenbaum, June 26, 1998.

p. 409: "She had come of . . . *The Divorcee*." Mick La Salle, *Complicated Women* (Thomas Dunne Books, 2000); also on TCM.

p. 409: "As a teenager . . . erotic perks." A.I. Jacobs, Feb. 1, 1997; A.I. LaRonge, Dec. 5, 1996.

p. 409: "Edie was aggressively . . . said one woman." A.I. anonymous, June 12, 2002.

p. 409: "Chauvinism . . . a surrogate son." A.I. Dorskind, April 1, 1998.

p. 409: "That attitude . . . higher salary." A.I. Rael, May 1, 1998.

p. 409–410: "Monica Lewis . . . female clients." A.I., July 31, 1997.

p. 410: "When Wasserman had. . . .Thackery said." A.I. Thackery, Sept. 20, 1997.

p. 410: "Shortly after it opened . . . Henry Hathaway." Ally Acker, *Reel Women, Pioneers of the Cinema*, (The Continum Publishing Co., 1991); also Cari Beauchamp, *Without Lying Down,* (University of California Press, 1999).

p. 410–411: "Most of the star directors. . . . until her death." Acker, *Reel Women*, pp. 16.

p. 411: "Waserman's studio had . . . my mother's involvement." A.I. O'Connell, May 14, 1998.

p. 411: "Hitchcock also relied . . . on the Universal lot." A.I. Adler, Dec. 15, 1998; also A.I. O'Connell, May 14, 1998.

p. 411: "There were hardly . . . roles," he said." A.I. Cannell, Jan. 18, 1999.

p. 411: "One who flourished . . . low-budget film." A.I. Tanen, July 7, 1998.

p. 412: "Hollywood is . . . Goldman." A.I. Goldman, April 17, 2002.

p. 412: "Even though women . . . in Hollywood." Figures from Prof. Martha Lauzen, at San Diego University.

p. 412: "One woman who . . . told a reporter." also Maneker, "Now for the Grann Finale," *New York*, Jan. 21, 2002.

p. 412: "But eventually . . . got distracted." A.I. Sheinberg, April 21, 1998.

p. 413: "In addition . . . magazine soon folded." A.I. Dorskind, Aug. 1, 1998;

p. 413: "As one man explained: . . . mail order service." A.I. anonymous, July 29, 1997.

p. 413: "By the early . . . Dorskind said." A.I. Dorskind, Aug. 1, 1998.

p. 413: "Wasserman's desire to . . . pursue a deal." A.I. Jay Stein, July 28, 1998.

p. 414: "But as he studied . . . as scary." A.I. Sheinberg, April 21, 1998.

p. 414: "Even so, Wasserman . . . necessary, prevailed." A.I. Buzz Price, Sept. 17, 1998.

p. 414: "At some subconscious . . . trying to buy it." A.I. Sheinberg, April 21, 1998.

p. 414: "Harcourt Brace . . . said Price." A.I. Buzz Price, Sept. 17, 1998.

p. 414–415: "In 1977, Waserman . . . $200 million." Kathryn Harris, "MCA Takes The Cautious Road, *Los Angeles Times*, Nov. 22, 1981.

p. 415: "That was frustating . . . said Sheinberg." A.I. Sheinberg, April 21, 1998.

p. 415: "Four years later . . . tipling its investment.' A.I. Harris, Nov. 22, 1981.

p. 415: "By then, . . . often anymore." A.I. Sheinberg, April 21, 1998; May 19, 1998.

p. 415–417: "Lew's men . . . the tension was there." A.I. Stein, July 28, 1998.

p. 417–418: "Transamerica Corp . . . several top executives." Putnam, *The Undeclared War*, pp. 336–345; Steven Prokesch, "Remaking the American CEO" in *The New York Times*, January 25, 1987.

p. 418: "Wynn had acquired . . . to Milken." Alex Ben Block, "Controlling the Media Game," reprinted in *Cleveland Plain Dealer*, Nov. 17, 1985; A.I. Sheinberg, April 21, 1998.

p. 418: "Wasserman learned . . . Anti-takeover measures." A.I. Sheinberg, Ibid.

p. 419: "Then, to make sure . . . go any further." A.I. Delaney, April 10, 1998.

p. 419: "To reinforce . . . still had fangs." A.I. Slusser May 8, 1998.

p. 419: "For years . . . would fare." Harris, "Lights! Camera! Regulation!" *Fortune Magazine*, Sept. 4, 1996.

p. 419–420: "He joined three . . . much to Wasserman's annoyance." MCA annual report 1980; A.I. Harris, Nov. 22, 1981.

p. 420: "In 1983, he . . . wanted $120." Ben Block, "Controlling the Media Game," *Cleveland Plain Dealer*, Nov. 17, 1985.

p. 420: "The merger talks . . . merger of its time." A.I. Sheinberg, Arpil 21, 1998.

p. 420–421: "For the former . . . their respective fields." Kramer's papers.

p. 421: "Edie Wasserman's . . . had a tough time." A.I. Goldberg, May 9, 2003.

p. 422: "Edie's longtime . . . Eye Institute." A.I. Krauskopf, June 7, 2000.

p. 422: "But a few weeks . . . April 7, 1984." "Doris Stein, who husband founded MCA, dead at 82," *Los Angeles Herald Examiner*, April 9, 1984.

p. 422: "The family held . . . from friends." A.I. Oppenheimer, Aug. 12, 1997.

p. 422: "There weren't many. . . .her by," said Christy." A.I. Christy, March 27, 2003.

p. 423: "That was not . . . rare Chinese works." Rita Reif, "Auctions," *New York Times*, April 11, 1986, ; also Christy.

p. 423: "I'd say her . . . Wasserman said." A.I. June 10, 1999.

p. 423: "True to her . . . of James Galanos." A.I. Oppenhimer, Aug. 12, 1997; A.I. Sandy Rosenbaum, a curator at Doris Stein Research and Design Center, LACMA.

p. 423–424: "To Edie, Doris . . . Goldberg noted." A.I. Goldberg, May 9, 2003.

p. 424: "In those days . . . just to have fun." A.I. Rex Reed, Jan. 30, 2002.

p. 424: "After Doris. . . . Christy explained." A.I. Christy, March 27, 2003.

p. 424: "As for Edie . . . in good taste." A.I. Goldberg, May 9, 2003.

p. 424–425: "There were no . . . on a particular idea." A.I. Dunne, Oct. 25, 2002.

p. 425: "Around 1982, . . . Studios after all." A.I. McDonnel, May 30, 2003.

p. 425: "She pushed her pet . . . Irma Kalish." A.I. Seltzer, July 15, 1997; A.I. Kalish, Sept. 9, 1997.

p. 425: "By the mid . . . friend, Edie said." Army Archerd, "Home is Close to Edie's heart," *Variety*, July 9, 1996.

p. 426: "A few weeks, . . . become her mission." "Wasserman, Koch, MPTF Silver Medallion Honorees," *Variety*, May 20, 1985.

p. 426: "It's her life." A.I. Wasserman, Nov. 3, 1999.

p. 426: "She'd hit up . . . which delighted Edie." A.I. Seltzer, July 15, 1997.

Chapter 39

p. 427: "In the spring of 1983 . . . stunning deal." Based on photos and archives at the Reagan Presidental Library.

p. 427: "Wasserman had already . . . he said." Harris, Nov. 22, 1981.

p. 427: "Lew as not . . . returning to the set." Meeting was May 26, 1983, according to records at the Reagan Presidential Library.

p. 427: "Wasserman was . . . knocking down." A.I. Sheinberg, April 21, 998.

p. 427–428: "The president . . . a record high." Lou Canon, *Role of a Lifetime.*

p. 428: "I think you . . . obtaining his goal." A.I. Waserman, Nov. 3, 1999.

p. 428: "There was a push . . . devastate Wasserman's company." A.I. Gomery, Feb. 6, 1997. Note: When MCA's annual reports from 1970 to 1983 didn't break out this figure, or report a percent increase from a year that did report the figure, the author estimated the number based on historical figures.

p. 428–429: "The networks . . . should be killed." Marvin Wolf, *Beating the Odds*, p. 453.

p. 429: "The studios were . . . getting anywhere.' A.I. Jack Valenti, June 5, 1997.

p. 429: "Reagan . . . had to stay." A.I. Gomery, Feb. 6, 1997.

p. 429: "When Valenti . . . And I don't tell." A.I. Valenti, June 5, 1997.

p. 429: "The reversal was strange . . . at the time." From Wolf, *Beating the Odds.*

p. 430: "He got a little . . . Ronald Reagan. . . ." Ibid.

p. 430: "Reagan also got cocky . . . and launder money." Canon, *Role of a Lifetime*, pp. 628–637.

p. 430: "Only a fool . . . might fail." A.I. Sheinberg, May 21, 1998.

p. 431: "Wasserman had grown . . . . snickered but Lew." A.I. Koenig, April 27, 1999.

p. 431: "The company's once . . . times," said Lewis." A.I. Lewis, March 31, 2001.

p. 431: "The IRS investigated . . . is procedures." A.I. Lewis, ibid; also MCA annual report.

p. 432: "James Garner . . . 37 percent." Garner on *60 Minutes*, Dec. 7, 1980.

p. 432: "The writer/producer . . . *Dollar Man.*" A.I. Gil Melle, July 29, 2002.

p. 432: "Veteran music composer . . . filed his suit." A.I. Ibid.

p. 432: "It was their policy . . . said Lewis." A.I. Lewis, March 31, 2001.

p. 432: "Harve Bennett . . . several more years." A.I. Melle, July 29, 2002.

p. 432: "As for Roy . . . before he died." A.I. Huggins, Feb. 24, 2000.

p. 432: "MCA is not an . . . and lost." A.J. Cervantes, Oct. 24, 1996.

p. 433: "Lew thought . . . well and good." A.I. Sheinberg, May 21, 1998.

p. 433: "Lew inculcated in . . . the same way." A.I. Jay Stein, July 28, 1998.

Chapter 40:

p. 433: "Ned Tanen . . . left after a year." A.I. Tanen, July 7, 1998,

p. 435: "He asked Frank Price . . . such as Tom Petty." A.I. Price, Dec. 2, 1999.

p. 435: "Wasserman's passion . . . to $96 million." MCA annual report 1982, 1983, 1984; also "Reshaping a Sluggish MCA," *Business Week*, August. 10, 1981.

p. 435–436: "Universal Studio's . . . on film locations." A.I. Dorskind, Feb. 26, 1997; also MCA annual report 1982–1984.

p. 436: "He began planning . . . from his competitors." Pamela Holllie, "MCA Looks to Florida," *New York Times*, July 28, 1981.

p. 436: "But he later thought better . . . spread the risk." A.I. Jay Stein, July 28, 1998.

p. 436: "Disaster, however . . . down very hard." A.I. Sheinberg, May 21, 1998. Also Hollie, "MCA Looks to Florida," July 28, 1981.

p. 437: "Sheinberg blustered . . . of dollars extra." A.I. Stein, July 28, 1998; A.I. Shein-berg, May 21, 1988.

p. 439: "Like many other companies . . . in those days." A.I. Sheinberg, May 21, 1998; A.I. Stein, July 28, 1998; Pollock, Aug. 16, 1998; also John Taylor, *Storming the Magic Kingdom* (Ballantine Books, 1987).

p. 439: "Wasserman's cherished theme . . . for park guests." A.I. RP Oct. 21, 1997.

p. 439: "Stein was growing . . . about the mob." A.I. Stein, July 28, 1998.

p. 440: "What most of MCA . . . was so thoughtful." A.I. Goldberg, May 9, 2003; also A.I. Barbara Greenspun, April 8, 1998.

p. 440: "Edie got the Las . . . . said Barton." A.I. Barton, March 31, 1997.

p. 440–441: "In fact . . . Teapot Dome oil reserves." *This Cleveland of Ours*, Vol. II, (S.J. Clarke Publishing, 1933), pp. 565–567; A.I. Jacobs, Feb. 1, 1997.

p. 441: "Bedkerman also . . . said one report." Editorial, *Cleveland Press*, March 5, 1932.

p. 441: "He had an interest . . . Thisteldown Race Track." Hank Messick, *The Silent Syndicate*, (New York: Macmillan, 1967), pp 13, 151, 163.

p. 441: "His realty company . . . two years." Two of his real estate companies were listed as applicant/owner on the Mayfair Casino's liquor license and deed of own-ership, according to County Cuyahoga records. Also "Henry Beckerman Dies," *Cleveland Plain Dealer*, Oct. 15, 1949.

p. 441: "After 1926, when . . . distilled illegal whiskey." A.I. LaRonge, Dec. 5, 1996.

p. 441: "He was almost . . . one reporter noted." Draft of Beckerman's obitituary, written Aug. 24, 1936 (from archives of *Cleveland Plain Dealer*.)

p. 441: "But few people . . . asked me." A.I. Curtis, Feb. 17, 2000.

p. 441: So whenever . . . bounce on his knee." A.I. Jackie Gerswhin, June 23, 1998; also A.I. anonymous, June 12, 2003; also A.I. Muriel Stevens, and Barbara Green-spun, publisher of *Las Vegas Sun*, April 8, 1998.

p. 442: "Edie loved to gamble . . . in a pinch." A.I. Gerber, Feb. 5, 1998.

p. 442: "In 1955, she . . . in my life." A.I. Gershwin, June 23, 1998.

p. 442: "That night . . . everyone intermingled." A.I. Curtis, Feb. 17, 2000; A.I. Leigh, Feb. 5, 1998; A.I. Gershwin, June 23, 1998.

p. 442–443: "After that, El Rancho. . . .Beldon's place." A.I. Stevens, April 8, 1998.

p. 443: "To Edie and many women . . . never had before." A.I. Stevens, Greenspun, April 8, 1998.

p. 443: "It was true . . . undo their efforts." A.I. Bergman, May 2, 2003; also Robert Friedman, "Senator Paul Laxalt, the Man Who Runs The Reagan Campaign," *Mother Jones*, Aug./Sept. 1984 also Del Tartikoff, *Electric Nevada*, 1996; Jim McGee, "Laxalt Named Mobster Special Assistant," June 14, 1987, *Miami Herald*.

p. 444: "During Prohibition . . . national crime syndicate." A.I. Messick, March 10, 1997; also Messick, *Silent Syndicate*.

p. 445: "The move left . . . from an inferno." Author, "Beckerman Jury Told of Land Firm," *Plain Dealer*, June 13, 1936.

p. 445: "So began the biggest . . . for arson." Based on dozens of news articles by the *Plain Dealer* and *Cleveland Press*.

p. 445: "Two days after . . . front page news." "Beckerman Says He Will Return

Soon," *Cleveland Plain Dealer*, Dec. 8, 1933; "The Fix that Failed," *Cleveland Press*, May 15, 1934.

p. 445: "After a friend . . . jury tampering." "The Fix that Failed," *Cleveland Press*, May 15, 1934.

p. 445–446: "Today, Beckerman . . . bank depositers." "Beckerman says He's Broke," *Cleveland Press*, July 17, 1934.

p. 446: "Yet, neither the . . . was acquitted." Ibid.

p. 446: "A week later . . . Henry's trial." A.I. Jacobs, Feb. 1, 1997; A.I. Heller, April 15, 1997.

p. 446: "MCA always . . . age 89." A.I. Gerber and Murray, July 29, 1997.

p. 446–447: "Now, in the Manhattan . . . self-censorship." Ronald Ostrow and Robert Jackson, "Presser an FBI (Target) and Informant), *Los Angeles Times*, June 6, 1984; also A.I. Bergman, May 2, 2003.

Chapter 41:

p. 447: "When Universal TV's . . . projection room." Wasserman saw every one of his films or TV pilots, he told *Forbes*, Nov. 1, 1974.

p. 447: "Created by Michael . . . moral ambiguity." IMDB.

p. 447–448: "Wasserman called . . . several Emmys." MCA annual report 1984, 1985.

p. 448: "It quickly became . . . *Miami Vice* set." David Robb, "Martin Bacow Long a Hollywood Shadow Figure," *Variety*, Feb. 15, 1984; Robert Wagman, "Vice in Miami—and beyond," *Los Angeles Daily News*, July 13, 1987; also Tren Yarborough, April 27, 1997.

p. 448: "By now, the federal . . . phone anytime." A.I. Stavin, Feb. 14, 1998; May 16, 2003.

p. 449: "What Stavin didn't . . . continued covertly." A.I. Stavin, Feb. 14, 1998; A.I. Martin, May 2, 2003; Canon, *Role of a Lifetime*, p. 628.

p. 449: "One of Secord's agents . . . Nichols was laundering money." A.I. Al Martin, May 2, 2003; June 19, 200; also Martin, *The Conspirators: Secrets of an Iran-Contra Insider*, (National Liberty Press).

p. 449–450: "As for MCA's association . . . build a case." A.I. Stavin, May 16, 2003.

p. 450: "Inside the Black Tower . . . their rivalry." A.I. Price, Dec. 2, 1999.

p. 450–451: "The two men . . . to their men." A.I. Pollock, Aug. 16, 1998; A.I. Price, Dec. 2, 1999; A.I. Antonowsky, Aug. 21, 1998.

p. 451: "George Lucas . . . Price's Goose." Ibid.

p. 451: "Some days. Sheinberg . . . spines." A.I. Sheinberg, May 19, 1998.

p. 452: "One day, a fistfight . . . one man." A.I. Alex Ben Block, May 7, 2001; A.I. Sheinberg, May 1998;

p. 452: "In 1982 . . . MCA's executive suite." MCA annual reports 1982–1986.

p. 452: "In 1985, the government . . . top artists." Henry Schipper, "Pisello Trial Gets Underway," *Variety*, March 30, 1988.

p. 452: "Before he went to prison . . . top artists." Knoedelseder Jr. "Salvatore Pisello," *Los Angeles Times*, May 4, 1986.

p. 452: "Grand juries in . . . sprig." Knoedelseder, "Probe Points to Mob Role in Record Deal," *Los Angeles Times*, March 3, 1986.

p. 453: "A budget record . . . and the mob." A.I. Rudnick, July 20, 1995; July 28, 1997.

p. 453: "During Pisello's . . . were deep." A.I. Rudnick, July 28, 1997; also *Stiffed*, p. 138.

p. 453: "The audit committee . . . no one was fired." A.I. Sheinberg, May 19, 1998; A.I. PT Aug. 29, 1996.

p. 453: In February 1986 . . . investigations." A.I. Rudnick July 28, 1997.

p. 453–454: "Edie concentrated . . . July 14 party." A.I .Goldberg, May 9, 2003.

p. 454–455: "That Saturday night . . . Givenchy gown." A.I. Link, July 12, 2002; also "Party, Party," *Cleveland Plain Dealer*, July 18, 1986; Frank Rose, "The Last Mogul," *Los Angeles Times Magazine,* May 21, 1995.

p. 455 "That was unusual . . . said Christy." A.I. Christy, June 20, 2002.

p. 455: "A month or so . . . joined MCA." A.I. Sheinberg, May 19, 1998.

p. 455–456: "Once again . . . with her husband." A.I. Goldberg, May 9, 2003.

p. 456: "Inside were pictures . . . just as exciting." Quote is taken from inside the 50th anniversary program, author's collection.

p. 456: "None of the . . . half-century career." "Wasserman Honored," *Variety,* Dec. 17, 1986; also A.I. Sheinberg, May 19, 1998.

p. 456–457: "Frank Sinatra . . . said one guest." A.I. ML, July 15, 2002.

p. 457: "She had been . . . that of her husband's." A.I. Goldberg, May 9, 2003.

Chapter 42:

p. 458: "That year, Wasserman . . . enlisted other donors." Confirmed by Mark Burson, executive director of Ronald Reagan Presidential Foundation, June 6, 2003.

p. 458: "Then, in early . . . Iran-Contra scandal." Canon, *Role of a Lifetime*, p. 644.

p. 458: "Strauss had sat . . . enjoying it." Robert S. Strauss, *Current Biography Year-book*, 1992, pp. 543–6; also Alan Murray, "Private to Public," *Wall Street Journal,* Oct. 2, 1998.

p. 458: "Reagan as insisting . . . Howard H. Baker, Jr." Canon, *Role*, pp. 640–646.

p. 459: "A few months . . . new set of hearings." Howard Baker, Jr. from The Howard Baker Jr. Center for Public Policy, University of Tennesee.

p. 459: "Everybody denied . . . both directions." A.I. Bones Howe, May 15, 2003.

p. 459–460: "MCA Records . . . so-called Network." A.I. Rudnick, July 28, 1997; also Chuck Phillips, "Payola Probe with no Payoff," April 19, 1996, *Los Angeles Times.*

p. 460: "Azoff had . . . eight platinum (1 million or more.)" MCA annual reports 1983–1987.

p. 460: "In May 1986, MCA . . . Jimmy Buffett." MCA annual report 1986.

p. 460: "It's shocking . . . Geffen Records." Michael Goldberg, "Grand Jury Investigates Mob Ties," *Rolling Stone*, May 8, 1986.

p. 460: "By 1986, the industry's . . . record industry dinner." Henry Schipper, "CAP and MCA Sever Indie Promot Ties," *Variety,* Feb. 28, 1986.

p. 460: "Cameras had caught MCA's . . . mafia guys." Azoff stated this in letter to CBS's Lawrence Tische.

p. 460: "MCA defended . . . independent promoters, too." Chuck Philips, "Payola Problem with No Payoff," April 9, 1996.

p. 460–461: "MCA stood out . . . and New York." A.I. Rudnick, July 28, 1997.

p. 461: "There is logical . . . erring on the side of logic." A.I. Jay Stein, July 28, 1998.

p. 462: "In 1981 . . . belonged to Lew." Garth Drabinsky bio.

p. 462–463: "Even so, Wasserman . . . spreading his risks." A.I. Stein, July 28, 1998; A.I. Sheinberg, May 19, 1998.

p. 463: "In the spring . . . influence-peddling." "What's Wrong," cover story, *Time*, May 25, 1987.

p. 463: "Then, Wasserman's . . . takeover bid." A.I. Sheinberg, May 19, 1998.

p. 463–464: Satisified that his MCA . . . and mercury." Mitchell Fink, "Hard to Swallow," *Los Angeles Herald Examiner*, Nov. 5, 1987.

p. 464–465: "A team of doctors . . . and their wives." A.I. Krauskopf, July 29, 1998; A.I. anonymous, June 12, 2002.

p. 465: "Wasserman's other family . . . force attorneys." *Fink, Hard to Swallow*; A.I. Rudnick, July 28, 1997; A.I. Stavin, May 16, 2003.

p. 465: "The specter of Lew's . . . dead man's empire." *US News and World Report*, Sept. 7, 1989.

p. 465–466: "But Wall Street . . . jumped from $48 to $52." A.I. Sheinberg, May 19, 1998; also stock quoted in July 10, 1987 story in *Wall Street Journal*.

p. 466: "FBI Agents. . . .covert operation." A.I. Stavin, May 16, 2003; also transcripts reported in "Just a Coupla Wiseguys Sitting Around Talkin," Part One and Two, *Spy* magazine, July and August 1989.

p. 467: "Further investigation . . . other political hot spots." A.I. Martin, May 2, 2003; also *Laissez Faire City Times*, Vol. 5 No. 46.

p. 467: "Stavin and other federal officers . . . to prove it." A.I. Rudnick, July 28, 1997; A.I. Stavin, Feb. 14, 1998; Martin, May 2, 2003.

p. 467–468: "On July 16, Wasserman had recuperated . . . near-death experience." *Business Week*, Feb. 29, 1988, from Studio archives.

p. 468: "*Variety* had already . . . and kept it." Draft of article dated July 17, 1987, found in Universal Studio archives.

p. 468: "Wall Street was already . . . Lew R. Wasserman." *U.S. News and World Report*.

p. 468: "On Aug. 1, 1987 . . . in front of my house." A.I. Pollock, Aug. 16, 1998.

Chapter 43:

p. 468–469: "One day . . . just been thwarted." A.I. Stavin, May 16, 2003.

p. 469: "Stavin's counterpart . . . unsuspecting prosecutor." "Arraignment of Pisello," *Daily Variety*, July 14, 1987; A.I. Rudnick July 28, 1997,

p. 470: "Edie and a recovered . . . event of the year." A.I. Raines, Oct. 9, 1998; about records: *Stiffed*, p. 35; A.I Goldberg, May 9, 2003. Note: The pontiff had visited North Ameica only once before.

p. 470–471: "At the same time . . . he must have known." A.I. Rudnick, July 28, 1997; Knoedelseder, *Stiffed*, pp. 326–327; Moldea, "MCA and the Mob," June 1988, *Regardie's*.

p. 471: "That week . . . dialogue with young people." MCA annual report 1987.

p. 472: "The Wassermans then . . . falling down a pipe." Item in Sept. 17, 1987, *Los Angeles Herald Examiner*.

p. 472: "A few days later . . . to the mob." Sept. 18, 1987 articles.

p. 472–473: "That's when Wasserman . . . formidable clout." A.I. Rudnick, July 28, 1997; Feb. 18, 1997.

p. 474: "On Black Monday . . . drops ahead." *Wall Street Journal,* Oct. 20,. 1987.

p. 474: "Rudnick, meanwhile . . . kept asking collegaues." A.I. Rudnick, Feb. 18, 1997, July 28, 1997.

p. 475: "On new Year's Eve . . . and Richard Secord." A.I. P.M., Aug. 2, 1998; also Canon, *Role of Lifetime,* p. 653.

p. 475: "Several high-ranking . . . enrich himself . . ." Meese had allegedly helped Wedtech Corp., his friend, attorney Wallach, and benefitted from the breakup of the Baby Bells; *Time,* May 1987; Note: Meese declined several interview requests.

p. 475: "They worried . . . own careers." "Two Top Justice Officials Quit," *Washington Post* March 30, 1988.

p. 475: "Weld said that his . . . in Meese's office." Weld as quoted in *ABA Journal,* Dec. 1, 1998.

p. 475: "Nevertheless . . . in charge." Ibid; "Meese Sees No reason to Step Down," *Washington Post,* March 31, 1988.

p. 476: "Back in Los Angeles . . . controlling labor relations." "Organized Crime Reaps Huge Profits from Pornographic Films," *New York Times,* Oct. 12, 1975; also 1984 report by the Los Angeles County Commission on Crime; and a confidential report to the California Legislature, obtained by author.

p. 476: "There was a lot of . . . RICO charges." A.I. Stavin, May 16, 2003.

p. 477: "One of these . . . he said." A.I. anonymous, June 6, 2003.

p. 477: "Sure enough . . . to the top." A.I. Rudnick, July 28, 1997.

P. 477: "In August 1988 . . . video case was eventually dropped." A.I. Stavin, May 16, 2003.

p. 477: "The sound of strings . . . he told me." Michael Orey, "Death of a Mob Probe," *American Lawyer,* July 1988; A.I. Dwyer, Jan. 18, 1997.

p. 478: "In March 1992, Stavin . . . was investigating." Known as The Inslaw Affair, Sept. 10, 1992 report.

p. 478: "In July 1988 . . . celebrates his birthday." Bakernia, University of Tennessee; MCA annual report 1989.

Chapter 44:

p. 479: "By 1989, the Japanese yen . . . the Pacific Rim." Report, Japanese Investment in *U.S. Real Esate Review,* Dec. 1989, Mead Ventures.

p. 479: "The giants were turning . . . shareholders that year." *Time,* Dec. 10, 1990.

p. 480: "At 76, Wasserman was . . . became financing." A.I. Tanen, July 7, 1998; A.I. Sheinberg, May 19, 1998.

p. 480: "Michael Ovitz . . . a stunning deal." Profile of Ovitz, A.I. Valenti, A.I. Tanen, July 7, 1998. Sony deal announced in *Variety.*

p. 480–481: "In late 1989 . . . Zen heaven." Background from Matsushita's website, corporate profile, The Founder; The Beginnings; Also "Who's Biting Whom?" *Economist,* Sept. 29 1990.

p. 482: "In November 1989 . . . were serious." A.I. Stein, July 28, 1998; A.I. Sheinberg, May 19, 1998. Also, Peter Boyer, *Vanity Fair,* Feb. 1991.

p. 482: "Once again . . . at our house again." A.I. Bergman.

p. 483–484: "The piece . . . unfairly damaged the company." *60 Minutes,* Nov. 19, 1989 story.

p. 484: "The story infuriated . . . or something." A.I. Sheinberg, May 19, 1998.

p. 484: "That week, Edie . . . with the Wasermans." A.I. Dunne, Oct. 25, 2002.

p. 484 "It ended a . . . controlled by them." A.I. Pollock.

p. 484: "Despite the bad . . . Foothill Road home." "Lights, Camera, Action," *Business Week,* Dec. 10, 1990.

p. 484–485: "The elegant but . . . have felt at home." A.I. Dunne, Oct. 25, 2003; A.I. Goldberg.

p. 485: "By all accounts . . . green tea." A.I. Herb Steinberg, Aug. 4, 1998.

p. 485: Papers reported . . . and $90." A.I. Danny Welkes, March 25, 1998; also A.I. WSJ, Sept. 25, 1990.

p. 485: "That translated . . . to $8.7 billion." *Wall Street Journal,* Oct. 25, 1990.

p. 485: "Ovitz had . . . said one report." Ibid, A.I. Pollock, Sheinberg.

p. 486: "Edie celebrated . . . his clever lyrics." A.I. Dunne, Boyer piece.

p. 487: Days later. . . . or $66 a share." A.I. Tanen, Pollock, Sheinberg, Steinberg.

p. 488: "Lew's sale . . . *Variety* declared." *Variety.*

Chapter 45:

p. 488–489: "Wasserman was ecstatic . . . Quasar brands." A.I. Sheinberg; "Lights Camera, Action," *Business Week.*

p. 489: "But then the global. . . .300 managers." *Wall Street Journal* piece.

p. 489: "In March 1992, Matsushita . . . for three months." A.I. Dan Slusser and reports from Agency France Presse, March 25, 1992 and March 31, 1992.

p. 489: "Meanwhile, Wasserman . . . said Sheinberg." A.I., May 19, 1998.

p. 490: "Edie . . . afraid of anybody." A.I. Dunne, Oct. 25, 2002.

p. 490: "The Wassermans still . . . alms and benediction." A.I. Stein, July 28, 1998.

p. 491: "Ned Tanen . . . directed it all." A.I. Tanen, July 28, 1998.

p. 491: "As Wendy Goldberg . . . take us in hand." A.I. Goldberg, May 9, 2003.

p. 491–492: "Indeed, he was genuinely . . . so long." A.I. Wasserman, June 10, 1999, Nov. 3, 1999.

p. 492: "In 1993, Wasserman . . . with ITT Corp." A.I Steinberg, Aug. 4, 1998; Harris, "Lights Camera! Regulation!" *Fortune,* Sept. 4, 1995, .

p. 492–493: "On Sept. 17, 1994, Wasserman . . . totally demoralized us." A.I. Sheinberg, May 19, 1998; A.I. Jay Stein, July 28, 1998; A.I. Slusser; A.I. David Weitzner.

p. 494–495: "If the Japanese . . . shut out of the loop." A.I. Sheinberg, Pollock, Slusser.

p. 495: "A few months later . . . for a total of $1 million." A.I. Dunne; also *Vanity Fair* April 1996, The Last Emperor, p. 313; A.I. Link.

p. 495–496: "Gradually, the Wasermans . . . personal stock fell lower." A.I. Tanen, July 28, 1998; A.I. Sheinberg, May 19, 1998.

p. 496: "We see him. . . .money, she added." A.I. June 7, 1997.

p. 496: "I asked Wasserman if that . . . citicize Bronfman." A.I. Waserman, Nov. 3, 1999.

p. 496: "Facts said it all . . . 250 recording artists." Seagram's annual reports 1995–1998; also *Wall Street Journal* pieces; *Los Angeles Magazine.*

p. 497: "What happened to Lew . . . more than enough." A.I. Sheinberg, May 19, 1998; A.I. Tanen, July 7, 1998.

p. 497–498: "So it was exhilarating . . . for the price of one." A.I. Judy Balaban; A.I. Dunne, Oct. 25, 2002; A.I. Sean Daniel; Clinton address on July 15, 2002.

p. 498: "The Wasermans and . . . for his $11 million legal defense." A.I. Wasserman, Nov. 3, 1999.

p. 498: "Lew helped me become president . . . for anything." Clinton, at Lew's memorial, July 15, 2002.

p. 499: "The hybrid called . . . $34 billion in debt." A.I. Pollock, May, 2002.

p. 499: "It all became too . . . of when." A.I. Wasserman, Nov. 3, 1999.

p. 499: "Instead, the industry . . . bargaining table." A.I.

p. 499: "I told some Park . . . who was lying." A.I. Herman, April 5, 2003.

EPILOGUE

p. 500: "He once said . . . new technology." A.I. Victor Tempkin.

p. 500: "He kept a laptop . . . and I understood." A.I. Wasserman, June 22, 1999, Nov. 3, 1999.

p. 501: "About the only people . . . giant figure." A.I. Curtis, Feb. 17, 2000.

p. 503: "By 2003, the landscape . . . horizontally . . ." Diller on Bill Moyers interview, April 25, 2003.

p. 503: "Has there ever . . . he asked me."A.I. Nov. 3, 1999.

p. 504: "Late 20th Century business . . . headline performances." Some of this from Sharp's obituary and essay on salon.com. Also *Boston Globe* piece.

p. 505: "Walt Disney . . . Tokyo-based corporation." Numbers based on individual annual reports from 2002.

p. 506: "Meanwhile Edie . . . spoil the surprise." A.I. Steinberg, Aug. 4, 1998; A.I. John McClean.

p. 508: "By the year 2001 . . . to show up." A.I. Balaban ; Goldberg; Rex Reed; off-record May 10, 2001.

p. 508 "Added film producer . . . they should." A.I. Cramer.

p. 508: "The last time I saw Wasserman . . . move without a cane." Wasserman Campus dedication, Jules Stein Eye Institue.

p. 509: "The end came . . . stars and leaders." Personal account of memorial.

p. 509: "I would fly anywhere . . . had felt like." Comments from Sweeney, July 15, 2002.

BIBLIOGRAPHY

Acker, Ally *Reel Women: Pioneers of the Cinema 1896 to the Present* New York: Continuum, 1991.

Bart, Peter (introduction), and J. Spencer Beck (ed.) and the Editors of Variety *The Variety History of Show Business* New York: Harry N. Abrams/A Variety Book, 1993.

Bilby, Kenneth *The General: David Sarnoff and the Rise of the Communications Industry* New York: Harper & Row, 1987.

Behlmer, Rudy *Inside Warner Bros. (1935-1951): The Battles, the Brainstorms, and the Bickering — From the Files of Hollywood's Greatest Studio* New York: Viking, 1985.

Biskind, Peter *Easy Riders, Raging Bulls: How the Sex-Drugs-and-Rock 'n' Roll Generation Saved Hollywood* New York: Simon & Schuster, 1998.

Brown, David *Let Me Entertain You* New York: William Morrow and Co., 1990.

Cagin, Seth, and Philip Dray *Hollywood Films of the Seventies: Sex, Drugs, Violence, Rock 'n' Roll & Politics* New York: Harper & Row, 1984.

Ceplair, Larry, and Steven Englund *The Inquisition in Hollywood: Politics in the Film Community 1930-1960* Berkeley: University of California Press, 1988.

Curtis, Tony, and Barry Paris *Tony Curtis: The Autobiography* New York: William Morrow and Co., 1993.

Cannon, Lou *President Reagan: The Role of a Lifetime* New York: PublicAffairs, 1991.

Dick, Bernard F., *City of Dreams: The Making and Remaking of Universal Pictures* Lexington: The University Press of Kentucky, 1997.

Dunne, John Gregory *The Studio* New York: Farrar, Straus & Giroux, 1968.

Eisenschitz, Bernard (Tom Milne trans.) *Nicholas Ray: An American Journey* London: Faber and Faber, 1990.

Felch, William Campbell, M.D. (text), and the Twenty-fifth Anniversary Book Committee *Vision for the Future: Jules Stein Eye Institute 1966-1991* Los Angeles: University of California, Los Angeles, 1992.

Finler, Joel W. *The Hollywood Story* New York: Crown Publishers, 1988.

Fisher, Eddie *Eddie: My Life, My Loves* New York: Harper & Row, 1981.

Fishgall, Gary *Pieces of Time: The Life of Jimmy Stewart* New York: Charles Scribner's Sons, 1997.

Fonda, Henry, as told to Howard Teichmann *Fonda: My Life* New York: NAL Books/New American Library, 1981.

Gabler, Neal *An Empire of Their Own: How the Jews Invented Hollywood* New York: Anchor Books/Doubleday, 1988.

Goldenson, Leonard H., with Marvin J. Wolf *Beating the Odds: The Untold Story Behind the Rise of ABC: The Stars, Struggles, and Egos That Transformed Network Television by the Man Who Made It Happen* New York: Charles Scribner's Sons, 1991.

Gomery, Douglas *The Hollywood Studio System* New York: St. Martin's Press, 1986.

Shared Pleasures: A History of Movie Presentation in the United States Madison: The University of Wisconsin Press, 1992.

Goodwin, Richard N. *Remembering America: A Voice From the Sixties* Boston: Little, Brown and Co., 1988.

Haber, Joyce *The Users* New York: Delacorte Press, 1976.

Hirschhorn, Clive *The Universal Story* London: Octopus Books, 1983.

Kelly, Thomas, with George Condon, Chuck Heaton, Marc Jaffe, Crisfield Johnson, and Mary Anne Sharkey *The Cleveland 200: The Most Noted, Notable & Notorious in the First 200 Years of a Great American City* Archives Press, 1996.

Kisseloff, Jeff *The Box: An Oral History of Television, 1920-1961* New York: Viking, 1995.

Knoedelseder, William *Stiffed: A True Story of MCA, the Music Business, and the Mafia* New York: HarperCollins Publishers, 1993.

Levy, Shawn *King of Comedy: The Life and Art of Jerry Lewis* New York: St. Martin's Press, 1996.

MacDonald, J. Fred *One Nation Under Television: The Rise and Decline of Network TV* New York: Pantheon Books, 1990.

Madsen, Axel *Stanwyck* New York: HarperCollins Publishers, 1994.

McCann, Graham *Cary Grant: A Class Apart* New York: Columbia University Press, 1996.

McDougal, Dennis *The Last Mogul: Lew Wasserman, MCA, and the Hidden History of Hollywood* New York: Crown Publishers, 1998.

Messick, Hank *The Beauties and the Beasts: The Mob in Show Business* New York: David McKay Co., 1973.

Moldea, Dan E. *Dark Victory: Ronald Reagan, MCA, and the Mob* New York: Viking, 1986.

Neff, James *Mobbed Up: Jackie Presser's High-Wire Life in the Teamsters, the Mafia, and the FBI* New York: Dell Publishing, 1989.

Paper, Lewis, J. *Empire: William S. Paley and the Making of CBS* New York: St. Martin's Press/A Thomas Dunne Book, 1990.

Powdermaker, Hortense *Hollywood: The Dream Factory, An Anthropologist Looks at the Movie-Makers* Boston: Little, Brown and Co., 1950.

Puttnam, David, with Neil Watson *The Undeclared War: The Struggle for Control of the World's Film Industry* New York: HarperCollins Publishers, 1997.

Puzo, Mario *The Last Don* New York: Random House, 1996.

Rains, Bob *Beneath the Tinsel: The Human Side of Hollywood Stars* Danville (IL): Three Lions Publications, 1999.

Reid, Ed *The Grim Reapers: The Anatomy of Organized Crime in America* Chicago: Henry Regnery Co., 1969.

Rose, Frank *The Agency: William Morris and the Hidden History of Show Business* New York: Harper Business, 1995.

Rosenfield, Paul *The Club Rules: Power, Money, Sex, and Fear - How It Works in Hollywood* New York: Warner Books/A Dove Book, 1992.

Scherman, David E. (ed.) *Life Goes to the Movies* Alexandria (VA): Time-Life Books, 1975.

Schwartz, Nancy Lynn *The Hollywood Writers' Wars* New York: Alfred A. Knopf, 1982.

Stone, Joseph, and Tim Yohn *Prime Time and Misdemeanors: Investigating the 1950s TV Quiz Scandal — A D.A.'s Account* New Brunswick (NJ): Rutgers University Press, 1992.

Smith, Sally Bedell *In All His Glory: The Life of William S. Paley, the Legendary Tycoon and His Brilliant Circle* New York: Simon and Schuster, 1990.

Stuart, Ray (ed.) *Immortals of the Screen* New York: Bonanza Books, 1965.

Sullivan, Neil J. *The Dodgers Move West* New York: Oxford University Press, 1987.

Taylor, John *Storming the Magic Kingdom: Wall Street, the Raiders, and the Battle for Disney* New York: Ballantine Books, 1987.

Tosches, Nick *Dino: Living High in the Dirty Business of Dreams* New York: Doubleday, 1992.

Turner, Lana *Lana: The Lady, the Legend, the Truth* New York: E. P. Dutton 1982.

Woodward, Bob *Wired: The Short Life and Fast Times of John Belushi* New York: Simon and Schuster, 1984.

ACKNOWLEDGMENTS

I'M MOST GRATEFUL TO MY SOURCES, who showed me patience and generosity. My apologies for not naming you all. I sincerely thank the great librarians at the main public libraries in Beverly Hills, Chicago, Cleveland, Los Angeles, and New York, as well as at the presidential libraries of John F. Kennedy, Lyndon B. Johnson, Jimmy Carter, and Ronald Reagan. The Hoover Institute at Stanford University, where Reagan's gubernatorial papers were kept for a time; the Western Historical Society; the Jewish Community Federation in Cleveland; Cleveland State University; the Jewish Federation of Las Vegas; the Los Angeles County Museum of Art; and the Jules Stein Eye Institute lent invaluable help. Without the professionals at the Margaret Herrick Library at the Academy of Motion Picture Arts and Sciences, I would not have been able to accurately paint several key scenes.

The representatives of the Hollywood unions instructed me in their histories; I hope I've done them justice. So too with the industry's management groups, notably the Motion Picture Association. *Variety*'s Peter Bart, his gracious assistant, Bashirah Muttalib, and Dan Edelson let me spend weeks reviewing the paper's archives. The editors at the *Hollywood Reporter*—Alex Ben Block, Matthew King, Scott Collins—also opened their archives and spurred me on. In an age when most city newspapers restrict access to their records, the Cleveland *Plain Dealer* and *Las Vegas Sun* were a delightful exception.

The then chair of the Department of Film at University of California Santa Barbara, Charles Wolfe, guided me while trustee Paul Lazarus became my early advocate. Dan Noyes, director at the Center for Investigative Reporting, advised me after my requests filed under the Freedom of Information Act went unanswered. Let's hope that the flow of information from our own government expands in years to come, rather than contracts.

Members of Jules Stein's family went extra miles on my behalf, notably Gerald Oppenheimer and Patsy Miller Krauskopf. The family of MCA executive Karl Kramer gave me his unpublished history of MCA, and band members of Kay Kyser, Lew Wasserman's first big client, shared their papers. Documentarian Steve Beasley lent tapes, while esteemed journalists Lou Cannon, James Neff, Dan Moldea, Marvin Wolf, Dennis McDougal and, P.J. Corkery magnanimously gave me contacts, insights, and direction.

I appreciate the kind help of Margaret Ross, Universal Studio's librarian, as well as that of Pamela Cheney, Treasurer of MCA, and her staff. The late Steve Allen allowed me to spend weeks combing through his vast personal library, which is now at the California State University at Northridge, site of the Los Angeles *Herald Examiner* archives and a gold mine for students of journalism. Radio star Jean Hayes, RKO actress Jane Russell, and Hollywood daughter Judy Balaban Quine demonstrated the definition of marquee glamour and class, while Robert Mitchum, Gregory Peck, and Abe Polonsky taught me something about old-studio style and myth-making.

Some of the reporting in this book was produced for stories that appeared in *Parade Magazine;* the *Los Angeles Times Magazine;* Salon.com; *Town & Country;* and the *Boston Globe.* My heartfelt thanks to my editors there.

To dear friends Gayle Lynds and Michael Collins, who generously read portions of the book; Joanne King for her organizational help; Ross Johnson for his rolodex; Joan Tapper for her editorial gifts; Daryn Eller and Mary Fischer for inspiration; Fred Klein for sound advice; Noel Greenwood for his thorough review; and Ray Briare for his astute, invaluable support.

Without the faith of my agent Paul Fedorko at Trident Media, and his able associate Elisabeth Weed, this book would never have landed in the hands of my editor Philip Turner, who to this writer was a dream come true. He and his talented colleagues at Carroll & Graf—Keith Wallman, Holly Beemis, Claiborne Hancock, Paul Paddock, Jennifer Steffey, Simon Sullivan, Judith McQuown, and Cole Wheeler—did the impossible while making it all seem like a most excellent adventure.

INDEX

ABOUT THE AUTHOR

KATHLEEN SHARP IS AN AWARD-WINNING JOURNALIST who covers California—including Hollywood—for the *Boston Globe*, Salon.com, and National Public Radio.

Her last book, *In Good Faith* (St. Martin's Press, 1996), detailed Prudential Securities's multi-billion-dollar scandal of the 1980s. *Publishers Weekly* called it "a shocking expose," while the *Wall Street Journal* wrote that it detailed "scurrilous actions," and *The New York Times Book Review* said it "showed the failure of a great name of American business."

Sharp has won five awards from the Society of Professional Journalists/Sigma Delta Chi, including first place for her investigative business stories and for her feature writing. She's been awarded the prestigious Business and Economic Journalism Fellowship to study toward her masters' degree at the Graduate School of Business at the University of Washington. She's written features for *Playboy, Parade, Town & Country, Vogue, Elle,* and *McCall's,* among many others.

She began her career reporting for the Seattle and Los Angeles bureaus of *Business Week* while also working at small newspapers. Sharp has contributed to *The New York Times,* covering business stories from the West Coast, and has covered Central California for the *Los Angeles Times.* She's also contributed stories to National Public Radio's "Morning Edition."

She lives with her family in Santa Barbara, California. Further information on her work and *Mr. & Mrs. Hollywood: Edie and Lew Wasserman and Their Entertainment Empire* can be found at her website, www.kathleensharp.com.